Glossator: Practice and Theory of the Commentary

Volume 9

Editor-in-Chief
Nicola Masciandaro (Brooklyn College, City University of New York).

Co-Editors
Ryan Dobran (Queens College, University of Cambridge).
Karl Steel (Brooklyn College, City University of New York).

International Editorial Board
Nadia Altschul (Johns Hopkins University).
Stephen A. Barney (University of California, Irvine).
Erik Butler (Emory University).
Mary Ann Caws (The Graduate Center, City University of New York).
Alan Clinton (University of Miami).
Andrew Galloway (Cornell University)
David Greetham (The Graduate Center, City University of New York).
Bruno Gulli (Long Island University).
Daniel Heller-Roazen (Princeton University).
Jason Houston (University of Oklahoma).
Ed Keller (Parsons, The New School for Design).
Anna Kłosowska (Miami University of Ohio).
Erin Labbie (Bowling Green State University).
Carsten Madsen (Aarhus University).
Sean McCarthy (Lehman College, City University of New York).
Reza Negarestani (Independent Scholar).
Daniel C. Remein (The University of Massachusetts Boston).
Sherry Roush (Penn State University).
Michael Sargent (Queens College and The Graduate Center, City University of New York).
Michael Stone-Richards (College for Creative Studies).
Eugene Thacker (The New School).
Evelyn Tribble (University of Otago).
Frans van Liere (Calvin College).
Jesús Rodríguez-Velasco (Columbia University).
Robert Viscusi (Brooklyn College, City University of New York).
Valerie Michelle Wilhite (Miami University of Ohio).
Scott Wilson (Lancaster University).
Yoshihisa Yamamoto (Chiba University).

GLOSSATOR

VOLUME 9

Pearl

Edited by

Nicola Masciandaro
&
Karl Steel

glossator.org

ISSN 1942-3381 (online)
ISSN 2152-1506 (print)
ISBN-13: 978-0692413159
ISBN-10: 0692413154

COPYRIGHT NOTICE

This work is Open Access, a print version of the online open-access journal *Glossator* (http://glossator.org). It is licensed under a *Creative Commons Attribution 3.0 United States License* (http://creativecommons.org/licenses/by/3.0/us/).

Nicola Masciandaro, Editor
Glossator: Practice and Theory of the Commentary
Department of English
Brooklyn College, CUNY
2900 Bedford Ave.
Brooklyn, NY 11210
glossatori@gmail.com

Cover image: Antonello da Messina, *The Virgin Mary Reading*. Public domain image. Source:
http://commons.wikimedia.org/wiki/File:Antonello_da_Messina_-_The_Virgin_Mary_Reading_-_Walters_37433.jpg

Contents

Karl Steel – "Innoghe": A Preface on Inexhaustibility ... i

1. **William M. Storm** – The Arbor and the Pearl: Encapsulating Meaning in "Spot" ... 1

2. **Kevin Marti** – *Pearl*, Fitt II ... 20

3. **Piotr Spyra** – *Pearl*, Fitt III ("More and More") ... 45

4. **Daniel C. Remein** – "Pyȝt": Ornament, Place, and Site – A Commentary on the Fourth Fitt of *Pearl* ... 61

5. **Noelle Phillips** – Meeting One's Maker: The Jeweler in Fitt V of *Pearl* ... 91

6. **James C. Staples** – "Mercy Schal Hyr Craftez Kyþe": Learning to Perform Redeeming Readings of Materiality in *Pearl* ... 109

7. **Paul Megna** – Fitt 7: Blysse / (Envy) ... 132

8. **Kevin Marti** – *Pearl*, Fitt VIII ... 154

9. **Walter Wadiak** – "Ther is no date": The Middle English *Pearl* and its Work ... 179

10. **Travis Neel** – Fitt X – More ... 198

11. **Monika Otter** – Enough (Section XI) ... 217

12.	**Kay Miller** – Fitt XII: Ryght	226
13.	**A. W. Strouse** – *Pearl*, Fytt XIII	251
14.	**Jane Beal** – The Jerusalem Lamb of *Pearl*	264
15.	**Tekla Bude** – Fitt 15 – Lesse	286
16.	**Karen Bollermann** – Out, Out, Damned Spot: *Mote* in *Pearl* and the Poems of the *Pearl* Manuscript	308
17.	**Karen Elizabeth Gross** – Seeing John: A Commentary on the Link Word of *Pearl* Fitt XVII	326
18.	**Bruno M. Shah & Beth Sutherland** – Theoretical Lunacy: Moon, Text, and Vision in Fitt XVIII	355
19.	**Anne Baden-Daintree** – *Delyt* and Desire: Ways of Seeing in *Pearl*	380
20.	**David Coley** – Fitt XX – "Paye"	400

"Innoghe": A Preface on Inexhaustibility

Karl Steel

We know that *Pearl* offers a picture of the "more and more" of God's grace. It gifts us with an extra stanza, 101 where we expected 100, as a formal sign that God is "never the lesse" (Fitt XV), always more than we could expect. *Pearl* tells us that God's infinite grace can never be used up, emptied, or satisfied, while also reminding us that, at least for now, we had better learn to be satisfied with our side of the river.[i] *Pearl* sees merely commercial economies, represented so neatly by the grieving jeweler, break open to make way for an unending generosity. *Pearl* teaches us that life, at its best, is anything but fair, and thank goodness for that.[ii]

Pearl gives us two ways of not being satisfied, then, the one insufficient, the other beyond sufficiency. We have the *dissatisfaction* of the jeweler, greedy, malcontent, jealous, sad at the death of what might be his daughter, marked as his only by his *not* having her, more than a bit envious that she's made such a good match; and then there's God's infinite *unsatisfiability*, always able to do more than what's required, always exceeding what's on order, whose eternal grace can keep on coming, because it's its own cause, its own power, its own necessity.[1]

---

[1] Anselm of Canterbury, *Cur Deus Homo*, Chapter V, in a dizzying attempt to save God from having something so compulsory as a *motive*: "God does nothing of necessity, since nothing whatever can coerce or restrain him in his actions. And when we say that God does something by necessity, as it were, of avoiding dishonor–which, in any case, he need not fear–it is better to interpret this as meaning that he does it from the necessity of preserving his honor. Now this necessity is nothing but his own changeless honor, which he has from himself and not from another, and on that account it is improper to call it necessity." In Eugene Fairweather, ed. and trans., *A Scholastic Miscellany: Anselm to Ockham* (Philadelphia: Westminster Press, 1956), 150. Also see Aquinas, *Summa Theologica,* http://www.newadvent.org/summa/2112.htm, 1a 2ae 112 art 1, "Is God alone the efficient cause of

But for a fuller picture of God's unsatisfiability, we must take another trip to the otherworld, travelling in the other direction: this guide also hails from the late fourteenth century, the Middle English translation of the *Vision of Tundale*, a representative medieval bestseller if ever there was one, with some 150 Latin manuscripts and translations into at least 12 other vernaculars. Tundale's a wicked Irish merchant, keen on collecting debts, who, after falling into a coma, travels first to hell and then, more briefly, into heaven. God's mercy, the vision says, "passud all thynge" (39; 813), while the demons, watching Tundale elude their grasp, complain that God "schuldust reward sone / Ylke mon aftur that he hathe done" (275-6), that God, in other words, should just do the right thing, and only that. God being God of course does more. The deeper Tundale's infernal journey, the deeper the pain: "That peyn hym thoght well more semand / Then all the peynus that he byforyn fand / That peyn passyd all odur peynus" (403-5; see also 760-64), and the more he encounters "sowlys in peyn withowttyn ende" (1128), "in peyn endles" (1163), who can do nothing but cry "welaway" (462; 1130), who can suffer "yett myght thei not fully dye" (1080).[2]

As might be expected, the justice of this unending punishment needed justification. Hugh of St Victor's *De sacramentis* explains that since sinners wanted to sin without end, they should be punished according to their will; while Aquinas heaps up a jumble of reasons, including that sin "offends God Who is infinite," and since "punishment cannot be infinite in intensity, because the creature is incapable of an infinite quality, it must needs be infinite at least in duration [requiritur quod sit saltem duratione infinita]."[3] Here, presumably, the antecedent, the unstated *it* of the Latin present

---

grace?," "Nothing can act beyond its species, since the cause must always be more powerful than its effect. Now the gift of grace surpasses every capability of created nature, since it is nothing short of a partaking of the Divine Nature, which exceeds every other nature. And thus it is impossible that any creature should cause grace."

[2] *Three Purgatory Poems: The Gast of Gy, Sir Owain, The Vision of Tundale*, ed. Edward E. Foster (Kalamazoo, MI: Medieval Institute Publications, 2004).

[3] Hugh of Saint Victor, *On the Sacraments of the Christian Faith* (*De Sacramentis*), trans. Roy J. Deferrari (Cambridge, MA: Mediaeval Academy of America, 1951), 468. Aquinas, *Summa Theologica*, ss 99, Art. 1, "By Divine justice, is an eternal punishment inflicted on sinners?" http://www.newadvent.org/summa/5099.htm.

subjunctive verb "sit," refers to the duration of both punishment *and* sinner, who endures without ever *fully* dying.[iii]

The same door that opens to infinite mercy also opens to infinite suffering: God is the sovereign, whose unregulated, self-generated goodness at once establishes and suspends the order of justice, with everything that follows from that.[4] But this operation, which, essentially, flips or reverse engineers Schmitt's *Political Theology* away from the secular and back towards the theological, makes God human, just as awesome and frightening as any other king.

God's inhuman infinity requires that we not be satisfied with that. To grasp God's *inhuman horror* more fully, we have to get him off his throne and sense the impossible, how he's invisibly and impalpably everywhere. God's time is beyond ours; his order beyond ours; his realm one that none of us, at least not here, can penetrate fully: you remember what happens to the *Pearl*-dreamer when he tries, in his frenzy, to slip across the river, while Tundale just as badly fails in trying to get into the furthest reaches of heaven. God offers a chance to get totally inhuman. He's so much more than a sovereign. He–or the divine it–operates at a scale that no human action, no human conceptualization, could ever satisfy. And yet this It still takes an interest, condemning us or saving us according to its own unlimited schedule, far beyond anything that we could think just.

Timothy Morton's *Hyperobjects*, on the topic of Very Large Finitudes, says that there's "a real sense in which it is far easier to conceive of 'forever' than very large finitude. Forever makes you feel important. One hundred thousand years makes you wonder whether you can imagine one hundred thousand anything."[5] A counterproposal: what the afterlife tells us is that our actions have consequences far beyond anything we could ever imagine. Something out there is taking an interest, disproportionate to our comprehension, but proportionate to Its own, rewarding or

---

[4] Carl Schmitt, *Political Theology: Four Chapters on the Concept of Sovereignty*, trans. George Schwab (Chicago: University of Chicago Press, 2005), 36, famously, "The exception in jurisprudence is analogous to the miracle in theology."

[5] Timothy Morton, *Hyperobjects: Philosophy and Ecology After the End of the World* (Minneapolis: University of Minnesota Press, 2013), Kindle location 1095.

condemning us according to calculations that we will enjoy, or suffer, undergoing without understanding, and—given that this is an eternity—without ever giving us an out. Without ever being satisfied that we will have done enough for It, in It.[iv]

Karl Steel is assistant professor English at Brooklyn College and the Graduate Center, CUNY. The author of *How to Make a Human: Animals and Violence in the Middle Ages* (Ohio State UP, 2011), more recent projects are on oysters, pets, feral children, and the cultural afterlife of Vikings among white supremacists. His website is www.medievalkarl.com. @karlsteel

End-notes (on commentary) by Nicola Masciandaro:
[i] This structural tension in the poem, between inexhaustibility and sufficiency, is analogous to the marginal situation of commentary, just as the dramatic encounter between dreamer-poet and Pearl Maiden takes place paradoxically by means of an impassible boundary, the river that flows–impossibly–between the incommensurable realms of time and eternity:

British Library MS Cotton Nero A.x., f. 38r (public domain image)

This commentarial correlation between the form and content of *Pearl*, between the drama of its dialectical narrative and the poetic production of the dream-vision as an expanding exegetical gloss on "that specyal spyce" (l. 938) of the Pearl, is captured in the deictic gestures of the Dreamer in the sequence of illustrations preceding the text. (On the phenomenological relation between commentary and spice/species, see Nicola Masciandaro, "Becoming Spice: Commentary as Geophilosophy," *Collapse VI: Geo/Philosophy* [2010]: 20-56). These manicular gestures, as Robert J. Blanch and Julian N. Wasserman observe, "narrate pictorially the Dreamer's psychological movement from receptiveness, to foolish error, to repentance" (*From Pearl to Gawain: Forme to Fynisment* [Gainesville, FL: University Press of Florida, 1995], 87). As such, they point the reader into participation with the difficult hermeneutic movement of the dream-vision towards divine grace, a movement passing by necessity through the twin sorrows, affective and intellectual, of grief and ignorance. As the real and symbolic organ of this movement, the indicating hand, in its figural capacity to enter the river which the Dreamer cannot, to perhaps be enough in the face of its own insufficiency, no less reflects the inexhaustible "grace of hermeneutics" defined by Michael Edward Moore "an experience of plenitude in the depths of reading" ("The Grace of Hermeneutics," *Glossator 5: On the Love of Commentary* [2011]: 163). In these terms, the paradox of divine grace, at once a too-much that seems never enough and a never-enough that seems too much, manifests in the form and process of that which seeks to understand and interpret it. Specifically, grace appears in commentary's plenitude or *copia* vis-à-vis its text and in the generativity of its error or wandering. Commentary strays, goes too far, says too much, but along a turning path that always finds a new way back into the unpossessable object of its attention and love, so that the voice of what possesses it may speak–before the end of time–a "A note ful new" (l. 879).

[ii] Life is not fair. But is it (not) beautiful, *fair*? This is a good question to pose to commentary as a form whose meaning and appeal are conspicuously in excess of its own content. As Nietzsche said, "All our so-called consciousness is a more or less fantastic commentary on an unknown, perhaps unknowable, but felt text" (Friedrich Nietzsche, *Daybreak: Thoughts on the Prejudices of Morality*, ed. Maudemarie Clark and Brian Leiter [Cambridge: Cambridge University Press, 1997], 78).

[iii] The principle of commentarial *copia* (on which see Hans Ulrich Gumbrecht, *The Powers of Philology* [Urbana: University of Illinois Press, 2003], 41-53) is thus also instanced by the doctrine of eternal hell, just as the impossible perfection of commentarial plenitude would be an infinite commentary on an infinitesimal text. Unable to satisfy divine justice in an immediate way, the damned soul suffers its sin *ad infinitum*, becoming a kind of endless commentary paradoxically deprived forever of the real presence of the eternal truth which its suffering glosses, as per the Dantean *contrapasso*, in which the nature of eternal justice is disclosed to the observer: "Così

s'osserva in me lo contrapasso" (*Inferno* 28.142). Correlatively, Augustine, commenting on John 5:25 ("he who hears my word and believes him who sent me, has eternal life"), envisions perfected being as final, face-to-face understanding of the original Word without gloss: "The fruit of faith [is] understanding, so that we may arrive at eternal life, where the Gospel would not be read to us, but he who has given us the Gospel now would appear with all the pages of reading and the voice of the reader and commentator removed" (*Tractates on the Gospel of John*, 22.2, quoted in Henri de Lubac, *Medieval Exegesis: The Four Senses of Scripture*, trans. E. M. Macierowski, 4 vols. [Grand Rapids, MI: Eedmans, 2000], 2.188-89).

iv Likewise, the commentator experiences (suffers and enjoys) insufficiency as the mysterious medium of satisfaction. This is more in keeping with the order of mystical theology than soteriology, according to which the essential hiddenness of God, in proportion to the infinity of spiritual desire, is the very condition of intimacy or union with the divine. Thus Mechthild of Magdeburg exclaims, "O blissful Estrangement from God, how lovingly am I connected with you!" (*The Flowing Light of the Godhead*, trans. Frank Tobin [New York: Paulist Press, 1998], 4.12). Augustine clarifies this paradox by pointing out that the presence of one's beloved does not diminish longing: "When we love another, even when we can see that person, we never tire of the presence of the beloved, but want him or her to be present always. This is what the psalm conveys by the words, *Seek his face always* [Psalm 104.4]: let not the finding of the beloved put an end to the love-inspired search; but as love grows, so let the search for the one already found become more intense" (Augustine, *Expositions of the Psalms*, trans. Maria Boulding, 6 vols. [Hyde Park, NY: New City Press, 2003], 5.186). And Eriugena elaborates upon this endless end in a manner that accentuates its sense of inevitable impossibility: "since that which human nature seeks and toward which it tends, whether it moves in the right or the wrong direction, is infinite and not to be comprehended by any creature, it necessarily follows that its quest is unending and that therefore it moves forever. And yet although its search is unending, by some miraculous means it finds what it is seeking for: and again it does not find it, for it cannot be found" (Johannes Scottus Eriugena, *Periphyseon*, PL 122:919, quoted in Bernard McGinn, *The Growth of Mysticism: Gregory the Great through the 12th Century* [New York: Crossroad, 1994], 118). Similarly, it is only through the Pearl's absence that the poet and his readers in turn become capable of being present to what she truly and really is—whatever she is—even and precisely if this capacity persists in a sufficiency that is never enough, across the time and space of a dreamy truth or visionary *if* as difficult as it is consoling:

> If hit be veray and soth sermoun
> That thou so stykes in garlande gay,
> So wel is me in thys doel-doungoun
> That thou art to that Pryses paye.
>   (1185-8)

I

THE ARBOR AND THE PEARL: ENCAPSULATING MEANING IN "SPOT"

William M. Storm

In 1955, Charles Moorman worried that "possible allusions to the Roman de la Rose, Boccaccio, Chaucer, Dante, and the Vulgate and utilizing possibly heretical theology, the medieval dream-vision, the elegy, and the *debat*" make *Pearl* "a critic's land of heart's desire," resulting in criticism that is varied, even contradictory, eventually becoming a "scholarly free-for-all."[1] *Pearl* has been read as allegorical,[2] parabolic,[3] and elegiac.[4] Other readings have focused on the poem as an image of the medieval church[5] or the medieval universe.[6] In addition, critics have seen the poem as an exploration of theology and aristocratic modes of worship.[7] And, *Pearl* has been

---

[1] Charles Moorman, "The Role of the Narrator in *Pearl*," *Modern Philology*, Vol. 53, no. 2 (1955), 73-81 (p. 73).
[2] D.W. Robertson, Jr., "The *Pearl* as a Symbol," *Modern Language Notes*, Vol. 65, no. 3 (1950), pp. 155-161; Priscilla Martin, "Allegory and Symbolism," *A Companion to the Gawain-Poet*, Arthurian Studies XXXVIII, eds. Derek Brewer and Jonathan Gibson, (Cambridge, U.K.: D.S. Brewer, 1997/2007), pp. 315-328.
[3] J. Allan Mitchell, "The Middle English *Pearl*: Figuring the Unifigurable," *The Chaucer Review*, Vol. 35, no. 1, pp. 86-111.
[4] Oscar Cargill and Margaret Schlauch, "The Pearl and Its Jeweler," *PMLA*, Vol. 43, No. 1 (1928), pp. 105-123.
[5] Ann R. Meyer, *Medieval Allegory and the Building of the New Jerusalem*, (Cambridge, U.K.: D.S. Brewer, 2003).
[6] Edward I. Condren, *The Numerical Universe of the* Gawain-Pearl *Poet*, (Gainseville: University of Florida Press, 2002).
[7] D.W. Robertson, "The 'Heresy' of *Pearl*," *Modern Language Notes*, Vol. 65, No. 3 (1950, pp. 152-155; Lawrence M. Clopper, "The God of the *Gawain-Poet*," *Modern Philology*, Vol. 94, No. 1 (1996), pp. 1-18; Lawrence Beaston, "The *Pearl*-Poet and the Pelagians," *Religion and Literature*, Vol. 36, No. 1 (2004), pp. 15-38; David Aers, "Christianity for Courtly Subjects: Reflections on the Gawain-Poet," *A Companion to the Gawain-Poet*, Arthurian

viewed as a poem on the nature of language use.[8] These readings are not exclusionary, fitting under the multiple headings that I listed and others I have not listed. Undoubtedly we might add to this list, bringing to light other readings of the meaning of *Pearl*. I do not intend to present a proscriptive reading of *Pearl* in this essay; in fact, I believe that the above readings will not be necessarily invalidated by this discussion.

Pearl is a poem of consolation, and it is a poem of theological concerns. It is also a poem that plays with language's imprecision; in addition, *Pearl* speaks to historical concerns and social upheaval. The poem provides a series of discussions between a bereaved Jeweler and heavenly-sanctioned instructress that allows readers to come to disparate, sometimes wildly disparate, interpretations. But this is also a poem of place, three specific places–the 'erber grene,' the paradisal garden, and the New Jerusalem–surrounded by sections of debate and instruction. What I would like to consider is how the arbor, the 'spotte' of the first section, institutes a conception of place that allows for various interpretations of the poem. But before the discussion of spot and arbor, I would like to consider the nature of Pearl and its/her relationship to the Jeweler, a relationship that will illustrate the complexities of reading the poem that might inspire such vastly different readings.

Pearl and the Jeweler

The first nine lines of the poem focuses the reader's attention on not only the subject matter of the poem but also the shifting qualities of that central item, the pearl:

Studies XXXVIII, eds. Derek Brewer and Jonathan Gibson, (Cambridge, U.K.: D.S. Brewer, 1997/2007), pp. 91-101; Jennifer Garrison, "Liturgy and Loss: Pearl and the Ritual Reform of the Aristocratic Subject," *The Chaucer Review*, Vol. 44, No. 3 (2010) pp. 294-322.

[8] Theodore Bogdanos, *Pearl: Image of the Ineffable. A Study in Medieval Poetic Symbolism*, (University Park, PA: Pennsylvania State University Press, 1983); Catherine Cox, "*Pearl's* Precios Pere: Gender, Language, and Difference," *The Chaucer Review*, Vol. 32, No. 4 (1998), pp. 377-390; David N. DeVries, "Unde Dicitur: Observations on the Poetic Distinctiones of the *Pearl*-Poet," *The Chaucer Review*, Vol. 35, No. 1, 2000, pp.115-132; Tim William Machan, "Writing the Failure of Speech in Pearl," *New Directions in Oral Theory*, Ed. Mark C. Amodio, (Tempe, AZ: Arizona Center for Medieval and Renaissance Studies, 2005), pp. 279-305.

> Perle, plesaunte to prynces paye
> To clanly clos in golde so clere,
> Oute of Oryent, I hardyly saye,
> Ne proved I never her precios pere.
> So rounde, so reken in uche araye,
> So smal, so smothe her sydez were,
> Queresoever I jugged gemmes gaye
> I sette hyr sengeley in synglure.
> Allas, I leste hyr in on erbere;
> (ll. 1-9)

These lines demonstrate the uniqueness of Pearl, and how in the Jeweler's career, he never found her equal. This specific use of language, the idea of "precios pere" and "sette . . . sengeley in synglure," enforces the Pearl's image as a transcendent being, as she was without equal and was set apart from the finest jewels. The Jeweler, though bereft of joy, recalls specific facts and the order of Pearl's makeup: "so rounde, so reken . . . so small, so smoþe." The order of his description reminds the reader of his profession as a jeweler; he starts with an overall impression of her shape and lovely appearance, moving to the minuter feature of her smallness and smoothness of sides, qualities that would show best under the focus of his loupe.

The opening description of the pearl, though, seems not to offer much beyond "very general terms, clos in gold and sette; the virtue of the pearl as a stone is described only in aesthetic and moral terms."[9] What color is a pearl? Pearls, one might answer, are an off-white color, something like ecru. But a pearl's color is just a reflection, as pearls are composed of layers of a translucent compound that reflect all the spectrum's colors. A pearl, in essence, contains all colors, just like white light, and reflects those colors back to the eyes. By containing all the colors, the pearl is pure light, and, by the criteria of St. Bonaventure, a perfect symbol for a soul. The use of a pearl in this context offers layered meaning, "pearls also existed as the common property of the iconography of heaven . . . [and] Pearls were always already traditional point of commerce

---

[9] Tony Davenport, "Jewels and Jewelers in *Pearl*," *The Review of English Studies*, New Series, Vol. 59, No. 241 (2008), pp. 508-520, at p. 511.

between the earthly and the heavenly."[10] *The Peterborough Lapidary* describes a pearl or *margarita*, as the "chef of al stons þat ben wyȝt & preciosse," which bring comfort because "it clensep him of superfluite of humours."[11] But the pearl of the poem is not simply a gem; "the gem must stand for something which the poet could represent as a pearl and at the same time as a maiden who had died in infancy and had been redeemed by Christ."[12]

Even the description of the pearl could be seen as "appropriate mainly to a precious stone, but the second both to a precious stone and to a girl (with sydez meaning 'flanks')."[13] The physicality of the description—we might imagine the Jeweler acting out the process of holding the pearl as he recounts her dimensions—speaks to the poem's "incarnational aesthetic, which is expressed through sensory imagery that culminates in a highly literalized vision of Jerusalem, is founded, in a haunting and recapitulative poetic, on a human body, and even more exactly, on a lost human body."[14] This body, of course, is "without spot," which could equally relate to issues of purity, including virginity.[15] Unlike the more defined jewels of the New Jerusalem, with meanings well-established in the lapidaries and in Biblical exegesis, the image of the pearl allows for "a strange origin combining natural processes with a sense of mystery and evanescence, and in its roundness and whiteness providing ideas of perfection of form and purity of colour."[16]

---

[10] Allen J. Fletcher, "Reading Radical Metonymy in Pearl," *Sacred and Secular in Medieval and Early Modern Cultures*, ed. Lawrence Besserman (New York: Palgrave, 2006) pp. 47-61 at p.55.
[11] *The Peterborough Lapidary, English Medieval Lapidaries*, eds. John Evans and Mary S. Serjeantson (London: Early English Text Series, 1933), pp. 63-118, at pp. 107 and 108.
[12] Marie Padgett Hamilton, "The Meaning of the Middle English *Pearl*," *PMLA*, Vol. 70, No. 4 (1955), pp. 805-824, at p. 805.
[13] A.C. Spearing, "Symbolic and Dramatic Development in *Pearl*," *Modern Philology*, Vol. 60, No. 1 (1962), pp. 1-12, at p. 3.
[14] Sarah Stanbury, "The Body and the City in *Pearl*," *Representations*, No. 48 (1994), pp. 30-47, at p. 37
[15] Nicholas Watson, "The *Gawain*-Poet as a Vernacular Theologian," *A Companion to the Gawain-Poet*, Arthurian Studies XXXVIII, eds. Derek Brewer and Jonathan Gibson, (Cambridge, U.K.: D.S. Brewer, 1997/2007), pp. 293-313.
[16] Davenport, "Jewels and the Jeweler in *Pearl*," p. 519.

Of course, this use of pearl brings up a number of meanings: "The symbol of the Pearl may be thought of on four levels. Literally, the Pearl is a gem. Allegorically, as the maiden of the poem, it represents those members of the Church who will be among the "hundred "in the celestial procession, the perfectly innocent. Tropologically, the Pearl is a symbol of the soul that attains innocence through true penance and all that such penance implies. Anagogically, it is the life of innocence in the Celestial City."[17] So for readers, we can be struck by the physical, economic, or spiritual qualities of the pearl. We might even hold all these ideas at once, or simply focus on one quality.

Such ideas might also be found with the jeweler who describes this missing pearl. The jeweler can be variously identified as an "appraiser of jewels, the retailer in precious gems, and the craftsman who cut and set them," which was not yet a guild within London's mercantile society, with jewelers found primarily on the continent.[18] The Jeweler's presence allows readers to make a series of connections, both theologically and economically. On the one hand, "God reassembles or recasts us a statute is reforged or as a jeweler, making a mosaic, puts the stones back together again,"[19] drawing reader's attentions to the conceptions of spiritual values of jewels and images of God within the framework of the poem. In fact, we might locate the biblical antecedents of our jeweler; "The 'jueler' referred to is the negotiator of Matt. 13. 45-46, who sold all of his jewels for a pearl of great price."[20] But there is also the economic value of having a jeweler appraising and searching for a lost commodity. Not only is the jeweler a primary figure within the poem, the "language of the jeweler's craft and trade precedes"[21] any other language within the poem. It is our first image, and so it immediately establishes the frame of reference for the remainder of the poem. Here, the Jeweler can evaluate not only the worth or *prys* of pearl, he can do so within a framework of some objective qualifications, which seem to

---

[17] Robertson, "The Pearl as a Symbol," p. 160.
[18] John M. Bowers, *The Politics of Pearl: Court Poetry in the Age of Richard II*, (Cambridge, U.K.: D.S. Brewer: Cambridge, 2001), p. 103.
[19] Caroline Walker Bynum, *The Resurrection of the Body in Western Christianity, 200-1336*, (New York: Columbia University Press, 1995), p. 30.
[20] Robertson, "The Pearl as Symbol," p. 158.
[21] Felicity Riddy, "Jewels in *Pearl*," *A Companion to the Gawain-Poet*, Arthurian Studies XXXVIII, eds. Derek Brewer and Jonathan Gibson, (Cambridge, U.K.: D.S. Brewer, 1997/2007), pp. 143-155, at p. 145.

increase his personal attachment to the item.[22] Even though the Jeweler may claim a personal relationship to the pearl, the use of a Jeweler forces larger, societal implications into the poem, aligning this figure with a "craft that had maintained a strong reciprocal relationship with the king, one redounding to the benefit of both parties, patron and artists alike."[23] The immediate description of pearl "in the first four lines, is an economic function."[24] This notion of aristocratic concerns allows that "*Pearl*'s use of the phrase "prynces paye" in both the opening stanza and the closing section demonstrates that royal and divine power both require individuals to subject their own desires to external judgment."[25] But this definition of the Jeweler as an actual jeweler presents issues too, not least of which is ownership; "Jewelers do not own jewels, or at least not permanently: jewels pass through their hands…brilliantly catches the temporariness of the relation between parent and dead child, as well as the latter's preciousness. The representation of the dead child as a pearl at the very beginning of the poem thus sets up a language that is used throughout to address ideas of human preciousness, value and loss."[26]

Thus far, we have seen that the pearl can stand for theological, spiritual, and economic values. At the same time, it might also be a metaphor for a deceased body. Then there is the jeweler who might be an actual jeweler, though he does not describe any technical terms and seems not to understand the transitory value of his position; or the jeweler might simply be a stock, biblical figure. These ideas are, once more, not exclusive readings. I believe that these first nine lines of the poem speak to issues that can be seen throughout the remaining 1203 lines of the poem; in fact, through the use of "pearl as the controlling image of the poem, the poet sets

---

[22] Nick Davis, "Narrative Form and Insight," *A Companion to the Gawain-Poet*, Arthurian Studies XXXVIII, eds. Derek Brewer and Jonathan Gibson, (Cambridge, U.K.: D.S. Brewer, 1997/2007), pp. 329-349, at p. 343.
[23] Bowers, *The Politics of Pearl*, p. 105.
[24] DeVries, "Unde Dicitur: Observations on the Poetic Distinctiones of the *Pearl*-Poet," p. 121.
[25] Garrison, "Liturgy and Loss: Pearl and the Ritual Reform of the Aristocratic Subject," p. 315.
[26] Riddy, "Jewels in Pearl," p. 145.

up in the reader's mind a willingness to believe in the fact of multiple meanings."[27]

Initial Spots of *Pearl*

In the first six stanzas of the poem, the *Pearl*-poet uses "spot," "spote," or "spotte" on ten separate occasions that fall into two categories: construction of interiority and construction of moral landscape. Line twelve, the first appearance of spot, reads: "Of þat pryuy perle wythouten spot"; a use repeated in line 24, "My privy perle wythouten spotte." "Privy," whose meaning is best approximated to the modern word "private," establishes a concept of possession and ownership; not only a physical ownership, but one that is internalized by the emotional and alliterative connection to Pearl. The uses of "privy" in Middle English vary: secret, concealed, confidential; private, personal, peculiar; unseen, invisible, imperceptible; and having to do with sex or procreation.[28] This use of "privy" in *Pearl* sets up a dichotomy between that which is personal and that which is public. The Jeweler's Pearl is not open for public consumption; it is only to be found in a kind of "domestic space," circumscribed by what readers imagine to be ivy covered trellises or walls of the arbor.[29] This idea of private consumption belies the ever-present issue that the Jeweler appears to be the least qualified person to understand fully the complexities of the Pearl. "Privy" also relates to the most intimate of human connections: the family, strengthening the idea of a father-daughter relationship. The first section also contains the construction of a moral landscape: "Syþen in þat spote hit fro me sprange" (ln. 13); "Þat spot of spysez mot nedeȝ sprede" (ln. 25). This use establishes a moral sphere of action; here, moral is used in the sense of perceptual or psychological. It is only in this spot, that of the arbor, where the Jeweler feels at peace, and it is only in this spot where he feels he can do anything. It is a landscape that allows him to live, though the Jeweler's life does not appear to extend further than this arbor. In fact, this initial conception of "privy" might be viewed in terms of

---

[27] Sylvia Tomasch, "A *Pearl* Punnology," *The Journal of English and Germanic Philology*, Vol. 88, No. 1 (1989), pp. 1-20, at p. 2.
[28] *Middle English Dictionary,* Part 7. Ed. Sherman M. Kuhn (Michigan UP, 1983), pp.1331-1334.
[29] Georges Duby, ed., *A History of Private Life*, Vol. 2, trans. Arthur Goldhammer (Belknap 1988), p.7.

the larger project of the poem: "*Pearl* does not let the public, outside world into the Dreamer's dream, which in the Pearl poet's case is wholly concerned with the Dreamer's own private crisis and its relationship to the Christian truths that are recorded in the Bible."[30] Of course, the very image of the pearl might complicate such a view, as "*Pearl*, in its luminescent, reflective structure and text, with its specular, saintlike intercessorial guide, is intended, I think, to serve as one of those mirrors for the *Pearl* audience."[31]

While "privy" establishes interiority and morality, spot, too, can be connected to blemishing and morality.[32] Critics maintain that the poem contains an intricate play "on *spot*, or *withouten spot*" to indicate Pearl's purity as well as a marker of the place of loss.[33] This use of with and without also "increases the possibility of a pun."[34] Complicating these well-established ideas, "spot" is but a deictic placeholder. It is a word that asks to have other words and concepts substituted for it. If taken in a strictly geometrical perspective, spot lacks dimension; in other words, spot needs a referent to establish both meaning and location. So how can there be two spots together or a spot without a spot? And the spot most often referred to is the pearl, which is itself, the poet claims, without a spot. What I refer to here is the problem of locating places of meaning—yes, spot seems to reference a specific piece of ground—but the qualities (physical and spiritual) of that location, and the physical construction of that location need clarification that the opening fails to address.

But a pearl is by its very nature round and difficult to grasp, as the Jeweler comes to find out. This inability literally to grasp the pearl can be equated easily with the idea of ineffability, the inability to grasp language for purposes of description. Just as the Jeweler cannot grasp Pearl neither can he properly describe it. There are similarly promising thoughts that note a "wholly semantic" dualism

---

[30] Sandra Pierson Prior, *The Pearl Poet Revisited*, Twayne's English Author Series No. 512, (New York: Twayne Publishers, 1994), p. 15.
[31] Josephine Bloomfield, "Aristotelian Luminescence, Thomistic Charity: Vision, Reflection, and Self-Love in Pearl," *Studies in Philology*, Vol. 108, Iss. 2, 2000, pp. 165-188, at p. 188.
[32] DeVries, "*Unde Dictur*: Observations on the Poetic *Distinctiones* of the *Pearl*-poet," p. 128.
[33] Stanbury, "The Body and City in *Pearl*," p. 39.
[34] Tomasch, "A *Pearl* Punnology," p.9.

of "spot," which simply refer to "defect" or "place."[35] Yet even by promising a complex play and duality, "spot" is still regarded by critics only as "place of stain and morality."[36] *Pearl*, I would like to suggest, manipulates the very language of space and place to construct and visualize an eschatological architecture, both the formation of an afterlife but also an architecture that promotes thoughts of the afterlife.

If spot is a marker of place, then what does it describe? "Spot's" use wants for specificity. The poet offers readers a seemingly serene landscape of a small arbor, and that arbor, ostensibly, fits into long-established modes of geographical description. Ralph Elliot believes that the poem never gives full weight to descriptions of place and space, relying rather on "topographical formulae and enumeration," which is a by-product of the metrical construction of the poem, resulting in "traditional *description loci*."[37]

Spot, with respect to place, seems to refer to the very place where the pearl was initially lost. Aiding the view of spot as place marker is spot's accompaniment by the qualifying "þat." Spot and "that" are inexorably intertwined, and translations of line 61, "Fro spot . . ." [From that spot] remarry spot and that. Joined by the demonstrative pronoun, "that," spot is a deictic gesture, pointing to the place where the Pearl was lost. The use of "that" adds "concreteness" to spot.[38] But the use of "that" denotes the speaker's spatial separation from the spot. Furthering this disconnect from the spot and the speaker, all actions that take place at the "spot" occurred in the past, which is noted by the use of the preterite. The speaker is removed from the spot by not only location but by time. How is it that he can refer to that spot when he is no longer there? His presence at the spot assures a proper description of the place, and yet his very description of the place promotes the idea that he is truly absent. Through his description and his feelings, readers can

---

[35] Morton Donner, "Word Play and Word Form in *Pearl*" in *The Chaucer Review*, Vol. 24, No. 2 (1989), pp. 322-331, at p. 323.
[36] W.A. Davenport, *The Art of the Gawain Poet*, (London, 1978), p.11.
[37] Ralph Elliot, "Landscape and Geography," *A Companion to the Gawain-Poet, Arthurian Studies* XXXVIII, eds. Derek Brewer and Jonathan Gibson, (Cambridge, U.K.: D.S. Brewer, 1997/2007), pp. 105-117, at p. 111.
[38] S.L. Clark and Julian Wasserman, "The Spatial Argument of *Pearl*: Perspectives on a Venerable Bead," *Interpretations*, Vol. 11, No. 1 (1979), pp. 1-12, at p. 5.

sense that he is emotionally tied to the place though not corporeally present.

The suspicion that the Jeweler is no longer at the spot has greater implications than scholars have considered previously. The acceptance of "spot" as marker of place and morality signals an understandable recognition of "that spot" being that spot within the arbor–that arbor where Pearl is buried. If that spot is indeed "the spot," then one can refer to it as a fixed temporal-spatial point of both physical and emotional importance. But what if spot cannot be fixed? What if, as noted above, the Jeweler appears to be removed from that spot?

As noted above, "spot" might simply refer to place; it is, as it were, a placeholder. This place, for the Jeweler, is the spot where he lost his valuable pearl. "Spot" is a word that wants for a degree of specificity; due to this ambiguity of "spot," it is not so difficult to see "spot" as a word that can be substituted for other words and other concepts. When we read spot, we substitute "arbor" for spot. We can also substitute "grave" for spot, and there is also the idea of "emotional loss" that can be read when "spot" appears. These various "spots" of meaning all have a seemingly logical place in the text. Substituting these concepts for "spot" works well because readers have the Jeweler as the guarantor of their validity. The Jeweler, however, is not present at the spot any more. While purporting to be present, he is truly absent. "Spot," at its very center of meaning, has a multitude of binaries. It is reasonable to assert that spot most assuredly relates to presence, because readers, just as the Jeweler and critics have, can reasonably point to that spot as the one where Pearl was lost. The absence of the Jeweler allows for "spot" to then become more acquainted with absence rather than presence. If this binary, that of presence/absence is inverted, then what, and who, is to say that all binaries are not inverted? This small point of "spot" speaks to concerns within the poem to use language to instruct. Spot also locates the larger issue of language's ability to enclose meaning in one spot, to inhibit it from deferring to other locations. Such concerns over actual location are not shared within the poem, "if the Dreamer fears that his pearl may have been "spotted" by her death, he never seems to doubt that she is, indeed, in the "spot" where he left her."[39] This description of the spot speaks to language use that borders between what is and what is not. When describing heaven the Jeweler must use the language of man, when describing life he must use the language of man, when describing this sacred space of the arbor he must use the language of man. And so we must be readily able to understand how he uses his language, the very words of space and place, to try and approach most nearly the language of the Divine.

We use language daily to orient ourselves, including the word and concept of spot, as a means to define one's own location. Geometrical concepts are well founded in the *Pearl* manuscript. For example, the pentangle on Gawain's shield, signifying that Gawain was "ay faithful in five and sere fyue syþez, / Gawan watz for gode knawen" (ll. 632-633). Each point in the pentangle relates to a series of five ideals: five senses, five fingers, five wounds of Christ, five joys of the Virgin Mary, and the five virtues of Chivalry. These five points serve as rhetorical devices, as Gawain breaks each of these ideals, dissolving the symbolic star on his shield and his reputation. And so with the Gawain precedent, we may look at how the concept of spot/point applies to *Pearl*. A spot, in geometrical terms, is most nearly related to the concept of a point. But a point needs something else to be anything. Point needs other geometric figures to relate to, to be compared to, to have distance measured to, etc. A point, if only by itself, accomplishes nothing; it is a single entity in a geometric world of vast nothingness. It is technically there, but when existence depends on the existence of other entities–and without those other points and figures, existence is only a technicality–can that be truly classified as existence? Point, either singularly or as a part of a collective, lacks dimension. Yet even though it lacks this necessary quality, we always return to point. It is always a place of arrival and departure; and so it is with *Pearl*, the Jeweler's journey begins and ends with that spot, that point–that pearl, that arbor.

The Arbor of *Pearl*

Even though the Jeweler's use of spot suggests an inability of language to name and encapsulate, he still attempts to fix that spot to a location, naming it as "þat spot þat I in speche expoun / I entred

---

[39] Katherine Terrell, "Rethinking the 'Corse in clot': Cleanness, Filth, and Bodily Decay in *Pearl*," *Studies in Philology*, Vol. 105, No. 4 (2008), pp. 429-447, at p. 435.

in þat erber grene" (ll. 37-38). *Pearl* begins in a garden. This fact is suggestive on many levels, not least of which is the idea of beginnings. Gardens are a place of beginning, but also of loss, confusion, and error. This green arbor of *Pearl* relates to a multitude of tradition, as gardens are polyphyletic in origin. All scholarship will rightly point to the arbor of the first section and show how its construction relates to the Garden of Eden, the *hortus conclusus* of the Song of Solomon, and even a cemetery. Yet even though this simple arbor is but a human construct and it relates to these particular tropes, the Jeweler's arbor holds qualities that modify the accepted forms of medieval gardens. Before readers can interpret the polygenetic influence on this garden, one must note how the arbor is treated in the poem. The arbor, in *Pearl*, stands as a place of order, fruitlessness, and purpose. Due to its competing roles and traditions, the arbor becomes an example of a sacred place; due to this instability in meaning, the arbor oscillates into the sacred, becoming a launching spot for the Jeweler's journey into the very heart of New Jerusalem.

The Jeweler's arbor is remarkable, which seems appropriate given the uniqueness of Pearl. The arbor, too, is unique because of its connection to order. Building establishes a bulwark in the midst of a "primeval disorder."[40] This arbor may appear to lack a proper order in the sense of the grand, cultivated gardens of Europe, but this is all that remains to the Jeweler. If one looks at the first section of the poem, there is little mention of anything outside of the arbor experience. When the Jeweler recounts his trade, it is in the past tense. His former life–the pearl and his trade–is but a memory; the world has faded away, and all that remains to the Jeweler is a small, green arbor where he lost his Pearl.

An *erber* "ranged in application from 'kitchen-garden' and 'cottage-garden' to 'grass-plot' and 'pleasure-garden,'" and even orchard, which is best defined as a "'kitchen-garden, etc., with one or more fruit-trees."[41] The description of the "erber-grene" is vague, but the manuscript illustration shows "Along the foreground, plants for one border; two rows of plants and one or two trees marking off other borders, and converging towards the background from left and

---

[40] Yi-Fu Tuan, *Space and Place: The Perspective of Experience* (Minneapolis, 2005), p. 104.
[41] C.A. Luttrell, "*Pearl*: Symbolism in a Garden Setting," *Neophilologus*, Vol. 49, Iss. 1 (1965), pp. 160-176, at p. 161.

right, to indicate, by their recession, the shape as a square or a rectangle; a curve, by a form of perspective, defining the limits of the erber–and beyond it trees in the distance."[42] But an arbor, as defined above, depends upon growth, specifically fruitfulness. This garden, however, seems trapped in an ambivalent existence, between death and life. Critics have questioned the relation between life and death in the arbor, whether one springs from the other.[43] However important that question is, the important fact of the debate is that the two are quite evidently related, and leads us to ask what the interplay of these two apparently disparate concepts appears to say about nature, about the nature of creation, and about the nature of this particular sacred place. What the question of death and life illuminates is this idea of fruitfulness. The garden appears to be fruitful. The narrator claims that it is a "spot of spysez mot nedez sprede" (ln. 25). Other possible evidence of the fruitful nature of the arbor is in the mentioning of flowers: "Blomez blayke and blwe and rede / Per schyne ful schyr agayn þe sunne" (ll.27-28). The poet also notes that "Flor and fryte may not be fede / Per hit doun drof in moldeȝ dunne" (ll. 29-30). Every image that the poet provides reinforces the lack of fruitfulness of the arbor. When the pearl trundles down from the Jeweler's hand, it lands in dead grass, a place where life does not exist. This lost Pearl, though, appears to bring life back to the arbor.

The arbor is, however, fruitless. Even at the mention of fruit, there is no tangible fruit to be picked. This absence of produce is underscored by the idea that this action takes place during the harvest: "In Auguste in a hyȝ seysoun, /Quen corne is coruen wyth crokeȝ kene" (ll. 39-40). The very use of August is suggestive of the difficulty of locating meaning within the poem. Critics have posited a number of August festivals and Christian holidays as the proper "seysoun," which all have significance to the poem: the Assumption of the Virgin, when people "brought medicinal plants from their kitchen or infirmary gardens to that the healing power of the herbs might be sanctified"[44]; Lammastide, the year's first harvest festival

---

[42] Ibid., p. 164.
[43] Edward Vasta, "*Pearl*: Immortal Flowers and the Pearl's Decay" in *The Middle English* Pearl: *Critical Essays*, ed. John Conley (South Bend: Notre Dame University Press, 1970), pp.185-202.
[44] Elizabeth Petroff, "Landscape in *Pearl*: The Transformation of Nature," *The Chaucer Review*, Vol. 16, No. 2 (1981), pp. 181-193, at p. 181.

"when the days were filled with sports and games"[45]; or Feast of the Transfiguration which "agrees closely with that of the other images in the herber as a type and a symbol of the glory of the resurrection."[46] These festivals celebrate both change and bounty, and so questions must be asked of the change and bounty of the arbor. The arbor's fruitfulness is only secure when it comes to flowers. Flowers do not provide any sustenance, and they do not sustain life. These flowers imitate the generative power of nature, but these fall short of the power to give life. Additionally, the coincidence of both life and death reinforces the ambivalent nature of the Jeweler's new world. He cannot escape death in the arbor, because even there death and life are so interlaced that the one must, and does, proceed from the other, which calls to mind the ever-present expression of obsequies, which stems from the creation narrative in Genesis 2:7: "And the Lord God formed man of the dust of the ground, and breathed into his nostrils the breath of life; and man became a living soul."

While the arbor does not appear to be successful with bearing fruit, it does serve a very real purpose. As noted above, the Jeweler remains outside of the scope of real life. All of his interactions with humanity have occurred in the past, and there does not appear to be any rationale for him to go into society. His world is contained in the arbor. The arbor provides for him an altar, as it were, to uphold the memory of his departed Pearl. The narrator describes his expectations for that place, as "Ofte haf I wayted, wyschande þat wele, / Þat wont watz whyle deuoyde my wrange / And heuen my happe and al my hele" (ll. 14-16). This arbor serves the same function as a church, a place where one goes for comfort. This place serves as his altar, but it also serves as a symbol of his hope for his precious pearl to be returned to him. The Jeweler's arbor fails him, as it does not bring the Pearl back; rather, the arbor serves as the starting point for his ethereal journey to the very gates of Heaven, separated from Pearl by the river of Heaven. The arbor, in essence, becomes a sacred place, joining in that tradition with the Gardens of Eden and the *hortus conclusus* of the Song of Songs.

---

[45] Michael Olmert, "Game-Playing, Moral Purpose, and the Structure of *Pearl*," *The Chaucer Review*, Vol. 21, No. 3 (1987), pp. 383-403, at p. 395.

[46] William J. Knightley, "*Pearl:* The 'Hyȝ Seysoun,'" *Modern Language Notes*, Vol. 76, No. 2 (1961), pp. 97-102, at p. 100.

Symmetrically speaking, the journey of the Jeweler should begin in this small garden, this arbor, as the poem and the Jeweler attempt to create a space for his own understanding of life. This garden for "Competent fourteenth-century readers must have recognized the *erber(e)* as the Garden of Eden."[47] Such a place is not simply paradise but also the place of humanity's first fall. The medieval audience believed Eden was but a place waiting to be found. When one crossed over a mountain, there Eden might be found waiting.[48] Of course, this garden is also a place of loss for the Jeweler, as it is the place where Pearl is thrust into the cycle of life that involves death and decay. But it is not just that gardens would be associated with the Garden of Eden: "While heaven is to be much superior to the first paradise located in the Garden of Eden, in the later Middle Ages the difference seems to have been thought to be a matter of degree rather than kind."[49] In addition to the Garden of Eden, reader's thoughts must also travel to the garden from the Song of Solomon. Though the Jeweler's garden relates to both the Garden of Eden and the *hortus conclusus* of the Song of Solomon, the *Pearl*-poet's modifies the commonly known frames of meaning for gardens and other standard literary tropes. The poet's freedom for modification stems from the joining of traditions, allowing for a flexibility of interpretation and use.[50] In medieval literature, the dichotomy of forest and garden captures the divide between what was considered the domains of action for the sexes. Whereas the knight must enter the forest to perform a task, women are left to remain in the garden. When men are faced with the conquering of the incredible in the vast stretches of wild that dominate the landscape, women are forced into roles of waiting in the garden, a place formulated to "stimulate . . . through the presence of flowers, spices, and aromatic herbs."[51]

But for whom are the flowers and the spices in the Jeweler's arbor intended? The garden is "Þat spot of spysez mot nedez

---

[47] Hamilton, "The Meaning of the Middle English *Pearl*," p. 807.
[48] Elizabeth A. Augspach, *The Garden as Woman's Space in Twelfth- and Thirteenth- Century Literature* (Lewiston: Edwin Mellen, 2004), p. 12.
[49] J.T. Rhodes and Clifford Davidson, "The Garden of Paradise," *The Iconography of Heaven*, ed. Clifford Davidson, (Kalamazoo: Medieval Institute Publications, 1994), pp. 69-109, at p. 73.
[50] P. M. Kean, *The Peal: An Interpretation* (London, 1967), p.31.
[51] Augspach, *The Garden as Woman's Space in Twelfth- and Thirteenth- Century Literature*, p. 1.

sprede" (ln. 25) filled with "Blomeʒ blayke and blwe and rede / Þer schyne ful schyr agayn þe sunne" (ll. 27-28). The aromatic charms of the arbor are not to induce a woman into love, but for a man to forget of his life, a lethean draught. These spices work as a kind of incense, "substances that apparently in the late Middle Ages was believed to be most typical of the fragrance of heaven," allowing churches–and other sacred places–"true foreshadowing of heaven."[52] The smells of *Pearl*'s arbor stem from "plants that appear to be really dried spices, springing from the pearl, and flowering, with neither their medicinal nor spicing qualities brought out by the poem, but beauty and aroma, which is not synaesthetic, as if the narrator was seeing and smelling things by his sense of taste, are metaphoric, of healing properties."[53] The Maiden, too, becomes an example of this medicinal quality, as her presence as a healing balm is noted with her description as "þat special spyce" (ln. 235). The absence of other vegetation, especially notable of the harvest season, "suggests something else missing here–order and regularity."[54] The lack of actual vegetation reminds readers not that there is a lack of order, but that this space does not seem to conform to natural laws of English landscape. These are flowers and spices that are "divorced from season and geography, and [have] no place in physical dimensions."[55] These flowers and aromas draw the reader's attention that this place symbolizes a "higher reality . . .[suggesting] where to look for consolation."[56] The facts of the garden push the Jeweler to recognize the higher order and reality for consolation; however, his grief cannot allow any such perspective.

While aroma provides incentive for the garden, this fragrance may also act as a form of entrapment. A major concept of the *hortus conclusus* relates to the possessive nature of the garden, i.e., who controls the door of the garden. The arbor of *Pearl*, however, lacks the very tangible lock and key; rather, the arbor provides a perhaps weightier concept of control: life and death. Whereas the medieval romances emphasize control of every aspect of life, the Jeweler's

---

[52] Clifford Davidson, "Heaven's Fragrance," *The Iconography of Heaven*, ed. Clifford Davidson (Kalamazoo: Medieval Institute Publications, 1994), pp. 110-127, at pp. 111 and 119.
[53] Luttrell, "*Pearl:* Symbolism in a Garden Setting," p. 170
[54] Petroff, "Landscape in *Pearl*: The Transformation of Nature," p. 184.
[55] Luttrell, "*Pearl*: Symbolism in a Garden Setting," p. 170.
[56] Petroff, "Landscape in *Pearl:* The Transformation of Nature," p. 187

weightier concerns show how illusory the control of the *hortus conclusus* is. The Jeweler understands how death's, in fact God's, mastery supplants any idea of dominance that humanity can try to display. This arbor is also a place of enclosure: "a locus in which the jeweler's bereavement and longing for the pearl are isolated and concentrated."[57] Our Jeweler, Pearl's father, attempts to control the world around him. The actions of the Jeweler are to remove himself from the world, making a space for worship, for vigil of the absent Pearl. The poem, mimicking this propensity, presents a "series of enclosure images rang[ing] from the simply enclosures of bodies, boxes, chests, graves, houses and arks, which are microcosms of the larger enclosures of temples and cities, to the special types of enclosures that are covenants, feasts and communities."[58] The Jeweler is not actively participating in the world; rather he is removed from all life. He seems to defy the logic that an individual cannot "be a subject of an environment . . . [only] a participant."[59]

While the Jeweler appears to be subject to the environment, he reminds readers that the Pearl is truly subject to her surroundings, noting that it is not just an arbor when he says, "To þenke hir color so clad in clot. / O moul, þou marrez a myry iuele, / My priuy perle wythouten spotte" (ll.23-25). Here is an example of "spot" as relating to purity, and the Jeweler's emotional response to the fact that his spotless pearl is now covered in the wet, dark ground of the Earth. The Jeweler does think of death quite often, and the fact that the only place he considers himself at peace is the flowery grave of his daughter speaks volumes to that concept. Pearl's short life never achieved the ability to take her part in the continuation of life. She dies too young, still a virgin; and yet, she displays a fruitfulness. Her virginity actually attracts Christ's attention to her: "In hys blod he wesch my wede on dese, / And coronde clene in vergynté, / And pyȝt me in perleȝ maskelleȝ" [On the throne he washed my clothing in his blood, / And crowned me pure in virginity, / And adorned me in spotless pearls] (ll. 766-768). Her life, though cut short, ensures her status as a favored subject in the kingdom of Heaven. Even though Pearl never reached sexual maturity, she still is able to give life, and the Jeweler misattributes her ability as a life-giver:

---

[57] Meyer, *Medieval Allegory and the Building of the New Jerusalem*, p. 171
[58] S.L.Clark and Julian N. Wasserman, "The *Pearl*-Poet's City Imagery," *The Southern Quarterly* XVI (1978), pp. 297-209, at p. 301.
[59] W.H. Ittelson, *Environment and Cognition* (New York, 1973), p.13.

> Of goud vche goude is ay bygonne;
> So semly a sede moȝt fayly not,
> Þat spryngande spycez vp ne sponne
> Of þat precios perle wythouten spotte.
> (ll. 32-35)

Even though Pearl never reached maturity, she is still human, and still is able to give her body to the Earth seemingly to perpetuate that beautiful spot of land. She is the source of happiness for the Jeweler, and she also guarantees the existence of life at that spot, as the beauty of the spices and flowers spring from her funeral mound, that small hill. The Jeweler points to a maxim "Of goud vche goude is ay bygone," and he believes that the beauty and life of the arbor stems from Pearl. Life does stem from Pearl, but it is not life. It is, once more, an imitating of life. This body in the ground does not give rise to fruit to sustain life, rather flowers and spices that promote fantasies of life. Even though the Jeweler claims that seeds could not fail to sprout from her body, the spice has gone to rot. These rotten spices and the aroma of flowers mask the death of the arbor, giving hope for life where none might exist.

These various garden tropes and traditions that inform the *Pearl*-poet's treatment of the arbor, and consequently affect our reading of the arbor, speak to the problem of multivalent traditions. When we read any kind of garden imagery, the text and the poet require us to think of all those form and tropes that inform that tradition. We must simultaneously think of the Garden of Eden or Error, the *hortus conclusus*, and grave imagery. Those past ideologies are fused with our present thoughts and ideas, forming a chronotope, which can be found to varying degrees "in all realms of the life of the world."[60] So while we can clearly recognize that the Jeweler is stuck in-between modes of thought, we must think with a multivalent mind so that these places of meaning are not lost upon us. Buildings, here the arbor, do not make arguments; rather, "they represent by structuring experiences in order to imply thoughts."[61] This is not a

---

[60] Mikhail Bakhtin, *The Dialogic Imagination: Four Essays by M.M. Bakhtin*, ed. M. Holquist, trans. C. Emerson and M. Holquist, (Austin: University of Texas Press, 1981), p.284.
[61] Andrzej Piotrowski, "Architecture and the Iconoclastic Controversy," *Medieval Practices of Space*, Eds. Barbara A. Hanawalt and Michal Kobialka, Medieval Cultures Series, Vol. 23, (Minneapolis: University of Minnesota Press, 2000), pp, 101-127, at p. 106.

blank landscape; the arbor is a place that has become differentiated from the space that surrounds it through the emotions and traditions attached to it. We do not enter into places without thoughts; we "enter into places armed with our cultural memories."[62] *Pearl* engages with the historical moment of fourteenth-century English society, balancing the traditions of gardens, theology, and economics. It is also a poem that asks readers to engage with the needs of spiritual and physical loss. The "erber grene" takes these traditions and layers them upon each other—much like the natural process of a pearl's formation—asking readers to engage with these various traditions to understand the poem's progression from the arbor to New Jerusalem and back.

William M. Storm is a lecturer at Marquette University. His research focuses on the ways medieval literature intersects with larger cultural and social concerns of the era. His dissertation focused on how heaven engages with discourses of space and place, art, and politics to present broader arguments on the nature of the afterlife. In addition, he remains interested in the ways that modern culture deploys various narratives of medievalism, and he explores that in a forthcoming piece that looks at the manipulation of medieval narratives for digital mediums.

---

[62] Clare A. Lees and Gillian R. Overing, "Anglo-Saxon Horizons: Places of the Mind in the Northumbrian Landscape," *A Place to Believe In: Locating Medieval Landscapes*, eds. Clare A. Lees and Gillian R. Overing, (University Park, PA: Pennsylvania State University Press, 2006), pp. 1-26, at p. 6.

II

PEARL, FITT II

Kevin Marti

Abstract: In Fitt II, the *Pearl*-narrator's account of his dream begins. He finds himself in Eden; he describes each of its features, which he says cause him to forget the grief of losing the pearl. Most of these features are more artificial versions of features of the *erber* described in Fitt I, but less abstractly geometrical versions of features of the heavenly city he sees later. Recurring key words underscore parallels among these three landscapes (and among the three subdivisions of each landscape) representing the stages of the resurrection in Christian Platonism.

Introduction

The landscape in which the narrator first finds himself after falling asleep is probably Eden.[1] Fitt II begins describing this first dreamscape and its effect on the dreamer. The stream described in the last stanza of the fitt separates Eden from a *Paradyse* (136) topped by *crystal klyffeȝ* (74; cf. 158-59).

Like most medieval literary dream visions, *Pearl* has a triadic structure: the narrator falls asleep in a first landscape and has a vision of a dreamscape that culminates in a vision-within-a-vision of a second dreamscape. Since the visions of both dreamscapes occur in the mind of the dreamer in the landscape in which he falls asleep, the three landscapes nest within each other like Russian dolls. These three main settings mirror each other: the features of the first setting are transformed into increasingly abstract and artificial features in the second and third settings; the Platonist[2] notion of the material

---

[1] In *Pearl: An Edition with Verse Translation* (Notre Dame: University of Notre Dame Press, 1995), William Vantuono inserts this heading for Fitts II-IV: "The Vision–Part One: The Terrestrial Paradise and the Pearl-Maiden."
[2] My commentaries on Fitts II and VIII use "Platonist" as an adjective to refer to the long stream of tradition whereby Plato's ideas were developed

world as a mirror of the realm of form or ideas[3] underlies this standard dream vision structure. The first setting in *Pearl* is the *erber*, described in Fitt I, and the third is the New Jerusalem. Many features of Eden, the second setting, are a more artificial version of features of the *erber* and anticipate even more abstractly geometrical features of the heavenly city as adapted from the description in the Apocalypse. The Eden Fitt II describes is a supernatural, ideal landscape, as is the earthly paradise described in the Anglo-Saxon *Phoenix* and Dante's *Divine Comedy*.

The fact that features of the Edenic landscape mostly described in Fitt II, the second setting in the poem, are the more abstract counterparts of features of the first setting and the less abstract counterparts of features of the third setting is consistent with the textual structure of nested, increasing abstraction in the major works of the dream vision tradition. The structure of three settings nested in order of increasing abstraction in *Pearl* mirrors the structure of the *Comedy* and of Chaucer's dream visions; it derives ultimately from the structure of the nested, increasingly abstract settings of the following ancient dream visions, which both indirectly and directly influenced medieval dream visions: Plato's *Dream of Er* influenced Cicero's *Dream of Scipio*, which was in turn widely available to medieval Europe as quoted in Macrobius's *Commentary on the Dream of Scipio*; Boethius's dream vision *Consolation of Philosophy* was also extremely influential. The textual structure of nested, increasingly abstracted figuration in these ancient and medieval dream visions models the increasingly dematerialized abstraction that characterizes the Platonist transit of the soul at death (*regressus animae*). In Christian Platonism the stages of the ascent of the soul at death and of the resurrection of the body at Judgment correspond with the stages of Platonist regression.[4] The increasingly abstract

---

and ultimately transmitted to late medieval Europe; that tradition includes texts scholars refer to as Neo-Pythagorean and Neo-Platonic.

[3] Herbert Grabes, *The Mutable Glass: Mirror-imagery in titles and texts of the Middle Ages and English Renaissance*, trans. Gordon Collier (Cambridge: Cambridge University Press, 1982), 75-76.

[4] These correspondences are not generally acknowledged in scholarship. Christian Schäfer discusses Christian Platonism in "The 'Churching' of Platonism as a Philosophical Challenge," in *Philosophy of Dionysius the Areopagite: An Introduction to the Structure and the Content of the Treatise* On the Divine Names (Leiden: Brill, 2006), 3-9. This essay uses "regression" to translate *regressus*, a term sometimes translated as "return" that describes a

settings in medieval dream visions therefore correspond with the stages of the ascent of the soul at death and of the resurrection of the body. (The body the soul inhabits after the final stage of the resurrection is an abstracted, spiritual form that retains the identity of the mortal body whose material, corporeal features have been shed; this conception of the resurrected body reconciles Platonist belief in a disembodied afterlife with Christian belief in an embodied existence after Judgment.) The stages of Platonist regression reverse those of procession (emanation), whereby the soul acquires an

---

process also often referred to as "reversion." Augustine supports the notion of regression he finds in Porphyry's *De regressu animae* (not extant) in *City of God*, bk. 10, ch. 30; unlike many other Platonists, who believe in an eternal cycle whereby the soul repeatedly descends to earth to take on a body again after repeatedly becoming incorporeal in its ascent to the heavens at death, Porphyry believes that the soul remains with God after death. Macrobius likewise affirms Porphyry's conception of regression in his *Commentary on the Dream of Scipio*, trans. William Harris Stahl (New York: Columbia University Press, 1952), 31-32; cf. 124-25. In lines 28-63 of *Paradiso* 4 Beatrice corrects the belief based on Plato's *Timaeus* that at death virtuous souls return to the celestial bodies from which they descended when they acquired a natural form at birth. She states that the fact that the souls appear to Dante within celestial bodies seems to confirm that belief, but that what he sees is a misleading condescension to his limited mortal capacity for perception, and that the words of the *Timaeus* may misrepresent Plato's own views. Thus Augustine and Dante transmit Platonist teaching about regression in the course of correcting or questioning it. The incremental decrease in corporeality Dante and his guides appear to experience as they rise through purgatory and paradise may also be a condescension to mortal perception based on the Platonist belief Beatrice discredits. The incremental increase in the gifts of the glorified body Manuele Gragnolati discerns in the course of the same ascent also appears to be based on the same Platonist belief; *Experiencing the Afterlife: Soul and Body in Dante and Medieval Culture* (Notre Dame: University of Notre Dame Press, 2005), especially 168, 174. Paul Rorem's foreword to Schäfer's *Philosophy of Dionysius* discusses "procession and return" as adapted by Ps.-Dionysius, Eriugena, Hugh of St. Victor, and Aquinas, xiii-xiv; Schäfer discusses "regression" and related terms on 36, 48, and 120, concluding on 151 that Ps.-Dionysius is a Christian Platonist. Jean A. Potter writes in her introduction to Eriugena's *Periphyseon: On the Division of Nature*, trans. Myra L. Uhlfelder (Indianapolis: Bobbs-Merrill, 1976), xxxviii: "Since all things were created in man and fell into their effects with his fall, so they are redeemed in him and will rise in his resurrection to reunite with their causes. The multiplicity of individuals returns to the unity whence it derived. Eriugena marks the stages . . . ."

increasingly corporeal form as it descends from the celestial bodies to earth; the procession of the soul corresponds with the procession of the numbers from the monad (One), which contains all numbers.[5]

In *Pearl*, as in the *Comedy*, there are three substages of ascent/resurrection (or the opposite in *Inferno*) within each of the three main settings, so the overall structure is a triad of triads typical of Platonist hierarchy.[6] Like the nesting upper, middle, and lower subdivisions of Dante's hell as well as of his purgatory and paradise, three nesting subdivisions comprise each of the three main settings of *Pearl*. The *Pearl* dreamer's visions of Eden, then the pearl maiden, and then her breast pearl in the first dreamscape parallel in that order his visions of the exterior of the heavenly city, then the procession of maidens within it, and then his own maiden within the procession in the second dreamscape.[7] Likewise his vision of the pearl enclosed in *golde* (2), then *gresse* (10), then *grounde* (10) in the *erber* parallels the sequence of three subdivisions within the first and second dreamscapes. Repeating key words and phrases mark off the boundaries of the three subdivisions of the first and second dreamscapes. References to the mind melting ("mynde moȝt malte," 224; "mynde to maddyng malte," 1154) create a parallel between the description of the breast pearl and the appearance of the maiden

---

[5] Macrobius, *Commentary on the Dream of Scipio*, 103-4, 126, 130, 133-37. Martianus Capella, *The Marriage of Philology and Mercury*, trans. William Harris Stahl and Richard Johnson, in *Martianus Capella and the Seven Liberal Arts* (New York: Columbia University Press, 1977), 2:264, 274-75. Vincent Foster Hopper, *Medieval Number Symbolism: Its Sources, Meanings, and Influence on Thought and Expression* (New York: Columbia University Press, 1938), 51-52, 96-98, 100. Jean A. Potter, introduction to Eriugena's *Periphyseon*, xxxiv.

[6] Hopper, *Medieval Number Symbolism*, 108-9. In the *Comedy* Dante's passage through the lower, middle, and upper sections of purgatory and paradise mark off three substages of ascent/resurrection, while his passage through upper, middle, and lower hell mark off three substages of a kind of reversal of that ascent/resurrection. Schäfer discusses examples of triadic structures in the works of Proclus and Ps.-Dionysius in *Philosophy of Dionysius*, 24-31, 43, 80-87; in 85-87 he applies the terms "scaling" and "Russian-doll-principle" to such triadic structures. Schäfer writes: "As in all Platonic writings, in Dionysius the Platonic Triad is present in every feature of the subjacent philosophical structure" (80). John E. Murdoch refers to "Platonic triplets" in *Album of Science: Antiquity and the Middle Ages* (New York: Scribner's, 1984), 333, 351.

[7] Here the Middle English *prosessyoun* (1096), applied to the group of maidens in the heavenly city, borrows from Platonist terminology.

in the procession, which respectively mark off the end of the third subdivisions of the second and third dreamscapes. Bird similes describing the dreamer (184, 1085) create a parallel between the first description of the maiden across the stream and the first description of the procession, which respectively mark off the beginning of the second subdivisions of the second and third dreamscapes. Fitt II mostly describes the first subdivision of the first dreamscape (up to the stream but before the vision of the maiden across it), and its features mirror features of the maiden and her breast pearl, the other two subdivisions of the same dreamscape, in addition to mirroring features of the *erber* and heavenly city. Like the *Comedy*, *Pearl* describes visions of a triadic Platonist hierarchy of stages each of which mirrors the other stages much as Ps.-Dionysius's triadic ecclesiastical hierarchy mirrors his triadic celestial hierarchy. That is, each of the three appearances of the pearl in the *erber* (in gold, grass, and ground) mirrors each of the three subdivisions of the first dreamscape (Eden, the maiden, her breast pearl), all of which in turn mirror the three subdivisions of the second dreamscape (the exterior of the city, the procession, the maiden within the procession). As in the *Comedy* in the hierarchy described in *Pearl* each level mirrors every other level as well as the macrocosm. As part of this larger pattern of nine nesting landscape subdivisions is a pattern of repeating words less structurally important than those cited above that mark off boundaries of subdivisions (224, 1154); repeating words that do not mark off boundaries instead draw attention to other parallel features among subdivisions. Since Fitt II mostly describes the first subdivision of the first dreamscape, words in Fitt II that recur in fitts describing one or more of the other eight subdivisions draw attention to many specific parallels among those subdivisions. In *Pearl* as in *Purgatorio* and *Paradiso* movement to a new setting or through a new subdivision of a setting is associated with an increase in the gifts of the glorified body: clarity, agility, impassibility, and subtlety (penetrability).[8] Earlier scholarship on the

---

[8] Manuele Gragnolati, *Experiencing the Afterlife*, especially 168, 174. Studies of the gifts of the glorified body include the following: Caroline Walker Bynum, *The Resurrection of the Body in Western Christianity, 200-1336* (New York: Columbia University Press, 1995), 131-32, 335-37; Nikolaus Wicki, *Die Lehre von der himmlischen Seligkeit in der mittelalterlichen Scholastik von Petrus Lombardus bis Thomas von Aquin* (Freiburg: Universitätsverlag, 1954), 202-37; Joseph Goering, "The *De dotibus* of Robert Grosseteste," *Mediaeval*

influence of scholastic teaching about these gifts in *Pearl* does not trace the stages of increase in the gifts evident in the course of the poem.[9] Words and phrases in Fitt II that recur in other subdivisions often highlight this overall pattern of increasing glorification.

The recurring key words and phrases that draw attention to parallels between the subdivisions of Eden described in Fitt II and other subdivisions contribute to a larger pattern of bracketing structures on different scales throughout *Pearl*. Key words that recur in the first and last lines of the whole poem and of most stanzas define both the fitt and the stanza as the main divisions and subdivisions respectively of the text of the poem. The way that recurring key words create brackets around the whole poem, individual fitts, and individual stanzas is of a piece with the bracketing structure of the alliterative scheme, two half-lines separated by a caesura. It is also consistent with the pairing of words and phrases in the same part of speech on the scale of the half-line, line, and pair of lines, all of which occur in Fitt II and throughout *Pearl*. And all of these bracketing structures mirror the nested bracketing effect created by a textual structure featuring gardens enclosing other gardens: the poem begins and ends in the *erber*, and right after that beginning and before that ending respectively is a description of Eden (Fitts II-IV) and the New Jerusalem (Fitts XVII-XIX), with the landscape of the vineyard parable (Fitts IX-X) at the center of the dialogue (Fitts V-XVI) located between the descriptions of Eden and the New Jerusalem.

The parallel features of the three nested main settings and their subdivisions gives them a structure similar to *rotae*, medieval diagrams of concentric wheel shapes widely used as memory aids.[10]

Studies 44 (1982): 83-101. The Latin term for these gifts, *dotes*, means "dowries" or "bridal gifts."

[9] Kevin Marti, "Traditional Characteristics of the Resurrected Body in *Pearl*," *Viator* 24 (1993): 311-35.

[10] For example, *rotae* were used to facilitate memory of the names and relationships among the elements, months, seasons, and planets, as noted by Murdoch: "Rotae and Circular Diagrams," in *Album of Science*, 52-61. As Murdoch observes on 52, the most influential collection of *rotae* is Isidore of Seville's *De natura rerum*; these circular diagrams were taken to be so central to the work that many of its early manuscripts bear the title *Liber rotarum*, and the diagrams made their way into manuscripts of the writings of Macrobius and William of Conches which, like those of Isidore, apply

The recurring words and phrases linking those settings and their subdivisions therefore serve a mnemotechnical purpose, as do the other bracketing structures over a range of scales throughout *Pearl*. The sequence of subdivisions of settings is a sequence of nested microcopies of the whole system which like many Platonist systems resembles a strange (fractal) attractor.[11]

Commentary

> Fro spot my spyryt þer sprang in space;
> My body on balke þer bod in sweuen.
> My goste is gon in Godeȝ grace
> In auenture þer meruayleȝ meuen.
> (61-64)[12]

The first line of Fitt II, like the first line of all of the fitts, contains the link word which is the most distinctive structural feature of the preceding fitt, here *spot*, which appears in the first and last lines of

---

medieval mnemotechnical diagrams to an understanding of Platonist tradition.

[11] Benoit B. Mandelbrot, "Fractal Attractors and Fractal ('Chaotic') Evolutions," in *The Fractal Geometry of Nature* (New York: Freeman, 1983), 193-99. Nested copies of larger structures within Platonist texts are common: A reworking of Nicomachus of Gerasa's *Introduction to Arithmetic* in chapter four of Iamblichus' *On Pythagoreanism* offers the principles underlying the next three chapters. The "mirroring at successive levels of identical structures" receives its first systematic application by Iamblichus, according to E. R. Dodds's introduction to Proclus's *Elements of Theology*, 2nd ed. (Oxford: Oxford University Press, 1963), xix-xx. Chapters one through three of Ps.-Dionysius' *On the Divine Names* serve as a "short prolepsis of the whole treatise," while chapters four ("copied almost completely from Proclus") and five contain successively shorter outlines of the entire work, according to Schäfer, *Philosophy of Dionysius*, 38, 116, 124, 133; Schäfer also notes on 173 that the *Divine Names* creates a foundation for the entire body of Ps.-Dionysius's work. Not only do individual Platonist texts contain nested epitomes of themselves, those epitomes are sometimes in turn reworkings of earlier Platonist texts, such that the same "mirroring at successive levels of identical structures" that characterizes individual texts (and many non-textual Platonist hierarchies) to some extent characterizes the larger body of texts that together comprise Platonist tradition generally.

[12] All quotations from *Pearl*, including the entirety of Fitt II, are from the edition by E. V. Gordon, *Pearl* (Oxford: Oxford University Press, 1953).

each stanza of the previous fitt, except for the first line of the first stanza. Variants on a link word connect the first and last lines of all but the first stanza of each fitt and link the first line of each fitt with the previous fitt, a structure called *concatenatio*. The sequence of twenty link words, together with the words recurring in the first and last lines of the entire poem, is of a piece with the alliterative and rhyme schemes throughout, such that link words often epitomize both schemes. In the first line of all stanzas but the first in Fitt I and in the first line of Fitt II *spot* is the first of the alliterating words. In the last line of all stanzas in Fitt I *spot* is the last rhyming word. The link word *adubbement* in Fitt II like *spot* in Fitt I interlinks rhyme and alliterative schemes by serving as the final rhyme word and then as the first alliterating word respectively in the last and first lines of successive stanzas. In *Pearl* link words often draw attention to the thematic gists of fitts. In the last lines of Fitt I *spot* means "blemish," whereas in its first lines *spot* means "location." The pearl is said to be *wythouten spot* in the last lines because it is located in what the first lines refer to as *þat spot(e)*, a grave; the intersection between the sense of location and the sense of blemish here suggests that mortality is a kind of blemish removed only at death. Because the link word from the previous fitt appears at the beginning of the next fitt, it interweaves the alliterative/rhyme schemes and thematic gists of adjacent fitts. Thus in Fitt II *adubbement* and its variants recall *wythouten spot* from Fitt I; like the lost pearl the dreamscape is without blemish. *Adubbement* in Fitt II refers to features of a landscape as if they are fine jewels, the landscape a jeweler's setting. The pearl maiden's presence in that richly ornamented landscape, first mentioned in line 161 of Fitt III, confirms her purity.

 The occurrence of *spot* in the first line of Fitt II also links the portions of the narrative featured in the first two fitts. The *spot* where the dreamer loses the pearl and where his spirit *sprang* is the same *spot* onto which the dreamer falls asleep, "On þat precious perle" (60). So the dreamscapes described in Fitt II and those that follow may be said to be somehow contained within the dreamer lying over the spot where the pearl disappeared.

 The occurrence of *sprang* here mirrors its occurrence in line 13 of Fitt I, where it describes the movement of the pearl *þurʒ gresse to grounde* (10), on this *spot*, at the moment of its loss. So the movement of the dreamer's spirit out of his body mirrors the loss of the pearl that *doun drof* (30), that *trendeled doun* (41) in the *erber*; both movements figure as the separation of the spirit from the body at death. Both occurrences of *sprang* also parallel the *spryngande spyceȝ* (35) from the earth over the spot where the pearl disappeared as well as the reference to "my Lady of quom Jesu con spryng" (453) in the heavenly city. The movement of Jesus out of Mary at birth mirrors the movements of the falling pearl, of growing plants, and of the ascending spirit of dreamer.

The absence of any article between *Fro* and *spot* conflates both meanings of *spot*: the dreamer's spirit ascends from the spot where his body sleeps over the pearl and his spirit separates itself from any spot in the sense of "impurity" or "defect."

The reference to the dreamer's *slepyng-slaȝte* ("sleeping-slaughter," 59) contextualizes the separation of spirit from body that follows as a dream of what the soul experiences during its ascent to heaven after death. And line 62 leaves no doubt that what follows is a dream. In medieval English dream visions a description of the narrator falling asleep sometimes separates the waking vision from the first dreamed vision, the first two of the three main settings; in line 275 of Chaucer's *Book of the Duchess*, "Y fil aslepe" is another reference to the narrator falling asleep between the waking vision and first dreamed vision.[13] Unlike Dante in the *Comedy*, the *Pearl* dreamer does not visit the otherworld bodily. The apostle Paul establishes the distinction between corporeal and incorporeal visits to paradise when regarding his own visit he writes that he does not know if it was in the body or out of the body (2 Corinthians 12). This narrator's body spends the entire dream *on balke*, on the *huyle* in the *erber* where he lost the pearl. Like the Green Chapel in *Sir Gawain and the Green Knight* this *huyle* from which the narrator visits the otherworld resembles a fairy mound because it grants access to *meruayleȝ*. The Green Chapel is associated with the Green Knight who appears as Arthur calls for *sum mayn meruayle* (94)[14] and who is an otherworldly transformation of Bertilak by Morgne la Faye (2446-55).

Of the *meruayleȝ* we first learn that they *meuen*. The nature of the movement the dreamer observes and experiences creates a pattern of increasing agility, culminating in the maiden's sudden

---

[13] Citation from Larry Benson et al., eds., *The Riverside Chaucer*, 3rd ed. (Boston: Houghton Mifflin, 1987).
[14] Citation from Malcolm Andrew and Ronald Waldron, eds., *The Poems of the Pearl Manuscript: Pearl, Cleanness, Patience, Sir Gawain and the Green Knight*, 5th ed. (Exeter: University of Exeter Press, 2007).

movement from the other side of the stream to the midst of the heavenly procession (1145-48) and in his own subsequent attempt to cross the stream (1153-1164).

> I ne wyste in þis worlde quere þat hit wace,
> Bot I knew me keste þer klyfeȝ cleuen;
> Towarde a foreste I bere þe face,
> Where rych rokkeȝ wer to dyscreuen.
> (65-68)

Medieval world maps frequently indicate the location of Eden, which is "connected to the rest of the world but set off from it," inaccessible to mortals.[15] As in the *Comedy* this dreamer enters Eden before attempting to enter heavenly paradise. The description of his vision of the maiden across the stream closely resembles the description of Dante's vision of Matelda across a stream in *Purgatorio* 28, evidence that the *Comedy* influenced *Pearl*. The fragrance (6), fluttering boughs (10) and leaves (17-18), and birds' song (14-15) described in the opening of that canto resemble their counterparts in the portrayal of Eden in Fitt II in *Pearl*.

The first of the described features of the dreamscape in which the narrator finds himself are the *klyfeȝ* that *cleuen*, called *rych rokkeȝ* and *crystal klyffeȝ* (74). The cliffs and pearl maiden are located across the stream described in the last stanza in Fitt II, and therefore in what the narrator takes to be *Paradyse* (137). What the cliffs cleave is unstated: A. C. Cawley suggests they cleave the sky;[16] Vantuono instead glosses *cleuen* as "were cleft." In any case *cleuen* anticipates *schere* (165) and *schorne* (213), which refer respectively to the brightness of the maiden as first glimpsed and then specifically to the brightness of her hair. The cliffs at the top of the dreamscape initiate a sequence of images of bright light sometimes related to cutting and/or gold associated with features at the top of a hierarchy.

The phrases "I bere þe face" and "wer to dyscreuen" emphasize the dreamer's sensory perception of the first dreamscape, which soon improves his mood and agility. As in the *erber*, whose fragrance puts him to sleep (57-60), perception of successive dreamscape features produces emotional and mental transformations in the

---

[15] Carolyn Dinshaw, "All Kinds of Time," *Studies in the Age of Chaucer* 35 (2013): 12.
[16] *Pearl; Sir Gawain and the Green Knight* (London: Dent, 1962).

dreamer. His first glimpse of the maiden leaves him "Wyth yȝen open and mouth ful clos" (183).

> Þe lyȝt of hem myȝt no mon leuen,
> Þe glemande glory þat of hem glent;
> For wern neuer webbeȝ þat wyȝeȝ weuen
> Of half so dere adubbemente.
> (69-72)

The rhyme scheme of the final quatrain of each stanza reverses that of the first two quatrains much as the rhyme scheme and line lengths set off the final five lines ("bob and wheel") from the rest of each stanza of *Sir Gawain*. As in that poem this concluding arrangement is often an independent clause that draws attention to something especially important. This quatrain describes the otherworldly quality of the light emanating from the cliffs. The nature of the light from these cliffs recalls the blooms that "schyneȝ ful schyr again þe sunne" in the *erber* (28) and anticipates the nature of the light emanating from the *Lombe-lyȝt* in the New Jerusalem, which is brighter than the sun or moon. The phrase *myȝt no mon leuen* anticipates the maiden's rebuke following the dreamer's second speech; alluding to the doubting Thomas story in the Gospel of John, she criticizes him for believing only what he can see (295-312). The last two lines of the stanza suggest that the landscape whose description follows is finer than the finest manmade tapestry; as the link word *adubbement* recurs in connection with the sequence of landscape features, it encourages the reader to visualize them as adornments, including jewels set on cloth. Charles G. Osgood cites other Middle English texts in which woven goods and landscapes are compared.[17] In this sense Eden anticipates the maiden's jewel-studded clothing in Fitt IV and that of the other maidens in the heavenly city (1099-104). *Of half* is one of a sequence of references to units of measure in statements of human inadequacy. Thus later the dreamer states that the human heart is incapable of feeling a tenth part of the joy the Edenic landscape inspires in him (135-36), that no one outside the procession can sing a single *poynt* of the maidens' song (891) and that no one who is not *wythouten mote* can enter a single *foot* into the heavenly city (970-72).

---

[17] *The Pearl: A Middle English Poem* (Boston: Heath, 1906).

The *glory* that *glent* from the crystal cliffs anticipates the jewels in the streambed that *glente purȝ glas* (114), the jasper that *glente* (1001) in the lowest foundation of the New Jerusalem, that city's wall of jasper that *glent* (1026) near the streets of gold compared to glass (1025), the city's gates that *glent as glasse* (1106), and the *glenteȝ* (1144) of the Lamb in that city.

Each final quatrain of each stanza of Fitt II focuses on a landscape feature that is somehow especially important because of its brightness: the cliffs in stanza one, the pearl gravel in stanza two, the otherworldly song of the birds with *flaumbande hweȝ* (90) in stanza three, the *bonkes* like *fyldor fyn* (106) in stanza four, and the jewel-studded streambed that makes the water gleam in stanza five. Likewise the final stanza of each of the first four fitts focuses on a landscape feature that is especially important because of its brightness: the *floury flaȝt* (57) in which the dreamer rests on the pearl in Fitt I, the stream in Fitt II, the maiden's face and figure in Fitt III, and the maiden's removal of her crown in Fitt IV. In this sense the structure of each stanza of Fitt II resembles the structure of each of the first four fitts.

> Dubbed wern alle þo downeȝ sydeȝ
> Wyth crystal klyffeȝ so cler of kynde,
> (73-74)

The *downeȝ sydeȝ* recall the *small . . . smoþe . . . sydeȝ* (6) of the lost pearl described in Fitt I and anticipate *smoþe* and *smal* as descriptive of the maiden (190) and the *quyte syde* of the Lamb in the heavenly city (1137); such recurring words reinforce the way images morph into other images as the dreamer moves from setting to setting. Just as the sides of the pearl are all *smal* and *smothe, reken in vche araye, alle* the sides of the hills have crystal cliffs. The little pearl lost on the *huyle* of the *erber* is transformed into crystal cliffs on hills, the first of several transformations. The *erber* within which are nested the two dreamscapes exhibits smaller-scale versions of features of those dreamscapes. The special nature of the cliffs, a property of crystal, is the fact that they are *so cler of kynde*, which explains the "glemande glory þat of hem glent" (70). Scholastic theology associates crystal with the clarity of the glorified body.[18] In *Pearl* these cliffs recall medieval use of crystal as windowed settings for

---

[18] Marti, "Traditional Characteristics," 320-25.

relics; in reliquaries the transparency of crystal draws attention to its association with the resurrected body. The crystal cliffs anticipate the *cler quyt perle* on the maiden's crown (207); the *cler* breast pearl she wears (227); the new song the procession of maidens sings *ful cler* (882); the *cler and quyt* beryl foundation of the heavenly city (1011); the walls and dwellings of the New Jerusalem, the main adornment of the hill in the second dreamscape, which are *sotyl cler* (1050); and the *red golde cler* of the Lamb's horns (1111). The heavenly city resembling crystal dominates its bright foundations and the hill under them much as the crystal cliffs here dominate the hills and bright forest. Fitt II features the beginning of a sequence of increasing increments of gifts of the glorified body associated with what the dreamer sees and with the dreamer himself. The gift featured first here (*so cler of kynde*; cf. *gold so clere*, 2) is clarity, the gift from which the other three gifts proceed in scholastic teaching.[19] So *cler* is one of the most important words linking the three main settings and their subdivisions. The phrase *sotyl cler* is one of many references in the poem to two or more gifts in relation to each other, in this instance subtlety and clarity.

> Holtewodeȝ bryȝt aboute hem bydeȝ
> Of bolleȝ as blwe as ble of Ynde;
> As bornyst syluer þe lef on slydeȝ,
> Þat þike con trylle on vch a tynde.
> Quen glem of glodeȝ agaynȝ hem glydeȝ,
> Wyth schymeryng schene ful schrylle þay schynde.
> (75-80)

Osgood cites many parallels between the features of these trees and those in Middle English adaptations from the paradisiacal landscapes in the literature of the Orient, including extreme brightness, unnatural colors, and silver leaves. The phrase *of Ynde* recalls *Out of oryent* (3) and anticipates *perleȝ of oryent* (82) and *coroun of perle orient* (255). The *blwe as ble of Ynde* of the trees recalls the *blwe* blooms (27) in the *erber* and anticipates the indigo blue (*ynde*) blended with purple in the twelfth foundation of the New Jerusalem, identified as *gentyleste in vch a plyt* (1015-16). The *Holtewodeȝ bryȝt* in Eden also anticipate the *tres ful schym* (1077) of the heavenly city. The

---

[19] Alexander of Hales, *Summa theologica*, 3a, q. 21, m. 7 (Quaracchi: Collegii S. Bonaventurae, 1924-1948); Marti, "Traditional Characteristics," 324.

fact that bright trees enclose crystal cliffs (*aboute hem byde3*) recalls the enclosure of the pearl in *gold so clere* (2) before its loss in the *erber* and anticipates the enclosure of the pearl maiden in clothing that is *Blysnande whyt* (163).

The trees are bright because their leaves reflect light. The simile comparing their leaves to *bornyst syluer* again recalls the *gold so clere* enclosing the pearl lost in the *erber* and anticipates the "brende golde bry3t / As glemande glas burnist broun" (989-90) in the description of the heavenly city that "schyrrer þen sunne with schafte3 schon" (982). So the silver-leaved trees are a bright setting for the hills comparable to the nested gold settings throughout *Pearl*. The simile *as bornyst syluer* is one in a long sequence of similes in the description of the first dreamscape which also includes *as blwe as ble of Ynde* (76), *As fode* (88), *As fyldor fyn* (106), *As glente þur3 glas* (114), and *As stremande sterne3* (115).

The phrase *on slyde3* (one word in MS.) which Malcolm Andrew and Ronald Waldron, Gordon, and Sarah Stanbury[20] read as two separate words meaning "slide over each other," contributes to the general parallel between dreamscape features and gifts of the glorified body, in this instance agility, an association reinforced by *con trylle*, which Gordon glosses as "quiver," and *glyde3*. In any case, *on slyde3* recalls *slode* (59) in the description of the narrator falling asleep after he *felle* in the *erber*. And the verb pair *glyde3* and *glode3* anticipates *glod* (1105), the verb describing the movement of the procession of maidens on the bright, golden streets of the heavenly city; it is a mode of locomotion more like gliding than walking and therefore a supernatural agility like that whereby the whole procession appears *sodanly* (1095, 1098) and whereby the pearl maiden who had just been near the dreamer appears suddenly within the procession (1147-52; Beatrice's sudden movement from Dante's side to the celestial rose in *Paradiso* 31 is a striking parallel). Just as the maidens' agility results from the clarity of the heavenly city, the reflected light from the leaves results from the agility of the leaves. Agility is also a function of clarity (and impassibility, the bliss resulting from an absence of noxious passions or other suffering[21])

---

[20] *Pearl* (Kalamazoo, MI: Medieval Institute, 2001).
[21] Aquinas, *Summa theologiae*, 3ae *Suppl.*, q. 82, a. 2, and *In epistolam I ad Corinthios commentaria*, ch. 15, lectiones 6 and 7; Bonaventure, *Breviloquium*, pt. 4, ch. 10, par. 1; Marti, "Traditional Characteristics," 327-29. An association between impassibility and bliss is suggested by Augustine, who

when the dreamer absorbs the maiden's brightness: "Suche gladande glory con to me glace" (171). *Quen* may suggest that the light these leaves reflect shimmers in part because of an intermittent light source. The brightness of the leaves is a reflection of the *glem of glodeȝ*. Israel Gollancz glosses *glodeȝ* as "bright shining clouds" based on Scandinavian cognates.[22] Reflected light from intermittent patches of brightness in a cloudy sky would impart a *schymeryng schene*.

> Þe grauayl þat on grounde con grynde
> Wern precious perleȝ of oryente:
> Þe sunnebemeȝ bot blo and blynde
> In respecte of þat adubbement.
> (81-84)

In this passage about the pearl gravel, like several similar passages, a landscape feature superior to sunbeams recalls the bright blooms against the sun in the *erber* and anticipates the superiority of the heavenly city to the sun and moon. References to the sun, moon, and stars in the poem are consistent with the comparison of the clarity of the glorified body to that of the sun, moon, and stars in 1 Corinthians 15 and in scholastic theology.[23] The specific features of this first dreamscape referred to as its *adubbement* are the sequence of bright features described near the end of each stanza listed above. The link word in Fitt II thus draws attention to the shared brightness of a sequence of different features in the same dreamscape. Then in the first two lines of Fitt III *dubbement* is linked to another listing of features first described in Fitt II: *doun, daleȝ, wod, water,* and *playneȝ*. In these ways the link word epitomizes the content of the fitt as it connects that content to the next fitt. The only pearls in Eden are *on grounde*, recalling the *grounde* (10) the pearl enters in the *erber* and anticipating the spear *grimly grounde* (654) that has caused Christ's side to bleed in the heavenly city. The phrase *con grynde* may hint that the disembodied spirit of the dreamer has weight as he treads

---

links *felicitas* with the physical weaknesses the resurrected body lacks in *Enchiridion* 91.

[22] *Pearl* (New York: Cooper Square, 1966). First published 1891 by David Nutt; citation is from Cooper Square edition.

[23] Aquinas, *Summa theologiae* 3ae *Suppl.,* q. 85, a. 2; Marti, "Traditional Characteristics," 321-23.

on the pearls, much as Dante's body moves the stones he treads on in lines 28-30 of *Inferno* 12. It is appropriate that the pearl gravel receives attention in the last quatrain as the most important feature in the stanza because pearls are spheres, along with circles the geometrical figures associated with God by way of the Platonist monad.[24]

> The adubbemente of þo downeȝ dere
> Garten my goste al greffe forȝete.
> So frech flauoreȝ of fryteȝ were,
> As fode hit con me fayre refete.
> (85-88)

Like the link word in the first line of Fitt III, the link word in the first lines of the third and fourth stanzas of Fitt II refers somewhat more generally to the collective features of the first dreamscape, though features mentioned in nearby lines are the context. "The adubbemente of þo downeȝ dere" clearly includes the entire first dreamscape, but the smell of fruit and the sight and sound of birds described in this stanza are the most obvious reason the dreamer forgets his grief, much as the smell of the flowers he sees and falls on at the end of Fitt I puts him to sleep. The phrase *frech flauoreȝ* describes the smell of the fruit in a way consistent with the simile comparing their effect on him to that of consuming food, reinforcing the parallel with the transformative effect of the smell of flowers in

---

[24] Kevin Marti, *Body, Heart, and Text in the* Pearl-*Poet* (Lewiston, NY: Mellen, 1991), 11, 17. Hopper, *Medieval Number Symbolism*, 73-74, 82-83, 96, 108, 138, 146, 149-50. God is represented in terms of circles in *Paradiso* 33, lines 115-41. Plato associates God with the sphere and circle in the *Timaeus*, trans. Benjamin Jowett, in *The Collected Dialogues of Plato Including the Letters*, ed. Edith Hamilton and Huntington Cairns (Princeton: Princeton University Press, 1961), 1164-65, 1169. Macrobius finds a correspondence between circles and spheres in bk. 1, ch. 17 and 21; in ch. 17 he discusses, with reservations, Cicero's equation of the outermost sphere of the cosmos with God; *Commentary on the Dream of Scipio*, trans. Stahl, 155, 157, 175-76. Nicomachus of Gerasa, who influenced many important medieval authorities on arithmetic (listed by Hopper, 98), compares the monad with God; *Introduction to Arithmetic*, trans. Martin Luther D'Ooge (New York: Macmillan, 1926), 95-96. Dietrich Mahnke calls the monad a "Verkörperung Gottes" in *Eine neue monadologie* (Berlin: Reuther, 1917); see especially 9, 16-18, 58-59.

Fitt I and anticipating the eucharistic reference in Fitt XX (1208-10). This synaesthetic experience, smell experienced as taste, resembles Dante's perception of the marble frieze of purgatory's first terrace in the form of sound and smell (*Purgatorio* 10, lines 58-63).

The smell of *fryteȝ* here (cf. *spyse* and *pereȝ*, 104) recalls the *fryte* (29) in the *erber* and anticipates the maidens brought as *newe fryt* (894) to God and the *twelue fryteȝ of lyf* (1078) in the heavenly city.

In *Pearl* the ability to acquire impassibility is a function of the ability to gradually see and hear (and sometimes smell) more and more abstract mirror images of the same things within a recursive system. Forgetting his grief is a function of the dreamer's gradual realization that the pearl under *grounde* (10) in the *erber* is also the crystal cliffs, the gravel *on grounde* (81) in Eden, the *faunt* that is *at the fote* (161) of the crystal cliff, and the pearls over the gates of the New Jerusalem. The pearl is not lost, but is rather set in an elaborately nested sequence of settings on different scales. So achieving emotional tranquility is a matter of learning to perceive the recursive stages of the ascent of the soul at death and of the resurrection of the body. In Fitt III the dreamer states that the same features of Eden described in Fitt II "Bylde in me blys, abated my baleȝ, / Fordidden my stresse, dystryed my payneȝ" (123-24), and that his joy increases the further he follows the stream:

> Doun after a strem þat dryȝly haleȝ
> I bowed in blys, bredful my brayneȝ;
> Þe fyrre I folȝed þose floty valeȝ,
> Þe more strenghþe of ioye myn herte strayneȝ.
> (125-28)

He then discovers "more of wele . . . in that wyse" (133) than he can describe, since a mortal heart could not experience a tenth part of that *gladneȝ glade* (135-36), and he concludes that *Paradyse* is across the stream, which is a "deuyse / Bytwene myrþeȝ" (139-40), a division between degrees of joy. As the dreamer follows the stream in Fitt III, his desire to cross it increases as he observes a landscape even more *fayr* than Eden, which had already become fairer (*feier*) the further he traversed it (103): "For if hit watȝ fayr þere I con fare, / Wel loueloker watȝ þe fyrre londe" (147-48). So an increase in the dreamer's joy as he follows the stream and looks across results from the increased brightness across the stream; the stream separates degrees of both joy and brightness. The *fyrre londe* across the stream recalls his statement about Eden that "Þe fyrre in þe fryth, the feier con ryse" (103) and anticipates 152-54: "Þe fyrre I stalked by þe stronde. / . . . For wo þer weleȝ so wynne wore." Movement alongside the stream in Fitt III is associated with an increase in the gifts of the glorified body much like movement towards the stream in Fitt II. The connection between joy and *fare* in 147 anticipates the movement of the maidens in the heavenly city: "So fare we alle wyth luf and lyste" (467). His joy increases again after he sees the maiden across the stream: "Suche gladande glory con to me glace / As lyttel byfore þerto watȝ wonte" (171-72); "No gladder gome heþen into Grece / Þen I" (231-32). He experiences the greatest degree of joy (impassibility) upon witnessing the maidens' own *mirþe* (1149) and the *Lombe delyt* (1141), Christ's joy despite his wounds in the heavenly city (1141-44), such that "Delyt me drof in yȝe and ere" (1153) and he attempts to cross the stream. The sight of the heavenly city *gart* him to consider crossing the stream (1151), much as the features of Eden *Garten* him to forget his grief (86). He then is dismayed to find himself back in the *erber* (1174-78) but later "yerned no more þen watȝ me gyuen" (1190). The stages of increased impassibility (and therefore joy) resulting from increasingly bright settings in *Pearl* are comparable with the incremental increases in the brightness of Beatrice's smile that signal increases in joy in successive heavens in *Paradiso*.[25]

A feature of the *concatenatio* of Fitt II draws attention to the value and splendor of the *adubbemente* that increases the dreamer's joy. In Fitt II and the first line of Fitt III *downeȝ* (73), *downeȝ dere* (85), *doun* (121), *dere* (72, 97, 108, 120, and 121), and *derworth* (109) recur in the same line as the link word *adubbemente* and its variants. These accompanying words help the link words integrate the main themes of Fitt II with the alliterative and rhyme schemes in each of its stanzas. Together with the link words they therefore contribute to the mnemotechnical scheme of the poem much as do recurring words linking its three main settings. The correspondence between features of the settings and the dreamer's apparently increasing possession of gifts of the glorified body, as in the *Comedy*, serves a similar mnemotechnical function.

---

[25] M. Barbi writes that "her smile, becoming ever more joyous, is the sign of their continual ascent from the lower heavens to the divine presence. . . ." Quoted by John D. Sinclair, *The Divine Comedy of Dante Alighieri: Paradiso* (New York: Oxford University Press, 1939), 29.

>   Fowleȝ þer flowen in fryth in fere,
>   Of flaumbande hweȝ, boþe smale and grete;
>   Bot sytole-stryng and gyternere
>   Her reken myrþe moȝt not retrete;
>   For quen þose bryddeȝ her wyngeȝ bete,
>   Þay songen wyth a swete asent.
>   So gracios gle couþe no mon gete
>   As here and se her adubbement.
>   (89-96)

The movement of the flock of birds through the forest contributes to a pattern of agility in Fitt II mostly consistent with the hierarchy of nature established in the first chapter of Genesis. The flying of the birds in stanza three continues a pattern that begins with the emanation of light from the cliffs in stanza one and the *glem* that *glydeȝ* through the *glodeȝ* (79) in stanza two. The latter movement of light, together with the apparent movement of the wind, contributes to the *schymeryng schene* (80) of the quivering leaves. The movement of light, wind, shimmering tree leaves, bright pearl gravel, and birds of flaming hues is followed by the walking of the human narrator in stanza four. The sequence of associations between clarity and agility in this fitt culminates in the flowing of the gleaming stream in stanza five. The *flaumbande hweȝ* of the birds recall the *rede* blooms (27) in the *erber* and anticipate the blood flowing from the Lamb in the heavenly city (1135-37). The birds that move *in fere* anticipate the "fryth þer fortwne forth me fereȝ" (98), the phoenix to which Mary is compared that *freles fleȝe* (431), the maidens who *glod in fere* in the heavenly city (1105), and the appearance of the dreamer's maiden *Among her fereȝ* (1150).

The last quatrain of stanza three makes it clear that the birds' appearance and song cause an emotion that cannot be felt by a human. The last two lines of the stanza elaborate on the statement in the second line that the narrator's ghost forgot its grief: the birds' appearance and song overcomes the grief by creating a *gle* that is *so gracios* that it is beyond human emotional capacity. The *swete asent* of the birds' song recalls the dreamer's statement that "þoȝt me neuer so swete a sange" as *the stylle stounde* in the *erber* (19-20) and anticipates the song of the maidens in the heavenly city (877-92). Hearing and seeing the birds makes the narrator's ghost impassible, incapable of suffering, the first in the sequence of incremental improvements in his mood. The *myrþe* of the birds' song that human instruments cannot reproduce anticipates the stream *Bytwene myrþeȝ* (140) as well as the maidens in the heavenly city who make *much of mirþe* (1149).

The third stanza includes several pairings of words in the same part of speech: *in fryth in fere, smale and grete, sytole-stryng and gyternere,* and *here and se.* Except for *sytole-stryng and gyternere,* which occupy the two halves of one line, these pairings are contained within half-lines.

> So al watȝ dubbet on dere asyse
> Þat fryth þer fortwne forth me fereȝ.
> Þe derþe þerof for to deuyse
> Nis no wyȝ worthé þat tonge bereȝ.
> (97-100)

Lines 99-100 invoke the ineffability topos, anticipating its invocation in response to the maiden's breast pearl (225-26).[26] What the human tongue cannot describe is the *derþe* of the *fryth,* including the many features of the forest called *der* already mentioned. Line 97 is summative: *al* of the features of the dreamscape are *dubbet on dere asyse.* The human inability to describe the *derþe* is a function of the human inability to experience the *gle* the appearance and song of the birds produce in the narrator's spirit. The pairing of *derþe* and MS. *worthe* bears on any decision to emend by adding a diacritical mark to the latter, as Andrew and Waldron, Gordon, and Stanbury do. The emphasis on the superiority of what the dreamer's spirit sees, hears, and feels to human perception and emotion anticipates the maiden's explanation of superhuman emotional relations within the heavenly court in Fitt VIII. It also recalls the statement about the pearl's superiority to all other precious stones that precedes the description of the *erber* where it was lost.

The narrator credits *fortwne* for conveying his spirit to the forest. The statement "þer fortune forth me fereȝ" recalls an earlier assertion: "My goste is gon in Godeȝ grace / In auenture" (63-64). The narrator's journey is credited to destiny, *auenture* as mediated from God by fortune in a scheme consistent with the beginning of Book Five of *Consolation of Philosophy. Godeȝ grace* is the counterpart

---

[26] Theodore Bogdanos, *Pearl, Image of the Ineffable: A Study in Medieval Poetic Symbolism* (University Park: Pennsylvania State University Press, 1983).

in *Pearl* to the divine intervention through Mary, Lucy, and Beatrice that initiates Dante's vision (*Inferno* 2, lines 43-104).

> I welke ay forth in wely wyse;
> No bonk so byg þat did me dereȝ.
> Þe fyrre in þe fryth, þe feier con ryse
> Þe playn, þe plontteȝ, þe spyse, þe pereȝ;
> And raweȝ and randeȝ and rych reuereȝ,
> As fyldor fyn her bonkes brent.
> I wan to a water by schore þat schereȝ–
> Lorde, dere watȝ hit adubbement!
> (101-8)

The dreamer walks *in wely wyse*, the superhuman counterpart for movement of the superhuman vision, hearing, and emotion he experiences; his agility and impassibility result from his perception of the dreamscape. He moves *ay forth*; no bank, no matter how big, hinders his motion. His unhindered movement in Eden contrasts with his and the pearl's movement that comes to a stop in the *erber*: *I felle* (57); *I slode* (59); *Þurȝ gresse to grounde hit fro me yot* (10); *hit doun drof* (30); *hit trendeled doun* (41). These references to movement anticipate the movement of the procession of maidens (*sodanly*, 1095, 1098; *glod*, 1105), the sudden movement of his maiden into the city (1147-48), and the dreamer's movement after viewing the heavenly city: *Delyt me drof* (1153), *I so flonc* (1165), *I sparred vnto þe bonc* (1169). The word *dereȝ*, which here means "hinders," connects the dreamer's agility here with the *derþe* of a *fryth* (98-99) which contains nothing that is not *der*. The superior clarity of the landscape, whose features shine like precious jewelry, facilitates the narrator's superhuman movement. Mary Vincent Hillmann emends *feier* to *feirer*[27] and Gordon retains *feier* as a possible form of *feirre*, the comparative of *feier*, both editors imply that the brightness of the landscape increases the further the narrator walks. The pairing of words in the same part of speech elsewhere is evidence for taking *feier*, like *fyrre*, to be an adverb. In this sense *feier con ryse*, so close to "No bonk so byg þat did me dereȝ," connects increasing clarity with increasing agility. The word *ryse* and other references to upward motion like *vp* (35, 177) and *spryngande* (35) are associated with agility in *Pearl*, much

---

[27] *The Pearl: Mediaeval Text with a Literal Translation and Interpretation* (Notre Dame: University of Notre Dame Press, 1961).

as the succession of settings encountered as Dante ascends is associated with agility and other gifts of the glorified body in *Purgatorio* and *Paradiso*.[28]

The catalog of landscape features ends with the stream whose *dere . . . adubbement* is the linking phrase at the end of stanza four and to whose description stanza five is dedicated. Gordon notes that the *reuereȝ* may be streams or "meadows along the bank of a stream." In 104-7 appears a sequence of increasingly bright and geometrical landscape boundaries that culminate in the even brighter *water* between Eden and paradise. The *rych reuereȝ* and golden *bonkes* of Eden and the gleaming stream dividing it from paradise anticipate the *reuer* "bryȝter þen boþe þe sunne and mone" (1055-56) that flows from under the throne of God in the heavenly city (cf. Apocalypse 22:1-2). Andrew and Waldron, like Gordon, compare the stream to that *reuer*, which also recalls the river of light Dante sees with jewel-like flowers representing humans on its banks (*Paradiso* 30, lines 61-69). The comparison of the *bonkes* to *fyldor* sustains the comparison of the landscape to tapestry; *fyldor* is gold thread often used in medieval embroidery (Osgood). The word *brent* in reference to the *bonkes* anticipates the phrase *brende golde bryȝt* (989) in the description of the heavenly city.

References to gold in *Pearl* are an important subset of the larger pattern of references to increasingly bright features, a sequence that connects features described in the *erber* with those in the dreamscapes by way of showing the dreamer that the pearl he thought lost is enclosed in a nested sequence of beautiful settings. The setting of *gold so clere* (2) mentioned before the description of the *erber* morphs into the gold *bonkes* of Eden (*as fyldor fyn*, 106), the maiden that shines "As glysnande golde þat man con schere" (165), her hair "As schorne golde schyr" (213), the heavenly city "al of brende golde bryȝt / As glemande glas burnist broun" (989-90), the

---

[28] Virgil explains in lines 88-93 of *Purgatorio* 4 that the ascent of Mount Purgatory becomes easier the higher one climbs. The relative speed and brightness of the angelic circles that invert the structure of paradise in lines 13-78 of *Paradiso* 28 makes it clear that the celestial spheres move more quickly and shine more brightly the higher they are located above the earth. The incremental increases in joy resulting from the increasing brightness of Beatrice's smile during the ascent of paradise, mentioned earlier, similarly associate successive settings with increases in clarity and impassibility.

city's "strete3 of golde as glasse al bare" (1025), its *golden gate3* (1106), and the Lamb with "horne3 seuen of red golde cler" (1111).

Lorde recurs at the beginning of two other lines, each set in one of the other two main settings: one describes the mirth made by the maidens in the heavenly city (1149) and in the other the narrator expresses the futility of resisting God's will after awakening in the *erber* (1199).

> The dubbemente of þo derworth depe
> Wern bonke3 bene of beryl bry3t.
> Swangeande swete þe water con swepe,
> Wyth a rownande rourde raykande ary3t.
> In þe founce þer stonden stone3 stepe,
> As glente þur3 glas that glowed and gly3t,
> As stremande sterne3, quen stroþe-men slepe,
> Staren in welkyn in wynter ny3t;
> For vche a pobbel in pole þer py3t
> Wat3 emerad, saffer, oþer gemme gente,
> Þat alle þe lo3e lemed of ly3t,
> So dere wat3 hit adubbement.
> (109-20)

The entire last stanza of Fitt II describes the stream which is the boundary between Eden and paradise, the most important landscape feature in the fitt. It mirrors larger structures on a small scale by way of mirroring cosmic structures (here stars in the sky, by way of a simile). The stream epitomizes the features of Eden described earlier in the fitt. The bright, precious stones of different colors which are its *adubbement* represent in the form of gems the different-colored, bright cliffs, trees, birds and banks of Eden. The light from the gems that in *alle þe lo3e lemed* recalls the *glemande glory* that *glent* from the crystal cliffs on *alle þo downe3 syde3* (70-74). The water that is *Swangeande swete* and that *con swepe* with a *rounande rour* such that the gems under it resemble *stremande sterne3* recalls the birds who sing *with a swete asent* and that *flowen* with *flaumbande hwe3* (89-94); the motion of the light from the cliffs (70); the *glem of glode3* that *glyde3* (79); the *grauayl* that *con grynde* which is brighter than the sun (81-84); the dreamer who *welke ay forth in wely wyse* (101); and the landscape features that *con ryse* (103-5). By recalling the different-colored, bright, moving features of nature in the preceding description of Eden, the stream flowing over precious gems underscores the parallel between Eden and the *erber*. The *erber* contains bright, multicolored blooms that *schyneȝ ful schyr agayn þe sunne* (27-28) and its description is preceded by a statement about *gemmeȝ gaye* (7). The movement of the bright features of Eden parallels that of the plants in the *erber* ("spryngande spyceȝ vp ne sponne," 35). It also anticipates the maidens that *con ryse* (1093), *glod* (1105) and *droȝ . . . forth* (1116) in the bejeweled heavenly city that *keued* (981), whose gates *glent as glasse* (1106) and whose *lombe-lyȝt*, like the river flowing from his throne, shines more brightly than the sun or moon (1045-48, 1054-56).

Each pebble in the stream is *pyȝt*, a term for setting or adorning with a jewel that reappears in 192, 205, 217, 229, and 241 (Stanbury). The gem-studded streambed anticipates the gem-studded clothing and crown of the maiden described in Fitt III. The reference to the streambed as "founce þer stonden stoneȝ stepe" anticipates the *foundementeȝ* (993; cf. *fundament*, 1010) of the heavenly city, each created from a different precious stone. Gordon and Stanbury note that *stepe* can be used regarding eyes in the sense "staring, glaring" or regarding jewels in the sense "brilliant," and Gordon observes that *staren* "is not exactly equivalent to 'shine,' but seems bound up with its application to stars"; both words hint at a connection between clarity and vision, anticipating the way vision of the breast pearl and of his maiden in the procession overwhelms the dreamer (223-28; 1147-55). Osgood cites parallels to this description of the streambed in paradisiacal landscapes elsewhere in medieval literature. The dreamer's ability to see stones so clearly through the stream anticipates his ability to see through gem-studded *sotyl cler* dwellings in the heavenly city: "The woneȝ wythinne enurned ware / Wyth all kynneȝ perré þat moȝt repayre" (1027-28). This similarity is reinforced by the parallel between the *bonkes* in Eden he compares to *fyldor fyn* (106) and the *streteȝ of golde* (1025) he mentions right before he describes the bejeweled dwellings of the city (1027-28).

The phrase *stroþe-men* is consistent with associations elsewhere in the poem between living humans and the earth. Gordon glosses *stroþe* as "earth, growth-covered earth." The statements "I am bot mokke and mul among" (905) and "Þy corse in clot mot calder keue" (320) contribute to the pattern. The phrase "quen stroþe-men slepe" invites comparison of the landscape the dreamer sees while asleep with the sky unseen by sleeping humans. It is also a verbal link at the end of the fitt describing Eden to the *slepyng-slaȝte* that ends the fitt describing the *erber*.

Kevin Marti is an associate professor of English at the University of New Orleans. His publications have focused on the Pearl Poet, Dante, and Chaucer.

III

Pearl, Fitt III ("more and more")

Piotr Spyra

The third concatenated stanza set in *Pearl* marks a departure from the noun-centered concatenation of the previous ten stanzas. The third fitt is organized around the words "more and more." Unlike "spot" or "adubbement," this raises an immediate question: more and more of what? The answer is going to come more from within the Dreamer than from without. The focal point here is no longer a physically defined spot, a sense of longing for something external to the narrator, or the beauty of the surrounding landscape but the maddening stream of thoughts and emotions that propel the Dreamer forward across the dreamscape in a frantic dash towards something he cannot quite identify. Forgetting the vertically aligned fall of the pearl down to the ground and the flowers that reach for the sun upwards along the same vertical axis, the narrator and his innermost desires now take on a distinctly horizontal orientation. Dashing across the otherworld, the Dreamer can perhaps hope for some kind of conclusive and comforting suspension of his frantic march onwards, yet cannot suspect what exactly will eventually arrest his movement and bring his spirit to a halt, both in the literal and metaphorical sense. The fitt is not only properly oneiric but altogether nightmarish in the way it approaches the quasi-resolution of the Dreamer's yearning for more and more effected by the appearance of the Maiden. Teasing him by providing apparent closure to his desire, the Maiden actually forecloses the possibility of satisfying it. As the ever-increasing expansion of the dreamscape predicated on the movement of the Dreamer clashes with the intensifying enclosure of his psyche around the more and more dangerously obsessive longing for both experience and joy, her initial appearance marks an important structural caesura in the poem, since it forces the narrator to stop, his immobility being a necessary prerequisite for the debate between the two characters that is to follow. It is the dynamics of movement that reveals the nightmarish face of the dream vision in stanzas 11-15.

Stanza 11

The fitt begins in a relaxed way, with a seemingly careless enumeration "of doun and dalez, / of wod and water and wlonk playnez" (ll. 121-122) that surround the Dreamer in this otherworldly landscape, qualifying all of them with the word "dubbement," the concatenated word of the previous fitt. These lovely downs and dales, the woodlands, the river, and the meadows, all soothe the aching heart of the narrator, which he explains in a number of paraphrases; they not only build up joy in him, but also ease his pain, suppress his anxiety and dispel his pains: they "bylde in me blys, abated me balez / forbidden my stresse, dystryed my paynez" (ll. 123-124). This sort of enumeration brings to mind Gawain's winter journey in another poem of the Cotton Nero A.x manuscript, *Sir Gawain and the Green Knight*, where the text lists in a curiously emotionless fashion all the manifold enemies of the knight, all the "wormez," "wolves," "wodwos," "bullez and berez, and borez," "and etaynez" (ll. 720-723) that he defeats on the way to his destination. In the Pearl-Poet's romance, this sort of enumeration serves to dismiss the threat posed by all these creatures and to stress the fact that winter itself takes on apocalyptic proportions, an enemy far less tangible but much more deadly. Here, in *Pearl*, a similar strategy is at work. The stanza opens with a clear reference to the previous fitt, which was all about the dazzling crystalline opulence of the landscape and its "adubbement," but immediately indicates that the focus will now lie elsewhere, acknowledging all the listed elements of the landscape but discounting them in order to point to something else that is going to preoccupy the narrator just as much as the beauty of the dreamscape, yet constitute real danger at the same time: his desire fuelled by the ocular splendor of his surroundings.

It is also interesting that the way the "doun and dalez" are mentioned here does not follow the regular pattern of description the poet likes to engage in. Speaking of *Sir Gawain and the Green Knight* Marie Borroff observed that there

> the narrator tends to see a given object or agent in relation to other objects or agents within a limited space. The resultant effect is one of fullness or crowding, with, at

times, a stereoscopic projection and depth in the imagined scene. (Borroff 1970, 134-135)

Her observation holds equally well for *Pearl*. However, unlike the description of the garden in fitt one, where the location of the various flowers is defined in relative terms (ll. 43-44), and unlike the relative positioning of the hills, cliffs, woods and the sky as outlined to the reader in fitt two, here the sentence proceeds step by step forwards in a simple line, without digressing even for a moment to comment on where the water meets the meadows or which direction to follow with one's eyes in order to spot the woods or the dales. The enumeration proceeds horizontally, and so does the passage that follows, outlining the effect of the sights on the Dreamer. There is absolutely no time to stop and reflect on what is going on here, and in this respect the opening of stanza 11 moves beyond merely recapitulating the thematic preoccupation of the previous fitt and ushers in the idea of a continuous motion forwards and ever forwards that predominates in *Pearl*'s third stanza set. This brings the readers a bit closer to understanding the phrase "more and more" when they finally get to it by the end of the stanza. Just like the lists of terrain features or their effects on the narrator, the whole fitt is going to provide them with more and more of the same.

From the lines that come next, we learn that the Dreamer followed in bliss "the strem þat dry3ly hạlez" (l. 125), his brains brimful with joy. At this point it is slowly becoming clear that this fitt is indeed more about his reaction to the experience of finding himself in the dreamscape than the otherworld itself. And the next two lines reinforce that impression, since we learn that the further the narrator traveled on, the more the strength of joy constrained his heart (l. 128: "his herte straynez"). No additional detail of the topography of the surrounding area is given here, and none is going to feature in the stanza's final four lines either, for there the narrator launches himself into a reflective meta-remark about the human condition, moving beyond his ocular obsessions for a moment. It becomes apparent, despite the detailed topographical description of the otherworld in fitt two, that what the initial phase of the dream vision in *Pearl* is ultimately about is the inner soulscape of the narrator and not the visual opulence of the lovely downs and dales, even if the latter serves to highlight the former. This accounts for the lack of descriptive detail with regard to the lands opening before the

Dreamer's eyes in stanzas 11-15, especially in comparison with stanzas 6-10.

The move from seeing to reflecting upon what is seen signifies an inward spiritual journey on the part of the narrator and indicates that his movement across this land of visual wonder is fraught with latent meaning, that "the dreamer who sees should also interpret" (Stanbury 1991, 21). With the numbing of his sensory faculties effected at the point of entry into the dream still in place, the narrator finds it difficult, however, to make sense of what he sees. Rather than attempting at an interpretation of the particulars of the scene, he only remarks that "fortune, as it tests a person, regardless of whether she sends him weal or woe, tends to provide him more and more of the same" (ll. 129-132). Andrew and Waldron argue that "the passage seems to be referring to the common human experience that strokes of both good and bad fortune 'come not in single spies / But in battalions' (*Hamlet* 4.1.78-9)" (Andrew and Waldron 2007, 60). This is a feasible explanation of the lines in question, but they strike one as somewhat out of place in this context and invite the main question that the fitt poses: more and more of what? Is it that the dreamer, transported to this miraculous land, has found there even more sorrow than before? This is certainly not the case, what with the numerous reminders about how joyful he is. The only alternative is that he is referring precisely to the joy and elation of finding himself in such a beautiful place and being nourished ("refete" – l. 88) by its exquisite radiance. There is something ominous, nevertheless, about calling this flood of joy a test. The rationale behind it may be that this general comment on the workings of fortune comes from without the vision proper, that it is expressed with hindsight, from a position of knowledge achieved only by the very end of the poem. That this is a test, may, nonetheless, be inferred from the general outlook on the Dreamer's predicament already provided by stanza 11. Leaving the frame of the garden and moving into an open space with no clear boundaries, the Dreamer can no longer hope for any comforting enclosure that would enable him to process his experience. Instead, he has to open himself to the unknown and interact with the unearthly environment of the otherworld. The stakes are high because, whatever happens to him, he knows he is going to face more and more of the same, whatever that might be. And, as the remaining part of the fitt will show, too much bliss can easily turn into a nightmare.

Stanza 12

The second stanza of this fitt provides an excellent example of the Pearl-Poet's mastery in effecting smooth transitions – not just between fitts, but also on a smaller scale, between individual stanzas. Having just learned that fortune tends to give us more and more of the same, we now find out that the amount of what we are experientially given by providence may sometimes be too much to bear. The Dreamer confesses that there was so much joy in him that even if he had the time to express it, he would not be able to. This innocuous remark, despite its honest candor and sense of rapture, brings us a step closer to the nightmarish section of the fitt, for it could just as well be a complaint about the overabundance of sensual and emotional stimuli. While it is hard to see anything truly frightening in it at this stage, once the reader reaches the next stanza these words are going to strike a somewhat ominous note.

It is worth returning to the word "constrains" ("straynez") here, as used in the previous stanza, for the narrator mentions his heart again. Earlier, he spoke of how the joy his "herte straynez," and now he explains that "vrþely herte myȝt not suffyse / to þe tenþe dole of þo gladnez glade" (ll. 135-136). This has traditionally been understood to mean that an earthly heart will not suffice to convey even a tenth part (dole) of the experience. "Dole," however, could also mean sorrow or grief, and thus we get yet another hint that there is something about this joy that could easily turn into a feeling that is much less pleasant. The same could be said of the word "straynez," for while constraining the sorrow-stricken thoughts of the Dreamer certainly serves him well and helps him forget about the pearl he had lost, it does imply some kind of violence done to his emotions. The same word also appears in the manuscript in the text of *Patience* (l. 234), where we see how the wild currents of the storm "strayned" the body of the prophet Jonah, and it is quite obvious there that the process was anything but pleasant.

The text only begins to elaborate fully on the negative side of the dream experience in the next stanza. Here, in stanza 12, what follows the statement about the inadequacies of the narrator's earthly heart is something far less sinister and more comically ironic. It is here that the Dreamer tries to interpret his surroundings and fails utterly in his attempts for the first time. As is the case throughout the poem, his guesses as to the nature of what he sees prove to be inordinately earth-bound and almost absurd in their triteness. A reader of *Pearl* who has gone through the whole poem will know that the river is something that is not to be crossed, a kind of a boundary between the world of mortals who can see things with their physical eyes only and the realm of heaven, where living mortals clearly do not belong and truth is communicated through spiritual sight. The river thus constitutes something of an ontological caesura that structures the entire dreamscape and communicates the sense of disjunction between the realms of heaven and earth. How pathetically trite then is the narrator's remark (ll. 139-140) that the river is most likely an artificial waterway ("a deuyse") constructed to join pleasure-gardens ("myrþes") located by the side of pools ("by merez"). Naturally, the reader unfamiliar with the rest of the poem may at this point actually share this assumption, but this only serves to prove that readers actually share all of the Dreamer's ocular and conceptual handicaps predicated upon his mortality, and that his lesson is also ours. This passage is the first in a series of fragments scattered throughout the poem in which the narrator time and again makes wildly inaccurate guesses or puts forward questions that are comically out of place, as when he asks the Maiden about her lodgings on the other bank (ll. 929-932); there, with no constructions in sight, he seems genuinely alarmed that she should be at the mercy of the elements. It is here, however, in stanza 12, that we find the first germs of this kind of thinking: the Dreamer's thoughts are clearly bound with notions of human artifice, and looking for canals or pleasure-gardens will get him nowhere, try as he might to understand the nature of the otherworldly lands with his limited earthly logic.

What is worth noting is that the poem puts the critics in the exact same position in which it puts the Dreamer. Many have tried to make sense of the topography of the otherworld, which produced readings such as Sandra Pierson Prior's. Prior argues that

> [a]lthough it is usual to read this river [the one running through the dream landscape] as one and the same with the river that flows from the Throne envisioned at the end of the poem, such an identification is never made in the poem and is, I believe, totally wrong. (Prior 1996, 61)

In an analogous manner, Wendell Stacy Johnson inquires about the exact location of the trees mentioned in stanza 90, trying to make sense of the phrase "aboute þat water" (l. 1077). Do they stand on the stream's edge or are they part of the heavenly city (Johnson 1970,

45)? What both Prior and Johnson are doing is not much different from the Dreamer's interpretive efforts in stanza 12. The fact is that finding himself in this otherworldly landscape the Dreamer has to construct its meaning from scratch, and the quality of his guesses and assumptions serves to illustrate a major point: as a mortal he is nowhere near grasping the true essence of reality. And—by the same token—critics are bound to make similar mistakes by engaging in the same kind of necessary, natural yet often limited readings of the otherworld's topography, focusing on the superficial layers of the textual material.

The following two lines (ll. 139-140) once again strike a note of irony if one is already familiar with the remainder of the poem. "I thought there was a walled city on the other side" are the narrator's words, and he is both right and wrong. Not knowing what is to come next, the reader may envision finding a medieval city on the other bank and thus share in the Dreamer's expectations, but the city to be revealed is neither medieval nor walled in the traditional sense, for it is the New Jerusalem, with its walls made of gemstones. Nor is it literally *there* on the other bank, for the Dreamer only manages to see it later in a spiritual vision and never actually spots it in the distance. This part of stanza 12 is crucial for understanding the later events in the poem, for it contains the first indication that the Dreamer will find it particularly difficult to think of a *city* in anything other than earthly terms; this will come to the surface when at some point he is going to refuse to accept that he can actually see the New Jerusalem, arguing that the city of Jerusalem is in Judea and simply cannot be anywhere else (ll. 921-922).

The transition from merely observing the dreamscape to interpreting it is crucial for the progression of the narrative, for it prepares ground for the later debate between the Maiden and the Dreamer. Still, the final two lines of stanza 12 (ll. 143-144) take us beyond the mood of speculation and the interpretative endeavors of the Dreamer aimed at making sense of what he sees: "Bot þe water watz depe, I dorst not wade, / and euer me longed ay more and more." This expression of visceral fear and its conflux with an increase in desire is already an ominous introduction to the terrors that the Dreamer confronts in the next stanza.

Stanza 13

John Gardner once noticed that the text of *Pearl* "incorporate[s] to an unusual degree elements of realistic dream psychology"

(Gardner 1975, 10). Stanza 13 serves well to illustrate this point. It is also unique when it comes to the way it opens. What the reader finds here is more and more of "more" itself. Unlike in the other stanzas of fitt three, the entire phrase "more and more"–and not just one "more"–appears here, and it follows directly the final "more and more" of stanza 12. This fourfold repetition of "more" may be seen as drawing our attention to something important just about to happen, something that the Dreamer will hardly be able to bear given his earthly heart.

What "more" qualifies here is the Dreamer's desire, for he explains that his longing to see the other bank grew with every moment, so beautiful was it to behold from his vantage point. When at some point he wishes to wade across, however, problems arise. With no suitable ford in sight, he wanders on, and the further he goes by the bank the more dangerous the prospect of reaching the other side turns out to be: "Bot woþes mo iwysse þer ware / þe fyrre I stalked by þe stronde" (ll. 151-152). Although it could be read as an expression of social anxiety, suggestive of the Dreamer's unease in the face of meeting the lord of the supposed pleasure-gardens (see Andrew and Waldron 2007, 61), "mo woþes" (more dangers) also suggests that with the narrator's every step the current is getting wilder, and the passage more risky. This part of the poem makes use of dream mechanics in a number of ways. First of all, it presents the Dreamer as prompted to move towards a certain destination that appears to be unattainable. The further he gets, the closer he ought to find himself to whatever it is he is after, but the distance he covers only reduces his chances of reaching the other bank. Moreover, the realization of this frustrates him; when he says that it seemed to him that he should not hesitate for fear of harm and finally make the attempt to wade across (ll. 153-154: "and euer me þo3t I schulde not wonde / for wo") and fails to deliver on his words, this sounds as if he was being systematically denied something by his dream experience. He is tempted into longing for the other side and its splendor and stopped short of ever getting there, and thus the intensity of its beauty and the resulting intensity of his desire prove to be a curse rather than a blessing. Being so close and yet so distant from the object of one's desire is very close to actual dream mechanics, and so is the fact that for some reason turning back never seems to be a feasible option for the Dreamer. What is a nightmare if not an experience of attempting either to reach something, or to escape from someone, and being locked up in a timeless stasis in which we are one small step away from attaining our goal, or only a hair's width away from the monster pursuing us, never quite able to achieve satisfaction or reach safety? What the vision has in store for the Dreamer is more than beautiful vistas or fascinating colors – it is also a mechanism for fuelling his desire with no option provided ever for satisfying it.

At this point is might be useful to try to define what exactly constitutes the nature of the narrator's desire. Naturally, it could be identified with a sense of possessiveness towards his pearl, the object of his desire, but in the context of fitt three and the exploration of the dreamscape in general, there is an additional–cognitive, or rather epistemological–level to it. As Barbara Kowalik puts it, the Dreamer has a "curious and searching spirit" (Kowalik 1994, 18), and he desires to know just as much as he craves to possess. The latter aspect of his longing to reach the other bank is at this stage in the poem still more prominent than the former. With the Maiden not yet in sight, he wishes to cross the stream not to hold her in his arms but simply to verify the various hypotheses he has just formulated in his mind. That this is the main stimulus driving him across the otherworld makes an important point about human nature and man's epistemological capacity, the Dreamer becoming something of an Everyman in this respect. Always struggling to provide answers to manifold questions yet failing to capture the essence of reality on the other side of the great divide between man and God, human reason is both a powerful epistemological tool and a source of inevitable fallacies, which the narrator's mistaken theory of canals and pleasure-gardens epitomizes, for despite what the narrator surmises, the flow of this particular river and the essence of divine nature can never be circumscribed by an earthly, mortal agent.

This desire to know, to explore and to domesticate the unfamiliar also emerges from the linearity of the narrator's movement. He keeps heading on along the bank of the stream, traversing an open space without any recognizable landmarks or limits to its vast expanse, possibly unable, and certainly unwilling to turn back. In this, *Pearl* is much different from the famous French allegorical poem *Roman de la Rose*, for its dream comes not within the confines of a *hortus conclusus*, but precisely upon leaving the garden and moving out into the open. While the *Roman* is a major source for the poem, the dominant inspiration in this section of the vision comes neither from its secular allegory, nor from the eschatological visions of the Book of the Apocalypse, but from down-to-earth dream mechanics. One need not even refer to Macrobius, the medieval authority on dreams and their classification and meaning, to make sense of the Dreamer's experience, for it is founded on the visceral fear of being suspended in a life-or-death situation rather than the magisterial exposition of different types of dreams that Macrobius offers in his *Commentary on the "Dream of Scipio."* After all, whether the Dreamer makes his move or not is a matter of life and death, and with every second he tarries he finds himself contemplating a more and more daunting task. What makes this experience so literally nightmarish is that, unable to decide either way, he simply carries on, torn apart—more and more—by his desire and fear for his own life.

This apparent enclosure of the Dreamer within the dynamics of his forward movement, so static despite all the vigor of his drive across the dreamscape, may also be seen as symbolic of his later position in the debate with the Pearl Maiden. He will often seemingly accept her arguments, follow her guidance and listen with great care and attentiveness, yet time and again he will utter words that will immediately prove he has moved nowhere. The best example of this is perhaps his question about the wound of the Lamb, which he is quite surprised at (l. 1138), or his questions about the lodgings of the Maiden. Although he keeps marching on, he is, after all, not getting closer to anything, and the linearity of his progression may, from this perspective, be seen as quite circular, leading nowhere but into the same dark alleys and corners of his mortal mind. A major change that will help him break out of this deadlock, arrest his movement and present him with something more is, however, just about to happen. Whether it will offer the Dreamer more of the same, or even more than that, is not yet clear when, with much suspense, he tells us that "a new matter came to [his] notice, which moved [his] mind ever more and more" (ll. 155-156).

Stanza 14

Stanza 14 is founded upon suspense. We learn that there is a young maiden on the other bank who is familiar to the Dreamer, but what she really is and how the Dreamer knows her is, and will remain, a mystery. This requires some commentary on the construction of the poem in general. The fact is that although numerous hints are scattered throughout the text that identify the

Maiden as the Dreamer's daughter, practically to the point of certainty, the nature of their relation is never defined explicitly, and the words "my father" or "my daughter" are never uttered. In this respect, the epistemological perspective of the reader mirrors that of the narrator, for just like the Dreamer, who can only get closer and closer to the truth about his vision without ever grasping it fully, the reader of the poem is bound never to acquire certainty as to the true nature of the Dreamer-Maiden relationship. This strategy, consisting in having both the poem's protagonist and readers face similar epistemological limitations, may account for the rather curious fact that this key detail of the story is in the end never overtly clarified.

The actual connection between the girl and the narrator remains therefore somewhat vague. Visually precise, the words of the text tell us much about what the girl looked like but little as to what that might mean – either for the Dreamer, or for us, the readers. The Maiden is found sitting under a crystal cliff, her mantle shining with a radiance not unlike that of the crystalline background that, rather than silhouetting her, seems to merge with her body. This communicates very well the idea that there is something uniquely special about the girl, and the lack of clear division between the Dreamer's perception of the Maiden and that of the landscape points to her being not only more than earthly words could express but ontologically more than one could ever make sense of. The image of the girl is then followed by the line "I knew hyr wel, I hade sen hyr ere" (l. 164), which seems to lead somewhere, promising a solution to this puzzle, but is cut short by another visual observation – that the girl shone like glistened gold that has been cut. Once again the Dreamer introduces the element of artifice into his interpretation of the otherworld. Right after he says that he could recognize her, he begins to describe her not in terms of the landscape, or as part of it, but as the work of a goldsmith. He puts special emphasis here not on the fact that she shone like gold, but that the gold she made him think of was worked on by a human hand. This serves as an introduction to the metaphor used extensively in the later debate of the Dreamer and the Maiden – that of the jeweler. Indeed, what the Dreamer is already beginning to do here is to see his daughter as his own creation, the product of his own metalworking, which by right belongs to him, for he is her originator. What he fails to notice is that the Maiden is truly one with the landscape (which fitt four will reinforce in its imagery), being something of its extension, which the imagery of radiance that she shares with it strongly suggests. Above all, however, this comparison with cut gold and the metaphorical self-identification of the Dreamer with a goldsmith or a jeweler makes little sense when juxtaposed with the image of a pearl. Pearls are not worked on but simply recovered from nature, made directly by God's hand. Stanza 14 bears witness to this confused and contradictory clash of metaphors communicating the inner struggle of the narrator's mind regarding the identity of the girl's true maker; while he may see her metaphorically as a product of metalworking, she is in fact a *pearl*, the creation of the ultimate Maker of all. It is quite ironic that this mistaken observation is ushered in by the words "I knew her well."

The stanza also engages the problematic of spiritual (mis-)recognition, an important issue both in the poem at large and the *Pearl* manuscript as such. Acts of recognition are for the Pearl-Poet distinctly visual, yet it takes more than good eyesight to make them epistemologically valid. As the Maiden says later in fitt six, she thinks little of a jeweler who believes everything he sees with his eyes (ll. 301-302). Seeing is not the same as knowing, and ocular inspection does not automatically lead to mastery over the perceived object. This emerges very clearly from an episode in *Pearl's* manuscript companion, *Cleanness*, where Christ's regal divinity is immediately recognized by the animals in the stable (l. 1087), even if the image of a poor baby they see does not visually suggest that in any way. The Dreamer's problem is that, conditioned by his mortality and possessiveness, he is guided by physical rather than spiritual sight and takes the girl for a product of a human, and not divine hand. This also connects with the altogether misguided attempts of the Dreamer to make sense of the dreamscape in the previous stanzas. And the final two lines once again bring us back to the desire to possess more and more and present it as intertwined with the Dreamer's visual efforts aimed at epistemological mastery over the perceived scene: "On lenghe I loked to hyr þere; / þe lenger, I knew hyr more and more" (ll. 167-168). The longer he looks, the more he believes he knows the Maiden. As the remainder of the poem will show, this belief is nothing but self-illusion. The only things the Dreamer can know are the things he already knows from his mortal life, and the Pearl Maiden is not really the same mortal person that he had lost, for she now belongs to the crystalline otherworld and not the garden-world of death and decay.

Stanza 15

The fitt's final stanza is again focused on the act of looking, this time in terms of an actual exchange of gazes. So far the Dreamer was the only agentive force in the otherworld, and the sole source of action in the poem. It is only here that we witness the first reaction of the dream landscape to his presence, channeled through the Pearl Maiden. Her gaze only comes late in the stanza, however. At first it is still all about the narrator's act of looking, and despite all the earlier excitement and joy at finding himself in the dream world, he now says that he was swept away by such a feeling of "gladande glory [...] / As lyttel byfore þerto watz wonte" (ll. 171-172). The gradual intensification of his feelings has evidently not ceased, and his desire to cross the river and reach the other bank is now stronger than ever before. His joy must therefore be qualified by a sense of irony, for as the dangers increased with his every step, finally precluding him from safely wading across the river, his decision not to run the risk and make the attempt is now something he will certainly regret. On the other hand, such a static conclusion of his spirit's journey along the bank is a necessary prerequisite for the debate to follow, for it allows the Dreamer and the Maiden to maintain the distance necessary to effect it. It must be noted, however, that although the Dreamer is not going to move until the very end of the poem, this does not imply emotional immobility, for his desire to be reunited with the Maiden will only grow ever more and more.

The confusion which the narrator feels at this particular moment is, as he says, partly due to the fact that he sees the girl in "so strange a place" (l. 175). This is a perfect example of looking without truly seeing. Not only is she radiant with an unnatural beauty that characterizes the whole of the mysterious landscape he traverses, but she is also separated from him by a river he cannot find the courage to cross – and these are signs he fails to interpret, blindly assuming that nothing has changed since the day he saw her last in the earthly world. In other words, he acknowledges the oddity of seeing her there yet does not see the significance of the peculiar circumstances of this encounter. His desire makes him blind to the overwhelming sense of difference between the girl he once knew and the maiden he now sees.

The climactic moment of the fitt comes when the Maiden finally returns the Dreamer's gaze. Yet instead of a recognition parallel to his, subtended by desire and possessive love, her cold gaze only pierces the narrator, and the word "stonge" communicates an experience that involves real pain, one that "stonge myn hert ful stray atount" (l. 179), which Andrew and Waldron translate as stinging "into bewildered excitement." Once again we witness in the Dreamer a mixture of joy and pain, but what is of crucial importance here is that his gaze is not really reciprocated. It is obviously returned physically, but the cold eyes of the Maiden "speak" for the landscape and the realm of heaven rather than the girl that once loved him in the earthly world. In other words, what we see here is the first reaction of the dreamscape to the Dreamer, the first mutual interaction between the two and the formational stage of the debate which will be organized around this very principle: that of the Dreamer desperately trying to reach the girl, not just in the physical but also in the emotional sense, yet never moving a jot towards reclaiming his pearl.

The imagery of stanza 15 includes more references to painful intrusions upon the Dreamer's heart. Not only is his heart stung, but when his desire almost pushes him to action, "baysment get myn hert a brunt" (l. 174). In the words of Andrew and Waldron's translation, "desire urged me to call her, but confusion dealt my heart a blow." And then the act of seeing her there "my3t make myn herte blunt" (l. 176). His heart is here first delivered a blow, then stunned and finally stung. These violent actions done to the narrator's heart are mentioned in almost every other line, as if with every beat of his heart his suffering increased. Quite obviously "heart" could be read here metaphorically, and we may speculate about the word's exact meaning, but it seems that its most literal meaning, suiting the nightmarish aesthetics of the vision, is also at work here.

Fitt three in general, and its final stanza in particular, points to the rather problematic understanding of spiritual vision addressed by the narrative of *Pearl*. Although fitt two opens with the narrator saying that from the spot in the garden "my spyryt þer sprang in space" (l. 61) and that "my goste is gon in Godez grace" (l. 63), in fitt three this spirit evidently functions as embodied. The Dreamer considers the physical dangers of wading across the river, interacts with the environment and finally elicits its response in the form of the Maiden's cold, stinging gaze. His heart is first constrained by the strength of joy in stanza 11, only to receive a whole barrage of blows in stanza 15. The heart is here to be identified with his earthly, mortal desire, and that is why it could barely suffice to tell the tenth of the story. Its leanings and motions are incompatible with the cold, crystalline and deathly otherworld of the vision. This contrast only reinforces the impression that the Dreamer can never fully belong in the dreamscape. Being mortal, all he can do is to face the unknown and to try to withstand the gaze of the Maiden, whom he knows yet cannot really recognize the way he should. The Maiden's voice, which will speak with the wisdom of the elect and of the Lamb, is a go-between in his exposure to the divine realm of existence. Likewise, the Maiden's gaze stands in for the gaze of the Lord, which the Dreamer could never bear in this life even for a moment. As his heart is stung more and more the longer he looks at her, which the final two lines of the fitt finally tell us, we realize more and more than ever before that *Pearl* is above all about the incommensurable duality of the two planes of reality and bears witness to the great gulf between heaven and earth.

References

Andrew, Malcolm, and Ronald Waldron, eds. 2007. *The Poems of the Pearl Manuscript.* 5th ed. Exeter: University of Exeter Press.

Andrew, Malcolm, and Ronald Waldron, trans. 2007. *The Poems of the Pearl Manuscript: A Prose Translation.* Exeter: University of Exeter Press.

Borroff, Marie. 1970. "Criticism of Style: The Narrator in the Challenge Episode." In *Critical Studies of Sir Gawain and the Green Knight*, edited by Donald R. Howard and Christian K. Zacher, 125-143. Notre Dame, IN: University of Notre Dame Press.

Gardner, John. 1975. Introduction and Commentary to *The Complete Works of the Gawain-Poet*, edited by John Gardner, 3-90. Chicago: University of Chicago Press.

Johnson, Wendell Stacy. 1970. "The Imagery and Diction of The Pearl: Toward an Interpretation." In *The Middle English Pearl: Critical Essays*, edited by John Conley, 27-49. Notre Dame, IN: University of Notre Dame Press.

Kowalik, Barbara. 1994. *Artistry and Christianity in Pearl.* Gdańsk: Wydawnictwo Gdańskie.

Prior, Sandra Pierson. 1996. *The Fayre Formez of the Pearl Poet.* East Lansing: Michigan State University Press.

Stanbury, Sarah. 1991. *Seeing the "Gawain"-Poet: Description and the Act of Perception.* Philadelphia: University of Pennsylvania Press.

Piotr Spyra is Assistant Professor in the Department of Studies in Drama and Pre-1800 English Literature at the University of Łódź, where he teaches medieval and early modern English literature. He is the author of *The Epistemological Perspective of the Pearl-Poet* (2014). His research interests revolve around Middle English poetry, medieval folklore as well as literary theory. He is also the founder and supervisor of Geoffrey Chaucer Student Society, an academic society aimed at promoting Middle English literature among students of English literature in Poland. Email: cyrillus@wp.pl

IV

"Pyȝt": Ornament, Place, and Site – A Commentary on the Fourth Fitt of *Pearl*

Daniel C. Remein

The refrain-words of Fitt IV of *Pearl* play on the varyingly pitched semantic valences of the word *pyȝt*, often in alliteration with the phrase *precios perle(ȝ)*, and–in two of the five stanzas–also with the word *pyece*. Attention to the function of *pyȝt* in the language of this section–especially in relation to the dynamics of a proliferation of ornament and desire as played out within the spatial dynamics of place or site–will provide the main conceptual thread of this commentary.

Two Preliminary Glosses

1. *more*, the link.

Before proceeding to discuss *pyȝt*, a preparatory excursus on the concatenating word from the previous fitt is necessary. The concatenating form of the poem places the word *more*, from the refrain on *more and more* in Fitt III, as the first word of the first stanza of Fitt IV.[1] While all the sections of the poem carry over such concatenation, the overflow of *more* beyond the bounds of its proper section, with its connotations of excess and desire, would seem to constitute a special paradigmatic case. The status of *more* as a

---

[1] For further description of the generative formal restraints of *Pearl*, see Malcom Andrew and Ronald Waldron, eds., *The Poems of the Pearl Manuscript* (Exeter: University of Exeter Press, 1999), 34. See also, E.V. Gordon, ed., *Pearl* (Oxford: Oxford University Press, 1953), xxxvi-xli, 87-90; and Marie Borroff, trans., *Pearl: A New Verse Translation*, (New York: Norton, 1977), 32-5. References to specific lines of *Pearl* within sections of the commentary given parenthetically in line numbers. All references to *Pearl*, unless otherwise noted, from E. V. Gordon, ed., *Pearl* (Oxford: Oxford University Press, 1953). References to glossaries from editions of *Pearl* given in the format, "Gordon, *Pearl*, sv."

comparative adjective reminds the reader that there is always "more" without answering the question "of what." This link thus threatens the reader with at least two exhilarating and terrifying aspects of the mechanics of desire. 1) As critic George Edmondson argues, in Lacanian terms, *Pearl* is a poem about desire not only in that it dramatizes the preemptory loss of the Real that constitutes the subject, but also in that the poem confronts the reader with "a desire—or rather a *desirousness*—in the makeup of the Other that, once perceived, disrupts the illusion of the Other as 'whole'."[2] There is always more; and yet the pearl can always circulate as symbol, signifier, and allegory for such a dizzying array of readings because it can mark the "traumatic *punctum* of the Other's desire."[3] *More* is *less* than you might think. This is in part why the dreamer opens the first stanza of Fitt IV with the exclamation of fear, "[m]ore þen me lyste my drede arose," even at the site/sight of what he will soon discern as the lost object of his desire, his pearl/maiden.[4]

2) Paradoxically, at the same time that it inserts the reader into a psychoanalytic logic, this instance of *more* (the semantic, thematic, and decorative importance of which modestly poses as a mere exigency of *concatenation*) insists on the facticity of a kind of phenomenological experience. This insistence follows from the way that the overflow of *more* into Fitt IV offers *more* as a substantive and perhaps even suggests the substantiality or materiality of *moreness*.

This substantialization of *moreness* will not only associate *more* with *pyȝt*, but will also set up Fitt IV to maintain the focus built up by the description of the dream-landscape in Fitt III—namely, the material dynamics of desire in a material and overwhelmingly ornamental landscape containing, among the "dubbement dere of

---

[2] George Edmondson, "*Pearl:* The Shadow of the Object, the Shape of the Law," *Studies in the Age of* Chaucer 26 (2004): 42, 52. According to Edmondson, this incompleteness of the Other is conditioned by what Lacan marks as S(Ø) (read *S, barred-O*), or the "signifier of the lack in the Other" (48).

[3] Ibid., 61.

[4] A number of critics comment on the dramatization of these mechanics of desire in this most basic form. Viz. Edmondson, "*Pearl:* The Shadow of the Object," 40-41, 52-55; and Ad Putter, *An Introduction to the Gawain-Poet* (London: Longman, 1996), 155-56. See also J.J. Anderson, *Language and Imagination in the Gawain-Poet* (Manchester: Manchester University Press, 2005), 26; Sandra Pierson Prior, *The Fayre Formez of the Pearl Poet* (East Lansing: Michigan State University Press, 1996), 161-62.

doun and daleȝ" (121), "[a] crystal clyffe ful relusaunt" (159). Far from a hazy immaterial dream, as A.C. Spearing characterizes it, the dream world offers, "a science fiction landscape: it is planetary or lunar in its strangeness, and has a technicolour harshness in its brilliance."[5]

2. *Pyȝt*

In recorded literary usage, the Middle English (ME) word *pyȝt*, past tense of ME *picchen*, had a highly variable semantic range–the result of a semantic fusion of at least two Old English (OE) verbs (possibly verbs distinguishing intransitive/transitive and/or causative/non-causative verbs from one or two homophonic stems, *píc* and *pytt*) as well as the likely influence (if not direct involvement in the fusion) of Latinate cognates.[6] This fusion may very well have

---

[5] A. C. Spearing, *The Gawain-Poet: A Critical Study* (Cambridge: Cambridge University Press, 1970), 143. See also, Theodore Bogdanos, *Pearl: Image of the Ineffable: A Study in Medieval Poetic Symbolism* (University Park: The Pennsylvania State University Press, 1983), 42.

[6] Gordon's glossary to *Pearl*, sv. *pyȝt*, records an etymology from unattested OE Class I weak verb **piccan* (pa. t. *pihte*). The *Middle English Dictionary* (MED, online at http://quod.lib.umich.edu/m/med/) offers the same etymology by comparison with attested cognates in Old Icelandic (*pikka, pjakka*) and other medieval Germanic languages (MED, sv. *picchen* (v.), etym). The *Oxford English Dictionary* (OED, online at http://www.oed.com/) entry for modern *pitch*, a reflex of ME *picchen*, records "etymology uncertain," noting that the word is "perhaps the reflex" of unattested OE class I weak verb **piccan* (OED, sv. *pitch, v*^{2}, etym). The situation in OE is particularly confusing because even in identifying a related noun or a verbal root one would have to first distinguish between *píc* and *pîc*. This latter means pitch, resin, or tar, and forms the stem for OE verb *pícian* (to cover in pitch)–and so constitutes a red herring in our discussion of *pyȝt* (Joseph Bosworth, *An Anglo-Saxon Dictionary,* ed. Thomas Northcote Toller and Alistair Campbell (Oxford: Oxford University Press), 1973, sv. *píc, pic,* and *pícian*; this work cited hereafter as Bosworth-Toller). The OED further suggests that **piccan* may itself have been a causative formation from a stem shared by the verb for which modern *pick* is the reflex, with the caveat that we do not know if the stem vowel was long (as that particular causative construction would have required) (OED, sv. *pitch* v.2). Until the *Dictionary of Old English*–a perhaps more systematic lexigraphical authority–is able to publish a *p*-fascicule, we can only lay out the complexities of the extant material. Indeed, Toller's *Supplement* deletes *pícan* ("to use a *píc*, to remove by means of a *píc*") and redirects us to the *Supplement* entry for *pýtan*,

been a superficial and incomplete homophonic convergence that may have undergone subsequent fission, or, at any rate, was temporary—as attested by Present Day English *pit, pitch, peak,* and *pike,* and even the ubiquitous near function-verb *put.* In any case, the result was that *pyȝt* represented the enfolding of a whole host of related senses into either a single verb or verbs so homophonic and varyingly spelled that the *Oxford English Dictionary* (OED), the *Middle English Dictionary* (MED), and critical glossaries of *Pearl* have a difficult time efficiently distinguishing them; these senses include: making a hole with a pointed tool, removing something from a hole with a pointed tool, thrusting or throwing a pointed tool towards a particular spot, thrusting something into the ground so as to place it, placing/pitching a tent or other structure, shaping a tool into a point,

---

meaning "to push, poke, thrust, put out the eyes" (Bosworth-Toller, Supplement, sv. *pícan*). Loosely speaking, phonetically, the ME verb *picchen,* with its medial palatal affricate, *could* be the reflex of a verb with a stem ending in a [k] that underwent gemination and subsequent palatization, or the reflex of a verb ending in [t] with an infinitive in *-ian* (also resulting in palatization). This is the case whether or not the OE verbs in question are causative, and regardless of how they were formed. It would seem *possible,* even probable, that the apparent semantic variability in ME *picchen* could result from the fusion of two distinct OE verbs. Relatively unique among European languages, "Old English causative pairs often develop into single double-functional verbs, that can be used both with an intransitive and causative meaning" (Luisa García García, "Morphological Causatives in Old English: The Quest for a Vanishing Formation," *Transactions of the Philological Society* 110.1 [22]: 123). However, the OED also notes the potential influence of post-classical Latin *picchiarre* (to pitch hay), an "apparently isolated attestation," and Anglo-Norman *piccher* (to drive in foundation piles)–and the relationship of such words to ME *picchen* must probably remain unclear in the same way as that of ME *pike* (presumably from OE *píc,* and, presumably a word suggesting a device with a certain pointed shape, used in the activity described by *piccher*–whether in detailing jewelry or metalwork or pitching a tent) (OED, sv. *pitch* v.2, etym; and sv. *pike* n.1, etym). Regarding the etymology of *pike* in relation to both Germanic and Latinate cognates, the OED notes that "[t]his group of words presents many difficulties both in Romance and Germanic; the pattern of borrowing within and between Romance and Germanic languages appears to have been particularly complex, with individual words and senses being borrowed in different directions and at different times, in many cases reinforcing pre-existing words or senses" (OED, sv. *pike* n.1, etym.).

and decorating/arraying/adorning an object.[7] This last sense may seem like a sweeping denotative shift, but in fact can be considered an instance of semantic narrowing/amelioration: adorning an object can be one potential result of a carful picking away at or pitting of a surface, an expert placement of jewels or other ornamentation, and/or the production of (an array of) small spikes (as in a crown). So what links the semantic field is not counterintuitive, but the slope is slippery; it can be put in terms of a slurry of homophonic Present Day English reflexes: to make a pit you might use a pike, which is, of course, peaked–but might also be pitched, which might mean that you have put that peaked pike in a pit; and similarly, to put a tent in place you might pitch a pike into a pit.

And it would seem that some, if not all of this wider semantic variability should be understood as simultaneously active in occurrences of *py3t* in *Pearl*–especially in its occurrences as the refrain word of this fourth fitt. O. D. Macrae Gibson points out that the function of *py3t* as a concatenating word stresses its capacity to mean both *arrayed* and *set*.[8] Gordon glosses the word as varying in sense throughout the poem between "set," "fixed," and "adorned" (in the past tense form *py3t*), and "set," "placed," "fixed," and "adorned (with gems)" (in the past participle form *py3te*).[9] Andrew and Waldron gloss the word under their entry for the dialectical form of the uninflected infinitive *pyche*, recording variations in sense in *Pearl* between "array," "dress," and "decorate," and, in *Sir Gawain and the Green Knight* and *Cleanness*, between "fasten," "strike," "stick," and "occupy."[10] Sarah Stanbury's student-aimed marginal glosses vary between "fixed," "decorated," "trimmed," and "embroidered."[11] The MED records occurrences of similarly inflected/conjugated forms of *picchen* in *Pearl* as examples of its primary and tertiary definitions. The primary definition is expansive, reflecting a sense of transitive thrusting, throwing, or less powerful setting-into-motion of an object–along a precise

---

[7] See note above.
[8] O.D. Macrae-Gibson, "*Pearl:* The Link Words and the Thematic Structure," in *The Middle English Pearl: Critical Essays*, ed. John Conley (Notre Dame: University of Notre Dame Press, 1970), 206-07; reprinted from *Neophilologus* 52 (1968): 54-64.
[9] Gordon, *Pearl*, sv. *py3t*.
[10] Andrew and Waldron, *The Poems of the Pearl Manuscript*, sv. *pyche*.
[11] Sarah Stanbury, ed. *Pearl* (Kalamazoo: TEAMS, 2001), at lines 117, 192, 204, 216.

trajectory—resulting in the firm placement of that object in an equally precise place.[12] The MED records the occurrence of *pyȝt* at line 216, in the third stanza of Fitt IV, as an example for the specific sense of "to set something firmly in place, fix, embed."[13] The secondary sense offered by the MED, concerning setting up and building (especially pavilions or tents), needs to be understood as a variation on the sense of setting or thrusting a stake or pole into the ground which metonymically comes to refer to setting up the tent of which the pole is a part. Thus, in the alliterative *Morte Arthur*, the men of the round table "pight pavis [shields] on port [port-side]" much as one pitches a tent or as a jeweler fixes, sets up, or thrusts the gems of an ornament into particular places.[14]

The "poetic" senses of *pyȝt* ("adorned" or "arrayed")—to which readers of *Pearl* often leap—must be understood as concepts of adornment intimately related to and derived from a semantic field that coordinates concepts of place and spatial relations as well as technologies of emplacement and related locating, aiming, and architectonic activities/technologies.

That we should be alert to how multiple regions of this semantic field may overlap in any given occurrence of the term in *Pearl* is reinforced by key occurrences of these terms across the *Pearl*-poet corpus.[15] When, in *Sir Gawain and the Green Knight*, the *Pearl*-poet describes Bertilak's castle as it first appears to Gawain, it is "pyched on a prayere [meadow], a park al about/ Wyth a pyked [spiked, peaked (?)] palace pyned [enclosed] ful þik."[16] We are not here told about any building materials or procedures, only of the place of the castle, and so it would seem that the "pyched" castle is referred to less as "built" than as "situated" or "set"—or, alternately,

---

[12] See MED, sv. *picchen* (v.), 1.

[13] MED, sv. *picchen* (v.), 1c.

[14] See Larry D. Benson, ed., *King Arthur's Death: The Middle English* Stanzaic Morte Arthur *and* Alliterative Morte Arthur (Exeter: University of Exeter Press, 1986), 325. Cf. MED, sv. *picchen* (v.), 2a.

[15] Even aside from the now commonplace attribution of the poems of the London, British Library MS Cotton Nero A.x (art. 3) to a single author, accounts of thematic development across the MS have long been commonplace in *Pearl*-criticism. E.g. Lynn Staley Johnson, *The Voice of the Gawain-Poet* (Madison: University of Wisconsin Press, 1984).

[16] Norman Davis, ed., *Sir Gawain and the Green Knight*, eds. J.R.R. Tolkien and E.V. Gordon, 2nd Edn. (Oxford: Oxford University Press, 1967), lines 768-9.

that this usage derives from a metaphorical application of the verb for pitching or erecting a tent to the construction of a more permanent type of structure. The word *pyked* occurs as well in the following line, part of a cross-line alliteration on *p-*, but with the seemingly quite clear sense of "peaked" or "spiked" in reference to towers or battlements. By comparison, consider the use of the word in the account of the rich man's banquet from the Gospel of Matthew as retold in *Cleanness,* in which the rich man invites the poor wretches into his house so that "my palys plat full be py3t al aboute."[17] The term is here used more clearly in its "poetic" sense, as "arrayed" or "adorned,"[18] an implicit metaphor raising the social and aesthetic rank of the feast of the poor guests to that of decorations in a rich man's palace.

Following this philological excursus, the refrain of *py3t* in this fitt should also be read as a direct echo of the refrain on *spot* in the opening fitt of the poem. *Py3t* provides the poem with parallel but alternative puns related to *place* and physical location. In the following glosses on each stanza of Fitt IV, *py3t* will mark an obsession with spatiality, location, and the threshold of the site– despite influential readings of the poem that favor the prejudices of the pearl-maiden's exegesis and argue that the dreamer moves towards "a love uncircumscribed by the limits of the physical world."[19] Insofar as she is *py3t,* she will remain circumscribed by a notion of spatiality.

181-192:

> More þen me lyste my drede arose.
> I stod ful stylle and dorste not calle;
> Wyth y3en open and mouth ful clos
> I stod as hende as hawk in halle.
> I hoped þat ghostly wat3 þat porpose;
> I dred ondende quat schulde byfalle,
> Lest ho me eschaped þat I þer chos,
> Er I at steuen hit mo3t stalle.

---

[17] Malcom Andrew and Ronald Waldron, eds., "Cleanness," in *The Poems of the Pearl Manuscript* (Exeter: University of Exeter Press, 1999), line 83.
[18] See Moorman's marginal gloss on this occurrence, Charles Moorman, ed., *The Works of the* Gawain-*Poet* (Jackson: University Press of Mississippi, 2009), line 83.
[19] E.g. Johnson, *The Voice of the Gawain-Poet,* 162. See also 170.

> Þat gracios gay wythouten galle,
> So smoþe, so smal, so seme slyȝt,
> Ryseȝ vp in hir araye ryalle,
> A precios pyece in perleȝ pyȝt.

The vertical trajectory of *drede* (dread) in line 181 is matched by the rising of the delayed subject of the stanza's final sentence: the "precios pyece in perleȝ pyȝt" (192). The *precios pyece,* however, is contrastingly placed within a decorative radial field, and rises in her "araye ryalle." The *dread* itself, were we to visualize it in its contrast to the *pyce,* would appear as dull in finish but not necessarily entirely unpleasant. It may be only an instance of litotes when the dreamer reports the dread arising "[m]ore þen me lyste"; but, even so, it marks the extent to which the dreamer's experience is here constituted by a play of *enjoyment* (as distinguished from "pleasure").[20] One *can* desire and enjoy desiring an arising of dread, *but only to a point.* Critics have suggested that the dreamer's fear of losing the maiden a second time, or, alternately, that his confrontation with some abstract paradox causes this dread;[21] however, the matching vertical trajectories of the maiden and the dreamer's dread would seem to couple the two together, and so confirm that it is indeed the maiden herself which appears as dreadful.

This vertical trajectory itself is not insignificant. The upward movement of the dread in contrast to the grounded position of the dreamer's body parallels the vertical movement of the dreamer's "spryt" in contrast with his heavy "body on balke" in the garden at the beginning of the poem (61-2). In her argument that the axes of spatial perception in the dream-world are more complex than those of the *erber* of the first fitt (giving the lie to the maiden's demand that the dreamer give up on trusting his physical senses), critic Sarah Stanbury notes that the dream-world includes horizontal and both upward and downward vertical trajectories–in contrast to an

---

[20] As medievalist L.O. Aranye Fradenburg writes, "Please protect us from *jouissance* by delivering as much *jouissance* as the *I* can bear and still be there to bear it." See *Sacrifice Your Love: Psychoanalysis, Historicism, Chaucer* (Minneapolis: University of Minnesota Press, 2002), 18.

[21] Viz. Edmondson, "*Pearl:* The Shadow of the Object," 50; Theodore Bogdanos, *Image of the Ineffable: A Study in Medieval Poetic Symbolism* (University Park: Penn State University Press, 70-1).

exclusively downward-moving vertical trajectory coupled with the immobilizing circular trajectory of the *erber*.²² This rising "araye ryalle" invokes an even more complicated spatiality, combining a circular or radial set of axes with vertical motion–demonstrating the possibility of a radial spatiality not bound to horizontal planar arrangement (as the flowers of the *erber*) and yet still sensibly substantial.

The simile describing the dreamer's stance and silence "as hende as hawk in halle" has been read in ways both more and less sympathetic to the dreamer–from marking a reasonable affectively induced paralysis to marking an unredeemed and possessive desire of the narrator signaled by his affinity with a violent bird of prey.²³ Although Bogdanos does discuss the image of the hawk as a reflection of "the dreamer's rapacious possessiveness toward the Maiden," he also points out that "this self-imposed simile" follows a conventional medieval humility topos and cultivates pathos on behalf of the dreamer.²⁴ As much as the hawk is a bird of prey, we should also keep in mind Bogdanos's reminder that the hawk is a "heraldic, noble bird."²⁵ As part of an elite, human hunting ritual, hawks (ME *hauk, hawk,* can refer to hawks or falcons, to any type of falcon used for hunting) are an high status,²⁶ extremely valuable bird (so much so that King David II of Scotland may have procured a gyrfalcon from a locale as exotic as Greenland before David II sent it to Edward III in the early fourteenth century).²⁷ As such, the hawk

---

²² Sarah Stanbury, *Seeing the Gawain-Poet: Description and the Act of Perception* (Philadelphia: University of Pennsylvania Press, 1991), 17, 19, 21.
²³ For sympathetic readings see: Anderson, *Language and Imagination in the Gawain-Poet,* 29; Spearing, *The Gawain-Poet,* 149; and, Spearing, "Symbolic and Dramatic Development in *Pearl,*" in *The Middle English Pearl: Critical Essays,* Ed. John Conley (Notre Dame: University of Notre Dame Press, 1970), 132, reprinted from *Modern Philology* LX (1962): 1-12. For a "predatory bird" reading, see Paul F. Reichardt, "Animal Similes in *Pearl,*" in *Text and Matter: New Critical Perspectives of the Pearl-Poet,* ed. Robert J. Blanch, Miriam Youngerman Miller, and Julian N. Wasserman (Troy, NY: Whitson Publishing Company, 1991), 19.
²⁴ Bogdanos, *Image of the Ineffable,* 73.
²⁵ Ibid.
²⁶ MED, sv. *hauk* (n.(1)).
²⁷ Kirsten A. Seaver, *The Frozen Echo: Greenland the Exploration of North America ca. A.D. 1000-1500* (Stanford: Stanford University Press, 1996), 82-85.

is also an animal that represents less unbridled predatory violence than an important medieval instance of ritualized human control of non-human animal violence and meat-eating–in the sort of ritual that Karl T. Steel discusses as a "fundamental tool" of human domination of animals in attempts to produce human distinctiveness.[28]

This hawk is not a salivating, wild, carrion bird, nor is it even a trained hawk diving after a sparrow; this hawk behaves as one "hende in halle." While Gordon glosses this particular occurrence of *hende* as "quiet, still," Andrew and Waldron are more sensitive to the word's more specifically courtly valences, offering "noble, gracious, courteous," in addition to the flatter sense of "meek, well-behaved."[29] The adjective appears later in this poem as a substantive, meaning, according to Andrew and Waldron, "gracious knight, lady," and to Gordon, "gracious one."[30] As its most primary sense, the MED offers "[h]aving the approved courtly or knightly qualities, noble, courtly, well-bred, refined, sportsmanlike."[31] Since the hawk in this simile is specifically "in halle"–perhaps the implied scene, since it is not a hawk on the hunt, is that of a rare hunting bird presented as a gift to a King in a lavish court setting–it would seem that these courtly valences apply. Chaucer's image of Troilus, riding with retinue through a valley "in wyse of curtasie" with "hauke on honed" is sufficiently courtly,[32] but a hawk *indoors*, is a bird of high nobility, well-controlled on another level entirely.

The dreamer's state as compared to a hawk that is "courtly" in a hall is important too in its implications not only for the dreamer's moral and spiritual attitude/status with respect to the pearl-maiden, but also for the relationships of place and space in this stanza visa-vis the rising of the pearl "in perleȝ pyȝt" (192). Along with the pearl comes an "araye ryalle," and so the rising of the pearl decorated or placed in pearls carries with it, by its very virtue of being "in perleȝ pyȝt," a whole set of courtly placements and relationships–

---

[28] Karl Steel, *How to Make a Human: Animals and Violence in the Middle Ages* (Columbus: The Ohio State University Press, 2011), 65.
[29] Gordon, *Pearl*, sv. *hende*; Andrew and Waldron, *The Poems of the Pearl Manuscript*, sv. *hende, hynde*.
[30] Gordon, *Pearl*, sv. *hynde*; Andrew and Waldron, *The Poems of the Pearl Manuscript*, sv. *hende, hynde*.
[31] MED, sv. *hende* (adj.), 1.a.
[32] Geoffrey Chaucer, *Troilus and Criseyde*, in *The Riverside Chaucer* 3rd. edn., ed. Larry D. Benson (Boston: Houghton Mifflin, 1987) 5:64-5.

transforming this site within the landscape into a set of vectors connecting a decorative or *pyȝt* space that radiates from the wonder-pearl mentioned below (221). As *courtly*, this array situates the dreamer as just such a hawk in a hall, among the other bright spheres of nacre.

Here, the ornament is primary, preceding and determining the subsequent social, moral, and figural space. This primacy of ornament overwhelms and unsettles the dreamer. So while the "dred" of this stanza might suggest, as one critic would have it, "fluctuating emotions," or a precise feeling of "uncertainty" as to the status of the maiden as living or dead,[33] it could also be read as a more overwhelming and much more unsettling phenomenon of worldly life, as suggested by Bogdanos' sense of the dreamer's encounter with an interplay of life and death, or Edmondson's sense of the dreamer's fundamental psychic trauma before the Thing.[34]

It is, however, more a crisis of how to react to this intensity of decoration than an inability to understand any particular figural content that poses an immediate problem and silences the dreamer. The dreamer "hoped þat ghostly watȝ þat porpose" (185). Andrew and Waldron read this line as, "I thought that quarry [porpose] was spiritual"–a continuation of the hunting metaphor from line 183, in which the dreamer remains a hawk and his metaphorical sparrow-prey is the maiden.[35] Gordon reads *porpose* as "significance" (ie. "I thought/hoped the significance of it was spiritual").[36] In either case, the dreamer, far from failing to be able to read figurally, as many critics allege (and as is surely the case in other instances), is here *all too eager* to supply an allegorical reading, to reduce the complexity of thing to sign, to sublimate an encounter with decorative aesthetics into *significance*. A sign fully reducible to (spiritual) significance would be easier to take in; but the maiden appears as perceptible in terms of a phenomenon of unavoidable complexity.

Readers should keep in mind that at this point in the poem, what the dreamer beholds is not a girl transformed into allegorical

---

[33] Putter, *An Introduction to the Gawain-poet*, 184.
[34] Bogdanos, *Image of the Ineffable*, 30; Edmondson, "*Pearl*: The Shadow of the Object," 51.
[35] Andrew and Waldron, *The Poems of the Pearl Manuscript*, n. line 186.
[36] Gordon, *Pearl*, sv. *porpose*.

meaning so much as a girl calcified–transformed to pearliness.[37] Critics have long recognized that the description of the pearl-maiden here as "[s]o smoþe, so small, so seme sly3t," echoes the description of the lost pearl in the first stanza; that first pearl is, "[s]o rounde, so reken in vche araye,/ So small, so smoþe her syde3 were" (5-6).[38] The explicit echo here to these lines thus not only lithifies or ossifies the pearl-maiden, but also paradoxically suggests that she simultaneously occupies the space of a human body, of a bewilderingly vast landscape, and of a small round pearl. While the maiden ostensibly has the shape of a recognizable human body, the description of her size as "so seme sly3t" recalls the description of the smallness of the pearl in the opening lines ("so small, so smoþe"). And, this description of the pearl-maiden also recalls the roundness of the pearl, in that this line is immediately followed by a description of the maiden rising in her "araye ryalle": she may have the shape of a human, but the nacre of her pearls exudes an incandescence all around her in a glowing spherical aura of ornamental vectors. The scene thus also implies a certain paradox of scale: the pearl/maiden is small, but arises in a fully royal array. The little pearl, on "bonke3 brade" (138), at the foot of what must be a huge "crystal clyffe" (159), rearticulates the whole landscape.

193-204:

> Perle3 py3te of ryal prys
> Þere mo3t mon by grace haf sene,
> Quen þat frech as flor-de-lys
> Doun þe bonke con bo3e bydene.
> Al blysande whyt wat3 hir beau biys,
> Vpon at syde3, and bounden bene
> Wyth þe myryeste margarys, at my deuyse,
> Þat euer I se3 3et with myn ene;
> Wyth lappe3 large, I wot and wene,
> Dubbed with double perle and dy3te;
> Her cortel of self sute schene,
> Wyth precios perle3 al vmbepy3t.

---

[37] See Putter, *An Introduction to the Gawain-poet*, 182: "The 'pearl' metaphors admit to the [dreamer's] loss, but deny that the lost object is human."
[38] E.g. Spearing, "Symbolic and Dramatic Development," 133.

It is striking that the first sentence of this stanza depicts the full appearance of the maiden in her movement down the bank via a metonymy which figures the supposedly singular pearl-maiden in terms of the multiplicity of pearls that she wears. If we read the metonymy literally before understanding its reference to the maiden, it offers a narrative of pricey and well-placed pearls moving along the bank, seemingly of their own accord, as if clustered together by nothing but their cumulative gravity. Relying on an inverted syntax (by no means uncommon) that makes the (object) noun-phrase of the sentence the entire first line, the stanza *first* places front and center, not the singular maiden, but the pearl*s*.

Arguing that Fitt IV corresponds with Fitt XVII in a chiastic diptych structure, and in accordance with a preoccupation with gems on the part of both stanza-groups, Britton J. Harwood argues that the instance of *pyȝte* in line 193 should probably be read as "chosen"–linked to the occurrence of *pyked* in line 1036 ("Þe portaleȝ pyked of rych plateȝ"), and so as marking the pearl-maiden as one of a special few chosen for a particular status in heaven.[39] But we cannot discount the *set/adorned* semantic field here either.[40] These pearls of line 193 then should be understood as pearls that have been selected from royal wealth, but also as pearls of royal wealth that are set/emplaced as mutually adorning. They constitute, for at least three lines, the center of the scene. Even when the maiden appears in the subordinate clause in line 195, this is only by virtue of a substantive usage of the adjective "frech" to mean something still relatively ambiguous, such as *the bright and pleasant one* (or, *new,*

---

[39] Britton J. Harwood, "*Pearl* as Diptych," in *Text and Matter: New Critical Perspectives on the Pearl-Poet*, eds. Robert J. Blanch, Miriam Youngerman Miller, and Julian N. Wasserman (Troy, NY: Whitson Publishing Company, 1991), 68-69.

[40] Andrew and Waldron do include a separate glossary entry for *pike, pyke* (v.), meaning "gather" or "peck," but list this occurrence of pyked at 1036 as meaning "adorned" (*The Poems of the Pearl Manuscript*, sv. *pike, pyke*). And Gordon similarly does include a separate entry for a verb meaning "pick, gather, get," but lists its occurrence in 1036 as meaning "adorned." Especially at 1036, it would make less sense to read the "portaleȝ" [gates] of the vision of the New Jerusalem to be *pyked*–as in *selected*–from "rych plateȝ" [precious panels], than to read *pyked* here as either a variant spelling of *pyȝt*, or, as the adjective for which this occurrence provides a citation for the MED, *pīked*–which can be used "of a gateway" to mean "furnished with pinnacles or finials." See MED, sv. *pīked* (adj.), a.

renewed, fresh, cheerful, youthful, etc)[41]—which could, without too much stretching, refer to the adornment and not to a person at all. In this stanza, the person arrives only as accessory to her ornaments.[42]

The maiden's gleaming white "beau biys" is the first element of the maiden's outfit that the succeeding stanzas also address. As Gordon notes at length, the maiden's clothing, especially the "abundance of pearls," constitutes a fashionable aristocratic dress from the second half of the fourteenth century.[43] We can guess that the "blysande whyt" *beau biys* [fine linen] is a synecdoche for the "[b]lysnande whyt" *bleaunt* described earlier (163), that is, a sort of loose topcoat reaching nearly to the ground with side-openings up to the waist, elbow-length sleeves, and long sharply tapered "lappeȝ" (detached strips, or hanging sleeves).[44] Through the side openings—which, as Gordon notes, are not depicted in the manuscript drawings of the maiden—the maiden's *cortel* is visible; "a closer-fitting garment than the *bleaunt;* it reached from neck to feet, and had close-fitting sleeves to the wrists."[45] Cut from the "self sute schene" [same bright raiment], the cortel is part of a matching outfit, distinguished from the outer garment by depth perception and the subtle shadows of the side-openings alone, producing an effect of elaborate ornamentation out of only the folds and layers of the same stuff—and, along with the *lappeȝ*, yielding the effect of indefinite depths of differently angled cuts of fabric overlapping as they flow around this walking young body. The result in the dreamer's field of perception is twofold: in part giving the sense that it is no woman at all, but a body built up from elaborate folds and cuts of matching fabric; in part offering mimetic flashes of a pearl, with strips and panels of white fabric swirling about and catching shades of the brightly colored ornamental landscape of the dream-world like nacre. For at least this stanza, the person disappears entirely behind the adornment of the person, who is now transformed into an ornament (what does she decorate?) that is itself ornamented in turn. The *bleaunt* is adorned with "myryeste margarys at my deuyse" (199), the

---

[41] See Gordon, *Pearl,* sv. *frech*; cf. MED, sv. *frēsh* (adj.).
[42] For a version of this argument less sympathetic to the dreamer, see Edward L. Condren, *The Numerical Universe of the Gawain-Pearl Poet: Beyond Phi* (Gainesville: University Press of Florida, 2002), 51.
[43] Gordon, *Pearl,* n. 228.
[44] Ibid., see also sv. *lappeȝ;* MED, sv. *lappes.*
[45] Gordon, *Pearl,* n. 228.

large loose sleeves are decorated on down with a double row of pearls (202), and the cortel (recalling us to the refrain) is "[w]yth precios perleȝ al vmbepȝte" (204).

Attempts to construe exactly how to picture the "myryeste margarys" on the *bleaunt* have yielded divergent critical readings. Gordon reads the apparently idiomatic expression *at my deuyse* by taking *deuyse* as meaning something between "opinion" (offered by previous glossers) and "desire"–giving us "as many (or as fine) as one (I) would (want to) think of."[46] Stanbury offers a marginal gloss for the phrase as "in my opinion," but also proposes that *deuyse* may refer to a heraldic emblem, citing several later medieval literary and visual art examples in which "an unmarried daughter could be represented as bearing the paternal arms."[47] The options are to read the line as meaning that the *bleaunt* is adorned with "the merriest pearls by my devising" [as in, pearls that are as fine as I could want], or, with "the merriest pearls, in the shape of my heraldic device." This latter possibility is an attractive one for readers invested in identifying the maiden as having been the daughter of the dreamer in life, and could also explain why these are the "myryeste margarys." While Gordon and Stanbury both gloss *myryeste* as a superlative modifier for visual beauty (ie. fairest, loveliest), Andrew and Waldron, as well as the MED, suggest a much more general sense more closely linked with the Modern English reflex *merry* than students of ME might come to expect (students of ME being so-often wisely well-conditioned by C. S. Lewis's wariness of the "dangerous sense")–glossing the word as a modifier for lighthearted cheerfulness or the cause of such light pleasure and happiness.[48] That is, the pearls here bring a light smile to the face of the dreamer. This is notable, because, as we see above, beauty itself in *Pearl* is often too intense of a stimulus to bring simple pleasure without overwhelming the perceiver (see my note to line 181).

---

[46] Ibid., n. 199.
[47] Stanbury, *Pearl*, marginal gloss on line 199, n. 199.
[48] Gordon, *Pearl*, sv. *myryeste*; Stanbury, *Pearl*, marginal gloss, line 199; MED, sv. *mirī(e* (adj.); Andrew and Waldron, *The Poems of the Pearl Manuscript,* sv. *myry.* The MED lists "mirthful, blithe," among the senses of the word, while Andrew and Waldron even include "bonny." See also, C.S. Lewis, *Studies in Words* (Cambridge: Cambridge University Press, 1960), 12-14.

Even if *deuyse* cannot be read following Stanbury, the affect that the pearl-dress produces in the dreamer seems distinct from his preceding "dred." Although the white outfit of this stanza can be read as symbolic of the bridal garment of the spouse of Christ in the Revelation, or as reminiscent of a baptismal robe,[49] these pearls here seem less apocalyptic. Here, the ornamentation makes the dreamer happy, blithe, mirthful, and cheery. In contrast to the poem's earlier depiction of the river as a prohibitive *deuyse* that partitions the landscape into separate sites and provokes the dreamer's anxiety (line 139), the devising of these merry pearls extends the site of the pearl/maiden's array so as to happily enfold the dreamer within it.

The pearls on the maiden's clothing are said to be *vmbepyȝt*: they are themselves set and fixed in place as much as they, in turn, place the viewer and articulate the affective space of the dreamer. [*V*]*mbepyȝt* is a truly remarkable word in this context, bearing a prefix with specifically spatial significance and suggesting the extent to which *pyȝt* already names a phenomenon of placement within in a set of certain spatial relationships. These pearls on the dress are, in fact, decorative to the extent that they are paradoxically *selected, set,* or *placed* in dynamic mutually decorative relationship. Folds and pearls flash in the sun and produce a site of cheer. Ornament defines the space, transforming the shifting and flowing folds of decorated garment from a roving sign of "dred" into a physically articulated and perceptible site.

205-216:

> A pyȝt coroune ȝet wer þat gyrle
> Of mariorys and non oþer ston,
> Hiȝe pynakled of cler quyt perle,
> Wyth flurted flowreȝ perfet vpon.
> To hed hade ho non oþer werle;
> Her here leke, al hyr vmbegon,
> Her semblaunt sade for doc oþer erle,
> Her ble more blaȝt þen whaleȝ bon.
> As schorne gold shyr her fax þenne schon,
> On schyldereȝ þat legheȝ vnlapped lyȝte.
> Her depe colour ȝet wonted non
> Of precios perle in porfyl pyȝte.

---

[49] E.g. Anderson, *Language and Imagination*, 28; Bogdanos, *Image of the Ineffable*, 69.

Continuing with a description of the maiden's attire and finally turning to her hair, this third stanza confirms Spearing's sense that the appearance of the maiden and her attire "follows the normal medieval descriptive method, of accumulation of detail rather than selection"–directed here, unlike elsewhere in the *Pearl*-poet's corpus, "to a single end, the intensification of pearl qualities."[50]

The crown itself has been taken figuratively as a sign of the maiden's residency in heaven,[51] as a more general crown of virginity, and, in combination with gold hair and white clothes, as a sign of the pearl-maiden's association with the Virgin herself.[52] But the crown, "such as a queen might wear,"[53] also registers as a marker of temporal royalty in a fitt that, as Spearing observes, offers "recurring ideas of royalty."[54] In his efforts to historicize the *Pearl*-poet's corpus precisely within the court of Richard II, John M. Bowers's argues (somewhat controversially)[55] that the maiden can be associated with Queen Anne (who died at 27, suddenly, and was highly beloved of the king) even as the poem praises the virginity of the succeeding child-bride Isabelle.[56] In the course of his argument, Bowers furnishes the example of a crown from Queen Anne's dowry, which he describes as "an elaborate twelve-part circlet with twelve golden lilies."[57] That crown is itself *pyȝt* with 132 pearls as well as other various gems, and bears up well to Bowers's

---

[50] Spearing, *The Gawain-poet*, 145; cf. Spearing, "Symbolic and Dramatic Development," 133.

[51] E.g. Anderson, *Language and Imagination*, 28; Robert J. Blanch, "Precious Metal and Gem Symbolism in *Pearl*," in *Sir Gawain and Pearl: Critical Essays*, ed. Robert J. Blanch (Bloomington: Indiana University Press, 1966), 90.

[52] E.g. Bogdanos, *Image of the Ineffable*, 69; cf. Sandra Pierson Prior, *The Fayre Formez of the Pearl Poet*, 54; John M. Bowers, *An Introduction to the Gawain Poet* (Gainesville: University Press of Florida, 1996), 117-120.

[53] Gordon, *Pearl*, n. 228.

[54] Spearing, "Symbolic and Dramatic Development," 133.

[55] See, Edmondson, "*Pearl:* The Shadow of the Object," 29-31: Edmondson offers a compelling set of reservations about Bowers' attempt "to rehabilitate *Pearl* along historicist lines" that, according to Edmondson, "retreats from what is arguably most affecting about *Pearl*: the fact that its work of mourning, whether understood as personal or impersonal, factual or allegorical, exceeds its immediate object." Edmondson refers to Bowers, *The Politics of "Pearl": Court Poetry in the Ages of Richard II* (Cambridge: D.S. Brewer, 2001).

[56] Bowers, *An Introduction to the Gawain Poet*, 115-119.

[57] Ibid., 115-116.

comparison of it to the description of the pearl-maiden's crown at 205-8: both are "highly pinnacled, flowerlike in design, and encrusted with pearls."[58] The look, as Bowers's notes, is indeed that of high royalty, "sade for doc oþer erle" [dignified (enough) for a duke or a earl] (211).[59]

Whether or not Bowers is entirely correct in associating the maiden with Queen Anne, the crown certainly lends a royal aura to the maiden (and marks a significant departure from the Revelation 14 source-text).[60] While the crown surely does thus associate the maiden with Mary, Queen of Heaven, its imbrication within royal fashion contemporary to the poem also serves to locate the *pyȝt* pearl/maiden firmly within worldly horizons of space and time—with two salient effects. 1) The specifically royal tenor of the maiden's courtly attire coupled with the prohibition of the *deuyse* of the river (139) reinforces her position within the logic of the text as the Lady of courtly Love within a frame of both the Provençal love-lyric and the love-dream (ie. of Dante). This figure is, for Sandra Pierson Prior, that which should act as a catalyst for conversion (*pace* Beatrice), but fails to do so in *Pearl*.[61] Following Edmondson (following Žižek following Lacan), the crown would contribute to the development of the maiden as a figure for the inaccessible and desire-perpetuating Lady Object within the "formalities of courtly love literature" in *Pearl*.[62] 2) The royalty of the maiden's crown also imbues a sense of royalty to the whole scene, transforming again the space between the dreamer and the pearl/maiden (including, or despite, the *deuyse*/barrier of the river), such that are all in view of the crowned maiden—placed in the array of the crown as elements of a courtly,

---

[58] Ibid., 116.
[59] Ibid.
[60] Ibid.
[61] Prior, *The Fayre Formez of the Pearl Poet*, 170, 174, 179.
[62] See Edmondson, "*Pearl*: The Shadow of the Object," 49, and 52: "[T]he lover 'fodolked of luf-dangere' (line 11); the elaborate code of conduct designed to contain and perpetuate desire; the merciless, vaguely mechanical Lady who assigns to her would-be lover a series of senseless ordeals—were a means of covering over the void at the heart of the symbolic order, of deflecting a traumatic encounter with *jouissance* while at the same time maintaining the illusion that such an encounter might actually take place."

and thus worldly, integral site.[63] The boundary of the river notwithstanding, the dreamer is within the site/sight of a crown, and so framed—at least for all social purposes—as within the same site as the pearl-maiden.

The description of the crown also further elaborates the poem's assumptions about the interrelation of concepts of place, space, and ornament. The enjambed alliteration between *py3t* (205), *pynakled,* and *perle* (207), underscores that the *Pearl*-poet is throughout exploiting a pun that relates adjectives for decorativeness with an adjective for shape that also happens to describe a likely morphology of actual plastic decoration (ie. decorated/peaked). Such space would at once dazzle and frighten with polyfocal and polytangible perceptual hooks.[64]

The crown's radial and perhaps threatening pinnacles of "cler quyt perle" presumably alternate with more receptively shaped "flurted flowre3," whose concave openings must contrast rhythmically with the terminal-pointing pearls, creating a discrete series (207-08). In turn, this discrete series is simultaneously interlinked as a "werle," (209)–a noun with an uncertain sense, sometimes glossed as "garland," but more convincingly as "circlet" (on comparison with OE *hwerfel,* "whirlpool," *hwirfling,* "orb, something round," and *hwerfan,* "to revolve").[65] And in addition to its symbolic and aesthetic implications, this *werle,* which recalls as well the dreamer's characterization of the pearl/maiden who "styke3 in garlande gay" (1186), also serves as a figure for the structure of a poem with interlinking groups of linked stanzas. Ian Bishop's seminal argument that *Pearl* is more like a necklace of linked units than a single round pearl (a figure still often-invoked in descriptions of the poem's form) settles on the term *corona* in order to describe

---

[63] As Bogdanos similarly indicates, "the Maiden's courtly attributes also tie her to the world and rob her of her pure transcendentality" (Bogdanos, *Image of the Ineffable,* 69).

[64] On the function of rhetorical ornamentation as "hooks," see Mary Carruthers, *The Craft of Thought* (Cambridge: Cambridge University Press, 1998), 117.

[65] See Gordon, *Pearl,* n. 209; Andrew and Waldron, *The Poems of the Pearl Manuscript,* n. 209. Gordon cites vague "etymological associations of the word," and records an alternate suggestion that *werle* derives from the stem of the verb "wear," citing Holthausen's proposal of OE **werels.* But Andrew and Waldron provide the attested OE words listed in the main text ßabove, which render the gloss of "circlet" as relatively sufficient.

the poem's formal structure.⁶⁶ As Bishop explains, the term was used by sixteenth-century English and Italian poets to refer to a crown or garland of sonnets linked by *concatenatio,* but it can also refer to a particular type of ecclesiastical chandelier consisting of a "gilded circle set with gems of pearls" (in which the circle symbolized the New Jerusalem and the pearls its inhabitants).⁶⁷ *Werle* offers us a nice vernacular term for the form Bishop describes. Aside from offering an alternative to Bishop's symbolically and religiously loaded term, *werle* felicitously suggests a revolving or "whirling" *motion* (rather than links locked in a circle) that captures a sense of the poem's thematic and prosodic movement. This functionality of the *werle* as a self-reflexive figure for the form of *Pearl* not only offers insight into the aesthetic world of the poem, but also offers an important counterexample to Lynn Staley Johnson's claim that the language of *Pearl* is concerned only with matters of faith and not with "the life of poetry."⁶⁸

Another hitherto unnoticed implication of Bishop's figuration lies in the paradoxical simultaneity *and* discontinuity of the series that arises from the alternating flowery flutes and pearly pinnacles of the *werle*. As a figure of the poem's structure, the *werle* thus also formalizes the problem of *spacing* as fundamental to its implicit phenomenology and aesthetics.⁶⁹ To be *pyȝt* or even *umbepyȝt* in an array or a continuous crown is to be fixed and set within certain ontological and perceptual limitations determined by one's spatial relationships and placement. There is here a relationship between pearls, but it cannot be articulated as wholly continuous or in any

---

⁶⁶ Ian Bishop, *The Pearl in Its Setting: A Critical Study of the Structure and Meaning of the Middle English Poem* (New York: Barnes and Noble, 1968), 30. For depictions of the poem as a pearl or a pearl in its setting, see Prior, *The Fayre Formez of the Pearl Poet,* 162; Prior, *The Pearl Poet Revisited* (New York: Twayne, 1994), 48; Anderson, *Language and Imagination,* 19; Bowers, *An Introduction to the Gawain Poet,* 104-06; Condren, *The Numerical Universe of the Gawain-Pearl Poet,* 63; Renée Wellek, "*The Pearl:* An Interpretation of the Middle English Poem," in *Sir Gawain and Pearl: Critical Essays* (Bloomington, Indiana University Press, 1966), 4; Gordon, *Pearl,* xl. Stanbury stands out as an exception in seeming to take Bishop seriously (*Pearl,* Introduction, 6).
⁶⁷ Bishop, *The Pearl in Its Setting,* 30-31.
⁶⁸ Johnson, *The Voice of the Gawain-Poet,* 209.
⁶⁹ When I write *spacing,* I do very much mean to invoke the work of Jacques Derrida on the grapheme, viz. Derrida, *Of Grammatology,* corrected edn., trans. Spivak (Baltimore: Johns Hopkins University Press, 1997), 68.

way unmediated. The relationship is, instead, *decorative*—a quality that emerges here as an alternative or by-pass to the ineluctable problem of continuity and discontinuity in understanding spatial relationships.

The Maiden's hair (following Gordon's emendation of MS *lere* to *here*) crowns her face,[70] enclosing it, in "gold so clere," just as a gold setting encloses the pearl from the opening of the poem (1-2).[71] The loose hair, "vnlappeʒ," is apposite the loose *lappeʒ* of the *biys* which encloses the pearl/maiden's whole body (197). At this moment the pearl-maiden is, of course, on the whole, a pearl, but also a pearl whose face appears as a separate pearl—and this on top of her appearance as a pearl wearing pearls on clothes and crown.

---

[70] Gordon, *Pearl*, n. 210; cf. Andrew and Waldron, *The Poems of the Pearl Manuscript*, 210 and n. 210; Stanbury, *Pearl*, line 210. Andrew and Waldron object to Gordon's emendation on the grounds that the emendation to *here* (hair) would ruin the "logical development of the poet's description," and would require reading *leke* awkwardly as past tense. Instead, reading *leke* as a form of ME *lake*, meaning a type of fine linen, they take *lere-lake* as a compound for "face-linen," which they translate as "wimple" (rendering the entire line as an adverbial clause: "her wimple entirely encompassing her"). There is, however, no way in which such a wimple could be thought to enclose *all* of the maiden at this point. First of all, it seems clear that that the maiden's face *is* visible to the dreamer. Second, there is no need to assume that the poet would follow a single linear progression of describing crown, face, and hair in strict order without ever mixing the subjects. In fact, given the poem's preoccupation with enclosing circlets, a description of the maiden's head might be expected to follow the circular path of the maiden's crown—first noting the golden hair enclosing the white face (as a pearl in a golden enclosure), then mentioning the face, then returning to the hair to fully enclose the pearl/face. *Louken* can certainly be used to discuss not only "surrounding," but also "enclosing" (see MED, sv., *louken* v. 1). In either case, the poet breaks up this supposed logic at line 213, doubling back and returning the hair again. So we cannot assume that *lere* cannot be *here* because a discussion of hair at line 210 would disrupt the style of the stanza. Third, by line 213, when the poet returns to the hair, we learn that unlike a face-linen, which could not enclose all of the maiden, the hair hangs "vnlapped" [unbound] lightly on the shoulders, and possibly further down. So the hair very much could be said to enclose much of the maiden's body, if not all. One might yet object to the awkwardness of reading *leke* in the past tense, yet, it seems much more likely to me that we can follow Gordon's emendation, read *leke* as simply a present tense form, and assume that the poet slipped up in maintaining consistency of tense.

[71] See Anderson, *Language and Imagination*, 27.

With her complexion "more bla3t þan whalle3 bon," [more flashing-white than whale's bone] (212), the maiden's face indeed lends her a quality of overall "ossification,"[72] for she has out-calcified even the pearls on her own gown and crown. But while critics tend to characterize the maiden's complexion, along with her other dazzling qualities of "death polished into plastic perfection,"[73] as signs of the pearl/maiden's entry into an Ideal order incommensurate with the scope of human language,[74] these qualities also suggest with some concreteness what the pearl/maiden has become other than merely one or another abstraction beyond human language. As multiple critics notice, the maiden's hair and face are here described with the same diction used previously to describe the ornamental landscape of the earthly garden and the dream world.[75] The hair is *schyr* like the shinning of the sun and the sharply shinning plants in the garden (28, 42). *Schyr* also recalls the bank of the river in the dream world "þat schere3," and the sharply shinning sun in the dream world "[q]uen glem of glode3 agayn3 hem glyde3/ Wyth shymeryng schene ful schrylle þay schynde" (79-70). The hair shines as "shorne golde," recalling the sharply angular "crystal klyffe3" and "bornyst syluer" foliage of the dream-world's *adubbement* (74, 77). This is not merely the maiden slipping into the Ideal at the cost of her humanity, but a becoming-landscape. Furthermore, the maiden is not merely one ornament among other ornaments *py3t* in the decorated landscape. Rather, she is both a *porfyl* [embroidered border] herself in the scene of the poem and one element among others set within a *porfyl*. As a kind of beatific lawn-ornament, she is become (an element of) place.

217-228:

>Py3t wat3 poyned and vche a hemme
>At honed, at syde3, at ouerture,
>Wyth whyte perle and non oþer gemme,
>And bornyste quyte wat3 hyr uesture.
>Bot a wonder perle wythouten wemme

---

[72] Bogdanos, *Image of the Ineffable*, 70.
[73] Ibid., 72.
[74] Edmondson, "*Pearl*: The Shadow of the Object," 51; Anderson, *Language and Imagination*, 27; and Putter, *An Introduction to the Gawain Poet*, 151, 185.
[75] E.g. Spearing, "Symbolic and Dramatic Development," 134; Bogdanos, *Image of the Ineffable*, 73.

> Immydde3 hyr breste wat3 sette so sure;
> A manne3 dom mo3t dry3ly demme,
> Er mynde mo3t malte in hit mesure.
> I hope no tong mo3t endure
> No sauerly saghe say of þat sy3t,
> So wat3 hit clene and cler and pure,
> Þat precios perle þer hit wat3 py3t.

Moving on from the pearl-maiden's *werle* and face, the description proceeds to focus on another, smaller circular enclosure, the *poyned* [wristband, ornamental cuff]. However, rather than turning out wheels within wheels, a game of "connect the dots" begins to play out between the pearls peaking the crown, those forming a design on the *biys*, and those encircling the *cortel*—now also running up and down each hem or seam of the garments. These ornaments parcel out the remainder of the divisions of the maiden's body, "[a]t honed, at syde3, at ouerture" (218), while making a show of the ostensible homogeneity and purity of the ornamentation as of "whyte perle and non oþer gemme" (219). This pearl/maiden has a vaguely human morphology, but we glimpse here only the shape of non-integrated parts—a hand, sides, etc.

That the garments of the maiden are also described as "bornyst quyte" is of course a redundancy, but not as a symptom of defective poetizing. The burnishable quality of the clothes suggests their aesthetic and material homogeneity with the lithified or ossified face of the maiden—as if the maiden and her clothes are all carved of one undifferentiated block of *whalle3 bon* (212). The cut gold of the maiden's hair and the nacre of the pearls with which she is *py3t* constitute the only differentiation in her coloring. Now the pearl/maiden has accrued great density and weight: "[t]he opulence of her vestment thickens and draws down to matter her spiritual identity—much like van Eyck's heavily draped and bejeweled angels."[76]

Bot—and much rests on this conjunction that opens line 221, as I will note below—all these qualities are overshadowed by the "[w]onder perle wythouten wemme/ Immydde3 hyr breste" (221-22). Why is the wonder-pearl wondrous and what is its relationship to the other pearls; and, how is the wonder-pearl *py3t*?

---

[76] Bogdanos, *Image of the Ineffable*, 69.

Critics tend to myopically emphasize the significance of the *wonder perle* to the extent of losing sight of the ekphrasis of the maiden's appearance that constitutes the rest of this fitt.[77] This pearl has thus been assigned allegorical and/or symbolic significance worked out as distinct from that of the maiden or the larger lost pearl/maiden of the poem–often by taking the maiden's auto-exegesis at her word (733-44), and reading the wonder-pearl in relation to the biblical figure of the "pearl of great price."[78]

But Spearing was right, I think, to follow René Wellek's breakthrough claim that the symbolism of *Pearl* "is not simple and cannot be solved by a one-to-one identification with some abstract virtue."[79] Spearing's dramatization theory, which influentially explores the pearl as a constantly shifting symbol, accordingly maintains that, "to attempt to distinguish the symbolic significance of this one pearl from that of the pearl-maiden herself would be to misunderstand, indeed to resist, the poet's methods."[80] On its own, however, the "wonder perle" does function, with some degree of certainty, as the poster child *par excellence* for the so-called "inexpressiblity topos" of *Pearl*.[81] J. Allan Mitchell provides perhaps the best account of this particular pearl in this regard: "…the pearl's otherworldly aspect is essentially non-cognitive and unrepresentable–though it is experienced, since the dreamer certainly encounters *something*."[82]

---

[77] E.g. Britton J. Harwood, "*Pearl* as Diptych," 68-69; Anderson, *Language and Imagination*, 28.

[78] E.g. Anderson, *Language and Imagination*, 28. See also, Marie Padgett Hamilton, "The Meaning of the Middle English *Pearl*," in *Sir Gawain and Pearl: Critical Essays*, ed. Robert J. Blanch (Bloomington: Indiana University Press, 1966), 38-9. Cf. Bishop, *Pearl in Its Setting*, 92-3.

[79] Wellek, "The *Pearl:* An Interpretation," 34.

[80] Spearing, *The Gawain-Poet*, 145.

[81] In addition to Bogdanos, *Image of the Ineffable*, see J. Allan Mitchell, "The Middle English *Pearl:* Figuring the Unfigurable," *Chaucer Review* 35.1 (2000): 86-111; Anne Howland Schotter, "Vernacular Style and the Word of God: The Incarnational Art of *Pearl*," in *Ineffability: Naming the Unnamable from Dante to Beckett*, ed. Peter S. Hawkins and Anne Howland Schotter (New York, 1984), 23-34; Ann Chalmers Watts, "Pearl, Inexpressibility, and Poems of Human Loss," PMLA 99 (1984): 26-40.

[82] Mitchell, "Figuring the Unfigurable," 92. Mitchell argues, in fact, that the incommensurability between temporal and figural logic is at the heart of the poem (88, 108).

Key to understanding the dreamer's specific expression of the pearl's ineffability is his insistence that "a manneȝ dom moȝt dryȝly demme,/ Er mynde moȝt malte in hit mesure" (223-24). The word *malte* here preserves an early/dialectical infinitive form, which primarily means "to melt" (with reference to ice, snow, wax, metal, food, etc.–a range strikingly similar to that of PDE *melt*), and comes to mean, figuratively, "to comprehend" (as Gordon as well as Andrew and Waldron gloss the word)–the implicit metaphor figuring the act of understanding as an action of the (hard) mind or heart *softening* or *growing tender* (ie. *melting*–and so being overcome by the prevailing argument, or, alternately, able to conform to its (metaphorical) shape).[83] So when the dreamer claims that one's judgment (*dom*) might incessantly consider (*demme*) the wonder-pearl before the mind might "malte in hit mesure" [soften to its measure] (224), his diction implies that comprehension of the wonder-pearl could only occur after a long effort–not an effort of disembodied cognition of the symbolic, but of felt physical perception (as softening/melting), an *aesthetic* activity.

The dreamer's declaration of the insufficiency of language as a mode of relation to the pearl (225-26), thus does not necessarily locate all of the unspeakable qualities of the pearl on the side of significance, even if the interpretation of the maiden herself (as noted above) seems to authorize the general trend of modern exegetes. Both Lynn Staley Johnson and Sandra Pierson Prior call attention to the importance of the knotty status of the pearl(s) of the poem understood in terms of the Augustinian distinction between things and/or signs.[84] Now, the wonder-pearl is a *res* used as a *signum,* while the other smaller pearls of the maiden's attire are things that may or may not also function as signs. Most criticism that focuses on the ineffability of the wonder-pearl implicitly assumes that its unendurable quality results from its singular status as a *signum*–specifically, from the incommensurability (with creaturely experience) of that *for which it is a sign*. But nothing in the reaction of the dreamer suggests that we entirely neglect the status of this pearl as also a *res* that must be apprehended first by the senses, a thing whose unspeakability may very well in fact result from its thingly qualities.

---

[83] MED, sv. *melten* (v.), 1a, 1b, 2a.
[84] Johnson, *The Voice of the Gawain Poet,* 169-70; Prior, *The Pearl Poet Revisited,* 45-6.

One would expect the sign concerned with the absolute spiritual status of the maiden to be itself, in the first case, sufficient and absolute. The wonder-pearl marks the space where "pearl" as a perfect sign of the maiden indistinguishably meets the maiden's thingly pearls. But–and now we return to the *bot* I mention above– the wonder-pearl appears amidst a multiplicity of pearls. It is introduced with the conjunction "bot" (221), contrasting it, as an exception, to all the other pearls of the attire. This pearl cannot be spoken of, it would seem, because it is "clene and cler and pure" (228), its concrete physicality sublimated into unrepeatable ideality. This pearl is perfect–it is, "wythouten wemme" (221), incomprehensibly sufficient. One might expect the singular and ideal wonder-pearl to be like the "precious perle wythouten spot" (e.g. 48), whose pun (as both "imperfection, mark, sin," and as "place, location") suggests that to be without imperfection (or to be so rendered by divine grace) also means that one no longer has earthly, physically spatial parameters or coordinates.[85]

But the *bot* that introduces the wonder-pearl establishes that the pearl is *pyʒt* only in negative relation to all the pearls coating the maiden's attire, with at least two important consequences. 1) The wonder-pearl is not self-sufficient, even if *by degrees* it is *more* than the other non-wonder-pearls. Its wonder emerges, at least in part, only by contrast with the numerous other pearls against which it appears as the mark of surplus or excess decoration. Its function is thus not independent of the multitude of smaller pearls. Even the significatory function of the wonder-pearl only emerges as significatory in its difference from the minor pearls. 2) For the same reasons, the wonder-pearl need not be *wondrous* because of its ostensible unendurable signified or because it is "liberated from the spatial constrictions of earthly grave-yards,"[86] but precisely because of its inherence within the problems of space to the extent that it functions as a site-articulating decoration. The iteration of the refrain

---

[85] Cf. Johnson, *The Voice of the Gawain Poet,* 168-69. In a significant divergence from Johnson, who argues that the dreamer is unable to read "spot" figuratively, I suggest here that he gets the pun, but does not find in it a consolation. For the most forceful precedent to Johnson's reading of the poem as highly orthodox *consolatio,* See Conley, "*Pearl* and a Lost Tradition," in *The Middle English Pearl: Critical Essays,* 50-72. My reading here thus takes *Pearl* as much more of a poem of mourning and loss; see Edmondson, "*Pearl*: The Shadow of the Object".

[86] Johnson, *Voice of the Gawain Poet,* 170.

in this stanza, "Þat precios perle þer it watȝ pyȝt" (228), constitutes the delayed subject of the sentence beginning at line 225, and so refers specifically to the wonder-pearl. The same sentence that asserts the ineffability of this pearl simultaneously and implicitly asserts that the wonder-pearl appears within the constraints of a pitched site in finite space, "sette so sure" (222). The wonder-pearl, too, is *pyȝt*. And, it is as a *pyȝt* thing that it constitutes a sight/site that "no tong moȝt endure" (225).

The wonder-pearl, it seems, raises the very question of the relation of finitude to spatiality and to place. It is overwhelming because it is the vector or node by which the dreamer is interpolated into the site-defining array. Representational speech will not suffice as a response because such representational speech cannot function factically as a spatial or locative relationship. And, this is productive of such dread (181) because the dreamer could only possibly respond to the wonder-pearl in its facticity (as the horizon/node interpolating him into a decorative site) by decorating in turn—by the frightening prospect of becoming *pȝyt* himself, merely another pearl in the "araye ryalle" (191). As Johnson explains of the dreamer, "the source of his problem is death."[87]

229-240:

> Pyȝt in perle, þat precios pyce
> On wyþer half water com doune þe schore.
> No gladder gome heþen into Grece
> Þen I, quen ho on brymme wore.
> Ho watȝ me nerre þen aunte or nece;
> My joy forþy watȝ much þe more.
> Ho profered me speche, þat special spece,
> Enclynande lowe in wommon lore,
> Caȝt of her coroun of grete tresore
> And haylsed me wyth a lote lyȝte.
> Wel watȝ me þat euer I watȝ bore
> To sware þat swete in perleȝ pyȝt!

The scope of the scene in the final stanza of the fitt widens out again to that of the landscape, but now with the maiden doubly situated, locating her as both "[p]yȝt in perle" (229), and moving down to the shore "[o]n wyþer half water" [on the other side of the water] (230).

---

[87] Ibid., 145.

That the maiden is again called a *pyece* here (a word that can refer to a human individual but carries a primary sense and an overwhelming connation of a fragment or partial *object*),[88] echoing the form of the refrain in the first stanza of this fitt (cf. 192), reinforces the sense in which she is placed in the landscape as an ornament or as fragment of a larger decoration. In that first stanza of Fitt IV this *pyece* is described in terms that recall the description of the jeweler's lost pearl from the first stanza of the poem as "[s]o smoþe, so smal, so seme sly3t" (190), and the refrain of *pyece* here calls up again that jewelry-ification of the maiden. While in the first stanza, the maiden, appearing, "[r]yse3 up in hir araye ryalle" (191), here, she moves "doun the schore," as if completing the swing of a pearl pendant. In this way, too, the happiness of the dreamer, "quen ho on brymme wore" (232), is linked explicitly with the maiden's appearance as situated within that landscape.

The dreamer himself articulates his intimacy with the maiden in familial terms, as, "me nerre þen aunte or nece" (233). A critical debate about the nature of this relationship was once intimately linked with a debate about whether to read *Pearl* as an allegory or as an elegy, with early adherents to the elegy-approach heavily invested in speculation about the biography of the poet and the historical death of an actual person.[89] For a while, Gordon seemed to have partly settled the debate, arguing that the dreamer's relation to the maiden must be that of a parent[90]—and arguing that, although it is probable that the poet drew on genuine experiences of sorrow, "to the particular criticism of the poem, this decision is not of the first importance."[91] Two relatively more recent critical efforts have both upset this consensus despite their widely divergent approaches—Bowers' historicizing effort to identify the maiden with

---

[88] MED, sv. *pece* (n.), 1, 7.

[89] The most prominent points of biographical speculation included those of Sir Israel Gollancz, in his edition of the *Pearl* (London: Nutt, 1891), and those of Ten Brink, Charles Osgood, and Mother Angela Carson. The best accounts of these early debates are those of Spearing, *The Gawain-Poet* 127-37; Wellek, "*The Pearl:* An Interpretation," 3-20; and Bowers, *An Introduciton*, 117-121.

[90] Gordon, *Pearl*, xiii.

[91] Ibid., xvi. Wellek continued to disagree with this, arguing that only personal loss and consolation could have generated the poem, ("*The Pearl:* An Interpretation," 23).

Queen Anne,[92] and Edmondson's psychoanalytic exploitation of the ambiguity implied by the phrase "nerre þen aunte or nece" to argue that the maiden, "(mis)recognized" from afar, emerges as, if not "the dreamer's exact double," then, "in the manner of object *a*, as an uncanny paradox."[93]

It is, in any case, as a very intimate relation that the maiden is thus able to solicit speech from the dreamer who, one stanza before, claimed an inability to speak before the wonder-pearl. The nature of this intimacy may not be unrelated to the maiden's total transformation, at this point, into a kind of high-status lawn ornament. If not the double of the dreamer, the maiden constitutes an integral element of the landscape and so—and in spite of the *deuyse* of the river—contributes to the array of wonder that environs the dreamer (an array that includes the pearl-gravel over which the dreamer has walked (81-82) as much as it does the pearly attire of the maiden that he cannot directly touch). The maiden is here all decoration when she provokes him to speak.

The localizable qualities produced here by decoration are all the more localizable in that this final stanza of Fitt IV echoes the refrain of Fitt III (*more*) yet another time as the narrator explains that "[m]y joy forþy watȝ much þe more." Here, *more* takes the position of the third repetition of this stanza's *b*-rhyme, resonating most immediately with line 232: *quen ho on brymme wore*. Most directly, this rhyme prosodically links an adjective describing *excess* (more) with a finite form of a being-verb (*wore*, pa. subj. sg. of *ben*), thus yoking together excess and *substantial being*. Additionally the rhyme directs us back more generally to the line describing the maiden's location, on the bank, where she takes her position in/as an array of adornment within the ornamental landscape. Despite the narrator's assertion of familial intimacy with the maiden, the prosody draws a perhaps stronger affective link between the narrator's joy, the substantiality of excess, and the maiden's position within an ornamentally configured spatiality. Here, recalling the herbal *huyl* and the flowers whose scent lures the dreamer to sleep in the first fitt of the poem (41, 57-60), the dreamer refers to the maiden as a *special spece* (a precious spice/herb)—a sort of olfactory ornament. So, even when separated from the maiden by the *deuyse* of the stream, the

---

[92] Bowers, *An Introduction*, 110-126. See also Bowers, *The Politics of "Pearl": Court Poetry in the Age of Richard II* (Cambridge: D.S. Brewer, 2001).
[93] Edmondson, "*Pearl*: The Shadow of the Object," 50.

dreamer is not by any means cut off from being set within this array where even the *atmosphere* is apparently ornamental in force.

Yet, for all these "artificial" elements that coalesce in and as this topos, the scene is not, it should be noted, *unnatural.* Nor is the modern *nature/artifice* opposition taken on, rationalized, debunked, or re-inscribed. It is simply side-stepped. The maiden is "enclyndande" (236)–a term that describes her posture of courtly greeting, but that also functions as a basic concept of medieval natural philosophy, referring to the *natural inclination* of beings in terms of both moral propensity and physical position within the cosmos.[94] For all the narrator's attempt to record the intensity of his response to the appearance of the maiden with a very slowed-down, incremental set of expanding visual and temporal frames, it is in the end very little that snags and entangles the narrator in the linguistic relations to the maiden that will occupy the central fitts of the poem. Here, decoration transforms affect into space and relative position, and the logic of the site drives the materiality of desire.

Daniel C. Remein is an Assistant Professor of English at the University of Massachusetts Boston. He is currently working on a book on the poetics of ornament in *Beowulf* and the Berkeley Renaissance, and he is the author of the chapbook *Pearl* (Organism for Poetic Research, 2012). Remein is also a co-editor of Eth Press: Posmedieval Poetries.

---

[94] See C. S. Lewis, *The Discarded Image* (Cambridge: Cambridge University Press, 1964, reprint 2005), 141: "[w]hat we call gravitation–for the medieval, kindly enclyning." See also, MED, sv. *enclinen* (v.), 1., 2a., 2b., 6., 8a., 8b. Play between these senses is particularly visible in Chaucer. Viz. Chaucer, "Boece," in *The Riverside Chaucer*, 3.m.2.3, 4.m.6.9, 5.pr.3.190; "House of Fame," 734; "Monk's Tale," B. 3092.

V

MEETING ONE'S MAKER: THE JEWELER IN FITT V OF *PEARL*

Noelle Phillips

In Fitt V of *Pearl*, the concatenating term *jueler* draws attention to the conflicted identity of the narrator/Dreamer, whose grief, loss, and frustration configure the poem's emotional landscape and propel the narrative forward. Because the relationship between the Dreamer and the Pearl Maiden is arguably the most significant aspect of *Pearl*, this particular fitt offers much that can illuminate our understanding of the poem as a whole. It is here that the Dreamer first explicitly uses the title of jeweler, an identity that is then challenged by the Maiden. The changing nature of the repeated word *jueler* is also echoed in the interpretive slippage of other words associated with jewelers, such as *cofer, perle,* and *juel.* Such shifting boundaries of signification allow the reader to see what the Dreamer/Jeweler does not: that his identity, as well as the Pearl Maiden's, cannot be defined in only one plane of existence and using only one set of terms or signifiers. Indeed, this resistance to singular meaning is characteristic of *Pearl* as a whole, as two of its editors state: "Allegorical significance and individualized character, grandiose meaning and local event, vertical and horizontal language, in a word, heaven and earth: in the *Pearl* poet these are at once joined and strangely broken off from one another."[1] As the heavenly and earthly interpretive paradigms slide into one another, the status of the Jeweler also shifts; the reader is never allowed to settle into one mode of reading, but instead is compelled to hold alternative hermeneutic models in mind simultaneously.

The ability to move between these opposing models and problematize their separation from one another is imperative to our

---

[1] Malcom Andrew and Ronald Waldron, eds., *The Poems of the* Pearl *Manuscript: Pearl, Cleanness, Patience, Sir Gawain and the Green Knight* (Liverpool: University of Liverpool Press, 2007), 17.

reading of *Pearl*; readers need not be restricted by these deceptively simple dualities. In his discussion of figurative typology in the poem, Allan Mitchell quotes Elizabeth Salter's assertion that *Pearl* is a poem of both "transformation and continuity" – of change as well as similitude.[2] Ideas, spaces, and objects are at once conflated and separated from one another in a process of reversals, negations, and semantic shifts, making it hard to sustain any black-and-white view of the poem as one structured by rigid dichotomies. In her treatment of *Pearl*, and in particular of the Jeweler/Dreamer, Helen Barr resists what she considers the traditional interpretation of the poem as a timeless world of oppositions featuring an "antagonistic polarity between the earthly and the heavenly, and between what is literal and what is figurative."[3] While she certainly does not reject the idea that *Pearl* highlights such dualities, she urges readers to see the poem also as enmeshed in complex networks of social and economic relationships that blur the boundaries between these structuring oppositions. Barr sees the narrator's self-identification as a jeweler as central to the poem's participation in contemporary social practices, arguing that this characterization "establishes a material consciousness right at the heart of the poem" and emphasizes the narrator's socially (and, extension, spiritually) ambivalent position. Jewelers could be wealthy merchants who regularly interacted with the aristocracy, but they were not aristocratic themselves; they were "both inside and outside aristocratic culture."[4] They occupied the uncomfortable nexus of wealth, power, and birthright, boasting possessions and certain social advantages yet having no noble family heritage or the privilege of leisure.[5] *Piers Plowman*, a contemporary poem with theological concerns similar to those of *Pearl*, explores the liminal status of merchants during the scene of Truth's pardon:

> Marchaunts in the margyne hadde manye yeres
> Ac no *A pena et a culpa* no Treuthe wolde hem graunt [...]
> Ac under his secrete seel Treuthe sente hem a lettre
> And bad hem bugge boldely what hem best liked

---

[2] Allan Mitchell, "The Middle English 'Pearl': Figuring the Unfigurable," *The Chaucer Review* 35.1 (2000): 87.
[3] Helen Barr, *Socioliterary Practice in Late Medieval England* (Oxford: Oxford University Press, 2001), 40.
[4] Barr, *Socioliterary Practice*, 44.
[5] Barr, *Socioliterary Practice*, 43-44, 48.

And seethe sullen hit ayeyn and save the wynnyng
And amende meson-dewes therwith and myseyse men fynde.[6]

Merchants here are relegated to the margins of the pardon and the margins of Christian society. They will not be included in the general pardon sent to Piers by Truth, yet Truth gives them a way out through a special letter under his "secrete seel" that promises them protection as long as they make up for their mercantile misdeeds by becoming more altruistic with their wealth. As a self-identified jeweler, the Dreamer occupies this mercantile and marginal space, and the difficulty he experiences in his interactions with the Maiden throughout the poem is due, in part, to his lack of a stable social identity, as Barr demonstrates. However, it strikes me that the shifting social positions of the Maiden and the Dreamer – the nature of their vexed relationship, in other words – is what makes the "antagonistic polarity" of their spiritual states and places that much more interesting. Barr's interpretation of the Dreamer/Jeweler as a socially liminal mercantile figure offers a way for readers to reconsider the larger dualities that structure the poem. While these dualities remain a presence throughout one's reading of *Pearl*, their stability and moral resonance are constantly changing.

Introducing the Jeweler

Before proceeding to a more comprehensive commentary on the narrator as jeweler in Fitt V, we must first consider the introduction to the narrator's role, which we find in the first stanza of the poem. Its place at the beginning does, as Barr argues, indeed establish a material consciousness in the reader's horizon of poetic expectations. The descriptions in this section reveal that the Dreamer is not just a man or a father, but an artisan, merchant, and/or collector of beautiful things. His attitude to his own jewel and the jeweled landscape reveals a "focus on courtliness mediated through the discourse of commodification."[7] In his fascination with his pearl and the jewels around him, he demonstrates his preoccupation with the social capital to be accrued through wealth and possession of objects. Ian Woodward, considering the

---

[6] *Piers Plowman* C:9:22-30. See also D. Vance Smith, *Arts of Possession: the Middle English Household Imaginary* (Minneapolis: University of Minnesota Press, 2003), particularly Chapter 4, "Merchants in the Margins."

[7] Barr, *Socioliterary Practice*, 45.

relationships between human subjects and physical objects, suggests that objects become extensions of our own identity and deeply associated with our own social portrayal: "try to picture Jimmy Hendrix without his guitar, Satchmo without a trumpet, Groucho Marx without a cigar, Charlie Chaplin without his cane, a bus conductor without his portable ticket machine."[8] A jeweler without his pearl is no longer a jeweler; his identity is effaced, and he must cultivate a new one or recover his precious stone. For both Barr and Woodward, objects carry deep social signification by marking one's membership in specific communities.

It becomes increasingly clear, of course, that the Dreamer, whether or not he possesses his jewel, does not actually understand true courtly behavior or how to participate in that particular community. Instead, he has misunderstood wealth and beauty as constituting courtliness. His rich and impassioned description of the pearl in the first several lines of the poem is supposed to be compelling because, the stanza suggests, he has expertise in such things: "Ne proued I neuer her precios pere... Queresoeuer I jugged gemmez gaye / I sette hyr sengeley in synglure" (4, 7-8). In these lines, the poet draws the reader's attention not primarily to the position of the Dreamer but to his most valued object: his pearl. The Dreamer judges the pearl's economic and social value by describing it as fit for a prince, surpassing even those exotic gems that come "oute of oryent"; its beauty and proportions (lines 6-7) are ideal. However, he also claims he can judge its more spiritual and metaphorical value when he tells us that he set her above all the rest because she is unique, precious, and pure (lines 7-8). He assesses gems; he determines their value. The Dreamer's focus on the beauty of his lost jewel, his sorrow at his loss, and his ability to judge its value all support Felicity Riddy's argument that *Pearl* "is positioned at the meeting-point between aristocratic and urban values which sanction acquisitiveness: the desire to own beautiful things, the taste to recognize and commission them, the leisure to enjoy them."[9] While the Dreamer, both here and later, uses his experience with jewels to affiliate himself with the courtly community, the reader should recognize the problems with deploying possessions and free

---

[8] Ian Woodward, *Understanding Material Culture* (London: Sage Publications, 2007), 152.
[9] Felicity Riddy, "Jewels in Pearl," in *A Companion to the Gawain-Poet*, ed. by Derek Brewer and Jonathan Gibson (Cambridge: D.S. Brewer, 1997), 150.

time as markers of nobility. In particular, leisure is important here. The Dreamer is not historically embedded as an urban-dwelling, hard-working merchant; instead, he is a wanderer who ends up falling asleep in the grass while looking for something, much like the narrator Will in *Piers Plowman*. Will's character is problematic in part because of his lack of a clearly defined social role in the community, and it seems that *Pearl*'s Dreamer is similarly troublesome if one considers the social and not just the symbolic valence of his position.

The question of how literally we can take the Dreamer's role as jeweler is a vexed one. Although scholars such as Barr, Riddy, and John Bowers have more recently explored historicized interpretations of the Jeweler and read *Pearl* as contingent upon specific systems of economic and social exchange, [10] most scholarship over the decades has deployed a symbolic interpretation of the jeweler figure. As I indicated earlier, I believe the social matrix hinted at in the poem's jewel and jeweler references can offer a useful way of connecting or complicating the text's more obvious spiritual dichotomies. Riddy emphasizes the poem's place within "an aristocratic luxury system,"[11] citing not so much its literary value but the way the poetic focus on jewels may have echoed the luxury goods that surrounded or even enclosed the codex itself. This example of an economic understanding of the poem does not, however, exclude a symbolic reading; in fact, one could say that it parallels the symbolic enclosure of the Maiden, as a "jewel" herself, within the divine landscape that now functions as her "cofer" or jewelry box. Bowers's work explores the broad semantic range of the word "jeweler," which could refer to makers, keepers, and deliverers of jewels, but also emphasizes the close links between jewelers and goldsmiths, who had a solid relationship of patronage and gifting with the king.[12] The goldsmith/jeweler association lends support to Bowers's argument that the "longstanding social tensions between artisan and patron serve as an almost subliminal subtext in *Pearl* for the contentions and misunderstandings" between the Jeweler and the Pearl Maiden.[13] Indeed, the fraught power dynamics

---

[10] See Riddy, "Jewels," 143-56, and John Bowers, *The Politics of Pearl: Court Poetry in the Age of Richard II* (Cambridge: D.S. Brewer, 2001).
[11] Riddy, "Jewels," 148.
[12] Bowers, *Politics,* 103-5.
[13] Bowers, *Politics,* 105.

between artisan and patron – the question of who owns the art produced, of who can determine the value of the art, who truly "makes" a beautiful jewel – are evident in the Dreamer/Jeweler's blindness, disappointment, and erroneous assumptions about what his relationship with "his" creation (his Pearl) was, and what it is supposed to be. As these brief examples demonstrate, the symbolic and socio-historical readings of the narrator are by no means mutually exclusive; in fact, they often support one another.

Tony Davenport responds to these recent historicized interpretations of *Pearl* with skepticism, arguing that *Pearl*'s lack of technical jewel vocabulary and the ambiguous nature of the title "jeweler" render a historical or social reading tenuous. He suggests that the wider cultural associations of jewels and jewelers – wealth, possession, luxury – offer a more useful way to understand the Dreamer, who is a "leisured being whose state of life is determined by possession and loss".[14] Despite Davenport's stated opposition to historicized readings, his position here is very similar to that taken by Felicity Riddy, discussed above. The Dreamer is not an artisan hard at work over the precious objects he shapes and sells; instead, he wants the pleasure and social elevation of owning and being associated with those objects. This "excess of possessiveness" is, Davenport argues, particularly evident throughout Fitt V, where the Dreamer's status as a jeweler is highlighted.[15] However, Davenport's own focus on the fraught nature of the term "jeweler" and the Dreamer's life of leisure actually reinforces the significance of some of the social readings he questions. As discussed above, the socially ambivalent position of jewelers with respect to their aristocratic patrons parallels the spiritually ambivalent position of the Dreamer with respect to the Maiden. Moreover, the Dreamer's failure to perform adequately as a jeweler indicates not just his failure as an artisan, but his inability to participate properly in the courtly circles with which he would be loosely associated, and by extension, the wider discourse of courtliness itself.

Susannah Fein has recently argued for yet another level on which we can understand the nature of the Jeweler: the

---

[14] Tony Davenport, "Jewels and Jewellers in *Pearl*," *The Review of English Studies* 59 no. 241 (2008): 513.
[15] Davenport, "Jewels," 513-4.

hagiographical.[16] Fein highlights features of several different medieval texts, including the Apostle John's hagiographies, illustrated Apocalypses, and lapidaries that connect St. John to jewels and judgers of jewels. For example, two stories from John's *Vita* involve the transformation or restoration of precious jewels, and the *North Midland Lapidary* and *Pearl* itself refer to John's naming of the stones that constitute the gates of Heaven. Fein suggests that the Dreamer functions as a shadow of St. John, and therefore becomes a figure whose insufficiencies are all too clear in the light of the apostle's sharp discernment and skill in valuation.

In Fitt I, therefore, the respective identities of both the Maiden and the Dreamer are initially configured according to their roles as jewel and jeweler, the made and the maker, but these identities are almost immediately destabilized. By Fitt V it becomes increasingly clear that the dichotomies associated with these roles (creator and created, organic and mineral, nature and humanity, pure and impure) are collapsing into one another. The power structures are reversed in this fitt as the jeweler, the one with the power to preserve, judge, and craft his jewels, cannot recognize what or where the Pearl is, nor can he recognize her true nature and value. This, in turn, implies either that he himself cannot be a jeweler, a judge of gems, or that the Pearl is not a real jewel. The identities of the Dreamer as well as the Pearl break down and the reader must begin reassembling them. Fitt V is a key moment in this process of breakdown and reconstruction as it begins to develop a vision of the Dreamer's ideal internal state – that is, the individual identity to which he should aspire.

Describing the Jeweler

Beginning at the formal level, Fitt V is framed or marked by a circular progression of adjectival phrases attached to *jueler* in the final line of each stanza: *joyless jueler, gentyl jueler, no kynde jueler, joyfol jueler, no joyfol jueler*. These phrases reinforce the ambiguous nature of this title and its relationship to the Dreamer's stalled spiritual and personal growth. The first stanza concludes with the Dreamer stating that he has "ben a joyless jueler" (252) since his pearl has been taken away from him. The second stanza's final line is the Maiden's comment that the Dreamer would be able to join her in her spiritual

---

[16] Susannah Fein, "Of Judges and Jewelers: *Pearl* and the Life of Saint John," *Studies in the Age of Chaucer* 36 (2014): 41-76.

reincarnation only if he "were a gentyl jueler" (264). In the third stanza, the concluding line is the Maiden's condemnation that "Thou [the Dreamer] art no kynde jueler" (276), and the final line of the fourth stanza is the Dreamer's assertion that if he joined the Maiden "byyonde thise wawes / I were a joyfol jueler" (287-8). The final stanza of Fitt V ends with the Maiden's hard statement that the Dreamer is deluded about his assumption that he can cross the river to join her: "That may no joyfol jueler" (300). While the Dreamer moves from joyless to joyful in his misrecognition of where the Maiden is and how she got there, the final stanza clarifies that a joyful jeweler – that is, the state in which the Dreamer imagines himself to be fulfilled – cannot move to the new spiritual life that the Maiden represents. Casey Finch's translation of this line in Andrew and Waldon's edition of *Pearl* changes the resonance somewhat: he translates the Middle English lines "þe þrydde, to passe þys water fre: / þat may no joyful jueler" (299-300) to "You last aver / You'll wade this water easily. / You can't at all, my joyless jeweler!" The possessiveness of the phrase "my joyless jeweler" implies a changing power dynamic that is not apparent in the Middle English line, although it offers an interesting reversal of the Dreamer's sense of possession over the Pearl. Moreover, the translation's change from joyful to joyless in line 300 prevents the fitt from circling back to the "joyful" jeweler of the first stanza. Such circularity is structurally important in *Pearl* and should not be dismissed.

The change of "joyful" to "joyless" in Finch's translation also releases the reader from the need to evaluate why a joyful jeweler is problematic. Why can not a joyful jeweler (that is, one who now sees that the Pearl is no longer lost) join his jewel on the other side of the river? The Maiden earlier condemned the Dreamer for losing his joy because he lost a gem (lines 265-6), and now she says that no joyful jeweler can cross the waves to be with her. The pattern of joyless/joyful in this fitt, as well as the Maiden's response to those feelings, suggests that the Dreamer's focus on his joy or lack thereof is ultimately self-centered; he is unable to see beyond his own pleasure. Moreover, as Fitt VI reveals, one can only cross the water by first crossing through the earth – that is, passing through the grave, as the Maiden admonishes: "Thy corse in clot mot calder keve" (320). The Maiden herself experienced this when she, as a pearl, fell to the earth, "thurgh gresse to grounde" (10), before appearing near the New Jerusalem on the other side of the water. Only by going through the dark earth and "drwyry deth"

(323), thus temporarily releasing the grasping desire for earthly pleasure and joy, can the spiritual seeker achieve the ultimate place of deeper spiritual happiness. The progression of the *jueler* adjectives reveals that it is the Dreamer himself who values being a joyful jeweler; the Maiden, on the other hand, values spiritually-inflected characteristics such as gentility, nobility, courtesy, and selflessness. In the concluding lines of the second and third stanzas, she offers the possibility of spiritual transition for the Dreamer if only he was a "gentyl jueler" (264), but then condemns his anger and misunderstanding, concluding that he must *not* be a "kynde jueler" (276). While *kynde* and *gentyl* are not quite synonymous, their semantic range has a significant overlap.[17] The distinction between these framing adjectives (joyful versus gentle/courteous) allows Fitt V to articulate two systems of value: one's own pleasure versus bringing pleasure to others through graciousness and gentility.

From the beginning of Fitt V, it is clear that the Dreamer does not comprehend the distinction between self-centered pleasure and other-centered pleasure, or, correspondingly, the difference between the pleasures of earth and the pleasures of the New Jerusalem. The fact that the Dreamer's joy as a jeweler is contingent upon his ownership of his pearl calls to mind a parallel scene of emotional distress in the apocalyptic Book of Revelation:

> And the merchants of the earth shall weep and mourn over her [Babylon]; for no man buyeth their merchandise any more: The merchandise of gold, and silver, and precious stones, and of pearls, and fine linen, and purple, and silk, and scarlet... And the fruits that thy soul lusted after are departed from thee, and all things which were dainty and goodly are departed from thee, and thou shalt find them no more at all. The merchants of these things, which were made rich by her, shall stand afar off for the fear of her torment, weeping and wailing.[18]

---

[17] For example, although *kynde* often refers to something that is natural, this sense of the word also extends to heredity. The *Middle English Dictionary*'s third entry for this word concerns birthrights, legitimacy, and inheritance – all issues that populate the medieval discourse surrounding gentility and nobility.

[18] Revelation 18:11-15 (King James Version).

As Fein argues (discussed above), the apostle John, who wrote the Book of Revelation, was represented in medieval hagiographies as a judge and even a creator of gems, and yet one who did not seek to keep or sell them for profit. His attitude to the jewels he judges is in opposition to the merchants he describes in Revelation. The actual physical value of the jewels was irrelevant to St. John; what was significant to his spiritual credibility was his ability to discern their value. The Dreamer, on the other hand, wants to own his jewel's value. Materialism and possessiveness are closely linked to his joyful- or joylessness. Like the Babylonian merchants, he bewails the loss of his wealth without realizing that his wealth was never his to begin with. He wants the Pearl near him because she brings him joy, and the reason she brings him joy is that her very existence allows him to think of himself as her creator, keeper, and protector. Because he presents himself as a jeweler – as one who crafts jewels, who determines their value, and who controls their public circulation – his state of emotional satisfaction is dependent on the status of his jewel(s).

Stanza I (Lines 241 – 252)

However, it is clear from the beginning of Fitt V that "the state of being a 'jueler' is one that the dreamer lays claim to but does not earn."[19] Upon seeing the Pearl Maiden, the Dreamer's first question in the opening lines of Fitt V is whether she actually is the pearl that he lost: "'O perle,' quoþ I, 'in perlez pyȝt / Art þou my perle þat I haf playned'" (241-2). He thinks he recognizes her, but is not quite certain. This moment of near misrecognition occurs immediately after the conclusion of Fitt IV, in which the Maiden removes her crown and greets him; she attempts to bridge the gap between them by voluntarily lowering herself in an act of true gentility or *kynde*. However, the Dreamer's selfish focus on his own joylessness (due to his supposed loss of a possession) renders him unable to recognize the Maiden's new status and respond with the appropriate gentility to her. Instead, he appears to accuse her of misleading him, of forcing him into sorrow while she herself enjoys the lavish fruits of the dreamscape garden: "Pensyf, payred, I am forpayned, / And thou in a lyf of lykyng lyghte / In Paradys erde, of stryf unstrained" (246-8). His resentment, which he also extends to the fate ("wyrde") that tore her away from him, is co-existent with his joy at

---

[19] Davenport, "Jewels," 509.

rediscovering the Maiden. These twinned emotions result in the passive-aggressive tone of this first stanza, which concludes not with the Dreamer's statement of his newfound joy, but of his previous joylessness.

Stanza II (Lines 253 – 264)

Because the Dreamer responds to the Maiden's gracious greeting with an inappropriate focus on his own emotions, in the second stanza of Fitt V the Maiden is compelled to reinforce her status by replacing her crown (255) and chastising the Dreamer for his inability to move past his own interpretive horizon and, by extension, his own selfishness. Not only can the Dreamer not interpret or "read" the Maiden correctly, but he is also unable to provide an accurate account of his own experience. The Maiden tells him that "ȝe have your tale mysetente" (257) – in his telling of his story, he has distorted it. While the Dreamer saw death and destruction in his pearl's departure, the Maiden's speech reveals that the signifiers of death are simultaneously signifiers of new life: the "cofer" (coffin) that he imagines has taken away his pearl forever is actually a different kind of "cofer" – a jewelry box, in which the pearl is safely preserved and "comly clente" (beautifully enclosed) (259). The Maiden then extends this interpretation of "cofer" to the garden itself as a place of heavenly, perfected enclosure, changed from the darkness of the earth to which the pearl initially fell. This idealized garden is the reality of the coffin the Dreamer imagines. The Dreamer's failure to recognize these semantic shifts is a consequence of his preoccupation with his own joyfulness and his related inability to participate in an exchange of appropriate gentility with the Maiden. She tells him reprovingly that the same kind of coffer or jewelry box would be available for him as well, if only he "were a gentyle jueler" (264).

Stanza III (Lines 265 – 276)

As the Maiden continues her speech in the third stanza, she clarifies to the Dreamer that not only does he not recognize the changed nature of the Pearl now, but he did not truly understand what the Pearl was before. He did not realize that the Pearl/pearl[20] in its previous form was like a transitory rose rather than an

---

[20] The Maiden implies that the pearl that he lost is not the same entity as the Pearl that he found.

unchanging jewel: "For þat þou lestez watz bot a rose / Þat flowred and fayled as kynde hyt gef" (269-70). The idea of the pearl being at once transitory and permanent is not unique in the medieval mystical tradition. The word *gemma,* the Latin root of the English word "gem" that the poem uses synonymously with "jewel," can refer to either a plant bud or a jewel – both the transitory and the permanent, in other words. Sara Ritchey points out that Hildegard von Bingen used both senses of the word together when she described the flesh of Christ in such terms, as both earthly and heavenly: "the word [*gemmae*] implied here that Christ's body is a living tree that forever buds new branches through the work of the virgins/virtues on earth, though in heaven he was festooned with jewels rather than leaves."[21]

Like the Pearl Maiden's body, Christ's body manifests at once in both planes: the temporal and organic, and the permanent and divine. It is therefore natural or "kynde," the Maiden implies, that the pearl disappeared into the ground only to be divinely re-formed. In the next line she uses the same term ("kynde") to describe the chest or box (the "kyste") that enclosed and transformed the earthly Pearl into the eternal "perle of prys" (272). Since the Dreamer has hastily and erroneously "called thy wyrde a thef" (273) – that is, blamed divine providence for taking his possession rather than recognizing the true nature of the pearl's transformation – he is "no kynde jueler" (275). He does not understand the true, pure, natural ("kynde") course of the pearl's existence, and therefore he cannot be a "kynde jueler" himself. He cannot be a judge of gems because he does not realize the full range of meanings that the pearl embodies, and which the Maiden has covered in a few short lines: the pearl as at once a transitory jewel, dead child, divine graciousness, and the Biblical representation of eternal value (the pearl of great price). Worse, he "blamez þe bote," or blames the cure (275); he is resentful about the Pearl's new spiritual incarnation because it means that he, as a mortal, has lost his bauble. Here, at the end of stanza three in Fitt V, the Dreamer and the Pearl Maiden are more distant from one another than they were at the beginning of the poem, when he could not see her at all. He expected to recover the possession he created, when in fact he is encountering one who now represents the God who created *him.*

---

[21] Sara Ritchey, *Holy Matter: Changing Perceptions of the Material World in Late Medieval Christianity* (Ithaca: Cornell University Press, 2014), 68.

Stanza IV (Lines 277 – 288)

The first lines of stanza four at first appear to be a reflection of the Dreamer's thoughtful acceptance of the Maiden's difficult words: "A juel to me þen watz þys geste / And juelez wern hyr gentyle sawez" (277-8). However, given the fact that the Maiden has just challenged the Dreamer's status as a jeweler, his insistence on focusing on her and her speech as jewel-like seems to be a stubborn resistance to that challenge. He does not want to feel disenfranchised; he still wishes to hold the power of judging gems. He has ignored the Maiden's condemnation of his abilities and, moreover, he has ignored an important moment in which she shows that he himself is a created thing and not the creator. When she accuses him of calling the "Wyrde" (fate or God) a thief several lines earlier, she describes the "Wyrd" as "þat oȝt of noȝt hatz made þe cler" – that is, God has made him, the Dreamer, out of nothing (274). While many earlier critics understood this line to refer to the pearl, Alfred Kellogg has shown through Middle English precedent and syntax that it must refer to the "Wyrd"'s creation of the Dreamer himself. The Maiden's offense at the Dreamer's attitude stems from the fact that the Dreamer accuses God of thievery – the very God who created the Dreamer out of nothing.[22]

The Dreamer's description of the Maiden's statements as gentle words ("gentyle sawez") in the fourth stanza therefore seems increasingly inappropriate the more one considers it. Like the friars in *Piers Plowman* who "glosed þe gospel as hem good likede"[23] – that is, who interpreted Scripture to suit their own desires – the Dreamer "glosses" the Maiden according to his wishes. Furthermore, just as he misreads his own jewel, the Maiden herself, he also misreads the "jewels" that constitute her words to him. While they are "gentle" in the sense that they reflect the Maiden's discursive courtesy and gentility, their message is anything but soft or easy. By this point in the poem, we cannot trust the Dreamer's ability to recognize appropriate gentility, and therefore his judgment of the Maiden's words as gentle – whatever semantic register this adjective occupies – is fraught with problems. He cannot accept her judgment of him, and therefore he reduces her speech to soft-spoken, lady-like

---

[22] Alfred Kellogg, "Note on Line 274 of the 'Pearl'" *Traditio* 12 (1956): 406-7.

[23] *Piers Plowman* C Prol: 58.

platitudes rather than a powerful spiritual condemnation and correction.

This reduction of the Maiden and her speech is even more pronounced in his use of the term "geste" in line 277, the first line of this stanza: "A juel to me then was thys geste." "Geste" can mean either "guest" or "story", from the French "geste" (as in the *chanson de geste*). The Dreamer is either referring to the Maiden as a guest who is a precious jewel to him (suggesting possessiveness), or to her words as a story, a fable. It is likely that both meanings of the word resonate; the second meaning suggests the dismissal of her statements as a flight of fancy, which parallels his general reduction of her authority, and the first is reinforced two lines later when he calls her "*my* blysfol beste" (emphasis mine). His resistance to her authority and her right to judge him continues beyond this fitt, becoming particularly clear in Fitt IX where he refuses to accept that she could be an actual queen in Heaven (492). His focus in Fitt V on the jewel-like nature of her speech and his refusal to fully recognize her judgments is his own missed opportunity; while this should have been the time that he examined his own perspective more thoroughly, he instead slides back into objectifying the Maiden, offering trite apologies (281), but essentially remaining spiritually stagnant. His attitude has not changed since the moment he met the Maiden and was enraptured with her beautiful jeweled appearance.

The remainder of this stanza foregrounds the Dreamer's lack of spiritual progress. His focus remains on his own state of emotional satisfaction as he shrugs off the Maiden's revelations by focusing on his ownership of the pearl and how its "recovery" has made him happy again: "My grete dystresse thou [the Maiden] al todrawes [relieves] /...I trawed my perle don out of dawes [I thought my pearl was lost] / Now haf I fonde hyt, I schal ma feste [rejoice]" (282-4). It is not the pearl's transformation that is important to the Dreamer, despite what the Maiden shared with him; it is the pearl's proximity to him and his control over it/her. He goes on to say, in his naïve gladness, that he will live with the pearl in the bright forest groves ("schyr wod-schawes") and love the God who has "broght thys blysse ner" to him (284-6). His focus on his own pleasure leads him to the arrogant conclusion that he will live with the Maiden in her new heavenly location after she has just told him he could not. His syntax also hubristically implies that he will love God *because* He has brought the Dreamer's "blysse" near. The Dreamer concludes this summary of his intentions by saying that if he were beyond the waves (that is, across the river), he would be a joyful jeweler.

Stanza V (Lines 289 – 300)
In the final stanza of Fitt V, the Maiden responds to the Dreamer's shallow self-centredness with anger and derision. Her response to the Dreamer does to him what his response did to her: it reduces his speech to insignificance. She begins by highlighting his foolishness by suggesting that he must be making a joke: "Wy borde [joke] ye men? So madde ye be!" (290). His words cannot be authentic. Following this, she tells him that he has spoken three things without knowledge of what he says: "Thre words has thou spoken at ene / Unavysed, for sothe, wern alle thre / Thou ne woste in world quat on dos mene / Thy worde byfore thy wytte con fle" (291-3). Her condemnation empties the Dreamer's speech of signification, essentially reversing his treatment of her. She concludes by naming each incorrect statement: that he believes she is in the valley because he can see her; that he will live with her there; and that he will pass through the water. All of these, she finishes, cannot be done by a "joyfol jueler" (300). The Maiden's recognition of how the Dreamer attempts to negate her speech, and her quick and cutting reversal of that negation, reinforce the power dynamic that was implied when she replaced her crown. While her former existence as his jewel demonstrated the Dreamer's power, skill, and judgment, her reincarnation from the transitory to the divinely permanent reveals the Dreamer's true inadequacies. Instead of the item he crafted or made, the Pearl is now the figure he aspires to become and a representative of the Divine Being who created him. The poem is a quest not just for spiritual recuperation and fulfillment, but for personal spiritual identity.

Jennifer Garrison emphasizes *Pearl*'s "explicit focus on interiority and emotional reform rather than social acts,"[24] an observation that speaks to the significance of individual identity in the poem – an issue that was not often considered in Middle English poetry. Although personal identity was not a foreign concept to a medieval reader, it did not hold the same value as it did in later centuries. More often the self was configured along the lines of the

---

[24] Jennifer Garrison, "Liturgy and Loss: *Pearl* and the Ritual Reform of the Aristocratic Subject," *The Chaucer Review* 44.3 (2010): 303.

community.[25] Identity, even in its most individual manifestations, was therefore considered to be formed externally rather than internally. The medieval tradition of moral exempla is an example of how identity formation was imagined on a practical level; an external model was required in order to sustain a sense of individual identity. While the Dreamer thinks that the Pearl Maiden's identity rests in his hands, it becomes clear that, in fact, she is the external model that should inform *his* identity. Rather than the made and the known, the Maiden is now a Lacanian Other who is at once ultimately unknowable but also desirable, whether that desire is understood as a need for God and redemption or for personal, human fulfilment. The Dreamer's desire to recover the Pearl transforms into a desire to be like her, and this desire is unachievable. Gregory Roper sees this kind of identity formation as a penance based on the subject's ability to follow a guiding model: the dreamer "must confront the weak self he has become and find a way to reshape that self on a new model, the one which the Pearl-maiden provides...he comes to a task which is not merely recovery of his pearl, but a recover of his own proper 'I'."[26]

The Dreamer therefore sees in the Maiden his own potential completion, although in Fitt V he still misunderstands the nature of that completion. At this stage, he still views the Maiden as something belonging to him, something functioning as an accessory that reinforces his role as a jeweler. He does not yet understand that his preoccupation with his so-called possession and the emotional satisfaction he gains from that are preventing him from attaining true spiritual transformation. Like the body of Christ as considered by Hildegarde von Bingen, the Pearl exceeds the categories of owned/owner, human/inanimate, and temporal/permanent. It is not the Dreamer's object; it is a "thing" in the sense used by Bill Brown, who defines thingness as "what is excessive in objects...what exceeds their mere materialization as objects or their mere utilization as objects - their force as a sensuous presence....the magic by which objects become values, fetishes, idols and totems".[27] This "excessiveness" in the pearl is what renders it out of the Dreamer's

---

[25] David Aers, *Community, Gender, and Individual Identity: English Writing, 1360-1430* (London and New York: Routledge, 1988), 4.
[26] Gregory Roper, "*Pearl*, Penitence, and the Recovery of the Self," *The Chaucer Review* 28.2 (1993): 165.
[27] Bill Brown, "Thing Theory," *Critical Inquiry* 28 (2001): 5.

control, despite his initial illusion of ownership. She becomes something beyond him, and something which he longs to become. Her identity is "non-cognitive and unrepresentable" to the Dreamer at this point, and therefore his words are doomed to fall short of encompassing his relationship to her.[28]

Since Fitt V concerns the complexity of the Dreamer's role as jeweler and a judger (or mis-judger) of gems, it is appropriate that the repeating word in next fitt is *deme* – to judge, or judgment. Fitt V revealed that while the Jeweler should be able to judge gems accurately, in reality he judges the Pearl incorrectly at every turn. His erroneous judgments problematize his self-proclaimed identity and highlight his loss of power. Fitt VI focuses on this idea of judgment and extends it beyond the Dreamer and the Maiden to God Himself as the ultimate judge of human worth. Because in Fitt V the Dreamer can only hope to make a pretense of true judgment and discernment in his own actions, he experiences harsh and accurate judgment by the Maiden in Fitt VI. It is clear that he can no longer rely on artifice, on glittering surfaces that actually conceal hollow misunderstandings; he must be judged and exposed before he can become the "kynde" jeweler that the Maiden wishes him to be.

Bibliography

Aers, David. *Community, Gender, and Individual Identity: English Writing, 1360-1430.* London and New York: Routledge, 1988.

Andrew, Malcolm and Ronald Waldron, eds. *The Poems of the Pearl Manuscript: Pearl, Cleanness, Patience, Sir Gawain and the Green Knight.* Liverpool: University of Liverpool Press, 2007.

Barr, Helen. *Socioliterary Practice in Late Medieval England.* Oxford: Oxford University Press, 2001.

Bowers, John. *The Politics of Pearl: Court Poetry in the Age of Richard II.* Cambridge: D.S. Brewer, 2001.

Brown, Bill. "Thing Theory." *Critical Inquiry* 28 (2001): 1-22.

Davenport, Tony. "Jewels and Jewellers in *Pearl*." *The Review of English Studies* 59 no. 241 (2008): 508-520.

---

[28] Mitchell, "The Middle English 'Pearl'", 92.

Fein, Susannah. "Of Judges and Jewelers: *Pearl* and the Life of Saint John." *Studies in the Age of Chaucer* 36 (2014): 41-76.

Garrison, Jennifer. "Liturgy and Loss: *Pearl* and the Ritual Reform of the Aristocratic Subject." *The Chaucer Review* 44.3 (2010): 294-322.

Kellogg, Alfred. "Note on Line 274 of the 'Pearl'." *Traditio* 12 (1956): 406-7.

Langland, William. *Piers Plowman: A New Annotated Edition of the C-text*. Edited by Derek Pearsall. Exeter: University of Exeter Press, 2008.

Mitchell, Allan. "The Middle English 'Pearl': Figuring the Unfigurable." *The Chaucer Review* 35.1 (2000): 86-111.

Ritchey, Sara. *Holy Matter: Changing Perceptions of the Material World in Late Medieval Christianity*. Ithaca: Cornell University Press, 2014.

Riddy, Felicity. "Jewels in Pearl." In *A Companion to the Gawain-Poet*, edited by Derek Brewer and Jonathan Gibson, 143-156. Cambridge: D.S. Brewer, 1997.

Roper, Gregory. "*Pearl*, Penitence, and the Recovery of the Self." *The Chaucer Review* 28.2 (1993): 164-186.

Smith, D. Vance. *Arts of Possession: the Middle English Household Imaginary*. Minneapolis: University of Minnesota Press, 2003.

Woodward, Ian. *Understanding Material Culture*. London: Sage Publications, 2007.

Noelle Phillips completed her PhD in English at the University of British Columbia in 2011 and was shortly afterwards awarded a two-year Social Sciences and Humanities Research Council of Canada Postdoctoral Research Fellowship at the University of Toronto's Centre for Medieval Studies. She is currently a sessional lecturer at UBC, a distance education tutor for Okanagan College, and an adjunct editor at the Piers Plowman Electronic Archive. Her publications and presentations focus on book history and Middle English literature.

VI

"Mercy Schal Hyr Craftez Kyþe": Learning to Perform Re-Deeming Readings of Materiality in *Pearl*

James C. Staples

Abstract: With its concatenating word "demen" (to judge, condemn, ordain), Fitt VI of *Pearl* demonstrates the complexity of judgment. Indeed, if we read *Pearl* too quickly, our own "deeming" might lead to a damning dismissal of the poem's possibilities. We should read and deem the poem, but also re-read and re-deem the poem, simultaneously learning how to re-read and re-deem the world. By becoming co-participants in the "deeming" that takes place, we learn that such acts of judgment (whether aesthetic judgments or the Last Judgment) do not necessarily coincide with wrath, but might be the spaces for both mercy and beauty.

Following the discovery and recognition of his lost pearl, the dreamer quickly learns that things are not as straightforward as they first appeared. The maiden has just criticized the dreamer on three accounts: he believes only what he sees, he thinks he will be able to dwell with the maiden in paradise, and he is sure he can cross the river. Fitt VI begins with the maiden providing her own glosses for these "þre wordez." The maiden's response, in an initial reading of this fitt, might seem counterintuitive or even coldhearted. She says that jewelers are not very good at their job if they make only aesthetic judgments, which she compares to doubting God's spiritual promises based on rational inquiries. If the dreamer insists on relying only on reason, he will never recognize the promise of eternal salvation. She then asks him to judge himself based on his accusations against God. If he wants to dwell in Paradise, he first needs to ask the permission of a judgmental God, and then he is capable of entering Paradise only once he suffers the dreary death he deserves. The dreamer gets upset and exclaims that the maiden is condemning him to sadness, and he is getting tired of the fluctuating movements of his mind from extreme delight to distress, from finding his pearl to losing her again. He would rather suffer a fall or exile than continue in the enduring sadness. The maiden proposes that by dwelling on this lesser sadness, the dreamer might actually miss out on greater things. He should forget about his feelings and stoically love God, because endurance is greater than impatience. She then argues that judging and accusing God will not make matters any better. The only thing that will help his fallen situation is to beg for mercy, because God is the judge of all things.

Perhaps, though, this summary of Fitt VI is too simplistic. A. C. Spearing has argued that a major narrative shift occurs at the end of Fitt V, where the development of the story transitions from a meditation on symbolism to a more straightforward theological explication: "For more than four hundred lines the pearl symbol undergoes no further development, and simpler, more explicit forms of exposition take its place."[1] If we follow Spearing's reading, we see that the dreamer has clearly failed to recognize the theological truths expressed within the symbolic world around him, so he needs a more straightforward remedy (like the gentle remedies that Lady Philosophy uses to treat Boethius).[2] But does the maiden offer the dreamer such a "more explicit...exposition"? Theodore Bogdanos critiques what he sees as Spearing's oversimplification of the discourse between the dreamer and his pearl: "Despite the generic function of the rational guide that the Maiden brings into the poem, can the reader...really expect her utterance to be more intelligible or less alien to the human sensibility? For, after all, her utterance is an extension of her symbolic substance as symbolic action in verbal form."[3] Bogdanos proposes that nothing in the poem can be read as straightforward, especially explications of theological revelation, as

---

I would like to thank Karl Steel and Nicola Masciandaro for commenting on previous drafts of this essay. In addition, I would like to thank Ryan McDermott for his assistance and encouragement in writing the essay, along with Zach Moir for his feedback and support.

[1] A.C. Spearing, *The Gawain-Poet: A Critical Study* (Cambridge: University Press, 1970), 152.

[2] "Sed quoniam firmioribus remediis nondum tempus est...hanc paulisper lenibus mediocribusque fomentis attenuare temptabo" (Boethius, *Consolatio Philosophiae*, ed. James J. O'Donnell [Bryn Mawr: Bryn Mawr Latin Commentaries, 1990], Book I, Prose vi, s.21).

[3] Theodore Bogdanos, *Pearl: Image of the Ineffable: A Study in Medieval Poetic Symbolism* (University Park: Pennsylvania State University Press, 1983), 83.

the critical tradition surrounding *Pearl* seems to support;[4] however, somewhat surprisingly, scholars quickly move past Fitt VI and its unsettling accounts of God's judgment in order to discuss the more pleasant sections of the poem.[5]

My summary above is only part of the meaning of these five stanzas. As the maiden reveals to the dreamer **Al lys in Hym** (360), and only when the dreamer (and we, the readers) recognize the poem's insistence on the complexity of God, of his Word (and words), can we learn to discover the promise of salvation in even the most discomforting images. Through our examining closely the many accumulated layers of the words (like jewelers deeming multilayered pearls), we find that the maiden's warnings and accusations might be read in a more forgiving or merciful light.[6] By the end of the fitt, with this transformative reading in mind, we learn that the final stanza may not be a warning from the maiden about a wrathful God, but instead an invitation, asking the dreamer to turn his eyes upon Jesus (**Deme Dry3ten**), to take part in the creative

---

[4] Sarah Stanbury points out that the central problem with the poem becomes a crisis of interpretation: "By centering perception on the dreamer, together with the primary interpretation of what is seen or heard, the poet exploits a technique of narrative engagement that subverts the Maiden's text on ocular skepticism without offering an alternative epistemological model, dramatizing rather a crisis of interpretation" (Sarah Stanbury, *Seeing the Gawain-Poet: Description and the Act of Perception* [Philadelphia: University of Pennsylvania Press, 1991], 17). See also Catherine S. Cox, "Pearl's Precios Pere: Gender, Language, and Difference," *The Chaucer Review* 32.4 (1998): 385; Jim Rhodes, *Poetry Does Theology: Chaucer, Grosseteste, and the Pearl-Poet* (Notre Dame: University of Notre Dame Press, 2001); Lawrence Beaston, "*Pearl* and the Pelagians," *Religion and Literature* 36.1 (Spring 2004): 15-38; Lawrence M. Clopper, "The God of the 'Gawain-Poet'," *Modern Philology* 94.1 (Aug, 1996): 1-18.

[5] This is most apparent in Sandra Pierson Prior's *The Pearl Poet Revisited*, where she jumps from line 264 to line 483 in her summary of *Pearl*'s plot. Sandra Pierson Prior, *The Pearl Poet Revisited* (New York: Maxwell Macmillan Int., 1994), 27.

[6] Anselm of Canterbury emphasizes how perspective relates to questions of justice: "For it can happen that one and the same thing is, from different points of view, both just and unjust, and for this reason, is judged by people who are not considering the matter with care, to be entirely just or entirely unjust" (Anselm of Canterbury, "Why God Became Man," *The Major Works*, ed. Brian Davies and G.R. Evans [Oxford: Oxford University Press, 2008], 273.)

process of composing an understanding of God through all of His creation (**and Hym adyte** [endyte]) and, simultaneously, composing an understanding of all of creation through Him (**Al lys in Hym to dyȝt and deme**).[7] To understand how such a judgment is possible, I suggest that we might both resist the desire to speed through the poem and resist trusting our first impressions too strictly (both of which, I argue, are contained in the maiden's initial critique of the dreamer: he **levez wel þat he sez wyth yȝe**).

1. Illogical Logic

We are first confronted with a decorated first-person nominative pronoun, **I**, belonging not to the first-person narrator of the poem as we might first assume, but to the maiden who is assumed to be the pearl. In fact, the maiden establishes her subjective self for the first time with this initial letter–**I**. Prior to this moment, the maiden has merely exercised her observations as a "me"–an accusative pronoun that places the subjectivity on the side of the narrator, whom she calls **juelere** (well, whom she *would* call a **juelere** if he would submit to certain conditions).[8] Here, though, the maiden announces herself with an elaborately decorated **I**, and here she takes on the role of judge, the jewel judging the jeweler, taking in her object of appraisal, and finding him to be of **"lyttel…prayse"** (300). He is nothing like the pearls (or pearly white fleece) of the Lamb: "As praysed perle His wedez wasse" (1112). If this were a

---

[7] Following Adam Zachary Newton, Noah Guynn argues similarly for the intersubjective participative act between reader, narrative, and character in reference to two medieval lays. Guynn summarizes Newton's argument as follows: "Narrative is a mode of moral instantiation that nonetheless resists totalization and abstraction. It evinces instead the uniqueness of actors, actions, and circumstances and the ethical obligations inherent in communicative exchange" (Noah Guynn, "Hybridity, Ethics, and Gender in Two Old French Werewolf Tales," in *From Beasts to Souls: Gender and Embodiment in Medieval Europe*, ed. E. Jane Burns and Peggy McCracken [Notre Dame: U of Notre Dame P, 2013], 160); see also Adam Z. Newton, *Narrative Ethics* (Cambridge: Harvard UP, 1995).

[8] Tony Davenport reveals the multiplicity of roles of a person called "jeweler" in the Middle Ages, where a jeweler is not necessarily a craftsman who shapes and sells jewels; a jeweler could also be an appraiser or even patron of gemstones. Tony Davenport, "Jewels and Jewellers in *Pearl*," *The Review of English Studies* 59.241 (2008): 513.

reckoning of the worth of jewelers, our jeweler would be found wanting.

But why exactly? How has this jeweler failed? He simply believes **wel þat he sez wyth yȝe**. Should a jeweler be condemned for making value judgments based on material conditions?[9] Wouldn't a good jeweler look at the surface of the objects of his trade before he examined any further qualities, such as the stones' virtues? Should we view the jeweler here as a figure of St. Thomas,[10] needing the undeniable evidence of a penetrative finger, a finger that has the ability to see an unseeable God (fingers, even without eyes, have the ability to see, according to Augustine).[11] The so-called Theophilus reminds us that jewelers must bore holes into pearls in order to use them properly for the edification of their fellow Christians. He tells us, in quite materialistic terms, that we conform to what we see: "But if a faithful soul should see the representation of the Lord's crucifixion expressed in the strokes of an artist, it is itself pierced."[12] Does piercing a pearl have a similar effect on the soul of the one who pierces it? (As we soon learn, ultimately the pierced pearl is the pierced Lamb, who must, as we recall, be pierced by the seeing finger of his yet-to-be-believing brother). So maybe the maiden's rebuke underscores that the jeweler has not yet extended his finger—maybe he has *only* seen *wyth yȝe*, and would be more praiseworthy if he also saw with his finger, fully engaging with material reality. Or maybe he should be more willing to believe things unseen. "You

---

[9] David DeVries points out the necessarily troubling foundation for a poem that sets out to tell the experience of a vision while simultaneously downplaying the role of the senses. He argues that the "ludic celebration of the play of language" serves to reveal both the failure and the triumph of the human subject within the text. David N. DeVries, "'Unde Dicitur': Observations on the Poetic 'Distinctiones' of the Pearl-Poet," *The Chaucer Review* 35.1 (2000): 130. Others note the apparent irony in the maiden's condemnation of the jeweler, e.g., Bogdanos, 85; Rhodes, 127; Beaston, 31; Stanbury, 17.

[10] Beaston suggests this comparison (Beaston, 31).

[11] Augustine argues that "sight" is used instead of "touch" because sight more generally refers to understanding: "Non ait: tetigisti me; sed: *vidisti me*; quoniam generalis quodammodo sensus est uisus.... Tange et uide? Nec tamen oculos ille habebat in digito" (Augustine, *In Iohannis Evangeliumli*, CXXI.5).

[12] Theophilus, *On Diverse Arts: The Foremost Medieval Treatise on Painting, Glassmaking and Metalwork*, trans. John G. Hawthorne and Cyril Stanley Smith (New York: Dover Publications, 1979), 79.

believed because you saw me," Christ tells Thomas–is this a rebuke?–and Christ then blesses us for belief without sight (*beati qui non viderunt et crediderunt*).[13] Maybe jewelers ought to judge with their eyes closed.

Or maybe we ought not move so quickly through the poem. Let us return to the why of the jewel's judgment–the jeweler **levez wel þat he sez wyth yȝe**. The traditional reading of this line confirms all of our transcendental thoughts about materiality–good Christians should not simply believe what they see–isn't faith the exact opposite?[14] (Why would it be necessary for me to articulate a faith in something that everyone has the ability to see?) A reading of line 301, then, supports this reading–the material world serves no purpose for post-resurrection Christians. Or maybe the maiden is saying the opposite–she finds a jeweler of little value who too quickly turns away from the materiality of the world.[15] Maybe the entire meaning of this line (and the poem?) rests on the understanding of the word "levez", which possesses the meaning of both "to believe" (as it does in the following line, and twice more in this stanza) and "to leave, to abandon" (a reading that makes much more sense in light of the profession of a jeweler).

Such a jeweler, who too quickly judges based on appearances, is also a jeweler who **leuez oure Lorde wolde make a lyȝe**–by examining the material world, God's creation seems to be lying. Reason becomes irrational, or maybe reason is always already

---

[13] John 20.29.

[14] As Hebrews 11.1 states in the Vulgate, "Est autem fides sperandorum substantia rerum argumentum non parentum." Stanbury refers to the maiden's speech as an exhortation to ocular skepticism, an exhortation that mimics the opening lines to Chaucer's *Legend of Good Women*: "Her terms, that he should not entirely trust what he sees and also that he should have faith in things even if he cannot see them, echo the Chaucerian commonplace" (Stanbury, 16). See also María Bullón-Fernández, "Byȝonde þe Water': Courtly and Religious Desire in 'Pearl'," *Studies in Philology* 91.1 (Winter, 1994): 47; J. Allan Mitchell, "The Middle English 'Pearl': Figuring the Unfigurable," *The Chaucer Review* 35.1 (2000): 95-6; Beaston, 31.

[15] Seeta Chaganti argues something similar: "*Pearl* acknowledges the necessity of physical remains in the process of approaching the holy. As the pearl maiden herself points out, in order to cross over into the realm of the heavenly Jerusalem, 'Þy corse in clot mot calder keue'" (Seeta Chaganti, *The Medieval Poetics of the Reliquary: Enshrinement, Inscription, Performance* [New York: Palgrave Macmillan, 2004], 115).

irrational, since reason always relies in part on what one **sez wyth yȝe**. The natural world that encompasses the dreamer reveals a nature that does not entirely obey its own laws–nature is unnatural. Reason is irrational. And God is a liar.[16] Or maybe the jeweler needs a better light to view things with his *yȝe*. The writer of John's first epistle reminds us: "God is light, and in him there is no darkness.... If we say that we have not sinned, we make him a liar, and his word is not in us."[17] Without the light of Christ, the jeweler suffers in darkness from the same literal-mindedness as the Sanhedrin, who fail to recognize how a temple can and cannot fall down and still be rebuilt; how a man can be a king while simultaneously not being a king.[18] The jeweler has not (yet) learned the importance of wonder, of enchantment. Jane Bennett argues, "To be enchanted is to be struck and shaken by the extraordinary that lives amid the familiar and the everyday. Starting from the assumption that the world has become neither inert nor devoid of surprise but continues to inspire deep and powerful attachments."[19] The dreamer is too modern. His world has become disenchanted. According to Bennett, such a person "ignores and then discourages the affective attachment to that world."[20] He needs the enchanting refrain where "sense become nonsense and then a new sense of things."[21] But we are getting ahead of ourselves. The dreaming jeweler must first recognize his problem. He's being **vncortoyse**. He's failing at being a courtly nobleman, or at least failing to recognize what a courtly persona might value,

---

[16] Robert Blanch and Julian Wasserman argue that the poems of the Cotton Nero A.x manuscript all relate to moments where God seems to disrupt his own laws. Citing Augustine and Aquinas, they argue that man's disruption of natural law results in sin, but God's disruption of natural law leads to the miraculous: "Generally speaking, then, a miracle represents an incident, either *praeter* or *supra naturam*, wherein the laws of nature and principles of reason are seemingly violated or held in suspension in order to generate wonder; the breaking and eventual transcendence of reason are the first steps on the journey of faith" (Robert J. Blanch and Julian N. Wasserman, *From Pearl to Gawain: Forme to Fynisment* [Gainesville: University Press of Florida, 1995], 46-7).
[17] 1 John 1.5-6, 10.
[18] Matthew 26.57-68.
[19] Jane Bennett, *The Enchantment of Modern Life* (Princeton: Princeton University Press, 2001), 4.
[20] Bennett, 3.
[21] Bennett, 6.

which, for a jeweler, should be a chief concern.[22] (But doesn't courtesy also rely on exterior judgments? On self-presentation?) His blameworthy, discourteous judgments of his Lord, the liar, relate to his accusation that the Lord's **hyȝt** (promise) cannot be true. Based on what the jeweler has seen, continues to see, and believes, Fortune always wins. **Fortune dyd your flesch to dyȝe**, and his flesh will die. Even the wheel of Fortune follows the logical law of noncontradiction.

But God does not follow such a law, or so the jeweler's eyes suggest. Or maybe God is a liar. The jeweler's beloved pearl/daughter died but is alive. She is both lost and found. Again the maiden brings up the jeweler's ocular beliefs–you **leuez noþynk but ye hit syȝe**–and the whole experience is **westernays** (literally dis-orienting. The confounding **hyȝt** of the Lord makes the jeweler feel like he's attending a church that uncomfortably "orients" itself toward the west.[23] A western orientation–another logical conundrum). Fortune says all must die. The maiden has died. The maiden lives. And the sun rises behind the jeweler as he takes his communion–the Lord rises again, and the jeweler, like the foolish virgins, has missed the whole affair.[24]

All because the jeweler relies on his eyes too much. All because he believes too strongly (the maiden criticizes him four separate times in this first stanza for incorrectly believing). The final blow

---

[22] I disagree with Bullón-Fernández's reading, where she argues that this accusation of the jeweler's being "vncortayse" refers specifically to a "religious courtesy", which she distinguishes from the courtly notions of courtesy arising in the later concatenation of "cortaysye" in Fitt VIII (Bullón-Fernández, 41-2).

[23] In his edition of *Pearl*, Sir Israel Gollancz speculates the following etymology for the word "westernays": "From the use of the word [*bestornez*] in the Romaunt of the Rose, it is clear, too, that popularly the word was used with the idea of 'turned towards the *west*'.... My opinion is that the poet of the 'Pearl' tried to naturalise *bestornez* in English by changing it to an understandable form, viz., *westornays* or *westernays*; it is to be noted that he required a *w* word for alliteration, and the sound of Fr. *ez* for rhyme; *widishins* would have satisfied the alliteration, but not the rhyme; it is doubtful, however, whether this word was known to our poet. *Ye setten hys wordez ful westernays* may be compared with a parallel from Middle High German, *den namen erwidersinnes las*, i.e., 'he read the name backwards, perversely'" (Sir Israel Gollancz, ed., *Pearl: An English Poem of the Fourteenth Century* [London: Geo. W. Jones at the Sign of the Dolphin, 1918], 115-16).

[24] Matthew 25.1-12.

from the maiden seems to the jeweler (and to us on a first reading) to be as cold as her calcified shell—she unites the jeweler to the father of sins, and this time explicitly through the pride that results from his too-rational beliefs.[25] She accuses him of excessive pride, the type of which drives him, like his ancestors before him, from goodness to evil: **And þat is a poynt of sorquydryȝe, / Þat vche god mon may euel byseme, / To leue no tale be true to tryȝe / Bot þat hys one skyl may dem.** But this same type of pride, **sorquydryȝe**, is the renown of Arthur's courts in *Sir Gawain and the Green Knight*. The Green Knight arrives, expecting to find "sorquydryȝe", but he only finds people cowering "for drede" (*SGGK*, 311-16). Courteous men exhibit their **sorquydryȝe**, but their **sorquydryȝe** makes them **vncortoyse**. Clearly, logic is not going to mean much here.

2. Jewels Judging Jewellers Judging Jewels

The first stanza ends with **dem** and the next stanza starts with **deme**. This act of judging ("deeming"), becomes the point around which Fitt VI revolves. Even before the keyword is mentioned at the end of the first stanza, the maiden has already begun judging, taking on the role of the appraising jeweler for herself (though her judgment takes the form of **hald**ing, and she holds his appraisal value as **lyttel**). The jewel judges the jeweler, and she judges him primarily for judging things too quickly, based on his **one skyl** (reason alone).[26] She begins the second stanza, though, by commanding him

---

[25] Many critics point out the apparent cruelty or lack of sympathy expressed in both the maiden's and God's judgment of the dreamer. Edward Condren argues, "The maiden judges his remarks harshly.... What she says is not actually offensive; indeed, her explanations of medieval Christian theology are apparently sound, according to those who have studied the matter. But she says it with a surprising lack of sympathy. Instinctively readers want to see her greet her father (if father he is) with the kind of warmth his bereavement yearns for.... But we get none of this. Instead, from her opening lines she levels at him charges that he is mistaken (257), mad (267), that he is 'no kynde jueler' (276), and that he speaks before thinking (292-94)" (Edward I. Condren, *The Numerical Universe of the* Gawain-Pearl *Poet: Beyond Phi* [Gainesville: University Press of Florida, 2002], 52-3); see also Bogdanos, 86; Spearing, 154.

[26] A.R. Heiserman argues for the aptness of the concatenation of "deme" in Fitt VI, where the jewel judges the jeweler: "Then as jewel chastized jeweler, the word became *deme*, a term whose several meanings—think, say, judge, expect—were wrung from its use in the linkages. Thus the aptness of the

to **Deme now þyself**! She has, again, turned the tables on the jeweler—before he makes judgments about the materiality of the jewel-like world around him, he should be judging his own jewel-like self. And more specifically, he should be judging his jewel-like **wordez**. And through the refrain of the word **deme**, an iteration that reveals more the gaps in meaning than the sameness of meaning, we learn that the words of the poem are just as multilayered as finely cultured pearls, inviting judgment from the highly trained eyes of a jeweler. W. A. Davenport argues that the repetition of **deme** "calls his judgment more and more into question.... The Dreamer's want of judgment is contrasted with the decreeing power of God...."[27] Andrew and Waldron argue in their edition that the repetition reveals a gap between the dreamer and his Creator: "The different meanings of the concatenating word *deme* (variously 'allow,' 'consider,' 'judge,' 'condemn,' 'ordain') draw attention to the gap between the Dreamer's fallible will and judgment and the power of God to ordain what will be."[28] Over and over again in *Pearl* scholarship, we see a jeweler rightfully judged by a just God. Spearing proposes the hard justice of God's final judgment, but argues that sympathy falls both with God and with the jeweler: "Our own thoughts and feelings should be engaged on both sides of the encounter; we shall recognize the absurdity of the Dreamer's position, and yet—because it is based on a completely natural human response, and because the Dreamer is 'I', not 'he'—we shall also share in his suffering."[29] The sympathy here seems to revolve entirely around judgment—we can sympathize with the maiden and God in their judgment of the subpar jeweler; we can sympathize with the jeweler in his distress at what appears to be an unfair treatment by a hard and just God. Or maybe the "justice" here comes from the turned tables—maybe the jeweler, the usual judge, finally learns what it feels like to be judged by the object of his judgment—the object-become-subject (through the **I**) judges the

---

concatenatio contributes to the very structure of the debate" (A. R. Heiserman, "The Plot of Pearl," *PMLA* 80.3 [Jun., 1965]: 169).

[27] W. A. Davenport, *The Art of the Gawain-Poet* (London: Athlone P, 1978), 43.

[28] Malcolm Andrew and Ronald Waldron, eds., *The Poems of the Pearl Manuscript: Pearl, Cleanness, Patience, Sir Gawain and the Green Knight* (Berkeley: University of California Press, 1979), 68.

[29] Spearing, 154.

subject-become-object. And we are expected to feel, through sympathy, this radical shift in roles.

"**Deme now þyself**", she commands, as if to say, "you've judged everything else long enough, pointed to the spots that mar the surfaces of the objects around you, and you have a giant plank sticking out of your own eye![30] Judge yourself for a change!" Consider the **wordez** that man **to God...schulde heue**, and judge your own when you did converse (**con dayly**) with Him. (Or perhaps this dalliance is more like a flirtation with God.) Richard Newhauser proposes an allusion to Job 6.26 in this judgment of words[31]–does the jeweler here speak like Job's overly judgmental companions, dressing up their eloquence only to rebuke, with the words flying away with the wind? *Ad increpandum tantum eloquia concinnatis et in ventum verba profertis.*[32] Maybe the jeweler's jewel-like words have little value. Maybe they only appear (to the eyes) to hold any merit because they have been dressed up, *eloquiae concinnatae*. Like his judgments of the jewel-like landscape, his judgment of the meaning of his own jewel-like words relies more on appearances than on anything else.[33]

The maiden specifies exactly which **wordez** she judges to be idle (which *verba* the jeweler *in ventum profert*), and these words do not immediately seem to relate to his accusation of God as a liar–they are that he shall cross the stream and live with the maiden in her jewel-like coffer: **Þou saytz þou schal won in þis bayly / ... / Þou wylnez ouer þys water to weue**. And such words are worthless because the jeweler wrongfully judges himself worthy to be kept in the company of fully developed pearls–pearls that reside "in cofer so comly clente / As in þis gardyn gracios gaye…" (259-60). In order to cross the stream, the jeweler must become a pearl, like the maiden, "þurȝ kynde of þe kyste þat hyt con close" (271). Because he has not yet been reborn through the womb-like grave

---

[30] Matthew 7.3.
[31] Richard Newhauser, "Sources II: Scriptural and Devotional Sources," *A Companion to the Gawain-Poet*, ed. Derek Brewer and Jonathan Gibson (Cambridge: D.S. Brewer, 1997), 272.
[32] Job 6.26.
[33] In reference to Job 6.26, Gregory the Great distinguishes between two false types of speech–flattery and rebuke. The jeweler seems to be guilty of both here: "Duo sunt genera locutionum importuna ualde et noxia generi humano; unum quod curat etiam peruersa laudare, aliud quod studet semper etiam recta corripere" (Gregory the Great, VII.xxxvii.57).

(which, as I describe below, might be more appropriately compared to an oyster), he cannot yet dwell with her. And he continues to call God a liar, because God has condemned man to death and yet man lives.

3. Seduction, Sadism, Salvation

Before he can cross the river, before he can enter into the luxurious jewelry box on the other side, he must suffer death: **Þy corse in clot mot calder keue**.[34] He must ask permission, he must be denied permission, and he must wait until he has been purged of any remnant of his material humanity: **Me þynk þe burde first aske leue– / And ȝet of graunt þou myȝtez fayle**.[35] Who knows what good it will do, but he might as well submit himself to God and ask for permission, only to be rejected. Is this extreme humiliation, as Tison Pugh suggests? Later, the maiden will demand, **Þe oȝte better þyseluen blesse, / And loue ay God, in wele and wo**, and Pugh argues, "Resistance is futile, as humans must abide by and endure God's judgments, no matter how arbitrary or unkind they appear. The only proper response to this hierarchical relationship is willed sufferance leading to abject submission and a complete acceptance of God's will."[36] God's judgments are quite dismissive, his expectations seem arbitrary, so the jeweler ought to prepare himself for humiliating suffering. According to the maiden, before anyone can cross the stream (**Er ouer þys dam**) God has judged (**Dryȝtyn deme**) that man must die a dreary death (**drwry deth boz vch man dreue**) because of something his forefather did (**Oure ȝorefader hit con mysseȝeme**). And the apple probably doesn't fall far from the tree. This is perfectly just, isn't it?

---

[34] Katherine Terrell offers a reading of the "corse in clot" in which the dreamer develops from viewing the grave of his pearl as a place of rot and decay to recognizing the grave as a "fertile place" for "spiritual renewal" (Katherine H. Terrell, "Rethinking the 'Corse in Clot': Cleanness, Filth, and Bodily Decay in 'Pearl'," *Studies in Philology* 105.4 [Fall, 2008]: 429-47).

[35] Cox argues that the dreamer's carnality "is the necessary step in the process of signification." She, however, argues that because the maiden establishes here a carnal/spiritual dualism, the dreamer must "transcend carnal origin" in order to "appreciate fully the spiritual" (Cox, 380). See also Bogdanos, 86.

[36] Tison Pugh, *Sexuality and its Queer Discontents in Middle English Literature* (New York: Palgrave Macmillan, 2008), 41-2.

Or maybe this kind of justice involves a little bit more play, a flirtatious back-and-forth that involves a subtle invitation followed by a coquettish rejection, followed by further invitations. Maybe this kind of abjection could be something the dreamer learns to enjoy (or already does). Maybe when the jeweler **con dayly** (did dalliance) with God, the **wordez** that the jeweler heaved **to God** were met with God's own flirtatious replies, and these replies come across as coy.

This scene of absolute judgment, of extreme humiliation and denial, might be nothing more than the rituals of courtship found in *fin'amors*. According to C. Stephen Jaeger, an erotic flirtation that resists sexual union is an "ennobling love," one that cultivates virtue in the two lovers: "In order to ennoble, love had to be a subject of virtue; it had to derive from virtue and in some sense also be its source. And so ennobling love had to manage sexuality, hold it in its place by severe discipline, or—the most ascetic position—banish it altogether, demonize it, lay heavy taboos on it."[37] And, as Jaeger suggests, the sexier the courtship process, the more praiseworthy the resistance, and the more refining the love is for the lovers.[38] The flirtatious back-and-forth between the jeweler and his coy God reflects Mechthild of Magdeburg's amorous frustrations with (and intensified desire for) her seductive lover-God. Describing the threefold favor of God, she argues that God shows to his Creation tenderness, sublime intimacy, and, finally, intense suffering: "I much prefer to remain in this [last] state than in the other two.... The nature of love is such that it...becomes full of longing in rejection."[39] The jeweler has been seduced by the beauty that God ever discloses to him in this dream landscape (and in the real world?), and then God denies complete access to the jeweler.[40] Following Mechthild, we

---

[37] C. Stephen Jaeger, *Ennobling Love: In Search of a Lost Sensibility* (Philadelphia, University of Pennsylvania Press, 1999), 7.

[38] Jaeger argues, "The more private and intimate, the greater the force transforming matter into spirit. The exaltation is all the more intense, the more it lends itself to ridicule" (Jaeger, 144).

[39] Mechthild of Magdeburg, *The Flowing Light of the Godhead*, ed. Frank Tobin (New York: Paulist Press, 1998), 249.

[40] Stanbury describes the Dreamer's ultimate attempt to cross the stream as an act of seduction: "The method of the dreamer's visionary process is vision itself, a faculty that is finally self-consuming when sense impressions seduce him to attempt to ford the stream, and he awakens" (Stanbury, 17). See also Cox, 385.

might recognize God's own desire in His denial, a desire for the jeweler to increase in his desire–this dalliance seems to be bordering on tantric sex. Such a pursuit of ecstasy, where one desires "to push sexual pleasure to its limit and beyond" is similar to what Jean Baudrillard discusses in *Seduction*: "In the absence or denial of the orgasm, superior intensity is possible. It is here, where the end of sex becomes aleatory again, that something arises that can be called seduction or delight. Or again, sexual pleasure can be just a pretext for another, more exciting, more passionate game."[41] Rather than immediately giving the jeweler what he wants, God withholds *jouissance* from the jeweler so that the jeweler can agonize (and bask) in his unsatisfied cravings.

Perhaps Julian of Norwich was right. Perhaps Adam's fall is a delightful *felix culpa*. Julian comforts us by reminding us, "I saw that he will that we wit he taketh no herder the falling of any creatur that shalle be saved than he tok the falling of Adam, which we know was endlessly loved and sekerly kepte in the time of all his nede, and now is blissefully restored in hye, overpassing joyes."[42] Like Mechthild, Julian reminds us that our fall keeps us turning toward God's love: "And than wene we, that be not alle wise, that all were noughte that we have begonne. But it is not so. For it nedeth us to falle, and it nedeth us to see it. For if we felle not, we shulde not knowe how febil and how wreched we be of ourselfe, nor also we shulde not fulsomly know the mervelous love of our maker."[43] Let us, then, join our voices with the angels and archangels, and with all the company of heaven, to sing with the Middle English Lyricist: "Blessëd be the tymë / That appil takë was, / Therefore we mown singen, / 'Deo gratias!'"[44]

And although the death might be dreary (**drwry**), the death is also a courtship gift (a **drwry**). The jeweler does not just have to die; the jeweler *gets* to die. In *Cleanness*, God grants (hetero)sexual lovers a love-gift in the form of a "drwry":

---

[41] Jean Baudrillard, *Seduction*, 1979, trans. Brian Singer (New York: St. Martin's Press, 1990), 18.

[42] Julian of Norwich, *The Writings of Julian of Norwich: A Vision Showed to a Devout Woman and a Revelation of Love*, ed. Nicholas Watson and Jacqueline Jenkins (University Park: Pennsylvania State University Press, 2006), 293.

[43] Julian of Norwich, 315.

[44] "Adam lay y-bownden," *Medieval English Lyrics 1200-1400*, ed. Thomas G. Duncan (New York: Penguin Classics, 1995), 145. I also allude to Rite Two of the *Book of Common Prayer* of the Episcopal Church.

> I compast hem a kynde crafte and kende hit hem derne,
> And amed hit in Myn ordenaunce oddely dere,
> And dy3t drwry þerinne, doole alþer-swettest,
> And þe play of paramorez I portrayed Myseluen.
> (*Cleanness*, 697-700)

God grants earthly lovers a **drwry** that is "doole alþer-swettest", so we can only imagine what kind of "doole" he grants to His own lovers! The jeweler gets to enter into an oyster-like "kyste", a transformative chamber that purges him of any material impurities and allows the jeweler to develop into a jewel. (And I would guess that this "doole" is not, as the jeweler first thinks, a **doel-dystresse**, unless, of course, that's what the jeweler is into.)

4. Producing Perfect Pearls

This "dom", the effect of the maiden's "deme," is not simply a value judgment (as her "halde" was at the beginning of the fitt), but a prescription (maybe a punishment or maybe a reward? It's still difficult for the jeweler to distinguish).[45] He accuses the maiden of condemning him to **dol,** which causes him, he thinks, to **dowyne**(n), or to dwindle into nothingness. The jeweler has not carefully considered his words, though, because when the maiden prescribes a **dol** for the jeweler, he seems to brush past the fact that the word **dol** can mean either a "sadness" or a "gift", and each of these *dols* could result from the two meanings of *demen* here (to prescribe a punishment or a reward). When the maiden **demez** the jeweler **to dol**, she could, in fact, be presenting him with a gift (like the "doole alþer-swettest" of *Cleanness*).

Moving into the third stanza, into the poetic "kyste" at the heart of Fitt VI, we discover the inner workings of the refining process. Within this central stanza, the jeweler finally begins to fight back. He has heard enough of the maiden's seemingly cold-hearted words, and he resists, but although he resists (or through his resistance?), we see that he not only has become the object of deeming and the object of the sentence, but also becomes even more clearly the object of appraisal–the jeweler becomes the jewel: **Demez þou me**? The jeweler's speech within Fitt VI, his first response to the maiden's

---

[45] In the *Middle English Dictionary*, entry 9 for "demen", most closely defining the use of "demez" here, includes both "To prescribe or impose (a penalty)" and "to…make an award (to sb.)."

accusations, physically figures the placement of a pearl within an oyster—he is a bit of material that has entered into the encasement of the maiden's discourse, and through such a "kyste", the jeweler might begin to develop into a refined pearl. But the jeweler does not yet understand how this refining development works. He does not understand the irritating resistance required for a pearl to develop.

The jeweler, utterly confused and beginning to fear the unquenchability of his desire, hurls questions at the maiden and demands some answers: **Now haf I fonte þat I forlete, / Schal I efte forgo hit er euer I fyne? / Why schal I hit boþe mysse and mete?... / What seruez tresor bot garez men grete,/When he hit schal efte with tenez tyne? / ... / When I am partlez of perle myne, / Bot durande dole what may men deme?** His questions, in some way, all ask the same thing: "Why do you keep me from getting what I want?" The jeweler desires to have his pearl, and God has said no. Sometimes desire should go unfulfilled, even (especially) when the object of desire is so alluring. He knows only two things for sure: he's in pain (which suitably coincides with a disruptive hole in the manuscript page), and, without his pearl, he has no reason to live. **My precios perle dotz me gret pyne. / ... / Now rech I neuer for to declyne, / Ne how fer of folde þat man me fleme.** The jeweler fears that he dwindles (**I dowyne**), and he thinks that this roadblock to his getting what he wants will cause him to lose the one element that gives him a sense of personal value, and it will cause him to fail before he becomes fully refined. **Schal I efte forgo hit er euer I fyne?**[46] He still believes that value comes from the ownership of external things, but he fails to recognize that the resistance to his desire, the unattainability of satiety, actually leads to his refining, to a growth that is actually the opposite of the dwindling that he fears.[47]

In order to explore the jeweler's misconceptions, we should hedge our bets regarding the meaning of the maiden's initial classification of a failed jeweler (one **þat leuez wel þat he sez wyth**

---

[46] I am taking the word "fynen" to mean "to refine", along the lines of "Fin'amors", rather than "to end", as it is generally understood in this context.

[47] W. R. J. Barron notes the comparisons in lines 327-30 between the jeweler's suffering and *fin'amors*: "Like the courtly lover who fails to recognize the power which separates him from his love, he accuses her of heartless indifference to his suffering" (W. R. J. Barron, "Luf-Daungere," quoted in Spearing, 121)

y3e), and we should turn to the material workings of the world for some evidence about the ways that a pearl becomes refined. The mineralogist G.F. Herbert Smith describes in 1912 the process of pearl development, with Freud's notions of sublimation apparently serving as a subtext: "Tortured by the intrusion of some living thing...or of a grain of sand or other inorganic substance, and without means to free itself, the mollusc perforce neutralizes the irritant matter by converting it into an object of beauty that eventually finds its way into some jewellery cabinet."[48] The medieval account of the formation of pearls relies even more on the interplay between the material and the spiritual, but duration (**durande doel**) and refinement (frequently linked to purging) are necessary for the process. Mary Carruthers has noted the ways that pearl-formation compares in the Middle Ages to the process of mnemonic development: "Creatures who make pearls [margeries] are also in marginal [marges] evidence. Medieval natural lore held that snails made pearls in their heads, which is where a reader should also be creating pearls of great price from the matters of the book."[49] Elsewhere, Carruthers compares the "hermeneutic irritants" of medieval discourses to "an irritant like that eventually producing a pearl."[50] Such irritants appear in the ludic wordplays and contrarieties within the dialogue between the maiden and the jeweler.[51]

Turning to the *Cambridge Lapidary*, we see elements of pearl-refinement that seem to relate directly to the jeweler's unsettling

---

[48] G.F. Herbert Smith, *Gem-Stones and their Distinctive Characters* (London: Methuen & Co, 1912), 294.

[49] Mary Carruthers, *The Craft of Thought: Meditation, Rhetoric, and the Making of Images, 400-1200* (New York: Cambridge University Press, 1998), 162.

[50] Carruthers makes this connection between hermeneutic irritant and pearl-formation in her reference to Catherine Brown's *Contrary Things*. Mary Carruthers, *The Experience of Beauty in the Middle Ages* (Oxford, Oxford University Press, 2013), 203, n. 67.

[51] Bogdanos points out the extreme highs and lows of the dreamer's emotional state, which further supports my reading of the dreamer-as-pearl, becoming refined within the heart of this fitt: "The Maiden's rebuke and the prospect of self-dissolution that faces him, if he dares cross to her realm, catapult the dreamer from exultant hope to plangent despair, thus continuing the poem's emotional dialectic between joy and disappointment. No metaphysical argument can persuade away his anguish at the realization that discovering the ideal can be more painful for imperfect man than losing it" (Bogdanos, 85-6).

situation. According to the lapidary, a newly conceived pearl (*naisel*), which always risks the dangers of a miscarriage (*donkes tone durement / La conche avorte de sa piere*), forms within the womb of a base oyster through the spiritually impregnating powers of a drop of heavenly dew (*rosee*):[52]

> Unes a conches en la mer,
> Qu'eschafotes solons clamer;
> E ceste par la rosee
> En la gravele gist baee:
> De la rosee ki descent
> Prent li naisel concevement;
> Un cerclez vient la dedenz
> De la rosee bel e genz.[53]

For a successful birth, a drop of dew (that could easily be mistaken for a rose) must enter into the open oyster through an act of penetration, and it must remain long enough within the oyster to lead to a large and praiseworthy pearl (*grosse et lee*). Comparably, a rose, which might as well be a drop of heavenly dew (*rosee*), has penetrated the dreamer, leading to an irritating (but joyful) development of a *naisel* that must develop over a full term. The jeweler experiences an ocular penetration similar to the dreamer in the *Roman de la Rose*, whose penetrative gaze becomes penetrated by the virile rosebud:[54]

---

[52] The standard description of a pearl's development in the Middle Ages compares remarkably to descriptions of the Incarnation of Christ. E.g., Mechthild of Magdeburg describes the Incarnation: "The sweet dew of the eternal Trinity gushed forth from the fountain of the everlasting Godhead into the flower of the chosen maid; and the fruit of this flower is an immortal God and a mortal man and a living hope of eternal life. And our Redeemer became a Bridegroom" (Mechthild of Magdeburg, 49).

[53] "The Cambridge Version: Introduction and Text," *Anglo-Norman Lapidaries*, ed. Paul Studer and Joan Evans (Genève: Slatkine Reprints, 1976), ll. 1187-94.

[54] As critics have noted, the presentation of the rose in *Roman de la rose* is decidedly phallic. Simon Gaunt argues, "At the end of the poem, Jean [de Meun]'s figurative language apparently enables an increasingly explicit account of sexual intercourse, but if it is always assumed, perhaps a little hastily, that the allusions to penetration (21607-42) refer to heterosexual sex, the description of grabbing the rose's stalk and shaking it… is less easy to

> El miroër entre mil choses
> choisi rosiers chargiez de roses
> qui estoient en un destor
> d'une haie bien clos entor;
> et lors m'en prist si grant envie
> que ne lessasse por Pavie
> ne por Paris que n'alasse
> la ou je vi la greignor tase.[55]

Roses (or is it *rosees*?) are absolutely necessary for the process of pearl-birthing, and the maiden, who is a pearl and a rose, holds the impregnating potential to fill the oyster of the jeweler's heart and mind with heavenly dew.

In the previous fitt, the maiden informed the dreamer that the material pearl he lost "watz bot a rose / Þat flowred and fayled as kynde hyt gef" (269-70). And for the rose to become a pearl, the rose must be enclosed in the oyster-like "kyste": "Now, þurȝ kynde of kyste þat hyt con close / To a perle of prys hit is put in pref" (271-72). The maiden/rose/dew must enter into the "kyste" that is an oyster, a grave (**clot**), a text, and, finally, the jeweler's heart/mind (which is also a **clot**-like oyster/grave). The maiden becomes the penetrator in this queer relationship, raising the maiden to a masculine *domna* and placing the jeweler into "the 'feminine' role of passivity and submission," a gender reversal that Jane Gilbert argues is "an entirely standard part of *fin'amors*."[56] For the jeweler to develop a pearl and to develop into a pearl–to conceive the *naisel* and to become the *naisel*–the jeweler must be receptive to the

---

translate into a stage in 'normal' heterosexual intercourse" (Simon Gaunt, "Bel Acueil and the Improper Allegory of the Romance of the Rose," *New Medieval Literatures* 2, [Oxford: Clarendon P, 1998], 71-72). See also Karl D. Uitti, "'Cele [qui] doit estre Rose clamee' (*Rose*, vv. 40-44): Guillaume's Intentionality," *Rethinking the* Romance of the Rose*: Text, Image, Reception*, ed. Kevin Brownlee and Sylvia Huot (Philadelphia: U of Pennsylvania P, 1992), 39-64.

[55] Guillaume de Lorris and Jean de Meun, *Le Roman de la Rose*, ed. Félix Lecoy (Paris: Honoré Champion Éditeur, 2009), ll. 1613-20.

[56] Jane Gilbert, "Gender and Sexual Transgression," *A Companion to the Gawain-Poet*, ed. Derek Brewer and Jonathan Gibson (Cambridge: D.S. Brewer, 1997), 58-62.

maiden's rosy penetration.⁵⁷ He must become an ever-ready womb and simultaneously desire to climb into the spiritual womb of the **clot** to be born again as a *perle of prys*.⁵⁸

But we must remember that the roses from Christ are not always recognizably pleasant; in fact, sometimes the rosy **drwries** (love-tokens) from Christ the Lover can actually seem **drwry** (dreary). The Blessed Henry Suso's life story is filled with roses–the rose actually becomes his identifying characteristic in iconography– but Suso's roses are Suso's sufferings. They are the sufferings that spill all over a spiritually masochistic saint by his overly generous lover, and, as a breathtaking youth explains to him, "This multitude of roses are the many different sufferings God intends to send him. He should accept them cheerfully from God and endure them in patience."⁵⁹ No wonder the maiden encourages the jeweler to humble himself completely to the judgments of God. The creation of a pearl might require **doel**, but it does not have to be **doel-dystresse**–the jeweler has, again, misjudged the situation. All the jeweler has to do is to endure patiently (he **nedez schal þole, and be not so þro**) and to continue loving God, his beloved lover, who desires His beloved jeweler to desire to submit himself (or is it raise himself?) to the status of a jewel. Sufferings and roses develop beautifully when endured patiently, and by enduring them patiently, like the purging effects of a refiner's fire, or, more aptly, an irritant that enters into the womb of an oyster, the jeweler will allow the *drwry drwry* of the pain-inducing rose/*rosee* to develop into a fully formed pearl, one that has become both *grosse* and *lee*.

---

⁵⁷ The sexual act that results from the penetration by this rose/*rosee* resists heteronormative categorization, since both images simultaneously suggest and challenge the binaries of passive femininity and active penetration. Although the images of dew and roses may traditionally suggest femininity, medieval authors frequently present both images as penetrative. Following the argument proposed by Simon Gaunt in n. 54 above, the maiden-as-rose is penetrative, even phallic. Further, the image of dew contains suggestions of insemination both in Mechthild's description of the Incarnation, described above as "sweet dew of the eternal Trinity [gushing] forth from the fountain of the everlasting Godhead into the flower of the chosen maid," and, relatedly, in the famous opening lines of the *Canterbury Tales*, where the "droghte of March" penetrates with virile force.
⁵⁸ John 3.1-15.
⁵⁹ Henry Suso, *The Exemplar, with Two German Sermons*, trans. Frank Tobin (New York: Paulist Press, 1989), 137.

5. Re-Deeming Readings

The maiden reveals two options, maybe resulting from the two meanings of *demen* and the two types of *dol* described above: one where the jeweler **lurez lesse** and one where he gains **þe mo**. His assumption that the **doel** that results from a **drwry drwry** is a **doel-dystresse** could very well result from the amount of noise (**dyne**) that such a logical misidentification screams at him. And when reading about God's judgment on mankind, the fall of man, and **deþ**, we, too, might have a hard time drowning out the probability that **doel** means "grief" in this context; however, as we have discovered, logic does not always serve us justly in our exploration of this otherworld/poem. If the jeweler and we learn to drown out the noise of the **doel-dystresse**, the very **doel** that would cause him to **dowyne,** the jeweler might actually begin to grow, to become refined, to gain **þe mo**, through a **dol** that is *alper-swettest.*

Suffering is part of the process, but the suffering is glorious and glorifying. And although the **doel** might lead to the dreamer's **anger** (which **gaynez þe not a cresse**), the exhausting goings and comings of God-the-lover–the moments that seem like absolute abandonment or heartless judgment–are nothing other than a passionate **daunce,** a dance between a doe-like jeweler and his roe-like lover. This roe has all of the energy of a youthful fawn, and he can dance all night if necessary. Bernard of Clairvaux delights in such a cervine description of the lover in the Song of Songs,[60] through which we learn that the lover is both a merciful savior and a just judge:

> While this bridegroom, in the ardor of his love, seems to rush eagerly into the embraces of the beloved, he nevertheless knows how to direct his steps, or rather his leapings, with prudent consideration, being wary as to where to place his foot. A comparison with the [roe] as well as with the fawn is therefore called for, since the latter expresses the desire to save and the former the decision to choose.[61]

---

[60] "Donec adspiret dies et inclinentur umbrae revertere similis esto dilecte mi capreae aut hinulo cervorum super montes Bether" (Song of Songs 2.17).
[61] Bernard of Clairvaux, "Sermon 55: How We Ought to Judge Ourselves Lest We Be Judged," *Sermons on the Song of Songs*, 2014, http://pathsoflove.com/bernard/songofsongs/sermon55.html.

God, the youthfully virile roe, might **braundysch and bray** alongside his dancing doe, but He has not chosen to dance with his beloved jeweler in a moment of thoughtless passion (though Passion obviously plays a key role in this union). God-the-roe, instead, has thoughtfully deemed the jeweler as his beloved, has decided to dance with the jeweler for as long as it takes for the jeweler to tire, and hopes that the exhausted jeweler will find comfort in the realization that his lover has everything under control (**When þou no fyrre may, to ne fro, / Þou moste abyde þat He schal deme**). And once the jeweler has finally fallen asleep, his lover will do everything possible to ensure that no commotion from the other dancing deer awakens His beloved, saying, *Adiuro vos filiae Hierusalem per capreas cervosque camporum ne suscitetis neque evigilare faciatis dilectam quoadusque ipsa velit.*[62]

So **Deme Drȝyten, euer Hym adyte!** The pearl instructs the jeweler–judge God all you want–or maybe something more like "consider Him and all the possibilities that he could provide for you–possibilities that you cannot even imagine for yourself"; or "regard him as your lover, and learn how everything works out in the end" (all will be well, and all will be well, and every kind of thing will be well, as Julian's loving God reminds her).[63] This judgment (*dom*) that has lurked so menacingly over Fitt VI is nothing other than the dominion of a lover who has the jeweler's well-being as his chief concern, and he never strays: **Of þe way a fote ne wyl He wryþe**. But if the jeweler continues to dwell in sorrow (a **sorȝe** that is a **doel-dystresse**), if he continues to ignore the wonder that he experienced on discovering the beauty of this dreamy landscape, if he worries about losing his pearl more than he remembers the temporary joy that the pearl brought him (and the greater joy that the pearl's beauty revealed to him in a more fulfilling lover), then his recompenses (**mendez** that are *dooles alþer-swettest*) will never **mounte**; they will only **dowyne**. And so will he. Grains of irritating earth must learn to read their own materiality and the material wor[l]d with open minds if they ever desire to achieve the **blyþe** that results from their nacreous transformation. The jeweler must **sech Hys blyþe ful swefte and swyþe**. This transformation is, in part, a reading practice that requires an epistemological shift (one that we

---

[62] Song of Songs 2.7.
[63] Julian of Norwich, 209.

the readers learn alongside the jeweler), a reading practice that is not straightforward, but that requires a bit of slanted, or queer, reading.[64] The epistemological shift that occurs from one reading to the next further instructs the reader on how to mentally perform the very redemption (or "re-deeming"?) of the material world that the poem describes. Reading the poem *Pearl* too quickly might result in a deeming that results in a damning dismissal of all of the possibilities the poem and its words offer to us (we must not **leve wel** [abandon too hastily] what we see **wyth yȝe**). We should follow the advice of Mechthild's *Flowing Light of the Godhead* and read the poem multiple times in order to more fully understand it. The introduction to Mechthild's book says, "[This book contains] many things unheard of that you shall understand if you read this book nine times in faith, humility, and devotion."[65] We should read the poem and we should deem the poem (like jewelers), but we should also re-read the poem and re-deem the poem, and from this process we will learn to read the world, re-read the world, and, simultaneously, re-deem the world. Such a reading practice might be the very **craftez** of **Mercy** that she shall **kyþe** to us. We become co-participants in the "deeming" that takes place in Fitt VI, where we learn through praxis that such acts of judgment (whether aesthetic judgments or the Last Judgment) do not necessarily coincide with wrath, but might in fact be the very spaces for both the enactment of mercy and the refinement of true beauty.

James C. Staples is an English PhD student at NYU, where he researches contemporary theories of desire, sexuality, and embodied experience through the defamiliarizing lens of medieval religious poetry.

---

[64] Sara Ahmed argues that a "queer orientation" to the world allows new ways of seeing and experiencing the world that "have been made unreachable by the lines of conventional genealogy" (Sara Ahmed, *Queer Phenomenology* [Durham, Duke University Press], 107).

[65] Mechthild of Magdeburg, 36.

VII

FITT 7: BLYSSE / (ENVY)

Paul Megna

Introduction

While medievals were unfamiliar with the term "emotional intelligence,"[1] they nevertheless were acutely invested in the ethical project of helping themselves and others cultivate a "healthy" emotional disposition through willful acts–a project that undergirds the modern "emotional intelligence movement."[2] Of course, any standard of "emotional intelligence," whether tacit or explicit, is a cultural construct and therefore biased towards the ideals of those with the privilege to construct culture. Indeed, medieval scholastic theologians (not unlike modern theorists of emotional intelligence) jealously guarded their privilege, not only to imply when and where their audience ought to experience a given emotion, but also to define emotion itself, as well as its role in the *psychomachia* of everyday life.[3] In the thirteenth and fourteenth centuries, scholastic

---

[1] Daniel Goleman, *Emotional Intelligence: Why it Can Matter More Than IQ* (New York: Bantam Books, 1995), 3–12. According to Goleman's mixed model, "emotional intelligence" is a complex network of competencies involving self-awareness, self-regulation, social skill, empathy and motivation. Although it has gained considerable popularity in both academic and popular circles, the concept of emotional intelligence has met with substantial criticism. See, for example, Edwin A. Locke, "Why Emotional Intelligence is an Invalid Concept," *Journal of Organizational Behavior* 26.4 (2005), 425–31.

[2] See Barbara Rosenwein, *Emotional Communities in the Early Middle Ages* (Ithaca: Cornell University Press, 2006), 1–31; Sarah McNamer, *Affective Meditation and the Invention of Medieval Compassion* (Philadelphia: University of Pennsylvania Press, 2010); 119–206 and Fiona Somerset, "Excitative Speech: Theories of Emotive Response from Richard Fitzralph to Margery Kempe," in *The Vernacular Spirit*, ed. Renate Blumenfeld Kosinski, Duncan Robertson and Nancy Warren (New York: Palgrave, 2002), 59–79.

[3] Simo Knuuttila, *Emotions in Ancient and Medieval Philosophy* (Oxford: Clarendon Press, 2004), 177–255.

theologians such as John Duns Scotus and William of Ockham increasingly espoused a voluntarist theology according to which emotions are indirectly controllable and, consequently, "one can learn to feel them in a proper manner by forming habits which change the conditions of the passions."[4] For voluntarists, acts of volition are capable not only of managing involuntary emotional reactions, but also of changing the subject's emotional disposition and, resultantly, her subsequent emotions. In this regard, their ideas live on to this day. Modern psychologists, for example, often treat phobia by prompting patients to willfully confront feared objects in order to gradually reduce their emotional aversion thereto.[5]

In medieval England, of course, explorations of the relationship between the will and emotion were certainly not the sole province of lofty, Latinate scholastics. With the skyrocketing of literacy rates in the thirteenth and fourteenth centuries, a new brand of devotional literature–Nicholas Watson's "vernacular theology"– flourished throughout England, much of which directly assesses the extent to which willful acts can dictate one's emotional disposition.[6] Given the prominence of voluntarist ideas in late medieval England, I understand Cotton Nero A.x–containing *Pearl, Patience, Cleanness* and *Sir Gawain and the Green Knight* (*SGGK*)–as a series of exemplary narratives designed to help their audience willfully construct an ethical emotional disposition. Yet these narratives tend to portray, not characters who un-problematically emote ethically, but ones who struggle to emote well: *Pearl*'s dreamer erratically swings from melancholia, to bliss, to dread, to envy and back to melancholia; characters in *Cleanness* are violently punished for their "unlawful" enjoyment; Jonah learns that patience amounts to willfully enduring anger at God; and Gawain is compelled by a love of his own life, and concomitant fear of losing it, to withhold the green girdle from

---

[4] Knuuttila, *Emotions*, 256–86.

[5] Thomas D. Parsons and Albert A. Rizzo, "Affective Outcomes of Virtual Reality Exposure Therapy for Anxiety and Specific Phobias: A Meta-Analysis," *Journal of Behavioral Therapy and Experimental Psychology* 39.3 (2008), 250–61.

[6] See Nicholas Watson, "Introduction: King Solomon's Tablets," in *The Vulgar Tongue: Medieval and Postmedieval Vernacularity*, eds. Nicholas Watson and Fiona Somerset (University Park: The Pennsylvania State University Press, 2003), 1–14; and Vincent Gillespie, "Vernacular Theology," in *Middle English: Oxford Twenty-First Century Approaches to Literature*, ed. Paul Strohm (Oxford: Oxford University Press), 401–20.

Bertilak on the third and final day of their "exchange of winnings game," though he eventually re-ingratiates himself both to Bertilak and denizens of his own homo-social habitus, Arthur's court, through two public displays of shame.[7] According to these narratives neither positive feelings (bliss, mirth and love), nor uncomfortable feelings (envy, fear, anger and shame) are extraneous bodily conditions to be avoided, obfuscated or repressed. Instead, they are valuable—if potentially dangerous—ecstasies and adversities to be worked through in order to achieve a more finely tuned emotional disposition. In compiling these narratives, Cotton Nero A.x vies to teach us, not only how (not) to willfully craft emotional relationships with terrestrial and celestial others, but also that the capacity to emote ethically is not an innate character-trait, but an art-form that we must deliberately cultivate through a lifelong process of trial-and-error. The pedagogical character of these narratives, therefore, accords well with scholastic and voluntarist devotional programs that hold willful acts capable of habituating the passions.[8]

The process of trial-and-error through which Cotton Nero A.x's characters struggle to emote well is nowhere more pronounced than in *Pearl*, much of which is spent detailing either the dreamer's mercurial emotional state or the pearl-maiden's critique thereof. Some critics argue that the dreamer successfully accomplishes the work of mourning over the course of *Pearl*.[9] Others read him as obstinately refusing, right up until the end of the poem, to auto-affect an identificatory shift from a melancholic, courtly lover of the pearl-maiden to a universalist, Christian lover of the corporate church.[10] While in some ways opposed, these two critical strains both presuppose that the pearl-maiden's didactic agenda is to coax the dreamer from a melancholic obsession with his lost love-object to an

---

[7] For in-depth analyses of the political uses of misogyny in *SGGK*, see Patricia Clare Ingham, *Sovereign Fantasies: Arthurian Romance and the Making of Britain* (Philadelphia: University of Pennsylvania Press, 2001), 107–36; and Randy P. Schiff, *Revivalist Fantasy: Alliterative Verse and Nationalist Literary History* (Columbus: The Ohio State University Press, 2011), 72–99.

[8] For Thomas Aquinas' scholastic account of the relation between passions and habit, see *Summa Theologica*, I-II, q. 59. a. 1–5.

[9] Ann W. Astell, "Mourning and Marriage in Saint Bernard's *Sermones* and in *Pearl*," in *The Song of Songs in the Middle Ages* (Ithaca: Cornell University Press, 1990), 121, 134–35.

[10] David Aers, "The Self Mourning: Reflections on *Pearl*, *Speculum* 68.1 (1993): 54–73.

acceptance of his loss. To the contrary, I argue below that the dreamer evinces exactly this brand of acceptance in the poem's seventh fitt and that the pearl-maiden subsequently does everything in her power to render the dreamer desirous, even envious, of her existence in a celestial world characterized, ironically enough, by a complete lack of envy. Envy, according to medieval preaching manuals, consists of "sadness about someone else's happiness and glee about someone else's ruin or adversity."[11] Of course, the pearl-maiden neither explicitly tells the dreamer to be sad at her happiness, nor implies that he ought to be. On the other hand, she neither tells him to be happy for her happiness, nor implies that worldly subjects are capable of such a sympathetic identification with heavenly bliss. Instead, she implies that terrestrial subjects ought to endure, or work through, their inevitable envy of the endless, communal bliss enjoyed by celestial subjects in order to comprehend, rather than transcend, the ontological gap between a worldly life replete with envious desires and a heavenly afterlife entirely bereft thereof.

Where jealousy involves "the sense that someone else is receiving more attention and affection from one's love object,"[12] envy entails discomfort with another's good fortune and is therefore a sort of anti-love. Unlike preaching manuals which unequivocally condemn envy, *Pearl* does not outlaw this anti-love and even encourages it insofar as it fuels a desire to perform the requisite good behavior in order to get to heaven. Rather than castigating envy as a necessarily sinful hatred of the good, *Pearl* proposes a point of identity between discomfort with another's good and the ethical project of eschewing sin. In *Pearl*, envy can be ethical. Envy, from the Latin *in-videre*, signifies a negative form of vision. Hence, the eyes of Dante's envious are sewed shut with iron wire.[13] Since *Pearl* characterizes the envy felt by a terrestrial, Christian devotee towards those already enshrined in heaven as potentially productive, we might therefore read the overt and complex visual aesthetics of *Pearl*'s depiction of the New Jerusalem as designed to overcome the

---

[11] *Fasciculus Morum: A Fourteenth-Century Preacher's Handbook*, ed. and trans. Siegfried Wenzel (University Park: The Pennsylvania State University Press, 1989), 149.

[12] Salman Akhtar, *The Comprehensive Dictionary of Psychoanalysis* (London: Karnac Books Ltd, 2009), 155.

[13] Dante Alighieri, *Purgatorio*, trans. Allen Mandelbaum (New York: Everyman's Library, 1995), Canto XIII, ll. 67–72.

logistical difficulties of envying celestial and therefore invisible others.[14]

Commentary, Part I: The Dreamer Speaks

By the beginning of *Pearl*'s seventh fitt, the dreamer has already been twice rebuked by his interlocutor, the pearl-maiden: first for presuming to be permanently, rather than temporarily, united with his lost object (257–76), and again for his melancholic reaction to her first rebuke, which she condemns as blasphemous (289 – 324). Fittingly, then, the sixth fitt's concatenation word is "deme," which can alternately mean judge, consider, ordain or condemn.[15] As with the poem's other fitts, the seventh begins by echoing the previous fitt's concatenation word:

> Thenne demed I to þat damyselle:
> "Ne worþe no wraþe vnto my Lorde,
> If rapely I raue, spornande in spelle."
> (361–63)[16]

Although the pearl-maiden assigns the right to make judgments exclusively to God in the final line of the sixth fitt–"Al lys in Hym to dyȝt and deme" (360)–, in the first line of the seventh fitt the dreamer adopts the position of the judge ("demed I"). Of course, his somewhat presumptuous judgment could certainly be taken as an example of the dreamer's continual misapprehension of the pearl-maiden's lessons, which A. C. Spearing and his followers find comic.[17] On the other hand, it can just as easily be read as an assertion of the categorical difference between the ontological position of the pearl-maiden, who openly speaks as God's proxy and can therefore easily respect his rightful place as universal judge, and the dreamer, whose distance from divinity forces him to constantly

---

[14] I am deeply indebted to Nicola Masciandaro for many of the points in this paragraph.

[15] *Middle English Dictionary*, s.v. "demen."

[16] All quotes from the poems of Cotton Nero A.x are taken from *The Poems of the Pearl Manuscript: Pearl, Cleanness, Patience, and Sir Gawain and the Green Knight*, 5th ed., eds. Malcolm Andrew and Ronald Waldron (Exeter: University of Exeter Press, 2007).

[17] A.C. Spearing, *The Gawain-Poet: A Critical Study* (Cambridge: Cambridge University Press, 1970), 149–52.

engage in a speculative, if not blasphemous, evaluations of God's will.

The dreamer's judgment is often translated into the jussive mood: "Let the Lord not be wrathful / If I hastily speak foolishly, stumbling in speech."[18] Such constructions are frequent enough in Middle English to amply justify this translation. It is possible, however, to read the statement in the deductive mood, signifying something like: "It is not worth my Lord's wrath . . . ." According to the former translation the dreamer meekly beseeches God not to be angry with him; according to the latter he confidently declares that God will not. This ambivalence is emblematic of the dreamer's terrestrial predicament. God monopolizes the right "to dy3t and deme," but often opts against making either the grounds or results of his judgments readily apparent to terrestrial subjects, leaving the dreamer to simultaneously speculate that God would not be angry with him for speculating and enjoin God not to be angry with him for speculating. The wrath of God, of course, is a recurring theme throughout Cotton Nero A.x, especially in *Cleanness* and *Patience*. Eric J. Johnson brilliantly argues that *Cleanness* and *Patience* equip their audience with a *modus timendi* (mode of fearing) according to which worldly subjects ought to perpetually dread God's judgment without presuming to know exactly what that judgment entails.[19] Likewise, Lawrence Clopper, David Wallace and David K. Coley all argue that the God of Cotton Nero A.x, for all his apparent anthropomorphism, is utterly foreign to the humans whose fate he controls entirely.[20] Clopper, for example, argues that Cotton Nero

---

[18] See, for example Casey Finch's translation in *The Complete Works of the Pearl Poet*, 3rd ed., eds. Malcolm Andrew and Ronald Waldron (Berkley: University of California Press, 1993), 361, ll. 367–69.

[19] Eric J. Johnson, "'In dry3 dred and daunger': The Tradition and Rhetoric of Fear in *Cleanness* and *Patience*," Ph.D. Dissertation, 2000, University of York, 65–90 (on *modus timendi*), 91–206 (on *Cleanness* and *Patience*).

[20] Lawrence M. Clopper, "The God of the *Gawain*-Poet," *Modern Philology* 94.1 (1996): 1–18; David Wallace, "*Cleanness* and the Terms of Terror," in *Text and Matter: New Critical Perspectives on the* Pearl*-Poet*, eds. Robert J. Blanch, Miriam Youngerman Miller, Julian N. Wasserman (Troy, NY: The Whitson Publishing Company, 1991), 93–104; David K. Coley, "Remembering Lot's Wife/Lot's Wife Remembering: Trauma, Witness, and Representation in *Cleanness*," *Exemplaria* 24.2 (2012): 342–63; and David K. Coley, "*Pearl* and the Narrative of Pestilence," *Studies in the Age of Chaucer* 35 (2013): 209–62.

A.x deliberately mis-anthropomorphizes God in order to demonstrate "that those who imagine God to be an irrational or arbitrary being suffer from a profound misconception of the absoluteness and otherness of God at the same time that they fail to recognize God's merciful, covenental relationship with mankind."[21] Whether or not Cotton Nero A.x as a whole inspires hope that it is possible to either understand or predict God's oscillation between wrath and mercy, it certainly depicts terrestrial existence as a continual and dangerous effort to do just that, an effort in which the dreamer partakes through his speculative judgment.

The dreamer excuses himself for his potentially unwise speech by describing the emotional condition from which it arose:

> "My herte watz al wyth mysse remorde,
> As wallande water gotz out of welle.
> I do me ay in Hys myserecorde."
> (364–66)

When read in tandem, the first two above-quoted lines constitute a simile through which the dreamer accounts for his melancholic disposition: Emptiness ("mysse") afflicted his heart with remorse ("remorde"), which flowed out uncontrollably through his speech, just as rushing water flows out of a well. Interestingly, however, the second two above-quoted lines make a very different simile: Just as rushing flows out of a well, the dreamer throws himself at God's mercy. Once again, the ambivalence of these lines expresses the maddening indeterminacy of all the dreamer's worldly actions. His emotional state compels him to simultaneously revel in sadness at worldly loss and to abandon himself to God's mercy. For the dreamer, however, this coincidence is by no means paradoxical–as long as his expressions of grief end in an appeal for God's mercy they cannot be sinful, since, according to his understanding of Christian soteriology at this point in the poem, it's better to have sinned and repented than to have never sinned at all.[22]

Malcolm Andrew and Ronald Waldron posit that these lines allude to Ps. 21:15: "I am poured out like water; and all my bones are scattered. My heart is become like wax melting in the midst of

---

[21] Clopper, "The God of the Gawain Poet," 1.
[22] The pearl-maiden thoroughly refutes this view in Fitt 12.

my bowels."²³ Just as *Pearl*'s dreamer alternately complains of his internal emptiness and entreats God to mercifully forgive the hasty speech his suffering engenders, the narrator of Ps. 21 oscillates between desperate complaints that God has forsaken him and dogged faith that the same God will deliver him from peril. Both narrators dramatize a worldly wavering between sinful despair at God's incomprehensibility and penitential faith in God's mercy. Indeed, Middle English devotional writings frequently associate both sinful and penitential emotions with effusive wells. The author of *Jacob's Well*, for example, likens the pre-penitential subject's body to "a schelde pytt" (a shallow pit), filled with "þe dedly watyr" of sin, and proposes to render it, through "long labour," a "deepe welle," flowing with the waters of God's grace.²⁴ According to *Jacob's Well*, therefore, the heart-well can either gush penitential desires or deadly sins. The dreamer's problem in *Pearl* is that he has no way of being certain exactly what gushes out of him when he emotes.

After throwing himself at God's mercy, the dreamer segues somewhat abruptly from his declarative, perhaps even performative, display ("I do me ay in Hys myserecorde"), to an imperative address directly to the pearl-maiden, enjoining her to stop rebuking him, comfort him and pitifully reflect on her culpability for his melancholic state:

> "Rebuke me neuer wyth wordez felle
> Þaȝ I forloyne, my dere endorde,
> Bot kyþez me kyndely your coumforde,
> Pytosly þenkande vpon þysse:
> Of care and me ȝe made acorde,
> Þat er watz grounde of alle my blysse."
> (367–72)

According to the *Middle English Dictionary* (*MED*), the dreamer's use of the adjective "felle" marks the pearl-maiden's "wordez" as violent, angry or cruel.²⁵ Under the same sub-definition (5b), the *MED* lists a line of *Cleanness* in which Daniel refers to the damning figures written on Belshazzar's wall as "felle saȝes" (1737), which suggests

---

²³ All Biblical quotation are from the Douay-Rheims edition.
²⁴ *Jacob's Well: An English Treatise on the Cleansing of Man's Conscience*, ed. Arthur Brandeis, EETS o.s. 115 (London: Trubner, 1900), 1–3.
²⁵ *MED*, s.v. "felle."

that the dreamer—like Daniel and unlike Belshazzar—has a sense of the damning nature of the celestial message that he receives, though he—unlike Daniel and like Belshazzar—seems to have no desire to heed it. Instead, he rearticulates his melancholic grief by defending his right to "forloyne," or wander astray. To exemplify its entry on "forloinen," the *MED* can only muster the above-quoted usage and two from *Cleanness*: The first describes God's knowledge that the antediluvian humans "forloyned fro þe ryȝt wayez" (282), which causes him to flood the world; and the second describes God's wrath at the Jews of Jerusalem who "forloyn her fayth and folwȝed oþer goddes" (1165), which causes him to allow Belshazzar's father, Nebuchadnezzar, to ransack Solomon's temple.[26] For the *Pearl*-poet, it seems, "forloyn"-ing can and often does mark an unforgivable crime worthy of God's wrath. Despite this ominous valance, *Pearl*'s dreamer tries to have his cake and eat it too, so to speak, when he asks to "forloyn" without being rebuked by "wordez felle." If these lines, once again, can be taken to signify the dreamer's aloof misapprehension of his relation to celestial others, they can also be read as a tacit admission of his grief's illegality and a not un-humble request that the pearl-maiden allow him to work through his grief, rather than eschew or repress it for fear of divine retribution.

The dreamer asks-demands for the pearl-maiden to comfort him "kyndely." The semantic valance of the Middle English "kynde," of course, is much wider than that of its modern counterpart, "kind." In addition to benevolence, it also signifies nature and the natural order.[27] In fact, "kynde" can even be used, as it is in *Piers Plowman*, as a name for God.[28] The dreamer's appeal to the pearl-maiden's kindness, then, suggests that the natural, even God-like, thing for the pearl-maiden to do is to give him the comfort he feels he deserves. Extending his request-injunction, he asks her to meditate with pity ("[p]ytosly") on the fact that she, who once was the "grounde" of all his bliss, has accorded him with "care," which can mean, among other things, sorrow, pain, fear, grief or lovesickness. The dreamer's ostensibly theological call for pity recalls the rhetoric of courtly love: If the male lover is tortured by lovesickness, it is only right that the female object show him pity by

---

[26] *MED*, s.v. "forloinen."

[27] *MED*, s.v. "kynde."

[28] See for example, *Piers Plowman: The A Version*, ed. George Kane (Berkeley: The Athlone Press, 1988), 10, 1–45; cf. B.9.1–60 and C.10.128–55.

reciprocating his love, be she willing or not, dead or alive. This is, of course, insidious logic. As David Aers points out, it is precisely through this courtly logic that Troilus at once ensnares Criseyde in the ethical responsibility to love him and eschews his own responsibility for his love-afflicted actions:

> [J]ust as Troilus blamed the imprisoned Criseyde for his grief, telling her she remains responsible for his survival, or for his death, even so the narrator in *Pearl* blames the dead human being, the ground of all his bliss, for abandoning him to his lonely mourning . . . . In this familiar courtly language the lost object fulfills the traditional feminine role of nurturing life source; she is the man's essential physician without whom his life becomes a disease, a nightmare of emptiness and tormented dreams, the state which was explored by Chaucer in *Troilus and Criseyde* and in the *Book of the Duchess* and, in its more self-righteously violent outcomes, by Shakespeare in *Othello*.[29]

The dreamer *tries* to force the pearl-maiden opposite himself in an uneven gender binary in which the lady is ethically obligated to auto-affect love for the male courtly lover, who is free to "forloyn" to his heart's content, ethically responsible for neither his own actions, nor, even more alarmingly, their effect on the lady's existence. But does he succeed in doing so?

Continuing his project of assigning the pearl-maiden culpability for his emotional state, the dreamer characterizes her as a source of intermittent and unpredictable pleasure and pain, not unlike the Boethian world:[30]

> "My blysse, my bale, ȝe han ben boþe,
> Bot much þe bygger ȝet watz my mon;
> Fro þou watz wroken fro vch a woþe,
> I wyste neuer quere my perle watz gon.
> Now I hit se, now leþez my loþe."
> (373–77)

---

[29] Aers, "The Self Mourning," 57.
[30] Ancius Boethius, *On the Consolation of Philosophy*, trans. Victor Watts (New York: Penguin Books, 2000).

The dreamer's "blysse"/"bale" dichotomy anticipates *SGGK*'s narrator's description of Britain's constant oscillation between "blysse and blunder" (18). Despite her heavenly status, the dreamer continues to conflate the pearl-maiden with *his* worldly emotions about her. Indeed, he calls her neither "the source of my bliss and bale," nor "the object of my bliss and bale," but simply "my bliss and bale." In so doing, the dreamer recalls *The Book Duchess*'s equally melancholic black knight, who identifies his lost love as "my worldes blysse."[31] Unlike Chaucer's black knight, however, the dreamer finds (temporary) happiness in being reunited with his lost love. While Aers reads the dreamer as obstinately clinging to a courtly worldview for his entire dream, the above-quoted lines hint at progress: "From the time you were delivered ('wroken') from each and every torment ('vch a woþe')," the dreamer says, "I was unaware where my pearl had gone." He initially did not know that the pearl-maiden had found such blissful relief, though he now does. When he expresses his own relief, then, the dreamer is not just reveling in being temporarily reunited with his lost love, but also in finally knowing something about where his lost pearl had gone. If he sometimes speaks as a courtly lover, utterly unconcerned with his lady's subjectivity beyond whether or not she assuages his discomfort, the dreamer struggles to establish a less self-centered, un-envious relation to the lady by expressing his happiness at hers.

Equipped with his newfound optimism, the dreamer tries to end his argument with the pearl-maiden. He does not exculpate her for her role in producing his worldly pain, but he reiterates his call for comfort in a manner simultaneously courtly and theologically astute:

> "And quen we departed we wern at on;
> God forbede we be now wroþe;
> We meten so selden by stok oþer ston.
> Þa3 cortaysly 3e carpe con,
> I am bot mol and manerez mysse;
> Bot Crystes mersy and Mary and Jon,
> Þise arn þe grounde of alle my blysse."
> (378–84)

---

[31] Geoffrey Chaucer, *The Book of the Duchess*, in *The Riverside Chaucer*, 3rd ed., ed. Larry D. Benson (Boston: Houghton Mifflin Company, 1987), 333, l. 209.

Although he begins by recalling the past, worldly love that he once shared with the pearl-maiden ("we wern at on"), the dreamer employs this recollection to justify his present desire for both parties to abandon their anger and accomplish something productive in the immediate future of their rare, even miraculous, meeting. As we've seen, in Cotton Nero A.x, wrath is a judgment of guilt, occurring when a subject—be it man or God—recognizes a transgression. When he calls for himself and the pearl-maiden to mitigate their anger, therefore, the dreamer expresses, at the least, his desire to stop blaming the pearl-maiden for the sadness her absence has caused. Despite this un-Troilus-like ambition, the dreamer does not abandon his courtly parlance. To the contrary, he acts most Gawain-like when he modestly declares himself deficient in both speech ("mol") and manners. Just as Gawain repeatedly declares himself rhetorically inept to Bertilak's lady (1241–47), the dreamer employs a hyperbolic self-deprecation in order to enjoin the pearl-maiden to expand his worldview by speaking her mind. If only Troilus, Palamon and Arcite did the same.

Having already opened himself up to his lady's sovereign discourse, the dreamer strikingly designates Christ's mercy, Mary, and John, rather than the pearl-maiden, as the ground of all his bliss. These lines (383–84) present a challenge both to critics who read the dreamer as comically doltish and theologically obtuse and to those who read him as progressing, over the course of *Pearl*, from a courtly lover to a corporate Christian. Falling somewhere in between these two views, Aers writes off the dreamer's act of re-grounding his bliss in Christian icons as "a purely tactical concession, a formulaic compromise to facilitate both the continuation of the conversation and his own concerns within it. Nevertheless," Aers concedes, "it does lead into a question that did not occur to Troilus, to Palamon and Arcite, to Othello, or to Leontes: a question about *her* life."[32] Although Aers pays too short shrift to the potential causal connection between the dreamer's invocation of John and his later vision of the New Jerusalem (culled, as it is, directly from John's account thereof in Revelation), he recognizes that, at this point in the poem, the dreamer makes a most un-Troilus-like acknowledgement of his lover's interiority by asking her to recount her personal history. But does this make the dreamer less a courtly lover than Troilus, or simply a more ethical courtly lover than

---

[32] Aers, "The Self Mourning," 64.

Troilus, one capable of willfully forging a more egalitarian, intersubjective love? As scholars of romance and hagiography often note, courtly discourse and Christian ideology are rarely, if ever, mutually exclusive in medieval texts.[33] While the dreamer's act of re-grounding his bliss in Christ, Mary and John can be read as a means to prolong his lavishly polite, almost flirtatious, conversation with the pearl-maiden, could not it also be understood as a sublime moment, albeit a rare one in *Pearl*, in which courtliness and holiness complement, rather than contradict, each other? Can we read the dreamer as neither clinging to a courtly ethos, nor transitioning to devotional one, but struggling to love the pearl-maiden in manner satisfactory to both? Do his efforts signify his desire (or the poet's) to un-problematically conflate these two distinct yet inextricably intertwined ideologies?[34]

If the dreamer evinces progress by trying to reconcile his courtly leanings with Christian devotion, he cannot easily disregard the emotional dissonance between himself and the pearl-maiden:

> "In blysse I se þee blyþely blent,
> And I a man al mornyf mate.
> 3e take þeron ful lyttel tente,
> Þa3 I hente ofte harmez hate."
> (385–88)

Here the dreamer back-peddles, even regresses, to a courtly complaint about the pearl-maiden's heavenly indifference to his worldly struggles. He cannot help but read within her over-determined happiness—she is blithely blended with bliss—a lack of compassion ("ful lyttel tente") for his burning pains ("harmes hate"). Yet he goes on to soften his accusation by reiterating his desire to avoid quibbling with her and learn from her instead:

> "Bot now I am here in your presente,
> I wolde bysech, wythouten debate,
> 3e wolde me say, in sobre asente
> What lyf 3e lede erly and late,

---

[33] Elizabeth Leigh Smith, *Middle English Hagiography and Romance in Fifteenth-Century England: From Competition to Critique* (Lewiston: Edwin Mellen Press, 2002), 1–36.

[34] Charlotte Gross, "Courtly Language in *Pearl*," in *Text and Matter*, 79–92.

> For I am ful fayn þat your astate
> Is worþen to worshyp and wele, iwysse;
> Of alle my joy þe hyȝe gate,
> Hit is in grounde of alle my blysse."
> (389–96)

Despite the pearl-maiden's apparent inability or unwillingness to share his pain, the dreamer dramatically asserts his happiness ("I am ful fayn") at her heavenly "astate." Though he makes no explicit mention of envy, the spectral possibility that he might be sad at the pearl-maiden's happiness lurks behind his assurances to the contrary. Indeed, his earlier distinction between his own mourning and the pearl-maiden's un-compassionate bliss arguably provokes his later insistence that he is gladdened by her high estate. If the latter statement of shared bliss partially offsets the former statement of emotional dissonance, it does not completely negate the dreamer's initial complaint. Indeed, the question remains: If he can be happy with her celestial happiness and sad at her terrestrial absence, why can't she be happy with her celestial happiness and sad at his terrestrial sadness? This is the dreamer at his most volatile—he swings from utterly dejected and introverted ("mornyf mate") to joyously blissful and extroverted in eleven lines flat (385–96). And yet his mood-swing is more willful than erratic. It is as though he insists on their shared happiness in a voluntarist effort to actualize it.

Commentary, Part II: The Maiden Speaks

Although he tends to eschew culpability for his grief, the dreamer nevertheless makes willful efforts to mitigate the pearl-maiden's anger, as well as his own, through courtesy; efforts that she vocally appreciates:

> "Now blysse, burne, mot þee bytyde,"
> Þen sayde þat lufsoum of lyth and lere,
> "And welcum here to walk and byde,
> For now þy speche is to me dere."
> (397–400)

The maiden begins by wishing for the dreamer to encounter bliss, or, more precisely, for bliss to encounter him. However ostensibly positive, her blessing (or blissing) is not the ringing endorsement it at first seems. First of all, it implies that the dreamer's best, if not only, hope for obtaining worldly bliss is pure luck—if bliss finds him. Second, it curiously trivializes, or at least temporalizes, the dreamer's immediately prior declaration that his bliss is grounded in her heavenly status. Through her vocalized hope for his future happiness, the pearl-maiden gently reminds the dreamer that, as a terrestrial subject, he cannot simply ground his bliss in her celestial status to ensure its permanence. Likewise, in welcoming the dreamer based on her appreciation of his "speche," she implies that his current bliss too is not only precarious, but also contingent upon her continued approval. Far from offended by the dreamer's courtly rhetoric, the pearl-maiden mandates that he sustain it.

Extending her rather passive-aggressive acclamation of the dreamer's apologetic proposal, the pearl-maiden praises his newfound meekness and retroactively diagnoses their previous antipathy as rooted in his pride:

> "Maysterful mod and hyȝe pryde,
> I hete þee arn heterly hated here.
> My Lorde ne louez not for to chyde
> For meke arn alle þat wonez Hym nere."
> (402–04)

The pearl-maiden's warning that a tyrannical mindset ("[m]aysterful mod") and high pride are hated in heaven all too clearly implies that the dreamer is in constant danger of evincing these attributes, even as it congratulates him for ceasing to do so. Through it, she recalls her previous scathing, even mean-spirited, tripartite rebuke of the dreamer's desire to cross the water separating them and live with her happily ever after (289–324). Spearing justifies the pearl-maiden's sharp retorts as characterized by "deliberate and necessary harshness," holding that the dreamer "has no hope of gaining further understanding unless he can be shocked out of his fool's paradise."[35] Of course, such harsh didacticism is everywhere in Cotton Nero A.x. Even so, if we consider her primary rhetorical agenda to guide the dreamer to a state of meek acceptance, it is difficult to explain why, after he has painstakingly evinced just such an acceptance, the pearl-maiden continues to lecture him that God hates pride. After all, she does so in the process of ostensibly praising him for finally exiting his prideful "fool's paradise." It is equally difficult, moreover, to miss

---

[35] Spearing, *The Gawain-Poet*, 150–51.

the blatant hypocrisy in her warning that God does not love those who "chyde," which can mean criticize, complain or grumble, but also rebuke–an action quite integral to her own didactic *modus operandi*. Yet if we consider the pearl-maiden's rhetorical aim to stoke the dreamer's envy by repeatedly, if implicitly, highlighting the radical difference between the temporariness and contingency of his bliss with the permanence and certainty of her own, these rhetorical choices become much more explicable.

If the pearl-maiden's reply contains plenty of scornful undertones, it also conveys a tantalizing promise that the dreamer will be rewarded with further revelations for his good behavior. Once again, however, she stresses that his mystical experience and perhaps even the state of his soul depends on his adopting the diminutive, passive and eerily blank emotional posture that is meekness:

> "And when in Hys place þou schal apere,
> Be dep deuote in hol mekenesse.
> My Lorde þe Lamb loues ay such chere;
> Þat is the grounde of alle my blysse."
> (405–08)

Of course, the pearl-maiden's mandate that the dreamer adjust his emotional disposition ("chere") to one of meekness is perfectly in line with Christian ideology, as is her opposition of meekness to pride: Following their Latin antecedents, Middle English preachers' manuals frequently cast "mekenesse" as the affective antidote for pride.[36] While her theology is perfectly doctrinal, in recalling a pride/meekness binary reminiscent of those contained in manuals used by confessors to prescribe certain behaviors and proscribe others, the pearl-maiden is perhaps more authoritarian than consolatory. For George Edmondson, the cumulative effect of the pearl-maiden's doctrine "is to underscore the radical incommensurability between the mediated, language-bound world of the dreamer and the realm of limitless *jouissance* beyond the river."[37] Hence, her injunction that the dreamer must continually

---

[36] See, for example, *The Book of Vices and Virtues*, ed. W. Nelson Francis, EETS o.s. 217 (London: Oxford University Press, 1942), 130–43.

[37] George Edmondson, "*Pearl*: The Shadow of the Object, the Shape of the Law," *Studies in the Age of Chaucer* 26 (2004): 29–64, at 55.

affect meekness and repress pride carries with it the implicit reminder that she, who has already achieved heavenly bliss, need not worry about such tricky cognitive and emotional adjustments. According to the vice/virtue system that opposes pride to meekness, the dreamer's relation to the pearl-maiden ought not be one of envy, but one of charity (*caritas*).[38] Yet how can he feel charitably towards an interlocutor who ceaselessly reminds him of that he is not even capable of comprehending her bliss and status?

For Edmondson, the pearl-maiden exemplifies Jacques Lacan's S(Ø): the signifier of the Other's desire. The Lacanian subject desires nothing more than to fulfill the desire of some Other, be it God, Justice or, for the courtly lover, the Lady. S(Ø), not unlike the related "objet *a*," signifies that unknown entity with which the subject could sate the Other's desire.[39] Hence, *Pearl* begins with a prince deriving pleasure from enclosing a pearl in gold.[40] The syntax of the pearl-maiden's description of her heavenly predicament exemplifies the primal fantasy of finding completion in completing the Other. Her bliss is grounded in the fact that her lord the lamb loves when his subjects evince devout and meek cheer. Her happiness is therefore based in God's reciprocal happiness with her meekness. Together, they form a closed circuit in which meekness motivates love, love motivates bliss, and bliss motivates meekness. Across the river, however, the dreamer remains in a world where meekness often leads to immense physical suffering and bliss often leads gluttony or lust. By enjoining the dreamer to be meek when he enters the lamb's presence, however, the pearl-maiden hints that he will someday cross the river into the land of plentitude and *jouissance*. Of course, the game of evoking a sublime afterlife in order to mandate earthly meekness and passivity–so reviled by Friedrich Nietzsche–is fundamental to Christian ideology.[41] The pearl-maiden's rhetoric is striking, not for its ingenuity, but for the uncompassionate coolness with which she juxtaposes her bliss to the dreamer's pain.

After laying down the law to the dreamer, the pearl-maiden begins to satisfy his request by recounting the details of her life after death:

---

[38] *Fasciculus Morum*, 175–99.
[39] Edmondson, "*Pearl*," 46–48.
[40] Edmondson, "*Pearl*," 40–43.
[41] Friedrich Nietzsche, *On the Genealogy of Morals*, ed. and trans. Walter Kaufman (New York: Vintage, 1967).

> "A blysful lyf þou says I lede;
> Þou woldez knaw þerof þe stage.
> Þow wost wel when thy perle con schede
> I waz ful ȝong and tender of age."
> (409–12)

The maiden begins her account firmly entrenched in a first person/second person dynamic with the dreamer, oscillating between "you" and "I." In so doing, she recalls the closed identificatory circuit between father and daughter in worldly life, but also emphasizes the ontological split currently separating them. Curiously, however, at the moment when she most clearly identifies herself as the dreamer's dead daughter, she names herself, not in the first person, but in the third ("thy perle"), suggesting both that she is currently a categorically different entity than that the dreamer mournfully remembers and that she is no longer *his* pearl. Used repeatedly throughout Cotton Nero A.x, "scheden" signifies splitting or sundering.[42] While it is most frequently employed to denote the separation of rain or snow from clouds, it is also used to describe Gawain's axe sundering the "schyire grece" between the skin and bone of the green knight's neck (425). The sudden violence of the green knight's decapitation recalls that which separated the infantile pearl-maiden from her father. Like the latter violence, moreover, the former proves to be temporary—what was "schede" will be made whole again.

Despite the opaque causality characterizing her initial description of the rupture that separated father from daughter ("thy perle con schede"), in the following lines we learn that the pearl-maiden is not severed by an unknown agency, but taken to marriage by the lamb:

> "Bot my Lorde þe Lombe, þurȝ Hys godhede,
> He toke myself to Hys maryage,
> Corounde me quene in blysse to brede
> In lenghe of dayez þat ever schal wage."
> (413–16)

Here, the I/you dynamic of the previous lines gives way to a him/me dynamic that details the mystical marriage between the lamb and

---

[42] *MED*, s.v. "scheden."

pearl-maiden. Of course, images of crowned virgins married to Christ in heaven are fairly frequent in Middle English literature. The Early Middle English treatise on virginity, *Hali Meiðhad*, for example, displays heavenly virgins forming a circle around the Godhead, surrounded by a larger circle of chaste widows and a still larger circle of faithful wives.[43] While the dreamer's account of his vision of the New Jerusalem (721–1153)–in which the pearl-maiden is one of 144,000 virgins surrounding the lamb–is certainly reminiscent of *Hali Meiðhad*'s account of Christ's polygamous marriage to all the women of heaven, the pearl-maiden's earlier description of her mystical marriage to Christ is strikingly monogamous. Indeed, when she relates that the lamb crowned her queen "in blysse to brede / In lenghe of dayez that ever schal wage," she might be saying, as the *MED* suggests, that she is to remain in a state of eternal, marital bliss, though she also might be saying that she and the lamb procreate ("brede") in heaven for eternity.[44] While I don't want to suggest that the pearl-maiden copulates with the lamb of God in heaven, I do find her choice of words telling, especially given her familiarity with the literalist and materialist hermeneutic with which the dreamer has approached his vision thus far.

Having forced the dreamer into the margins of his own narrative, the pearl-maiden continues to describe her mystical union with the lamb, further blurring the ontological line between herself and God and emboldening that between herself and the dreamer:

> "And sesed in alle Hys herytage
> Hys lef is. I am holy Hysse.
> Hys pyese, Hys prys; and Hys parage
> Is rote and grounde of alle my blysse."
> (417–20)

Upon marrying the lamb, the pearl-maiden is put in possession ("sesed") of his entire inheritance ("herytage"). Here, legal language is employed to describe the pearl-maiden's transformation into heaven's queen. Patricia Margaret Kean notes that the legality with which the innocent pearl-maiden is saved contrasts the surplus grace required to save those stained by sin, suggesting to both audience

---

[43] *Hali Meiðhad*, ed. Bella Millett, EETS o.s. 284 (London: Oxford University Press, 1982).
[44] *MED*, s.v. "breden."

and dreamer, once again, a categorical difference between the dreamer and herself.[45] Inverting her earlier, third-person self-identification as the dreamer's pearl, the pearl-maiden now refers to herself as the lamb's loved one ("[h]ys lef"). She then asserts that she is "holy Hysse," a punning phrase that implies both that she is entirely (wholly) in his possession and that she is sanctified (holy) as a result. The next line—in which she evokes the lamb's value ("pyese"), nobility ("prys") and inheritance ("parage")—can be read in apposition to the prior line, meaning that the pearl-maiden herself constitutes God's value, nobility and inheritance. On the other hand, it can also be read as the subject of the final line of her speech, meaning that the lamb's value, nobility and inheritance are the ground of all her bliss. Following Edmondson, I would argue that neither meaning is correct, but that, in evoking both together, the pearl-maiden once again enacts the potent fantasy in which the subject finds completion and bliss in providing the lacking Other that which he lacks. But the subject for whom this fantasy is realized is the pearl-maiden and, by explaining how the dreamer's worldly loss is tantamount to her heavenly marriage, she renders the dreamer's tragic narrative of which he is the protagonist a comedy of which she is the protagonist and he plays an inferior male lover that she casts off for a better man . . . or lamb. If the pearl-maiden's account of her death and mystical marriage does not explicitly enjoin the dreamer to envy her, it offers him no clear route to finding charitable happiness in her bliss. To the contrary, it brings him face-to-face with the fact that his bliss was sacrificed for hers and God's superior bliss—both incomprehensible and unavailable to him—even after he has already made vocal attempts to move on by grounding his bliss, first in Christ, Mary and John and then in her incomprehensible heavenly estate. To put the matter colloquially, the pearl-maiden, at least as I read her, deliberately rubs it in—"it" being her static, eternal bliss.

Conclusion

Whether or not she does so in an effort to rouse the dreamer out of a state of acceptance and into one of envy, her speech has exactly that effect on him. In the beginning of the eighth fitt—whose perhaps ironic concatenation word is "cortayse"—the dreamer

---

[45] Patricia Margaret Kean, *The Pearl: An Interpretation* (London: Routledge, 1967), 187–88.

explicitly expresses his dissatisfaction, or at least disbelief, that the pearl-maiden has usurped Mary as the queen of heaven (421–32). This, in turn, inspires the pearl-maiden to launch into the parable of the vineyard in order to once again draw attention to the ontological chasm between earthly subjects, like the dreamer, who cannot help but experience envy and heavenly subjects, like herself, whose bliss multiplies with the recognition of the bliss of others (501–72). Indeed, the dreamer glimpses the pearl-maiden for the last time immersed in a huge crowd of pearl-laden virgins (1129–52). His vision of the New Jerusalem offers the dreamer, as Sarah Stanbury brilliantly argues, a fantasy of returning to the female body, which promptly evaporates the moment he tries to actualize it.[46] As Aers reminds us, the dreamer causes his vision to collapse around him by acting on a literalist interpretation thereof.[47] I am less eager than Aers and Spearing to blame the dreamer for his hermeneutic shortcomings and I think *Pearl* itself is too. The lesson that the pearl-maiden ultimately bestows on the dreamer is that life is an ever-fluctuating series of thoughts, experiences and emotions. The terrestrial subject cannot simply choose not to be envious because she "knows" envy is a sin, but she can practice, again and again, working through her sinful emotions and thoughts in an effort to produce more positive ones. There is no end to this struggle except in death and no skipping directly thereto. In the end, then, the pearl-maiden does not teach the dreamer how to feel, but forces him to develop the ability to willfully learn from his feelings and, in so doing, to take responsibility for them.

The difficulty of emotional life is omnipresent in Cotton Nero A.x, as is a profound appreciation of bliss, be it worldly or heavenly. Just as *Pearl*'s dreamer oscillates between "blysse and bale" and *SGGK*'s narrator describes Britain as a bastion of "blysse and blunder," the narrator of *Patience* instructs us to "[b]e preue and be pacient in payne and in joye" (525), calling patience "a nobel poynt þaȝ it displese ofte" (531). Amidst all its graphic depictions of human suffering, there is even bliss in *Cleanness*, though the bulk of it is either prelapsarian (260) or paradisiacal (177–79). In Cotton Nero A.x, the project of living well is reducible to neither a pure pursuit of pleasure, nor a world-denying abstinence therefrom. Living well

---

[46] Sarah Stanbury, "The Body and the City in *Pearl*," *Representations* 48 (1994): 30–47, see especially 33.
[47] Aers, "The Self Mourning," 58.

involves working through emotions, negative or positive, strategically. Had *Pearl*'s dreamer awoken immediately after grounding his bliss in Christian ideology and knowledge of his lost loved one's celestial bliss, it would be easy enough to read the poem as a sort of morality play in which the dreamer exemplifies how to grieve well. The pearl-maiden, however, is more interested in keeping the dreamer grieving, envious and altogether upset than alleviating his grief. Ironically enough, it is by vividly depicting a world beyond emotional fluctuation that the pearl-maiden keeps the dreamer's moods swinging.

Paul Megna is a doctoral candidate in English at the University of California, Santa Barbara. His dissertation, *Emotional Ethics in Middle English Literature* argues that Middle English texts conceptualize emotional judgements as integral to the process of ethical decision making. He has an article on *Piers Plowman* in *Exemplaria* 25.2 (2013) and one forthcoming in *The Yearbook of Langland Studies* 29 (2015).

VIII

PEARL, FITT VIII

Kevin Marti

Abstract: Fitt VIII reveals much information about larger textual structures in *Pearl*. Its Christian Platonist adaptation of 1 Corinthians 12 envisions Paul's metaphor of the body of Christ in terms of circles of different sizes. At this transition in the dialogue the dreamer reveals and the maiden addresses his confusion of heavenly for earthly hierarchy; she explains that her crown in no way detracts from Mary's or other maidens' crowns. A statement about each maiden wishing others' crowns were worth five crowns contributes to a symmetrical, nested arrangement of references to Five, Three, and Two within the dialogue.

Introduction

Fitt VIII serves as a transition between important sections of *Pearl*. Like similar transitions in Dante's *Divine Comedy*, where for example the plan of hell is revealed in *Inferno* 11 between visions of upper and middle hell, Fitt VIII offers a concise overview of the larger structures it bounds.

To understand how Fitt VIII serves as a transitional structure it is first necessary to understand how the nesting arrangement of the three main landscapes in *Pearl* (addressed in my commentary on Fitt II in this volume) is mirrored in the nesting arrangement of the fitts devoted to those landscapes. The setting of the first and final fitts of *Pearl* in the *erber* as well as the setting of the fitts just following the first fitt (II-IV) and just preceding the final fitt (XVII-XIX) in Eden and the New Jerusalem respectively creates nested pairings of corresponding portions of the text. The central dialogue section (Fitts V-XVI) is in turn nested within the descriptions of Eden and New Jerusalem, and within the dialogue is nested the paraphrase of the parable of the vineyard (IX-X), another landscape at the center of the poem. This nesting arrangement of landscapes as a textual structure mirrors on a larger scale the pairs of link words in the first and last lines of most stanzas and the pairs of words that appear in the first and last lines of the entire poem as well as other similar textual bracketing structures on different scales (including pairs of half-lines in each line and pairs of words in the same part of speech within some lines).

Within this nesting textual structure Fitt VIII is the last fitt of the dialogue section that precedes the central paraphrase of the vineyard parable which divides the dialogue into two halves. The recursive, scaling, circular geometry described in Fitt VIII resembles the geometry of the pentangle in *Sir Gawain and the Green Knight* in a transitional passage (619-55) between portions of that poem devoted to the first two of its three main settings (Arthur's court, Bertilak's castle, and the Green Chapel).

Since most of the dialogue section addresses matters regarding the pearl maiden's relationship to the heavenly court, it seems appropriate that it is the centermost textual structure just as the vision-within-a-vision of the heavenly court is nested at the center of the visions of Eden and of the *erber*: the dreamer dreams of Eden while he sleeps in the *erber*, then he is granted a vision of the New Jerusalem from his position in Eden. The dialogue begins in Fitt V with two speeches by the dreamer (241-52, 279-88) about the maiden's identity, his reasons to believe she is there, and his plan to join her. After each of these speeches the maiden criticizes it in a speech of her own (257-76, 289-324). A third speech by the dreamer (325-36) and one by the maiden (337-60) in Fitt VI address his ability to assess her status.

Fitt VII, whose link word is *blysse*, begins with the dreamer's statement that the pearl has been both his *blysse* and his *bale* (373) and the *grounde of alle my blysse* (372) and ends with his question and the maiden's response about her current *astate* (393-420). The maiden replies that the *grounde of alle my blysse* is *My Lorde þe Lamb*, specifically *Hys prese, hys prys, and hys parage* (407-8, 419). The discussion of *blysse* in Fitt VII lays the groundwork for the focus of Fitt VIII, whose first word is *Blysful*. Fitt VIII continues the discussion of the maiden's *astate* with particular attention to the inability of members of the heavenly court to resent or envy each other. My commentary on Fitt II traces stages of decrease in the dreamer's grief (increase in impassibility and therefore joy) and of increase in his agility (and presumably his subtlety) in response to increasingly bright, agile, and subtle landscapes; as in the *Comedy* the dreamer appears to acquire incremental increases in the gifts of the glorified body (clarity, impassibility, agility, and subtlety) as he passes through landscapes associated with greater increments of those gifts.[1] Fitt VIII features Mary as *myryest May* (435), the most impassible of maidens; she anticipates the Lamb who is the most impassible figure of all, with *glenteȝ gloryous glade* despite his wounds at the climactic finale of the dreamer's vision of the heavenly city (1141-44), and whose sight and sound increase the dreamer's joy: "Delyt me drof in yȝe and ere" (1153). The importance of the gifts of the glorified body in the depiction of characters in *Pearl* has been described before,[2] but not the incremental increase in these gifts associated with each stage of the dreamer's journey; my commentaries on Fitts II and VIII draw attention to these incremental increases, which support the notion that the *Comedy* influenced *Pearl.*

Like his paraphrases of the vineyard parable in Matthew's gospel and of the description of the heavenly city in the Apocalypse, in Fitt VIII the poet makes 1 Corinthians 12 consistent with the recursive, self-similar, scaling geometry of Platonist procession (emanation) and regression (reversion, return).[3] He does it in part by

---

[1] Manuele Gragnolati, *Experiencing the Afterlife: Soul and Body in Dante and Medieval Culture* (Notre Dame: University of Notre Dame Press, 2005), especially 168, 174. In the *Comedy* the association between settings and different increments of gifts of the glorified body is most obvious in the description of the angelic circles in *Paradiso* 28. The concentric angelic circles move more quickly and shine more brightly the closer they are to the central point, inverting the hierarchy of agility and clarity of the nine celestial spheres they mirror (lines 22-39). A pattern of increases in the brightness of Beatrice's smile as she and Dante ascend from heaven to heaven reflects a corresponding pattern of increases in impassibility. Dante experiences an incremental increase in these gifts each time he rises to a new celestial sphere.

[2] Kevin Marti, "Traditional Characteristics of the Resurrected Body in *Pearl,*" *Viator* 24 (1993): 311-35.

[3] Near the end of his *Republic* Plato's comparison of the eight whorls Er sees in his dream to "boxes that fit into one another" shows that their structure is recursive, self-similar, and scaling; trans. Paul Shorey, in *The Collected Dialogues of Plato Including the Letters*, ed. Edith Hamilton and Huntington Cairns (Princeton: Princeton University Press, 1961), 840-41. In the dream of Scipio described in bk. 6, sec. 17 of Cicero's *Republic* the recursive, self-similar, scaling structure of the nine concentric spheres of the cosmos is similar. Macrobius describes a similar structure in chapters 17-22 of bk. 1 of his *Commentary on the Dream of Scipio*, especially in his comparison of the

adding to his Pauline source the circular image of a ring on an arm or a finger and an implicit circular image of a crown on the head. Fitt VIII prepares for the paraphrase of the vineyard parable by explaining the distribution of heavenly reward in terms of scaling, circular recursion: a *rawe* of workers figures as a circle because the first hired are paid last, each receiving a circular penny (545-48).

Because the Platonist foundation for the poet's handling of recursion in numbers, in the geometry of the circle and sphere, and in the body is more obvious in Fitt VIII than elsewhere in the poem, this commentary will continue the discussion begun in my commentary on Fitt II of the correspondence between the stages of the vision and the stages of the ascent of the soul at death and the resurrection of the body in Christian Platonism. My commentary on Fitt II defines and cites sources for various Platonist concepts applied to Fitt VIII here. The absence of negative emotions among members of Christ's body results from their advanced stage of regression, the Platonist process whereby the soul gradually acquires a dematerialized state during its ascent after death; this process underlies the Christian Platonist scheme of resurrection.

The link word *courtaysye* and its variants build on the maiden's statement that the dreamer is *vncortayse* for lacking the faith to believe what he cannot see (303). The recurrence of *courtaysye* in Fitt VIII creates a pattern that shows how differently the dreamer and maiden understand the meaning of the word. E. V. Gordon notes that the application of the secular ideal of *courtaysye* to theology predates *Pearl* (xxxii-xxxiii).

Among its other observations, then, this commentary brings particular focus to small-scale mirror images in Fitt VIII of larger poetic structures and to Platonist traditions that clarify those images.

Commentary

> 'Blysful', quod I, 'may þys be trwe?
> Dysplese3 not if I speke errour.[4] (421-22)

---

concentric spheres to concentric circles in ch. 21; trans. William Harris Stahl (New York: Columbia University Press, 1952), 155-84, especially 175-76. Dietrich Mahnke traces the notion of concentric spheres from the ancient Greeks to the German romantics in *Unendliche Sphäre und Allmittelpunkt: Beiträge zur Genealogie der mathematischen Mystik* (Halle: Niemeyer, 1937); pages 144-215 discuss medieval sources of the tradition.

[4] All quotations from *Pearl*, including the entirety of Fitt VIII, are from the edition by E. V. Gordon, *Pearl* (Oxford: Oxford University Press, 1953).

These opening lines respond to the previous stanza, in which the maiden answers the dreamer's query regarding her *astate* (393), the *stage* of her *blysful lyf* (409-10). By echoing the link word of Fitt VII, *blysse*, the first line of Fitt VIII focuses even more attention on the central concern of the prior fitt, especially the maiden's statement about her *maryage* to *my Lorde þe Lambe* (413-14), whereby he "Corounde me quene in blysse to brede / In lenghe of dayeȝ þat euer schal wage" (415-16). In Fitt VII the maiden wishes *blysse* for the dreamer, stating that he is welcome to walk and stay here "For now þy speche is to me dere" (397-400); improvement in his use of language appears to increase his agility and impassibility (and therefore bliss). The statement is related to the sequence of incremental improvements in the impassibility of the dreamer, recalling how walking through Eden and gazing at paradise while walking along the stream increase his bliss and anticipating the greatest bliss, the *Delyt* from the sight and sound of the heavenly city that prompts his attempt to cross the stream (1153).

The most important word in the question that begins Fitt VIII is *trwe*: the dreamer asks the maiden whether what she has just stated can be true. In her response *trwe* (460) describes relations among members of the body of Christ that justify the *stage* of her *blysful lyf.* The meaning of *trwe* shifts from "accurate" to "steadfastly" (Gordon). She uses it to describe an ideal relationship among body parts in terms of a relationship among three circles of three different sizes. Both occurrences of *trwe* prepare for her later assertion that "al is trawþe that he con dresse" (495) in response to the dreamer's objection that being made queen on the first day is *to dere a date* (493). Her invocation of *trauþe* follows her statement that "Þer is no date of hys godnesse" (493). In the first line of Fitt VIII, then, *trwe* introduces an extended treatment of balanced relationships within a circular, recursive, self-similar structure that mirrors the pentangle in *Sir Gawain*, likewise identified as a symbol of *trauþe* (626). The fitt shows that the *trawþe* governing the geometry of the body of Christ orders its disorder, suiting it for paradise.

After the dreamer questions the maiden's statement about the degree of her bliss he expresses concern that his speech not displease her, a line echoed in the third line of the last stanza: "Bot my speche þat yow ne greue." In this and other ways the first and last stanzas of Fitt VIII, spoken by the dreamer, mirror each other and frame the three central stanzas in which the maiden describes the lack of suffering in heaven. The first and last stanzas begin with a single word spoken by the dreamer followed by *quod I*. The resulting circular form of Fitt VIII mirrors the circular form of the entire poem, whose first and last lines contain the words *pay(e)* and *perl(eȝ)*. The dreamer's expressed concern that he not displease her reflects his memory of her critical response in 289-324 to his speech in 279-88; his subsequent speech begins with a parallel expressed concern that his words not anger God (362-63). In the one-stanza speeches that begin and end Fitt VIII the dreamer shows an inability to understand the recursive, scaling, microcosmic hierarchy of the heavenly court; he therefore does not understand that he did not lose the pearl in the *erber* and that he cannot cross the stream prior to death. The middle three stanzas of Fitt VIII are the maiden's first attempt to correct his misunderstanding of hierarchy. Her next attempt is her paraphrase of Matthew's vineyard parable after Fitt VIII.

> Art þou the quene of heueneȝ blwe,
> Þat al þys worlde schal do honour?
> We leuen on Marye þat grace of grewe,
> Þat ber a barne of vyrgyn flour;
> Þe croune fro hyr quo moȝt remwe
> Bot ho hir passed in sum fauour?
> (423-28)

These two questions by the dreamer provide the reasoning behind his first question in this stanza. The maiden's assertion that she is married to Christ makes him wonder if she has displaced Mary as queen of heaven. The first of these two questions goes to the thematic heart of the fitt; *quen* and/or *kyng* and variants accompany the link word *cortaysye* and its variants in the first and last lines of most stanzas and elsewhere in Fitt VIII. As in many fitts here the link word and accompanying words highlight the difference between the earthly perspective of the dreamer and the heavenly perspective of the maiden. Other obvious examples are *Jerusalem* in Fitt XIV and *mote* in Fitt XVI, which draw attention to the dreamer's confusion regarding the earthly and heavenly cities with the same name. In her speech here and in her paraphrase of the vineyard parable the maiden attempts to show him that he does not understand hierarchy because he confuses earthly *courtaysye* with heavenly *courtaysye*.

The *blwe* color of the heavens recalls the *blwe* which is one of the three colors of the blooms of the *spyseȝ* growing from the *spot* where the pearl was lost in the *erber* (27) as well as the "Holtewodeȝ . . . / Of bolleȝ as blwe as ble of Ynde" in Eden (76), where the dreamer also encounters *spyse* (104).

The phrase *al þys worlde* in the first stanza mirrors *in worlde* (476) in stanza five. It anticipates *alle þys worlde* (824) in Fitt XIV, where it refers to the sins of mankind paid for by the *Lombe . . . trwe* (822) who "Hymself ne wroȝt neuer ȝet non" (825). The phrase *in worlde* (476) recalls the similar phrase regarding Eden's location ("I ne wyste in þis worlde quere þat hit wace," 65) and the maiden's complaint about the dreamer's first speech, that he understands not one of his three statements ("Þou ne woste in worlde quat on dotȝ mene," 293). It anticipates the maiden's statement that her *blysse* exceeds that gained by anyone *in þe worlde* (579) and that thanks to Christ's sacrifice nothing *in þe worlde rounde* (657) stands between humans and the *blysse* that Adam's sin made inaccessible. In other references the *worlde* becomes *broun* at the end of the day in the vineyard parable (537) and the maiden describes her death as a departure from the *worlde wete* (761); she counsels the dreamer to forsake the *worlde wode* (743) as she has done. The reference to the *worlde rounde* aligns the sequence of shifting meanings of *worlde*, including "mankind" and "earth," with its spherical geometry, much as the spherical pearl is aligned with a sequence of shifting meanings. The references to *worlde*, especially *al þys worlde* (424) in relation to Mary and Christ, reflect the Platonist conception of both God and the created world that mirrors him as spheres.[5]

The phrases *grace of grewe* and *of vyrgyn flour* recall the references to growing plants and their blooms in the *erber* (27-28) and anticipate the trees that miraculously produce fruit all year in the heavenly city (1077-79). The Incarnation and the grace it makes possible figure here as a plant-like growth, the product of virginity associated in the *erber* with blooms over the maiden's grave. The plant growth in heaven is an unnatural, perfect blooming that is static, moving, and growing at the same time.

The references to plant growth in the *erber*, Eden and the heavenly city figure forth the Incarnation as a miraculous transformation of all nature.

---

[5] Kevin Marti, *Body, Heart, and Text in the* Pearl-*Poet* (Lewiston, NY: Mellen, 1991) 17.

The implication in this first stanza that the maiden has inappropriately removed Mary's crown, like the reference to her being made queen at such a young age in the last stanza (474), is linked to the *worlde* that is *rounde*. The round crown symbolizes rulership over the world, including over vegetation, so the crown features floral decoration (208), recalling the blooms of the *erber*.[6]

> Now, for synglerty o hyr dousour,
> We calle hyr Fenyx of Arraby,
> Þat freles fleȝe of hyr fasor,
> Lyk to the Quen of cortaysye.'
> (429-32)

Like the final quatrains of many stanzas in *Pearl*, including all stanzas in Fitts II and VIII, this final quatrain condenses the themes of the first two quatrains. The dreamer thinks the *synglerty* of Mary precludes the possibility of any other queen in heaven. His inability to comprehend the nature of that *synglerty* recalls his difficulty understanding the relationship between other *gemmeȝ gaye* and the pearl lost in the *erber*: in the first stanza of the poem he says he "sette hyr sengeley in synglere" because "Ne proued I neuer her precios pere." The dream helps him to comprehend that loss by showing that *synglerty* does not rule out the possibility of a *pere* (cf. *parage*, 419). These references to singularity, recalling the first one describing the *rounde* (5) pearl, follow mention of the *worlde* elsewhere called *rounde*, references preparing for the explanation of the relationship of One to Five two stanzas later. His misunderstanding of singularity results from his misunderstanding of the relationship between the monad (One) and the numbers that in Platonist tradition are contained by and proceed from the monad. The unique *dousour* of Mary in heaven recalls the fragrance of blooms in the *erber* that puts the dreamer into a *slepyng-slaȝte* (59) and the fragrance from the fruit of Eden that has the effect of food on the dreamer (87-88).

---

[6] Vegetation metaphors, particular those involving seeds and flowers, figure prominently in medieval theological discussion of the gifts of the glorified body, especially in Aquinas' understanding of the seed metaphor in 1 Corinthians 15. The seeds that flower in Dante's *Paradiso* reflect Aquinas' teaching; Caroline Walker Bynum, *The Resurrection of the Body in Western Christianity, 200-1336* (New York: Columbia University Press, 1995), 232-40, 302.

Malcolm Andrew and Ronald Waldron as well as Charles G. Osgood note that the identification of the phoenix with Mary is an unusual variation on its conventional association with Christ;[7] this variation in this first stanza is consistent with the shift of focus from female to male authority in the course of Fitt VIII. The reference to *Arraby* indicates that the phoenix and Virgin, like the pearl, are *Oute of oryent* (3). Both are created *freles* by their *fasor*, their flawlessness associated with agility (*fleʒe*). Mary Vincent Hillmann notes a parallel focus on the phoenix as the creator's beautiful work in the Anglo-Saxon homily *Phoenix*.[8] Andrew and Waldron emend *freles* ("flawless" or, according to Israel Gollancz, "immaculate of form") to read *fereles* ("without equal"), but both words are consistent with the context; *fereles* contrasts with *fere*, which recurs elsewhere (89, 884, 616, 1105).[9] Osgood notes that the phoenix is also a symbol of the resurrection of Christ and man. Fire, the subtlest, brightest, and most agile of the four elements is associated with the glorified body in the *Comedy* (in lines 118-20 of *Paradiso* 33 and in the bright appearance of Beatrice and other souls in spheres of paradise above the moon, whose glorification anticipates their resurrection), and is consistent with the immaculate form of Mary.

The Anglo-Saxon *Phoenix* bears on *Pearl* in other ways as well. In it the land the phoenix inhabits in the Orient resembles Eden as described in Fitt II. Both are changeless landscapes featuring a plain, waterways, and beautiful fragrance. Like the pearl maidens the phoenix sings a song humans cannot sing.[10]

In *Pearl* the reversal of the rhyme scheme of the first two quatrains of each stanza in its final quatrain is the prosodic mirror image of the reversal of the order of the hiring of three groups of vineyard workers when they form a line to be paid (545-48). That reversal is of a piece with the reversal in word order whereby link words typically serve as both the first alliterating word and the final

---

[7] Malcolm Andrew and Ronald Waldron, *The Poems of the Pearl Manuscript: Pearl, Cleanness, Patience, Sir Gawain and the Green Knight*, 5th ed. (Exeter: University of Exeter Press, 2007). Charles G. Osgood, *The Pearl: A Middle English Poem* (Boston: Heath, 1906).
[8] *The Pearl: Mediaeval Text with a Literal Translation and Interpretation* (Notre Dame: University of Notre Dame Press, 1967).
[9] Israel Gollancz, ed., *Pearl* (New York: Cooper Square, 1966). First published 1891 by David Nutt; citation is from Cooper Square edition.
[10] "The Phoenix," in *Anglo-Saxon Poetry*, ed. and trans. R. K. Gordon, rev. ed. (London: Dent, 1954), 240, 242.

rhyming word in a stanza and whereby the order of link words and the recurring words that accompany them is sometimes reversed in adjacent lines (for example, in 432-33 and 444-45 the order of the link word variants on *cortaysye* and the accompanying words *Quen/kyndom* is reversed).

> 'Cortayse Quen', þenne sayde þat gaye,
> Knelande to grounde, folde vp hyr face,
> 'Makeleȝ Moder and myryest May,
> Blessed bygynner of vch a grace!'
> (433-36)

In this fitt one reflection of larger poetic structures is the maiden's sequence of vertical movements in 434-37: She kneels *to grounde*, she *folde vp hyr face*, and *ros ho vp*. (The maiden's gesture of obeisance is clear in *Knelande to grounde*, less so in *folde vp hyr face*, which A. C. Cawley glosses as "her face upturned,"[11] Sarah Stanbury glosses as "folds her face in her hands,"[12] and Hillmann translates as "her face concealed.") The sequence mirrors at this transition a sequence of vertical movements down and up throughout the poem, including: the pearl that *fro me sprange* (13), *doun drof* (30) and *trendeled doun* (41); the dreamer that *felle* (57) and whose spirit *sprang* (61) in the *erber*; the features of Eden that *feier con ryse* the further the dreamer walks (103); his walk along the stream until he sees the maiden (*Doun . . . I bowed*, 125-26); their ascent to the *heued* of the stream (*Bow vp*, 974); the descent of the heavenly city (*keued*, 981); the *prosessyoun* (1096) of maidens compared to the moon that *con rys* (1093); the ascent of the maiden from the stream to the heavenly city (1145-48); and the dreamer's plunge into the stream (1153-63). This sequence of vertical movements resembles a sequence of Platonist processions or regressions, discussed in my commentary on Fitt II.

The first quatrain of the maiden's three-stanza response to the dreamer's speech is a prayer to Mary. Her first two words reverse the order of the link word and *Quen* (*Quen of cortaysye*) that ends the preceding stanza. She begins her response to the accusation of having usurped Mary's position by praying to her and simultaneously showing obeisance with a bodily gesture. The first line identifies the maiden as the speaker after a linking phrase

---

[11] *Pearl, Sir Gawain and the Green Knight* (London: Dent, 1962).
[12] *Pearl* (Kalamazoo, MI: Medieval Institute, 2001).

identifying the person she addresses, much as the first line of stanza one identifies the dreamer as the speaker following identification of his audience in the link word. The prayer and gesture demonstrate her subjection to Mary before she addresses the dreamer.

The reference to the maiden as *þat gaye* recalls the *gemmeʒ gaye* (7) among which she is judged prior to the *erber* description and the *gardyn gracios gaye* (260) the dreamer first sees her in just across the stream from Eden; it anticipates the *garlande gaye* (1186) which is the heavenly city in which the dreamer finally sees her dwell and in which Christ is a *gay juelle* (1124). The *garlande gaye* she inhabits is contrasted with the *doel-doungoun* (1187) inhabited by the dreamer, based on the Platonist notion of the body as prison.[13] The recurrence of *gaye* draws attention to the transformational symbolism whereby a jewel morphs into crystal cliffs (74), gravel (81), a maiden, the heavenly city, and Christ. The earthly pearl is thus transformed in stages into a more and more heavenly pearl.

Makeleʒ Moder and myryest May are attributes of Mary conventional in Middle English poetry, as Osgood notes. Within the hierarchy of impassibility in *Pearl* Mary is the *myriest May*. In the poem *makeleʒ*, a conventional punning word as in the Middle English lyric "I Sing of a Maiden," means "mateless," "matchless," and/or "spotless."[14] Line 436 recalls line 425: all grace begins and grows from Mary in the form of Christ because her position is paradoxical. Both virgin and mother, she creates her own creator.

> Þenne ros ho vp and con restay,
> And speke me towarde in þat space:
> 'Sir, fele here porchaseʒ and fongeʒ pray,
> Bot supplantoreʒ none wythinne þys place.
> (437-40)

The fact that the raising of the maiden's face anticipates that of her body (cf. *folde vp hyr face* in 434 and *ros ho vp* in 437) prepares for her explanation of the relationship between the head and body of Christ two stanzas later. It may also anticipate her later instruction to the dreamer that he "Bow up towarde þys borneʒ heued" (974) in order

---

[13] Pierre Courcelle, "Tradition platonicienne et traditions chrétiennes du corps-prison," *Revue des études latines* 43 (1966 for 1965): 406-43.
[14] From gloss on *makeles* in line two of "I Sing of a Maiden" by Thomas J. Garbáty, ed., *Medieval English Literature* (Lexington, MA: Heath, 1984), 661.

to see the heavenly city, after which both he and she move upwards on opposite sides of the stream until they reach the *heued* or source of the stream (974-80). In *Pearl* vertical movement occurs in relation to hills: the dreamer *felle* and the pearl *doun drof* on the *huyle* in the *erber*; both the pearl and his spirit spring from him on the *huyle* in the *erber*; the lowering of the maiden's body followed by the raising of her face and then whole body occurs at the *fote* of the *crystal clyffe* where he first sees her (159-61); the movement of dreamer and maiden towards the *heued* of the stream is clearly upwards; the city descends onto the hill (980-81); the procession *con ryse* in that city (1093); and the maiden joins it on the hill (1147-48). These vertical movements up and down mirror each other on different scales.

Gollancz calls line 439 "an idiomatic way of saying 'many find here the prey they seek,'"; *prey* appears to refer to heavenly reward. The verb pair *porchaseȝ and fongeȝ* links the two halves of one line.

> Þat emperise al heuenȝ hatȝ,
> And vrþe and helle, in her bayly;
> Of erytage ȝet non wyl ho chace,
> For ho is Quen of cortaysye.
> (441-44)

The final quatrain of stanza two explains why there are no *supplantoreȝ* in heaven. Like the final quatrain of the other stanzas in this fitt, this quatrain emphasizes the top of a hierarchy by adding a new resonance to the linking word or phrase. The final quatrain of the first stanza in this fitt shows that Mary is queen of courtesy by virtue of the *synglerty* she shares with the phoenix. The final quatrain of this second stanza justifies the same title by specifying the scope of her *bayly*, which encompasses *al heuenȝ* as well as the noun pair *vrþe and helle*. Osgood calls *emperise* "One of the commonest mediaeval epithets of the Virgin"; like *courtaysye*, here *emperise* reflects established theological application of a secular concept.[15] The plural noun in the phrase *al heuenȝ* recalls *quene of heueneȝ* (423) and suggests a scheme of multiple heavens consistent with *Paradiso* and the Apostle Paul's account in 2 Corinthians 12. The word *non* (443), literally "no one," contributes to the pattern of references to One (for example, in lines 293, 378, 551, 557, 860, 864, 953) and to

---

[15] Andrew and Waldron indicate both secular and theological applications of *courtaysye* in the works of the Pearl poet, 311.

conditions without exception, including other occurrences of *non* (215, 455, 544, 700, 812, 825) throughout the poem. Like the final quatrain of the previous stanza, this quatrain emphasizes the uniqueness of the *courtaysye* possessed by someone whose court surpasses all others.

This final quatrain is a good illustration of the flexibility of the alliterative scheme in *Pearl.* Line 441 combines an alliterating initial *h* with alliterating initial vowels (*e* in *emprise* and *a* in *al*); by convention all vowels alliterate with each other. In 442 the alliterating initial vowels in *And, and,* and *in* are unusual; conjunctions and prepositions alliterate less frequently than other parts of speech. Line 443 is structured according to patterns of assonance (*erytage* and *ȝet; Of, non,* and *ho; erytage* and *chace*) rather than alliteration. Line 444, like the final lines of the first and especially the third stanzas, features a scheme of near-alliteration wherein the initial consonants of *ho, Quen,* and *cortaysye* represent different sounds that nonetheless resemble each other.

> 'The court of þe kyndom of God alyue
> Hatȝ a property in hytself beyng:
> Alle þat may þerinne aryue
> Of alle the reme is quen oþer kyng,
> (445-48)

Just as 433 reverses the order of *Quen* and *courtayse* in 432, 445 reverses the order of *Quen* and *cortaysye* in 444 except "king" substitutes for "queen" in *kyndom.* The shift from *Quen* to *kyndom* anticipates the first occurrence of *kyng* in the poem three lines later, in the noun pair *quen oþer kyng.* The noun pair recurs at the end of stanza four, where the phrase *kyng and quene* accompanies *courtaysye*; at the end of stanza five *courtaysé* pairs with *kyng.* So the royal words accompanying the link word *courtaysye* and its variants shift from *Quen* to *kyndom* to *quen oþer kyng* to *kyng and quene* to *kyng.* But *kyndom,* unlike the other royal words in this list, is in the first line of its stanza, a shift from *Quen* in the first line of the preceding stanza. In the first line of stanza four the reference to *Saynt Poule* continues the shift towards masculine authority. And in the first line of stanza five the dreamer's two separate references to himself as *I* place the dreamer himself in this succession of male authorities mentioned instead of the Queen. These shifts in the words referring to persons accompanying the link word *courtaysye* correspond with a similar, gradual shift in gender reference within the other lines in the stanzas. The gradual shift in emphasis by way of variations in link words and accompanying words is therefore a kind of *précis* or epitome of the content of the entire stanzas these words begin and end; the link words, as noted, also establish the alliterative scheme in the first lines and the rhyme in the last lines. In this sense the themes and structure of each stanza are an extension of those in its first and last lines, each of which resembles a Platonist terminus[16] and serves an important mnemotechnical role.

The phrase *court of þe kyndom of God alyue* shifts the emphasis from the *cortaysye* of the queen to the court as kingdom. *God alyue*, who is king, is the living God; the pairing of *Jesu* and *my Lady* in 453 is consistent with the shift towards male authority in the stanza. All of stanza four describes the structure of the body of *Jesu Kryst* (458); the title *Kryst* added in this second occurrence of *Jesu* emphasizes his authority even more. So *God alyue* is the resurrected, living Christ and also the individual believers who are members of his body. *God alyue* also signals a shift in focus from the pearl maiden's relationship to Mary to the relationship between the resurrected Christ and the members of his body.

The phrase *property in hytself beyng* (446, glossed as "special virtue inherent in itself" by Cawley) suggests something exclusive to and inherent in the nature of the court. The technical term *property*, like *pretermynable* (596, Osgood, liii), *poynt deterymynable* (594), and *prosessyoun* (1096) reflect medieval adaptation of Platonist terminology.[17] The phrase applies to a feature of heaven that receives a precise numerical (450-51) and geometrical (465-66)

---

[16] In Platonist cosmology all geometrical figures proceed from their termini (a line from a point, a surface from a line, and a solid from a surface) just as all numbers proceed from One (the monad) and just as human souls proceed from celestial bodies in the course of acquiring a corporeal shell during their descent to earth. Macrobius, *Commentary on the Dream of Scipio*, 96-101, 106-107, 124-37. Martianus Capella, *The Marriage of Philology and Mercury*, trans. William Harris Stahl and Richard Johnson (New York: Columbia University Press, 1977): 2:35, 264-66.

[17] Christian Schäfer discusses the importance of Platonist technical terminology among authors of the third through sixth centuries; some of this terminology was transmitted, directly or indirectly, to medieval authors writing much later. *The Philosophy of Dionysius the Areopagite: An Introduction to the Structure and the Content of the Treatise* On the Divine Names (Leiden: Brill, 2006), 4.

description. As stanza four shows, the relationships among the members of this court figure as relationships among body parts of the resurrected Christ. The two references to *alle* in 447-48 contribute to the technical precision of the description. To understand the special *property* of this court is to understand how statements in these two adjacent lines containing *alle* mirror each other: just as all new arrivals to the court through death or resurrection become kings or queens, each member of the court is king or queen of all of the members of the court. Presumably the distinction between king and queen is determined solely by the gender of each new arrival, such that the earthly superiority of king over queen does not apply to new arrivals, who are each others' equals. But Mary, the *meryest May*, ranks above the pearl maiden though both wear a crown. And the next stanza implies that as head of the body of the church Christ ranks above its other members even if an arm or a finger wears the counterpart of a crown in the form of a ring. The shift in Fitt VIII from *Quen*, with an emphasis on Mary, to *kyng*, with an emphasis on Christ, also establishes the superiority of Christ over Mary. So in this most egalitarian of royal courts a hierarchy nonetheless prevails. The unique *property* of the court here anticipates the description of the unique *properteȝ* (752) of the pearl maiden herself following her reference to the breast pearl as *lyke the reme of heuenesse clere* in connection with its presence *inmyddeȝ my breste* (740).

The dreamer's vision of the heavenly city in Fitts XVI-XIX like that in its Apocalypse source includes only one king, Christ at the center of his throne (835; cf. Apocalypse 5:6), and makes no reference to Mary, but the poet changes the sex of the other inhabitants of the city who appear with Christ: they are male in the Apocalypse (14:4) but female in *Pearl* (869-72, 1099-100). The maiden's reference to the "Lambeȝ vyueȝ . . . As in þe Apocalyppeȝ hit is sene" (785-87) and her statement that each soul in the city "Is to þat Lombe a worthyly wyf" (846) are consistent with this change. But her assertion that all new arrivals in the city are made *quen oþer kyng* (448) and the reference to *aldermen* (1119) show that Christ is not the only male in the city.

> And neuer oþer ȝet schal depryue,
> Bot vchon fayn of oþereȝ hafyng,

> And wolde her corouneȝ wern worþe þo fyue,
> If possible were her mendyng.
> (449-52)

The second quatrain of stanza three explains an aspect of the property of this court that is of a piece with the fact that all new arrivals are king or queen over all others: the fact that a new arrival can *neuer* (like *alle* and *non, neuer* allows for no exceptions) *depryve* any other member. No matter how many new arrivals are made king or queen, the kingship or queenship of individual members of this court remains undiluted, including Mary's queenship.

The reference to Five in line 448 integrates this passage into a symmetrical pattern of references to Five, Three, and Two that create a sequence of nested structures within the dialogue section.

Lines 450-52 describe an aspect of the emotional state of these court members resulting from their shared regal status. If any member's *mendyng* were possible, each member would wish that each other member's crown were worth five crowns (Osgood glosses *þo fyve* as "five of those"). The value of each of their crowns reflects their current state of virtue, which cannot be surpassed. Andrew and Waldron note that this figurative use of Five is idiomatic and also occurs in *Troilus and Criseyde*. The parallel statement in 849-50 (the only other occurrence of *fyf/fyue* in the poem) that each maiden wishes each other maiden were five maidens, like this one, is consistent with impassibility, here expressed as the incapacity to experience any decrease in bliss: "Bot vchon enle we wolde were fyf-- / Þe mo the myryer, so God me blesse." The joy of the members of this court increases with each new arrival: "Þe mo þe myryer" (850), with Mary always the *myryest May* (435). The statement in 1114-15 describing court members' subtlety is consistent with both references to Five: though there are many of them, there is no overcrowding ("Þaȝ þay wern fele, no pres in plyt").

These statements reflect the basis of medieval resurrection theology in Platonist regression, a fact generally unacknowledged by scholars; the relations among court members reflect the relationship between the numbers and the monad, which contains all numbers and exists outside the material constraints of space. The parallel between wishing each member's crown were worth five crowns and wishing each pearl maiden were five maidens is based on the Platonist understanding of the procession of numbers from the spherical or circular monad and of the head as a spherical microcosm of both the body and the universe. These teachings were transmitted to the medieval West by Chalcidius in his commentary on Plato's *Timaeus*.[18]

There is a similar parallel between two statements regarding the relation of One to Three, again one in each half of the dialogue: "Þre wordeȝ hatȝ þou spoken at ene: / Vnavysed, for soþe, wern alle þre. / Þou ne woste in worlde quat on dotȝ mene . . ." (291-93; cf. *þrydde*, 299) and

> In Ierusalem þus my lemman swete
> Twyeȝ for lombe watȝ taken þare,
> By trw recorde of ayþer prophete,
> For mode so meke and al hys fare.
> The þryde tyme is þerto ful mete,
> In Apokelypeȝ wryten ful ȝare . . . .
> (829-34)

Both are statements about the relation of One to Three as a principle of textual structure; in both *þrydde/þryd* occurs along with reference to One (*ene, on*) and Two (*Twyeȝ*). The fact that the three assertions (*wordeȝ* as microcosms of statements) that comprise the dreamer's opening statement, all spoken *at ene*, are all false is a function of the fact that he does not understand a single one of them. Likewise the fact that Christ's sacrifice at Jerusalem is truly recorded by two prophets means that the third record, in the Apocalypse, must be true as well. So the same relation of the monad to a number that governs the hierarchy of the maidens governs textual hierarchy. Related to the dreamer's inability to understand one of his own words is the human inability to sing a single *poynt* sung by the heavenly court (891) or enter a single *fote* into that court (970); these are conditions without exceptions.

Contributing to this same symmetrical pattern are four references to the relationship between One and Two, two references in each half of the dialogue (in 483 and 555 of the first half and in 674 and 949 of the second half), as a way of explaining the nature of heavenly reward. These are the only places where *two* occurs in the

---

[18] *Timaeus*, trans. Benjamin Jowett, in *Collected Dialogues of Plato*, 1173. Chalcidius, *Timaeus: A Calcidio translatus commentarioque instructus*, ed. J. H. Waszink, in *Plato latinus*, ed. Raymond Klibansky (London: Warburg Institute, 1962), 4:40, 228.

poem. In the first, the dreamer expresses his amazement that despite her having *lyfed not two ȝer in oure þede* (483) the maiden is made queen *on þe fyrst day* (486). In the second, some vineyard workers complain that each worker is paid a penny (*vchon inlyche a peny*, 546), including those that worked *bot on oure* (551), restated in 555 as *not houreȝ two*, a clear parallel to *not two ȝer* (483). In the third, the maiden's reference to *Two men* underscores the similar access to Christ enjoyed by both the *ryȝtwys man* and the *harmleȝ hapel* (674-76). In the fourth, the maiden explains that the dreamer confuses *moteȝ two*, the Old and New Jerusalems, in terms of the relationship between *þat on* (cf. *at ene*) and *þat oþer* in two lines with paired prepositional phrases: "In þat on oure pes watȝ made at ene / . . . . In þat oþer is noȝt bot pes to glene" (949-55).

These references to Five and Three together with a pair of references to Two in each half of the dialogue create nesting structures within the dialogue that mirror the nesting landscape structures framing the dialogue which, as the Introduction explains, are of a piece with bracketing effects associated with recurring words and phrases.

> Bot my Lady of quom Jesu con spryng,
> Ho haldeȝ þe empire ouer vus ful hyȝe;
> And þat dypleseȝ non of oure gyng,
> For ho is Quene of cortaysye.
> (453-56)

Like the other final quatrains in Fitt VIII this one stresses hierarchical importance, here as in the first two as an aspect of the status of Mary. *Bot* indicates that what follows qualifies what precedes it, and this final quatrain makes it clear that the special authority Mary exercises over this otherwise egalitarian court derives from the fact that "Jesu con spryng" from her. The phrase *con spryng* recalls the fact that the dream began after the pearl *sprange* (13) from the dreamer and the dreamer's spirit *sprang* from his body (61); the dreamer's experience, like Dante's, mirrors Christ's resurrection and ascent to heaven. It also recalls the *spryngande spyceȝ* that "vp ne sponne / Of þat precios perle" (35-36) in the *erber*. The court members' feelings about each other described in the preceding lines are consistent with their feelings about the authority bestowed upon the queen of courtesy: it *dypleseȝ non.* Christ is *ful hyȝe*, the top of the vertical hierarchy of upward and downward movements.

> Of courtaysye, as sayt3 Saynt Poule,
> Al arn we membre3 of Jesu Kryst:
> As heued and arme and legg and naule
> Temen to hys body ful trwe and tryste,
> (457-60)

Stanza four adapts the scheme of *courtaysye* developed thus far in Fitt VIII such that here the link word epitomizes a paraphrase of 1 Corinthians 12: the hierarchy in the court of heaven is consistent with Paul's metaphor of the relation of Christ to individual Christians based on the relations among more and less exalted body parts. This use of a brief paraphrase of one biblical passage to introduce a lengthy paraphrase of another biblical passage resembles the use of a paraphrase of the Beatitudes to prepare for a paraphrase of the Jonah story in *Patience*. *Al* here recalls *alle* in 447-48: all new arrivals are king or queen of the entire realm because all are members of Christ. Much as the first three stanzas explain Mary's special authority in terms of the bodily relation of mother to child in childbearing, this stanza explains relations among individual Christians in terms of their common share in Christ's body. Though *naule* has been taken to refer to a finger- or toenail, most editors translate it as "navel,"[19] so that it contributes to a pattern of central figures that include the pearl in the middle of the maiden's breast (221-22, 740) and the Lamb in the middle of the throne (835). But probably the reference is deliberately ambiguous; *naule* ends a line that moves from the head to the extremities.

This stanza offers parallels with the description of the pentangle in *Sir Gawain*: *courtaysye* (653) is one of the five virtues associated with the fifth point of the pentangle and *trwe* is cognate with the *trawþe* (626) the entire pentangle represents. While *fynger* in 466 is a closer parallel to the *fyue fyngres* (641) associated with the second point of the pentangle, *arme and legg and naule* parallel the wounds of Christ (642) associated with the third point and *heued* may correspond with the *fyue wyttez* (640) of the first point. The adjective pair *trwe and tryste* might as easily apply to the interconnectedness of

---

[19] For example, Cawley, Gollancz and Hillmann translate it as "navel," as does William Vantuono in *Pearl: An Edition with Verse Translation* (Notre Dame: University of Notre Dame Press, 1995). Osgood disagrees without offering a specific alternative, and Gordon takes it to mean "nail." Andrew and Waldron translate it as "belly."

the five groups of five things represented by the pentangle. Gordon's emendation of MS. *tyste* to *tryste* ("faithfully"), unlike Osgood's emendation to *tyȝte*, is (as Gordon notes) consistent with the frequent appearance of *true and tryste* in Middle English, but William Vantuono argues that *tyste* in the sense of "joined" or "woven together" fits the context. The phrase describes connections among parts of the body of Christ in language that could also describe the setting of a jewel, anticipating the references to Christ being *as trwe as ston* (822), to the dreamer's *trwe entent* (1191) after he returns to the *erber*, and to the *trw recorde of ayþer prophete* (831) that confirms Christ's sacrifice in Jerusalem. Within the general pattern of word pairings 459 stands out, with four nouns each joined to the next by *and*, two nouns in each half-line. The word *ful* (like *al*, *neuer*, and *non*) refers to a condition without exception, much as do the phrases *wythouten spot* in Fitt I and *wythouten mote* in Fitt XVI.

The reference to the relationship of the *heued* to the body here parallels references to relationships between the *heued* or *hed(e)* and other things where the word recurs. The *heued* (974) of the stream, its source, is the vantage point for the vision of the heavenly city. The maiden's crown is described in terms of the absence of other *werle* or circle on her head: "To hed had ho non other werle" (209). The dreamer's reference to "My hede vpon þat hylle" (1172) associates his head with the place where the pearl was lost.

> Ryȝt so is vch a Krysten sawle
> A longande lym to the Mayster of myste.
> Þenne loke what hate oþer any gawle
> Is tached oþer tyȝed þy lymmeȝ bytwyste.
> (461-64)

The word *vch* continues the pattern of words specifying a condition without exception. Just as the pearl is "So rounde, so reken in vche araye" (5), "vch a Krysten sawle" is a "longande lym to the Mayster." Each Christian soul serves as a body part; the maiden refers not only to the body of the *Mayster* but also the body of the disembodied dreamer (*þy lymmeȝ*). Osgood and Gollancz take *myste* to mean *myȝte* "might," but *myste* in the sense of "spiritual mysteries" (Gordon, Vantuono) is more consistent with 1 Corinthians 12. The maiden's instruction that the dreamer *loke* to the structure of his own body is consistent with the references to the effect of seeing the dreamscapes on the dreamer (for example, 85-86, 121-48, 169-84,

1153-56). The *hate oþer any gawle* he is told to look for does not exist here, another condition without exception. No member of the heavenly court feels any resentment towards any other member, any more than one of the dreamer's limbs can resent another limb. The technical language of 464, which includes the adjective pair *tached oþer tyȝed* and is consonant with a jeweler's craft, resembles the technical language used to describe the pentangle in *Sir Gawain*, an *endeles knot* (630) each of whose lines "vmbelappez and loukez in oþer" (628). The members of the body of Christ are as interdependent and as mutually intertwined as the lines and points of the pentangle. The previous stanza's assertion that each maiden wishes each other maiden's crown were worth five crowns is consistent with this parallel, since each of the five points of the pentangle is associated with a group of five things. The interdependence of parts of the recursive, scaling geometry of the pentangle mirrors the interdependence of parts of Christ's body.

> Þy heued hatȝ nauþer greme ne gryste,
> On arme oþer fynger þaȝ þou ber byȝe.
> So fare we alle wyth luf and lyste
> To kyng and quene by cortaysye.'
> (465-68)

Like the other final quatrains in this fitt this one focuses on the top of a hierarchy, here the *heued*, just mentioned in 459. Unless the *heued* is one of the *lymmeȝ*, from the middle quatrain to the final quatrain there is a shift from a focus on relationships among limbs to a focus on relationships between head and limbs. An analogous shift occurs between the middle and final quatrains of stanza three, from relationships among members of the court of heaven in general to the specific relationship between Mary and the other members. Middle English words for "head" and "brains" link all three of the poem's main settings: The narrator falls down and sleeps with his *hede vpon þat hylle* (1172) in the *erber* because the odor from the blooms reaches his *herneȝ* (58). Moving alongside the stream fills his *brayneȝ* with bliss (126). He sees the crown on the maiden's *hed* (209) in his vision of her from Eden. The two references to *heued* in this stanza clarify relationships in the New Jerusalem, which the dreamer views after arriving at the *heued* (974) of the stream.

The head's ability to feel *nauther greme ne gryste* parallels the lack of *hate oþer any gawle* among the limbs, a further development of the handling of emotional relationships in this court by way of yet another in a sequence of noun pairs that includes *arme oþer fynger*, *luf and lyste*, and *kyng and quene*. The *luf and lyste* among court members contrasts with *hate oþer any gawle* and with *greme ne gryste*. Vantuono glosses *lyste* as "happiness," consistent with seeing Fitt VIII as developing the treatment of *blysse* in Fitt VII. *So fare we alle* contributes to the sequence of conditions without exception. The word *fare* suggests that the court members' movement is a function of their emotional relationships,[20] especially in light of the occurrence of the word as part of the description of the dreamer's experience of Eden (*I con fare*, 147; cf. 129); *fare* also refers to the demeanor of the Lamb in Jerusalem (832). The conception of the spherical head as microcosm of the body underlies the reference to the *byȝe* on arm or finger which causes the head no resentment. This relationship comes by way of the equivalence of the sphere and the circle with the monad and God in Christian Platonism. In this passage the implicit circular crown on the head and the circular rings on two smaller scales worn by the arm or finger are consistent with Platonist schemes of emanation (procession) and regression. Here each Christian is a monad, a microcosm of the group of all Christians comprising the body of Christ, so that like Christ and Mary each member of the heavenly court wears a crown. This fitt describes a heavenly hierarchy resembling a bodily hierarchy in which the superiority of Christ and Mary is complicated through a nested involution of circles within circles; the equal status of all members of the Christian body results from the fact that each resembles the head. As part of this microcosmic figuration each maiden figures as a pearl but also bears many pearls as ornaments with the most important one in the middle of the breast. The tripartite hierarchy of different-sized circles here parallels the hierarchy of three ranks of nobility referred to in 489-92, where the dreamer contends that the rank of *countes* or *lady* suits the maiden better than *quene*; his statement that the maiden was *nerre þen aunte or nece* (233) is similar. The relationships within the triad of circles of different sizes in this paraphrase parallel the relationships among the three nested main settings in *Pearl*.

---

[20] Augustine offers a similar explanation for the absence of envy among Christians in heaven, following a discussion of their bodily movement; he observes that in a human body the finger does not want to be the eye, in *City of God*, bk. 22, ch. 30.

'Cortaysé', quod I, 'I leue,
And charyté grete, be yow among,
Bot my speche þat yow ne greue,
                    (469-71)

As mentioned, 471 echoes 422 in a way that creates a frame for the maiden's discussion of emotional relationships in the heavenly city, and here the dreamer elaborates further on the theme. A difference from stanza one is the dreamer's use of the plural pronoun *yow* in 470 and 471 (cf. *þou* in 423) before switching back to the singular pronouns *þyself* and *þe* in 473 and 474. There is then a sequence of persons he is concerned not to displease with his words, from *my Lorde* (362) to the pearl maiden (421-23) to the collective members of the court (470-71). The sequence culminates in the use of the link word *paye* with reference again to Christ in the sense of "please" regarding the dreamer's movement in Fitt XX; there the dreamer states: "Hit payed hym not þat I so flonc / Ouer meruelous mereȝ . . . (1165-66).

The fact that *Cortaysé* in 469 differs in spelling from all other occurrences of the link word might be attributed to the influence on the scribe of *charyté* in the next line. Whether the spelling of *Cortaysé* is scribal or not, together with *charyté* it creates a unique noun pair. It is important to consider this unique spelling of the link word in the context of the spelling of the other occurrences of the link word closest to it which may represent an important shift emendation can obscure. In the manuscript *cortayse* appears in 480 and 481, in which lines Gollancz emends to *cortaysye*, though Cawley, Gordon, Stanbury and Vantuono emend in both lines to *cortaysé*. The emendation to *cortaysye* in 480 and 481 makes the word consistent with the rhyme scheme, whereas the more common emendation creates a shift from *cortaysye* in 469 to *cortaysé* in the final three occurrences of the link word. Emendation of one kind or the other in 480 and 481 makes sense since the adjective *cortayse* is inconsistent with the rhyme scheme and syntax. But the manuscript spellings of the last four occurrences of the link word are anticipated by the manuscript spelling of the link word in 433 and may reflect a broad shift towards greater consonance with *charité*. Such a shift creates a new, concluding resonance for the link word with the key Christian concept of *caritas*. It is noteworthy that this concluding and perhaps summative resonance occurs within a speech by the dreamer rather than the maiden. Lines 469-70 constitute a concession to the maiden's argument right before the dreamer again questions it, a concession missing from the first stanza.

Only line 472, overlooked by the scribe, is missing from the poem's unique manuscript.

> Þyself in heuen ouer hyȝ þou heue,
> To make þe quen that watȝ so ȝonge.
> What more honour moȝte he acheue
> Þat hade endured in worlde stronge,
> And lyued in penaunce hys lyueȝ longe
> Wyth bodily bale hym blysse to byye?
> What more worschyp moȝt he fonge
> Þen corounde be kyng by cortaysé?
> (473-80)

Despite the progress in the dreamer's understanding of the maiden's status indicated by the first lines of the fifth stanza, in the last two quatrains of the stanza he begins a further development, continued in the first stanza of the next fitt, of the objection to the maiden's queenship he raises in the first stanza. Line 473 contributes to the pattern of references to vertical movement in the poem, and *heue* recalls the maiden's sharp criticism of the dreamer's language early in the dialogue ("Deme now þyself if þou con dayly / As man to God wordeȝ schulde heue," 313-14), lines that rebuke the dreamer for improperly sending his words upwards. Though she makes it clear in the previous fitt that the Lord himself took her in marriage and crowned her queen despite her tender age (412-15), he accuses her of having inappropriately made herself queen. It is an especially striking example of the obtuseness of this dreamer. The phrase *so ȝonge* here recalls her words *ful ȝong and tender of age* (412) and anticipates his statement of her age as *not two ȝer* (483).

The masculine pronouns in what follows (*he*, 475; *hys*, 477; *hym*, 478; *he*, emended by Gollancz, Gordon, Osgood and Stanbury from *ho*, 479) consolidate the shift from feminine to masculine referents in the course of the fitt as described above, climaxing with *kyng* at the end of the fitt.

The gist of the dreamer's objection here and in the next stanza is that someone not yet two years old who could not know God or pray to him could not possibly have higher status in heaven than someone who has undergone great suffering through a long life of penance. Rather than being made queen upon arrival in heaven, he posits, she should occupy a lower rank of nobility. The notion he invokes that *bodily bale* on earth makes possible heavenly *blysse* is a medieval theological commonplace, whereby a *tempus flendi* (time of weeping) on earth makes possible a *tempus ridendi* (time of laughing) in heaven, and vice versa.[21] Here this invocation of orthodox doctrine brings to a kind of climax the multifaceted treatment of emotion in Fitts VII and VIII for which the references to the noun pair *bale* and *blysse* in 373 and 478 serve as a kind of frame. The notion that *blysse* is something one can *byye* prepares for the treatment of achieving salvation in terms of labor for money in the paraphrase of the vineyard parable that follows. The final two occurrences of the link word (480, 481) are associated with the notion of earned reward the dreamer outlines here. He says that to be crowned king in heaven after a lifetime of penance is an appropriate form of courtesy and that if what the maiden says is true the courtesy of heaven is too easy to achieve. The second line of Fitt IX, "3yf hyt be soth that þou cone3 saye," recalls the question "may þys be trwe?" in the first line of Fitt VIII, in another of the ways the lines near its beginning and end create a frame for Fitt VIII.

Kevin Marti is an associate professor of English at the University of New Orleans. His publications have focused on the Pearl Poet, Dante, and Chaucer.

---

[21] Kevin Marti, "Dante's 'Baptism' and the Theology of the Body in 'Purgatorio' 1-2," *Traditio* 45 (1989/90): 169-90.

IX

"THER IS NO DATE": THE MIDDLE ENGLISH *PEARL* AND ITS WORK

Walter Wadiak

The Parable of the Vineyard (Matthew 20: 1-16) tells us that the first shall be last and the last shall be first. As narrated by the maiden in the Middle English *Pearl*, the parable has an obvious application. The maiden, an infant who "lyfed not two yer" (483), is "last" in the sense that she worked for the least amount of time in the vineyard of the world, and so she gets paid first in the coin of heavenly bliss. Indeed, she is the queen of heaven, however much the Dreamer may object. The maiden's high station in this way constitutes a challenge to conventional ideals of social order, one that draws implicitly upon the radical social vision of the Book of Matthew from which the parable is drawn. Just as the meek shall inherit the Earth, the lowest will be the most exalted in heaven. *Pearl* as a whole dramatizes this upending of the social order indirectly but forcefully in its picture of a daughter who confidently instructs her own father in Christian doctrine. The Parable of the Vineyard is central to the maiden's argument that human categories for determining authority and worth do not apply in heaven, and her narration quite explicitly yokes this claim to a vision of social justice in which "pore men her part ay pykes / Thagh thay com late and lyttel wore" [poor men always get their share / though they come late and work little] (573-74). Yet if the parable in one sense challenges medieval ideas about social order, it seems at the same time to reaffirm those ideas in ways that mirror other aspects of the poem. A lord, identified in the parable with God, pays peasants a wage that he determines, and when some are dissatisfied he dismisses their objections. Stated so baldly, it would be hard to imagine a story more expressive of the "quiet hierarchies" that (on one view) emerged out of the medieval synthesis of feudalism and Christianity.[1] What then can we make of a parable that seems to function so ambiguously in the story for which it provides a structural and thematic center?[2] Can we see a politics–conservative or otherwise–at work in the parable at *Pearl*'s core?

Another way of putting this would be to ask whether we can use the Parable of the Vineyard to place *Pearl* in its historical context–to "date" the poem. For it is no coincidence that "date" is the linkword of the section that marks the parable's opening in *Pearl*. The parable is, after all, about the measurement of time and, by extension, the question of what time might be worth in both material and spiritual terms. The workers who "threte" (561) or complain about the payment of a full day's wage to those who have worked for only a few hours are in effect claiming that time has not been measured properly. The lord's reply in effect makes a claim for a different way of measuring time. Yet "date" is also relevant to Fitt IX in its potential identification with historical time since it is precisely here–in the picture of the discontented workers–that *Pearl* comes closest to articulating the urgent concerns of the tumultuous decades in which the poem's writer lived and worked. Given that Fitt IX is explicitly about work–depicting the lives of those who "wrythen and worchen and don gret pyne" (511)–we might well ask whether the parable can tell us anything about how the poem itself works as an aesthetic reimagining of historical tensions. For many readers, *Pearl* is a poem that seeks an escape from history, so that the poem's attitude is essentially "defensive."[3] Yet Fitt IX, in its insistence on "date," complicates such a view, suggesting rather that

---

[1] This famous phrase is from Robertson, *Preface*, 51. Bowers, *The Politics of Pearl*, also makes use of the phrase in arguing that a world of such hierarchies "could only perhaps be realized in an official literary dream such as *Pearl*" (136). Yet Bowers's own reading suggests that the poem is in fact intensely engaged with the historical tensions that Robertson sees the medieval world as being innocent of.

[2] On the Parable of the Vineyard as the structural and thematic heart of *Pearl*, see Wood, "*Pearl*-Dreamer and the *Hynne*," Marti, *Body, Heart, and Text*, 83-99, Putter, *Introduction*, 168-77, and Andrew and Waldron, *Pearl*, 34-5.

[3] Muscatine, "Style as Defense," argues that *Pearl* expresses "allegiance to high-medieval feudalism" (37). See also Bowers, "*Pearl* in Its Royal Setting," for an argument that the poem is specifically royalist, even perhaps a product of the Ricardian court.

the poem needs history even as it offers us a vision of the apocalyptic end of that history. In this respect, the poem harbors surprising resemblances to the more explicitly topical literature of the last decades of fourteenth century, such as *Piers Plowman*.[4]

We can already catch a glimmer of the tensions that will motivate Fitt IX in the first line: "That cortaysé is to fre of dede / Yf hyt be soth that thou cones saye" (481-82). The maiden, the Dreamer asserts, has been given too great a gift in being made heaven's queen. The economy of heaven, like that of feudalism, depends upon gift-giving, but gifts can be problematic, either too much or not enough. The heavenly economy is, moreover, a competitive sphere in which, as the maiden admits, "fele here porchases and fonges pray" (439) [many here ask for and receive possessions]. While "porchases" may be things given, they are preeminently things possessed, and even in Middle English a "porchase" carries associations with the world of effortful and acquisitive self-interest that the Parable of the Vineyard will realize more fully.[5] Even as the maiden banishes the specter of discord in heaven with her assertion that there are "sopplantores none" (440) to be found there, the possibility of conflict is inscribed in its very negation.

The question of economic justice will be posed in terms of the maiden's age–her own personal "date"–yet the drama that unfolds from that immediate question speaks to some of the most pressing social conflicts that made up the poem's historical context, as we will see. It is thus important that the Dreamer's objection to the maiden's rank in heaven is based on his sense of the unfairness of such a situation: "Thou lyfed not two yer in oure thede; / Thou cowthes never God nauther plese ne pray / Ne never nawther Pater ne Crede" (483-85). These lines are of course the textual basis of the traditional identification of the pearl-maiden as the poet's (or a patron's) two-year-old daughter, who is either dead or perhaps a novitiate (and thus dead to the world).[6] What is clear is that "two

---

[4] Bowers, "Politics of *Pearl*," was among the first to make this claim in a sustained way. Other notable explorations of the poem's interest in late-medieval social realities, particularly with reference to the narrator's use of the Parable of the Vineyard, include Helen Barr, "Pearl–Or the Jeweler's Tale," and Watkins, "'Sengeley in Synglere'."

[5] See *MED*, s. v. *purchās(e* (n.) (1a).

[6] The phrase "in oure thede" inspired Carson to imagine the pearl-maiden as a foreigner in whom the poet might have been romantically interested ("Aspects of Elegy"), but Vantuono notes that such a reading is rendered

yer" is an insufficient period, in the Dreamer's view, for the maiden to have merited the exalted rank of a queen: "I may not traw, so God me spede, / That God wolde wrythe so wrange away" (487-8). Such a rank is "to dere a date" (492), a pronouncement that marks the section's first use of its linkword. "Date" as the Dreamer here uses the word, variously glossed by readers as "limit," "rank," and "fixed position," carries a meaning that has to do with boundedness, as the maiden's reply–"ther is no date of Hys godnesse" (493)–will confirm in the next line. But the notion of God's mercy as having "no date" is also, significantly, a claim for a God who operates outside of history.[7] Such a claim is far from innocent, I am suggesting, in a set of stanzas that seek an escape from the very historical tensions to which they also point.

Because there is "no date" to God's goodness–no temporal context as well as no measurable limit–it also follows (as the maiden now asserts) that God can do no wrong: "For al is trawthe that He con dresse / And He may do nothynk bot ryght" (495-6). Such a statement seems on its face a most conventional theological sentiment, perfectly in line with the conservative politics of *Pearl* as a whole. In fact, even at the level of theology, the poet is struggling to reconcile competing ideas, so the maiden's claim here evokes without fully addressing a familiar problem in medieval theology: Are God's actions good because He chooses to do only good, or is a given act good simply because He wills it?[8] The question is relevant

---

doubtful by the maiden's own earlier remark that she was "ful yong and tender of age" (412) when the Dreamer lost her (*Pearl*, 129).

[7] Set against this background of the urgency of human time, the maiden's assertion that God's mercy has "no date" is more than just a claim that God's mercy escapes all limit. It is also, as several readers have noted, a pun on the timeless nature of the divine realm to which the maiden belongs, an eternal present that (as Boethius asserts) transcends time. For Mitchell, the juxtaposition here of human "date" and divine timelessness undercuts "the *historicizing impulse* of figural interpretation" ("Figuring the Unfigurable," 99), radically calling into question the poem's ability to provide adequate analogies for the divine by drawing from the realm of human experience.

[8] The latter position–voluntarism–had strong support in the late-thirteenth and fourteenth centuries, notably from Duns Scotus and William of Ockham. Recent research, moreover, has suggested that the *Pearl*-poet was likely aware of the work of Ockham and his Oxford contemporaries. If so, we might read the maiden's remark here as a masterpiece of equivocation. On the one hand, we could plausibly interpret her assertion as falling into the voluntarist camp: all is "trawthe" that God ordains simply *because* He

not just because it informs Pearl's surprisingly precarious sense of what constitutes just authority, but also because God's authority looks a great deal like the more tangible economic power of the "lorde" whose vineyard will be the site of the poem's most explicitly realized conflict. We might even say that the poem's inability to answer a complex theological question—to what extent does God obey a recognizable moral law?—helps motivate its turn toward parabolic discourse as a site of useful if fraught analogies:

> "As Mathew meles in your Messe,
> In sothfol gospel of God almyght,
> In sample He can ful graythely gesse
> And lyknes hit to heven lyghte.
> 'My regne,' He says, 'is lyk on hyght
> To a lorde that hade a vyne, I wate."
> (497-502)

As Mary Raschko points out, the analogy here is not to the vineyard as heaven, but more specifically to God as the source of authority. In Raschko's words, "the idea that heaven is like a man and something he owns, rather than something he does, concentrates the comparison with heaven in the vineyard owner himself, enhancing his moral authority and preparing the reader to blame those who question or contradict him."[9] That authority is allied both to Matthew—who tells the parable—and to God Himself, presumably the "He" who begins speaking at line 499. Yet if the "He" is meant to express a timeless truth, the stanza that begins by insisting on the atemporality of the divine ends by making God Himself speak like a late-medieval Englishman, a stylistic choice highlighted by the colloquial interjection "I wat" and even by the strangely offhand word—"gesse"—that the maiden uses to describe God's presumably

---

ordains it. But this statement is carefully balanced with a reassuring sense of God's conformity to moral law: "He may do nothynk bot ryght." The second assertion—which might seem merely to restate the first—in fact differs in its subtle implication that God's power is limited to the extent that it cannot deviate from the good, which is in turn potentially if not automatically accessible to human knowledge. Read thusly, the maiden's remark encapsulates the tension in *Pearl* between consolation and divine unknowability. For a recent discussion of *Pearl* as a drama of the will, see Jessica Barr, *Willing to Know*, 122-151.

[9] Raschko, *Rendering the Word*, 101.

firm knowledge about the nature of heaven.[10] If the parable on the one hand promises to bring the authority of God, Matthew, and the unnamed "lorde" of the vineyard into a kind of overwhelming alignment, this alignment will at the same time prove vulnerable to the historical contingencies opened up by parabolic discourse. This is just to say that the kind of knowledge that the parable offers will be historically conditioned. This sense of history's pressure is if anything bolstered by the lord's claim in the parable that he is "goud" (568) and thus incapable of cheating anyone, a statement that at least potentially invites us to judge this lord by earthly standards, even as it evokes a world of historical struggle in which other lords can and do cheat their workers.[11]

In fact, we know already from its status as the linkword that "date" will be central to the argument of Fitt IX, though the maiden has begun by insisting upon the date-lessness of God's beneficence. "Date" appears right away in the urgent guise of the swiftly passing seasons:

> Of tyme of yere the terme was tight
> To labor vyne was dere the date"
> (503-4)

The "tyme of yere" alluded to is probably September, the traditional month for harvesting grapes. As Lynn Staley Johnson remarks, the date is significant for the poem's Christian message in that

---

[10] ME "gesse" can mean "considered opinion," but only something that is "withouten gesse" is "beyond a doubt." One might be wrong, for instance, to "gesse" that Criseyde is beyond all reproach, as the narrator of Chaucer's *Troilus and Criseyde* does (Book 1, lines 286-87). To "ful graythely gesse" is to guess very carefully, but the poem stops short of recommending its guesswork as a sure foundation for knowledge of the divine, even as it suggests the *suitability* of the parable it now introduces. See *MED*, s. v. *gesse* (n.) (a).

[11] One could certainly argue, alternatively, that the lord's statement here is an expression of the total freedom of divine prerogative: in other words, that God never *could* cheat anyone simply because He is God. At the same time, the lord raises the possibility that he is bound by some form of law, asking rhetorically whether it is *louyly* ("lawful" 565) to pay as much as he wants. Much hinges on whether we choose to take these words at face value, and how far we are to go in identifying the lord in the parable with God. As in the maiden's discussion of God's inability to do wrong, the exact nature of the theodicy being proposed is unclear.

184

September sees the sun move into Libra, the sign of judgment and a stark reminder of the Last Judgment itself. Yet John Bowers reminds us that this "tyme of yere" is also when agricultural workers had the best chance of securing high wages from landowners; the time is "tight" in more ways than one for owners whose grapes might rot on the vine if they are not harvested.[12] Such a reading is strengthened by the immediately following line: "That date of yere wel knawe thys hyne" (505), where "hyne" can be translated roughly as "servants."[13] What the "hyne" know, on this reading, is how to extract the highest wage possible from the "lorde" who needs their services. Indeed "hyne" will appear again by the poet near the poem's end, when the Dreamer refers to the "homly hyne" (1211) who exist in what one editor calls a "harmonious hierarchical relationship" with God.[14] Yet the "hyne" of the parable are not nearly so securely feudal—not at all the things of the household that "homly" implies. Milling about the marketplace, they sell their services freely to the highest bidder. And like medieval merchants, they know how to make their time pay. They know well that, in the maiden's words, "to labor vyne was dere the date," and that their labor is accordingly valuable.

Yet the possibility of conflict is averted for now, with the workers agreeing to a wage that, as Bowers notes, would have been "outrageously low even before the arrival of the Black Death":

> The lorde ful erly up he ros
> To hyre werkmen to hys vyne
> And fyndes ther summe to hys porpos.

---

[12] Johnson notes that the days of September are marked by shortening hours offering "diminished opportunity for human activity." ("The *Pearl* Dreamer and the Eleventh Hour," 8). In that respect, the September date also recalls the movement toward harvest as a time of reckoning—an idea that has already been evoked by the poem's opening "in Auguste in a hygh seysoun / quen corne is corven wyth crokes kene" (39). For the point that the vintage-time offered the best chance for workers to press their demand for higher wages, see Bower, "Politics of *Pearl*," 425.

[13] Stanbury, in her TEAMS edition, gives "households" here on the argument that *hyne* "refer broadly to members of a household ... rather than to laborers" (note to line 505). Yet the *hyne* clearly occupy a subordinate role in this line, as also at lines 632 and 1211. Other editors, including Anderson and Andrew and Waldron, translate the word as "laborers."

[14] Stanbury, *Pearl*, note to line 1211.

> Into acorde thay con decline
> For a pené on a day, and forth thay gos."
> (505-510)[15]

To consider the "pené on a day" as a real penny, as Bowers does here, is to complicate a tradition in *Pearl* criticism that would read the penny in purely allegorical terms. A direct translation of the Biblical *denarius*, the penny to which the workers agree also recalls variously the Eucharist, the mass-penny, and most richly of all, perhaps, the Pearl of Great Price itself, which the penny resembles in its circular shape.[16] But readings that stress the theological meaning of the penny may fail to appreciate the full complexity of its symbolic work—the way in which it signifies difference as well as similarity. A symbol of the Eucharist and thus, by extension, of the community of the faithful, the penny will ironically be the cause of discord as the parable develops. Where the pearl evokes a world of aristocratic luxury and limitless excess, the penny's resolutely economic nature will be evident in the fact that it is not enough. If heaven is an aristocratic idyll where everyone is not only "fayn of otheres hafyng" (450) but wishes that others had *more*—five times as much, as the maiden asserts in the next line—the penny by contrast introduces us to an economy of scarcity in which competition is the rule. Or again, if the penny is what one reader calls a "two-dimensional" reminder of the "three-dimensional" pearl, it is worth noticing, too, what this suggests about how *Pearl* registers the loss of meaning inherent in the movement from one symbol to another to yet another.[17] In this sense, the penny foregrounds the problematically mediated nature of the poem's allegorical work. A symbol of a symbol, the penny measures the distance between what the poem wants to say about the nature of heaven and the everyday analogies to which it resorts in its vernacularizing of contemporary theological discourse. If the penny is salvation, it is also, in its inescapably material form, a thing of the world rather than of God, as the Jesus of Matthew's gospel will remind the Pharisees shortly

---

[15] Bowers, 426n20.
[16] See, respectively, Ackerman, "Pearl-Maiden and the Penny," Gatta, "Transformation Symbolism," and Wilcox, "Constructing Metaphoric Models."
[17] Wilcox, "Constructing Metaphoric Models," 14.

after reciting the Parable of the Vineyard.[18] The maiden's narration of the parable works to heighten rather than occlude this historical register of meaning, as will shortly become clear.

Indeed, the possibility of historical conflict, temporarily forestalled when the workers–in an interesting and singular locution[19]–"declyne" (509) into an agreement with the lord, gets raised again in the lines that follow:

> Aboute under the lorde to marked tos
> And ydel men stande he fyndes therate.
> 'Why stande ye ydel?' he sayde to thos,
> 'Ne knawe ye of this day no date?'
> (513-16)

The mention of "under"–about 9 AM–begins a series of references to the specific time of day that contribute to the sense of urgency that underlies this parable. The possibility of idleness can of course be read against the approach of death–the end of day–as an indication of the need to repent. The lord's pointed question to the idle workers in this sense carries a double meaning. "Ne knawe ye of this day no date" could mean "Don't you know the time of day?" as well as "Don't you know that this day has a limit (date)"? In that case, the lord's question would amount to a reminder of the danger of spiritual idleness. Yet the problem of "ydel" laborers who will not work for less than their preferred wages will be familiar to any reader of *Piers Plowman*. A series of laws like the 1388 Statue of Laborers attempted to fix wages at pre-plague levels, but the charge of idleness echoes through the last half of the century.[20] The lord's harsh

---

[18] Matthew 22:21.

[19] The *MED* lists only one instance in which "declyne" might mean "to come to an agreement." See MED s. v. *dēclīnen* (v.) (3b). The sense is presumably one of "falling into an agreement," perhaps with an intriguing glance at the primary literal meaning, "to turn, turn away, go away," which hints that something is being deflected in this moment.

[20] One such idle worker memorably tells Piers Plowman to "go pissen with his plowgh" (6. 155). See Langland, *Vision of Piers Plowman*, 102. Bowers cites John Gower's castigation of idle workers in his *Vox Clamantis*: "For the very little they do they demand the highest pay" (qtd. in *Politics of Pearl*, 44). Gower puts the point even more finely just after the passage cited by Bowers: "They are sluggish, they are scarce, and they are grasping" (*Major Latin Works*, 208-9).

reminder to the workers can thus simultaneously be read alongside contemporary struggles over the right of peasants to dispose of their labor as they saw fit. This struggle is in fact built into the basic situation of the parable, which imagines agricultural workers as free agents:

> "'Er date of daye hider arn we wonne,'
> So was al samen her answar soght.
> 'We haf standen her syn ros the sunne
> And no mon byddes uus do ryght noght.'
> 'Gos into my vyne, dos that ye conne,'
> So sayde the lorde and made hit toght.
> 'What resonabele hyre be naght be runne,
> I yow pay in dede and thoghte.'
> (517-24)

The workers carefully defend themselves against the charge of idleness—understandably, since those who refused to work might be punished for their lack of employment as early as 1349.[21]

The lord's reply, with its promise of "resonabele hyre" (523), resonates with contemporary debates over what might constitute a just wage. At least one manuscript of *Piers Plowman* uses the same phrase—"resonabile hire" (*Passus* 3, 256)—to describe the moderate wage "that laborers and lowfolk takeþ of hir maistres" (255), differentiating this wage from "mesurelees" (246) reward.[22] The *Pearl*-poet's use of this term is yet another clue that he not only knows about but actively engages with the social and economic developments treated more explicitly by overtly topical writers such as Langland. Unlike Langland, the *Pearl*-poet does not engage directly with the labor-shortage in the second half of the fourteenth century as the primary cause of this conflict. If anything, the parable suggests "a situation of unemployment, in which surplus laborers wait eagerly for work and defend themselves from the charge of idleness."[23] Certainly the picture of workers who have been standing

---

[21] For a discussion of the social causes and implications of the 1349 Ordinance of Laborers as well as the closely related 1351 Statute of Laborers, see, Palmer, *English Law in the Age of the Black Death*, 17-21.

[22] See Cambridge University Library MS Dd.1.17, available online at *Piers Plowman Electronic Archive.*

[23] Raschko, *Rendering the Word*, 106.

in the market since before dawn would tend to support this view. The lord also has no trouble recruiting men or getting them to agree to his terms, however much they may quibble with the payment after the fact:

> Thay wente into the vyne and wroghte
> And al day the lorde thus yede his gate
> And nw men to hys vyne he broghte
> Welnegh wyl day was passed date.
> (525-528)

Yet the problem of "idleness," while it seems antithetical to a situation of labor-surplus, is implied by the simple fact that the lord, like his Biblical precursor, needs to return repeatedly to the marketplace in search of new laborers. The poet expands on Matthew, moreover, in staging the lord's forays into the marketplace as opportunities for dialogue between the lord and the workers. The tone of these encounters gradually becomes more confrontational, until the last such encounter, at "evensonge," the poet's term for the "eleventh hour" of the Biblical parable:

> "At the date of day of evensonge,
> On oure byfore the sonne go doun,
> He sey ther ydel men ful stronge
> And sade to hem, wyth sobre soun,
> 'Wy stonde ye ydel thise dayes longe?'
> Thay sayden her hyre was nawhere boun.
> 'Gos to my vyne, yemen yonge,
> And wyrkes and dos that at ye moun.'
> (529-536)

Even before the encounter begins, the stanza ratchets up the tension by describing the men as not only "ydel" but "ful stronge"–fully capable of the work they seem to be avoiding. This time the lord speaks aggressively, "wyth sobre soun," in a way that makes his displeasure clear and repeats the charge of idleness at line 533. The workers' reply is significant on several levels. By saying that "her hyre was nowhere boun," they are asserting–as in previous encounters with the lord–that they are not idle by choice. This information would have been important for the lord to know, since one stipulation of contemporary labor laws was that workers could not be hired away from a landowner with a previous claim on their services.[24]

The use of the word "boun" is charged here, evoking a world in which many peasants are in fact not securely bound to a single feudal lord in relationships of permanent dependence. More broadly, we might see the peasants' claim that they are "nawhere boun" in relation to the poem's well-known obsession with images of binding and enclosure.[25] Fitt IX is especially rich in these images. Binding is what the workers do to the vines when they "kerven and caggen and man hit clos" (512)–cut and tie and secure them. It is also what the lord does when he secures a contract with the workers–"made it toght" (522)–and then makes it firm by his promise of ready payment. The poem's efforts to imagine the Dreamer's pearl itself as securely fastened in its "setting"–the New Jerusalem–arguably has a defensive subtext, one in which objects (and people) are bound and stationary rather than mobile. Peasants who are "nawhere boun" and must be made secure offer perhaps the most politically charged instance of this interest in stasis.

Here it is also intriguing to consider the potential status of the "yemen yonge" (535) whom the lord commands to go and work. That the men are "yonge" is significant because labor legislation stipulated that all able-bodied men under the age of 60 and without independent means must work.[26] The term "yemen" is more difficult, in part because at least one editor emends it to "ye men." Yet assuming the dominant reading in which "yemen" is written as one word, the lord's mode of address may speak indirectly to late-medieval anxieties about social hierarchy that underlie so much of

---

[24] Cf. Bowers, *Politics of Pearl*, 48.

[25] The narrator famously begins by wishing he could enclose his pearl in a proper setting: "Perle, plesaunte to pryncez paye / To clanly clos in golde so clere" (2). The garden or *hortus conclusus* images that follow continue this theme, and later heaven itself will be described as a "cloystor" (969). Harwood remarks that in particular "stanza-groups V and XVI are unified by the topos of enclosures" (*Pearl as Diptych*, 68). Staley, "Pearl and the Contingencies of Love," concludes from the poem's repeated emphasis on enclosure that the pearl-maiden is an oblate, possibly Isabel, the third daughter of Thomas of Woodstock, who entered the House of Minoresses when she was only a small child.

[26] The text of the law, including the stipulation that all "within the age of threescore years" must work, can be found in Baker, *England in the Later Middle Ages*, 161-62.

this poem. A yeoman might be a hired laborer, and the term could be used contemptuously of an inferior. Increasingly by the late fourteenth century, however, a yeoman could also be a fairly substantial figure, ranking directly below a squire and holding land in his own right. The narrator of *A Gest of Robyn Hode*, for instance, begins his legend by proudly asserting that his hero was "a gode yeman" (3), and the action opens on a scene in which Robin comically but ably mimics the manners of the aristocracy.[27] We know, moreover, that it was precisely such figures—those peasants who had seen their fortunes rise in the aftermath of the Black Death, rather than the poorest of the agricultural labor force—who were the main impetus for the Rising of 1381.[28] In calling the workers yeomen, the lord is acknowledging indirectly what is so threatening about them: their social indeterminacy.

This last confrontation between the lord and the idle workers marks the high-point of the section's tense drama—a drama that will continue to unfold in the next fitt when the workers prove dissatisfied with the lord's payment. Yet at the end of Fitt IX, the "date" of the poem is already clear. We are at the Biblical eleventh hour, what the poet calls "the date of day of evensonge, / On oure byfore the sonne go doun" (529-30). Scriptural commentary on the parable identifies this time of day with the last of the five ages of man, the time stretching from Christ to the present in which medieval Christians lived.[29] The ages-of-the-world model thus assumes that medieval people were living in a time near the end of the world, in which calamities like the Black Death were a sign of the impending Apocalypse. *Pearl* is not alone in providing late-medieval readers with an image of the End of Days though its image of the New Jerusalem is among the most startling of such representations. Even before the Dreamer sees the splendors of God's eternal city, however, we get a hint of what is to come as Fitt IX winds to a close:

---

[27] See *MED* s. v. *yēman* (n.) (1d) and (1e) but also (2) "a member of the landholding class below the rank of squire." In the last sense, the term could be used as an honorific coming after a name, a fact which suggests the rising status of yeomen in the course of the later Middle Ages. For *A Gest of Robyn Hode*, see Knight and Ohlgren, *Robin Hood*, 80-168.

[28] Justice, *Writing and Rebellion*, 13-66, makes the case that the rebels of 1381 were as a group surprisingly literate and upwardly mobile.

[29] Raschko, *Rendering the Word*, 81-2.

> Sone the worlde bycom wel broun,
> The sunne was doun and hit wex late.
> To take her hyre he mad sumoun;
> The day was al apassed date.
> (537-40)

The summoning to which the lord calls his workers is the starkest reminder yet in this poem of the inevitability of judgment and has been read as a message for the Dreamer (who may himself be in his "eleventh hour").[30] On the level of Christian history, the coming of night marks a final escape from history, as "date" and its problems are finally left behind in a vision of the Day of Judgment.

Are we to conclude, then, that "the parable that keeps on harping on the importance of 'date' ends up by shrugging off its relevance"?[31] It is true that there is something circular about the logic of the maiden's argument. After beginning by asserting that God's mercy has "no date," the maiden introduces us in Fitt IX to a world seemingly alive with the texture of historical life and the urgency of swiftly passing time, only to revert at the end of the fitt to a reminder of what lies beyond history, when the world itself will be "al apassed date." On such evidence, we might conclude that the poem raises the possibility of history–of "date"–only to turn our gaze from it, directing our view instead to the heavenly city that lies outside of time. Something like this process is indeed well underway by the time the maiden has finished with the parable. The laborers, after complaining of the unfairness of being paid the same amount regardless of how long they have worked (549-56), simply disappear from the parable after their complaint has been made, at which point the unnamed "lorde" becomes, inexplicably, "Kryste" at line 569. Even the possibility of distinguishing the parable from its exegesis seems to have disappeared in this moment, and with it the possibility of historical reading. A similar turning-away from history is enacted in the maiden's comparison of herself, at lines 577-84, to the "pore men" (573) whom Christ promises will always have their reward. It is as though the specter of those "that swange and swat for longe

---

[30] For the argument that "the poet's emphasis upon time implies that the dreamer himself is in his eleventh hour," see Johnson, "The *Pearl* Dreamer and the Eleventh Hour," 10.
[31] Putter, *Introduction*, 171-72.

yore" (586)—of those who toil in the vineyard of the world—is raised only to be disregarded as irrelevant.

The parable is after all, we are now reminded, not about history and its work but a specific response to the Dreamer's objections regarding a young girl's rank in heaven. The space for historical experience that had seemed to be opened up by the parable is reduced once more to a quibble over the pearl-maiden's biological age. "Evensonge," so easy to read in terms of the medieval belief that we are living near the end of the world—that "evensonge" is now—turns out to be not a direct reflection of our own historical experience but a highly personal metaphor that the maiden applies to her own situation: those who come to the vineyard at this late hour are those who died young. Even the accounting of time provided by the maiden's interpretation—in its refutation of the more traditional association of "evensonge" with those at the end of life—muddles chronology in a way that violates our sense of proper temporality.[32]

Yet the poem is not, perhaps, quite done with "date." As we approach heaven near the poem's close, we notice that its walls are adorned not only with pearls and other gems but also with "dates," specifically, the birth-dates of "Israel barnes" (1040). Heaven itself may be a timeless realm—a city basking in the light of a sun that never sets (1069-71)—but just outside, indeed on the very walls of heaven, the history of the Exodus is written. It would be easy, of course, to read this as a trivial slip on the part of the poet, who after all is merely following Biblical tradition.[33] Yet it is symptomatic of a poem that ends with a fall back into history. For we know of course that the "date" or limit of the Dreamer's experience will assert itself as a boundary that cannot be crossed—the river or "strem" (1162) that the Dreamer tries and fails to traverse at the poem's end, only

---

[32] Robertson defends the maiden's interpretation as orthodox, averring that her reading is "consistent with Medieval exegetical tradition" ("'Heresy' of *The Pearl*," 155), yet Putter, 174, follows Bogdanos's suggestion that we have here "an illogical syllogism, which in its absurd dialectic incarnates another inscrutable principle governing God's mercy: his view of time" (*Image of the Ineffable*, 96).

[33] As Stanbury notes in her edition, the account of the names on heaven's gates is from Revelation 21: 12, but the detail that their birthdays are also written there derives from Exodus 28 (note to line 1041). Since his account mostly follows that of Revelation closely, the addition arguably marks a deliberate and self-conscious choice on the poet's part.

to awaken back into historical time. Having experienced the bliss of "Goddes present" (1193)–both God's presence and his *present*–the Dreamer will be "kast of kythes that lastes aye" (1198)–cast out of the land that endures beyond time, in a movement that repeats the first exile from the garden, the moment of humanity's fall into history.[34] And the reason for his exile is not just disobedience but specifically the crime of (like the workers in the parable) wanting more than he has: "Bot ay wolde man of happe more hente / Then moghten by ryght upon hem clyven" (1195-6). Still of the world, the Dreamer cannot escape the desire for more of divinity than will actually cleave to him, and it is this very desire that plunges him back into the historical time of the fallen world, where the only "always" is ironically the reality of unfulfilled desire.

So history will return, after all, even if it does so now in the reassuringly static guise of ritual. This is of course the Mass to which the maiden refers when she introduces the Parable of the Vineyard: "as Mathew meles in your Messe" (497). It is this ritual enacted in and through history, even more than the Word itself, that provides access to the divine in the poem's Eucharistic theology.[35] Yet when the narrator, no longer the Dreamer, ends by reassuring us that we encounter Christ in the form of bread and wine "uch a daye" (1210), his formulation cannot help but evoke that other day so central to the poem's drama: the day of the parable in which human history, with all its toils and travails, messily unfolds. The poem that gestures towards God's eternal present–a place beyond all date–simultaneously dramatizes history as inescapable.

---

[34] The meaning of "present" as "the present time" is attested in *MED*, meaning 3(a). The entry cites Chaucer's translation of Boethius's *Consolation of Philosophy* for the notion of "present" as "God's eternal present (without past or future)."

[35] We do not need to read the poem as a Eucharistic vision to recognize the importance of the poem's final return to the ritual act that achieves timelessness from within time itself. Cf. Philips, "Eucharistic Allusions," and especially Marti, *Body, Heart, and Text*.

WORKS CITED

Ackerman, Robert W. "The Pearl-Maiden and the Penny." *Romance Philology* 17 (1963-4), 615-23.

Anderson, J. J., ed. *Sir Gawain and the Green Knight; Pearl; Cleanness; Patience.* Rutland, VT: Tuttle, 1996.

Andrew, Malcolm, and Ronald Waldron, eds. *The Poems of the Pearl Manuscript: Pearl, Cleanness, Patience, and Sir Gawain and the Green Knight.* London: Edward Arnold, 1978. Third ed. Exeter: University of Exeter Press, 1996.

Baker, Derek, ed. *England in the Later Middle Ages.* [Portraits and Documents]. Dallas, TX: Academia, 1993.

Barr, Helen. "Pearl–Or The Jeweller's Tale." *Medium Ævum* 69 (2000), 59-79.

Barr, Jessica. *Willing to Know God: Dreamers and Visionaries in the Later Middle Ages.* Columbus, OH: Ohio State University Press, 2010.

Bogdanos, Theodore. *Pearl: Image of the Ineffable: A Study in Medieval Poetic Symbolism.* Pennsylvania: Pennsylvania State University Press, 1983.

Bowers, John. "*Pearl* in Its Royal Setting: Ricardian Poetry Revisited." *Studies in the Age of Chaucer* 17 (1995), 111-55.

–. "The Politics of Pearl." *Exemplaria* 7 (1995), 419-41.

–. *The Politics of Pearl: Court Poetry in The Age of Richard II.* Cambridge: D. S. Brewer, 2001.

Carson, Mother Angela. "Aspects of Elegy in the Middle English *Pearl.*" *Studies in Philology* 62 (1965). 17-27.

Chaucer, Geoffrey. *Troilus and Criseyde.* Ed. Stephen A. Barney. New York: Norton, 2005.

Gatta, John. "Transformation Symbolism and the Liturgy of the Mass in *Pearl.*" *Modern Philology* 71 (1974): 243-56.

Gordon, E. V., ed. *Pearl.* Oxford: Clarendon Press, 1953.

Gower, John. *The Major Latin Works of John Gower.* Trans. Eric W. Stockton. Seattle: University of Washington Press, 1962.

Harwood, Britton J. "The *Pearl* Dreamer and the Eleventh Hour," in Robert J. Blanch, Mirian Youngerman Miller and Julian N. Wasserman, eds., *Text and Matter: New Critical Perspectives of the Pearl-Poet.* Troy, NY: Whitston, 1991. 61-78.

Johnson, Lynn Staley. "The *Pearl* Dreamer and the Eleventh Hour," in Robert J. Blanch, Mirian Youngerman Miller and Julian N. Wasserman, eds., *Text and Matter: New Critical Perspectives of the Pearl-Poet.* Troy, NY: Whitston, 1991. 3-15.

–. "*Pearl* and the Contingencies of Love and Piety," in David Aers, ed., *Medieval Literature and Historical Inquiry*. Woodbridge, Suffolk: D. S. Brewer, 2000. 83-114.

Justice, Stephen. *Writing and Rebellion: England in* 1381. Berkeley: University of California Press, 1994.

Knight, Stephen and Thomas Ohlgren, eds., *Robin Hood and Other Outlaw Tales*. Kalamazoo, Mich.: Medieval Institute Publications, 1997.

Langland, William. *The Vision of Piers Plowman: A Complete Edition of the B-Text*. London: J. M. Dent, 1984.

Marti, Kevin. *Body, Heart, and Text in the Pearl-Poet*. Queenston, Ontario: Mellen Press, 1991.

Middle English Dictionary. Edited by H. Kurath, S. M. Kuhn, and R. Lewis. Ann Arbor: University of Michigan Press, 1957-2001. Online edition, *Middle English Dictionary Online*.

Mitchell, J. Allen. "The Middle English *Pearl*: Figuring the Unfigurable." *Chaucer Review* 35 (2000): 86–111.

Muscatine, Charles. "The *Pearl* Poet: Style as Defense," in *Poetry and Crisis in the Age of Chaucer*. Notre Dame: University of Notre Dame Press, 1972. 37-69.

Palmer, Robert C. *English Law in the Age of the Black Death, 1348-1381: A Transformation of Governance and Law*. Chapel Hill and London: University of North Carolina Press, 1993.

Piers Plowman Electronic Archive, last modified June 19, 2014, http://piers.iath.virginia.edu/.

Phillips, Heather. "The Eucharistic Allusions of *Pearl*." *Medieval Studies* 47 (1985), 474-86.

Putter, Ad. *Introduction to the Gawain-Poet*. London: Longman, 1996.

Raschko, Mary. *Rendering the Word: Vernacular Accounts of the Parables in Late Medieval England*. Ph.D. diss., UNC-Chapel Hill, 2009.

Robertson, D. W., Jr., *Preface to Chaucer*. Princeton: Princeton University Press, 1962.

–. "The 'Heresy' of *The Pearl*." *Modern Language Notes* 65 (1950), 152-55.

Stanbury, Sarah, ed., *Pearl*. Kalamazoo, Mich.: Medieval Institute Publications, 2001.

Vantuono, William, ed., *The Pearl Poems: An Omnibus Edition*, 2 vols. New York / London: Garland, 1984.

Watkins, John. "'Sengeley in Synglere': *Pearl* and Late Medieval Individualism." *Chaucer Yearbook* 2 (1995), 117-36.

Wilcox, Miranda. "Constructing Metaphoric Models of Salvation: Matthew 20 and the Middle English Poem *Pearl.*" *Studies in the Bible and Antiquity* 3 (2011): 1–28.

Wood, Anne Douglas. "The *Pearl*-Dreamer and the *Hynne* in the Vineyard Parable," *Philological Quarterly* 52 (1973): 9-19.

Walter Wadiak is Assistant Professor of Medieval Literature at NTU-Singapore. He has written about Chaucer and Middle English romance, and his forthcoming book, *Savage Economy*, explores how later English romances refashion the "noble gift" into a tool for imagining new forms of late-medieval and early-modern community.

FITT X – MORE

Travis Neel

Introduction

Fitt X concludes the Parable of the Laborers in the Vineyard (Matt. 20: 1-16) begun in Fitt IX. The Fitt begins in the middle of a fairly close translation of the gospel text including Christ's aphoristic moralization of the parable (541-572). The Maiden, identifying herself with the last laborers to arrive in the vineyard, explains that the parable demonstrates how grace has granted her more reward in Heaven than could have been expected through a judgment of justice (577-588). The Dreamer responds to the Maiden, mimicking the complaint of the first workers in the vineyard and suggesting a Scriptural precedent for expecting Heavenly reward to be determined in some measure by earthly merit (589-600). Fitt X concludes with the Dreamer's insistence that the parable – and by extension the Maiden's status in Heaven – represents an excessively unjust system of payment.

The Dreamer's response to the Maiden's explication of the parable has often been presented as evidence for his theological simplicity, his intellectual solipsism, or an outright act of resistance.[1] Closer attention to other contemporary references to the Parable of the Laborers in the Vineyard, however, reveals that the Dreamer

---

[1] Lynn Staley, *The Voice of the Gawain Poet* (Madison, WI: University of Wisconsin Press, 1984), and Sandra Pierson Prior, *The Pearl Poet Revisited* (New York: Maxwell Macmillan, 1994). Both David Aers and Jim Rhodes have proposed slightly different readings, arguing that the Dreamer is neither naïve nor ignorant but simply representative of alternative theological positions. For Rhodes, the Dreamer and Maiden engage in a Bahktinian dialogic in which each has authoritative though contrastive positions. For Aers, the Dreamer's resistances to the Maiden's instruction mark him as a figure of heterodoxy. See Jim Rhodes, *Poetry Does Theology: Chaucer, Grosseteste, and the Pearl-Poet* (Notre Dame, IN: University of Notre Dame Press, 2001), 126-128; David Aers, "The Self Mourning: Reflections on *Pearl*," *Speculum* 68, no. 1 (1993): 54-73.

may, in fact, be giving voice to a commonly held interpretation of the text – one that recognized the importance of worldly works within the economy of spiritual reward. The Parable of the Laborers in the Vineyard appears in a number of other Middle English texts. These works often incorporate materials from the rich traditions of exegetical and homiletic comment on the parable, including Origen, Augustine, Gregory the Great, the *Glossa Ordinaria*, and Nicholas of Lyra.[2] The parable makes regular appearances as the gospel reading for Suptuagesima Sunday in surviving Middle English sermon collections.[3] While these sermons often make explicit references to the traditions established by Origen, Augustine, Gregory, and others, they often betray the particular concerns of their late-medieval English lay communities in interpreting and applying the scriptural text. Drawing from a variety of contemporary Middle English sermons, Mary Raschko's recent work has shown a prevalent emphasis on the reciprocal relationship between earthly works and heavenly reward in vernacular preaching.[4] Perhaps the most famous insistence that the parable demonstrates such a relationship is Thomas Wimbledon's *Redde racionem villicacionis tue*

---

[2] For an extensive listing of the available sources on the Parable of the Laborers in the Vineyard see Wailes, 138.

[3] For the best and most recent treatment of the parables within vernacular English writings of the period, see Mary Raschko, "Rendering the Word: Vernacular Accounts of the Parables in Late Medieval England." PhD Dissertation (University of North Carolina at Chapel Hill, 2009). Important foundational treatments are offered in G.R. Owst, *Literature and Pulpit in Medieval England: A Neglected Chapter in the History of Enlish Letters and of the English People* (Cambridge: Cambridge University Press, 1933) and Stephen L. Wailes, *Medieval Allegories of Jesus' Parables* (Berkeley: University of California Press, 1987). Middle English sermons touching on the parable can be found in the following collections: Woodburn O. Ross, ed., *Middle English Sermons, Edited from British Museum MS Royal 18 B. xxiii*, EETS o.s. 209 (London: Oxford University Press, 1940), 40; Anne Hudson, ed., *English Wycliffite Sermons*, Vol I (Oxford: Clarendon Press, 1983), 37/378-383; Anne B. Thompson, ed., *The Northern Homily Cycle*, TEAMS Middle English Texts Series (Kalamazoo: Medieval Institute Publications, 2008), 14/83-93; Cigman, ed., *Lollard Sermons*, EETS o.s. 294 (Oxford: Oxford University Press, 1989), 8/80-92; and Susan Powell, ed., *John Mirk's Festial, Edited from British Library MS Cotton Claudius A.II*, EETS o.s. 334 (Oxford: Oxford University Press, 2009), 15/60-66.

[4] Raschko, 86-87.

preached at Paul's Cross in 1388.⁵ Wimbledon's sermon, which takes the Parable of the Laborers in the Vineyard as its protheme, mobilizes the text in a defense of the tri-partite organization of labor among priests, secular rulers, and laborers. The sermon draws on the Matthew text to show how all will be called on the day of judgment to render an account of how they have lived: "And so eueri man trauayle in his degre; for whanne þe euen is come þat is þe ende of þe world, 'þanne euery man shal take reward, good oþer euyl aftir þat he haþ trauayled here.' Prima Corinthios iij."⁶ A so-called Lollard sermon makes the connection more explicitly:

> Þis gospel techeþ vs to wirche faste and be not idel while we been here wandrynge in þis wei, for þe hure of þe hiȝe blisse of heuene þat God haþ bihiȝte to alle suche; and also to haue a tristi hope: þouȝ we haue misspendid oure tyme, ȝet naþeles, and we ben founde his trewe seruantes in oure laste age, we schullen haue þe same reward of euerlastyng blisse.⁷

The relationship between earthly work and spiritual reward is made clear here: in order to hope for a reward that has already been promised (bihiȝte), the faithful must demonstrate themselves to have been true servants through diligent work.⁸

The reference to the labor in the vineyard also crops up in Middle English poetry to emphasize the place of earthly works in determining divine judgment. In *Dives and Pauper*, for example, Pauper quotes from the parable in order to explain how all will be asked to account for their lives on the day of judgment:

---

⁵ Thomas Wimbledon, Wimbledon's Sermon: Redde Rationem Villicationis Tue: A Middle English Sermon of the Fourteenth Century. Ed. Ione Kemp Knight (Pittsburgh: Duquesne University Press, 1967).
⁶ Wimbledon, 68/114-118.
⁷ Cigman, ed., 80/5-10.
⁸ Ibid., 92/411-415. The sermon offers a detailed schematic of a tripartite workforce beset by three enemies, each with three corresponding attributes, who try to spoil the vineyard by catching the workers in idleness. It concludes with a final exhortation that God may help the workers "to wirche so wiseli in þis world oure werkis in þis vyne, eche man in his estaat þat he stant inne, þat we moun like þe Lord þerwiþ and be alowed [þ]e peny" (88-92/283-415; 92/428-431).

For þan Christ schal seyn to euery man & woman: Tolle quod tuum est et uade [Mt. 20: 14], Tac þat is þin and þat þu hast deseruyd & go þin way, to heuene ȝif þu haue do wel & to helle ȝif þu haue don omys and nout amendyt þe.⁹

What is interesting here is how the storyworld of the parable has been subsumed into the words spoken by the lord of the vineyard. Pauper does away with the need to interpret the parable allegorically or to parse the meaning from Christ's aphoristic morals. Rather, he takes seriously the simile that begins the parabolic exploration of how the kingdom of heaven is like a man who hires laborers to work in his vineyard and renders the parable as the spoken words of Christ. Stripped of its integumental vehicle in this way, the parable offers Pauper a straightforward gloss of the Book of Daniel and a prophecy of what Christ will say on the day of judgment.

This context of contemporary engagement with the parable in Matthew is crucial to a reading of the exchange between the Dreamer and the Maiden at the structural center of the *Pearl*-poem. Far from Pauper's straightforward adoption of the Matthew text as a gloss for the operations of divine judgment, the *Pearl*-poet's attention to the parable underscores what some have read as the central crux of the poem: "a direct confrontation between earthly and heavenly values."[10] The *Pearl*-poet neither glosses over the literal level of the story nor allows the literal to be entirely subsumed into a moral or anagogical reading. Rather, the *Pearl*-poet distends the parable, adds to it, and dwells on its potential to produce more than one reading. The combination of structural and verbal repetitions aligning the two interlocutors with characters from the parable brings the tension between the desire for just reward and the superfluity of divine grace into confrontation with each other not only within the storyworld of the parable but also within the dream vision itself. The concatenation of the word *more* in Fitt X further underscores this tension, suggesting something larger, greater, additional, longer in duration, stronger, more complete, or more important within and

---

[9] Priscilla Heath Barnum, ed., *Dives and Pauper*, Vol I, Part II. EETS o.s. 280 (OUP, 1980), 250.
[10] Malcolm Andrew and Ronald Waldron, ed., *The Poems of the Pearl Manuscript: Pearl, Cleanness, Patience, Sir Gawain and the Green Knight*, 4th ed. (Exeter: University of Exeter Press, 2002), 79.

simultaneously beyond both the parable and the exchange in Fitt X.[11] Through the repetition of *more* and its verbal variants in addition to the structural repetitions of the relations between lord and laborer, God and Maiden, Maiden and Dreamer, and God and Dreamer, Fitt X discloses more and more within the Parable of the Laborers in the Vineyard and in the parable's relation to its readers.

541-542: The date of þe daye þe lorde con knaw / Called to þe reue: Lede, pay þe meyny / Gyf hem þe hyre þat I hem owe

The concatenated word of Fitt IX, *date*, begins Fitt X as the object of the periphrastic verbal construction, *con knaw* (began to know or recognize), which takes *þe lorde* as its subject. The centrality of *þe lorde* at the outset of Fitt X is suggestive. It is *þe lorde* who determines when the time is right for settling accounts at the end of the day, who summons the reeve to gather the laborers, who owes the laborers their recompense, who worries about being reproached, who pronounces that the wage for each will be a penny, and who asserts that the penny is simultaneously the perrogative of their covenant (562) and what pleases him to offer as a gift (565-6). As in the Matthew account, Christ identifies himself with *þe lorde* from the parable (569). Medieval readings of the parable interpret the householder as both Chirst and God. In Wimbledon's sermon, the householder is glossed as Christ, himself: "To spiritual undirstondyng þis housholdere is oure lord Iesu Crist, þat is heed of þe houshold of holi chirch."[12] The sermon in BL Additional 41321 seems to have the Godhead in mind as the figural householder: "Þis housholder þat þis gospel spekeþ of is oure Lord God, whiche haþ an housold of þre stagis – þat is heuene, erþe, and helle."[13]

544: And fyrre, þat non me may reprené

The *fyrre* (furthermore, MED 6d) of this line evinces the excess of this moment in the Maiden's recounting of the parable. While the *Pearl*-poet's account of the Matthew text cannot be called a literal translation of the Vulgate, it remains a fairly close paraphrase of the

---

[11] Middle English Dictionary (MED), "more" definitions 1a, 2a, 3b, 4b, 5a, 6a, 7a, and 8a.
[12] Ibid., 61/13-15.
[13] Cigman, 81/11-13.

scriptural text. This line, however, seems to emerge *ex nihilo* and draw particular attention to the *pleny* of line 549.

545-548: Set hem alle vpon a rawe / And gyf vchon inlyche a peny. / Bygyn at þe laste þat standez lowe, / Tyl to þe fyrste þat þou atteny.

The word "peny" was a common Middle English translation for biblical and classical monetary units, here rendering the Latin *denarius*.[14] John Bowers, who reads the *Pearl*'s distention of the parable as a comment on late fourteenth century English labor practices and economic realities, suggests that a penny a day would have been in accordance with the legal requirement of a just wage established by the 1388 Statute of Laborers.[15] Bowers sees the *Pearl*-poet's treatment of the parable as a fantasy wish-fulfillment of the English landed gentry, who would have envied the householder's ability to rigorously enforce the terms of a labor contract and maintain the final word over negotiations while still seeming benevolent and generous to last laborers. He suggests that *Pearl* be read within the context of "a traditional literary disdain toward *vileins*" that "unanimously took the part of the landed gentry in these social contests."[16] The Maiden's gloss (573-588), which I treat below, offers an alternative to the literal reading of the penny, suggesting that it signifies another system in which "vch mon payed inlyche" (603). For now, though, it suffices to note that the language of the parable – here, *gyf vchon inlyche* – will be repeated by one of the interlocutors of the dream vision.

That the first shall be last and the last shall be first is one of the aphoristic morals attached to the parable by Christ (Matthew 20:16). As the final part of the instructions given by the owner of the vineyard to his reeve, this utterance has not yet gained the force of prophecy, but it will be repeated again in *Pearl* at lines 570-572 and reiterated by the Maiden as both the lesson of the parable and a justification for her position in Heaven.

---

[14] Middle English Dictionary (MED), "peni" definition 2a.
[15] John Bowers, Politics of Pearl: Court Poetry in the Age of Richard II (Cambridge: D.S. Brewer, 2001), 47.
[16] Ibid., 44. He adds further, "At immediate issue here is the lord's absolute right to enforce labor contracts and to determine the wage-level for the laborers hired for the summer harvest" (46).

549-554: And þenne þe fyrst bygonne to pleny / And sayden þat þay hade trauayled sore / Þese bot on oure hem con streny / Vus þynk vus oȝe to take more. / More haf we served, vus þynk so, / Þat suffred han þe dayez hete,

The first laborers complain that they have worked longer and therefore deserve more recompense than the last laborers to arrive. They suggest that just payment might be proportional to the relative difficulty of the laboring or to the time spent in the vineyard ("þat þay hade trauayled sore" (550) and "suffred han þe dayez hete" (554)). The *Pearl*-poet draws particular attention to the division among the workers by inserting the householder's concern that he might be reproached (544), offering a lengthier account of the laborer's complaints than is attested in the Matthew text, and repeating the structure of the complaint in the Dreamer's response to the Maiden's gloss of the parable (589-600). Unlike the author of *Pearl*, though, medieval sermons on the parable attempt to obscure any potential for reading discord among the laborers. The protheme to Wimbledon's sermon concludes with a paraphrase of the lines that open Fitt X, rendering the Matthew text: "Whanne þe day was ago, he clepid his styward and heet to ȝeue eche man a peny." [17] Wimbledon's sermon does not continue the parable beyond these lines, avoiding the complaint of the workers and the aphorisms offered at the conclusion of Matthew's account. This seems like a good strategy considering that Wimbledon's sermon is largely a defense of the divisions of feudal labor along a tripartite model.

Other medieval sermons, however, retain the complaint of the laborers and work hard to account for it within a moral and anagogical reading of the parable. The sermon for Septuagesima Sunday in Anne Hudson's collection of English sermons follows the example offered by Gregory the Great's homily on the parable by insisting that the *grucchynge* of the laborers be understood as a "wondrying in sowle, and þanking of Godis grace þat he ȝaf so myche ioye to men for so luytel traueyle."[18] The sermon transforms the complaint of the laborers into a moment of joy and appreciation for the householder's magnanimity, but it proves difficult for even so short a sermon as this one to maintain in the face of the parable's closing exchanges. Only a few lines later, continuing its explanation of the parable's closing moments, the text defends the response of

---

[17] Wimbledon, 61/13-15.
[18] Hudson, 382/105-106.

the vineyard owner by reproving the *grucchynge* of the laborers: "Ne non of hem schulde gruccen aʒeynes goodnesse of þis iuste Fadir, for he may ʒyuen of his owne more þan any man may disserue by mannys riʒtwisnesse, or euenehed of any chaffare."[19] It is clear that *grucchynge* has returned to its more common sense in this defense of the lord's magnanimity, but it is unclear how the two readings of the *grucchynge* are meant to relate to one another. The Septuagesima sermon in BL Additional 41321 also strains to give a positive reading of the laborer's complaint and, like the sermon in Hudson's collection, relies on Gregory's transformation of the worker's complaint to do so: "þis grucchynge is not ellis but a wonderful merveilynge in mannes soule or mannes þouʒt of þe grete mercy, bounte, and grace of oure Lord, þat rewardeþ eche man iliche."[20] Unlike the sermon in Hudson's collection, however, the BL Additional 41321 sermon has room to entertain alternative readings. Suggesting, "Or ellis it mai be vnderstonde þus, as anoþer glose seiþ", the sermon interprets the complaint of the laborers again, but this time it declares that the laborers unjustly reproach the owner of the vineyard.[21] The text reads, "For to him þat cam first, hee quytt him his couenaunt, and more myʒte he not axe, bi lawe ne bi resoun; and him þat came laste, he rewardide him of his grace."[22] Not only is the complaint of the first laborers unreasonable, it is unlawful. Clearly, the laborer's *grucchynge* has returned no longer as the marvelous wondering of its earlier transformation but as the envious and covetous moaning that, as the sermon reminds its audience, has no place among the blessed.

555-556: Þenn þyse þat wroʒt not hourez two, / And þou dotz hem vus to conterfete.´

The complaint that the last laborers worked only one hour in the vineyard (551) is amended here to two hours. This divergeance from the Matthew text, where Matthew 20:12 has the last laborers working only one hour, recalls that the Maiden "lyfed not two ʒer in oure þede" (483).

In line 556, the confrontation between earthly and heavenly values takes on the language of counterfeiting: "and you do

---

[19] Ibid., 382/109-112.
[20] Cigman, 84/159-162.
[21] Ibid., 85/173; 173-185.
[22] Ibid., 85/176-179.

counterfeit us to them." The MED identifies this passage as the sole exemplar of definition 1c for *countrefeten*, "to be like (sb.), be equal to", but the tone of this moment in the parable suggests that *conterfete* carries the connotative weight of its other denotations as well.[23] At the very least, there is a sense of false simulation or the attempt to pass off an inferior object as more worthy or valuable.[24] I would suggest, as well, that the *Pearl*-poet might have been calling to mind the legal sense of *countrefeten*, which denoted contrivances in plots of deception, murder, and treason.[25]

557-8: Þenne sayde þe lorde to on of þo / 'Frende, no waning I wyl þe ȝete

The Lord's response to the complaining workers is difficult to parse from the outset. Both the language and syntax of his initial utterance has proven difficult for editors of the poem, who have relied on the *Pearl*-poet's fidelity to the text in Matthew to justify their respective interpretations. The difficulty resides in line 558 with the word *waning*, which appears in the manuscript as *wanig*. The word has commonly been understood as a noun from the verb *wane* (OE *wanian*), meaning "grow less" or "decrease." Andrew and Waldron suggest that the line be read as, "Friend, I do not wish to make any reduction (of what is due) to you."[26] Citing both the *Lindisfarne Gospels* (Mark 5:38) and *Owl and the Nightingale* (line 311), David Fowler proposes that the word be read instead as a form of the Old English *wā nung*, meaning "lamentation." Thus, Fowler has proposed that the line be rendered: "Friend, I will allow thee no lamentation."[27] While Fowler's reading makes sense of the line without the supplementation Andrew and Waldron provide and without stretching the obvious connotation of ȝete (to permit, to allow), even Fowler concedes that his reading diverges from the Vulgate line: *Amice, non facio tibi injuriam*, which finds a closer parallel in Andrew and Waldron's translation.

---

[23] MED, "*countrefeten*" definition 1c.
[24] MED, "*countrefeten*" definitions 4 and 5.
[25] MED, "*countrefeten*" definition 6. See also the definitions for *countrefeten* and *contreven* in John A. Alford, *Piers Plowman: A Glossary of Legal Diction* (Cambridge: D.S. Brewer, 1988), 36 & 38.
[26] Andrew and Waldron, note to lines 553-9, pg. 79.
[27] David C. Fowler, *MLN*, 74 (1959), 582.

559-564: Take þat is þyn owne, and go. / And I hyred þe for a peny agrete, / Quy bygynnez þou now to þrete? / Watz not a pené þy couenaunt þore? / Fyrre þen couenaunde is no3t to plete; / Wy shalte þou þenne ask more?

The householder's response to the worker's complaint insists on the terms of their agreement at the time he hired each group of workers. According to the owner of the vineyard, to ask for more than the agreed-upon penny would be to claim more than was stipulated in their agreement of a penny in exchange for a day's labor (509-510). The repetition of the word *couenaunt* in consecutive lines reinforces not only the conditional terms of the workers' agreements with the vineyard owner but also the legal force of their contract.[28]

565-566: More, weþer louyly is me my gyfte / To do wyth myn quatso me lykez

If the payment of a penny to the first workers is justified by the terms of their agreement, the payment of a penny to the last wokers is justified by what pleases the vineyard owner to offer as a gift. Howard H. Schless and Richard Firth Green have suggested that this appeal to "quatso me lykez" echoes the attention given to the "princes paye" in the poem's opening and closing lines, which invoke an absolutist legal maxim *quod principi placet, habet legis vigorem* (the prince's pleasure has the force of law).[29]

567-568: Oþer ellez þyn y3e to lyþer is lyfte / For I am goude and non byswykez

The Gollancz edition of the poem notes that lines 565-568 echo the Wycliffite Bible "Whether it is not leueful to me to do that that

---

[28] For a discussion of the language of contracts and covenants in *Sir Gawain and the Green Knight* that has much to recommend for the reader of *Pearl*, see Robert J. Blanch and Julian N. Wasserman, "Medieval Contracts and Covenants: The Legal Coloring of Sir Gawain and the Green Knight," *Neophilologus* 68 (1984): 598-610. For a more general introduction to English contracts, see chapters 18-21 in John Baker, *An Introduction to English Legal History*, 4th Ed. (Oxford: Oxford University Press, 2002).

[29] Howard H. Schless, "Pearl's 'Princes Paye' and the Law," The Chaucer Review, Vol. 24, No. 2 (Fall, 1989), 183-85; Richard Firth Green, *A Crisis of Truth: Literature and Law in Ricardian England* (Philadelphia: University of Pennsylvania Press, 1999), 373-374.

Y wole? Whether thin iȝe is wicked, for Y am good?"[30] The parallels are certainly striking since the lines from *Pearl* read, "or else your eye is lifted to evil (*luper/lyper*) / For I am good and not a cheat." The line in the parable seems to recall an earlier moment in Matthew describing the eye as the lamp of the body, warning that "if thine eye be evil, thy whole body shall be full of darkness" (KJV Matthew 6:24). *Pearl*'s addition of "and non byswykez" to the simple Latin, *ego bonus sum*, from Matthew 20:15 seems to have a dual function. Primarily, the verb *biswiken*, seems to be used here in its primary sense meaning to cheat, deceive, or mislead and its closely overlapping denotation of being misled by the devil, the world, or the flesh.[31] These two definitions seem apropos to the Matthew text's reading of the eye as a lamp of the body as well as the householder's assertion that he is not defrauding the workers. Additionally, the word *biswiken* denotes the taking away or withholding of what is owed, which echoes the householder's insistence of treating his agreement with the workers as a covenant or contract.[32] When read concurrently, the literal, theological, and quasi-legal denotations of *biswiken* provide the range of the householder's defense of his actions.

569-572: Þus schal I, quoþ Kryste, hit skyfte / Þe laste schal be þe fyrst þat strykez, / And þe fyrst þe laste, be he neuer so swyft, / For mony ben called, þaȝ fewe be mykez.

Having concluded the parable in the gospel of Matthew, Christ offers two aphoristic statements by way of explanation. As so often happens in the gospel accounts, the narrative quickly moves from Christ's speech to the next narrative moment without anymore of a tranisition than the simple particle, *and* (*kai/ et*). The word signals the end of one narrative moment and links it to the next, but the precise nature of their contiguity is never quite clear in Matthew's account. Often the particle functions merely to mark sequence; sometimes Matthew employs it to evoke the poetry of the Hebrew Scripture by rhythmically punctuating the prose; and at other times the particle suggests a more nuanced relationship between what comes before

---

[30] Gollancz, Sir Israel, ed. And trans., *Pearl, Edited with Modern Rendering, Together with Boccaccio's Olympia*, 2nd Ed. (London: Chatto and Windus, 1921), 144.
[31] MED, "*biswiken*" definition 1 & 2.
[32] MED, "*biswiken*" definition 4.

and what follows: causal, logical, ascensive, or adversative.[33] In this case, what follows is a short narrative scene in which Jesus takes the twelve disciples to Jerusalem and prophesies his betrayal, crucifixion, and resurrection (Matthew 20: 17-19).[34] The sequence from parable to the salvific moment of Christian theology is mirrored in the medieval homiletic tradition, where the Parable of the Laborers in the Vineyard prompts two seemingly paradoxical lines of doctrine. On the one hand, medieval audiences were reminded that God offers the penny of eternal bliss equally to all. On the other hand, medieval preachers and exegetes stressed that this penny could not be gained by idleness: while the gift of grace could not be earned, work – both of the spiritual and bodily variety – was the surest path into the vineyard where the penny could be given.

The two moral statements Christ offers for the parable appear in the Vulgate and throughout English Bible translations through the seventeenth century, but a number of modern English translations based on Nestle-Aland's *Novum Testamentum Graece* omit the final clause of Matthew 20:16 (*multi sunt enim vocati pauci autem electi*), citing a more reliable manuscript tradition.[35] While some modern editions may no longer include this second aphorism, it is clear that the status of the *electi* in Matthew 20:16 was a concern for the *Pearl*-poet and his contemporaries. The Parable of the Wedding Feast (Matthew 22: 1-14; Luke 14:16-24), recounted in *Cleanness*, provides

---

[33] Stephanie Black argues that the basic function of kai in Matthew is continuative, but she allows that other low level semantic values remain possible. Stephanie Black, Sentence Conjunctions in the Gospel of Mathew: Kai, De, Tote, Gar, Oun, and Asyndeton in Narrative Discourse, Library of New Testament Studies, Book 216 (NY: Bloomsbury T&T Clark, 2002), esp. 111-113. See also A.T. Robertson's treatment of Greek particles in Robertson, A Grammar of the Greek New Testament in the Light of Historical Research (NY: Hodder & Stoughton, 1914).

[34] This is Christ's third prediction of his crucifixion in each of the synoptic gospel accounts (Mark 10:32-34 and Luke 18:31-34). The first appears at Matthew 16:13-23, Mark 8:27-33, Luke 9:18-22, and John 6:67-71; the second occurs at Matthew 17:22-23, Mark 9:30-32, and Luke 9:43-45.

[35] I discovered this difference when investigating the conjunction (*For*), which translates the *enim* of the Latin Vulgate and is consistent with the Wycliffite Bible, the Douay-Rheims Bible, the Geneva Bible, and the King James Version of the Bible. The American Standard Version, the New International Version, and the Revised Standard Version follow Nestle-Aland's *Novum Testamentum Graece* in omitting the second aphorism.

a much bleaker lesson that "fele arn to called" (162) while the *Northern Homily Cycle* glosses the two aphoristic morals separately so that the Parable of the Vineyard seems to offer two distinct opportunities for instruction.[36]

573-576: Þus pore men her part ay pykez, / Þaȝ þay com late and lyttel wore, / And þaȝ her sweng wyth lyttel atslykez, / Þe merci of God is much þe more.

The final lines of this stanza offer one more explanation for the parable but this time through the words of the Pearl Maiden herself. The Maiden's explanation seems superfluous if not altogether redundant, but A.C. Spearing has argued that the Pearl-poet consistently offers explicit exegesis for the audience so that they might experience a similar process of symbolic interpretation that the Dreamer undergoes.[37] For Spearing, the poem presents a lesson of how to read medieval symbolism by interpreting its figural meaning for the reader as the Dreamer moves through his vision. Here, the Maiden makes more explicit the connection between the vineyard and the reward of everlasting bliss: the kingdom of Heaven is like a vineyard in that even poor men may recieve their part of the compensation though they arrive late and are little or unimportant. Even should they be spent (*atslykez*, OE æt + slican,) with little labor (sweng), they receive the lord's mercy. The repetition of *lyttel* in the Maiden's gloss is yet another reminder of the small pearl lost by the jeweler in Fitt I.

577-584: More haf I of joye and blysse hereinne, / Of ladyschyp gret and lyuez blom, / Þen alle þe wyȝen in þe worlde myȝt wynne/ By þe way of ryȝt to aske dome. / Wheþer welnygh now I con bygynne / In euentyde into þe vyne I come / Fyrst of my hyre my Lorde con mynne / I watz payed anon of al and sum.

The Maiden's explanation likens her queenship in Heaven to the rewards given to the laborers who entered so lately into the vineyard and looks ahead to the concatenated line of Fitt XII. In explaining her status in Heaven, the Maiden returns once more to the language of the parable. She explicitly identifies herself with the

---

[36] *Northern Homily Cycle*, 84/60-79 and 90/331-432.
[37] A.C. Spearing, "Symbolic and Dramatic Development in *Pearl*", *Modern Philology* 60, no. 1 (Aug. 1962): 12.

laborers hired at *euensonge* (529), recalling not only the group of laborers to enter the vineyard last and receive their payment first but also the youth of the Jeweler's child (483). The Maiden's interpretation of the parable as an explanation for her own position in Heaven deviates from the two dominant threads of interpreting the hours of the day within the parable as either the ages of man or the ages of the world, but D. W. Robertson has identified a precedent in the twelfth century exegete Bruno Astensis for the Maiden's explanation.[38]

The Maiden identifies the penny given to the workers of the vineyard as the eternal reward of heavenly bliss. In the *Northern Homily Cycle*, the penny of the parable is glossed in a way that directs attention toward the reward in Heaven awaiting those who have worked towards God's will on Earth: "That es the joye that lastis aye./ For a penye es rounde and hase nane ende/ Swa es the blisse where we sall lende/ If we be lymes of Hali Kirk/ And Goddes will therin will wirke."[39] For the Maiden, however, the penny represents a pure and absolute gift of grace that permits her more bliss and joy than could be won or earned through a judgment of *ryȝt*, which encompasses not merely legal justice but also moral right, desert, entitlement or prerogative, as well as duty and obligation.[40] The image of the penny evokes a series of iconic resonances, most notably the gift of the Host at Mass. At the center of the poem, though, the penny juxtaposed with the repetitions of the first who are last and the last who are first also recalls both the structure of the poem, where the last line echoes its first, and the central image of the pearl, so small and so round (5/6).

585-588: ȝet oþer þer werne þat toke more tom, / Þat swange and swat for long ȝore, / Þat ȝet of hyre noþynk þay nom, / Paraunter noȝt schal to-ȝere more.´

The Maiden recognizes that there are others who spent more time or did more labor in the vineyard. Her perspective here at the end of her explanation of the parable contributes one more layer of

---

[38] For an account of the traditional interpretation of the hours in the parable, see J. A. Burrow, *The Ages of Man: A Study in Medieval Writing and Thought* (Oxford: Clarendon Press, 1988), esp. 59-66. D. W. Robertson, "The 'Heresy' of the *Pearl*," *Modern Language Notes* 65, no. 3 (1959): 152-155.
[39] *Northern Homily Cycle*, 88/222-226.
[40] MED "right" definitions 3, 5, 4b, 6a, 7.

interpretation to the story in Matthew: namely, how the last workers in the vineyard would have experienced the householder's magnificence. The Maiden's recognizes that others labor more to receive what she was given "anon of al and sum" (584). The last workers in the vineyard may also have shared this recognition, and perhaps they, like the Maiden in these lines, would have shown sympathy for those who receive nothing for their additional work (*hyre*) and may not for a long time (*to-ȝere more*).

589-594: Then more I meled and sayde apert / ˜Me þynk þy tale vnresounable / Goddez ryȝt is redy and euermore rert, / Oþer holy wryt is bot a fable. / In sauter is sayd a verce ouerte / Þat spekez a poynt determynable

Both the parable and the Maiden's explanation present a difficult response to the Dreamer's questions posed at the end of Fitt VIII: "What more honour moȝte he acheue / þat hade endured in worlde stronge, / And lyued in penaunce hys lyuez longe...?" (475-477). While his response to the Maiden attests that by the middle of the poem the Dreamer is not quite prepared for the revelation of divine magnanimity, the reader has good cause to sympathize with him. Andrew and Waldron note, "[His] failure to understand derives partly from the difficulty of the concepts involved, but mainly from the intensity with which the Dreamer grieves for loss and desires its restoration. The immediate effectiveness of logical argument when set against the intensity of deep feeling is limited, even when the logic has divine authority."[41] As the Dreamer's response recalls the objection of the first laborers in the vineyard, the reader is reminded not merely of the language of the parable but also of the extreme weight of the Dreamer's earthly attachments and his desire to make more meaning out of them in the concluding stanza of Fitt X.

The Dreamer asserts that the Maiden's tale is unreasonable because it renders Holy Scripture a mere fable. While the parable is, in fact, a fable in the sense that it presents "a short fictitious narrative meant to convey a moral," it is clear that the Dreamer has the word's other denotations in mind.[42] In part, his response is a reaction to the structure and function of parables as forms of

---

[41] Andrew and Waldron, 35.
[42] MED "fable" definition 1b. Fable is also defined as "a false statement intended to deceive" and "an idle or foolish tale." MED definitions 2a and 3a.

narrative that rely on excesses, superluity, and slippage thereby requiring elaboration, explication, or glossing. Jesus explains that his parables are offered to listeners so that "seeing they may see, and not perceive; and hearing they may hear, and not understand" (Mark 4:12). Stephen Wailes notes the wide range of meanings that the Greek loan word *parabola* can take in its Scriptural associations – particularly through the Vulgate's use of *parabola* for a variety of figurative expressions, and in his treatment of medieval exemplarity, J. Allan Mitchell suggests that patristic and medieval readers would have understood parables as belonging to part of the tradition of classical rhetoric typified by Quintilian's *Institutio Oratoria*, which distinguished the parable from the paradigm. [43] Mitchell writes, "The success of paradigms typically depends on their simplicity – brevity, clarity, and plausibility. The parable, by contrast, differs in that it compares things whose likeness is 'far less obvious.' An enigmatic figure, the parable is more provocative than directly persuasive because it challenges an audience to think through the terms of the comparison being made rather than to apply it immediately in action without reflection."[44] This description seems appropriate to the Parable of the Laborers in the Vineyard, which proposes at its outset that the Kingdom of Heaven "is lyk on hyȝt / to a lorde þat hade a uyne" (501-502). What the terms of that comparison are seem, at least from the outset, to be as obscure and arbitrary as the householder's equation of the first workers with the last. Rather than the mysterious mechanisms of the parable, the Dreamer prefers the "verce ouerte" (593), that is clear, manifest, revealed.[45]

595-600: Þou quytez vchon as hys desserte, / Þou hyȝe Kyng ay pertermynable. / Now he þat stod þe long day stable,/ And þou to payment com hym byfore, / Þenne þe lasse in werke to take more able, / And euer þe lenger þe lasse þe more.

The Dreamer provides a quotation from the Psalter to demonstrate both his preference for overt Biblical authority and his insistence that Divine reward takes account of earthly works. His invocation recalls once more the inversion of the relationship

---

[43] Wailes, 3-4; J. Allen Mitchell. *Ethics and Exemplary Narrative in Chaucer and Gower* (D.S. Brewer: Cambridge, 2004), 118.
[44] Mitchell, 118.
[45] MED "overt" definition 1b and 1c.

between the Jeweler and his Pearl, who "cowþez neuer God nauþer plese ne pray, / Ne neuer nawþer Pater ne Crede – / And quen mad on þe fyrst day!" (484-486). Now, speaking to the lost child made queen, the Dreamer appeals to the very Psalter his child had never been old enough to read in order to reply to her Scriptural glossing. *Pearl*'s translation of is quite close to the Psalm: "God hath spoken once; twice have I heard this; that power belongeth unto God. / And unto thee, O Lord, belongeth mercy; for thou renderest to every man according to his work" [*semel locutus est Deus duo haec audivi quia potestas Dei et tibi Domine misericordia quia tu redes unicuique iuxta opera sua*] (Psalm 62:11-12 / V Psalm 61:12-13).

The Dreamer's opening, "Then more I meled and sayde apert" (589), suggests a tension in his relationshi to both the Maiden and her revealed authority over Scriptural interpretation. On the one hand, his preference for clear and open speech is reflected in his quotation of the Psalter and the claim that his speech in these final lines is plain, uncovered, overt, frank, or open.[46] On the other hand, closer attention to the language of his speech reveals the kind of quasi-legal discourse that the househoder had invoked when defending his reward to the laborers in the vineyard. Spencer has been the most recent scholar to draw close attention to the difficulties presented by "pertermynable" (596), a word that seems only to survive in this one iteration.[47] Gordon's edition of the poem amends the word to *pretermynable* and suggests that it could be an abbreviation for *praeterminabilis*. His note explains, "it is usually interpreted as 'pre-ordaining,' and assumed to represent a scholastic Latin *praeterminibalis*, rendering Greek προοριζειν, the usual word in the New Testament for 'pre-ordain.'"[48] Andrew and Waldron follow P.M. Kean's suggestion that *per* is an intensifying prefix and declare that the emendation to *pretermynable* is unnecessary and does not correspond to the meaning of the Psalm text.[49] Spencer reads the latinate vocabulary of the Dreamer's response at the end of Fitt X – "ryȝt", "determynable", "quytez", and "pertermynable" – as

---

[46] MED "apert" definitions 1a, 2, 3a, 3b, and 4a.
[47] H. Leith Spencer, "*Pearl*: 'God's Law' and 'Man's Law,'" *Review of English Studies* 59, no. 240 (2008): 317-341.
[48] E.V. Gordon, ed., *Pearl* (Oxford: The Clarendon Press, 1953), 65-66.
[49] M.P. Kean, *The Pearl: An Interpretation* (London: Routledge and Kegan Paul, 1967), 191; Andrew and Waldron, note to line 596, pg. 81.

bombastic and an attempt to assert clerkly authority.⁵⁰ From the combination of the approximately synonymous verbs in line 589 to the precise terminology with which he frames his response, the Dreamer seems to stage one final attempt to assert the authority of his experience and learning over the Maiden. In so doing, he turns to a Latinate vocabulary to argue for a reward that accounts for earthly works. It is an appeal that recalls both the workers of the parable and the Maiden's statement that she enjoys more bliss than any might win "By þe way of ryȝt to aske dome" (580).

The Dreamer's response, especially his final insistence that those who worked for the shortest time seemed to earn more in proportion than those who worked longer, finds an analogue in an anonymous lyric in Harley MS. 2253. The lyric paraphrases the parable in four twelve-line stanzas before offering a final 12-line gloss:

> Þis world me wurcheþ wo;
> rooles ase þe roo,
>   y sike for vnsete,
> ant mourne ase men doþ mo
> for doute of foule fo,
>   hou y my sunne may bete.
> Þis mon þat Matheu ȝef
> A peny þat was so bref,
>   Þis frely folk vnfete,
> ȝet he ȝyrnden more,
> ant saide he come wel ȝore,
>   ant gonne is loue forlete.⁵¹

The Harleian narrator's grief for the man who worked more is analogous to the *Pearl* Dreamer's desire for a payment that "quytez vchon as hys desserte" (595). But as the Maiden shows, the Parable of the Laborers in the Vineyard reveals that the grace of God promises so much more.

---

⁵⁰ Spencer, 323.
⁵¹ G.L. Brook, ed., *The Harley Lyrics: The Middle English Lyrics of MS. Harley 2253* (Manchester: Manchester University Press, 1948), 43/49-60. A more recent edition and translation is available in Susanna Greer Fein, ed., *The Complete Harley 2253 Manuscript*, Vol 2, Translated by Fein, David Raybin, and Jan Ziolkowski, TEAMS Middle English Texts Series (Kalamazoo, MI: Medieval Institute, 2014).

Travis Neel is a PhD Candidate in the Department of English at The Ohio State University. He is currently writing a dissertation entitled "Forms and Figures of Friendship in the Chaucer Tradition."

XI

Enough (Section XI)

Monika Otter

The linking word "enough" occupies a pivotal place in the structure of *Pearl*, in the thematic strand of linking words that denote quantities, measures, deadlines ("more and more," "date" "never the less"). It marks the juncture between desire and copious fulfillment, between want and surplus, but, perhaps most crucially, between the Dreamer's quantitative, earthly reasoning and the Pearl's transcendent vision of limitless abundance.

Enough is semantically ambivalent to the point of paradox. In *Pearl*, the word marks several paradoxes, not easy to pry apart since they are all interconnected. At the most fundamental thematic level, Sandra Pierson Prior notes that the word plays up the ambiguous relationship between the Dreamer's necessary desire for heaven and his equally necessary resignation to his earthly loss, his contentment (*paye*) with what he can have here: a tension that is crucial to the poem's ethos, indeed arguably its central conflict.[1]

Secondly, Section XI takes advantage of the built-in semantic complexity of the word *enough*. It sits on the dividing line between "too little" and "too much," want and excess, a lack to be remedied and a generous excess, inopia and copia; it remedies a lack and piles on overabundant riches, fills and overfills a gap. There is a world of difference between worrying whether there is "enough to go around," "enough to make ends meet" (as in the Dreamer's anxious questions) and a generous invitation to a plentiful feast, where there is "enough for everybody," "enough and to spare," which is what Pearl seems to have in mind.

In Middle English usage, this contrast between superfluity and mere adequacy seems particularly evident, because the use of *enough* meaning "abundant"/"abundantly" is more amply represented than

---

[1] Sandra Pierson Prior, *The Pearl Poet Revisited* (New York: Twayne, 1994), 38.

in other historical periods. In the Oxford English Dictionary (OED), with its longer diachronic reach, that semantic paradox is muted. In the Middle English Dictionary (MED) the entire entry is structured around it –justly, given the wealth of citations:

> *inough,* n: a. Abundance; a great deal; b. a sufficiency, enough.
> *inough,* adj.: a. Plentiful, generous, abundant, great, plenty of. . . .; b. sufficient, adequate, satisfactory.
> *inough,* adv. a. very much, extremely, a great deal; b. enough, sufficiently.[2]

Of course, *Pearl* is one of the sources mined for citations, and occurrences of the word from Section XI are evenly sprinkled across the abundant/adequate divide–a little arbitrarily, for the distinction is not always clear, and some instances might fit equally well under "abundant" and "adequate."

This uncertainty points to another feature of *enough* as a quantifier: it is not simply the middle point of a sliding scale, halfway between "too little" and "too much"; it is not simply Goldilock's "just right." It partakes of both sides, the want and the excess. It takes on the coloring, the connotations of one or the other, or both.[3] It brings together, glancingly and uncertainly, two measurements that are not on the same linear scale. It functions a bit like a "Kippbild," those squinting ("multistable") images such as the celebrated rabbit/duck or "My Wife/My Mother-in-Law," that can be seen as one integrated image or another, but not both simultaneously.[4]

---

[2] *The Electronic Middle English Dictionary*, Middle English Compendium (MEC), University of Michigan. Last updated 24 April 2013. <http://www.quod.lib.umich.edu>. Accessed November 20, 2014. *The Oxford English Dictionary Online*, Oxford University Press, updated Sept. 2014. <http://www.oed.com>. Accessed November 20, 2014.

[3] See my essay "Sufficientia: A Horatian Topos and the Boundaries of the Self in Three Twelfth-Century Poems," *Anglo-Norman Studies* 35 (2012): 247; and William J. Asbell, Jr., "The Philosophical Background of Sufficientia in Boethius's Consolation, Book 3," in *New Directions in Boethian Studies*, ed. Noel Howard Kaylor, Jr., and Philip Edward Phillips, Studies in Medieval Culture 45 (Kalamazoo: Medieval Institute, 2007), 3-16.

[4] I am grateful to Manuele Gragnolati for pointing out the Kippbild connection. See the website of the Multistable Images project at the Institute of Cultural Inquiry, Berlin (<https://www.ici-berlin.org/past-core-

Illuminating recent discussions of "enoughness" and "sufficiency" can be found in environmental studies, where they relate to the concept of sustainability. Sarah Darby lays out a working definition:

> Sufficiency can be broadly defined in two ways: one is qualitative, implying wealth and plenty; sufficiency means that a purpose is achieved, a need is satisfied, and some sort of optimal state has been reached: 'enough is as good as a feast'. By implication, 'enough' is something to be celebrated and relished. It is subjective in nature and so is normally used in relation to an individual....
>
> The second type of definition is quantitative, implying a clear *threshold* of acceptability: do we have enough food for the day? Is the rainfall this spring sufficient to allow the crops to grow to harvest? .... Is 450 ppm of carbon dioxide in the atmosphere sufficiently low to prevent runaway global warming from occurring? Quantitative sufficiency thus implies 'floors' (enough for a necessary purpose) and 'ceilings' (too much for safety or welfare, in the short or long term). It is more objective in nature, using absolute points of reference.[5]

But even though Darby stresses a "qualitative" component to *enough*ness, and even while the environmentalists stress the complexity of the concept, their considerations still remain firmly on a quantitative plane. In *The Logic of Sufficiency*, Thomas Princen suggests that sufficiency is a matter of "management," or finding an ideal quantity that would do justice to a number of competing claims, from environmental sustainability to provision of goods and services and a level that is not merely adequate or "second best" but truly satisfactory. He speaks of managing, maximizing, planning,

---

projects/multistable-figures-and-complementarity/>); and E. H. Gombrich, *Art and Illusion: A Study in the Psychology of Pictorial Representation,* Bollingen Series XXXV.5, 11th ed. (Princeton: Princeton University Press, 2002), 5.

[5] Sarah Darby, "Enough is as Good as a Feast–Sufficiency as Policy," *Proceedings, European Council for an Energy-Efficient Environment, Summer Study, 4-9 June 2007.* 111. <http://www.eceee.org/library/conference_proceedings/eceee_Summer_Studies/2007/Panel_1/1.255/paper>). See also Thomas Princen, *The Logic of Sufficiency* (Cambridge: MIT Press, 2005), 6-10.

efficiency[6] – all terms concerned with the finding of an optimal *quantity*.

Pearl, by contrast, challenges her father and her readers to think beyond a quantitative, measured, finite world; in fact, she seems oblivious to the fundamental misunderstanding between her and her father, who struggles to wrap his finite mind around the infinite enoughness that defines heaven. This disagreement, in turn, strains the poet's power of expression, his *copia dicendi*, since he, too, has only the language of finite quantities to express it; he can, strictly speaking, represent only the Dreamer's part of the dialogue and must fall short of representing Pearl's. His strategy is, first, to exploit the duality of a quantitative *enough* that the MED illustrates so plentifully, playing up abundance against fear of shortfall; and, secondly, paradoxically, by reinscribing a finite idea, of commensurateness and proportionality, in this section and the next, with the linking phrase "by ry3te," just as we thought we had left the ideas of justice and the measurements of the finite world behind.[7]

Stanza li (lines 601-612) must, by the rules of this poetic game, take up the last line of the previous segment. So we begin by reprising the Section X idea of "more or less," and the Dreamer's concerns about commensurability. He conceives of fair pay as a proportional recompense directly predicated on a measured length of working time–or, expanded metaphorically, of lifetime: the concern is that a child who died young has not "labored in the vineyard" long enough to merit the same reward as someone who has struggled through a full life span. The "more and lasse," "lyttel oþer much" (line 604), is instantly negated by pointing out that we are now talking about another realm altogether, "Godez ryche" (line 601). The dichotomy

---

[6] Princen, *Logic of Sufficiency*, 18.

[7] The edition I am using primarily is "Pearl," in *The Poems of the Pearl Manuscript*, eds Malcolm Andrew and Ronald Waldron, 5th ed. (Exeter: University of Exeter Press, 2007), 53-110. I am also consulting "Pearl," in *Middle English Literature*, eds. Charles W. Dunn and Edward T. Byrnes (New York: Harcourt Brace Jovanovich, 1973), 339-75; and to a lesser extent A. C. Cawley and J. J. Anderson, ed., *Pearl, Cleanness, Patience, Sir Gawain and the Green Knight* (London: Everyman, 1978). I am retaining, for convenience, Dunn and Byrnes's continuous numbering of the stanzas throughout the poem (so that Section XI comprises Stanzas li-lv); but I am also giving the line numbers for each stanza, since Andrew and Waldron, as well as many other editions, do not have this feature.

is softened and bridged by two devices: first, an appeal to human categories of generosity (*fraunchyse, large*) as opposed to stinginess. Bliss is not withheld ("reparde," line 611); the *cheuentayn* is "no chyche" (line 606), and perhaps the folksy character of that word, with its onomatopeic-sounding repeated consonant clusters, reinforces how human the concept of "stinginess" is. Secondly, the stanza begins a chain of water images that continues throughout the section. Water is an obvious and immediately visualizable metaphor for overflowing plenty, and also, in its uncountable fluidity, an antidote to the Dreamer's urge towards the countable and discrete (this many pennies for this many hours of work). The stanza ends by introducing the refrain of the last line, more stable in Section XI, as has been noted, than it is in most of the sections.[8] Where other segments delight in greater or smaller variations of the final line, here the refrain "For þe grace of God is gret inoghe" is varied only once in the five stanzas.

Stanza lii (lines 613-24). Exceptionally, the first line of this stanza does not reprise the key word. Whether that is a deliberate variation of the pattern is hard to say, but other instances of such violations (such as the supernumerary stanza in the "never the less" segment, XV) are more overtly meaningful. The word "now," a similar sound but no doubt a weaker echo than the word "enough" would be, takes on the task of concatenating the stanzas. Whether that maneuver is meant to carry a punning meaning analogous to the supernumerary "never the less" stanza is not clear.[9] But it puts much emphasis on the word *now*, as a turn to a different sort of reasoning. Pearl now takes on her father's argument point by point, like a professional debater ("þou motez," "þou sayz"), and accuses him of intentionally confusing ("mate," line 613) the issue.[10] As the temporal nature of "now" perhaps signals, we are also back to a finite mode of reckoning: Pearl begins by restating her father's question (or implied argument) about [?] whether Pearl's pay has been excessive: "þat I my peny haf wrang tan here," since she came "to late" (lines 614-15). The first line of her rebuttal (617) leaves us momentarily in a

---

[8] Prior, 38.
[9] Andrew and Waldron, note to lines 613-14.
[10] Gloss in Dunn and Byrnes; alternatively, "defeat" (as in "check-mate") or "shame" (as Andrew and Waldron gloss it). All are supported by clear instances in the MED, s.v. *maten.*

semantic suspension, before we can decide whether the *bourne* she asks about is the word for "man" (s.v. *bern* in the MED), or for "water course, stream" (s.v. *bourn* in the MED), reminding us of the water theme, before the ambiguity is resolved in the next line: we are talking about a hypothetical man, "have you ever met a man who...." (The French-derived *bourn* = "boundary" is, according to the OED, not attested until the sixteenth century, but since the river in *Pearl*'s landscape *is* an absolute boundary, one would not be far off if one heard that meaning vibrating in the background also.) Temporal terms abound in this stanza (*abate* [remain, last], *sumtyme, ofte, alder*), further reinforcing the finite, measured way of thinking–only to reassert the superabundance of grace in the refrain of the final line.

Stanza liii (lines 625-36). Surprisingly, the next stanza turns the *enough* back to a meaning of mere adequacy or sufficiency, rather than abundance: "But innoghe of grace hatz innocent," the innocent (who died in infancy) has "enough grace." This inaugurates the argument that continues into Section XII: everyone deserves full "pay," and pay is not proportional to working time; is a free gift of abundant grace rather than the claiming of a right acquired by having put in "enough" time. Nonetheless the Innocent deserve it more, "by right." In parallel with this return to proportionality and relative measures, the semantic element of finite time is again strongly asserted in this stanza: "as sone as," "by lyne" (in due course, in order, line 626); end of day and end of life: the day already "carries dark within it" ("with derk endente" line 629); death descending (line 630). As in the previous section, especially stanza xlviii, Pearl stresses the vineyard owner's right to do what he wants with his money ("why schulde he not...," line 634). Her emphatic "yis" in line 635 signals a surprising turn of argument: she goes so far as to assert that the last-arrived should be paid first–"for þe grace of God is gret innoghe" for such an apparent reversal of due process. This twist in the argument is deliberately counter-intuitive. It would have been relatively easy to grasp a simple negation of proportionality, an absence of finite quantities, as the crucial feature that sets heaven apart from earth. But, in true Pseudo-Dionysian fashion, Pearl proceeds to unsettle and deconstruct the understanding we thought we had arrived at. Pseudo-Dionysius, whose thought, whether directly or indirectly, is a strong presence in the poem, insists on saying *and* unsaying, on asserting *and* negating, on radically disrupting earthly ideas of hierarchy even as he constructs the most hierarchical heaven imaginable (in his *Celestial Hierarchy*). Pearl has already taken her father through this paradoxical mode of reasoning in Section VIII: all the elect are queens in heaven, but that does not make them "supplantorez" of *the* Queen of Cortaysye (line 440). Here in Section XI she repeats the process with regard to quantity, enoughness, and abundance, with regard to grace and right. Heaven is the realm in which, incomprehensibly and ineffably for us, grace is limitless, but justice, merit, "right" and other quantifiable notions of equability, are equally contained in it, without contradiction.

Stanza liv (lines 637-48). The "innoghe" that heads up this stanza is semantically relatively weak, simply asserting that the matter is sufficiently well known. What we and the Dreamer are reminded of is the genesis of the conceptual separation in the preceding stanza: like so much else, it is a result of the Fall, in which Adam forfeited "blysse parfyt" (line 638). We all were repaid for that decision: "al wer we dampned for that mete." While all editors gloss *mete* as "food" (i.e., Adam eating the apple), the homophones meaning "boundary," "suitable, fitting," "appropriately" or "copiously" (MED) also resonate in that rhyme word, and all are relevant to the context. (Andrew and Waldron's index lists all three, with interesting citations from the other Nero A.x poems: so all meanings were clearly available to this particular audience and writer.) The only thing that is limitless or copious here is the eternity of the punishment ("withoute respyt," line 644). Line 645 emphatically turns this idea around with the repeated "bot": it is the conjunction "but," but also the near-homophonic and homographic *bote*, "remedy" (MED). The remedy is liquid and abundant, water and blood. Its fluidity is perhaps also depicted in the especially rich concatenation of sound correspondences of this line: *ryche ran rode roghe* form not only a four-member alliterative chain, but what Gerard Manly Hopkins would have termed a "vowelling off"; the only major non-alliterating word in the line, "blod," rhymes with "rode," and even the function words *on* and *so* are tied in phonetically (both have the /ɔ/ vowel that dominates in this line, and *ran* and *on* are near-rhymes). This is the only stanza in which the refrain is varied, with the mildly surprising verb *wex*: if God's grace is abundant and "gret inoghe," how can it *grow*?[11] But the verb is also

---

[11] Prior, 38.

entirely appropriate here. It captures the copious shedding of liquid in the previous lines (*waxen* in the sense of welling forth). More importantly, it marks a precise point in time (assisted by *firste* in line 638 and *as-tyt* in line 645). The redemption, which made abundant grace available, happened at a precise historical moment, one that crucially interrupted the timeline from Creation to Doomsday, creating an all-important before-and-after; and it also disrupts eternity, here in the form of shutting down the eternity of "helle hete" referred to in lines 643-44.

Stanza lv (lines 649-60). The first line (649) confirms our reading of *wex* in line 648, as a voluminous pouring forth: "innoghe þer wax out of þat welle/ Blod and water." Even the wound is described as "brode" (line 650) participating in the semantic thread of copiousness. The imagery continues to rely on water and blood—not new or unique to this section, and unsurprising in itself. But the combination and condensation of the images is bold and at times startling. The stanza economically condenses an image of the crucifixion with the harrowing of hell. Even more economical is the formulation in line 654: the water, equated with baptism, "follows" the spear (John 19:34). A causal connection is indicated, albeit an abbreviated one that omits several logical steps: *because* Christ's body was pierced, baptism became possible. (If one is not already familiar with the theology, one will ask, "but how does one cause the other?", and the explanation would involve a number of intermediary steps between cause and—ultimate—effect, here elided.) But we are also invited to picture not so much the spear being thrust into Christ's side, but its being withdrawn, so that blood and water "folʒe" ("follow"–and a near-homophone of "flow"). The visual effect is striking (we can certainly visualize the stabbing motion, but who has ever paused to imagine the spear being pulled back?), and in its unusualness manages to condense a whole string of theological reasoning into less than two lines. The idea of a withdrawal is taken up in line 658: salvation consists of Christ *withdrawing* any obstacles between us and bliss. ("now ther is noght.... bytwene uus and blysse bot that he wythdrough"). The sudden reversal of the semantics of copiousness is a little startling. It may remind us of the first stanza of Section XI, were God "laues his giftes" (607) and does *not* withhold ("reparde," line 611). Where grace has so far been figured as a limitless pouring forth and piling on, it is suddenly re-thought as a clearing of space, an emptiness that is also an opening for new pourings-forth (water and blood follow the withdrawn spear): equally generous but visually very different.

While this final stanza in one way interrupts the continuity of thought from Section XI's *enough* to Section XII's *by ryghte*, it also acts as a pivot between them. The crucifixion/harrowing of hell image we are left with at the end of Section XI is both the wellspring (literally) and the logical resolution of the Pseudo-Dionysian paradox the section sets up, to be continued in Section XII. Readers are challenged, first, to think beyond their own quantitative, literal, "just" but ungenerous conception of reward and punishment: the reign of God is a space of copiousness, where stingy calculations are irrelevant. This opposition, however, does not immediately create a paradox, an ineffability, or even a mental discomfort. It is not difficult, or unpleasing, to think that quantitative thinking is simply negated in heaven. In fact, first-time readers (such as college students) who have made only this first step often find it hard to account for the Dreamer's difficulty with that notion, and his opposition to it comes across as small-minded. Pearl, indeed, sets us up to think so, in Section V, where she chides him for being an "unkind jeweler." But of course his discomfort is deeper than that. He is sensing, and the poem is naming, a genuine disjuncture between a finite world of measurements and time, and a qualitatively different realm that is *not* merely a negation of our world, but both its negation and its fulfillment. Pearl's apparent inability, or indifference, to fully grasp what troubles her father underscores the fundamental divide between their ways of thinking. The poem cannot fully name this disjuncture, or the nature of that other world, and therefore resorts to a different sort of bafflement. Just as we thought we had grasped the limitlessness of heaven, the poem reinscribes the notion of proportional justice, but–it hints–in a different and unfathomable way.

Monika Otter teaches medieval literature and translation studies at Dartmouth College. She has written on medieval historiography, hagiography, romance, and medieval Latin poetry.

FITT XII: RYGHT

Kay Miller

§1. Grace innogh the mon may have
That synnes then new yif him repente
Bot wyth sorw and syt he mot hit craue
And byde the payne therto is bent. [661-64]

§1.1 'mon may'

While it may seem trite to comment on such an apparently pragmatic instance of alliteration, the effect here is to draw focus from the concatenating phrase to the central theme of fitt XII: the conditional nature of grace's attainability for any living person.

The auxiliary 'may' introduces a conditional mood that predominates in this fitt, as seen in ll. 669 'the gyltyf may ...'; 694 'Thou may hit wynne ...'; and 703 '... thou may be innome'. The uncertainty of the sinner's salvation is contrasted to the future and present grammatical certainties of the righteous, who 'schal se [God's] face', and above all, the innocent, who 'is ay saf by ryght'.

From the twelfth century, grammar had gained a theological significance as a means of representing and understanding God, his being and his actions.[1] Modistic queries about ordained and potential actions of God gained particular significance in the wake of the condemnation 1277, Bishop Tempier's measure to restrict the discussion of 'dangerous' Aristotelian ideas at the University of Paris. Article 147 of the condemned theses proposed that 'the absolutely impossible cannot be done by God.'[2]

The condemnation of this article provoked more potentially heretical speculation, since if God is able to do the impossible, if he

---

[1] E. J. Ashworth, "Review of *The Mirror of Grammar: Theology, Philosophy and the 'Modistae'* by LG Kelly" *Speculum* 80 No.2 (2005): 603.

[2] Edward Grant, "The Condemnation of 1277, God's Absolute Power, and Physical Thought in the Late Middle Ages", *The Nature of Natural Philosophy in the Late Middle Age*s (Washington: CUA Press, 2010), 53-4.

has *potentia absoluta* (short of "logical contradiction"[3]) then no divine promise is certain to be kept. As Thomas of Buckingham ventured, 'the basic tenets of faith might be mere contingencies.'[4]

Fitt XII of *Pearl* engages in a negotiation between a philosophical climate of skeptical inquiry, and the 'mystical certainty'[5] that, in the fourteenth century, acted as a counterweight to the destabilising effects of rationalism. Across the fitt, as I hope to show, Pearl constructs an argument that aims to reconcile, and ultimately subjugate, reason to revelation, though without ever making any guarantees concerning individual salvation.

§1.2 'thenne new'

In fitt XII Pearl refines her previous argument, and discusses not just sinners-by-default – that is, all mankind - but the particular and individualised post-baptismal sinner. The uncertain nature of God's grace is shown to hang on humanity's imperfection – one salvation, through baptism, evidently is not enough for us. Structurally, this fitt begins on an argumentative backlash, as if in imitation of the subject's own return to sin. It might be argued that Pearl's guardedly provisional and legalistic language in this fitt (see §10.1) is founded on the instability of the human nature, but her portrayal of the forces of judgement is not designed to instil confidence - even if the sinner repents, Pearl allows only that he *may* have grace.

§1.3 'yif him repente'

Etymologically, a tautologous combination of the Latin *re* (again) and *paenitere* (to regret or cause to regret),[6] to repent essentially means to re-regret. The buried implication in this word of swimming against the tide, of beginning at a disadvantage, reinforces the backtracking movement suggested by the sinner's doubly undermined (by himself and Adam) grace.

---

[3] Grant, "The Condemnation of 1277", 53.
[4] John M Bowers, "*Patience* and the Ideal of the Mixed Life." *Texas Studies in Literature and Language* 28 (1986): 4
[5] David Knowles in Bowers, "*Patience* and the Ideal", 4.
[6] "repent, v.". OED Online. June 2014. Oxford University Press. <http://www.oed.com/> (accessed July 30, 2014).

Coinciding with the conditional mood of Pearl's speech, an eternally prior loss of security is established, although repentance is also forward-looking, as an 'undertaking to reform in future.'[7]

The temporal and unfinished nature of the sinner manifests as a perpetual entrapment in a state of pain. *Paenitere* has its root in *poena* (penalty, punishment, 'unpleasant consequence'),[8] which Pearl depicts as a necessary and expiatory aspect of repentance – 'the payne therto is bent', l. 664 - in line with scholastic views.[9] That said, pain is not by necessity productive. Harm done by an individual is inevitably re-felt in the form of repentance, damnation, or in the course of living, as expressed by Augustine: 'every disorder of the soul is its own punishment.'[10] The only certainty presented is that the sinner will be caught up in the repercussions of sin.

This idea of recursive sin and pain can also pertain to the jeweler's grief as a self-perpetuating moral and emotional disorder.

§1.4 'Bot ... hit'

Syntactically, there is some ambiguity as to whether the sinner is supposed to crave grace or repentance. The former might seem likely if one considers that 'sorw and syt' and craving are synonymous with sincere repentance, although in that case, 'and' would seem a more appropriate conjunction than 'but'.

On the other hand, Pearl's apparent understanding of repentance as expiatory belongs to a scholastic outlook whereby grace is the 'efficient cause' of contrition.[11] Repentance, then, is a gift (a 'benignity') from God: '*ignorams quoniam benignitas Dei ad paenitentiam te adducit*'.[12] By this logic, the sinner must first have grace in order to get grace through repentance. If it is repentance itself that the sinner must crave, this gives the 'but' more purpose,

---

[7] ibid.
[8] "poena, n.". OED Online. September 2014. Oxford University Press. <http://www.oed.com> (accessed December 05, 2014).
[9] Renn Dickson Hampden, *The Scholastic Philosophy considered in relation to Christian Theology* (London: Simpkin, Marshall and Co.,1848) 248.
[10] Augustine, trans. F.J. Sheed, *Confessions* (Indianapolis/Cambridge: Hackett Publishing Company, 2007) I.xii.19
[11] Thomas Aquinas, *Summa Theologiae*. <http://dhspriory.org/thomas/english/QDdeVer28.htm> (accessed December 4, 2014). I-II.28.viii, s.c.4.
[12] Romans 2:4 (Latin Vulgate) in *Douay Rheims Bible Online*. <http://www.drbo.org> (accessed July 30, 2014).

marking 'sorrow and grief'[13] as a further condition attached to the proviso 'yif him repente', rather than a continuation of it.

This exacting process indicates a key proposition of this fitt: that grace is only attainable for those to whom God grants it. Even when earned by sorrow, grief and pain, it can only be given as a favour.

§1.5 'sorw and syt'

This contemporary hendiadystic phrase means 'to lament, to express regret or anger...vexation or moral evil'. It is also recognised as a term for labour pains.[14] If this sense is implied alongside the more straightforward reading of sorrow and grief then it emphasises the productive nature of repentance, or of craving repentance, as labour through which salvation may be delivered.

To extend the metaphor, the saving grace potentially obtained through sorrow is figuratively a child. This has an obvious significance as a reference to Christ as an infant messiah; the effecting of salvation through Christ's innocence will be the fitt's climactic movement. The image also pertains to Pearl and others like her who died in infancy and a state of innocence; Pearl herself is cast as a possible agent of salvation for the jeweler (see §2.2).

§1.6 'craue'

According to the OED, crave has a possible root in the Germanic *kraft*, to force or extract, 'to demand ... with authority or by right'. In l. 663 crave is used in the sense, 'to earnestly beg, as a gift or favour'.[15] The Germanic root suggests a relevant ambiguity between rights and favours; whether the guilty have any rights in this passage has been debated with reference to ll. 701-8 (see §10.2).

§2. Bot resoun of ryght that can noght raue
Saues evermore the innossent.
Hit is a dom that never God gave,
That euer the gyltles schulde be shente. [665-68]

---

[13] J. J. Anderson, *Sir Gawain and the Green Knight, Pearl, Cleanness, Patience* (London: Everyman,1996) 26.
[14] "sorw and sytr". MED. April 2013. University of Michigan. http://quod.lib.umich.edu/m/med (accessed July 30 2014).
[15] "crave, v.". OED Online. (accessed 30 July, 2014).

§2.1 'Bot'

In fitt XII the word 'but' occurs four times: ll. 663, 671, 695 and 705. Here, in anaphoric parallel with the instance in l. 663, the word introduces a new strand to Pearl's argument, contrasting the relations to grace of the 'gyltyf' and of the 'gyltles'.

The innocent enjoy a fundamentally different status to the guilty, since their right to safety is already established. The comparison drawn here is reasonable insofar as the states of guilt and guiltlessness are contrasted in this fitt, but it also forces attention to the source of their difference. It has been established in fitts X and XI that to live is more or less by necessity to be guilty, and that Pearl, the embodiment of innocence, is thus because she died young. This is confirmed in l. 700, which applies specifically to the living: 'non lyvyande to the is justyfyet'. The contrast is not between those who acted justly and those who did wrong, but between those who did and did not have an opportunity to sin. In that sense, it is not a fair comparison. Pearl's repetition of the conjunction 'but' gives a sense of superfluity to the second sub-clause: the innocent are a class of their own.

§2.2 'resoun'

Translators have interpreted 'resoun' either as an abstract concept – Osgood's 'fair consideration,' Vantuono's 'cause of justice' – or else as 'Resoun', 'a quasi-personification of justice', as described by Andrew and Waldon.[16] The former approach is consistent with the fitt's legalistic tone (see §10.2) stressing as it does the process of 'coming to a correct decision', guided by 'rectitude of judgement'.[17] To favour the personified Reason is, as a reader, to take this discriminatory faculty away from the human thinker, and to set it up as a semi-divine authority - Andrew and Waldon even take 'resoun' to refer to directly to God.[18] In fact, Reason has long standing as a literary personage in her or his own right.

To personify 'resoun' seems appropriate, in part simply because its grammatical status as the subject of the clause confers the action (saving) not on a thinker but on the faculty. Furthermore,

---

[16] William Vantuono, *The Pearl Poems: An Omnibus Edition, Volume 1* (New York: Garland, 1984), 256.

[17] H. L. Spencer, "God's Law and Man's Law", *Review of English Studies* 59 (2008): 331.

[18] Vantuono, *The Pearl Poems: An Omnibus Edition, Volume 1*, 256.

Reason is a character that an informed reader might well expect to see in a dream-poem, since the reason-figure has a generic heritage extending back to Lady Philosophy in Boethius's *Consolatione*, and beyond that to Augustine's *Soliloquia*.[19]

The female Reason in Jean de Meun's portion of the *Roman de la Rose* is a particularly likely model for Pearl's Reason; *The Roman de la Rose* has an evident influence on *Pearl*, and de Meun's Reason is is used as a prototype for Pearl herself:

> She seemed like a person of high estate. By her appearance and her face it would seem that she was made in Paradise, for Nature would not have known how to make a work of such regularity. Know, if the letter does not lie, that God made her personally in his likeness and in his image, and gave her such advantage that she has the power and the lordship to keep man from folly, provided he be such that he believe her.[20]

This description is echoed in *Pearl*, fitt 13:

> Quo formed the thy fayre fygure?
> That wroght thy wede, he was ful wys.
> Thy beauté com never of nature... [747-49]

While I will discuss the implications of this allusion in the description of Pearl shortly, I will first pursue the nature of the reason-figure, and the purpose it could serve in Pearl's argument. Primarily, Reason is a figure in God's image, but made for the edification of humanity – de Meun draws on the Biblical creation of mankind (Gen. 1:26-28) in his description of her.[21] Reason as he appears in Piers Plowman (where he is male) 'shal rule [the king's] reaume and rede [him] the best.'[22] In the *Roman de la Rose*, taking after Lady Philosophy, she shows an enlightened understanding of

---

[19] Lynch, *The High Medieval Dream Vision: Poetry, Philosophy and Literary Form*, 68.

[20] Charles Dahlberg ed., *The Romance of the Rose* (Hanover and London: the University Press of New England, 1971), 73

[21] Dahlberg, *The Romance of the Rose*, 368.

[22] William Langland, *Piers Plowman*, ed. Derek Pearsall (Exeter: University of Exeter Press, 2008) 4.9.

the Wheel of Fortune and its inconstancy, and of the workings of Nature.[23]

In short, the reason-figure has 'lordship' and understanding of the ways of the mortal world, and, equipt with this understanding, tends to despise mortal preoccupations. Augustine's *Ratio*, a prototypical reason-figure insofar as it remains an abstraction, urges him to 'flee the senses. The body is a trap.'[24] A fourteenth-century vision of *Ratio* is portrayed in the poem *Parvule, cur ploras*, where she oversees man's humiliating journey through his ages, from infancy to death.[25] The poem is presented on a Wheel of Life, with Christ pictured at the centre; any implication of spiritual salvation is left to that image, and goes unmentioned by *Ratio*.

This type of reason-figure is used by Pearl to represent the strict concept of justice that automatically exempts the innocent from danger. If we continue to take prompt post-baptismal death as a condition of innocence, then Reason is well-placed to know that the innocent do not belong to the realm of mortality, and should not incur its penalties.

Salvation for the living is not in Reason's purview. However there are, debatably, two further guiding figures in this fitt, Wisdom (see §8.1) and Christ, who help Pearl to explain that concept.

As noted earlier, Pearl is also a variant of the reason-figure. She conforms to the description Lynch gives in her overview of this trope in her 'attempts to inform and cure [the dreamer's] diseased imagination' and in helping to lead him to a 'revelation' that will foster 'moral and psychic wholeness.'[26] She departs from type, however, in that her role is more mystical than philosophical. Reason is only the first rung of her argument; she is aiming for the ineffable.

Josephine Bloomfield points out that Pearl can be seen in terms of Pseudo-Dionysius's conception of hierarchy, whereby God's truth is relayed through guiding figures possessed of superior understanding.[27] Pearl herself makes use of a Dionysian hierarchy of intermediaries in this fitt in order to move her argument towards

---

[23] Dahlberg, *The Romance of the Rose*, 91-137.
[24] Lynch, *The High Medieval Dream Vision: Poetry, Philosophy and Literary Form*, 53.
[25] Mary Dove, *The Perfect Age of Man's Life* (Cambridge: CUP, 1986),96.
[26] Lynch, *The High Medieval Dream Vision*, 68-69.
[27] Josephine Bloomfield, "Stumbling towards God's Light", 394-95.

a moment of revelation. This series of surrogates begins with Reason and ascends to Christ.

§2.3 'ryght'

As Vantuono points out, 'ryght' can either be understood as signifying justice – 'just and equitable treatment' - or the 'justifiable claim' accorded to privilege.[28] Depending on which definition of is followed, 'resoun' is either the application of 'abstract right'[29] or an enforcer of God's hierarchy - or, as Pearl might argue, both, since the two cannot be separated. As with most catch-words (see §3.1), the meaning of 'ryght' varies. In l. 672 it signifies security, in other stanzas - 'by ryght' - it denotes privilege or justice. The fact that the innocent are 'ryght' (safe) by right typifies the occasional use, in Pearl, of semantic ambiguity to imply tautology (see §6.4) and to suggest a confounding inflexibility in how things are: right is a right, for those who are right.

§2.4 'the innossent'

'Innocent' is from the Latin root *in* (not) + *nocere* (to hurt or injure). The word, understood to mean 'harmless', also suggests the meaning 'unharmed', which accords well with the Old Testament usage of *innocente* to signify 'cleanness'.[30]

The innocent are harmless and also unharmed by God in that they are preserved from sin. In dying young, Pearl was protected from the possibility of sinning. This exemption can only be a privilege, as much as the preservation of the harmless is surely a matter of justice. Even the sense in which death in infancy is experienced as harm - as the sacrifice of a blameless life - carries the honour of *imitatio christi*.

Innocence, for Pearl, has an equivalent status to that of virginity in Jerome's anti-Jovinian defense of the hierarchy of heaven - notably, Pearl appears later as one of 144, 000 virgin brides of Christ. According to Jerome's scheme, 'Christ loves virgins more than

---

[28] Vantuono, *The Pearl Poems: An Omnibus Edition, Volume 1*, 257.
[29] Spencer, "God's Law and Man's Law", 331.
[30] ibid., 329.

others,' and those who are enabled to go through life unstained have been granted 'a greater grace from God.'[31]

The question of hierarchy is significant throughout *Pearl*, and especially in this passage, where the superior rights of the innocent are so strongly emphasised. As I argued before, Pearl's use of allegorical guides in this fitt suggests a Dionysian model of hierarchy whereby spiritual superiors raise us "towards a truth ... which is simple and one,'[32] so that hierarchy is a means towards the end of enlightenment. Bloomfield argues that the poem as a whole gestures to such a unifying process, though, as I hope to show in examining this fitt, such a resolution is never quite achieved, and the austere Jeromian model of hierarchy never surmounted.

§2.5 'saues'

Modal auxiliaries are no longer needed here: reason 'saves' – not may save, not shall save – the innocent. As Pearl's presence on the far side of the river indicates, the innocent are 'always safe'; set outside life and time, they are safe in 'God's all seeing now'[33] while the outcome for sinners remains contingent. It should be noted that to save is not only to rescue but also to preserve or protect.[34]

In short, what has been set up grammatically and explicitly in the first stanza is a double standard.

§2.6 'evermore...never...ever'

The correspondence of these chronological superlatives emphasises the certainty of the innocent's position, and its constancy alongside temporal fluctuation. The verbal pattern through ll. 666-68, where '[n]ever' moves from the first half-line to the second then back to the first enacts a pantomime of dialogism in Pearl's monologic argument. All Pearl's positives and negatives reinforce a single point, but are nevertheless in conceptual opposition to each other, so that her argument seems to close in on all sides, a multifaceted absolute. This rhetorical technique conspicuously

---

[31] Josephine Bloomfield, "Stumbling toward God's Light: The *Pearl* Dreamer and the Impediments of Hierarchy" *The Chaucer Review* 45, No. 4 (2011), 392.
[32] Bloomfield, "Stumbling towards God's Light", 395.
[33] Dove, *The Perfect Age of Man's Life*, 94.
[34] "save, v.". OED Online. (accessed August 01, 2014).

represses a question which haunts the fitt: why are only the innocent made innocent, and not the rest?

§3. The gyltyf may contryssyoun hente
    And be thurgh mercy to grace thryght
    Bot he to gyle that neuer glente
    As inoscente is saf and ryghte. [669-72]

§3.1 'hente...thryght...glente'

Three contrasting movements are described in these lines. Definitions of 'hente' include, to lay hold of, seize or catch, to get to, arrive at, reach or to occupy[35] - the final sense is adhered to by most translators, and seems fitting given the metaphors of grace as place in ll. 678-81, 693-94 and l. 719. Glossed this way, the verb suggests an active approach of and arrival at the state of contrition, which in turn confers some power on the 'gyltyf' – a sense of control over their destiny stronger than that depicted in l. 675: 'the ryghtwys man schal se hys face'.

'Thryght', however, consigns the guilty to the passive and undignified position of having been 'thrust' into a state of grace by a superior power. This lackadaisical impuissance is far from suggesting grace as 'a quality possessed by human beings', 'an individual virtue or excellence which is regarded as divine in origin' - grace here is exclusively 'a quality of God',[36] for which the guilty seem essentially unworthy.

Conversely, the use of 'glente' to describe a non-existent slip into 'gyle' describes a glancing motion so subtle that its secondary application is to the movement of light. The use of this term apophatically reinforces the fitt's implication that the innocent and the guilty are not so much contrasting examples (as suggested by the rhyming opposition of 'hente' and 'glente') as irrevocably different and incomparable.

§4. Ryght thus I knaw wel in this cas
    Two men to save is god by skylle. [673-74]

---

[35] "† hent, v.". OED Online. (accessed July 30, 2014).
[36] "grace, n.". OED Online. (accessed July 30, 2014).

§4.1 'god by skylle'

'Early editors', Vantuono writes, 'rendered 'good', but Hillman's 'God'... seems preferable.'[37] As with many individual words in this fitt, this ambiguity of meaning leaves room for doubt as to the overall claim Pearl is making about the supremacy of privilege or of justice. The OED defines 'skylle' as 'reason as a faculty of the mind', 'discretion in relation to special circumstance' and/or 'that which is reasonable, proper, right or just.'[38] In conjunction with this word, 'Good' would suggest the principle of just behaviour, as guided by reason. 'God' in the same place would convey that the salvation of two types is a matter of divine discretion, and that his will is the only reason necessary.

Vantuono's translation, '[If] God, by agreement, is to redeem two men ...'[39] is questionable in introducing an element of contingency into a 'case' that Pearl 'know[s] well', and where the outcome is 'certain' (see l. 685). His 'by agreement' implies either that redemption is entirely a matter of theoretical debate, if the agreement is a matter of theological consensus, or else, if the agreement is between God and man, that God has struck a deal. This is an interesting translation insofar as it suggests the existence of a contract or guarantee for the righteous, whoever they are. The thesis of this fitt is never that God might renege on his offer of salvation, as Thomas of Buckingham imagined, but that only the innocent can be sure of their status. Vantuono's translation seems to posit that God is not a totally free and unpredictable agent, but is bound by 'the rights of his true subjects'[40] - God is held to his own 'skylle'.

The use of the word 'skylle' here also portrays 'resoun' unambiguously as a property of the mind. It puts personified Reason into retirement in preparation for Wisdom (see §8.1).

§5. The ryghtwys man schal se hys face,
    The harmles hathel schal com hym tylle. [675-76]

---

[37] Vantuono, *The Pearl Poems: An Omnibus Edition, Volume 1*, 674.
[38] "skill, n.1". OED Online. (accessed July 30, 2014).
[39] Vantuono, *The Pearl Poems: An Omnibus Edition, Volume 1*, 47.
[40] Spencer, "God's Law and Man's Law": 321.

§5.1 'harmles hathel'

Defined in the OED as a 'man of worth',[41] and in the MED as a man, warrior or nobleman,[42] the word is derived from the Old English *athel*, meaning ancestry/origin or nobility. The term may therefore be used in a humble sense, but has connotations of nobility which here, as the alliteration emphasises, are interlinked with harmlessness, which is the prize and the cause of high status within the hierarchy of souls.

§6. The Sauter hyt sas thus in a pace:
"Lorde, quo schal klymbe thy hygh hylle,
Other rest withinne thy holy place?"
Hymself to onsware he is not dylle:
"Hondelynges harme that dyt not ille,
That is of hert both clene and lyght,
Ther schal hys step stable stylle."
The innocent is ay saf by ryghte. [677-84]

§6.1 'The Sauter hyt sas'

Aside from her use of facilitating reason-figures, Pearl always backs up her argument with scriptural authority, which is treated as proof since the Bible is, as stated by Aquinas, an example of supernatural illumination, bearing 'the stamp of God's own knowledge.'[43] This first allusion to the Bible sets a precedent, to be followed in the overall structure of the fitt, of looking to revelation - in the forms of God's word, and of Christ - in order to justify reason.

§6.2 'hymself to onsware'

This passage paraphrases parts of Psalms 14 and 23, the contents of which correspond closely at points. The poet's decision to replicate the psalms' question and answer format is in accordance with the pincer motion of Pearl's argument in this fit, as described earlier (see §2.6). The personified Psalter answers his own question with certainty and promptness: he 'is not dylle'.

---

[41] "† hathel, n.". OED Online (accessed July 30, 2014).
[42] "hathel". MED. April 2013.(accessed July 30 2014).
[43] Armand Maurer, *Being and Knowing: Studies in Thomas Aquinas and Later Medieval Philosophers* (Toronto: Pontifical Institute of Medieval Studies, 1990), xii.

To pose a question and then immediately respond to it is to ostentatiously debar an answering party from the discourse – it is notable that this is a fitt where the jeweler does not speak. The impression given is both of unassailable control (by Pearl, by the Psalter), and of an unresolved aporia located in the space where another voice might have broken in.

Writing about Psalm 23, Sumpter discusses the probable roots of its 'question-answer-confirmation' structure in torah-entrance liturgy, wherein questions are posed to, and answered by, a priest. However, following Botha, he argues that the intended effect here is purely rhetorical, and that the psalm should be read as a post-exilic reassertion of the believers' right to Israel.[44] The adaptation of these verses in *Pearl* likewise exhibits a self-answering dialectic of salvation: the chosen may speak with and for God to answer their own question, which is in fact antiphonic to the answer, with no intervening uncertainty (see §6.4). The appearance of a dialectical structure (a form favoured by scholastics, and based on reason) is belied by mystical oneness. The fault-line exists for those who are outside the establishment of salvation - like the wordless jeweler.

§6.3 'of hert both clene and lyght'

This image of the beatific vision elides Psalm 23.4 ('*innocens manibus et mundo corde*') with Matthew 5:8 ('*beati mundo corde quoniam ipsi Deum videbunt*').[45] The latter is also paraphrased in *Cleanness* and in *Patience*:

> The hathel clene of his hert hapenes ful fayre
> For he schal loke on oure Lorde with a loue chere[46]

> Thay ar happen also that arn of hert clene,
> For thay her Savyour in sette schal se with her yyen [47]

Although Pearl specified that 'the ryghtwys man schal se hys face,' the *Pearl* poet evidently associates the beatific vision specifically with

---

[44] Philip Sumpter, "The Coherence of Psalm 24", *Journal for the Study of the Old Testament* 39 No. 1 (2014): 35, 39. Sumpter uses the alternative psalmic numbering system.
[45] Ps. 23:4, Matt. 5:8 (Latin Vulgate)
[46] *Cleanness* ll. 27-8.
[47] *Patience* ll. 23-4.

the state of cleanness, which here indicates innocence, since the 'clene and lyght' heart is a property specifically of those who 'did no harm.' The use of 'hathel' in *Cleanness* corresponds with the phrase 'harmles hathel' in *Pearl*, suggesting that the poet has a specific vocabulary associated both with the beatific vision and the state of cleanness, and that in the context of his *oeuvre* this passage, though ostensibly applied both to the innocent and the righteous, truly belongs to the innocent.

Pearl returns to Ps. 23:4 in the next stanza when describing the righteous man, 'That takes not her lyf in vayne, Ne glaveres her nieghbor wyth no gyle.' Her vacillation between separate books and chapters of the Bible is another example of how her impenetrable discourse incorporates breaches, distances, even 'gyle' - although her different sources back each other up, the fact that she does not stick to a single passage gives her argument a somewhat selective tone. The Psalter is perhaps the book of the Bible with which a lay reader might be expected to have the greatest familiarity - fudging the sense of it by combining it with Matthew 5:8 may be a calculated attempt to discomfit the reader.

§6.4 'Ther schal hys step stable stylle'

'Stable' here is a verb – meaning 'to render steadfast,' 'to ordain permanently'[48] – but use of its adjectival form – meaning secure, stationary, not liable to change – has been recorded from the thirteenth century.[49] The adjective 'stylle,' meanwhile, has a homophone in the verb 'stille' - to make or become still.[50] While grammatically this phrase is not quite subject to the syntactic ambiguity described by Morton Danner as a feature of *Pearl*,[51] a shadow sense is implied of something like 'his stationary step shall become still there', suggesting paradoxically but accurately that the 'harmles hathel' has always stepped, and stopped, in the holy place, with neither action nor jeopardy.

The self-confirming double meanings of this line are examples of the same kind of paronomastic tautology seen in the poet's play

---

[48] "† stable, v.1". OED Online (accessed August 02, 2014).
[49] "stable, adj.". OED Online (accessed August 02, 2014).
[50] still, v.1". OED Online (accessed August 02, 2014).
[51] Morton Danner, "A Grammatical Perspective on Word-Play in Pearl" *The Chaucer Review* 22 No.4 (1988).

on the word 'ryght' (see §2.3). Overdetermination and instability of meaning are suggested at the same time. This use of language reflects the way that Pearl conveys an intractable message which she simultaneously renders questionable and confusing, denying her audience the security that is vouchsafed to the innocent.

§7. The ryghtwys man also sertayn
Aproche he schal that proper pyle,
That takes not her lyf in vayne,
Ne glaveres her nieghbor wyth no gyle. [685-88]

§7.1 'Aproche'
Kind words butter no parsnips.

§8. Of thys ryghtwys sas Salamon playn
How Koyntise onoure con aquyle;
By wayes ful streght he con hym strayn,
And scheued hym the rengne of God awhyle,
As quo says, "Lo, yon lovely yle!
Thoy may hit wynne if thou be wyghte."
Bot hardyly, wythoute peryle,
The innocent is ay saf by ryghte. [689-96]

§8.1 'Koyntise ... he'
Other possible emendations of the manuscript's 'How oure con aquyle' include 'How kyntly on[o]re con aquyle'; 'How kyntly oure [kyng him] con aquyle'; 'How kyntly oure [Koyntise hym] con aquyle'; 'Hym Koyntise oure con aquyle.'[52] To favour a reading that names 'Koyntise' (Wisdom) seems appropriate since ll. 689-92 paraphrase Wisdom 10:10: 'She conducted the just [righteous man], when he fled from his brother's wrath, through the right ways, and shewed him the kingdom of God, and gave him the knowledge of the holy things ...'[53] With or without a direct mention, the figure of Wisdom would be evoked here, just as the personified Reason is alluded to in l. 665, whether or not 'resoun' is taken primarily to signify an abstract concept.

---

[52] Vantuono, *The Pearl Poems: An Omnibus Edition, Volume 1,* 47.
[53] Wisdom 10:10 (Douay Rheims Version).

As Andrew and Waldon point out, it is not necessary, when favouring the 'Koyntise' reading, to emend 'he' to 'ho' in order to restore Wisdom to the feminine identity she takes on in the Book of Wisdom, since the change of sex 'facilitates the "common medieval identification" of Wisdom with Christ.'[54] 'Quoyntise' is also used as a synonym for Christ in *Patience* l. 39.[55]

There is cause to connect Wisdom not only with Christ, the ultimate revelation-figure, but also with Reason. Wisdom is 'the unspotted mirror of God's majesty, and the image of his goodness';[56] Reason is also made in God's likeness. Wisdom bestows

> true knowledge of the things that are: to know the disposition of the whole world, and the virtues of the elements; The beginning, and ending, and midst of the times, the alterations of their courses, and the changes of seasons; The revolutions of the year, and the dispositions of the stars; The natures of living creatures, and rage of wild beasts, the force of winds, and reasonings of men, the diversities of plants, and the virtues of roots; And all such things as are hid and not foreseen, I have learned: for wisdom, which is the worker of all things, taught me.[57]

Wisdom shares Reason's lordship, her knowledge of nature, her synchronic perspective on time, and her mission of guiding humanity (see §2.2). Although there is no obvious allusion to the Book of Wisdom in de Meun's description of Reason, the resemblance of Reason to Wisdom may well have occurred to the Pearl poet.

Wisdom, however, goes beyond Reason in having a stake in salvation. She is sent 'out of thy [God's] holy heaven … that she may be with me [Solomon], and may labour with me, that I may know what is acceptable with thee.'[58] Pearl introduces Wisdom as a figure who shows the righteous man heaven, and advises him on getting there: 'thou may hit winne if thou be wyghte.' Wisdom is like

---

[54] Vantuono, *The Pearl Poems: An Omnibus Edition, Volume 1*, 258.
[55] Anderson, *Sir Gawain and the Green Knight, Pearl, Cleanness, Patience*, 298.
[56] Wisdom 7:26 (Douay Rheims Version).
[57] Wisdom 7:17-22 (DRV).
[58] Wisdom 9:10 (DRV)

Reason, with the addition of faith and hope. Wisdom is also a tropological representation of Christ.

§8.2 'thys ryghtwys'
The allusion to Wisdom 10:10 is also interesting in terms of its thematic connection to Psalm 23. The 'righteous man' in Wisdom 10:10 is Jacob, who was licensed by God to inherit his brother Esau's birthright - it is from Esau that Jacob is fleeing when Wisdom comes to show him 'the rengne of God.' Meanwhile, Psalm 23 refers to *faciem Dei Jacob* (the face of the God of Jacob).[59] This link in subject matter suggests a coherence underlying Pearl's appeal to these different scriptural passages, which in turn might appear to reflect some hinted consistency between Reason and Wisdom.

One significant thing about the God of Jacob is that he does not necessarily play by the rules, according to earthly standards. Although Jacob was the second-born of twins, his mother Rebekah was told 'two nations are in thy womb, and two peoples shall be divided out of thy womb, and one people shall overcome the other, and the elder shall serve the younger.'[60] While it to some extent challenges notions of earthly hierarchy and order, the story of Jacob ultimately demonstrates God's favouritism, and his unpredictability. The God of Jacob is the God of the chosen, and their inexplicable rights.

Another connection between Psalms and the Book of Wisdom is that the latter was supposed to be written by Solomon, the son of David, from whose ancestral line Jesus came.

§8.3 'As'
Wisdom, already an allegorical figure, now incorporates another imagined persona through this simile. The glimpsed 'lovely yle' ('distant province')[61] is in a state of mirage-like uncertainty conveyed by 'may'; that this provisional utopia is only a figure of speech puts the possibility of reaching 'the rengne of God' at an even further distance from reality. The movement towards revelation in this fitt is still incomplete.

---

[59] Ps 23:6 (LV).
[60] Gen. 25:3 (DRV)
[61] Charles G. Osgood, *The Pearl* (Boston: D. C. Heath, 1906) 72.

§9. Anende ryghtwys men yet sas a gome,
David in Sauter, if ever ye sey hit:
"Lorde, thy servaunt draw never to dome,
For non lyvyande to the is justyfyet." [697-700]

§9.1 'yet says a gome'
Even allowing for the demands of form, it is jarring to have David introduced here as if for the first time, since parts of the Psalter have already been discussed in this fitt. Pearl's monologue is increasingly well-populated with spiritual guides, to the extent that David is tripled: posing a question, answering himself, and popping up again as 'a gome.' That multiple figures are made out of one source reflects Pearl's tactic of summoning many allegorical and scriptural authorities - Solomon, David, Reason, Wisdom, Christ - in order to build an argument which is all hers. Her presence represents the implacable morality behind an argument which, for all its modulations, is essentially unaltering: 'the innocent is ay saf by ryght'.

Behind Pearl, of course, is the poet, whose deployment of scriptural figures adds to the visionary authority of *Pearl*, while also tactfully highlighting the difference in status between poetry and scripture, potentially inserting another breach, another spiritual obstacle, between the reader and revelation.

§9.2 'if ever ye sey hit'
This is another slightly odd intrusion, which must read as either naive, patronising or sarcastic. It might be taken as read that the jeweler is familiar with the Psalter, ownership of which was relatively common among the laity by the fourteenth century,[62] although his familiarity with the Bible and Christian doctrine varies significantly over the course of the poem. I would argue that the most stubborn spiritual problem faced by the jeweler is not ignorance but doubt; the dream scenario allows him to confront the faultlines in his faith by encountering scripture as if for the first time.

§10. Forthy to corte quen thou schal com,
There alle oure causes schal be tryed,

---

[62] Claire Donovan, *The de Brailles Hours* (London: The British Library, 1991), 26.

Alegge the ryght, thou may be innome
By thys ilke spech I have asspyed -- [701-4]

§10.1 'to corte'

The image of the court case, and the legal language used in this stanza - 'corte', 'causes', 'tryed', 'alegge', 'innome'[63] - reify the idea of judgement, which has been contemplated at a distance throughout the fitt. This is, theologically and dramatically, the fitt's climactic passage, referencing both doomsday and the crucifixion, and bridging the breach between the innocent and the guilty.

§10.2 'Alegge the ryght, thou may be innome'

This line has been interpreted in several ways. To Gollancz the sense is 'Renounce your claim, [and] you may be received...', meaning that if the defendant renounces his claim to righteousness, accepting David's statement, taken from Ps. 142:2, that 'no man living shall be justified' in God's sight, then he may be received into grace.

To Osgood, the meaning is 'Claim your privilege, [and] you may be received...', suggesting that the defendant should use David's words ('this ilke spech') as evidence in his favour, and that by proving he could not have lived guiltlessly, he may establish that he should be spared condemnation. According to this reading the guilty, like the innocent, have rights.

Everett and Hurnard have made a convincing case that 'alegge' is in the conditional subjunctive rather than the imperative, and that 'innome' is a legalistic term meaning cornered, trapped or 'refuted in argument.'[64] Their rendering of the line is, '[If] you claim to be righteous, you may be trapped,' in light of the guilt testified to by David.

Everett and Hunard's reading is the most consistent with Pearl's argument throughout the passage, and with her pointed grammatical provisionality: if 'alegge' is in the subjunctive, it adds another layer of hypotheticalism to what is already a conditional statement ('thou may be innome'). It also seems more characteristic of her didactic approach to warn the jeweler of a potential pitfall than to tell him what he should do.

---

[63] D. Everett; Naomi D. Hurnard, "Legal Phraseology in a Passage in Pearl" *Medium Aevum* 16 (1947): 13.
[64] Everett and Hurnard, "Legal Phraseology", 13.

Osgood's rendering is interesting in that the defendant uses 'skylle' to plead his case. This is in accordance with H.L. Spencer's politicised reading of *Pearl* as a poem which reflects a king's obligations to his subjects.[65] To continue with a more theologically oriented reading, the idea of putting forward one's imperfection in one's own defense is not a simple matter of legal sophistry: trusting God to play fair, and to offer everyone the chance of salvation, can only be a matter of faith.

§11. Bot he on rode that blody dyed,
    Delfully thurgh hondes thryght,
    Gyve the to passe, when thou arte tryed,
    By innosens and not by ryghte. [705-8]

§11.1 'Bot'

This word is instrumental in Everett and Hurnard's argument against Osgood's interpretation, since if there is any possibility that the defendant might plead his 'privilege' successfully, then this would contradict the stanza's closing declaration that souls are saved by Christ's innocence, 'and not by ryght.'

To split hairs briefly, an apparently inappropriate 'but' would not be unprecedented in this fitt (see §1.4). In the first stanza, Pearl uses the conjunction to force a link between parallel cases. If we accept Osgood's reading, ll. 703-08 would read with the following sense: if you claim your privilege, you may be received, *but* may Christ let you pass through his innocence and not by your right. The effect of the sub-clause would be to simultaneously allow the possible effectiveness of the defendant's claim and to dismiss it on the grounds that such claims ultimately depend on Christ's intervention. To allow reason to reach the theologically correct conclusion, but with religious mysticism still playing the decisive part, would be consistent with Pearl's methods in this fitt.

I have expounded this rather unwieldy reading in order to illustrate the syntactic status of innocence in this fitt as something which is both essential and superfluous. It is Pearl's salient point, and explains how the sinner may be saved, but is also external to any reasoning or debate about the moral status of the living.

---

[65] Spencer, "God's Law and Man's Law", 321.

§11.2 'Gyve'

The mood of the stanza's closing statement remains subjunctive. Osgood, Everett and Hurnard take it to express the volitional 'may Christ let you pass'; Anderson interprets it as yet another provisional statement: 'Christ should allow you to go free...'[66]

§11.3 'thurgh hondes thryght'

This very specific and isolated image of Christ's torture brings the reader into an encounter with the physicality of the crucifixion that replicates the methods of affective piety, a devotional practice that involved contemplating, often in great detail, the torments of Christ on the cross.[67] This type of contemplation encouraged a visceral connection between worshippers and Christ; at this moment in the poem the connection between innocence and guilt, effected by the crucifixion, is central.

The phrase summons two words already used in this fitt: 'hondelynges' (with [his] hands), l. 681, and 'thryght' (thrust) l. 670 (see §3.1). The former refers to the hands of the harmless, the latter is applied to the movement through which the guilty might arrive at grace. Here these words are used again in order to conflate the movement through which the guilty are saved, with the violent motion with which Christ's harmless hands were pierced by nails. This image invests the formerly hapless sinner with responsibility for a truly harmful action (this is also where the harmless become the harmed - see §2.4), and summons the central Christian paradox that humanity is saved by its own violence. At this point the privilege of the innocent becomes the privilege of the guilty. This reconciliation of the two strands of Pearl's argument is a moment of revelation - revelation in the form of Christ as God incarnate - which supersedes concepts both of justice and privilege.

§12. Ryghtwysly quo con rede,
    He loke on bok and be awayed
    How Jesus hym welke in arethede,

---

[66] Anderson, *Sir Gawain and the Green Knight, Pearl, Cleanness, Patience*, 27.
[67] Stephen J. Shoemaker, "Mary at the Cross, East and West: Maternal Compassion and Affective Piety in the earliest L*ife of the Virgin* and the High Middle Ages" *The Journal of Theological Studies* 62, No. 2 (2011), 571.

And burnes her barnes unto hym brayde. [709-12]

§12.1 'Ryghtwysly quo con rede'

In his determination to make *Pearl* adhere to iambic tetrameter, Gollancz identifies this line's slightly awkward metre:[//] Rýght / wsyslý // quó / con réde.[68] The initial caesura, necessary even if one has a more flexible understanding of the poem's metre, highlights a change of tone at this point in the fitt, moving from the dramatic climax of judgement and sacrifice to a simpler biblical narrative (see §12.3).

As in stanzas three and four, the catch-word 'ryght' is adapted into 'ryghtwys,' though the concept of righteousness was torn apart in the preceding stanza. The weak caesura that Gollancz locates between 'ryght' and 'wys,' dividing the word into its constituent parts, may reflect this.

The '-wys' part of 'ryghtwys' may be derived either from the adjective 'wise', or the noun signifying 'a manner... of doing.'[69] Here Pearl encourages her audience not just to read righteously, as part of religious observance, but to read in the right way, taking the correct lesson from the text, and to read wisely, with an understanding of the 'rengne of god' (which Wisdom revealed), and how it belongs to the innocent.

§12.2 'he loke on bok'

This appeal to the biblical source, and exhortation to consult it, is evidently a rhetorical gesture since Pearl's account draws from Matt. 19:13-15 and Mark 10:13-16, as well as from Luke 18:15-17, upon which it is primarily based.[70] Having freely paraphrased several passages of the Bible, Pearl's instruction here that we 'look at the book' ourselves emphasises her use of this story as the final instance of supernatural illumination on which her argument is founded.

§12.3 'welke ...brayde'

The change into the past tense gives this narrative a sense of historical authority. Notably the other scriptural voices in this fitt,

---

[68] Israel Gollancz, ed. and trans. *Pearl* (London: Chatto and Windus, 1891), 38.
[69] "righteous, adj., n., adv., and int.". OED Online. (accessed July 30, 2014).
[70] Anderson, *Sir Gawain and the Green Knight, Pearl, Cleanness, Patience*, 286.

David and Solomon, spoke in the present tense: 'sas Salamon playn', 'yet says a gome.' Christ's cameo is established as prior to the debate conducted by Pearl; his actions and words (which, as might be expected of the *logos*, reinforce each other) are the centre and source of Pearl's argument.

§13. For happe and hele that fro hym yede
 To touch her chylder thay fayr hym prayed.
 His dessypeles wyth blame let hem bede,
 And wyth her resounes ful fele restayed. [713-16]

§13.1 'resounes'
 The concept of reason recurs here as something which must fall short of what is divinely right.

§14. Jesus thenne hem swetely sayde:
 "Do way, let chylder unto me tyght;
 To suche is hevenryche arayed."
 The innocent is ay saf by ryght. [717-20]

§14.1 'Jesus ... sayde'
 Christ asserts that heaven is made for the innocent, showing innocence to be at the centre of God's scheme for humanity - to question their place is to question heaven itself.

 In the previous stanza, the 'rights' of the guilty were ultimately dismissed. Here all of the meanings of 'ryght' - safety, justice, privilege - are combined, and made synonymous with innocence. Significantly, the poem's only instance of broken concatenation occurs between fitts XII and XIII. While various numerological readings and codicological emendations have been put forward, I would suggest that 'Jesus', the first word of the following stanza, is in conceptual concatenation with 'ryght.'

 In following Pearl's ascending hierarchy of guides, from Reason to Christ - from reason to right - it should be remembered that this poem is not one that ever grants total resolution. The testament of Christ gives us a brush with Dionysian enlightenment, but his words are paraphrased, and the final line brings us back to Pearl as the sole speaker in this fitt. She remains in place as the poem's reason-figure, standing between the jeweler and God, as a help and an impediment. The jeweler is kept in the realm of uncertainty.

WORKS CITED

Anderson, J. J., ed. *Sir Gawain and the Green Knight, Pearl, Cleanness, Patience* (London: Everyman, 1996).

Ashworth, E.J., "Review of *The Mirror of Grammar: Theology, Philosophy and the 'Modistae'* by L.G. Kelly" *Speculum* 80 No.2 (2005): 602-4.

Aquinas, Thomas, trans. Dominican House of Studies, *Summa Theologiae*. <http://dhspriory.org/thomas/english/QDdeVer28.htm> (accessed December 4, 2014).

Augustine, trans. F.J. Sheed, *Confessions* (Indianapolis/Cambridge: Hackett Publishing Company, 2007).

Bloomfield, Josephine, "Stumbling toward God's Light: The *Pearl* Dreamer and the Impediments of Hierarchy" *The Chaucer Review* 45, No. 4 (2011): 390-410

Bowers, John M., "*Patience* and the Ideal of the Mixed Life." *Texas Studies in Literature and Language* 28 (1986): 1-23.

Donner, Morton, "A Grammatical Perspective on Word-Play in Pearl" *The Chaucer Review* 22 No.4 (1988).

Donovan, Claire, *The de Brailles Hours* (London: The British Library, 1991).

Douay Rheims Bible and Latin Vulgate in *Douay Rheims Bible Online*. http://www.drbo.org (accessed July 30 2014).

Dove, Mary, *The Perfect Age of Man's Life* (Cambridge: CUP, 1986).

Everett, D.; Hurnard, Naomi D., "Legal Phraseology in a Passage in Pearl" *Medium Aevum* 16 (1947): 9-16.

Gollancz, Israel, ed. and trans. *Pearl* (London: Chatto and Windus, 1891).

Hampden, Renn Dickson, *The Scholastic Philosophy considered in relation to Christian Theology* (London: Simpkin, Marshall and Co., 1848).

Langland, William, *Piers Plowman*, ed. Derek Pearsall (Exeter: University of Exeter Press, 2008).

Lynch, Kathryn L., *The High Medieval Dream Vision: Poetry, Philosophy and Literary Form* (Stanford, California: Stanford University Press, 1988).

Maurer, Armand, *Being and Knowing: Studies in Thomas Aquinas and Later Medieval Philosophers* (Toronto: Pontifical Institute of Medieval Studies, 1990).

Middle English Dictionary. April 2013. University of Michigan. <http://quod.lib.umich.edu/m/med/>.

Osgood, Charles G., ed. *The Pearl* (Boston: D. C. Heath, 1906). ed. and trans., *The Pearl: An anonymous English Poem of the Fourteenth Century* (Cambridge, Mass.: The Riverside Press, 1907).

Oxford English Dictionary, *OED Online*. <http://www.oed.com> (accessed July 30, 2014).

Shoemaker, Stephen J., "Mary at the Cross, East and West: Maternal Compassion and Affective Piety in the earliest *Life of the Virgin* and the High Middle Ages" *The Journal of Theological Studies* 62, No. 2 (2011), 570 - 606.

Spencer, H.L., "God's Law and Man's Law", *Review of English Studies* 59 (2008): 317-41.

Sumpter, Philip, "The Coherence of Psalm 24,. *Journal for the Study of the Old Testament* 39 No. 1 (2014): 31-54.

Vantuono, William, *The Pearl Poems: An Omnibus Edition, Volume 1* (New York: Garland, 1984).

Kay Miller is a Learning Mentor at Bacon's College, London. She holds an MA in Medieval Literatures from the University of York.

XIII

Pearl, Fytt XIII

A. W. Strouse

We play at Paste–
Till qualified, for Pearl–

        –Emily Dickinson

"We see – Comparatively" according to Emily Dickinson (534, ll. 1). So, Dickinson advances a poetic credo of glossing, a practice that she refers to more explicitly when she writes:

> A Book I have – a friend gave me –
> Whose Pencil – here and there –
> Had notched the place that pleased Him –
> At rest – His fingers are –
>   (360, ll. 13-16)

Dickinson would have us interpret through comparison–by way of synonym, analogy, and type. In fact, over one-third of Dickinson's poems partake of a comparative method: many of her works are "meta-poetic glosses" that reflect upon the conception of the simile.[1] Dickinson's vein of comparison is decidedly spiritual, especially in her "We see," where she argues that the large things of this world, when translated through a spiritual lens, appear quite tiny. This interpretative process makes "A furrow–Our Cordillera– / Our Apennine–a Knoll" (ll. 7-8). Earthly travails, like mountain chains, seem vast from a human perspective; but, viewed from the heavens, they are microscopic, inconsequential.

I'd like to thank the editors of *Glossator* as well as Wendy Tronrud for their assistance with this commentary.

[1] See Shirley Sharon-Zisser, "To 'See–Comparatively': Emily Dickinson's Use of Simile" *The Emily Dickinson Journal*, 3.1 (1994): 59-84

This sentiment rhymes with the advice given by the Pearl in Fytt XIII when she recounts the parable of the precious pearl, which exceeds all earthly value and represents heaven's riches. Actually, Dickinson's work shares many points of resemblance with *Pearl*, and her comparative method mimics, in some ways, medieval practices of exegesis. Dickinson's mode of seeing partakes of a medieval-ish, allegorical sensibility. Here I will describe some connections between Dickinson and medieval glossing; then I will gloss Fytt XIII with Dickinson.

Through allegoresis, Dickinson finds, first, that the flesh represents the spirit; and, reading further, she imagines that the spirit supersedes the flesh. Her poem "We see" shucks off the husk and advances the kernel. The literal, though immanent, is rapturously transcended. Through spiritual interpretation, the soul is spared "Some Morning of Chagrin" at doomsday (ll. 14). Dickinson's critical approach, as a mode of Christian mysticism, takes Christ as the grounds of its beseeching. In sotto voce, Dickinson alludes to the Crucifixion when she imagines that worldly suffering ("the Anguish") is a sign "for His Firmament" (ll. 10-11). Christ's Passion, a perfect realization of human pain, is its very annulment. Through a Christological readerly posture, Dickinson spiritualizes the worldly, even to the point of ruthless trivialization. Creation is a "book," written by its Creator, Who subsequently "Had notched the place that pleased Him."

Dickinson participates, then, in what Kathleen Biddick has termed the "typological imaginary."[2] As Biddick points out, the (medieval, clerical) worldview is rooted in a comparative reading practice that regards the Hebrew Bible as the "Old Testament." Judaism, from this perspective, is a type for the Christian anti-type, so that Christians understand the Old Testament as typologically equivalent with the Gospels. As Biddick says, this equivalence generates anxiety, because it makes Judaism and Christianity synonymous and hence reversible.[3] Christians, Biddick argues,

---

[2] See Kathleen Biddick, *The Typological Imaginary: Circumcision, Technology, History* (Philadelphia: U of Pennsylvania P, 2003), particularly p. 1-8.

[3] This reversibility is, according to Jeffrey S. Librett, impicit in Erich Auerbach's formulation of the *figura*; see *The Rhetoric of Cultural Dialogue: Jews and Germans from Moses Mendelssohn to Richard Wagner and Beyond* (Stanford: Stanford UP, 2000), 12, ff. Librett argues that with figural interpretation, as opposed to allegorical interpretation, "neither the prefiguration nor its fulfillment... loses its reality" (13). Biddick's contention

arrest the possibility of reversion through a supersessionary logic, which sees Christianity as breaking from and supplanting Judaism. Christians "cut off" the Jewish type, a formulation that is commonly articulated through metaphors of circumcision. Thus Saint Augustine in his *Tractatus adversus Iudaeos* explains that Christians no longer perform literal circumcision because "veterem hominem circumcidimur, non in exspoliatione corporis carnis" (2; "we are circumcised by cutting off the old man, not by mutilating the flesh of our bodies"). Augustine "sees comparatively," finding the "old man" of Judaism as a type for Christian truth, a prefiguration whose content is abnegated by "cutting it off."

Dickinson herself is aware—if not necessarily critical—of the anti-Jewish implications of her Christian comparative seeing. In her "Your Riches – taught me – Poverty," Dickinson celebrates the paradoxical value system enabled by allegoresis, which takes "the first" as "the last," (299). Dickinson attempts to relate to the Divine by way of the earthly, an interpretative method that she describes as her will to "estimate the Pearl" (ll. 30). This spiritual expedition, in which carnal "riches" are excised in favor of pure, spiritual wealth, is articulated as a process of excising what Augustine called the "old man" of Jewish literalism. Dickinson's "estimation" requires, she notes, that she remove from the soul the "stint" and "blame" that "but be the Jew" (ll. 19-20). Dickinson's comparative poetics is not innocent of the anti-Jewish posture that inflected medieval exegesis.

Dickinson also intimates a circumlogical dimension to her comparative sensibility. She describes her method of glossing in terms of a phallic figure that is suggestively "segmented." Dickinson's comparative vision in "We see" opens with an image of a tower, thus:

> We see – Comparatively –
> The Thing so towering high
> We could not grasp its segment
> Unaided – Yesterday–
> (ll. 1-4)

Like the medieval trope of circumcision–the mechanism, as Biddick establishes, through which Jewish type becomes translated into and

---

is that the supercessionary logic of Christian doctrine in fact alters the reality of the prefiguration; Christians assume the inferiority of the literal type.

then amputated from Christian anti-type–Dickinson's divided tower is the hinge upon which her comparison turns. It facilitates the supercessionary logic of a "Yesterday" that now is understood in light of "This Morning's finer Verdict" (ll. 5). Meanwhile, Dickinson's slashes mark the gloss as a cut. Through slashing, Dickinson transitions from type to antitype (like the "furrow" that is a "Cordillera"). The apparently seamless, seemingly innocent gesture of the hyphen incarnates the scissoring by which the spiritual is excised from the letter.

Arguably, the poem's final stanza complicates this analysis. The last two lines are ambiguous, if not cryptic: "The waking in a Gnat's – embrace – / Our Giants–further on–" (ll. 15-16). These lines may be emblematic of what Shirley Sharon-Zisser calls "another type of simile that Dickinson uses to foreground language at the expense of knowledge," a kind of "free play of signifiers at the expense of a transcendental signified" (70). If indeed Dickinson has dropped out of a transcendental mode and entered into a more ambiguous, riddling mood, then perhaps she has superseded supersession altogether and escaped the ethical-political problems of her medievalish glossing. More likely, Dickinson ends her poem with these enigmatic lines in order to skirt the cheap sentimentality–the "don't sweat the small stuff" philosophy–that her poem flirts with.

In any case, it is not the agenda of this commentary to see Dickinson as beyond, above, or after the medieval. Rather, the hope would be to fulfill comparison's potential for reversibility (to see, for example, "Our Apennine" as a "knoll," while holding the Apennine, too, in the mind, in itself, without reference to its anticipated antitype). I want to situate Dickinson in relation to the medieval without historical cutting, allowing each one to dock into the other. Medieval commentators perhaps permitted just such exegetical shuttling in secular contexts. They often glossed Virgil's *Aeneid* with passages from Boethius's *De consolatione philosophiae*, and Boethius likewise was frequently understood in terms of Virgil.[4] At a certain level both of these works could be taken as allegories for Christian salvation; but, read in relation to one another, neither work necessarily supersedes the other. This critical method of interrelated glossing would inlay literary works into an interconnected net, with each

---

[4] See Christopher Baswell, *Virgil in Medieval England: Figuring the Aeneid from the Twelfth Century to Chaucer* (Cambridge UP, 1995), 120-30.

work, jewel-like, reflecting other works, their facets gleaming with gloss-reflections.

To undertake a gem-tactics of uncut annotation, this commentary would gloss *The Pearl,* Fytt XIII, with passages from Scripture and with poems by Emily Dickinson.[5] Passages from Dickinson will be provided in-text using brief comments that explicate how both Dickinson and the Pearl-Poet might meet in the prism of the figure of the pearl. Biblical allusions and philological issues are treated in footnotes, which also offer paraphrases and treat textual matters.

This commentary is not an exegesis but an edition. I do not aim to elaborate fully all of the points of comparison between Dickinson and *Pearl* in order to establish a typological, one-to-one equivalence. The point, instead, is to create through parataxis an invitation for the reader to dwell in the possibility of a harmony between the two poets. This possibility I see as something of an antidote to supercessionary readings. The juxtaposition of Dickinson and *Pearl* would facilitate, through the wormhole of glossing, a naïve reading that credits poetry for its power to possess readers with the unhistorical. Indeed, the amateur reader represents my gloss's target audience. What follows is a kind of course-packet for those uninitiated into the field of *Pearl*/Dickinson studies. I borrow the commentaries found in the standard classroom editions of *Pearl,* in order to open up these texts to further glosses. This edition, however, is followed up by some further thoughts on how Dickinson's "pearl" ambiguously negotiates between the literal and the figurative as a vexed sign that, like Dickinson's dashes, hangs on to both sides of the divide.

---

[5] All Biblical citations are from the King James Version. Dickinson's poems are from *The Complete Poems of Emily Dickinson,* ed. Thomas H. Johnson (New York: Little, Brown and Company, 1960), 84, 214, 320. Fytt XIII is cited from Malcolm Andrew and Ronald Waldron, *The Poems of the Peal Manuscript:* Pearl, Cleanness, Patience, Sir Gawain and the Green Knight (Berkeley: U of California P, 1979), 87-90. Line and folio numbers follow Andrew and Waldron and run continuously with the rest of the poem. Marginal commentaries borrow from Andrew and Waldron, and marginal glosses and paraphrases are from J.J. Anderson, *Sir Gawain and the Green Knight, Pearl, Cleanness, Patience* (London: Everyman, 1996), 28-30.

XIII[6]

721	'Ry3t[7] con calle to Hym Hys mylde	*called; gentle (disciples)*
	And sayde Hys ryche no wy3 my3t wynne	*kingdom; man*
	Bot he com þyder ry3t as a chylde	
	Oþer ellez neuermore com þerinne.[8]	*or else*
	Harmlez, trwe, and vndefylde,[*]	*guiltless*
725	Withouten mote oþer mascle of sulpande[9] synne:	
	Quen such þer cnoken on þe bylde,[10]	*knock; dwelling*
	Tyt schal hem men þe 3ate unpynne.[11]	*quickly; unfasten*
	Þer is the blys þat con not blynne	*cease*
730	Þat þe jueler so3te þur3 perré pres	*a precious stone*
	And solde alle hys goud, boþe wolen and lynne,[12]	
	To bye hym a perle was mascellez.[13]	*that was spotless*

---

[6] Andrew and Waldron note that the concatenation is supplied by *mascellez perle*, and that there is some play on *mascellez* ("spotless") and *makellez* ("matchless"), as in 781-4.

[7] The MS has "Jesu," which would be the only instance in which the poem breaks the pattern of concatenation. Andrew and Waldron argue, based on the poem's formal regularity, that "Jesu" must be a scribal substitution for "Ry3t."

[8] Lines 1-4 refer to the episode in which Christ's disciples ask Him who is the greatest in the kingdom of heaven. Christ calls a child to Him ("calle to Hym Hys mylde"), and then He replies, "Verily I say unto you, Except ye be converted, and become as little children, ye shall not enter into the kingdom of heaven," (Matthew 18:3).

[*] Note that the poet employs tricolons in the fifth line of stanza one and again in the fifth line of stanza two. These tricolons would seem to mimic poetically the shape of the Trinity.

[9] The word's etymology is obscure, but it may be related to German dialect *sulper, solper* (bog, mud), sölpern to soil, sully (*OED*).

[10] "Without spot or stain of polluting sin" (Anderson).

[11] A reference to Revelation 3:20, "Behold, I stand at the door, and knock: if any man hear my voice, and open the door, I will come in to him, and will sup with him, and he with me."

[12] "And sold all his goods, both woolen and linen" (Anderson).

[13] Christ teaches that "the kingdom of heaven is like unto a merchant man, seeking goodly pearls: / Who, when he had found one pearl of great price, went and sold all that he had, and bought it" (Matthew 13:45-46). The Pearl-Poet translates the "merchant" of the Gospels into a dealer of cloth ("wolen and lynne"). Cloth production was the driving force of the English economy during the late fourteenth century, as discussed in Eileen Power, *The Wool Trade in English Medieval History* (London: Oxford UP, 1942). Notably, the Jewish Law forbids clothes that contain both wool and linen (see Lev. 19:19

'This makellez perle, þat boȝt is dere,
Pe joueler gef fore alle hys god,[14]
735 Is lyke þe reme of hevenesse clere—
So sayde the Fader of folde and flode— *land, sea*
For hit is wemlez, clene, and clere,* *spotless, pure*
And endelez rounde and blyþe of mode,[15]
And commune to alle þat ryȝtwys were. *common*
740 Lo, euen inmyddez my breste hit stode: *exactly in the middle of*

Her breast is fit for pearls,	Like a breath, the pearl exists
But I was not a "Diver"–	in the Pearl's chest–"Lo, even
Her brow is fit for thrones	inmyddes my breste hit stode,"
But I have not a crest.	she says (ll. 740). The Pearl
Her heart is fit for *home*–	goes on to describe her pearl
I–a Sparrow–build there	not as a literal necklace, but as
Sweet of twigs and twine	a spiritual sign of God's love.
My perennial nest.	Dickinson, too, tells us that
	"Her breast is fit for pearls,"
	and she similarly means a
	figurative pearl, admitting "But
	I was not a 'Diver'" (84, ll 1-2).
	Dickinson, like a "Sparrow"
	(ll. 6) builds a nest in the heart
	that is "sweet of twigs and
	twine." Dickinson, like the
	Pearl-Poet, exploits the power
	of alliteration to create
	spiritual poem-pearls from air,
	as birds twine together twigs.

---

and Deut. 22:11). As Karl Steel notes, the point of this law is about maintaining purity and avoiding mixture. Thus it applies readily to the Pearl's advocacy for spiritual purity.

[14] "This matchless pearl, which is dear bought, for which the jeweler gave all his goods, is like the realm of bright Heaven" (Anderson).

[15] Andrew and Waldron provide a lovely explication: "The pearl's shape is thus seen to symbolize the perfection and infiniteness of heaven. It may be argued that the poem itself, with its meticulously proportioned construction, imitates this formal perfection."

My Lorde, þe Lombe þat schede Hys blode,
He pyȝt hit þere in token of pes.   *set; peace*
I rede þee forsake the worlde wode   *advise you to; mad*
And porchace þy perle maskelles.'

I taste a liquor never brewed–
From Tankards scooped in
   Pearl–
Not all the Vats upon the
   Rhine
Yield such an Alcohol!

Inebriate of Air–am I–
And Debauchee of Dew–
Reeling–thro endless summer
   days–
From inns of Molten Blue.

When "Landlords" turn the
   drunken Bee
Out of the Foxglove's door–
When Butterflies–renounce
   their "drams"–
I shall but drink the more!

Till seraphs swing their snowy
   Hats,
And Saints–to windows run–
To see the little Tippler
Leaning against the–Sun–

Dickinson calls herself an "inebriate of Air" who drinks "from Tankards scooped in Pearl." Dickinson thus distills "air" into the pearl-brew of poetry. Fytt XIII, too, reflects on how poetry is ornamented breath, or air inlaid with "pearl." [Steel: The overall point is that the E.D. and Pearl are both meta-poetical works about creation, at least when read alongside one another.]

The pearl "is lyke the reme of hevenesse clere; / So sayde the Fader of folde and flode" (XIII, ll. 735-6). Here, "hevenesse clere," refers to the next life, but also to the literal air of the heavens. This is the vault of heaven that God "sayde" into existence in Genesis I, when He (as Holy Spirit) first created the air, land, and sea. The pearl, then, is like the clear air of the sky, like the speech of God as he fabricated the elements–it is a kind of divine poetry, a stylization of air that turns the ether into the celestial heavens (just as Dickinson conflates these two kinds of air when she announces the parallels between butterflies and seraphs; ll. 9-16).

745 'O maskelez perle in perlez pure,   *wears; of great value*
     Þat beres,' quoþ I, 'the perle of prys,
     Quo formed þee þy fayre fygure?   *for you*
     Þat wroʒt þy wede he watz ful wys;[16]
     Þy beauté com neuer of nature–   *from*
750 Pymalyon paynted never þy vys,   *Pygmalion; face*
     Ne Arystotel nawþer by hys lettrure
     Of carped þe kynde þese propertéz;[17]
     Þy colour passez þe flour-de-lys,   *surpasses*
     Þyn angel-hauyng so clene cortez.
755 Breue me, bryʒt, quat kyn offys[18]
     Berez the perle so maskelles?'[19]

We play at Paste–
Till qualified, for Pearl–
Then, drop the Paste–
And deem ourself a fool–

The Shapes–though–were
    similar–
And our new hands
Learned *Gem*-Tactics–
Practicing *Sands*–

The Jeweler compares God to the artist Pygmalion and to the scientist Aristotle, finding Him superior to both. This shares an understanding of God's pearl– his poetry–as both an aesthetic object and a kind of philosophy, but transcendent ones [Steel: Has God left behind the material or simply been better at it? Given the rich aesthetic effects of the poem, I have to say it's probably the former. God is better than Aristotle and Pygmalion: he's not devalued what they do, but rather does what they do better than they do it. I think that materiality of the Pearl, so material even in Paradise, is a key quality of the poem, and

---

[16] "And he who made your clothes was most skilful" (Anderson).
[17] "Nor did Aristotle in his writings speak of the nature of these attributes" (Anderson).
[18] As Andrew and Waldron note, the MS is unclear, with some editors reading *ostriys* ("oysters") and others *of triys* ("of peace").
[19] "Your angelic bearing (is) so perfectly refined. Tell me, beautiful one, what kind of office does the pearl so spotless hold?" (Anderson).

> perhaps a place to introduce a bit of conflict between your gloss and the E.D. poem]. Earthly art and science do not measure up to the truth of the Pearl, a division at play as the Pearl struggles to teach her student, the Jeweler, about her place in Heaven.
>
> Dickinson similarly notes that Christian salvation can be a pedagogical problem. "We play at paste," she says, "Till qualified for pearl" (320, ll. 1-2); in other words, man, made of clay, play-acts his journey toward salvation, only to find that, when he becomes worthy of Heaven, the pasty life of mortals will have been foolish.

	'My makelez Lambe þat al may bete,'[20]	
	Quoth scho, 'my dere Destyné,	
	Me ches to Hys make, alþaȝ unmete	
760	Sumtyme semed þat assemblé.[21]	
	When I wente fro yor worlde wete[22]	*dismal* (lit. *wet*)
	He calde me to Hys bonerté:	*blessedness*
	"Cum hyder to Me, My lemman swete,	*beloved* (*one*)
	For mote ne spot is non in þee."	*stain; none*
765	He gef me myȝt and als bewté;[23]	*gave; power; also*
	In Hys blod He wesch my wede on dese,	
	And coronde clene in vergynté,[24]	

---

[20] "My matchless Lamb, who may make amends for everything" (Anderson).

[21] "Chose me as His bride, although at one time that union would have seemed unfitting (i.e. while she was still alive)" (Anderson).

[22] Andrew and Waldron suggest that *wete* emphasizes the contrast between the world of flower and flesh and the world of eternity.

[23] The lines echo the Song of Songs 4:7, "Thou art all fair, my love; there is no spot in thee."

[24] "In His blood He washed my clothes on the dais (i.e. where His heavenly throne was), and crowned me pure in (my) virginity" (Anderson).

	And py3t me in perlez maskellez.'²⁵	set
	'Why, maskellez bryd, þat bry3t con flambe,	
770	Þat reiatéz hatz so ryche and ryf,²⁶	
	Quat kyn þyng may bè that Lambe	kind of
	Þat þee wolde wedde unto Hys vyf?	as His wife
	Ouer alle oþer so hy3 þou clambe	climbed
	To lede wyþ Hym so ladyly lyf.	so queenly a
775	So mony a comly onvunder cambe²⁷	
	For Kryst han lyued in much stryf,	
	And þou con alle þo dere outdryf,	
	And fro þat maryag al oþer depres,	
	Al only þyself so stout and styf,	
780	A makelez may and maskellez.'²⁸	

Dickinson's comparisons often turn upon the figure of the pearl. In the lines that make my epigraph, for example, Dickinson's "pearl" represents a spiritual realm that is somehow superior to "paste." She accesses this pearl only after she has first become "qualified." "Pearls" are exclusively for the elect–not intended for the proverbial swine. They belong to those whose good works earn them heavenly credentials. Then, these certified paste-players "drop the paste, / And deem ourself a fool" (ll. 3-4). Notably, the shift in number from plural "we" to singular "a fool" mimics the supercessionary formula by which individual Christians are subsumed into the Divine. Dickinson transliterates the philosophical awkwardness of the mystical *imitatio Christi* into the ambiguously numbered "ourself." Meanwhile the "paste" of the type is "dropped" for the "pearl" of the anti-type. But Dickinson resists, to some extent,

---

[25] Compare to Isaiah 61:10, "I will greatly rejoice in the Lord, my soul shall be joyful in my God; for he hath clothed me with the garments of salvation, he hath covered me with the robe of righteousness, as a bridegroom decketh *himself* with ornaments, and as a bride adorneth *herself* with her jewels."

[26] "Why, spotless bride, who shines so brightly, who has such rich and abundant royal honours" (Anderson).

[27] Anderson reads *annunder*.

[28] "So many lovely ladies (lit. many a lovely one under comb) have lived in great hardship for Christ, and you are able to drive out all those worthy ones and exclude all others from that marriage, yourself being the only one sufficiently firm and resolute, a peerless and spotless maiden" (Anderson). Andrew and Waldron point out that *comly onvunder cambe* is a periphrasis, and that similar constructions are found in *Pearl* at ll. 116 and 1110. They suggest that the Dreamer is characteristically incredulous.

complete supersession. Her poem turns back, rereading the original "paste" as a necessary prerequisite for spiritual advancement: "the shapes, though, were similar," she reminds us (ll. 5). By "playing," we have learned to "practice" our gem-tactics. Dickinson's comparative figuration operates through "dropping," but finally returning to and rereading her "paste."

This movement of supersession and then reversal is the trajectory, too, of several other "pearls" in the Dickinson corpus. The enchanting "I started Early –Took my Dog" undertakes a spiritual journey from earth to heaven; but at its narratological volta the poem turns back to reflect upon the worldly, a turn affected by the moment when "my Shoes / Would overflow with Pearl" (520; ll. 19-20). Writing elsewhere that "She rose to His Requirement – dropt / The Playthings of Her Life," Dickinson suggests that the soul must "rise" to a higher calling and leave behind the earthly (732; ll. 1-2). But, as Dickinson intimates in the concluding stanza of that poem, these "playthings" live on, with spiritual lives of their own, even despite the allegorical comparison that apparently has evacuated them of meaning: "as the Sea / Develop Pearl, and Weed," (ll. 9-10). Like Saint Paul, Dickinson "puts away childish things" (1. Cor. 13:11). But her pasty and playthings, once "dropped," remain replete with resonance.

The pearl reflects a desire for access to that otherworldly realm of meaning beyond the physical. As the Jeweler communes wistfully with his deceased daughter, praying for knowledge of the life to come, Dickinson's "pearl" is charged, too, with love-longing for transubstantiation, as in her prayer to raindrops: "Myself Conjectured were they Pearls – What Necklaces could be" (794; ll. 7-8). And her hope for the grass is that it "thread the dews all night, like pearls," (333; ll. 9). The pearl announces a poetic sensibility that craves allegoresis, of a unity with the world that would produce spiritual transcendence. The pearl enables a mystical shift from the literal to the spiritual when Dickinson asks "Did the harebell loose her girdle / To the lover bee" (213; ll. 1-2). Dickinson's carnal research agenda–her prurience about pollination–is translated into a spiritual domain when, with a parallel question, she asks "Did the 'Paradise' – persuaded – / Yield her moat of pearl" (ll. 5-6). The pornography of bee/flower sex becomes translated into a spiritual deflowering when the soul, yielding up its virginal "pearl," is seduced by Paradise. The convoluted reversibility of typology, however, inspires Dickinson to recognize the ambiguity inherent in

Christian figuration: "Would the Eden," she asks, "*be* an Eden?" (ll. 7). If the literal is transcended, what remains of meaning? If, in fact, spiritual purity ends in an eroticized merging with the divine, how does one credit such a state without recourse to the letter? Dickinson's "pearl" must be the flag of a poetic disposition that desires to hold the contraries of type and anti-type, both together at once, transcended and yet reversed. It is this inability to let go—this inseparable cleavage between spiritual and earthly, despite all attempts at excision—that haunts the typological imaginary and that motivates the dreamer of the *Pearl*.

The pearl, too, embodies Dickinson's critique of the way in which modernity relies upon a Christian supercessionary logic in order to delineate its break with and supremacy over the past. "What once was 'Heaven'" Dickinson laments, "Is 'Zenith' now" (70; ll. 17-18) The regime of modern science "sees comparatively" and usurps old, religiously inflected signs. Science re-reads the world and empties it of spiritual content. Dickinson's vexed hope for a reversal, again, lies with the pearl:

> I hope the Father in the skies
> Will lift his little girl –
> Old fashioned – naughty – everything –
> Over the stile of "Pearl."
>
> (ll. 29-32)

A. W. Strouse researches and teaches medieval literature at the City University of New York. He is the author of *Retractions & Revelations* (Jerk Poet, 2014) and *My Gay Middle Ages* (punctum books, forthcoming).

XIV

THE JERUSALEM LAMB OF *PEARL*

Jane Beal

Near the conclusion of part XIII of *Pearl*, the Dreamer asks the Pearl-Maiden, "Quat kyn þyng may be þat Lambe / Þat þe wolde wedde vnto hys vyf?" (ll. 771-72) [What kind of thing may be that Lamb / that he would wed you as his wife?]. The Dreamer follows this question with an objection to her claim, as he understands it, to be the only bride of Christ – over all other women, however beautiful or virtuous they may have been in life. The Pearl-Maiden answers by clarifying the communal inclusivity of her spiritual marriage to Christ, alluding to John's spiritual vision of the New Jerusalem, and remembering the Crucifixion itself. Her answer, which makes up all of part XIV of *Pearl*, emphasizes the symbolic representation of Christ as Lamb and the theme of redemption made possible through Christ's death. Although the Dreamer's question appears to be motivated by an earthly jealousy, the Pearl-Maiden attempts to lift his understanding into a heavenly realm. Her words specifically foreshadow the vision the Dreamer will experience of the New Jerusalem and the bleeding Lamb later in the poem. Her explanation acts as both invitation and preparation, not only for the Dreamer, but also for the readers of *Pearl*.

The five stanzas of part XIV of *Pearl* can be read in relation to their literary and cultural contexts. To facilitate deeper understanding of the Pearl-Maiden's speech in these stanzas, this essay considers the complex interweaving of such important Christian theological ideas as the Bride of Christ, the Lamb of God, and the Crucifixion of Jesus as well as the prophecy of Isaiah concerning Christ and the Revelation of John regarding the Lamb on the throne at the time of the Last Judgment. Although the Dreamer's sorrow has complicated and challenged his prior understanding of his Catholic faith, the Pearl-Maiden's reminders of heaven, which she further develops in part XV, awaken in him a desire to enter heavenly places. Admittedly, at this stage in his spiritual journey, the Dreamer's primary desire is to go up in order to be with her, the young woman he loved and lost,[1] but his heart is also slowly awakening to a desire to be with Christ.

Bride of Christ

The Pearl-Maiden first revealed her spiritual marriage to Christ to the Dreamer at the end of part VII of *Pearl*: "I watȝ ful ȝong and tender of age / Bot my Lorde þe Lombe þurȝ hys godhede, / He toke myself to hys maryage ... I am holy hysse" (l. 412-14, 418) [I was very young and of tender age / But my Lord the Lamb through his divinity / took me to himself in marriage ... I am wholly his]. She affirms this again in part XIII, when she declares: "My makeleȝ Lambe þat al may bete," / Quod scho, "my dere destyné, / Me ches to hys make" ("My matchless Lamb who beats out all," / said she, "my dear destiny, chose me as his mate") (l. 757-59). She asserts her marriage for a third time in the first stanza of part XIV, this time explaining that she is not the Lamb's only wife (rather, she is one part of the corporate bride of Christ). In so saying, she alludes to Revelation 21 directly, which describes the New Jerusalem as a bride:

> "Maskelles," quod þat myry quene,
> "Vnblemyst I am, wythouten blot,
> And þat may I wyth mensk menteene;
> Bot 'makeleȝ quene' þenne sade I not.
> Þe Lambes vyueȝ in blysse we bene,
> A hondred and forty [fowre] þowsande flot,
> As in þe Apocalyppeȝ hit is sene;
> Sant John hem syȝ al in a knot.
> On þe hyl of Syon, þat semly clot,
> Þe apostel hem segh in gostly drem
> Arayed to þe weddyng in þat hyl-coppe,
> Þe nwe cyté o Jerusalem. (l. 781-92)

> ["Flawless," said that merry queen,
> "unblemished am I, without spot,

---

[1] On the nature of the relationship between the Pearl-Maiden and the Dreamer, see Jane Beal, "The Pearl-Maiden's Two Lovers," *Studies in Philology* 100:1 (Winter 2003): 1-21. Available at http://muse.jhu.edu/journals/sip/summary/v100/100.1beal.html.

and that may I in humility maintain.
But 'matchless queen' I did not say.
The Lamb's wives in bliss we are,
14[4],000 in company,
as is seen in the Apocalypse:
St. John saw them all together.
On the hill of Zion, that seemly group,
the apostle saw in a spiritual dream,
arrayed for the wedding on that hilltop,
the new city of Jerusalem."]

As in part VII, so in part XIII and here: in each instance in which the Pearl-Maiden claims to be married to Christ, the Dreamer has difficulty understanding and accepting the reality of her new marital status. It is as if he does not know, cannot remember, or is actively denying, because of his grief over the Pearl-Maiden's loss, what contemporary medieval readers might expect him to know as a Christian about the Bride of Christ, the *sponsa Christi* of Christian theology, from the Bible, the exegesis of Church Fathers, and the tradition of Catholic contemplative spirituality.

The tradition of imagining spiritual marriage to Christ in the Middle Ages has its roots in the Hebrew Bible and the Christian New Testament.[2] It was developed within the early church, particularly by the example of Augustine and the theory of sexual hierarchy articulated by Jerome in *Against Jovinian*, which emphasized the chaste ideal in a sexually immoral world; it was further emphasized in medieval virgin martyr legends.[3] Allegorical

---

[2] For direct Old Testament references to God as Bridegroom and Israel as Bride, see, for example, Isaiah 54 and 62, Ezekiel 16, and Hosea 1-3. For New Testament references to Christ as the Bridegroom, see how Jesus is depicted as referring to himself as such in the Synoptic Gospels (Matthew 9:15, Mark 2:19, Luke 5:34), the parable of the wise and the foolish virgins (Matthew 25:1-13), John the Baptist's recognition of Jesus as the bridegroom (John 3:27-30), the apostle Paul's allegorical meditation on marriage, especially as it is a picture of the relationship between Christ and the Church (Ephesians 5:21-32), and Revelation 21.

[3] In the tenth century, Hrotsvita of Gandersheim would write a number of plays celebrating the same plot: virgins resist attacks on their purity by vile men and are, miraculously, preserved in both life and chastity with the consequence that the men are frequently converted to Christianity (though often only after first being made to look ridiculous). As Karen A. Winstead

commentaries on the Song of Songs, beginning with Origen in the second century, infused Christian contemplation with a sensual and passionate language for imagining the soul's union with the divine.[4] By the twelfth century, Bernard of Clairvaux could celebrate the spiritual marriage of the soul to Christ extravagantly in his sermons on the Song of Songs without objection from his monastic audience to any conflict between the literal and spiritual sense of his text.

Bernard of Clairvaux, in his second sermon on the Song of Songs, provides an allegorical exegesis of the kiss mentioned in the first verse of that great epithalamion, which shows a clear set of connections, a continuum of relation, between *lectio divina*,[5] meditation on the senses of scripture, experiences of contemplative prayer, and the desire to pass through the stages of purgation and illumination to unification with God:

> All the prophets are empty to me. But he, he of whom they speak, let him speak to me. Let him kiss me with the kiss of his mouth ... His living and effective word is a kiss; not a meeting of lips which can sometimes be deceptive about the state of the heart, but a full infusion of joys, a revelation of secrets, a wonderful and inseparable mingling of the light from above in the mind on which it is shed, which, when it is joined with God, is one spirit with him ... O happy kiss, and wonder of amazing self-

---

has shown in her anthology, *Chaste Passions: Medieval English Virgin Martyr Legends* (Ithaca, NY: Cornell University Press, 2000), the stories of virgin martyrs had wide currency in England between the thirteenth and fifteenth centuries, with such famous saints as St. Lucy, St. Cecilia, St. Margaret, St. Agnes, and St. Katherine being just a few of those that were well-known. The Pearl-Maiden has been compared to at least one of these virgin martyrs, St. Margaret. See James Earl, "Saint Margaret and the Pearl Maiden," *Modern Philology* 70 (1972): 1-8.

[4] See E. Ann Matter, *The Voice of my Beloved: The Song of Songs in Western Medieval Christianity* (Philadelphia, PA: University of Pennsylvania Press, 1992) and Ann Astell, *The Song of Songs in the Middle Ages* (Ithaca, NY: Cornell University Press, 1995).

[5] Divine reading is discussed in further detail in the section of this essay focused on the Revelation of John (below).

humbling which is not a mere meeting of lips, but the union of God with man!⁶

In these words, Bernard reveals his own extensive practice of *lectio divina*, his own meditation on Scripture, and through his allegorical exegesis of the Song of Songs, shows how it led to an understanding of intimate, contemplative prayer–in which he could hear the voice of God–and the "kiss" experienced in this state that leads to the union of God with man.

Similarly to Bernard of Clairvaux, many medieval Christian women left written records that show that their own contemplative prayer life led, in a striking number of cases, to distinctive visions of their souls being married to Christ. Contemplative women who recorded their experiences of spiritual marriage include Angela of Foligno, Catherine of Siena, Birgitta of Sweden, Margery Kempe, and Teresa of Avila, among others.[7] While their spiritual visions met with a mixed reception by their contemporaries, rarely were they dismissed as heretical or unorthodox by the Church because of a clear tradition establishing precedent for their visions in scripture and church exegetical tradition.

Spiritual devotion to Jesus, and visionary experiences of spiritual marriage to him in prayer, can better be understood as part of the overall movement of affective piety in the Church in the later Middle Ages. Affective piety was the compassionate, co-identifying,

---

[6] Bernard of Clairvaux, *Selected Works*, trans. and forward by G.R. Evans, introduction by Jean LeClercq, Classics of Western Spirituality (New York: Paulist Press, 1987), 216-17.

[7] For discussion of this phenomenon in cultural context, see Bernard McGinn, *The Flowering of Mysticism, 1250-1350* (New York: Crossroad Publishing Company, 1998), the third volume in his series on the Presence of God; R. N. Swanson, *Religion and Devotion in Europe, c. 1215-c.1515* (Cambridge: University of Cambridge Press, 1995, rprt. 1997), esp. chap. 5 "Devotion"; Monica Furlong, *Visions and Longings: Medieval Women Mystics* (Boston: Shambala, 1997); Elizabeth Alvilda Petroff, ed., *Body and Soul: Essays on Medieval Women and Mysticism* (Oxford: Oxford University Press, 1994), and Steven Fanning, *Mystics of the Christian Tradition* (London: Routledge Press, 2001), esp. chap. 4 "The Western Church in the Middle Ages." For a discussion of spiritual marriage in another late-medieval, West Midlands text, see Heather Reid, "Female Initiation Rites and Women Visionaries: Mystical Marriage in the Middle English Translation of 'The Storie of Asneth,'" in *Women and the Divine in Literature Before 1700*, ed. Kathryn Kerby-Fulton (Victoria: University of Victoria, 2009), 137-152.

emotional response of believing Christians to the sufferings of Christ on the Cross, which, through scripted (and unscripted) prayers, hymns and lyrics, as well as interpretations of Augustine's writings and applications of Franciscan theology, encouraged contemplatives to imagine themselves beside Mary, the weeping mother of Jesus, at the foot of the Cross.[8] As Sarah McNamer has argued, late medieval meditations on the Passion are "richly emotional, script-like texts that ask their readers to imagine themselves present at scenes of Christ's suffering and to perform compassion for that suffering victim in a private drama of the heart."[9] McNamer sees this as a specifically historical and gendered experience of believing women, devoted to the suffering humanity of Christ, one in which loving and being loved by God was experienced not as a theological concept, but a lived reality.

Pearl aligns with this understanding of the gendered experience affective piety, with the female Pearl-Maiden showing a greater ability to meditate on Christ's Passion as well as, ultimately, to enter into a spiritual marriage with Christ,[10] experiences which are denied the male Dreamer, at least temporarily. (Of course, it must be acknowledged that the Pearl-Maiden is represented in the poem not only as a real person, infinitely precious to the Dreamer's limited

---

[8] See Rachel Fulton, *From Judgment to Passion: Devotion to Jesus and the Virgin Mary, 800-1200* (New York: Columbia University Press, 2005).

[9] Sarah McNamer, *Affective Piety and the Invention of Medieval Compassion* (Philadelphia: University of Pennsylvania Press, 2010), 1. Two related studies relevant for consideration of *Pearl* in the context of late-medieval contemplative devotion are Barbara Newman, "What Did It Mean to Say "I Saw"? The Clash between Theory and Practice in Medieval Visionary Culture," *Speculum* 80 (2005): 1-43 and Seeta Chagnati, *The Medieval Poetics of the Reliquary: Enshrinement, Inscription, Performance* (New York: Palgrave Macmillan, 2008), esp. chap. 4, "Enshrining Form: *Pearl* as Inscriptional Object and Devotional Event."

[10] It is worth noting that while most literary scholars see the Pearl-Maiden's loss as her death, one scholar has argued that her loss represents her enclosure in the religious life. See Lynn Staley, "*Pearl* and the Contingencies of Love and Piety," in *Medieval Literature and Historical Inquiry: Essays in Honor of Derek Pearsall*, ed. David Aers (Cambridge: D.S. Brewer, 2000), 83-11. In this case, when the Dreamer sees the Pearl-Maiden and hears her description of spiritual marriage, it follows that her spiritual marriage could equally well be before death in visionary contemplation. However, most medieval Christians expected to enter into the wedding feast of the Lamb, promised in Revelation, after their death, not before.

perceptions, but also, simultaneously, as an allegorical figure of multivalent meaning appearing for the edification of readers.) More importantly, these studies (noted above) show that spiritual devotion to Jesus, the suffering Christ on the Cross, was closely related to the contemplative journey into God and unification with the divine imagined as spiritual marriage. Thus it should come as no surprise that the Pearl-Maiden's revelation of her spiritual marriage to Christ is intimately connected to her highly imagistic, even visionary meditations on his Passion.

Lamb of God

In the second stanza of part XIV, the Pearl-Maiden reveals that she will meditate on Jerusalem. She has already spoken, in the first stanza, of the "nwe cyté o Jerusalem" (l. 792), the heavenly Jerusalem, an allusion to Revelation 21. Now she will speak of the historical Jerusalem. In so doing, she participates in a tradition of contemplative meditation on scripture and erudite Christian commentary on it, especially Augustine's well-known *De Civitate Dei* (*The City of God*), which contrasts Rome and Jerusalem, meditating on both the historical and the heavenly Jerusalem in the process.[11]

> "Of Jerusalem I in speche spelle.
> If þou wyl knaw what kyn he be,
> My Lombe, my Lorde, my dere Juelle,
> My Ioy, my Blys, my Lemman fre,
> Þe profete Ysaye of hym con melle
> Pitously of hys debonerté:
> 'Þat gloryous gyltleȝ þat mon con quelle
> Wythouten any sake of felonye,
> As a schep to þe slaȝt þer lad watȝ he;
> And, as lombe þat clypper in hande nem,
> So closed he hys mouth fro vch query,
> Quen Jueȝ hym iugged in Jerusalem.' (l. 793-804)

---

[11] Revelation 21 relates to Ezekiel 40:1-4 and 48:35, which similarly prophesies the coming of the New Jerusalem. In *De Civitate Dei* 20.19.17, Augustine gives commentary on the New Jerusalem, calling it the *visio pacis* ("vision of peace") for all Christian pilgrims. For further detail, see the entry on the "New Jerusalem" in *A Dictionary of Biblical Tradition in English Literature,* ed. David Lyle Jeffrey (Grand Rapids, Mich.: Wm. B. Eerdmans Publishing Co., 1992), 546-48.

["Of Jerusalem I will speak a while.
If you will know what kind he is –
my Lamb, my Lord, my dear Jewel,
my Joy, my Bliss, my generous Love –
the prophet Isaiah spoke of him,
compassionately of his graciousness:
"That glorious Guiltless One that men quelled
without any justification of felony:
like a sheep to the slaughter he was led there,
and, as a lamb that is taken in hand to be shorn,
so he closed his mouth to each question,"
when the Jews judged him in Jerusalem."]

Though the Pearl-Maiden says she will speak of Jerusalem (and indeed she does), her focus now is specifically on the death of the Messiah, which Isaiah predicted, that took place in this historical Jerusalem. But before she gives a paraphrase of Isaiah 53:7, she multiplies her love-names for her Bridegroom: "My Lombe, my Lorde, my dere Juelle, / My Ioy, my Blys, my Lemman fre." Notably, the first is "My Lombe."

The title *agnus Dei*, or Lamb of God, originates in John's Gospel, which depicts the moment when John the Baptist sees his cousin Jesus coming down to the Jordan to be baptized and declares: "Behold the Lamb of God who takes away the sins of the world!"[12] This title, "Lamb of God," is used a second time in the gospel (John 1:36). Later, John's Revelation expounds upon the evocatively imagistic connection between Christ and the Lamb, referring more than twenty-five times to the Lamb, though this Lamb of Revelation has lion-like qualities and sits enthroned at the Last Judgment.[13]

The identification of Jesus with the Lamb in the New Testament draws on the Jewish tradition of the Paschal Lamb. Jewish Law (*torah*) required that the lamb be a one-year old male lamb, without flaw, defect or blemish, offered as a sacrifice on Passover.

---

[12] John 1:29. In the final stanza of part XIV, the Pearl-Maiden will directly allude to this moment.

[13] For discussion of Christ as Lamb, see Robert C. Neville, *Symbols of Jesus: A Christology of Symbolic Engagement* (Cambridge: Cambridge University Press, 2001), esp. Ch. 2 "Jesus the Lamb: Blood Sacrifice and Atonement," 60-92. See also Andreas J. Kostenberger, L. Scott Kellum, and Charles L. Quarles, *The Lion and the Lamb: New Testament Essentials from the Cradle, the Cross, and the Crown* (Nashville, Tenn: B&H Academic, 2012).

Passover, the high holy day that commemorates the Exodus of the Jewish people under the leadership of Moses from slavery in Egypt;[14] it was the feast being celebrated in Jerusalem at the time of the Crucifixion of Jesus. *Pearl*, which scholars have sometimes associated with the Advent or Christmas season, actually uses Paschal (Easter) imagery predominantly.[15]

The image of the Lamb is central to the Christian liturgy of Easter, but the association of it is linked to the Jewish prophecy of Isaiah from the Old Testament that the Pearl-Maiden paraphrases: "He was oppressed, and he was afflicted, yet he opened not his mouth. Like a lamb that is led to the slaughter, and like a sheep that before its shearers is silent, so he opened not his mouth."[16] Christian tradition ties this passage to those moments in the Gospels during the trial of Jesus when he was silent in the face of accusation (Matt. 26:43, Mark 14:61, Luke 22:67).

The image of Jesus as the Lamb is present not only in biblical, literary, and liturgical traditions, but also in visual ones, for it was widely reproduced in medieval art in manuscripts, stained glass windows, and architectural carving as well as other media. Indeed, some literary scholars have argued that it is likely that the Pearl-Poet had seen and meditated deeply on the images of the *agnus Dei* and that these images, not scripture alone, directly influenced the imagery of *Pearl*.[17]

---

[14] For further detail on Christian understanding and incorporation of Passover in the liturgy of the Church, see *Illuminating Moses: A History of Reception from Exodus to the Renaissance*, ed. Jane Beal (Leiden: Brill, 2014), esp. Ch. 5, "Moses and the Paschal Liturgy," by Luciana Cuppo-Czaki. *Illuminating Moses* also expounds on the relationship between Moses and Jesus, who was regarded by Christians as a "second Moses."

[15] For discussion of the Easter season in relation to the symbolism of the poem, see Jane Beal, "The Signifying Power of *Pearl*," *Quidditas: The Journal of the Rocky Mountain Medieval Association* 33 (2012), 27-58.

[16] Isaiah 53:7.

[17] See Rosalind Field, "The Heavenly Jerusalem in *Pearl*," *Modern Language Review* 81 (1985): 7-17; Muriel Whitaker, "'Pearl' and Some Illustrated Apocalypse Manuscripts," *Viator* (1981): 183-96; and Nancy Ciccione, "*Pearl* and the Bleeding Lamb," *Approaches to Teaching the Middle English Pearl*, ed. Jane Beal and Mark Bradshaw Busbee (New York: MLA, forthcoming). A particularly striking image from a related medium comes from a panel of the Ghent altarpiece (1432 AD). Whitaker and Ciccione both note that the manuscript illustrations depicting a bleeding *agnus Dei*, as the poem *Pearl* does (l. 1135-36), are comparatively rare.

Crucifixion of Jesus

The Pearl-Maiden refers to Jesus as both her Lamb and her "lemman," which in Middle English means "lover."[18] The intimacy of the Pearl-Maiden's relationship to Christ, as his Bride, is signaled by the word "lemman," but Christ's role as lover is directly linked to Christ's fulfillment of the role of the unblemished Lamb of God. This can be seen earlier in the poem when the Pearl-Maiden first describes her spiritual marriage. The Lamb first calls her "my lemman swete" (l. 763), and then washes her clothes in his blood (l. 766), an image with its source in Revelation 12:11. In both Revelation and *Pearl*, the blood of the Lamb represents the blood Christ shed on the Cross. For in Christian theology, the suffering and death of Christ, endured at the Crucifixion in order to provide an atoning sacrifice for sin, unites fallen humanity to a pure and perfect God: it is what makes the Pearl-Maiden's marriage possible; it is the ultimate revelation of Christ's love.

It should therefore come as no surprise that in the third stanza of part XIV, the Pearl-Maiden describes Christ's Crucifixion.

> "In Jerusalem watȝ my lemman slayn
> And rent on rode wyth boyeȝ bolde.
> Al oure baleȝ to bere ful bayn,
> He toke on hymself oure careȝ colde.
> Wyth boffeteȝ watȝ hys face flayn
> Þat watȝ so fayr on to byholde.
> For synne he set hymself in vayn,
> Þat neuer hade non hymself to wolde.

---

[18] See Middle English Dictionary, s.v. "lemman," http://quod.lib.umich.edu/m/med/.

> For vus he lette hym fly3e and folde
> And brede vpon a bostwys bem;
> As meke as lomp þat no playnt tolde
> For vus he swalt in Jerusalem." (l. 805-16)

> ["In Jerusalem was my Love slain
> and torn on the cross with bold boys;
> to bear all our sorrows willingly,
> he took on himself our cold cares.
> With buffets was his face laid open
> that had been so fair to behold.
> Because of sin he made himself empty,
> who had never had any inclination to sin himself.
> For us he allowed himself to be scourged and bowed
> and stretched upon a cruel beam.
> As meek as a lamb that utters no complaint,
> for us he suffered in Jerusalem."]

The Pearl-Maiden's description is particular, focusing on the Cross ("rode"), the buffeting of Christ's face ("Wyth boffete3 wat3 hys face flayn"), and the scourging ("He lette Hym fly3e"), noting in addition the moment when Jesus gave up his spirit ("folde") after being stretched out upon the torturous cross-beam ("brede vpon a bostwys bem"). It is notable that this is not a historical summation of the betrayal by Judas, the desertion of the disciples, the trial by night, the walk to Calvary, or the events that took place at the foot of the Cross with John, Mary or others such as is found in the Gospels. The Pearl-Maiden's particular focus here is on Christ's suffering on the Cross. It is less in keeping with a historical account and more with mediation consonant with contemplative devotion and affective piety.

For the Pearl-Maiden is clearly expressing a compassionate, co-identifying, emotional response to Christ's suffering. Her description is so vivid it is almost as if she were present at the foot of the Cross herself. She imagines herself there, and through her description to the Dreamer, invites him to behold the Crucifixion with the eyes of his heart as well.

At the conclusion of the stanza, the Pearl-Maiden characterizes Jesus as humble lamb ("meke as lomp")[19] who makes no complaint. The humility and silence the Pearl-Maiden notes are both important here because they are exemplary, worthy of imitation, especially for one entering the contemplative life who wishes to draw near to God in prayer.[20] The Pearl-Maiden is inviting the Dreamer to think, to imagine, the way a Christian contemplative does. She is subtly leading the Dreamer forward toward the greater visions that will be revealed later in the poem. Will the Dreamer come to see Christ as Lamb and Lover as the Pearl-Maiden does?

Prophecy of Isaiah

In her speech to the Dreamer, the Pearl-Maiden is, in many ways, like a medieval preacher. She paraphrases scripture in her own vernacular words, she shows the relationship between Old Testament prophecy and New Testament fulfillment, and she appears to seek, through her exegetical exposition, to affect the heart and mind of her listener.[21] This becomes further evident in the fourth stanza of part XIV:

> "In Jerusalem, Jordan, and Galalye,
> Þer as baptysed þe goude Saynt Jon,
> His wordeȝ acorded to Ysaye.
> When Jesu con to hym warde gon,
> He sayde of hym þys professye:
> 'Lo, Godeȝ Lombe as trwe as ston,
> Þat dotȝ away þe synneȝ dryȝe
> Þat alle þys worlde hatȝ wroȝt vpon.

---

[19] Here, as elsewhere in the poem (e.g., l. 1046 "Lombe-liȝt"), the poet uses "lomp" as a *double entendre*, referring to Jesus as both the Lamb and the Lamp (or Light of the World).

[20] In the Middle Ages, humility was considered the first rung of the the ladder of contemplation that ascends into God. See, for example, Bernard of Clairvaux, *De gradibus*, in *Select Treatises of Bernard of Clairvaux: De Diligendo Deo and De gradibus humilitatis et superbiae*, ed. W.W. Williams and B.R.V. Mills (Cambridge University Press, 1926).

[21] Jane Chance discusses the Pearl-Maiden as preacher in her essay, "Allegory and Structure in *Pearl*: The Four Senses of the *Ars praedicandi* and Fourteenth-Century Homiletic Poetry," in *Text and Matter: New Critical Perspectives of the Pearl-Poet*, ed. Robert J. Blanch, Miriam Youngerman Miller, and Julian N. Wasserman (Troy, NY: Whiston, 1991), 31-59.

Hymself ne wroȝt neuer ȝet non;
Wheþer on hymself he con al clem.
Hys generacyoun quo recen con,
Þat dyȝed for vus in Jerusalem?'" (l. 829-40)

["In Jerusalem, Jordan, and Galilee,
where the good Saint John baptized–
his words agreed with Isaiah.
When Jesus went toward him,
he said of him this prophecy:
'Lo, God's Lamb, as true as stone,
that does away the heavy sins
that all this world has wrought.'
Himself, he never wrought any,
but on himself he can take all.
His generation who can reckon,
who died for us in Jerusalem?'"]

In this passage, the Pearl-Maiden recalls the ministry of John the Baptist in the geography of the Holy Land: Jerusalem, the Holy City; Jordan, the river where John baptized Jesus, and Galilee, the land where Jesus was raised from childhood to manhood. She then memorializes the moment when Jesus walked toward John to be baptized, and she paraphrases John's words ("Behold the Lamb of God who takes away the sins of the world"), noting how they accord with the prophecy of Isaiah 53 concerning the Suffering Servant (Jesus, according to Christian interpretation). But the Pearl-Maiden does more than paraphrase: she expands her source with her own metaphor. Specifically, she adds that God's Lamb is "as trwe as ston."

This simile is apt in the context of *Pearl* for it highlights the jewel-stone motif that rolls throughout *Pearl*.[22] Christ is also elsewhere called a "Jewel" (l. 795 and l. 1124); so is the Pearl-Maiden herself (ll. 23, 249, 253, 277), and so are souls in heaven (l. 929). The simile may also constitute an allusion to the idea that Christ is the stone that the builders rejected but who has become the

---

[22] For discussion, see Johnson, Wendell Stacey, "The Imagery and Diction of *The Pearl*: Toward an Interpretation," *English Literary History* 20 (1953): 161-80. Rpt. Conley, 27-49.

Cornerstone.[23] Certainly the Pearl-Maiden's words further develop the symbolic imagery used in the poem to represent Christ.

In this stanza, as in the previous one, the Pearl-Maiden emphasizes the Christian theological point that the Lamb's death is for "synne" (cf. l. 811 and l. 824) and "for vus" (cf. l. 816 and 829). She paraphrases Isaiah 53:8 when she asks, "Hys generacyoun quo recen con?" In the context of the original biblical passage, this question (a statement in Isaiah) is filled with pathos, for the Suffering Servant dies without issue, without child or heir, which was considered a tragedy in ancient Israel. Yet in the new context of *Pearl*, the question in Middle English may have another resonance, implying that Christ's "generation" – his offspring – cannot be reckoned, not because there are none, but because they are so many! Christ, through his death, regained all the children of God for heaven.

This, of course, is what Christian salvation means: to receive forgiveness from sin, the mercy of God, and entrance into heaven to live eternally with God and all the saints and the angels. The Pearl-Maiden appears to want the Dreamer to remember this. For she will go on to describe heaven (in part XV) before obtaining permission for the Dreamer to behold heaven in a vision that he sees with his own eyes.

It is worth observing that the Pearl-Maiden is, from a late-medieval perspective, a most unusual preacher: not male, but female; providing exegesis not on earth, but apparently from heaven; not from a pulpit, but in a vision. A medieval English member of the religious orders with a license to preach in the fourteenth-century might have shared similar, orthodox insights about this passage from John's gospel. But the Pearl-Maiden's "angelic bearing" (l. 754), her unique beauty and shining appearance, coupled with her articulation of knowledge – that should have been beyond her reach as one who knew neither the Lord's Prayer nor the Creed (l. 485) before her death – makes the force of her sermon all the more powerful to the Dreamer and the readers of *Pearl*. For she has apparently gained her understanding not from traditional catechizing, but from intimate relationship to Christ.

---

[23] See Psalms 118:22, Matthew 21:42, Mark 12:10, and Acts 4:11.

Revelation of John

In many ways, part XIV is "bookish," concerned as it is with the complex hermeneutical relationship between Old Testament prophecy, New Testament fulfillment, and translation of both into vernacular English poetry. The section's final stanza is especially so, elaborating on the Revelation of John and referring to the written record of it ("recorde"), the book of Revelation itself ("Apokalypeȝ"), and the opening of the book with seven seals ("Lesande þe boke with leueȝ sware / Þere seuen syngnetteȝ wern sette in seme") by Christ the Lamb sitting in the midst of the throne.

> "In Ierusalem þus my lemman swete
> Twyeȝ for lombe watȝ taken þare,
> By trw recorde of ayþer prophete,
> For mode so meke and al hys fare.
> Þe þryde tyme is þerto ful mete,
> In Apokalypeȝ wryten ful ȝare;
> Inmydeȝ þe trone, þere saynteȝ sete,
> Þe apostel Iohn hym saȝ as bare,
> Lesande þe boke with leueȝ sware
> Þere seuen syngnetteȝ wern sette in seme;
> And at þat syȝt vche douth con dare
> In helle, in erþe, and Jerusalem." (l. 830-41)

> ["Thus in Jerusalem my sweet Love
> twice as a lamb was taken there,
> by the true record of another prophet,
> in a manner so meek–thus all his fare.
> The third time completes all.
> In the Apocalypse written full clearly,
> in the midst of the throne, where the Saints sit,
> the Apostle John saw him plainly,
> opening the book with square leaves,
> where seven seals were set in the seam.
> And at that sight all shall bow,
> in hell, in earth, and in Jerusalem."]

The Pearl-Maiden's deep meditation upon scripture, evident in her learned discourse, reflects a practice among contemplatives of the medieval period known as *lectio divina* or divine reading. This practice fostered the ability to interpret the layers of meaning in scripture: literal (or historical), allegorical (or spiritual), moral (or ethical in application), and anagogical (or revelatory of things to come). It makes sense to reflect on this practice, and Christian contemplative hermeneutical approaches, before examining the final stanza more closely.

The practice of *lectio divina* was encouraged by the early Church Fathers: Augustine, Jerome, Ambrose, and Gregory as well as Origen and Cassian. Divine reading was actually a series of practices that could include beginning in silence, reading aloud, meditating, praying, contemplating and eventually applying the truths of scripture. Such intensive reading helped train contemplative Christians to read scripture for its multiple meanings. The four recognized levels of scriptural interpretation compelled the devout to pursue contemplative reading that could foster deeper understanding of biblical passages. The four levels are aptly summed up in a Latin phrase: *litera gesta docet; allegoria quod credas; moralis quid agas; quo tendas anagogia* ("the literal (sense) teaches deeds; the allegorical what to believe; the moral what to do; the anagogical where to go").[24] To derive the meaning from these senses required time and thought, which the founders of the monastic orders, particularly Saint Benedict, fully recognized. To accommodate *lectio divina*, Benedict's Rule permitted two hours of private scripture readings to monks, but three during the season of Lent; St. Caesarius of Arles likewise permitted two hours of private readings to nuns in his Rule.[25]

By the twelfth century, the stages of *lectio divina* were codified in a letter to a fellow monk by Guigo II, a Carthusian monk, and the letter circulated as a treatise known in Latin as the *Scala Paradiso* or the *Scala Claustralium*.[26] Guigo advised that the *lectio divina* include

---

[24] This medieval phrase occurs in various places, including a sermon of Jacobus de Fusignano, a Dominican friar and later bishop (fl. 1280s-1330s), in Siegfried Wenzel, *The Art of Preaching: Five Medieval Texts and Translations* (Washington, D.C.: The Catholic University of America Press, 2013), 60-61.

[25] Beryl Smalley, *The Study of the Bible in the Middle Ages* (Notre Dame, Ind.: University of Notre Dame Press, 1964, repr. 1978), 29.

[26] It was later translated into Middle English under the title *Ladder of Foure Ronges*. For an edition, see the one included in Barry Windeatt, *English Mystics of the Middle Ages* (Cambridge: University Press, 1994), 248-52; see also Guigo II the Carthusian, "Ladder of Monks" and "Twelve

reading, meditation, prayer, and contemplation. His letter begins in this fashion:

> When I was at hard at work one day, thinking on the spiritual work needful for God's servants, four such spiritual works came to my mind, these being: reading; meditation; prayer; contemplation. This is the ladder for those in cloisters, and for others in the world who are God's Lovers, by means of which they can climb from earth to heaven. It is a marvelously tall ladder, but with just four rungs, the one end standing on the ground, the other thrilling into the clouds and showing the climber heavenly secrets. This is the ladder Jacob saw, in Genesis, that stood on the earth and reached into heaven …
>
> Understand now what the four staves of this ladder are, each in turn. Reading, Lesson, is busily looking on Holy Scripture with all one's will and wit. Meditation is a studious in searching with the mind to know what was before concealed through desiring proper skill. Prayer is a devout desiring of the heart to get what is good and avoid what is evil. Contemplation is the lifting up of the heart to God tasting somewhat of the heavenly sweetness and savor. Reading seeks, meditation finds, prayer asks, contemplation feels …
>
> Reading puts, as it were, whole food into your mouth; meditation chews it and breaks it down; prayer finds its savor; contemplation is the sweetness that so delights and strengthens.[27]

For Guigo, then, as well as other Christian contemplatives in monastic environments, the practice of *lectio divina* connected his earthly experience with heavenly realities, as Jacob's dream of the ladder did for him at Bethel (Genesis 28). The stages of *lectio* were active, entailing commitments to seek, find, ask, and feel, and they

---

Meditations," trans. Edmund Colledge and James Walsh, *Cistercian Studies Series 48* (Kalamazoo, Mich.: Cistercian Publications, 1979).
[27] This translation is by Julia Bolton-Holloway. See "*The Ladder of Four Rungs*: Guigo II on Contemplation," http://ww.umilta.net/ladder.html.

were metaphorically akin to eating because they provided food for the soul.[28]

It is especially notable that Guigo anticipates that both those living inside the cloisters, oath-bound to the monastic life, and those living outside of them, as lay Christians in the world, would practice *lectio divina*: "This is the ladder for those in cloisters, and *for others in the world who are God's Lovers,* by means of which they can climb from earth to heaven" (emphasis added).

While the *Pearl*-Poet's status as a monastic or lay Christian is unknown, the visionary poem *Pearl* gives strong evidence that he practiced divine reading, for he paraphrases scripture throughout the poem, using it to compose, create, and interweave the four levels of meaning that he found in the Bible into his dream vision. Furthermore, the Dreamer's ascent through three ever rising landscapes – the earthly garden, the paradisial dreamscape, the heavenly vision of Jerusalem – act metaphorically like Jacob's ladder, the *scala paradiso* connecting earth to heaven and heaven to earth. The apotheosis of the poem, the grand vision of the New Jerusalem based upon Revelation 21, shows just how deeply the poet has meditated on scripture. But the Pearl-Maiden's revelations in part XIV demonstrate that she has gone before the Dreamer and scaled the stages that lead to heaven, with Christ's help, to become the Bride of Christ; she then comes to the Dreamer, Beatrice-like,[29] and lead him upward. She is actively pursuing this purpose at the conclusion of part XIV.

In the final stanza, the Pearl-Maiden again calls the Lamb "my lemman swete," echoing and repeating Christ's own words to her earlier before he washed her clothes in his blood: "Cum hyder to me, *my lemman swete,* / For mote ne spot is non in þe" (l. 763-64, emphasis added).[30] The concatenation word, "Jerusalem" (meaning "City of Peace"), is repeated in the first and last line of the stanza – as it has been in every stanza – and will be once more in the first line of part XV, when Christ is called, "Jerusalem Lombe" (l. 842). The image presented of the Lamb in part XIV, however, is not the Lamb

---

[28] See Michael Casey, *Sacred Reading: The Ancient Art of Lectio Divina* (Liguori, MI: Liguori/Triumph Publications, 1996) and chapters 3-6 in Guglielmo Cavallo and Robert Chartier, eds., *A History of Reading in the West* (Oxford: Blackwell Publishing Ltd., 1999).
[29] Beatrice is one of Dante's guides in *The Divine Comedy*.
[30] This passage alludes to Song of Songs 4:7-8.

led to the slaughter in the earthly city, but the Lamb with the book with seven seals in the heavenly city. This Lamb is depicted in Revelation 5-7 as being seated in the midst of the heavenly throne with a scroll, sealed with seven seals, which he alone is worthy to open.

In medieval iconographic tradition, the scroll was represented as a codex with seven signets and the Lamb resting or standing upon it.

Conclusions

In part XIV of *Pearl*, the Pearl-Maiden answers the Dreamer's question: "Quat kyn þyng may be þat Lambe / Þat þe wolde wedde vnto hys vyf?" (What kind of thing may be that Lamb / that he would wed you as his wife?) (ll. 771-72). She does so through a complex meditation on her role as Bride of Christ, Christ's role as the Lamb of God, and the Crucifixion of Jesus in the historical Jerusalem as well as the prophecy of Isaiah concerning the Suffering Servant (Jesus) and the Revelation of John regarding the Lamb on the throne at the time of the Last Judgment. Her explanation reveals that the spiritual practice of *lectio divina* and meditation on the four layers of meaning in scripture inform her understanding and that she seeks to similarly inform the Dreamer. She is preparing him for a future vision of the New Jerusalem. Indeed, the last line of the final stanza, "In helle, in erþe, and Jerusalem" (l. 841), suggests a ladder leading from death, through earthly existence, and into heaven.

Just as the Pearl-Maiden with the Dreamer, so the poet with his readers is issuing an invitation in the dream-vision poem to a deeper understanding of divine things. This is made manifest in subsequent parts of the poem and its conclusion, when the awakened Dreamer reveals his transformed understanding of Christ, whom he now regards not only as his Lord, but his Friend (l. 1204), and in the poet-narrator's reference to the Eucharist, which all believers partake of in the communal Mass.

Overall, part XIV acts as a foundation and preparation for future understanding, reinforcing knowledge of the relationship between the historical Jerusalem and the heavenly one and, most importantly, the Lamb's atoning sacrifice in the first and lordship in the second. The images of the Lamb that the Pearl-Maiden describes are iconic and meant, in the private contemplation of the heart, to draw readers closer to the love of God. Regardless of where readers are in their spiritual journey, they are invited to ascend higher into heavenly realms.

References

Astell, Ann. *The Song of Songs in the Middle Ages*. Ithaca, NY: Cornell University Press, 1995.

Beal, Jane, ed.. *Illuminating Moses: A History of Reception from Exodus to the Renaissance*. Leiden: Brill, 2014.

Beal, Jane. "The Signifying Power of *Pearl*." *Quidditas: The Journal of the Rocky Mountain Medieval Association* 33 (2012): 27-58. http://humanities.byu.edu/rmmra/pdfs/ 33.pdf.

Beal, Jane. "The Pearl-Maiden's Two Lovers," *Studies in Philology* 100:1 (Winter 2003): 1-21. Print. http://muse.jhu.edu /journals/sip/summary/v100/100.1beal.html.

Bernard of Clairvaux. *Selected Works*. Trans. and forward by G.R. Evans, introduction by Jean LeClercq. Classics of Western Spirituality. New York: Paulist Press, 1987.

Bolton-Holloway, Julia, trans.. "*The Ladder of Four Rungs*: Guigo II on Contemplation." http://www.umilta.net/ladder.html.

Casey, Michael. *Sacred Reading: The Ancient Art of Lectio Divina*. Liguori, Mich.: Liguori/Triumph Publications, 1996.

Cavallo, Guglielmo and Robert Chartier, eds.. *A History of Reading in the West*. Oxford: Blackwell Publishing Ltd., 1999.

Chagnati, Seeta. *The Medieval Poetics of the Reliquary: Enshrinement, Inscription, Performance*. New York: Palgrave Macmillan, 2008.

Chance, Jane. "Allegory and Structure in *Pearl*: The Four Senses of the *Ars praedicandi* and Fourteenth-Century Homiletic Poetry." In *Text and Matter: New Critical Perspectives of the Pearl-Poet*. Eds. Robert J. Blanch, Miriam Youngerman Miller, and Julian N. Wasserman. Troy, NY: Whiston, 1991. 31-59.

Ciccione, Nancy. "*Pearl* and the Bleeding Lamb." In *Approaches to Teaching the Middle English Pearl.* Ed. Jane Beal and Mark Bradshaw Busbee. New York: MLA, forthcoming.

Earl, James. "Saint Margaret and the Pearl Maiden." *Modern Philology* 70 (1972): 1-8.

Fanning, Steven. *Mystics of the Christian Tradition.* London: Routledge Press, 2001.

Field, Rosalind. "The Heavenly Jerusalem in *Pearl.*" *Modern Language Review* 81 (1985): 7-17.

Fulton, Rachel. *From Judgment to Passion: Devotion to Jesus and the Virgin Mary, 800-1200.* New York: Columbia University Press, 2005.

Furlong, Monica. *Visions and Longings: Medieval Women Mystics.* Boston: Shambala, 1997.

Guigo II the Carthusian. "Ladder of Monks" and "Twelve Meditations." Trans. Edmund Colledge and James Walsh, *Cistercian Studies Series 48.* Kalamazoo, Mich.: Cistercian Publications, 1979.

Jeffrey, David Lyle, ed.. *A Dictionary of Biblical Tradition in English Literature.* Grand Rapids, Mich.: Wm. B. Eerdmans Publishing Co., 1992.

Kostenberger, Andreas J., L. Scott Kellum, and Charles L. Quarles. *The Lion and the Lamb: New Testament Essentials from the Cradle, the Cross, and the Crown.* Nashville, Tenn.: B&H Academic, 2012.

"Lemman," Middle English Dictionary (online) - (accessed 23 July 2014).

Matter, E. Ann, *The Voice of my Beloved: The Song of Songs in Western Medieval Christianity.* Philadelphia, Penn.: University of Pennsylvania Press, 1992.

McGinn, Bernard. *The Flowering of Mysticism, 1250-1350.* New York: Crossroad Publishing Company, 1998.

McNamer, Sarah. *Affective Piety and the Invention of Medieval Compassion.* Philadelphia, Penn.: University of Pennsylvania Press, 2010.

Neville, Robert C.. *Symbols of Jesus: A Christology of Symbolic Engagement.* Cambridge: Cambridge University Press, 2001.

Newman, Barbara. "What Did It Mean to Say "I Saw"? The Clash between Theory and Practice in Medieval Visionary Culture," *Speculum* 80 (2005): 1-43.

Petroff, Elizabeth Alvilda, ed.. *Body and Soul: Essays on Medieval Women and Mysticism.* Oxford: Oxford University Press, 1994.

Reid, Heather. "Female Initiation Rites and Women Visionaries: Mystical Marriage in the Middle English Translation of 'The Storie of Asneth.'" In *Women and the Divine in Literature Before 1700.* Ed. Kathryn Kerby-Fulton. Victoria: University of Victoria, 2009. 137-152.

Smalley, Beryl. *The Study of the Bible in the Middle Ages.* Notre Dame, Ind.: University of Notre Dame Press, 1964, repr. 1978.

Staley, Lynn. "*Pearl* and the Contingencies of Love and Piety." In *Medieval Literature and Historical Inquiry: Essays in Honor of Derek Pearsall.* Ed. David Aers. Cambridge: D.S. Brewer, 2000. 83-11.

Swanson, R.N., *Religion and Devotion in Europe, c. 1215-c.1515.* Cambridge: University of Cambridge Press, 1995, repr. 1997.

Wenzel, Siegfried. *The Art of Preaching: Five Medieval Texts and Translations.* Washington, D.C.: The Catholic University of America Press, 2013.

Windeatt, Barry. *English Mystics of the Middle Ages.* Cambridge: Cambridge University Press, 1994.

Winstead, Karen A.. *Chaste Passions: Medieval English Virgin Martyr Legends.* Ithaca, NY: Cornell University Press, 2000.

Whitaker, Muriel. "'Pearl' and Some Illustrated Apocalypse Manuscripts." *Viator* (1981): 183-96.

Jane Beal, PhD is a writer, educator, and literary scholar. She has authored *John Trevisa and the English Polychronicon* (ACMRS, 2013), edited *Illuminating Moses: A History of Reception from Exodus to the Renaissance* (Brill, 2014), and with Mark Bradshaw Busbee, co-edited *Translating the Past: Essays on Medieval Literature in Honor of Marijane Osborn* (ACMRS, 2012) and *Approaches to Teaching the Middle English Pearl* (MLA, forthcoming). Her book, *The Signifying Power of Pearl*, is under review. She has served as a professor at Wheaton College and Colorado Christian University, teaching literature and creative writing, and a midwife in the U.S., Uganda, and the Philippines. She currently teaches at the University of California, Davis, where she is working on a new book about love and redemption in the mythology of J. R. R. Tolkien. She also writes poetry, fiction, and creative non-fiction. To learn more, see http://sanctuarypoet.net.

XV

FITT 15 – LESSE

Tekla Bude

Fitt 15 asks the reader to imagine the possibility of bliss as a logical or numerical problem. How does one understand heaven and God's grace through quantitative judgments? How do the rational operations of comparison, proportionality, and noncontradiction work when applied to the idea of perfection? Is it possible to compare one form of happiness or blessedness to another? Although these questions were part of Christian theology from its earliest instantiations, their deliberation took a decidedly analytical cast in the thirteenth and fourteenth centuries, as scholastic philosophy debated the nature and validity of Pelagianism, predestination, charity, and operant grace under the new infusion of Aristotelian thought brought about by translations of the *Logica Nova* in the 12th century.[1] Fitts 13-15 are concerned with these ideas, and Fitt 15 in particular addresses soteriological numerosity through a poetic adaptation of Revelation 7:1-17.[2]

---

[1] William J. Courtenay, *Schools and Scholars in Fourteenth-Century England* (Princeton: Princeton University Press, 1987); William J. Courtenay, *Capacity and Volition: A History of the Distinction of Absolute and Ordained Power* (Bergamo: Pierluigi Lubrina, 1990); Henrik Lagerlund, 'The Assimilation of Aristotelian and Arabic Logic up to the Later Thirteenth Century,' in *Medieval and Renaissance Logic*, ed. Dov M. Gabbay and John Woods (Amsterdam: Elsevier, 2008), 281-346; Lloyd A. Newton, ed., *Medieval Commentaries on Aristotle's* Categories (Leiden: Brill, 2008); Katherine H. Tachau, *Vision and Certitude in the Age of Ockham: Optics, Epistemology and the Foundations of Semantics, 1250-1345* (Leiden, 1988); Thomas Williams, 'Ockham's Repudiation of Pelagianism' in *The Cambridge Companion to Ockham*, ed. Paul Vincent Spade. (Cambridge: Cambridge University Press, 1999) 350-373.

[2] Richard K. Emmerson and Bernard McGinn, eds., *The Apocalypse in the Middle Ages* (Ithaca and London: Cornell University Press, 1992); Ann Raftery Meyer, *Medieval Allegory and the Building of the New Jerusalem* (Cambridge: D.S. Brewer, 2003); A. C. Spearing, *The* Gawain *Poet: A Critical*

In Fitt 13, the Narrator had assumed that the Pearl-Maiden's divine marriage displaced others: 'So many a comly onvunder cambe,' he says, 'and for that maryage al other depres' (ll. 775, 778). In other words, he imagines the space, and the joy, of heaven in terms of a figure that accords to topographical reason.[3] This is the beginning of a logical, and numerological, formulation of salvation that spurs the Narrator toward a dialectic engagement with the Pearl-Maiden. The Narrator's assumption at the opening of Fitts 13 and 14 is that grace works logically, like finite space, that it is rational, or indeed that it can be accounted for through language.[4] In response to this initial assumption, the Pearl-Maiden appropriates the terms of logic and reason – borrowing from Aristotle's *Categories* – in order to prove them insufficient to discuss the grace she experiences as the Bride of Christ, and it is with the Pearl-Maiden's response to the Narrator that Fitt 15 begins.

Study (Cambridge: Cambridge University Press, 1970), 165-6; Sarah Stanbury, *Seeing the* Gawain-*Poet: Description and the Act of Perception* (Philadelphia: University of Pennsylvania Press, 1991);
[3] Compare the Pearl-Maiden to Julian of Norwich, who was granted a vision into heaven in the Ninth Revelation of her Long Text, was granted a vision into heaven which was both hierarchical and democratizing:

> I saw thre hevens, and alle of the blissed manhed of Criste. And none is more, none is lesse, none is higher, none is lower, but even like in blisse[...] and I behelde with grete diligence for to wet how often he wolde die if he might. And sothly the nomber passed my understanding and my wittes so ferre that my reson might not, nor cold not, comprehende it ne take it.

Julian is wrestling with many of the same issues accounted for by *Pearl*: immediate knowledge and unity with God, the internal logical contradiction of celestial hierarchization, and the singularity of a perfect sacrifice. (See Julian of Norwich, *The Writings of Julian of Norwich: A Vision Showed to a Devout Woman and Revelation of Divine Love*, ed. Nicholas Watson and Jacquline Jenkins [University Park: Pennsylvania State University Press, 2006], 195-197).
[4] Rita Copeland and Ineke Sluiter, *Medieval Grammar and Rhetoric: Language Arts and Literary Theory, AD 300-1475* (Oxford: Oxford University Press, 2010); Donatus, *Ars Grammatica*, in *Grammatici Latini*, Vol. IV, 355-402; Priscian, *Institutiones Grammaticae*, in *Grammatici Latini*, Vol. 2, 1-597. Carin Ruff, 'Latin as an Acquired Language,' in *The Oxford Handbook of Medieval Literature*, Ralph Hexter and David Townsend, eds. (Oxford: Oxford University Press, 2012), 47-62.

Aristotle's *Categories* and medieval commentaries on them were some of the first texts studied by any medieval student of philosophy. A short text, its fifteen chapters focus on ten categories of being and language that can be applied to almost all words: substance, quantity, qualification, relatives, location, time, position, ownership, action, and affection. Although some words – like syncategorematic terms – exist outside of these categories, the text understands language to work logically and methodically: if a word can be placed in one category, it cannot belong to another without a fundamental change to its meaning. Medieval discussions of Aristotle's *Categories* tended to hold, as Aristotle and his commentators did, to logical proofs for their argumentation. The *Categories* had a wide influence on the medieval understanding of words, but also of substance, accident, and subjecthood, and they serve as the basis for the Narrator's understanding of grace and perfection at the beginning of *Pearl*. In both content and form, Fitt 15 applies the *Categories* to the landscape of *Pearl*, an implementation of logic that causes real problems when describing the infinitude of heaven.

> Thys Jerusalem Lombe had neuer pechche
> Of other huee bot quyt jolyf
> That mot ne masklle moȝt on streche,
> For wolle quyte so ronk and ryf.
> Forthy vche saule that hade neuer teche
> Is to that Lombe a worthyly wyf.
> (ll. 841-6)

The opening lines of Fitt 15 employ the well-worn metaphorics of color to invoke the idea of sinlessness: white is the symbolic color of purity, and the Lamb of God is white.[5] Furthermore, *pechche*, or

---

[5] Robert Blanch, 'Games Poets Play: the Ambiguous Use of Color Symbolism in *Sir Gawain and the Green Knight*,' *Nottingham Medieval Studies* 20 (1976): 64-85; Peter Dronke, 'Tradition and Innovation in Western Colour-Imagery,' in *The Medieval Poet and His* World (Rome: Edizioni di Storia e Letteratura, 1984), 55-104; John Gage, *Color and Meaning: Art, Science, and Symbolism*, (Berkely: University of California Press, 1999); 'Though your sins are as scarlet, they will be as white as snow; though they are red like crimson, they will be like wool'. '*Si fuerint peccata vestra ut coccinum, quasi nix dealbabuntur; et si fuerint rubra quasi vermiculus, velut lana alba erunt*' (Isaiah 1:18).

'patch,' and its sonic resonance with the French *péché*, or 'sin' would not have been unfamiliar to a writer as well-versed in medieval Romance as the *Pearl*-poet, further stressing the contrast of white with blamelessness and of patches to sin. The *teche*-less human soul, a match for the Lamb's purity, is worthy of becoming Christ's mystical bride.

But white (*albus*) is also one of those terms fundamental to medieval philosophy, used as an exemplar in discussions of accidents and the qualities of substances.[6] Accidents refer to attributes like quantities (four, five), qualities (mortal, white), relatives (double, half), times (yesterday), and so forth; they are present in subjects, but do not have a real existence apart from them.[7] White, (*albus*) in particular held a place of importance in medieval philosophy, often used as the exemplar of an accident, a placeholder for thinking about the properties of accidents in general.[8] Medieval philosophy was not only concerned with subjects and predicates or with substances and accidents. The *Categories* were foundational for medieval philosophy because the text could also be interpreted as a work of grammar and logic.[9] To the logician's mind, the *Categories* presented subjects and predicates as the building blocks of syllogisms and propositional statements, rather than as descriptors of substances that actually existed.

Following Aristotle, medieval logicians and metaphysicians alike defined four classes of categorical statements which comprised

---

[6] Color is present in body, therefore in individual bodies, for if there were no individual body in which it was present, it could not be present in body at all. Thus everything except primary substances is either predicated of primary substances, or is present in them, and if these last did not exist, it would be impossible for anything else to exist. See, for instance, William J. Courtenay, *Ockham and Ockhamism: Studies in the Dissemination and Impact of His Thought* (Leiden: Brill, 2008), 68ff.

[7] Aristotle, *Categories* and *De Interpretatione*, trans. and ed., J. L. Ackrill (Oxford: Clarendon Press, 1963), I.5

[8] 'Some things, again, are present in a subject, but are never predicable of a subject. For instance, a certain point of grammatical knowledge is present in the mind, but is not predicable of any subject; or again, a certain whiteness may be present in the body (for colour requires a material basis), yet it is never predicable of anything.' Aristotle, *Categories* and *De Interpretatione*, trans. and ed., J. L. Ackrill (Oxford: Clarendon Press, 1963), I.2.

[9] Lloyd A Newton, ed. *Medieval Commentaries on Aristotle's* Categories (Leiden: Brill, 2008).

the building blocks of argumentation. These are the universal ('All men are white'), the particular ('Some men are white'), the indefinite ('A man is white'), and the definite ('This man is white'). From these types of statements, and with the addition of negating terms, logicians were able to build the propositions fundamental to syllogisms and sophistic rhetoric. They also developed theories of supposition, restriction, amplification, and modality, defining how predicates range over a domain of individuals and whether qualities ascribed to a subject always apply to that subject.[10] The first stanza of Fitt 15 sets up the idea of sinlessness as a series of propositions, logical statements which proceed from one idea to the next. One might construct the following syllogism, for instance, about the wives of the Lamb:

> All souls which are *techeless* are *worthyly wyves*.
> This particular soul is *wythoute teche*.
> Therefore, she is a *worthyly wyf*.

Of course, *Pearl* is more than a series of simple syllogisms, and reducing it to propositional logic requires ignoring the metaphors, symbolism, and diction that make this poem singular among medieval literary productions. However, the Narrator's questions take the form of logical statements, and the Pearl-Maden's responses operate within dialectical discourse, requiring readers to, at least at first, take seriously the logical formulae in operation here: the Lamb is white (which equates to perfection); if he were not, he would no longer be the Lamb. To the extent that this poem operates allegorically, the term *quyt* is not only a description of the Lamb, but an accident universally applicable to all subjects (*vche saule*) in pursuit of purity.

Take, for instance, the word *ryf* (l. 844), which means 'plentiful' or 'abundant', and is applied to the *quyte* earlier in the line. In one

---

[10] John Duns Scotus was the first medieval philosopher to use modality as a means of allowing for alternative possibilities at a given time. This allowed him to posit interesting things about predestination and the absolute and ordained powers of God. For Scotus, even though God knows the future and predestines it; it is still contingent. the only difference is that 'God's activity all takes place in a single individual moment or *nunc* that never passes into the past' (Calvin G. Normore, 'Duns Scotus's Modal Theory,' in *The Cambridge Companion to Duns Scotus*, ed. Thomas Williams [Cambridge: Cambridge University Press, 2002], 129-31).

sense, this is the *Pearl*-poet engaging in an ineffability topos: white is abundant in whiteness. But, logically, what does it mean for whiteness to be 'abundant' in itself? Can qualities be diminished or intensified and still remain the qualities in question? Is it possible to be more white than white? As it turns out, fourteenth-century philosophers, following Nicole Oresme, used the idea of the latitude of forms to explore this very issue.

> And thagh uch day a store He feche
> Among uus commes nouther strot ne stryf,
> Bot uchon enlé we wolde were fyf.
> The mo the myryer, so God me blesse,
> In compayny gret our luf con thryf
> In honour more and neuer the lesse
> (ll. 847-852)

As the first stanza ends, the Pearl-Maiden describes heaven in a series of logical propositions that operate parallel to the metaphor of pearl-white wool developed in the first half of the stanza.[11] But her description of heaven results in a paradox: if the Jerusalem Lamb and his brides are already white, without *teches* – metaphorically and literally without blemish – how is it possible for their honor to become greater? How can something that is already perfectly white become more perfectly white?

These questions echo a line of philosophical inquiry that began in earnest in Paris in the late thirteenth century, and continued in Oxford the fourteenth: what is the real categorical distinction between quantity and quality? Can qualities be quantified? Aristotle had said no: quantities and qualities were different types of things, and could not be combined or confused with each other. In chapter 6 of the *Categories*, Aristotle holds to the rigorous separation of qualities and quantities:

> A quantity does not admit of a more and a less. Four-foot for example: one thing is not more four-foot than another. Or take number: we do not speak of a three as more three than a five, nor of one three as more three than another three. Nor yet is one time called more a time than another. Nor is there a single one, among those we listed, as to

---

[11] Terence Parsons, *Articulating Medieval Logic* (Oxford: OUP, 2014), 7.

which a more and a less is spoken of. Hence a quantity does not admit of a more and a less.[12]

With a few notable exceptions, medieval theologians and logicians agreed that quantity and quality were irrevocably different, arguing against metabasis, or the transition of methodology from one science to another (in this case, the possibility of enumerating just how 'white' something was). While in traditional logic something may be white, whiter, or whitest, this difference was inherently unquantifiable. William Ockham, Nicole Oreme, and the Oxford Calculators posited the opposite: that qualities could be quantified.[13] As employed by late scholasticism, this idea lead to that of the latitude of forms, wherein 'any quality which admits of variation and involves the intuitive idea of intensity – that is, such notions as velocity, acceleration, and density' could be expressed quantitatively.[14] The latitude of a form described how much of a quality something possessed, and philosophers discussed primarily how this quality was lost or intensified (*remissio* or *intensio*). That whiteness, for instance, which is explored in lines 841-846, could admit of intensification or diminution is not merely poetic wordplay; rather, Fitt 15 asks the reader to imagine the latitude of forms applying to *quyte*ness, and also to heavenly *honour* (l. 852) and *blysse* (l. 863). This does not imagine the qualities at play as classical *qualia*, which in most medieval philosophy could not be quantified, but rather, as qualities that might possibly admit of measurement.

Does *Pearl*'s hermeneutic allegiance lie with the concept of the latitude of forms? The first lines of this stanza gesture toward a particulated, measurable cohort of heavenly wives, where *uch day* the bridegroom brings more maidens to heaven, *uchon* wishing she were *fyf*, thus making infinite merriment *myryer*. Heaven is also imagined as a space that adheres to mathematical topographies. However, the lack of quantification in this same stanza (*mo the myryer*) and the purely qualitative and comparative *in honour more and never the lesse*

---

[12] Aristotle, *Categories*, I.6.
[13] Steven J. Livesey, 'William of Ockham, the Subalternate Sciences, and Aristotle's Theory of *Metabasis*', *The British Journal for the History of Science*, 18:2 (1985), 127-45; Livesey, 'The Oxford Calculatores, Quantification of Qualities, and Aristotle's Prohibition of Metabasis', *Vivarium*, 23:1 (1986), 50-69;
[14] Carl B Boyer, *The History of the Calculus and its Conceptual Development* (New York: Dover, 1949), 73

of the final line suggest that enumeration is not necessarily the only aspect of *Pearl*'s heavenly landscape.

Lesse is a particularly powerful end-word for this series of stanzas because it is relational (unlike *fewer*, which would denote discrete, calculable entities).[15] At the same time, while *lesse* ends every stanza of Fitt 15, the longer phrase *neuer the lesse* does as well, and this phrase has the capacity to modify the comparative function of *lesse*. *Neuer*, it should be noted, cannot be the subject or the predicate of a proposition, and as such is a type of word medieval scholars called *syncategorematic:* a word which contributes to the formal structure of a proposition, but which operates outside of the distinctions of Aristotle's *Categories*. The introduction of *neuer* before *lesse* places the *lesse sous rature*, reinterpreting it to mean any number of things: *nevertheless* (besides), *neuer lesse* (always more), as well as *neuer lesse* (always fewer, a quantifiable amount, rather than less, an unquantifiable comparative term).

> Lasse of blysse may non vus bryng
> That beren thys perle vpon oure bereste,
> For thay of mote couthe neuer mynge
> of spotlez perlez that beren the creste.
> (ll. 853-856)

Scholars are divided over whether Fitt 15's six stanzas are intentional, or the result of an editorial or authorial mistake.[16] The numerology of Cotton Nero A.x as a whole supports the inclusion of all six stanzas: with the sixth stanza in Fitt 15, *Pearl* runs to 101 stanzas, the same number as in *Gawain*. Edward Condren's monograph on the *Pearl*-poet notes that the sixth stanza in Fitt 15 is of numerical importance to the poem – and Cotton Nero A.x as a whole.[17] Condren's study notes not only the number of stanzas of

---

[15] *Pearl* uses this language elsewhere; compare 15's use of *lesse* with Fitt 3 (*more and more*), 10 (*more*), and 11 (*inoghe*).

[16] Charles Osgood proposed, for instance, that the second stanza of Fitt 15 is otiose, whereas Andrew and Waldron propose that all of Fitt 15's stanzas are intentional. Malcolm Andrew and Ronald Waldron, *The Poems of the Pearl Manuscript: Pearl, Cleanness, Patience, and Gawain and the Green Knight* (Exeter: University of Exeter Press, 2002), 94; Charles C. Osgood, ed. *The Pearl* (Boston and London: Heath, 1906).

[17] Edward I. Condren, *The Numerical Universe of the Gawain-Pearl Poet* (Gainesville: University Press of Florida, 2002).

Pearl and *Gawain*, but also goes further: *Pearl* and *Purity* both have 12 extra lines than a round number (and 1200 and 1800 = 3000) and *Patience* and *Gawain* have 31 extra lines (and 500 and 2500 also = 3000).[18] He also notes that the manuscript's total line numbers adhere to the Golden Ratio (that is, a:b::b:c, and a+b=c). But here Condren should be regarded a little more carefully. The numbers are close to the Golden Ratio, but not nearly as exact as to allow us to reject or accept a stanza from *Pearl* based on his calculations. For instance, if *Pearl* contains its current number of 1212 lines, *Purity* 1812, *Patience* 531, and *Sir Gawain and the Green Knight* 2351, then *Purity* + *Patience* = a (2343), *Pearl* + *Gawain* = b (3563), and the totality of the manuscript = c (5906), a:b::b:c is not exact (a:b = 0.6576 and b:c=0.6033, a difference of 8.60% from the mean). Taking away a stanza from *Pearl* would not only make the poem itself a round number (at 1200 lines), but it would also affect the Golden Ratio calculation by an almost insignificant amount (a:b = 0.6598 and b:c = 0.6025, a difference of 8.61% from the mean).

However, the *Pearl*-poet is obviously concerned with number and magnitude, and Fitt 15's particular concern with numerosity makes an extra stanza here both appropriate and ironic. When, for instance, line 853 suggests that none of the Brides of Christ may have *lasse* of bliss, this suggests that *blysse* exists as part of the qualitative, rather than quantitative role of medieval categories of language and/or being. If in some hypothetical heaven, the maiden were to become less blessed, would she also lose her status as a *worthyly wyf?* This brings us back, once more, to the latitude of forms: a person may become more or less hirsute and remain just as much a person as they were before; the same person may not become more or less alive and remain a human being.[19] Is bliss the former type of quality, or the latter? This stanza suggests that to lessen the Pearl-Maiden's degree of *blysse* is impossible without changing her substance, and that her state of pearl-white spotlessness is literally the *least* blessed she can possibly be.[20] The six-stanza form of Fitt 15 performs the

---

[18] See also Cary Nelson, *The Incarnate Word: Literature as Verbal Space* (Urbana: University of Illinois Press, 1973).
[19] Tanay, 79.
[20] F.A.C. Mantello and A.G. Rigg, *Medieval Latin: an Introduction and Bibliographical Guide* (Washington, DC: Catholic University of America Press, 1996) 355-6.

superfluity of perfected bliss; any diminution of it would return Fitt 15 back to the mundane, normal formal structure of the other fitts.

> We thurȝoutly hauen cnawyng;
> Of on dethe ful oure hope is drest.
> (ll. 859-60)

The Pearl-Maiden's paradoxical status as perfectly, and yet least, blessed redounds again in these lines, as her knowledge is defined as *thurȝou*: complete knowledge of perfection, the sum total of all possible knowledges about the *perle* (l. 854), the *Lombe* (l. 861), and his *dethe* (l. 860); this is the epistemic equivalent of infinite aggregation, as all knowledges of particulars eventually lead to the singularity, which is an understanding of salvation. These lines juxtapose the *ful*ness of hope with Christ's sacrifice, a contrast between the immeasurable infinite and the idea of singularity, *on dethe* serving as the basis of all accounting.[21]

A similar idea appears in Julian of Norwich's *Revelations*, which contemplate *less*eness, blessedness, and the death of Christ. Near the beginning of the Short Text, Julian describes her spiritual vision as something like a pearl: a small object the size of a hazelnut.

> [The Lord] shewed me a litille thinge the quantite of a haselle nutte, lygande in the palme of my hande, and, to my understandinge, that it was as rounde as any balle. I lokede theropon, and thought: 'Whate maye this be?' And I was answerde generaly thus: 'It is alle that is made.' I merveylede howe that it might laste, for methought it might falle sodaynlye to nought for litille. And I was answerde in mine understandinge: 'It lastes and ever shalle, for God loves it.'[22]

Only a few lines later, Julian notes that when she is 'substantiallye aned' (united in substance) to God she will have 'full reste' and 'varray blisse,' which is essentially what is happening in *Pearl* in lines

---

[21] For discourses of medieval accounting, see Rosemary O'Neill, *Accounting for Salvation in Middle English Literature* (PhD diss, University of Pennsylvania, 2009).

[22] Julian of Norwich, *Writings*, 69.

859-60.²³ This was a common technique in the medieval period: as the worshipper ascended from meditation to the higher rungs of contemplation, one common maneuver was to reduce the object of meditative fixation away from complex images and narratives down to their smallest form.²⁴ This abnegation of imagination provided for the operation of the affective powers of the soul. *Pearl* repeatedly toys with the distinction between meditation, with its reliance on narrative, description, and images, and contemplation, with its desire to break free from the imagination for the sake of the lapidary object. These issues are not unique to *Pearl*, or Julian, and indeed are commonplaces of mystical texts, especially those in the pseudo-Dionysian tradition.²⁵ *On the Divine Names,* Chapter 5, discusses the possibility of number as it relates to heaven:

> Every number preexists uniquely in the monad, and the monad holds every number in itself singularly. And every number is united in the monad; it is differentiated and pluralized only insofar as it goes forth from this one. All the radii of a circle are brought together in the unity of the center that contains all the straight lines brought together within itself. These are linked one to another because of this single point of origin and they are completely unified at this center. As they move a little away from it they are differentiated a little, and as they fall farther they are farther differentiated. That is, the closer they are to the center point, the more they are at one with it and at one

---

[23] Julian of Norwich, *Writings*, 69.
[24] Michelle Karnes, *Imagination, Meditation, and Cognition in the Middle Ages* (Chicago: University of Chicago Press, 2011); Mary Stallings-Tany, ed. *Meditaciones vite Christi, olim S Bonauenturo attributae*, Corpus Christianorum Mediaevalis vol. 153 (Turnholt: Brepols, 1997), chap 49, ll 45-53.
[25] This includes Robert Grosseteste and Albertus Magnus' translations and commentaries on the pseudo-Dionysian corpus, as well as Aquinas and Bonaventure, who cite him and praise him throughout their work. In addition to this, late medieval mysticism was frequently reliant on the *via negativa*. This includes mystics such as Marguerite Porete, Meister Eckhart, Johannes Tauler, Jan van Ruusbroec, *The Cloud of Unknowing*, and Nicholas of Cusa.

with each other, and the more they travel away from it the more they are separated from each other.[26]

Pearl suggests that *on dethe*, like the pearl itself, is the monad which serves as the basis of number, it is the singular thing on which infinitude rests.[27]

> And with him maidens hundrethe thowsande,
> And fowre and forty thowsande mo.
> (ll. 869-70)

The specific number of maidens is borrowed from John's Revelation in 7:1-7, which tallies 12,000 from each tribe of Israel for a total of 144,000, although here there are twelve groups of twelve thousand virgins each. Notably, this number is later changed to 100,000: '*Hundreth thowsandes I wot there were*,' the Narrator remarks in Fitt 19 (l. 1107). Why this discrepancy? Part of the reason is metrical, but part of the point of Fitt 15 is a negation of the power of specific enumeration. This account is numerically true in the same sense that '*the mo the myryer*' (l. 850) is true and in the same way that the maiden says '*uch on enle we wolde were fyf* (l. 849). That is, both 100,000 and 144,000 maidens are type of perfection, a form of *neuer the lesse* which presents itself as quantitative but is in fact qualitative. Having already negotiated the coincidence of opposites in the infinitesimal/infinite in lines 859-60, *Pearl's* numerical contradiction proposes the coincidence of quantity and quality.

> A hue fro heuen I herde thoo
> Lyk flodez fele laden runnen on resse;
> And a thunder browez in torrez blo.
> That lote, y leve, was never the les.
> (ll. 873-876)

This stanza continues the Johannine revelation which comprises stanzas three through five, although it greatly elaborates on the

---

[26] Pseudo-Dionysius, *The Divine Names*, in Pseudo-Dionysius, *The Complete Works*, (Mahwah: Paulist Press, 1987), pp. 99-100.
[27] For more on the monad, see Peck, Russell A. 'Number as Cosmic Language,' in *Essays in the Numerical Criticism of Medieval Literature*, ed. Caroline D. Eckhardt (London: Associated University Press, 1980), 15-64.

quality of the song sung by the throng of the blessed in the Biblical account. This is also one of very few references to hearing in *Pearl*, and is the only sustained call to attend specifically to the text's sonic environment. Until this point in *Pearl* and particularly in Fitt 15, the balance between quantitative and qualitative measurement has been held in tension: the *spotlez perlez* of the heavenly brides representing the potential for both enumeration and its impossibility. Pearls are metonymies for completion, but are also counting-stones (*calculi*), individual entities.

This stanza departs from the language of *discreta* in what will be a twenty-five-line comparative analysis of musical sound. First, the text focuses on music as *flodez, thunder,* and *torrez* which *run* and *brow*, undifferentiable and totally unified. This *hue* manifests as a continuous, which makes it fundamentally different from the divisible sound which comprises spoken language. St Augustine's description of music as *rhythmus continuus* had broad implications when thinking about the nature of time, motion, and number as it applied in a musical context.[28] Dorit Tanay notes the importance of this way of thinking to late medieval sound-science, where the very idea of continuity was considered antithetical to the idea of the particle. 'Nothing continuous,' she notes, was thought to be

> composed of indivisibles. A line cannot be composed of points, the line being continuous and the points indivisible, for the extremities of two points can be neither one.[29]

This idea again is borrowed from Aristotelian physics and categories, which forbade the metabasis of continua (which were qualitative) and discrete numbers (which were quantitative). From Zeno (d. ca. 430 BC) onward, discourses of measurement dealt with the coincidence of opposites (also known as dichotomy), that is, how infinity might be constructed of infinitesimals, as part of a discourse on movement and change. Zeno's paradox is famous, and illustrative of the point: in order to cover a distance from point A to

---

[28] Allan Fitzgerald and John C. Cavadini, eds., *Augustine Through the Ages: An Encyclopedia* (Grand Rapids: Eerdmans, 1999), 473.

[29] Dorit Tanay, *Noting Music, Marking Culture: The Intellectual Context of Rhythmic Notation, 1250-1400* (American Institute of Musicology: Hänssler-Verlag, 1999), 103.

point B, first Socrates must cross from point A to halfway to point B (point C). From C to B, one must pass half of that distance (point D), and from D to B, half that distance again. This same halving of the distance can be done *ad infinitum*, and therefore, Zeno posited, Socrates will never reach his goal. In fact, he posited, all movement whatsoever is impossible. In order to resolve Zeno's paradox, one must understand that the series ($½ + ¼ + 1/8 + 1/16 + 1/32 \ldots = 1$); that is, that an infinite sum of infinitely smaller fractions, in this case, results in a rational number. This was an unsettling problem for medieval mathematicians, who, apart from a few figures (like Tewkesbury, Oresme, or the Oxford Calculators) considered Zeno's paradox to be highly problematic, if not insoluble.[30] Augustine's description of musical temporality depended this type of continuity, wherein its parts must also be continua, and never infinitesimals. The revelatory opening of *Pearl*'s musical awareness operates within the classical numero-metrical vein.

However, in the late thirteenth and early fourteenth centuries, a new type of mathematical thought was introduced into music theory through the use of the latitude of forms. John Tewkesbury's *Quatuor principalia musicae* suggests that music might be both continuous and discrete. 'There is no doubt that music is made up of both quantities,' he said, '*musica plana* is constituted in one way and *musica mensurabilis* in the other.'[31] Tewkesbury differentiates between two types of music in his description of musical divisibility. The first, *musica plana*, or plainsong, is continuous. The second, *musica mensurabilis*, mensurable music or polyphony, is discrete. This difference arises from the quality of plainsong and polyphony in the context of both theory and in performance. Plainsong, with its long melismatic phrases and its independence from concerns about voicing and harmony, concerns

---

[30] Elzbieta Jung and Robert Podkonski, 'Richard Kilvington on Continuity,' in *Atomism in Late Medieval Philosophy and Theology*, ed. Christophe Grellard and Auråelien Robert (Leiden: Brill, 2009), 65-84.

[31] *Quatuor principalia musicae*, CS IV:254; *Cum omnis quantitas aut est continua aut discreta...* (following Boethius)... *in utraque quantitae musicam esse constitutam non est dubium; sed aliter plana et aliter mensurabilis musica se habet.* Dorit Tanay, *Noting Music, Marking Culture: The Intellectual Context of Rhythmic Notation, 1250-1400* (American Institute of Musicology: Hänssler-Verlag, 1999), 115.

the raising and lowering of the voice [...] which consist in continuous quantity. Such a quantity begins with a finite magnitude, but decreases to infinity. For if we take a line of a foot long [...] it can be divided equally in two, and its half can be cut in half again. And in turn its half can be divided in half, and no limit can ever be set to dividing a magnitude.[32]

Tewkesbury's *musica plana* and the *torrez* of sound are theoretically different from mensurable music, because plainsong is infinitely divisible into continua which never become infinitesimals, that is, their *lote is neuer the lesse* – never the smallest in size. When *Pearl* first represents Saint John's sonic revelation, he experiences it as a continual entity.

> A note ful new I herde hem warpe
> To lysten that watz ful lufly dere.
> As harporez harpen in her harpe,
> That nwe songe thay songen ful cler,
> In sounande notez a gentyl carpe;
> Ful fayre the modez thay fonge in fere.
> Ryȝt byfore Godez chayere
> And the fowre bestez that Hym obes
> And the aldermen so sadde of chere,
> Her songe thay songen, neuer the les.
> [...]
> Nowthelese non was never so quoynt,
> For alle the craftes that ever thay knewe,
> That of that songe myght synge a poynt
> Bot that meyny the Lombe that swe

---

[32] *Quatuor principalia musicae*, CS IV:254; *Elevationis namque vocum et depositionis certa limitatio, per pondera et per mensuram ut in cordarum extentione inventa est, ut patet in Secundo principale cap. 2, ex quibus, plana musica et ejus proportiones exordia sumpserunt quae in continua consistun quantitate, de quibus dictum est superius. Quae quidem quantitas incipit a magnitudine quae finita est, sed decrescit in infinitum. Nam si sit vel pedalis linea vel cujuscumque alterius modi, potest in duo aequa dividi, ejusque medietas in aliam medietatem secari. Rursusque ejus medieta in aliam medietatem dividi, ut nunquam dividendi magnitudinem ullus terminus fiat.* Dorit Tanay, *Noting Music, Marking Culture: The Intellectual Context of Rhythmic Notation, 1250-1400* (American Institute of Musicology: Hänssler-Verlag, 1999), 115-16.

> For thay arn bo3t, fro the vrthe aloynte,
> As newe fryt to God ful due,
> And to the gentyl Lombe hit arn ajoynt,
> As lyk to Hymself of lote and hwe.
> (ll. 879-96)

A new type of sound appears on the musical landscape in the fourth and fifth stanzas, one that aligns itself with Tewkesbury's *musica mensurabilis* and discrete sound. As the apostle John begins to distinguish notes within the rushing *flodez* and *torez* of song, he gains the capacity to elaborate on its qualities: the song is *showted scharpe*, (l. 877) and consists of *mode3* – a technical term which implies a growing ability to analyze aural experience. Some elements of this song are still beyond his reach. For instance, St. John remains incapable of singing it himself – he isn't *quoynt* (l. 889) enough to sing a *poynt* (l. 893) of it – and some of its elements remain ineffable, a reality which becomes apparent when the one of the most self-reflexive lines in all of medieval poetry is invoked to describe the song (*A note ful new I herde hem warpe / as harporez harpen in her harpe*) – but this *nwe songe* contrasts with the music of the earlier stanza by adhering to the language of divisibility and differentiation. Gone are the *flodez*, and in their place are *notez* and *poyntez*. Compare St. John's second description with Tewkesbury's *musica mensurabilis*, which uses the concept of infinitesimals to inscribe the timespace of song: *Musica mensurabilis*, which is prolonged by numbers, extends through time in discrete quantity. For every measured note or sound lasts for the number one, two, or three. Although it can increase by doubling or trebling to infinity, as will be shown below, it decreases to the finite, that is, to unity.[33]

There is a new idea here, namely, that brevity might be measurably compared to duration – that is, that categorical opposition could be described in terms of the latitude of forms described by Scotus, Johannes de Muris, and others, by dividing continuities into countable parts.[34]

---

[33] Dorit Tanay, *Noting Music, Marking Culture: The Intellectual Context of Rhythmic Notation, 1250-1400* (American Institute of Musicology: Hänssler-Verlag, 1999), 115-16.

[34] "A whole system based on hierarchy and compartmentalization began here to give way to increasingly daring generalizations which led eventually to the modern notion of variety and diversity as simply the full unfolding of

Certainly, points and continuities refer to mathematical, analytical, and quantitative ideas, but the term *poynt* also has a long and storied history in medieval mysticism, appearing as a central element of texts from pseudo-Dionysius' *Celestial Hierarchies* to Julian of Norwich's *Revelationes* and *The Cloud of Unknowing*, treatises which connect the concept of littleness and *lesse*-ness to language, devotion, and meditation. For instance, the *Cloud* suggests that 'bot a litil worde of o silable' is the best mantra for a sung devotion, 'for ever the schorter [a word] is, the betir it acordeth with the werk of the spirite.'[35] That is, the more that speech is unlike language that unfolds over time – the more it is like the quantum event of musical time – the more power it has to draw the body from its corporeality and into the metaphysical realm. For the *Cloud*-author, language, song, and the human mind are all unfold in quantifiable time: words, ideas, and music occur in discrete temporalities (and are marked by philosophy, knowledge, and also rupture from divinity). On the other hand, angelic awareness is a product of continuous time (expressed in holy love, mysticism, and unification with the deity). This second type of awareness is not natural to humans, and requires a shift beyond anthropological types of thought. How do understandings of quanta, time, and measurability affect its language and music? The *Cloud*-author looks to the same sorts of discussions of infinity and the infinitesimal, of the relation of mathematics to song, as *Pearl* does in this section.[36] The *Cloud*, for instance, attempts to deconstruct sensory perceptibles, concerning itself not with particular sense-modalities, such as hearing or vision, but instead with time, and, in particular, with musical time. Was time itself composed of discrete and numerable atomic units, or was it absolutely continuous, subdividable into infinity, as John of Tewkesbury and others posit?[37]

---

an essentially homogeneous formative principle.' Dorit Tanay, *Noting Music, Marking Culture: The Intellectual Context of Rhythmic Notation, 1250-1400* (American Institute of Musicology: Hänssler-Verlag, 1999), 87.

[35] Patrick J. Gallacher, ed., *Cloud of Unknowing*, (Kalamazoo: TEAMS Middle English Texts, 1997), ll. 500-01.

[36] The *Cloud*-author's dedication to apophaticism and proximity to pseudo-Dionysian thought is not at issue here. The *Cloud of Unknowing* encourages the reader to cast herself into a space of ignorance – of the world, of the word, and of God – in order to attain to the realm of spiritual enlightenment.

[37] The Oxford *calculatores* of the fourteenth century would examine the problems of the temporal and spatial aspects of angelic existence from a

Contemplation 'is the schortest werke of alle that man may ymagyn,' says the *Cloud.* Indivisible, it is the fundamental building block of time, 'neither lenger ne schorter then is an athomus; the whiche athomus, by the diffinicion of trewe philisophres in the sciens of astronomye, is the leest partie of tyme.' Contemplative time is 'so litil that, for the littilnes of it, it is undepartable and neighhonde incomprehensible.'[38] The concept of the infinitesimal is analogous to the incomprehensible and illogical nature of contemplation itself, yet it still follows the mathematical logic of astronomical science. It is not illogical; it is merely incomprehensible. The *Cloud* connects this atomic understanding of time to language and devotion. The contemplative takes 'bot a litil worde of o silable' as her prayer. Why? 'For it is betir then of two, for ever the schorter it is, the betir it acordeth with the werk of the spirite.'[39] The shorter a word is – the more it is unlike language that unfolds over time, and the more it is like the quantum building block of the 'athomus' – the closer it is to the operational time of grace. This is a temporality for which the mystic is morally accountable, and this time-account is linguistic:

> This is that tyme of the whiche it is wretyn: Alle tyme that is goven to thee, it schal be askid of thee how thou haste dispendid it. And skilful thing it is that thou geve acompte of it; for it is neither lenger ne schorter, bot even acording to one only steryng that is withinne the principal worching might of thi soul, the whiche is thi wille. For even so many willinges or desiringes – and no mo ne no fewer – may be and aren in one oure in thi wille, as aren athomus in one oure. And yif thou were reformid bi grace to the first state of mans soule, as it was bifore sinne, than thou schuldest evermore, bi help of that grace, be lorde of that stering or

---

different perspective, their work does not deal specifically with angels. See David Keck, *Angels and Angelology in the Middle Ages* (Oxford: Oxford University Press, 1998), 112; Edith Sylla, 'Medieval Quantifications of Qualities: The Merton School,' in *Archive for History of Exact Sciences* 8 (1971): 7-39; John Murdoch, 'From Scoial into Intellectual Factors: An Aspect of the Unitary Character of late medieval Learning,' in *The Cultural Context of medieval Learning*, ed. John Murdoch and Edith Sylla, (Boston: D. Reidel, 1975), 271-348.

[38] Patrick J. Gallacher, ed. *The Cloud of Uknowing.* (Kalamazoo: TEAMS Middle English Texts, 1997), ll. 301-315.

[39] *Cloud,* ll. 500-1.

of thoo sterynges; so that none yede forby, bot alle thei schulde streche into the soverein desirable and into the heighest wilnable thing, the whiche is God.[40]

By making time discrete, every moment of a person's life can be counted, and accounted for; every willful action of the soul is granted its own time, and these times in the aggregate 'stretche,' or form the continuity of life out of discreta. *The Cloud of Unknowing*, structures human thought as an aggregate operation of the will. The infinite calculus of this will approaches God. The dimensions of musical temporal possibility shift from qualitative to quantitative in Fitt 15 of *Pearl*.[41]

There is one further excursis that bears on the faculties of the soul and the application of virtue in relation to this passage and the *fowre bestes* of line 886. Obviously, the four animals referred to in this passage can be interpreted as those of the eschatological beasts of Ezekiel 1.4-14 as well as Revelation 7:11. Each creature is shaped like a man, but with four faces: a human, a lion, and ox, and an eagle – symbology which is applied to the four evangelists, Matthew, Mark, Luke, and John, respectively – but which was also used by St Jerome as an allegory for the mind of man: the human face is man's rational function, the lion its affective, the ox the appetitive, and, finally, the eagle the *synderesis*, or what medieval theologians called 'the spark of the conscience.' What exactly is this faculty of the soul? Jerome introduces *synderesis* in his discussion of Cain: Synderesis is 'that spark of conscience wheich was not extinguished even in the breast of Cain... and by which we discern that we sin.'[42] *Synderesis* never errs, and operates in abstract principles, which is what distinguishes it from *conscientia* or conscience. Conscience may err, and may be dampened down or destroyed over time. From Philip the Chancellor (ca 1235) to Bonaventure and Ockham, most theologians dealt with *synderesis/conscientia*, sometimes attributing its power as affective, other times as rational or intellective; conscience was, at any rate, and important area of study in the 13th-15th

---

[40] *Cloud*, ll. 301-315.
[41] *Pearl* ll. 873-6, above.
[42] 'Even when a person does not feel guilty about having done something which is wrong, he may still regret the consequences... this residue is the 'spark of conscience." Timothy C. Potts, *Conscience in Medieval Philosophy*, (Cambridge: Cambridge University Press, 1980), 10-11.

centuries.[43] By drawing on the symbology of the evangelists/faculties of the soul in this passage, the *Pearl*-poet calls to mind not only the harmonization of the gospels, but also the collaborative work of the human soul as mental and rational as well as visceral and emotional, at the heart of which is the *synderesis*, or the unitary *punctum* of discerning truth from falsehood. The *lesse* which ends every verse of this section contracts and plays with the language not only of musical time, but of ethical space.

Pearl may not consciously present the latitude of forms *contra* categorical qualities in its description of sounds, but two very different languages of numerical analysis occur between these two stanzas as they apply to the music of heaven, the properties of contemplation, and the time of the soul.

> 'Neuer the les let be my thonc,'
> Quoth I, 'my perle thaȝ I appose;
> I schulde not tempte thy wyt so wlonc,
> To Krystez chambre that art ichose.
> [...]
> Now, hynde, that sympelnesse cones enclose,
> I wolde thee aske a thynge expresse,
> And thaȝ I be bustwys as a bose,
> Let my bone vayls neuerthelesse.
>   (ll. 901-12).

The final stanza of Fitt 15 continues the dialogue between the Maiden and the Narrator in what Andrew and Waldron see as a shift from 'rebellious pride to obedient humility.'[44] The ecstatic stanzas of the Johannine revelation force the Narrator to recognize himself as a poor debater, and even though he continues to ask questions about

---

[43] There are many who comment on the conscience, but Philip the Chancellor wrote the first treatise on conscience around 1235. His basic concerns are to describe that the *synderesis* is a series of general principles of virtue that can never be mistaken, whereas *conscientia* is applied *synderesis*, and may err. Following him, Bonaventure, Ockham, Scotus, and Aquinas all weighed in on the relationship of *synderesis* to *conscience*, viewing *synderesis* as more or less intellectual (Aquinas considered it more intellectual Bonaventure less so) or as more or less dynamic (Scotus viewed the *synderesis* as a dynamic principle, whereas others were prone to reserve dynamism for the conscience). See Potts, *Conscience*, 104ff.

[44] Andrew and Waldron, *Pearl Manuscript*, 97.

the spatial aspects of heaven in Fitt 16, it is as a schoolchild rather than a dialectician. Even here, he shows his lack of understanding: had the Narrator paid closer attention in Fitt 15, he would have realized that physical spatiality is unimportant, an inherent reduction of heaven into the space of the categorical logics of quantity and quality akin to the *poynt*. Instead, the import of heavenly space is its ability to produce mental images; the spiritual impact of imagining heaven as spatial provides a referential base for contemplation.

Concluding Remarks

The Pearl-Maiden's response in Fitt 15 elaborates on the discussion begun in Fitt 11, with its end-line of reassuring sufficiency: *for the grace of God is gret inoghe* (l. 612), but in Fitt 15, the Pearl-Maiden's language shifts from the positive descriptions of Fitts 12-14 to language which is increasingly apophatic. Fitt 15 contrasts the idea of sufficiency with the idea of plenitude, where the *lesse* (and *neuer the lesse*) which end each stanza mean simultaneously the inability to change, and the possibility for the total destruction of identity if any change occurs: if the song of heaven is *neuer lesse*, it must continue *ad infinitum*, but if it does admit of diminution, it will cease to be heavenly song. In order to contemplate both of these forms of *lesse*, Fitt 15 relies on two distinctions. The first distinction is between logic/grammar/language on the one hand and being/ontology on the other. The second distinction is between a qualitative understanding of *lesse*-ness (relative change) and a quantitative understanding of it (the logic of infinitesimals). This debate takes a number of different forms throughout the Fitt, from thinking about language, to contemplating mathematical continuity, and from there to imagining the mathematical underpinning of musical performance. It then returns, at the end of the stanza, back to the simplicity (line 909) of the pearl-metaphor. Though the pearl has proven to be generative of complex logical and ontological referentiality, the Narrator's desire for simplicity at the end of this stanza suggests a turn away from heavy philosophical labor towards contemplation. A well-formed categorical proposition is either true or false, but not both. One gets a hint, here, that this does not hold for *Pearl*.

Pearl has been called a 'study in numerology,' a common thread in criticism which endures despite the poem's generic fluidity.[45] But the numbers which suffuse *Pearl* should not be thought of in terms of the number of maidens in the New Jerusalem nor in the number of lines of stanzas or Fitts which comprise the poem or the manuscript as a whole. Instead, the deep structure which focuses the intellectual or poetic drive of *Pearl* is its tendency to critique and then sublimate the tensions between an categorized, rational, and numbered world with an affective realm beyond – or prior to – the world of enumeration. It is this procedural dance which imbues the poem with its circularity and what Zeeman calls the poem's 'discursive gap' and the Pearl-Maiden's demand for submission.[46] The poem requires a hermeneutic leap away from satisfying philosophical tenets, which are not actually all that satisfying, and towards the potential surfeit of illogic. It does this by combining, in Fitt 15, the discourses of *continua* and *discreta* along with the positive language of philosophical inquiry with the *via negativa* of apophasis and ineffability.

Tekla Bude is Kathleen Hughes Junior Research Fellow at Newnham College, Cambridge.

---

[45] Nicolette Zeeman, 'Medieval Religious Allegory: French and English' in Rita Copeland and Peter T Struck, *The Cambridge Companion to Allegory* (Cambridge: Cambridge University Press, 2010), 148-161.

[46] Zeeman, 'Religious Allegory,' 158.

XVI

OUT, OUT, DAMNED SPOT: *MOTE* IN *PEARL* AND THE POEMS OF THE *PEARL* MANUSCRIPT

Karen Bollermann

Of the many noted and notable aspects of poetic artistry on display in the Middle English poem *Pearl*,[1] one of the subtlest is the pervasive deployment of a semantic dialectic.[2] Not only does each fitt develop a tension of meanings inherent to its concatenating word, but definitional play infuses instances of these words in other fitts. Just as the Dreamer's levels of understanding are built up in spirals of learning,[3] so too are the reader's apprehension and

---

[1] All references to *Pearl*, as well as references to *Cleanness, Patience*, and *Sir Gawain and the Green Knight*, are taken from the critical editions of these poems found in *The Poems of the Pearl Manuscript*, Malcolm Andrew and Ronald Waldron, eds. (Exeter: University of Exeter Press, 1996); my textual translations are based on this edition. With regard to *Pearl*, I will refer to the two main characters as the Dreamer and the Maiden. For general statements on the poem's poetic artistry, see, for example, A. C. Spearing, "Poetic Identity," p. 41; Felicity Riddy, "Jewels in *Pearl*," p. 147; H. N. Duggan, "Meter, Stanza, Vocabulary, Dialect," pp. 232-238; and, Nicholas Watson, "The *Gawain*-Poet as a Vernacular Theologian," pp. 297-298, all in *A Companion to the Gawain-Poet*, Derek Brewer and Jonathan Gibson, eds. (Cambridge: D. S. Brewer, 1999).

[2] Britton J. Harwood, "*Pearl* as Diptych," exploits the concept of a semantic dialectic, but in a far different, more structurally restrictive manner than in the present article; in *Text and Matter: New Critical Perspectives of the* Pearl-Poet, Robert M. Blanch, Miriam Youngerman Miller, and Julian N. Wasserman, eds. (Troy, NY: The Whitston Publishing Company, 1991), pp. 61-78.

[3] Watson, "Vernacular Theologian," acknowledges, but rejects, the view of many that the Dreamer, to varying degrees, does not learn anything, p. 299, while Nick Davis, "Narrative Form and Insight" (in *A Companion*), finds that the Dreamer both learns and does not learn, p. 344. Helen Cooper, "The Supernatural" (in *A Companion*), discusses the Dreamer's journey to understanding, pp. 279, 285; and, Priscilla Martin, "Allegory and Symbolism" (in *A Companion*), remarks on the Dreamer's growing understanding, pp. 316, 323, 325. Lynn Staley Johnson, "The *Pearl* Dreamer and the Eleventh Hour," finds the Dreamer in need of last-minute

appreciation of lexical meaning informed by refinements of word usage across the poem. Thus, to better understand the meaning of Fitt XVI's concatenating word *mote(les)*, one must not only tease out its valences within the fitt, but must also engage with those fitts (all earlier) that participate in the process of its meaning-building: Fitts I, XIII, XIV, and XV. The first of these prior fitts, which concatenates on *spot*, establishes the simplest, most literal understanding of *mote* as either a spot, stain, blemish or a location, place. The latter three fitts expand and enrich the dialectic of meanings of *mote* that are fully realized in Fitt XVI. Thus, in the process of explicating Fitt XVI, I will attend to the above-noted earlier fitts, with the particular goal of developing a locus of meanings for *mote* in *Pearl*. Following that, I will expand this investigation into *mote* by considering its twelve total appearances in the other three poems of the *Pearl* manuscript. As we shall see, religious valences predominate in the first three poems (*Pearl, Cleanness*, and *Patience*), while secular valences (including to the hunt) cluster in the last poem (*Sir Gawain and the Green Knight*). Finally, of these four poems, *Pearl* (and only *Pearl*) evinces an additional meaning of *mote* (once as a noun, and once as a verb), denoting conflict, argument, or strife. While *mote* appears only three times (and prosaically) in works by Geoffrey Chaucer, this final type of *mote*, with its legal overtones, occurs not infrequently in William Langland's *Piers Plowman*.[4]

---

instruction, p. 11, while Jane Chance, "Allegory and Structure in *Pearl*: The Four Senses of the *Ars Praedicandi* and Fourteenth-Century Homiletic Poetry," concludes that, as a result of successful learning steps, the Dreamer returns from his vision "educated, illumined," pp. 38, 43; both in *Text and Matter*.

[4] All references to Chaucer's works are taken from *Chaucer's Major Poetry*, Albert C. Baugh, ed. (Englewood Cliffs, NJ: Prentice-Hall Incorporated, 1963); all references to *Piers Plowman* are taken from *Piers Plowman: The C-Text*, Derek Pearsall, ed. (Exeter: University of Exeter Press, 1999). For the general practice of using Chaucer and Langland as companion authors for reading the *Pearl*-poet's corpus, see, for example, David Aers, "Christianity for Courtly Subjects: Reflections on the *Gawain*-Poet" (in *A Companion*), pp. 91-101; Spearing, "Poetic Identity," pp. 35-51; Riddy, "Jewels," p. 149; and, Watson, "Vernacular Theologian," p. 295.

Meanings of *mote* and its close synonyms and antonyms

The two dominant and competing meanings of *mote* in *Pearl* (and especially in Fitt XVI) are those denoting spot, stain, or blemish[5] and those denoting location, place,[6] or, more specifically, city/citadel (through metonymy, a moat signifies that which it surrounds).[7] The negative *moteles*, however, applies only to the former definitional set, as in spotless, stainless, blemishless,[8] or, when formulated as *wythouten mote*, without spot/stain/blemish;[9] neither means without location or place. The only other negative usage is idiomatic: *not a mote/myte*, not a bit/jot.[10]

Mote and *moteles* find several important analogues throughout the poem. *Spot*, the concatenating word of Fitt I, signifies both of the above dominant meanings,[11] and *spotlez* is synonymous with *moteles*;[12] *wythouten spot*, however, may mean either *spotlez* or of indeterminate location.[13] *Maskle* and *maskellez* (a shared concatenator of Fitt XIII) refer only to spot, stain, or blemish and to spotless, stainless, or blemishless, respectively;[14] there is no spatial implication to either. On the other hand, although *makelez* (Fitt XIII's other concatenator) means matchless or peerless (literally, without mate)[15] and so is asynonymous with the preceding terms,

---

[5] *MED*, *mot*, *mote* (n.(1, defs. a and d)).
[6] *MED*, *mot*, *mote* (n.(3, def. 1c)).
[7] *MED*, *mote*, *mot* (n.(1, defs. b and c).
[8] *MED*, *moteles* (n.), from *mot* (n.(1)). Note that *moteles* is misidentified as a noun; it, like its analogues *spotles* and *maskelles*, is an adjective.
[9] *MED*, *mot*, *mote* (n.(1d)).
[10] *MED*, *mot*, *mote* (n.(1c)), including the idiomatic *mountaunce of a litel mote*, found in *Patience*.
[11] See *MED*, *spot* (n.(1, defs. 3, 4b, and 5)).
[12] *MED*, *spotles* (adj.).
[13] See *MED*, *spot* (n.(1, def. 3)). While this definition does not compass a negative location, the Glossary entry in Andrew and Waldron, *The Poems*, notes that the two senses of blemish and location are "perhaps combined in *wythouten s[pot]*" (p. 348).
[14] For *maskel*, see *MED*, *maskel* (n.(def. a)); in general, *maskel* and *mote* often occur together, in either order, as in *maskel or mote*. For *maskelles*, see *MED*, *maskelles* (adj.); note that all of the listed textual citations to this word are from *Pearl*.
[15] *MED*, *makeles* (adj., def. a, and also b).

the Dreamer confuses it with *maskellez*, for which error he receives correction.[16]

Mote in Fitt XVI

Here follows my translation of Fitt XVI, bracketed by a brief summary of the immediately preceding and subsequent material.

Fitt XV: About Christ in the New Jerusalem, with a long paraphrase from Revelation. In the final stanza, the Dreamer acknowledges the differences between himself and the Maiden, and begs her to consider his humble request.

Fitt XVI

Stanza 1

913 "Nevertheless, shining one, I beseech you,
if you can see to it that it be done,
915 as you are glorious without blemish (*galle*; syn. of *maskel*),
do not reject my piteous request:
Have you no dwelling (*wonez*) within a castle's wall (*castel-walle*)
nor manor (*maner*) where you may sup and live?
You tell me about Jerusalem, the royal realm,
920 where noble David was installed on the throne,
but by these woods it is not situated –
it's in Judea, that noble place (*note*).
As you are completely spotless (*maskelez*),
your dwelling (*wonez*) must be **without spot** (*wythouten mote*).

Stanza 2

925 "This **spotless** (*motelez*) company you speak of,

---

[16] In general, only Christ and Mary are *makeles* (see, e.g., l. 757 and l. 436, respectively), though, once, the Pearl of Price is referred to as both *makellez* (l. 733) and *maskelles* (l. 744). When the Dreamer mistakenly refers to the Maiden as *makeles* as well as *maskellez* (l. 780), the Maiden clarifies that, while she is indeed *maskelles* and one of heaven's queens, she never averred that she was a "*makelez quene*" (l. 784); that title inheres only to Mary. For additional contemporary references to Mary as *makeles*, see Lyrics 10 and 54 in *One Hundred Middle English Lyrics*, rev. edn., Robert D. Stevick, ed. (Urbana, IL: University of Illinois Press, 1994); and, Lyric 77 in *Medieval English Lyrics, 1200-1400*, Thomas G. Duncan, ed. (London: Penguin Books, 1995).

so great a company of thousands in a crush,
a great city (*cetê*), as you are so many,
you must have, without doubt.
So comely a group of lovely jewels
930 would be done badly should [they have to] lie outside,
yet by these banks where I stroll,
I see no dwelling (*bygyng*) anywhere about.
I think you only come and linger [here]
to gaze on the beauty of this lovely stream.
935 If you have sturdy dwellings (*bygyngez*) elsewhere,
direct me now to that fair **citadel** (*mote*)."

Stanza 3

"That **citadel** (*mote*) you speak of in Judea,"
that precious spice then said to me,
"That is the city (*cytê*) that the Lamb visited
940 in which to suffer pain for man's sake;
understand [it] as the old Jerusalem,
for there was the old sin destroyed.
But the new [Jerusalem], which came down from God's messenger,
the apostle gave an account of it in Revelations.
945 The Lamb who is without [any] black spots (*spottez*)
has ferried His fair host there;
and, as His flock is without blemish (*flake*),
so is His **citadel** (*mote*) **without spot** (*withouten moote*).

Stanza 4

"Plainly [I] speak of two **citadels** (*motez*),
950 though both are called Jerusalem,
which to you means nothing more than
'city of God' or 'vision of peace.'
In that one, our peace was achieved –
the Lamb chose it [in which] to suffer with pain;
955 in that other, there is nothing but peace to glean
which shall last forever without end.
That is the city to which we press
after our flesh is laid to rot;
there, glory and bliss shall ever increase
960 for the company that is **without spot** (*withouten mote*)."

Stanza 5

"**Spotless** (*Motelez*) maid, so meek and mild,"
I then said to that lovely flower,
"Bring me to that pleasant burg (*bylde*)
and let me see your blissful bower."
965 That shining one said, "God will prevent that –
you may not enter within His castle (*tor*).
But, from the Lamb, I have appealed you
for a sight of it, through great favor.
From without, to see that perfect cloister
970 you are permitted, but [you may go] within not one step –
to wander its walks you have no ability,
unless you were clean, **without spot** (*withouten mote*).

Fitt XVII (beginning)

"If I this **citadel** (*mote*) shall reveal to you,
come up toward this river's head;
975 I, opposite you on this side,
shall go, until you are in view of a hill."

The Dreamer then does this and sees the New Jerusalem; its description follows.

Note, in Fitt XVI, that *mote* in its unmodified form refers only to a location, a citadel. *Moteles* occurs twice, once in reference to the Maiden's heavenly companions and once in reference to the Maiden herself, where it reinforces her prior description in the first stanza as *maskelez*. All other occurrences of *mote* in the fitt are modified by *withouten*. This phrase forms the final two words of Stanzas 1 and 3-5; they do not occur at the end of Stanza 2, as would be expected, as a result of the fitt's central preoccupation, discussed below.

That this fitt concentrates the dialectic, previously developed in the poem to this point, between location-spot and blemish-spot is evident from the sheer repetition of place/structure words (e.g., *wonez, maner, Jerusalem, bygyng, cyté, burg, tor*, occurring a total of 27 times) and spotless/purity words (e.g., *withouten mote/galle/flake/spottez, maskelles, motelez*, occurring a total of 10 times). Indeed, it is only the spotless – the Lamb, the heavenly elect, and the Maiden – who occupy these spots. This central connection is made express in the Maiden's final words (in this fitt) to the Dreamer: You may look, but you cannot touch, as you are not one of us. Additionally, in terms of this fitt's concatenatory structure, citadel lies, literally, at its heart, while the heavenly company enclose and infuse it, and the Maiden (fittingly, in her role as guide-instructrix) frames them both, as the following schematic reveals:

Stanza 1: ...
           923 *you [Maiden] spotless*
           924 *your dwelling without spot/speck/stain*
Stanza 2: 925 <u>spotless/stainless company</u>
           ...
           936 **citadel**
Stanza 3: 937 **citadel**
           ...
           947 <u>His flock without blemish</u>
           948 **His citadel** without spot/speck/stain
Stanza 4: 949 **citadels**
           ...
           960 <u>company without spot/speck/stain</u>
Stanza 5: 961 *spotless/stainless Maiden*
           ...
           972 without spot/speck/stain

Line 948 deserves special attention for two *mote*-worthy reasons: It is overladen; and, it acts as the fulcrum on which the two halves of the fitt balance. In the original, the line reads: "So is Hys mote withouten moote." This highly unusual doubling of a concatenator in a single line crystallizes the importance of the New Jerusalem, its status as the locus of spotless purity, and the larger role of spiritual purity in the poem. Note as well that, in this fitt, four *mote* words/word-forms precede this line, and four follow it. Ultimately, if we are to understand what it means to be without blemish, we must always turn our inward eye to Christ's kingdom in heaven; there, and only there, is spotlessness perfected. Lastly, the final two lines of Stanza 1 (ll. 923-24) parallel the final two lines of Stanza 3 (ll. 947-48), but with an important difference: As the lines of the former refer only to the Maiden, the dwelling in which she is presumed to reside is not yet specified as <u>the</u> citadel which is the central concern of the fitt; in the complementary lines of the latter, both the host and their citadel are identified as belonging to the Lamb. Thus, the only *mote* line that stands outside this heavenly synchrony is the final line of the fitt, wherein it is revealed that the Dreamer cannot participate in this dynamic unless he too is pure.

Despite this moral and actual warning and the Dreamer's eventual disregard of it, the (possibly surprising) numerical superabundance of place words over spiritual-condition words in this fitt accords well with its specific poetic context: The three preceding fitts articulated lessons about the two Jerusalems, the actions of Christ and the Lamb within each, and the nature of the divine (non-)hierarchy;[17] the succeeding three fitts recount the Dreamer's unmediated experience of the New Jerusalem, the Lamb, and the heavenly host. In this regard, Fitt XVI marks the turning point in the apex of the dream-vision, the transition from theological instruction to esoteric knowledge.[18]

The anomalous nature of the immediately preceding fitt (XV), with its surfeit of stanzas, has been the subject of much scholarly debate.[19] Beyond focused attempts to reconcile its irregularity, it has often been implicit or explicit in offering schemata for the overall structure and movement of the poem.[20] Without expressing any

---

[17] On issues of divine hierarchy in the poem, see generally Brewer, "Introduction," pp. 14-15, 17; Watson, "Vernacular Theologian," pp. 303-304; and, Davis, "Narrative Form," p. 344. Josephine Bloomfield, "Stumbling toward God's Light: The Pearl Dreamer and the Impediments of Hierarchy," *The Chaucer Review* 45.4 (2011): 390-410, offers a thorough analysis of the issues and problems of hierarchy in the poem; she also analogizes, *pace*, *Pearl* to Julian of Norwich's *Shewings*, though she finds the Dreamer, unlike Julian, "only an accidental spiritual pilgrim," pp. 400, 407.

[18] A useful counter-example is the first (short) version of Julian of Norwich's *Shewings*, in which her visions are related without theological explication, and the second (long) version, in which she theorizes the spiritual meaning of her visions. See *The Shewings of Julian of Norwich*, Georgia Ronan Crampton, ed. (Kalamazoo, MI: Western Michigan University, Medieval Institute Publications, 1994), "Introduction," pp. 1-23, especially pp. 1-3. On Julian's text as relevant to the *Pearl*-poet generally, see Watson, "Vernacular Theologian," pp. 295-296; with specific attention to her use of *poynt*, see Davis, "Narrative Form," p. 336.

[19] For an overview of the major lines of contention, see the note to ll. 841-912 in Andrew and Waldron, *The Poems*, p. 94.

[20] On the numerical structure of *Pearl* generally, see, e.g., D. S. Brewer, "Introduction" (in *A Companion*), p. 18; and, Martin, "Allegory and Symbolism," p. 319. Chance, "Allegory and Structure," finds a tripartite division of the poem, framed by the opening and closing fitts, which reflects the three senses of non-literal reading, p. 33. Harwood, "Diptych," posits a

views on Fitt XV's stanzaic surplus, I would argue that it both serves as the crisis point in the poem's inner conflict—the theological debate between the Dreamer and the Maiden—and marks its resolution. Prior to Fitt XV, the Dreamer has repeatedly challenged the Maiden's doctrinal lessons, very often in a way that reveals his inferior understanding.[21] In Fitt XV, the debate ends: There is little additional conversation between the Dreamer and the Maiden, and she offers no further religious instruction to him. Indeed, the final lines of Fitt XV inaugurate a different relationship between the two. The Dreamer is now a humble petitioner who makes one request, knowing his very question may be unworthy of response. The Maiden is no longer the didact, becoming instead the granter of boons: First, she considers his request; and, then, she facilitates its fulfillment as both procurer of favor (the final stanza of Fitt XVI) and guide (the first stanza of Fitt XVII). From this point forward, the Dreamer's instruction is experiential, visual, and unmediated.

Regarding this transition, one may ask: Does the poem offer a critique of purely didactic theology, in favor of experiential spirituality?[22] Or, does the Dreamer's failure to truly understand the latter suggest that, while it may be the higher form of knowing, all we humans can hope to aspire to is to understand and internalize what we are taught? At any rate, it seems clear that a sound grounding in theology, at least for the Dreamer, was insufficient

---

diptych structure for the poem, with Fitts 10-11 as the central pair, all others paired in descending/ascending order, p. 61. For the most recent detailed numerical analysis of *Pearl* and its companion poems, which includes significant discussion of earlier scholarship in the same vein, see *The Epistemological Perspective of the* Pearl-*Poet*, Piotr Spyra (Farnham, Eng.: Ashgate, 2014).

[21] See, e.g., Aers, "Courtly Subjects," p. 101; Richard Newhauser, "Sources II: Scriptural and Devotional Sources" (in *A Companion*), pp. 268-269; Cooper, "The Supernatural," pp. 283-285; Martin, "Allegory and Symbolism," pp. 324-325; Davis, "Narrative Form," pp. 331, 342; and, Bloomfield, "Stumbling toward God's Light," pp. 390, 405.

[22] See Newhauser, "Sources II," p. 268. Charlotte Gross, "Courtly Language in *Pearl*" (in *Text and Matter*), remarks on the Dreamer's "paucity of progress," reflected in his repeated inappropriate use of courtly/romance language, p. 85. Spyra, *Epistemological Perspective*, finds no real dialogue between the Dreamer and the Maiden, such that, at the end, the Dreamer has learned nothing, pp. 27, 34.

preparation for his ecstatic vision.[23] The Dreamer's repeated learning failures are reminiscent of both Jonah's (in *Patience*) and Gawain's (in *Sir Gawain and the Green Knight*) similar failures;[24] it may well be, in the poet's estimation, that cycles of failure constitute the human experience, in response to which all we can do is brush the dirt (*mote*) off ourselves and keep trying to improve and to understand.[25]

In this pursuit, we are not without help, for, within our fallen world, there remains one token of our prelapsarian past, one symbol to guide us in our mortal struggle toward spotlessness: the pearl. That the pearl is indeed such a symbol is attested to in Fitt XIII, where the Maiden refers to it as not only *maskellez*, but also *makellez* (l. 733). Recall that *makeles* may only otherwise properly describe Christ/the Lamb and Mary. The Maiden goes on to explain the pearl's participation in divine singularity: It is like the realm of pure heaven, according to God, because it is flawless, pure, and bright, endlessly round, of gentle spirit, and common to (shared by) the righteous (ll. 735-39).[26] It is symbolic of heaven and its perfection, the only terrestrial object deserving the description of matchless, an orb that, literally, reflects light and, symbolically, reflects the unity and purity of original creation, unable to be either sullied or

---

[23] On the results of the vision itself, see Watson, "Vernacular Theologian," p. 305. On the Dreamer's misapprehension of the river as a spiritual boundary separating the pure from the impure, see Paul F. Reichardt, "Animal Similes in *Pearl*" (in *Text and Matter*), p. 19; this focus on category separation so as to avoid contamination is a central concern of *Cleanness*.

[24] On the Dreamer's, Jonah's, and Gawain's failures, and their similarities to each other, see Cooper, "The Supernatural," pp. 278-279; Watson, "Vernacular Theologian," pp. 300, 310; Martin, "Allegory and Symbolism," pp. 316, 319; Newhauser, "Sources II," 262, 268, 270-271; and, Spyra, *Epistemological Perspective*, pp. 35-47. On the cyclical patterns of human existence as reflected in poetic structure, see Davis, "Narrative Form," p. 338.

[25] For a similar conclusion, see Watson, "Vernacular Theologian," p. 293. Bloomfield, "Stumbling toward God's Light," concludes that "the poet seems to be encouraging his audience on their own spiritual journey," p. 410.

[26] Tony Davenport, "Jewels and Jewelers in *Pearl*," *The Review of English Studies*, n.s., 59 (Sept. 2008): 508-520, 511, notes that the "virtue of the pearl ... is described only in aesthetic and moral terms."

improved by mankind.[27] Consider, in this regard (and across all of the manuscript's poems), the pearl's unique position in the divine and created order:

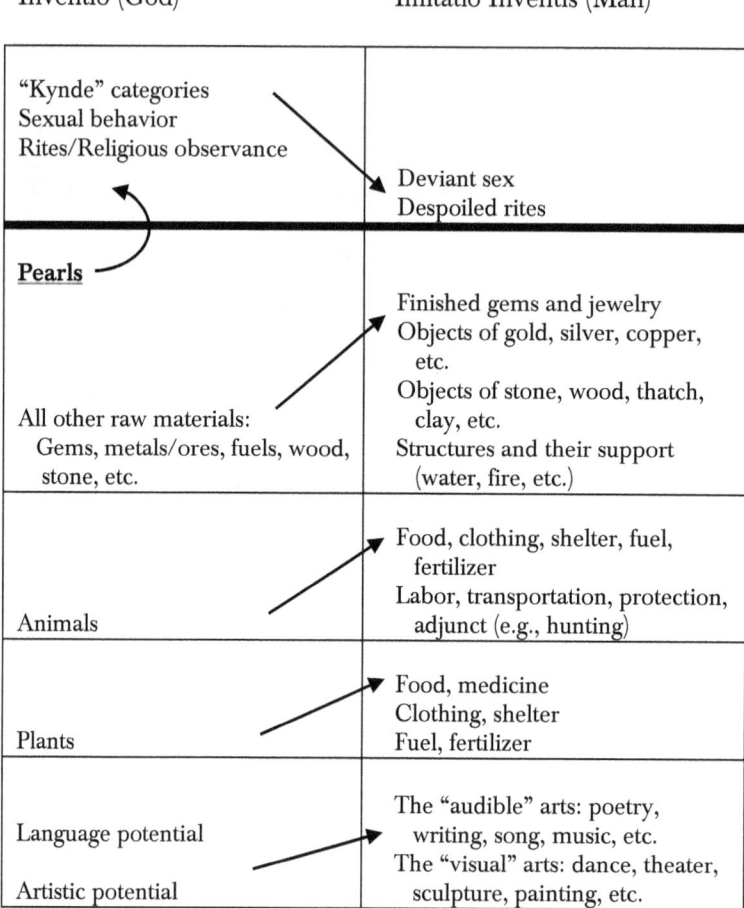

Inventio (God) — Imitatio Inventis (Man)

Inventio (God)	Imitatio Inventis (Man)
"Kynde" categories Sexual behavior Rites/Religious observance	Deviant sex Despoiled rites
Pearls All other raw materials: Gems, metals/ores, fuels, wood, stone, etc.	Finished gems and jewelry Objects of gold, silver, copper, etc. Objects of stone, wood, thatch, clay, etc. Structures and their support (water, fire, etc.)
Animals	Food, clothing, shelter, fuel, fertilizer Labor, transportation, protection, adjunct (e.g., hunting)
Plants	Food, medicine Clothing, shelter Fuel, fertilizer
Language potential Artistic potential	The "audible" arts: poetry, writing, song, music, etc. The "visual" arts: dance, theater, sculpture, painting, etc.

With regard to all of God's creation, mankind is able to improve on the many raw gifts given; with regard to higher things, to divine law,

---

[27] It may become bespattered, but can be cleaned; it may be set into gold or clothing, but is not altered in order to be so mounted (unlike gemstones, for example). On this unique quality of the pearl, see Spearing, "Poetic Identity," pp. 41-42.

action by mankind can, however, only lead to corruption.[28] The sole terrestrial exception is the pearl, which human action cannot improve. It alone of all creation participates in and reflects the divine.[29]

The *Mote* Problem

One of the larger problematics in the poem as a whole is that of location. Where exactly does the poem open and close? In a garden; at a gravesite?[30] And, where is the dream garden into which the Dreamer first enters?[31] What land(scape) does the Maiden occupy? As she is always on the far bank, is the river a sort of moat-*mote*, walling off this 'heavenly' space from the larger dream space? And then, there is the more specific problem of distinguishing the city-*mote* of the Old Jerusalem from that of the New Jerusalem. Finally, in all of these spaces, what does it mean to be *mote-d* or *moteles*? To be stained or unstained? Are some of these spaces both *moteles* and *withouten mote*?

Fitt I, with its concatenation on *spot*, serves as the entry into this problematic. Note that, unlike Stanza 2 of Fitt XVI, all five stanzas of Fitt I end with the phrase *withouten spot*.[32] In the first two stanzas, it is a *priuy perle* that is without (a) spot; in the final three stanzas, the *perle* is *precios*. Each of the fitt's four opening-stanza *spot* references (as well as its carry-over into the first line of Fitt II) seems clearly to denote a location: the place in the *erber* where the Dreamer has lost his pearl, mourns its loss, contemplates its potentially productive 'after-life', and, ultimately, falls into his dream-sleep. It would be

---

[28] This is a central preoccupation of *Cleanness*; see, generally, Watson, "Vernacular Theologian," p. 309.

[29] As medieval lapidaries attest, pearls are engendered from heavenly dewdrops. Davenport, "Jewels and Jewelers," analogizes the spiritual processes the Dreamer must go through, post-vision, to the growth of a pearl: "a speck [*mote*] in the process of shaping its own spiritual nacre," p. 520. For another statement on the pearl's unique association with purity, see *Cleanness*, ll. 1117-1132. In this sense, the pearl represents God's art, while polished, faceted gemstones are artful; see Davis, "Narrative Form," p. 333. For an extended discussion of jewels in *Pearl*, see Riddy, "Jewels," pp. 143-155; see also Martin, "Allegory and Symbolism," pp. 322-323, 328.

[30] See Newhauser, "Sources II," p. 267.

[31] See Newhauser, "Sources II," p. 267; Cooper, "The Supernatural," pp. 284-285; and, Martin, "Allegory and Symbolism," pp. 323-324.

[32] In this fitt, *spotlez* does not occur.

easy to read *withouten spot* as an equally specific reference to the pearl's physical appearance, its blemishless quality.[33] If we accept the pearl as a metaphor for a deceased young child, it would likewise refer to her innocence, her sinless state at death.[34] It is also possible, however, to read *withouten spot* as denoting a location problem: The Dreamer states that he has lost this pearl because it slipped from his hand; he even castigates the soil for mucking it up. If he is indeed at the spot where he lost it, he ought to have been able to find it; if it is a gravesite, then he is at an empty spot, knowing not in what new spot his lost child now resides. And, while *precios* marks this pearl as special, costly, and/or unique, *priuy* may suggest, in addition to private or personal, hidden, and so, without a known location.[35]

In this sense, Fitt XVI represents part recapitulation of and part movement beyond Fitt I.[36] In Fitt I, the lost pearl's location is unknown – it may be in the ground of a flowerbed, or in a grave; Fitt XVI addresses two locations as well (the Old and New Jerusalems). Whereas the two sites of Fitt I are indistinguishable, those of Fitt XVI are clearly elucidated. Furthermore, while the Old Jerusalem is literally 'on the ground' (i.e., in Judea), the New is accessible only through the grave. Additionally, the pearl of Fitt I is lost, locationless (*withouten spot*), homeless (*priuy*). In Fitt XVI, the Dreamer several times asserts that the Maiden must have a home somewhere nearby, as indeed she does; she is neither lost nor homeless. Indeed, the Dreamer remarks that it would not be mete for the heavenly host to lie outside, a reversal of the condition of the lost pearl of the poem's opening.

The connections between Fitts I and XVI extend beyond the parallels of the semantic synonymy between *spot* and *mote*, the preoccupation with dual locations, and the appropriateness of inside and outside, as additional motifs from Fitt I recur in Fitt XVI. Spices and flowers, some of which are specifically enumerated, form part of the lost pearl's setting in the former, while, in the latter, the

---

[33] See Andrew and Waldron, *The Poems*, p. 54, note to ll. 12-60.

[34] As *Pearl*, ll. 483-485, suggests. See, e.g., Brewer, "Introduction," pp. 2, 7, 21; Malcolm Andrew, "Theories of Authorship" (in *A Companion*), p. 25; Riddy, "Jewels," p. 154; and, Watson, "Vernacular Theologian," p. 306.

[35] For a similar reading of *spot* and its problems in this fitt, see Davis, "Narrative Form," p. 337.

[36] Harwood, "Diptych," however, pairs Fitt XVI with Fitt V, on the basis of a shared "topos of enclosures," p. 68, a reading with which the present author disagrees.

Maiden herself is Spice (l. 938) and Flower (l. 962). Likewise, the earlier motifs of gleaning and the harvest and of rot and decay are reiterated in this later fitt (ll. 955, 958). Finally, as the Dreamer's emotional tenor has shifted from a chaotic range of strong feelings in Fitt I to a calm curiosity in Fitt XVI, the comfort that Christ brings, not accessible to the Dreamer in the former, is now available to him, in the form of a vision of the New Jerusalem, in the latter. Thus, by virtue of this pre-vision, the totality of Fitt I has been transformed in Fitt XVI, a necessary precondition to the coming vision of the New Jerusalem.

This pattern of recapitulation with transformation extends throughout the remainder of the poem, a process inaugurated in the final (surplus) stanza of Fitt XV.[37] As mentioned above, Fitt XV marks the end of the Maiden's instruction of the Dreamer; note that all of Fitt XIV and the first five stanzas of Fitt XV consist entirely of the Maiden's speech, her final and most important lesson. While Fitt XIII teaches that the Pearl is a symbol of Heaven, Fitt XIV begins the process of distinguishing the Old Jerusalem from the New; the New Jerusalem is the focus of Fitt XV. By Fitt XIV, the Dreamer now knows that the Old is not to be found in the 'land' he now occupies, such that he requests a vision of the New, which wish is granted. Not only does Fitt XVI hearken back to, while also moving beyond, Fitt I, but the subsequent fitts do likewise, as follows:

- Fitt XVII (the end of the Dreamer's conversation with the Maiden) :: Fitt IV (the beginning of his conversation with her)
- Fitt XVIII (the astounding beauty of the city) :: Fitts II and III (the astounding beauty of the dream 'paradise')
- Fitt XIX (the sight of the Maiden causes the Dreamer to want to cross the River) :: Fitt V (the sight of the Maiden causes the Dreamer to want to cross the river)
- Fitt XX (after the abrupt end of the vision, the Dreamer realizes he cannot enter the heavenly kingdom until after death) :: Fitt VI (the Maiden tells the Dreamer that he cannot enter her realm until after death)

---

[37] Harwood, "Diptych," believes the poem doubles back after Fitt X; in his reckoning, Fitt XVI ought to be paired with Fitt V, pp. 61, 68. As my argument makes clear, I disagree with both statements.

Thus, not only does the final line of the poem 'return' us to the poem's beginning, but the final five fitts have all been preparing us for this return, a return not so much to the beginning, but to a new, and hopefully improved, beginning.[38]

Mote in the rest of *Pearl* and elsewhere in the *Pearl* Manuscript

Beyond this focused attention to *mote* in Fitt XVI of *Pearl*, it may prove instructive to consider its additional uses and contexts throughout the poem, as well as in the other three poems that comprise the *Pearl*-manuscript. Within *Pearl*, *mote* occurs as follows:

<u>Fitt XVI (wherein *mote* is the concatenating word)</u>
- spot/speck/stain – ll. 924, 948, 960, 972
- citadel – ll. 936, 937, 948, 949
- spotless/stainless – ll. 925, 961

<u>Elsewhere in *Pearl*</u>
- spot/speck/stain – ll. 726, 764, 843
- citadel – ll. 142, 973 (concatenating carry-over into Fitt XVII)
- spotless/stainless – ll. 899
- argument/conflict/strife – ll. 613 (verb), 855 (noun)
- phrase "not a myte (mote)" – l. 351

Combining these uses of *mote* reveals the following frequency distribution:
- spot(less)/stain(less): 53%
- citadel: 32%
- argument/conflict/strife: 11%
- phrase: 5%

As the above illustrates, the two dominant meanings of *mote* on display in Fitt XVI accurately reflect the term's meaning within the poem as a whole: In 85% of cases, *mote* refers either to spot, stain, blemish (or the lack thereof) or to location (specifically, citadel). Note, however, that, whereas in Fitt XVI, citadel (and other

---

[38] Bloomfield, "Stumbling toward God's Light," finds that the Dreamer "seems finally able to see himself potentially as a spiritual pearl ... though he cannot yet be described as 'enlightened'," p. 409.

structural terms) took precedence over blemish (for reasons elucidated above), the overarching semantic emphasis attributed to *mote* in *Pearl* is the quality of being stained or unstained.

This primacy of meaning extends to the manuscript's two other religious poems, where, though *mote* occurs rarely, it most often refers to purity or the lack thereof:

Cleanness
- spot-/speck-/stainless – l. 556 (= 100% frequency)[39]

Patience
- spot/speck/stain – ll. 268, 299 (= 50% frequency)
- citadel – l. 422 (= 25% frequency)
- phrase "mountaunce of a lyttel mote" – l. 456 (= 25% frequency)

Such is not the case, however, in the manuscript's final poem, wherein secular meanings predominate:

Sir Gawain and the Green Knight
- citadel – ll. 635, 764 (specifically, a moat), 910, 2052 (= 57% frequency)
- hunting horn/horn blast – ll. 1141, 1364 (= 29% frequency)
- phrase "not a mote" – l. 2209 (= 14% frequency)

Importantly, not only are there <u>no</u> usage references to stain/blemish or purity, but all of the citadel references are to strictly secular locales. In the preceding three poems, when *mote* is used to denote a locale or citadel, the reference is specifically religious/Biblical.

Chaucerian and Langlandian *Motes*

For comparison purposes, let us consider uses of *mote* in the works of two major contemporary figures: those of Geoffrey Chaucer and of William Langland. Across the Chaucerian corpus, *mote* only occurs three times: once in a phrase ("naught a moote"), once proverbially ("motes in the sunne-beem"), and once in

---

[39] This line reads as follows: "Withouten maskle oþer mote, as margeryeperle." Not only is this a direct echo of the pearl and the Maiden in *Pearl*, but the passage in which this line appears (ll. 545-556) recapitulates ll. 971-972, and surrounding context, of Fitt XVI.

reference to a hunting horn ("a gret horn blew thre mot").[40] Neither *moteles* nor *withouten mote* appears in Chaucer's works, and, clearly, *mote* is neither common to his lexicon nor vested with any spiritual significance.

Despite the overtly religious and didactic nature of Langland's *Piers Plowman*, *mote* does not take a spiritual register in that text either (all versions, though citations are only given for the C-text). Rather, as much of *Piers Plowman* is devoted to the dialogic pursuit of truth and justice, the most frequent use of *mote* (and related word-forms) activates its connotation of debate, argument, or strife, often with specifically legal overtones. Twice, *mote* appears in verb form, meaning to plead a legal case (I, l. 172; III, l. 197); twice, as the gerund *motyng*, meaning the pleading of a case (IV, l. 132; IX, l. 54); twice, as the compound *mo(e)t-halle*, meaning the court where cases are pled (IV, ll. 148 and 163); and twice, as the noun *motyef*, meaning the subject matter of a (scholarly) debate (XV, l. 130; XVI, l. 231). The only two other uses of *mote* refer to a defensive moat around a building or structure (VII, l. 233; XXI, l. 366).[41] Again, neither negative form of *mote* occurs. For Langland, while *mote* (and related forms) is not uncommon in his text, it is generally circumscribed by legal understandings and processes.

Finally, a scan of two volumes of (roughly contemporaneous) Middle English lyrics, including many devotional lyrics, reveals that *mote*, *moteles*, and *withouten mote* do not readily occur; rather, words meaning clean, pure, bright, etc., are more often used. Thus, in the wider ambit of major works by important authors of the time, as well as in other poetic compositions (secular and devotional), the poems of the *Pearl*-manuscript stand out as uniquely *mote*-worthy as a signifier for purity (or its lack), and none more so than *Pearl* (and Fitt XVI) itself.

---

[40] *Troilus and Criseyde*, III, l. 1603; *The Canterbury Tales*, "The Wife of Bath's Tale," l. 868 (compare to *Patience*, l. 268, where Jonah entering the whale's mouth is likened to a "mote in at a munster dor," the small particle one sees when sunlight shines in through an open door); and, *The Book of the Duchess*, l. 349, respectively.

[41] *Mote* appears in the B-text, in a passage not found in the C-text, as part of a paraphrase of the Latin Matthew 7:3: "a mote in thi brotheres eye."

Final thoughts on *mote*

It ought not escape our attention that the poem's focus on *mote* (and its negatives) comes just before the Dreamer's vision of the New Jerusalem. Although, prior to Fitt XVI, the larger project of distinguishing the pure and the impure, as well as of apprehending our physical spot (be it the world of the garden/gravesite, of the dream garden, or of the heavenly kingdom) had been developed in various ways, it is only in Fitt XVI that these notions come together. Quite literally, our quality of spotted- or spotlessness determines both our location and our condition in the world, the recognition of which can (and ought to) motivate reparative and restorative spiritual movements. Without such efforts, we are doomed, both in this world and the next; with them, we too may become a pearl of price to the Prince. It is, then, no joke to proclaim, "Out, out, damned spot!"

Karen Bollermann is a Visiting Scholar with the Department of English at Texas A&M University. She holds a Ph.D. in Old English Literature, as well as a J.D./M.B.A. She has published articles in a number of medieval studies journals, and is a co-editor of *Religion, Power, and Resistance from the Eleventh to the Sixteenth Centuries: Playing the Heresy Card* (Palgrave Macmillan, 2014). She is engaged in continuing research on Old and Middle English literature, as well as on twelfth-century English political and intellectual history.

XVII

SEEING JOHN: A COMMENTARY ON THE LINK WORD OF *PEARL* FITT XVII[1]

Karen Elizabeth Gross

For some, Fitt XVII is a letdown. After the uncanny landscapes and emotionally fraught reunion earlier in the poem, *Pearl*'s presentation of the Heavenly Jerusalem is an "authority-ridden vision [that] seems rather flat."[2] Critics complain that it is derivative of the Book of Revelation and not a real theophany: the description is "decidedly secondhand," and "John's vision is authoritative and reliable, but the narrator's own dream is subject to doubt."[3] The Dreamer relies upon John's script, and when he deviates most "his reason and self-control also begin to fade."[4] This slavish translation from Revelation is taken as proof that *Pearl* recounts not a contemplative experience but a meditative one, a sequence of thoughts inspired by reading the Bible, not by having an encounter with the divine.[5] Perhaps Fitt

---

[1] I would like to thank Karl Steel, Tara Williams, and the editors of *Glossator* for their generous advice as well as the staff of Watzek Library, Lewis & Clark College, Portland, Oregon. This essay was completed before it could benefit from Susanna Fein, "Of Judge and Jewelers: *Pearl* and the Life of St. John," *Studies in the Age of Chaucer* 36 (2014): 41-76.

[2] John Finlayson, "*Pearl*: Landscape and Vision," *Studies in Philology* 71 (1974): 314-43 (333).

[3] Sandra Pearson Prior, *The Fayre Formez of the Pearl Poet* (East Lansing: Michigan State University Press, 1996), 16-17, 66. See also Ann Chalmers Watts, "*Pearl*, Inexpressibility, and Poems of Human Loss," *PMLA* 99 (1984): 26-40 (29-32); P. M. Kean, *The Pearl* (London: Routledge and K. Paul, 1957), 210-12.

[4] Jennifer Garrison, "Liturgy and Loss: *Pearl* and the Ritual Reform of the Aristocratic Subject," *Chaucer Review* 44 (2010): 314.

[5] Denise Louise Despres, *Ghostly Sights: Visual Meditation in Late-Medieval Literature* (Norman: Pilgrim Books, 1989), 115. J. J. Anderson also suggests that the reading of Revelation here is colored by the Dreamer's experience of meditative texts and images used in affective piety (*Language and Imagination in the Gawain-Poems* [Manchester and New York: Manchester University Press and Palgrave, 2005], 69-70). Ad Putter, more sympathetic, still sees this reliance on Revelation as proof of the Dreamer not being a

XVII's close correspondence to Revelation attests to a medieval taste for demonstrating deference to scripture as well as an enthusiasm for pastiche that many modern readers no longer share. But if Homer can occasionally nod, then here, most critics would have us believe, the *Pearl*-Poet snoozes as deeply as his Dreamer.

I am unsatisfied by the suggestion that the description of Heavenly Jerusalem is deliberately flat in order to displace the poem's emotional crescendo to the crossing of the river. Nor do I fully accept those interpretations that make Fitt XVII a referendum on the Dreamer's moral state, arguing that the poet intended us to be bored by the description in order to underscore the Dreamer's obtuseness and his separateness from the celestial celebrations before him. I tend to believe that the modern readers, rather than the Dreamer, are the ones who don't get it. Instead of either using this passage to evaluate the spiritual state of the narrator or judging these verses aesthetically according to the rest of the poem, I shall consider Fitt XVII mainly in isolation, particularly its link word. In a poem almost devoid of proper nouns—even Pearl is introduced first as a gem and remains an ambiguous symbol—John's name ringing as a refrain is all the more conspicuous, particularly as it is linked with that other refraining name, Jerusalem. Several scholars have already carefully documented how the *Pearl*-Poet responds to John's Revelation in a larger context of mystic vision.[6] I am here more concerned with what John himself would have meant to a fourteenth-century reader as well as writer. Who was "the apostle John" for a medieval English audience? How is John a vernacular

---

mystic: "At what for Dante and many medieval mystics was to be the culmination of their visionary experience, the Dreamer only sees...what John saw.... It is no exaggeration to say that this section of *Pearl* is largely a string of quotations from this biblical text. By the end of it, we know no more about the City of God than what we could have read for ourselves in the Bible. Perhaps this is a disappointment, but it is indicative of the modesty of a poet who did not presume he could see any further than his audience" (*An Introduction to the "Gawain"-Poet*, [London and New York: Longman, 1996], 194).

[6] Along with Finlayson ("*Pearl*: Landscape and Vision"), see Ann R. Meyer, *Medieval Allegory and the Building of the New Jerusalem* (Cambridge: D. S. Brewer, 2003), and Theodore Bogdanos, *"Pearl": Image of the Ineffable, A Study in Medieval Poetic Symbolism* (University Park, Penn.: The Pennsylvania State University Press, 1983), esp. 99-142.

authority? And is seeing with John a defensive strategy or a liberating move for the poet?

John and the Pure *Auctor* of Vision

In *Pearl* John is identified as the author of the "Apocalypsis," and both the Dreamer and the Pearl-Maiden cite him as an authority on the New Jerusalem. John the Apostle was in fact a scriptural *auctor* several times over, for a gospel, three epistles, and the Book of Revelation were attributed to him.[7] While scholars today doubt that the same person wrote all five texts, medieval exegetes believed that John composed Revelation while exiled on the Isle of Patmos, banished by Emperor Domitian. Cast as a message to the seven churches of Asia, Revelation describes a sequence of unfolding visions of the end times, including the opening of seals, the blowing of trumpets, and the pouring of abominations from bowls. Sinister yet enigmatic threats such as the Whore of Babylon and the Beast are ultimately overthrown. *Pearl* makes no use of this terrifying iconography of judgment and punishment, instead borrowing from Chapter 21's description of the final vision of the New Jerusalem, where the saved shall dwell with God. Unlike many other visions of the afterlife, the dreamer does not engage in infernal tourism nor receive a preview of the end times' torments; rather his concerns are the fate of one particular soul.

However, John's ability to glimpse heavenly secrets long predated Patmos. At the Last Supper John is described as "lying on Jesus' breast" (John 13:23-25), a special tenderness that Peter encourages John to exploit by asking the Lord which of the Apostles would betray Him. Like many medieval commentators, St. Thomas Aquinas interpreted this physical intimacy as a symbol for John's "knowledge of mysteries, which were made known to him by Christ, and especially for the writing of this Gospel. He says he was lying close to the lap of Jesus, for the lap signifies things that are hidden."[8]

---

[7] There was also an apocryphal *Book of John the Evangelist* associated with the Cathars; see the translation by M. R. James, *The Apocryphal New Testament* (Oxford: Clarendon Press, 1924), 187-93.

[8] "secretorum notitiam, quae ei Christus revelabat, et specialiter in conscriptione huius Evangelii, unde dicit quod *recubuit in sinu Iesu*: per sinum enim secretum significatur; supra I, v. 18: *unigenitus, qui est in sinu patris ipse enarravit*" (St. Thomas Aquinas, *Commentary on the Gospel of St. John*, trans. Fabian R. Larcher, O.P., and James Weisheipl, O.P., 3 vols. [Albany: Magi Books, 1998], 3.28-29, ch13.1804).

Often artists would depict this moment as John actually slumbering on Christ's bosom, suggesting that his access to divine mysteries came through dreams. Hence why this scene sometimes appeared in Anglo-Norman illustrated Apocalypses as an explanatory prelude to the vision of the end, for several manuscripts situated Revelation within John's *vita*.[9]

FIG. 1 Cambridge, Corpus Christi College, MS 20, f. 1. By permission of Master and Fellows of Corpus Christi College, Cambridge

[9] For a table of Apocalypse manuscripts containing scenes from the Life of St. John the Evangelist see Appendix II in Nigel Morgan, *The Lambeth Apocalypse: Manuscript 209 in Lambeth Palace Library* (London: Harvey Miller, 1990), 269-70. The usual moments that were illustrated included the resurrecting of Drusiana, the changing of the stones, the raising of the youth as well as the criminal, and the empty tomb.

Cambridge, Corpus Christi College, MS 20 makes the association even stronger: here John's nap at the feast is visually linked to Revelation, with the dining table carried through into the next panel as the prow of the ship depositing John at Patmos, thereby causally connecting sleep and vision as we read these images from left to right (FIG. 1).

Thus, even among the Twelve Apostles, John held a special status, rivaled perhaps only by Peter in prominence. Early on John exhibited a special sight, allowing him to recognize Jesus's divine nature while in human form, and his Gospel is considerably more preoccupied with the unearthly side of Christ than the Synoptic texts. Thus Origen refers to John's book as "the firstfruits of the Gospels," for the Lord "reserves for the one who leaned on Jesus' breast the greater and more perfect expressions concerning Jesus."[10] John was present at a number of key moments of Christ's revelation of his divinity, including the Transfiguration (Matthew 17:1-9, Mark 9:2-8, Luke 9:28-36) and the empty tomb on Easter morn (John 20:1-10). For this clarity of vision, piercing even the secrets of heaven, John was likened to the eagle, which the bestiaries explained "is named [*Aquila*, or 'eagle'] for its keenness (*acumine*) of sight"; eagle chicks proved their nature by "vigorously maintain[ing] a calm focus of vision, a steady gaze at the light cast by the sun" while dangling from their parents' claws.[11] In most portraits John is depicted with his totem eagle, not only in Evangelist portraits in Bibles but in

---

[10] Origen, *Commentariorum in evangelium Johannis* 1.21-22, as found in Origen, *Commentary on the Gospel According to John*, trans. Ronald E. Heine, 2 vols., Fathers of the Church 80 (Washington D. C.: Catholic University Press of America, 1989), 1.37.

[11] "Aquila ab acumine oculorum vocata.... Asseritur quoque quod pullos suos radiis solis obiciat, et in medio aeris ungue suspendat. Ac si quis repercusso solis lumine intrepedam oculorum aciem inoffenso intuendi vigore servaverit, is probatur quod veritatem naturae demonstravit" (quoted from Willene B. Clark, *A Medieval Book of Beasts: The Second-Family Bestiary: Commentary, Art, Text, and Translation* [Woodbridge: Boydell Press, 2006], 166-67 [ch. 52]). As Debra Hassig notes, the eagle was also an emblem for baptism and the renewal of the flesh: *Medieval Bestiaries: Text, Image, Ideology* (Cambridge: Cambridge University Press, 1995), 81-82; for a Middle English instance, see *An Old English Miscellany Containing a Bestiary, Kentish Sermons, Proverbs of Alfred, Religious Poems of the Thirteenth Century*, ed. Richard Morris, EETS os 49 (1872; Woodbridge: Boydell and Brewer, 1997), 3-4.

Books of Hours as well, which often included synopses of the Gospels (FIG. 2).

FIG. 2 Georges Trubert (active Provence 1469-1508), Book of Hours Los Angeles, J. Paul Getty Museum, MS 48 f. 13. Digital image courtesy of the Getty's Open Content Program.

So prominent was this image that it even crept into iconophobic settings, the example in London, British Library, MS Royal 1 C VIII being the only known miniature in all surviving Wycliffite Bibles.[12] According to Isidore of Seville, John's gift of heavenly wisdom confirms his name's etymology, "in whom is grace" or "grace of the Lord": appropriate for "the disciple whom Jesus loved," as he referred to himself in his Gospel.[13] Another sign of this especial favor is that it was to John that Jesus entrusts his mother after his death (John 19:27), so that he becomes Mary's surrogate son. We should assume that the *Pearl*-Poet and his audience would have most frequently encountered John in this role *in loco filii*, as represented in the ubiquitous motif of the Virgin and John at the base of the Crucifix, blue and red-clad figures flanking the cross in numerous panels, windows, illuminations, alabasters, and sculptural groups on Rood screens in churches throughout Europe. (Among surviving late medieval English examples in parish churches are the Rood screen and glass in Sts. Peter and Paul at East Harling, the remains of the Rood screen at St. Agnes at Cawston, and the painted wood panels in St. Catherine in Ludham, now in the chancel arch.) John's custody of Mary was also emphasized in the widely known liturgical sequence *Johannes Iesu Christo multum*.[14]

Returning to *Pearl*, John as the patriarch closest to Christ and dreamer of heaven's secrets is an appropriate authority to confirm the veracity of the Dreamer's account of heaven. At first glance, the Dreamer's fidelity to a text by the most privileged of the Apostles seems a protective move. His humble deference to John's Apocalypse balances his audacity of citing Scripture in Middle English and claiming to see the Celestial Jerusalem while still a layman. The repeated insistence that John is the author of this passage, not himself, and the dreamer's implicit imitation of John, resembles somewhat the defensive strategy that Spiritual

---

[12] Kathleen E. Kennedy, *The Courtly and Commercial Art of the Wycliffite Bible*, Medieval Church Studies 35 (Turnhout: Brepols, 2014), 68-72.

[13] *Etymologies*, VII.ix.11, in *The "Etymologies" of Isidore of Seville*, trans. Stephen A. Barney, et.al. (Cambridge: Cambridge University Press, 2006), 169.

[14] Nancy van Deusen, "*Verbum dei deo natum* and its Manuscript Context," 55-79 (65), and Lori Kruckenberg, "Music for St. John the Evangelist: Virtue and Virtuosity at the Convent of Paradies," 133-60 (142-44), both in *Leaves from Paradise: The Cult of John the Evangelist at the Dominican Convent of Paradies bei Soest*, ed. Jeffrey F. Hamburger (Cambridge, Mass.: Harvard University Press for Houghton Library, 2008).

Franciscans and even at times Wycliffite writers resorted to.[15] In this sense John's presence in Fitt XVII is unremarkable. Yet there are a number of further correspondences between *Pearl* and John as represented through his cult and legend that suggest that the poem's emphasis on John is not simply authorial citation.

Like the Dreamer, after his vision John does not remain in heaven nor retreat to a cloister but instead returns to a full, active life. Post Patmos, John is kept especially busy raising people from the dead. Most famously he revives his friend Drusiana, whom he commands to wake up and fix his lunch.[16] But he also, while reprimanding some apostates, resurrects a recently married youth to serve as a credible witness on the pains of hell; another time, as if surviving a poisoned draught were not enough to convince an obdurate pagan, John performed the further miracle of reviving the two criminals who had died drinking from the same chalice.[17] Thus, in the context of *Pearl*, a poem agonizing over loss, John repeatedly reminds us that death can be overcome through faith and love.

He himself is the best proof of this, as John is the one apostle who does not die. There is no account of John's martyrdom, and hagiographies describe him as living to an old age. When his allotted years expired, John was either left to sleep beneath the earth or else was taken bodily into heaven, perhaps to where Enoch and Elijah rest. Scriptural support for this miracle was drawn from John 21:21-23, when Peter, just learning that he is to follow Christ to death by crucifixion, asks what will happen to John; Jesus replies, "So I will

---

[15] Kathryn Kerby-Fulton, *Books under Suspicion: Censorship and Tolerance of Revelatory Writing in Late Medieval England* (Notre Dame: University of Notre Dame Press, 2006), 214-15, 222-23.

[16] "And whanne he come into the cite, Drusiane his frende that hadde gretli desired his coming was born dede.... And thanne the apostell comaunded to sette downe the bere and vnbynde the body and saide: 'Oure Lorde Ihesu Crist arere the, Drusian, arise vp and go into thi hous and make redi my mete'" (*Gilte Legende*, ed. Richard Hamer, Early English Text Society os 327 [Oxford: Oxford University Press, 2006], 1.50-51). Perhaps the most well-known incident after his writing of the Apocalypse, the raising of Drusiana was the subject of a play by Hrotsvit of Gandersheim (*Calimachus*) and of numerous images in *predellae* and manuscripts, as well as in the North Dome mosaic of the Duomo of Venice (c.1100-25); Giotto's Peruzzi Chapel in Santa Croce, Florence (c.1320); and later Filippino Lippi's fresco for the Strozzi Chapel, Santa Maria Novella, Florence (c.1502).

[17] *Gilte Legende*, 1.50-57.

have him to remain till I come, what is it to thee?" Dante famously scorned this legend in the *Paradiso* when he has the Evangelist himself chide the Pilgrim for his astonishment at not seeing John's body, assuring that his corpse is rotting on earth with the rest of us.[18] But in doing so Dante was once again bucking authority, for even St. Jerome at times declared that John simply "fell asleep" and was spared death.[19] (St. Augustine, however, expressed skepticism on this point.)[20] John's shrine in Ephesus corroborated this legend of assumption or dormition, as it was claimed that when later visitors dug up John's grave in search of relics, all that were found were his sandals. Soon afterwards, holy white dust miraculously bubbled forth from the burial mound on his feast day, thought by some to be crystallization of the slumbering Apostle's breath. This *manna* was itself an eagerly sought relic, pilgrims collecting the powder in *ampullae* for prophylactic uses.[21]

While doubtful that the *Pearl*-Poet would have journeyed to Ephesus himself, particularly as in 1308 it had ceded from Byzantine to Turkish control, he most likely was familiar with this legend, as it was discussed in commentaries and hagiographies, as well as *Mandeville's Travels*. A John whose body was incorrupt makes for a striking contrast with the Pearl "withouten spot" that at the same

---

[18] *Paradiso* 25.124-29: "In terra è terra il mio corpor, e saragli / tanto con li altri che 'l numero nostro / con l'etterno proposito s'agguagli. / Con le due stole nel beato chiostro / son le due luci sole che saliro, / e questo apporterai nel mondo Vostro" [On earth my body is earth, and it will be there with others until our number equals the eternal purpose. Only the two lights that ascended (Christ and the Virgin Mary) have the two stoles in the eternal cloister, and you shall take this back to your world] (*Paradiso*, ed. and trans. Robert Durling [Oxford: Oxford University Press, 2011]).

[19] *Adversus Jovinianum* 1.26, although in *De viris illustribus*, IX, Jerome states clearly that John died.

[20] *In Johannis Evangelium* 124.2, as in St. Augustine, *Gospel of John, First Epistle of John, and Soliloquies*, trans. John Gibb and James Innes, for *A Select Library of Nicene and Post-Nicene Fathers of the Christian Church*, 1st ser., ed. Philip Schaff (New York: 1888), 7.447-48. St. Thomas Aquinas also demurred on this crux, cataloguing the contrasting views of Sts. Augustine, John Chrysostom, and Jerome: *Commentary on the Gospel of John*, 2646-57.

[21] Maggie Duncan-Flowers, "A Pilgrim's Ampulla from the Shrine of St. John the Evangelist at Ephesus," in *The Blessings of Pilgrimage*, ed. Robert G. Ousterhuot (Urbana: University of Illinois Press, 1990), 125-39.

time "to rot is runne" (26) and "doun drof in mode3 dunne" (30).[22] The Dreamer has an unflinching obsession with the pearl decaying in the mound, turning moldy ("To þenke his color so clad in clot! / O moul, þou marrez a myry juele" [22-23]). This morbid image of a rotten discolored pearl that sends forth spices and flowers from its decay is a strange variation on the Evangelist's mound containing untouched corpse, breathing forth white *manna*.[23] Both mounds simultaneously signify the presence and absence of their occupants.

John's body was inviolate also in the sense that tradition held that he was a virgin. Having been called away from his wedding feast, John was presumed to have remained chaste. In his prologue to John's Gospel, St. Jerome remarks that Christ called John *de nuptis*, a phrase usually interpreted to mean that John became a disciple at his own wedding, presumed to be the Marriage at Cana (John 2:1-11): Jesus may have granted wine to the guests, but he took the groom with him. Interpreting the bridegroom as John also implies that he was key in initiating Christ's ministry, for the transformation of water into wine at Cana was His first miracle, performed out of affection for both His mother and His hosts. Jerome cited John's example in *Adversus Jovinianum* (1.26), for of all the Apostles John "remained a virgin, and on that account was more beloved by our Lord."[24] John's intactness granted him a number of special privileges with Jesus, over Peter in particular: John was the one who lay on Christ's breast; he was the swiftest to the Easter sepulcher; he identified the resurrected Lord when the Apostles were fishing, for "the virgin alone recognized a virgin." John's virginity was even responsible for his incorruptible body: "Hence we have a proof that virginity does not die, and that the defilement of marriage is not washed away by martyrdom, but virginity abides

---

[22] All quotations from *Pearl* are taken from Malcolm Andrew and Ronald Waldron, eds., *The Poems of the Pearl Manuscript: "Pearl," "Cleanness," "Patience," and "Sir Gawain and the Green Knight,"* 5th ed. (Exeter: University of Exeter Press, 2007).

[23] *St. Erkenwald* also engages with the motif of the pristine corpse; for a recent defense of shared authorship, see Marie Borroff, "Narrative Artistry in *Saint Erkenwald* and the Gawain-Group: The Case for Common Authorship Reconsidered," *Studies in the Age of Chaucer* 28 (2006): 41-76.

[24] Translation from St. Jerome, *Letters and Select Works*, trans. W. H. Fremantle, in *A Select Library of Nicene and Post-Nicene Fathers of the Christian Church*, 2nd ser., eds. Henry Wace and Philip Schaff (New York: Charles Scribner's Sons, 1912), 6.365-66.

with Christ, and its sleep is not death but a passing to another state."[25] John's virginal state may in part explain the frequent medieval visual tradition of depicting him nearly alone among the Apostles as an unbearded youth except for in scenes explicitly post-Patmos when he is an old man. (This reputation of John being "supremely devoted to chastity" may also account for Gawain's swearing by St. John when declaring to his host's wife that he has no mistress [1788-91].[26])

Pearl's obsession with intactness makes John, the Apostle most associated with purity, a good fit. The Pearl Maiden repeatedly is described as spotless (12, 24, 36, 48, 60), and it is for her cleanness that the Lamb has called her to be his bride: "Cum hyder to Me, My lemman swete, / For mote ne spot is non in þe" (763-64). Furthermore, her purity grants the Maiden access to divine mysteries, for the innocent are distinguished from the merely righteous (681-83, 721-320). What Jerome said of John applies as well to the Pearl Maiden: "The virgin expounded mysteries which the married could not."[27]

Thus, John in his *vita* resonates with the Pearl Maiden as much as with the Dreamer. As a mortal who in this life glimpses the New Jerusalem, John is an authoritative forerunner for the Dreamer. And as a man of resurrections, John promises the renewal the Dreamer desires for his Pearl. Yet as a virgin granted special favor with the Lord, including access to celestial mysteries as well as a burial mound prolifically fecund, John prefigures the Pearl-Maiden. And as the Apostle who was allowed to see God without a martyr's death, he becomes a comforting figure making the possibility for salvation

---

[25] St. Augustine is less strident than Jerome on this point, noting that "There are some who have entertained the idea–and those, too, who are no contemptible handlers of sacred eloquence–that the Apostle John was more loved by Christ on the ground that he never married a wife, and lived in perfect chastity from early boyhood. There is, indeed, no distinct evidence of this in the canonical Scriptures: nevertheless it is an idea that contributes not a little to the suitableness of the opinion…that that life was signified by him, [namely] where there will be no marriage" (*In Johannis Evangelium*, Tractate 124.7 from St. Augustine, *Gospel of John, First Epistle of John, and Soliloquies*, trans. John Gibb and James Innes, for *A Select Library of Nicene and Post-Nicene Fathers of the Christian Church*, 1st ser., ed. Philip Schaff [New York: 1888], 7.452).

[26] Andrew and Waldron, eds., *The Poems of the Pearl Manuscript*, 272, n1788.

[27] *Ad Jovinianun*, 1.26 (6.366).

open for all, not simply the most heroic. Of course, Revelation's description of heavenly glories makes John's presence inevitable in *Pearl*, but even aside from his vision of the New Jerusalem it is hard to imagine which biblical patriarch or matriarch would better suit the concerns of the poem.

John the Vernacular *Auctor*

As an Apostle with five scriptural books attributed to him, John certainly qualified as an *auctor* far removed from the vagaries of the vernacular. At first the gulf between Latin scripture and Middle English alliterative verse appears great. We are used to thinking of Middle English as having a lowly, tertiary status behind Latin and French. This tension between Middle English and Latin especially becomes heightened by Lollardy's polemical translations of the Bible, and Archbishop Arundel's reactive Constitutions of 1409 bespeak of a fraught contest in late medieval England about how the vernacular can be a vehicle for scripture and its exegesis.[28] Yet scholars have tempered this picture of a stark binary of Latinity and vernacularity as well as a draconian regime of censorship.[29] Furthermore, while in the wake of different heresies church and royal prohibitions may have forbid translations of the Bible, there was never a complete restriction: For example, the Bible was entirely translated into French by the mid-thirteenth century, and it widely circulated in both France and England.[30] Certainly the *Pearl*-Poet is in good company with Chaucer and Langland as a Middle English author including biblical verse into his own, not to mention the popular fourteenth-century paraphrases of scripture in works such as *Cursor Mundi* and the *Prick of Conscience*. Therefore, while the citing of John so incessantly in Fitt XVII may be a deferential move

---

[28] Nicholas Watson, "Censorship and Cultural Change in Late-Medieval England: Vernacular Theology, the Oxford Translation Debate, and Arundel's Constitutions of 1409," *Speculum* 70 (1995): 822-64.

[29] Fiona Somerset, "Professionalizing Translation at the Turn of the Fifteenth Century: Ullerston's *Determinacio*, Arundel's *Constitutions*," in *The Vulgar Tongue: Medieval and Postmedieval Vernacularity*, eds. Fiona Somerset and Nicholas Watson (University Park: Pennsylvania State University Press, 2003), 145-57 (152-54); Alastair Minnis, *Translation of Authority in Medieval English Literature: Valuing the Vernacular* (Cambridge: Cambridge University Press, 2009), 26-27; and Kerby-Fulton, *Books under Suspicion*, 397-401.

[30] Frans Van Liere, *An Introduction to the Medieval Bible* (Cambridge: Cambridge University Press, 2014), 194-95.

on the poet's part, we should not assume that it was motivated by fear of seeming to overstep his bounds as a vernacular writer.

Moreover, we should remember that Revelation was one of the most accessible parts of the Bible for an English lay audience. After the Psalter, the Apocalypse is the earliest book of scripture to be rendered in the vernacular.[31] There were translations into both Old French and Anglo-Norman, in prose and verse.[32] Revelation was also translated into Middle English prose twice, both times from French rather than Latin. These Middle English versions circulated independent of the Lollard Bible, although later they were incorporated into the Wycliffite translations.[33] There is even evidence that Revelation, as well as the Gospel of John, were so popular in Middle English that they were part of a small handful of scriptural texts speculatively copied as readymade booklets, available for binding into customers' collections at a moment's notice.[34] Accompanying commentaries were also translated. To some extent, then, we should think of Revelation as a vernacular book, and sometimes even a vernacular poem.

We should also think of it as an illustrated book.[35] While Revelation has a rich visual history in a variety of media, in the thirteenth century a distinctive tradition of Anglo-French illumination of the Apocalypse developed, which can roughly be divided into two iconographic groups, those with illustrations that accompany the Berengaudus commentary and those that are keyed to a French prose gloss.[36] The Berengaudus commentary on Revelation, already circulating widely in England in the twelfth

---

[31] James H. Morey, *Book and Verse: A Guide to Middle English Biblical Literature* (Urbana and Chicago: University of Illinois Press, 2000), 351-53.

[32] For an edition of the prose see Léopold Delisle and Paul Meyer, *L'Apocalypse en français au XIIIe siècle (Bibl. Nat. Fr. 403)*, Société des Anciens Textes Français v. 44 (Paris: Didot, 1901).

[33] Elis Fridner, "Introduction," in *An English Fourteenth Century Apocalypse with a Prose Commentary, Edited from MS Harley 874 and Ten Other MSS* (Lund: C. W. K. Gleerup, 1961), xxv-xxx.

[34] Kennedy, *Courtly and Commercial Art*, 42, 46-51.

[35] And sometimes even a picture book: a few Anglo-Norman Apocalypses are almost completely illuminations, such as New York, Pierpont Morgan Library, MS 524 and Oxford, Bodleian Library, MS Auct. D. 4. 17.

[36] Suzanne Lewis, "Exegesis and Illustration in English Apocalypses," in *The Apocalypse in the Middle Ages*, eds. Richard K. Emmerson and Bernard McGinn (Ithaca: Cornell University Press, 1992), 259-75 (259).

century in unillustrated copies, interpreted the text from the standpoint of the Church Universal. While monastically focused in its commentary, this version of the Apocalypse was often commissioned and owned by lay folk, albeit aristocratic ones. These manuscripts frequently have a large image spanning across two columns, which dominates the page, creating a meditative, sequential unfolding of the Apocalypse. Often John is presented as a proxy for the reader, anxiously watching events unfold, but remaining outside the image's frame (FIG. 3).

FIG. 3 Dyson Perrins Apocalypse, Los Angeles, J. Paul Getty Museum, MS Ludwig III, f. 5. England (most likely London), c. 1255-60. Digital image courtesy of the Getty's Open Content Program

In contrast, the thirteenth-century French prose gloss on the Apocalypse was translated from the commentary to the *Bible moralisée* (which in turn was a Latin redaction of the *Glossa ordinaria*) and was influenced by the mendicants.[37] Manuscripts of Revelation

---

[37] For the mendicant elements of the prose commentary, particularly in its references to preachers, see Lewis, "Exegesis and Illustration in English Apocalypses," 254; J. C. Fox, "The Earliest French Apocalypse and

with this gloss generated their own complex network of iconographic families, roughly divided between the cycle of 69 illustrations known as the Corpus-Lambeth Stem (so named for "core" manuscripts London, Lambeth MS 75 and Cambridge, Corpus Christi MS 394), and the slightly later (c.1280-1330), more copiously illustrated group sometimes called the metrical Apocalypses, as the biblical text has been rendered into Anglo-Norman verse with the same accompanying French prose gloss.[38] Besides the use of French, the didactic vernacular gloss provided an interpretive paradigm that was more suitable for a lay, as opposed to monastic, audience. As Suzanne Lewis observes, "Whereas the older [Berengaudus] commentary invites contemplative spiritual meditation, the French prose gloss rallies the reader to deal with [Revelation's] moral imperatives as a series of practical remedies to contemporary problems"; the miniatures likewise adapt to these different roles, those of the Berengaudus cycle suggesting allegorical, theological readings, while the pictures of the Corpus-Lambeth cycle figure John's vision as a series of visualized sermons with "pictorial exempla."[39] The *mise-en-page* tends to reflect this change, as images are similarly presented as a choppy series of interruptions to the text, sometimes only spanning a single column (FIG. 4).

Commentary," *Modern Language Review* 7 (1912): 445-68 (454); Delisle and Meyer, *L'Apocalypse en français au XIIIe siècle*, I.ccxiv-ccxxii.

[38] Aileen H. Laing, "The Corpus-Lambeth Stem: A Study of French Prose Apocalypse Manuscripts," *Manuscripta* 21 (1977): 18; Sammye Lee Justice, "The Illustrated Anglo-Norman Metrical Apocalypse in England," Ph.D. diss. (Princeton University, 1993).

[39] Lewis, "Exegesis and Illustration in English Apocalypses," 263-65. See also Suzanne Lewis, "'Apocalapses' in Text and Image: from Translation to Transformation in Fourteenth-Century Vernacular Apocalypses," in *Tributes to Nigel Morgan. Contexts of Medieval Art: Images, Objects, and Ideas*, eds. Julian M. Luxford and M. A. Michael. (London: Harvey Miller, 2010), 141-47.

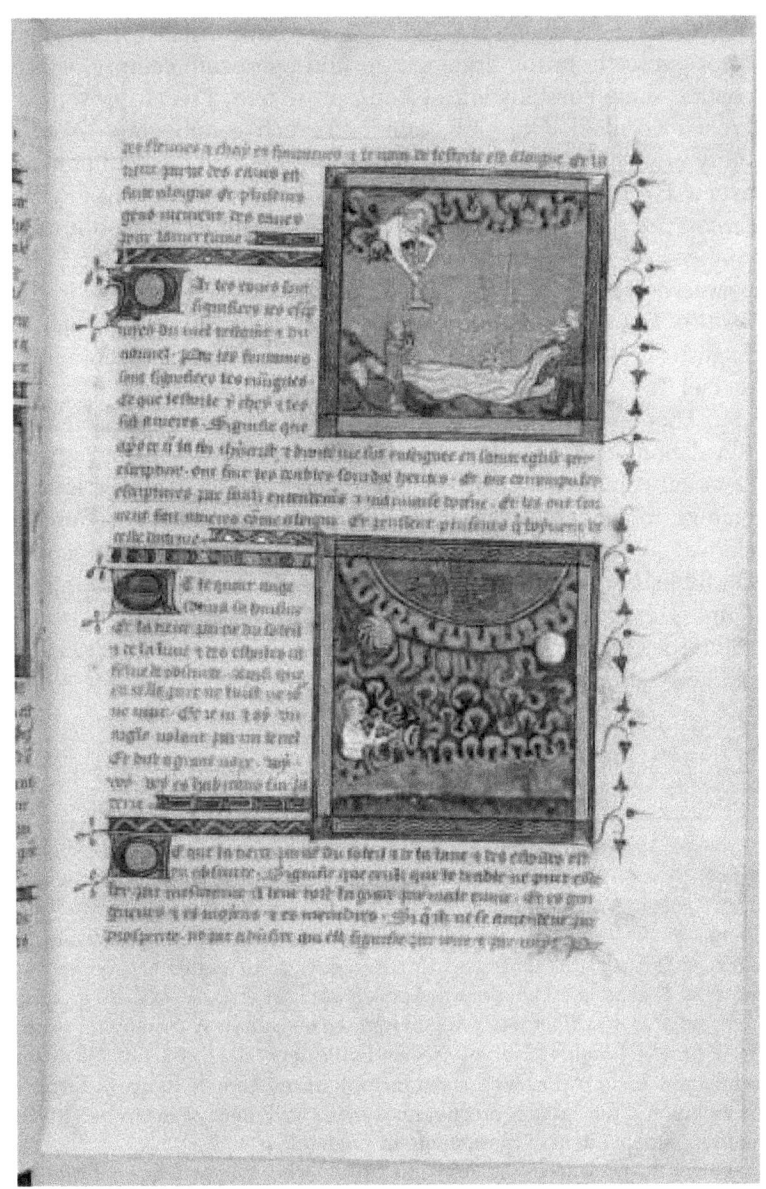

FIG. 4 Yates Thompson Apocalypse. London, British Library, Yates Thompson MS 10, f. 14. France, Central, c. 1370-90. Courtesy of The British Library.

Combined, there are over 50 surviving English illustrated Apocalypses from the thirteenth to mid-fourteenth century, which contain some combination of Latin prose text, French prose text, French versified text, and Latin or French commentary. Nearly thirty more examples of illustrated Apocalypses in this tradition are extant by French or Flemish artists, mostly relying on English prototypes and from places with strong political and artistic connections to England, namely Normandy and Lorraine.[40] So pervasive were these illuminated books that, as Lewis notes, "In the *Manière langage*, a collection of dialogues used to teach French to English speakers, French was described as the language 'des angels du ciel.'"[41]

Therefore, we should think of the *Pearl*-Poet's experience of Revelation as possibly that of a vernacular book, with textual as well as visual commentary, that often circulated on its own as a luxury manuscript rather than as the final book of a volume of mostly clerical preserve. As much as John and his Apocalypse would signify the Bible they would also elicit associations with elite consumption. *Pearl* is a finely wrought piece of craftsmanship akin to these glamorous books.[42] Both Rosalind Field and Muriel Whitaker have pointed out correspondences between iconography from some

---

[40] Nigel Morgan, "Some French Interpretations of Illustrated English Apocalypses c.1290-130," in John Matthew, ed., *England and the Continent in the Middle Ages: Studies in Memory of Andrew Martindale, Proceedings of the 1996 Harlaxton Symposium*, Harlaxton Medieval Studies VIII (Stamford: Shaun Tyas, 2000), 137-39. But see also the addendum to this argument that Morgan makes in "The Bohun Apocalypse," in *Tributes to Lucy Freeman Sandler: Studies in Illuminated Manuscripts*, eds. Kathryn A. Smith and Carol H. Krinsky (London: Harvey Miller Publishers, 2007), 91-110 (95 n20): while the Latin Apocalypses made in France seem to borrow English iconography, the French prose copies made in France seem to be almost entirely independent of those made in England.

[41] Lewis, "'Apocalapses' in Text and Image," 141-42, quoting Paul Meyer, "La manière de langage qui enseigne à parler et à écrire le français," *Revue critique d'histoire et de littérature* 12 (1873): 382.

[42] Felicity Riddy discusses Apocalypses association with lavish craftsmanship in "Jewels in Pearl," in *A Companion to the "Gawain"-Poet*, eds. Derek Brewer and Jonathan Gibson (Cambridge: D. S. Brewer, 1997), 143-55 (146-47).

Anglo-Norman Apocalypses and images in *Pearl*.⁴³ Sarah Stanbury has remarked generally about the ways that both the illustrated Apocalypses and *Pearl* represent the sensory process of seeing.⁴⁴ And, as Barbara Nolan observes, the poet reveals a fascination with the technical aspects of manuscript production: "In his description of the apocalyptic vision, the poet even chooses words drawn from the illuminators' craft. Not only is the city 'brende golde'; the horns of the Lamb are 'red golde cler'; and the wall of jasper gleams as 'glayre,' the white of egg used in making illuminations."⁴⁵

Most of the manuscript examples these critics draw upon are from the Berengaudus family. One of the most striking aspects of these codices is the depiction of John as an animated spectator in the margins. Often he is shown as peering through a window, separated from the celestial events by a frame (FIG. 3).⁴⁶ While some art historians have shied away from calling this figure of the watching John the "voyeur" motif, in the context of *Pearl* voyeurism seems an appropriate descriptor.⁴⁷ The Pearl Maiden promises to share with

---

⁴³ Rosalind Field, "The Heavenly Jerusalem in *Pearl*," *Modern Language Review* 81 (1986): 7-17; Muriel A. Whitaker, "*Pearl* and Some Illustrated Apocalypse Manuscripts," *Viator* 12 (1981): 183-96.

⁴⁴ *Seeing the "Gawain"-Poet: Description and the Act of Perception* (Philadelphia: University of Pennsylvania Press, 1991), 24-31.

⁴⁵ Barbara Nolan, *The Gothic Visionary Perspective* (Princeton: Princeton University Press, 1997), 200.

⁴⁶ For discussion of this device as a metaphor for mystical vision, see Suzanne Lewis, "The English Gothic Illuminated Apocalypse, *lectio divina*, and the Art of Memory," *Word & Image* 7 (1991): 1-32 (esp. 2-13); and Cynthia Hahn, "*Visio Dei*: Changes in Medieval Visuality," in *Visuality before and beyond the Renaissance*, ed. Robert S. Nelson (Cambridge: Cambridge University Press, 2000), 169-96 (esp. 183-86).

⁴⁷ Peter K. Klein, who first applied the term "voyeurism" to the iconography of John gazing through the window ("From the Heavenly to the Trivial: Vision and Visual Perception in Early and High Medieval Apocalypse," in *The Holy Face and the Paradox of Representation*, eds. Herbert L. Kessler and Gerhard Wolf [Bologna: Nuova Alfa, 1998], 247-78) has renamed it as the "external witness motif" ("Visionary Experience and Corporeal Seeing in Thirteenth-Century English Apocalypses: John as External Witness and the Rise of Gothic Marginal Images," in *Looking Beyond: Visions Dreams, and Insights in Medieval Art and History*, ed. Colum Hourihane, Index of Christian Art Occasional Papers XI (Philadelphia: Index of Christian Art Department of Art & Archaeology Princeton University in association with Penn State University Press, 2010), 177-202. Richard K. Emmerson also quibbled with

the Dreamer a glimpse of the New Jerusalem, but there is a sense that he is furtively spying (on his own dream!), as he "lurked by launces so lufly leved" (978), skulking in the bushes in order to watch the procession. (Cotton Nero A.x. has its own marginal voyeurs, foliate faces peering out of the capitals; three of these four grotesqueries are in *Pearl*.)[48]

The other families of illustrated Apocalypses related to the vernacular prose gloss, the Corpus-Lambeth Stem and the metrical Apocalypses, also provide suggestive comparisons with *Pearl*. The Corpus-Lambeth Apocalypses often do not have the spying John, nor do they generally have large depictions of the Heavenly City, such as that in the Trinity Apocalypse (Cambridge, Trinity College, MS.R.16.2). However, the Corpus-Lambeth's more broken layouts, with column-width illustrations in a subordinate position to surrounding text (FIG. 4), creates a *mise-en-page* that resembles that used in vernacular romances.[49] And in the metrical family of Apocalypses the visual narrative is dilated so that almost every event receives its own illumination.[50] I find that this shifts the images from seeming to provide a synthetic interpretation of the biblical text, serving as separate visual glosses with their own integrity, to becoming illustrations more tightly keyed to the text. Often in Anglo-Norman Apocalypse illuminations John can seem a romance hero, encountering on his journey magical beasts, battles with knights, a damsel in distress, a dangerous temptress, and elaborate feasts.[51] Combining these narrative and visual elements with the

---

the use of "voyeurism," arguing that it misrepresents John's vision as illicit: "Visualizing the Visionary: John in his Apocalypse," in *Looking Beyond*, ed. Hourihane, 148-76 (156).

[48] The other face appears in *Sir Gawain and the Green Knight*: Paul F. Reichardt, "Paginal Eyes: Faces among the Ornamented Capitals of MS Cotton Nero A.x. Art. 3," *Manuscripta* 36 (1992): 22-36.

[49] Lewis, "'Apocalapses' in Text and Image," 143.

[50] Justice, "The Illustrated Anglo-Norman Metrical Apocalypse in England," 5.

[51] George Henderson, "Studies in English Manuscript Illumination–Part 2: English Apocalypse 1," *Journal of the Warburg and Courtauld Institutes* 30 (1967): 104-37 (116-17); M. Dominica Legge, *Anglo-Norman Literature and Its Background* (Oxford: Clarendon Press, 1963), 236-39; R. Freyhan, "Joachimism and the English Apocalypse," *Journal of the Warburg and Courtauld Institutes* 18 (1955): 211-44 (225-26). While not calling John a romance hero, Suzanne Lewis describes how John becomes a character

verse format of the Anglo-Norman translation, we once again can see how Revelation in fourteenth-century England may just as much have resembled vernacular romances as Scripture—a duality evidenced as well by the *oeuvre* of a poet who wrote both biblical poetry (*Cleanness, Patience*) and Arthurian romance (*Sir Gawain and the Green Knight*).

John the *Auctor* of Gemology

John was considered an authority not only of the glories of heaven but of the splendors of the earth. As the fourteenth-century Middle English *Bok of Stones* explains,

> The appocalipse witnesseth vs þat god loued so moche my lord seint Iohn þe euangelist þat he did lede him be his aungel to se þe priuities of paradys; and also be a uision he sigh þe grete paradys as a Cite. There he sigh þe twelue stones that God named, and the xj stones þat hymselfe / named be the wille of God þat were þe foundement of þe heuenly kyngdome.[52]

Sometimes in biblical exegesis these stones would be interpreted symbolically, as Nicholas of Lyra does in his commentary on the Apocalypse (1329), in which he reads the layers of gems as the "twelve articles of faith concerning Christ—six pertaining to his divinity and six to his humanity."[53] But Revelation's jewels would also be understood literally as the earthly stones, so that John was also cited as an *auctor* in works of natural philosophy, particularly lapidaries. One branch of Anglo-Norman gem books has even been dubbed the "Apocalyptic Lapidary," as it is dedicated solely to the stones of Revelation as well as two other heavenly gems (the pearl of the gates and the diamond adamant of the foundation).[54]

---

within Revelation in *Reading Images: Narrative Discourse and Reception in the Thirteenth-Century Illuminated Apocalypse* (Cambridge: Cambridge University Press, 1995), 20-25.

[52] *The Middle English "Boke of Stones": The Southern Version*, ed. George R. Keiser, SCRIPTA 13 (Brussels: Omirel, 1984), 4; also edited in *English Mediaeval Lapidaries*, eds. Joan Evans, and Mary S. Serjeantson, EETS os 190 (London: Oxford University Press, 1933), 18.

[53] *Nicholas of Lyra's Apocalypse Commentary*, trans. Philip D. W. Krey (Kalamazoo: Western Michigan University Press, 1997), 226-28.

[54] *Anglo-Norman Lapidaries*, eds. Paul Studer and Joan Evans (Paris: Librairie Ancienne Édouard Champion, 1924), 260-76. As they remark in their

England was particularly fascinated with the properties of gems. The oldest known vernacular lapidary is in Old English, and lapidaries were enormously popular in Anglo-Norman as well as Middle English; moreover, many Latin manuscripts of gem lore appear to be of English provenance.[55] As George Keiser observes, this prevalence of lapidarial knowledge meant that romance writers as well as the *Pearl*-Poet could assume an audience well versed in the properties of stones.[56] The virtues associated with each of Fitt XVII's gems have already been documented.[57] For now, I simply want to emphasize that the lapidary tradition provides yet another vernacular context for John as an *auctor*. And part of this lapidarial context was the conviction that stones, if not precisely alive, had animate properties; as several scholars have recently reminded us, medieval understandings of the environment perceived stone as possessing inclinations and virtues.[58]

John's hagiography further links him with precious stones. According to the Golden Legend, John became scandalized when he saw a philosopher order his disciples to grind jewels into powder as proof of their contempt for wealth. Appalled at the waste–those gems would be better served as alms–John miraculously

---

Introduction, "Nowhere, indeed, did the lore of jewels enjoy greater popularity than in Anglo-Norman England" (viii). Cf. Joan Evans, *Magical Jewels of the Middle Ages and the Renaissance*, rprnt. (1922; New York: Dover, 1973), 73-78. The Longleat manuscript of the Apocalyptic Lapidary contains the following lines on pearl: "Margarita: Unium ad colurs toutis maniers/ E engendré de la rosee del ciel" (*Anglo-Norman Lapidaries*, 7, 275).

[55] London, British Library, MS. Cotton Tiberius A.iii, dating to the eleventh century: see Evans and Serjeantson, "Introduction," in *English Mediaeval Lapidaries*, xi.

[56] Keiser, "Introduction," in *The Middle English "Boke of Stones,"* vii-x, citing E. V. Gordon, "Introduction," in *Pearl* (Oxford: Clarendon Press, 1953), xxxiv-xxxv.

[57] Robert J. Blanch, "Precious Metal and Gem Symbolism in *Pearl*, in *"Sir Gawain" and "Pearl": Critical Essays*, ed. Robert J. Blanch (Bloomington and London: Indiana University Press, 1966), 86-97.

[58] Valerie Allen, "Mineral Virtue," and Kellie Robertson "Exemplary Rocks," both in *Animal, Vegetable, Mineral: Ethics and Objects*, ed. Jeffrey Jerome Cohen (Washington D.C.: Oliphant Books, 2012), 123-52 and 91-121 respectively, and Cohen's own "Stories of Stone," *postmedieval* 1 (2010): 56-63, the arguments of which will be expanded in his forthcoming *Stories of Stone: An Ecology of the Inhuman* (Minneapolis: University of Minnesota Press, 2015).

reassembled the jewels from the dust, leading to the conversion of two wealthy youths, who sell their possessions to follow the Apostle. However, they soon have second thoughts, as seeing their former servants dressed more splendidly than themselves fills them with regret. Disgusted, John transforms driftwood and seashells into gold and gems, sending them to the jewelers to verify their worth. Later John inveighs against wealth, taunting the youths for the heavenly glories they have forsaken through their eagerness to grasp the gems of this world; the miraculously resurrected newlywed corroborated the Evangelist's account, describing how through their backsliding "thei hadd loste the euerlasting palais of ioye that bene made of precious stones and of mervailous light and full of all delites."[59] Abashed, the repentant youths re-pledge their faith, and John restores the shells and sticks to their original forms. These miracles would have been familiar not only through legendaries but also as celebrated in the well-known liturgical sequence *Verbum dei deo natum*.[60]

While the ultimate message of this set of miracles is the worthlessness of material wealth compared to spiritual treasure, this legend further links John with precious gems and depicts jewelers as his allies, confirming the saint's miracles. John may be austere, but he is no iconoclast. He balks at the willful destruction of the beautiful stones and acknowledges that they have market value in this world. (One wonders what his reaction would have been to the rebels grinding John's of Gaunt's jewelry in mortars during the Peasants' Revolt).[61] Moreover, heaven is described in comfortingly legible signifiers of luxury and wealth. The New Jerusalem is an even better version of these earthly splendors. St. Eligius may be the patron saint of goldsmiths and jewelers (including, presumably, the Dreamer),[62] but through his *vita* John has ties to those professions as well.

---

[59] *Gilte Legende*, 1.52, lines 87-89. In the Middle English version, the seashells and driftwood are instead stones from a riverbed.
[60] Felix Heinzer, "Explaining the Bread of True Intelligence: John the Evangelist as Mystagogue in the Sequence *Verbum dei deo natum*," 89-90, 97 (81-99) and Erika Kihlman, "Commentaries on *Verbum dei deo natum* in Fourteenth- and Fifteenth-century Manuscripts," 127 (101-31), both in *Leaves of Paradise*, ed. Hamburger.
[61] Riddy, "Jewels in Pearl," 152.
[62] St. Eligius is perhaps most familiar to readers of Middle English as the subject of the Prioress's oath (*Canterbury Tales* 1.120). A translation of his *vita* by Dado of Rouen can be found in *Medieval Hagiography*, ed. Thomas Head

In a context more directly pertinent to the *Pearl*-Poet, the Evangelist was further associated with jewelry. St. Edward the Confessor, who held a special devotion to St. John, was importuned for alms by a humble pilgrim at the dedication of a church to the Evangelist; as the king had already emptied his purse he gave his ring to the beggar, who turned out to be none other than St. John in disguise.[63] The pilgrim's ring became the Confessor's saintly emblem, as in the Wilton Diptych, where he supports a kneeling Richard II. In Westminster scenes of Sts. Edward and John together decorated sacred spaces (e.g. the Confessor's shrine, illuminated manuscripts of the saint's *vita*) and secular ones (particularly the Painted Rooms in Westminster Palace ordered by Henry III).[64] As Paul Binski notes, while the Confessor "was not widely portrayed outside royal circles," there was a special devotion to him by the successive abbots of Tewkesbury; the Tewkesbury connection leads to Edward le Despenser (d. 1375), who shared his name with the Confessor and who, among other titles, was Lord of the Manor of

---

(New York and London: Routledge, 2001), 137-68 (trans. Jo Ann McNamara). Taddeo Gaddi has some delightful *predellae* (c.1360; now at the Prado Museum in Madrid) depicting St. Eligius before King Clothar and at work when he is called to his ministry.

[63] Aelred of Rievaulx, *Vita Sancti Edwardi*, translated in *The Life of Saint Edward, King and Confessor, by Blessed Aelred, Abbot of Rievaulx*, trans. Jerome Bertram, FSA (1990; Southampton: Saint Austin Press, 1997), 81-86 (for the miracle of the pilgrim's ring). Aelred seems to be responsible for inserting this legend into Edward's hagiography: Frank Barlow, "Introduction," in *The Life of King Edward who Rests at Westminster attributed to a Monk of Saint-Bertin*, ed. and trans. Barlow, 2nd ed. (Oxford: Clarendon Press, 1992), xxxviii, n.107. This incident is also recounted in *"La Vie d'Edouard le Confesseur," by a Nun of Barking Abbey*, ed. and trans. Jane Bliss, Exeter Medieval Texts and Studies (Liverpool: Liverpool University Press, 2014),146-52, and briefly told in *Gilte Legende*, 1.56-57.

[64] See *Age of Chivalry: Art in Plantagenet England 1200-1400*, eds. Jonathan Alexander and Paul Binski Exhibition at the Royal Academy of Arts, London, 1987 (London: Weidenfeld and Nelson and the Royal Academy of Arts, 1987), 214 (#35, the panel painting of St. Edward and the pilgrim, c.1370) and 341 (#330-39, copies of the Painted Chamber). Matthew Paris also illustrated this legend in his *La Estoire de Seint Aedward le Rei* (Cambridge, University Library, MS Ee 3.59, fols. 29r and 30r): reprinted in Cynthia Hahn, *Portrayed on the Heart: Narrative Effect in Pictorial Lives of Saints from the Tenth through the Thirteenth Century* (Berkeley: University of California Press, 2001), 250-51.

Tewkesbury and was commemorated at the monastery there.⁶⁵ And Despenser points to the *Pearl*-Poet's milieu.⁶⁶

Thus, along with being the Evangelist of eschatological sight John was a vernacular authority on gem lore. He was an associate of gems and jewelers. And he was a courtly saint, one closely identified with English monarchs as well as the great magnate at the center of the social and political milieu of the *Pearl*-Poet. As his holy-day (December 27) coincided with the Christmas season, St. John would be part of courtly feasts, as is the case in Bertilak's home in *Sir Gawain and the Green Knight* (1020-24). Michael J. Bennett and John Bowers among others have done much to disabuse us of the idea of *Pearl* as a provincial poem and instead to see the poet's concerns as deeply adumbrated by the Ricardian court.⁶⁷ Felicity Riddy and Helen Barr have in particular discussed the Dreamer's profession of jeweler and how the poem's relation to elaborate, wrought objects heightens these courtly associations.⁶⁸ Now we can add the prominence of John to this evidence, for the refrain of Fitt XVII would conjure for the fourteenth-century audience more than simply a biblical elder but an active saint with ties to precious gems as well as the English monarchy.

John an *Auctor* of Gender-Role Reversal

John further authorizes the Dreamer to speak of heaven as a man. By the fourteenth century, visionary authorship was a role more and more employed by women. Richard Rolle aside, while many men authored works of advice for contemplation (e.g. the *Cloud*-author, Walter Hilton) or served as amanuenses guaranteeing a vision's orthodoxy, accounts of a personal experience with God

---

⁶⁵ Binski, *Age of Chivalry*, 214.
⁶⁶ Ann R. Meyer, "The Despensers and the "Gawain" Poet: A Gloucestershire Link to the Alliterative Master of the Northwest Midlands," *Chaucer Review* 35 (2001): 413-29.
⁶⁷ Michael J. Bennett, *Community, Class and Careerism: Cheshire and Lancashire Society in the Age of "Sir Gawain and the Green Knight"* (Cambridge: Cambridge University Press, 1983) and John Bowers, *The Politics of "Pearl": Court Poetry in the Age of Richard II* (Cambridge: D. S. Brewer, 2001); see also H. L. Spencer, "*Pearl*: 'God's Law' and 'Man's Law'," *Review of English Studies*, n.s. 59 (2008): 317-41, and John Watkins, "'Sengeley in synglere': *Pearl* and Late Medieval Individualism," *Chaucer Yearbook* 2 (1995): 117-36.
⁶⁸ Riddy, "Jewels in Pearl," 143-55; Helen Barr, "Pearl—or, 'The Jeweller's Tale,'" *Medium Aevum* 49 (2000): 59-79.

were as often from female visionaries, such as St. Catherine of Siena, Mary of Oignies, and, a generation after the *Pearl*-Poet, Margery Kempe.[69] Moreover, the works of Continental female mystics, including St. Bridget of Sweden, the beguines, and St. Hildegard of Bingen, had a renewed currency in fourteenth-century England.[70] It is too much to call the Dreamer's visionary status an act of transvestism—although it is curious to think that the other great apocalyptic Middle English poem of the fourteenth-century, *Piers Plowman,* opens with its male dreamer going about in disguise. (Must male visionaries somehow step outside their normal social role as a requisite for sight?) But within this late medieval general feminizing of mystical vision, the emphasis upon John could serve as a reminder that men have access to contemplative vision as well.

The Dreamer's claiming of a position that by the late fourteenth-century had become more feminized seems part of a larger pattern of gender-switching in *Pearl.* The Dreamer has not a male angel guide, as John had, but a laywoman explicating Scripture and assuming the functions of cleric.[71] Moreover the 144,000 virgins in the Lamb's train are transformed from men to women: Revelation specifically identifies them as "those not defiled with women" (Rev 14:4).

John himself embodied this fluidity of roles, as one of his epithets was the *sponsa* of Christ. This was a term he shared with Mary Magdalene, and both became types for the contemplative life.[72] Commentators often puzzled over the significance that John was especially marked as "the disciple Jesus loved," pondering how

---

[69] John Coakley, *Women, Men, and Spiritual Power: Female Saints and Their Male Collaborators* (New York: Columbia University Press, 2006).

[70] Kerby-Fulton, *Books under Suspicion,* 188-203, 247-56; Jennifer N. Brown, *Three Women of Liège: a Critical Edition of and Commentary on the Middle English Lives of Elizabeth of Spalbeek, Christina Mirabilis and Marie d'Oignies* (Turnhuot: Brepols, 2008).

[71] Kevin Gustafson, "The Lay Gaze: *Pearl,* the Dreamer, and the Vernacular Reader," *Medievalia et Humanistica* ns 27 (2000): 57-77 (66-67). I would add that not only is the Maiden presented as a clerkly figure, but she is not explicitly a personification (e.g. Ecclesia, Truth) that a reader would associate with exposition; she is a young laywoman.

[72] Jeffrey F. Hamburger, *St. John the Divine: The Deified Evangelist in Medieval Art and Theology* (Berkeley: University of California Press, 2002), 152. Martha and Peter were their counterparts as the active life.

exactly the Lord would have a special favorite.[73] As Thomas Aquinas summarizes,

> For the present, it is enough to say that John was more loved by Christ for three reasons. First, because of the cleanliness of his purity: for he was a virgin when chosen by the Lord, and always remained so.... Secondly, because of the depth of his wisdom, for he saw further into the secrets of God than others.... Thirdly, because of the great intensity of his love for Christ: "I love those who love me" (Prv 8:17).[74]

While Origen shied away from recognizing an especially close intimacy between Christ and John, interpreting the Evangelist's lying on the bosom as a sign for "resting on more mystical things," [75] Aelred of Rievaulx was more bold, implicitly identifying John as Christ's bride:

> [O]ur Jesus himself, lowering (himself) to our condition in every way, suffering all things for us and being compassionate towards us, transformed it by manifesting his love. To one person, not to all, did he grant a resting-place on his most sacred breast in token of his special love, so that the virginal head might be supported by the flowers of his virginal breast, and *the fragrant secrets of the heavenly bridal-chamber* might instill the sweet scents of spiritual perfumes on his virginal attachments more abundantly because more closely.[76]

As mentioned above, Christ and John would frequently be depicted together, with John tenderly asleep on Christ's chest, as in this

---

[73] Augustine, *In Johannis Evangelium*, Trac.124.4-7; Jerome, *Ad Jovinianum*, 1.26. John Boswell notes that Jesus' naming of John as custodian of his mother replicates what would happen between spouses: *Same-Sex Unions in Premodern Europe* (New York: Vintage, 1995), 138-39.
[74] Thomas Aquinas, *Commentary on the Gospel of John*, ch.13.1804.
[75] Origen, *Commentariorum in evangelium Johannis*, 32.264-79, translated from *Commentary on the Gospel According to John*, 2.391-94.
[76] *Speculum Caritatis* 3.40.111, translated from Aelered of Rievaulx, *The Mirror of Charity*, trans. Elizabeth Connor, Cistercian Fathers Series 17 (Kalamazoo: Cistercian Publications, 1990), 299 (emphasis added).

elegant carving from Constance (ca. 1300; FIG. 5).[77] Nearly thirty examples of this sculptural group survive.

FIG. 5 Christ and Saint John the Evangelist, 1300-1320. Germany, Swabia, near Bodenese (Lake Constance), early 14th century. Polychromed and gilded oak; 92.7 x 64.5 x 28.8 cm. The Cleveland Museum of Art, Purchase from the J. H. Wade Fund 1928.753

It is hard not to read this pair as eroticized, Jesus's head tilted gently towards "the disciple he loved," one hand protectively on his

---

[77] Eleanor S. Greenhill, "The Group of Christ and St. John as Author Portrait: Literary Sources, Pictorial Parallels," in *Festschrift Bernhard Bischoff zu seniem 65. Geburtstag dargebracht von Freunden, Kollegen und Schülern*, eds. Johanne Autenrieth and Franz Brunhölzl (Stuttgart: Anton Hiersemann, 1971), 406-16.

shoulder while the other holds John's hand, fingers extended caressing the palm. Their weight leans in towards each other, emphasized by John's drapery folds as well as the angle of Christ's shoulder. John's beardlessness as well as deep-carved curls and full lips slightly feminize him next to Jesus. Other eroticized images of Jesus and John include scenes of Jesus chucking John on the chin (a shorthand gesture for romantic intimacy) and embracing him.[78] A late fifteenth-century German representation goes so far as to dress John's luxuriously long hair in a bridal chaplet and seat him at a wedding feast beside Christ as groom.[79] Virgin and visionary, John became especially popular in convents, nuns identifying with him as fellow *sponsae Christi*.[80] Once again, we see John as a double for both the Dreamer and the Maiden, the former as living visionary, the latter as virginal bride of Christ.

In Conclusion: Remembering John

As a final rejoinder to some of the earlier-cited criticism of Fitt XVII as tedious, I suggest that the monotony of the Dreamer's account of the Heavenly Jerusalem generates an incantational rhythm to these lines. As P. M. Kean noted, Fitt XVII is the most interlocked in all of *Pearl*.[81] Perhaps this does create the most static section in the entire poem. But it is appropriate that among all the motion and energy in *Pearl*, soon to culminate in the procession of praise, that heaven should simultaneously be a point of stillness. The regular refrain of Fitt XVII keeps us still as well, forcing us to linger and look. The almost clinical catalog empties away the Dreamer, not in order to leave us without an emotional purchase on this scene but to make room for our own reactions to this splendor, for we must bring our own emotions to this vision in order to cement it in our memories for our salvation. Certainly English illuminated Apocalypses were useful as books of memory, with their images suitably vibrant, violent, and emotional for easy recall and with their series of unusual objects that could provide frames on which to hang

---

[78] Carolyn D. Muir, *Saintly Brides and Bridegrooms: The Mystical Marriage in Northern Renaissance Art*, Studies in Medieval and Early Renaissance Art History (Turnhout: Brepols, 2013).
[79] In Öffentliche Bibliothek der Universität Basel, MS A.vi.38, fol.4r, reproduced in Hamburger, *St. John the Divine*, plate 25.
[80] Hamburger, *St. John the Divine*, 95-164.
[81] *The Pearl*, 210.

other lists (e.g. Four Horsemen, Seven Seals).[82] While Cotton Nero A.x's illustrations do not seem to lend themselves well as prompts for a memory image, Fitt XVII does provide a verbal *figura* for a memory palace, with each of its layers clearly demarked by stones of different colors. Repetitive images might make for a confused memory storehouse, but repetitive language can help with memorizing, especially when in verse and with link words. Thus Fitt XVII may be so constructed for aiding readers trained in medieval mnemonic practice to create their own visualization of the Celestial Jerusalem, and through internalization of the place allow themselves to be present. Like the Dreamer, we may be lurking on the other side of the river, but John shares with us his aquiline sight, allowing us to see the New Jerusalem in all its lapidarian splendor.

Karen Elizabeth Gross is Associate Professor of English at Lewis & Clark College in Portland, Oregon. She has written about Boccaccio, Petrarch, Chaucer, Mary Magdalene, and hunting manuals. Her research interests include medieval humanism and the interactions between literature and the visual arts.

---

[82] On illuminated Apocalypses, see Lewis, "The English Gothic Apocalypse, *lectio divina*, and the Art of Memory," 13-32.

XVIII

Theoretical Lunacy: Moon, Text, and Vision in Fitt XVIII

Bruno M. Shah, O.P. & Beth Sutherland

Introduction

Much has been made of *Pearl*'s exquisite form.[1] Each fitt provides a gateway into the poem, revealing a new angle from which one might enter. This process of reading, whereby each facet succeeds the last without replacing it, generates the glimmer for which the poem is so renowned. Each stanza-set adds to the sheen, often by reimagining its central motif, generating "the" pearl anew. How does a pearl come to be? According to medieval lapidaries, pearls were thought to be formed from "droplets of dew or rain." They were believed to hold healing properties and were often ground down and used in Arabic medicine. The fifteenth-century *Peterborough Lapidary* praises the pearl as "the chief of al stones."[2] Indeed, the pearl is an exceptional sort of gem, not forged alone beneath the earth by heat and pressure. A pearl is a response to something alien. Medievals may not have understood the biochemistry behind these stone-like miracles, but they sensed the improvisational, malleable nature of their beauty.[3] However

---

[1] "Pearl, indeed, is perhaps the most completely self-enclosed of all medieval dream-poems: the most perfect in its artistry, pearl-like in its circularity of structure, so 'smothe' that its surface gives no purchase for any attempt to lever apart the real and the imagined" (A. C. Spearing, *Medieval Dream-Poetry* [Cambridge: Cambridge University Press, 1976], 120).

[2] R. A. Donkin, *Beyond Price: Pearls and Pearl-Fishing: Origins to the Age of Discoveries* (Philadelphia: American Philosophical Society), 259–260.

[3] Regarding medieval metaphors of resurrected, glorified, and heavenly embodiment: "...they are revealing exactly because they are offhand and oblique, for images often carry speculation or intuition or hunch far beyond what the technical terms at the disposal of medieval theorists–terms such as eidos, substantia, persona–can bear" (Caroline Walker Bynum, *The*

mineral, pearls cannot come to be without the agency of an organic creature. A microscopic intruder works its way into the pillowy interior of a clam's shell. It scrapes and irritates the soft flesh. The clam registers this particle as a disruption but has to contend with its presence. To do so, it encases it within a combination of organic and inorganic material: nacre, which is composed of calcium carbonate and conchiolin. It wraps the particle within many layers of this translucent substance, and this layering produces the iridescence: the more layers, the more remarkable the luster.

This response neither ejects nor eclipses the strange presence. Rather, it builds upon it, conforming to and elaborating upon its shape while transfiguring its substance—and doing so with material through which light can pass. Where there is light, there is the possibility of vision. The pearl illuminates the small bit of matter even as it hides it. This combination of alarm at the unknown, the penetration of light, and the proliferation of glossy matter receives special (re)consideration in Fitt XVIII. The link-word "moon" works its way into the poet's mind. A pearl forms around the object, both critiquing and consuming it. Or perhaps the image of the moon throws yet another layer of nacre over the larger pearl that is the poem itself. Using the moon as a point and medium of vantage (in XVIII), the poet examines the interplay of light and matter as a means of displaying how poetry might unveil the indescribable realities of heaven.

Our commentary follows the physical process of pearl-formation. As co-authors, we have responded to one another's insights, each allowing his/her thoughts to be colored by the other's. We take our inspiration from the collaborative, accretive growth of a pearl. Countless layers enwrap the mysterious bit of heaven at the poem's core: the Apocalypse of John delivers the vision elaborated by a dream (triggered by human grief), glossed by the Maiden, recounted by the poet, and interpreted by generations of scholars. The Dreamer is outside of the city, then outside of his dream. We, outside of the poem, wrap our own layers of meaning around it, but always with words through which the poem's own light must pass.

Resurrection of the Body in Western Christianity, 200-1336 [New York: Columbia University Press, 1995], 7–8).

There is no dissection, no scaffolding. At best, we share in the pearl by contemplating and responding to it.[4]

Stanza I

Drawing on Scripture, this section explores the tension between particularity and sameness. How does the heavenly city resolve or reconcile the individuality of souls with the inseparability implied by "one Body"? In what way are the discrete "components" of heaven held together and evaluated? The Pearl Maiden offers a mysterious alternative to the Dreamer's possessive, earthly ideal of togetherness. Yet she does so solidly within the revelatory landscape of a prior vision (and text). The Dreamer's vision in XVIII is both embedded within and eruptive beyond the Apocalypse of John, which the *Pearl*-poet glosses. "As John hym wrytes yet more I syye", says the Dreamer (XVII). Only as this commentary concludes shall more be said about this "more." For now, it is well to recognize that it is not the Maiden but the city that is crowned, in this instance, with four sides of three gates, "The portales pyked of rych plates, / And uch yate of a margyrye, / A parfyt perle that never fates" (1037–39, cf. 205). Here is manifested the true pearl of great price that does not fade or die–the house of David, the Body of Christ, the Church of God, all-resplendent (cf. Eph 2.20-22).[5] As a gloss on Apocalypse 21.21, the poet's reading is remarkably incisive. The Douay-Rheims Bible translates, "And the twelve gates are twelve pearls, one to each: and every several gate was of one several pearl." The "several" is an interpretive transformation (cf. *et singulæ portæ erant ex singulis margaritis*), trying to make sense of a peculiar image: that each gate (*porta*) is a pearl, and each of the gates is of a single pearl (which is the literal sense of the Greek as well).[6] In distinguishing "margyrye" (a synonym of "pearl") from "perle," the poet appears to distinguish

---

[4] For the Middle English, we have relied on J. J. Anderson's edition. *Sir Gawain and the Green Knight, Pearl, Cleanness, Patience*, ed. J. J. Anderson (London: Everyman, 1996), 39–41.

[5] In dynamic parataxis, Psalm 89 [88].37 declares the following about the final and all-incorporating enthronement of David: "And his throne as the sun before me: and as the moon perfect for ever, and a faithful witness in heaven."

[6] Consider that each of the Twelve Tribes of Israel is named "Israel." See 1 Kings 18.31; cf. Genesis 48–50. "Israel" is the new name that Jacob receives after he contends overnight with an angel and is not defeated (see Genesis 32.28). Jacob as well as each of his sons and their tribes is Israel.

the former from the latter as part from integral whole. The true and "parfyt perle that never fates" is that mysterious substance in which each gate and each gate's pearl (read: "margyrye") fully participates. The particular ascription with which the Dreamer had designated the Pearl Maiden, "perle," is now applied to the perfect, transcategorial reality that emits the "parfyt" and "unfating" (undying) light of glory, even as it assumes an edifice's body.

For *Pearl*, however, true beauty is registered, not in terms of objects but in terms of relationality. As A. C. Spearing has noted, the entire poem is about relationships, and the way "the impact of the more than human upon the human" causes a "reassessment of human values." For Spearing, the *Pearl*-poet does not make absolutely clear the Maiden's identity. She is very reasonably understood to be the Dreamer's daughter; and yet, the poet does not want to foreclose other possible relationships (e.g., one between romantic lovers). This indeterminacy "enabled the poet to write a poem not about one particular relationship, but about human relationship in general." Accordingly, the dreamed envisioning of the Maiden leads to a beholding of an eschatological city.[7]

The city's relations between parts and integral whole are (self-evidently) personal. Each gate (which is a pearl) is named with each of "Israel's sons." "Uchon [portale] in scrypture a name con plye / of Israel barnes, folewande her dates, / That is to say, as her byrth-whates; / The aldest ay fyrst thereon was done" (1039–42). It is the name that is the unique index of value–precisely because it is the interval between word and visage, parent and child, beauty's transcendent call and the image's particular response. A pearl crowns each gate and so does a name. The all-surpassing worth of the substantive object (daughter, pearl, heaven) gives way to the crowning mystery in terms of personal relationality. The poet underscores this mystery of relationality. The Maiden is never properly named, even as the relationship with her that the Dreamer-as-father figures proves essential to the vision's trans-earthly drama. Either, then, the idolized Maiden is irreducibly unnameable (as in, e.g., the postmodern Eco's *The Name of the Rose*),[8] or she is only

---

[7] See A. C. Spearing, "Pearl," in *The Gawain Poet: A Critical Study* (New York: Cambridge University Press, 1970), 147.
[8] Mention of postmodernity and the "unnameable other" also brings to mind Lévinas; though for him, there is no correspondence between the

nameable by the One whose selfsame Name is above all other names (as in, e.g., the premodern and near-contemporary Beatrice of Dante). Regardless of whether or not the person as more and other than an object can be named, though, it is stunning that its relations can be figured.

There exists a remarkable parity between each of the gates and pearls and sons of Israel. Each is of measureless worth. And yet, they are ordered according to "birth" (cf. Gen 48.38; 1 Cor 15.23). In figuring that which lies beyond all earthly standard of measure (the justice of heaven), the scriptural and poetic authors nevertheless maintain standards of arrangement and order that are described in mundane terms (order of birth). This ordering, though, surpasses the Christian father's medieval moralism. Even after appreciating his pearl's bliss, the father disputes the rank of her splendor, giving voice to the age's theodicial questions about the status of children who die before the age of reason. The Maiden now lives as a veritable queen. But, the Dreamer reasons–himself having entered a kind of limbo–she had not sufficiently employed intelligent freedom to merit her place in heaven, having lived "not two yer in oure thede" ("but two years in our land," 483). Without "penaunce" how could she afford "blysse to byye" (477–78)? In fact, she was never even old enough to pray or recite the Lord's Prayer and Creed (484–85). Why does she enjoy such surpassing rank as to be comparable to Mary, the virgin mother, who, against all other human persons (save her divine-human son), possesses "synglerty" most truly (see 425–28; cf. 8)? It is here, peering into that most spotless of spots, that the Dreamer can begin to envision for the reader (even if he cannot appreciate for himself) the just ordering of persons that is heaven's beautiful and integral arrangement. It is a place whose walls and borders do not obstruct, where no one evaluates another's appearance as more or less worthy than one's own; where every beatified soul is a king or queen, and "uchon fayn of otheres hafyng" (see 445–52; cf. 784–86, 847–50).

Heaven evaluates persons in relational–not objective terms. A person's worth is found in the justifying call of God, which furthermore resounds when shared and celebrated between others. Address is the purest place. Salvation obtains within the dia-logical stretch between callings and namings. This is the register of

---

terms of the relation, and this asymmetry is fundamental specifically to the constitution of ethics, as first philosophy.

scriptural valuation, which reveals the glory of the sons and daughters of God (cf. Rom 8.19), those elected or called into the divinity's family. The baptismal call of the eternal Word's selfsame beauty is transmitted from heaven through preachers, Holy Writ, and their glossators, exhorting individuals "To bye... a perle was mascelles" ("to purchase an immaculate pearl")–one's personal call from glory on high to live forever, in accord with the words that are written in the Book of Life, which are the names of the holy ones (line 732; see Apoc 21.27). It is the conceit (in both senses) of revelatory poetry, whether canonical or not, that seeks to speak this distance between the mutually transcendent terms of personal relation. Indeed, it is the carrying-over work of revelatory meta-phor that *Pearl* so sublimely accomplishes.

Stanza II

Stanza two continues to explore the transfiguration of particular objectivity into relational, unitary being. It shifts focus from names and persons to optics and light. Here, poetry encroaches upon the brink of what can be imagined (rendered into images). It does so by taking the translucency of heaven's roads to both perceptual and conceptual extremes. The Douay-Rheims translators render the corresponding Scripture, "And the street of the city was pure gold, as it were transparent [*perlucidum*] glass. ...And the city hath no need of the sun, nor of the moon, to shine in it. For the glory of God hath enlightened it, and the Lamb is the lamp thereof" (Apoc 21.21, 3). The *Pearl*-poet gives this transparency a literal sense, imagining material reality as suffused and transfigured by God's light.

The first line picks up the link-word "moon" only to abandon it. The New Jerusalem has neither sun nor moon because Christ himself illumines the city; he is the "lambe-lyght" by which all things are seen. Yet God does not merely emanate light (like the sun), and he certainly does not reflect it (like the moon, though medievals probably did not know this). God is the ground and wellspring of light, itself the physical phenomenon which formally conditions sight and, by literal and metaphorical extension, knowledge. As the Light beyond light, God relates all created phenomena to himself as their originating creator. And so, physical light, though a creature, seems to reveal God's nature in a special way, becoming a central poetic motif in language about the divine. Natural light seems almost as original as its supernatural origin. "Let there be light," God says upon creation of heaven and earth (Gen 1.3). Amongst all physical phenomena, light appears the most auto-originary. It just is. It seems inseparable from the energies that produce it. The poet seems to appreciate this quasi-divine quality of light, and utilizes it as a means of figuring divinity. In this way, he is theologically Johannine, taking cues from the Gospel that figures the divinity of Christ in terms of light. This makes sense, as the poet would likely have associated the evangelist with Apocalypse, following the text's conceit regarding its own authorship. John describes Christ as "the true light, which enlighteneth every man that cometh into this world" (John 1.9). He portrays Jesus as stating, "I am the light of the world: he that followeth me, walketh not in darkness, but shall have the light of life" (John 8.12). For John, true life can be found only in Christ, and that life is the light of humanity (John 1.4). Depicting the "trone" where "hyghe Godes self" sits, the *Pearl*-poet takes the reader to the source of all light. Yet God does not give as the world gives, and the world's wisdom is foolishness in his sight (John 14.27, 1 Cor 3.19). God does not reducibly illumine as physical light illumines, notwithstanding the analogicity between Creator and creation.

Light transcends the metaphorical in John's hands (without leaving it behind). Poetic projects that "translate" revelatory, apocalyptic realities into semi-imaginable terms often use their conceits paradoxically. In her essay on inexpressibility in *Pearl*, Anne Chalmers Watts characterizes this imperative neatly: "words say that words cannot say." Yet they "must ever maintain a reality outside these verbal and imaginative constructions that say they cannot say."[9] Christ cannot be interpreted according solely to one's everyday experience of natural light. His is an-other light altogether, gestured at by physical light. Christ may be the "true light," come into the world to enlighten humanity, but that does not mean he is discerned as illuminative. "He was in the world, and the world was made by him, and the world knew him not" (John 1.10). What else fails to comprehend the light? "And the light shineth in the darkness, and the darkness did not comprehend it" (John 1.5). This is not (or, at least, not merely) the seething darkness of a dualism pitting evil against good in opposite-but-equal cosmic combat. While it refers primarily to the impaired vision (and by implication, cognition) in a postlapsarian world–like all poetic figures–it recursively operates on

---

[9] Ann Chalmers Watts locates the content of *Pearl* within the larger context of contemplative praxis. Ann Chalmers Watts, "Pearl, Inexpressibility, and Poems of Human Loss," *PMLA* 99.1 (1984): 26, 29.

a literal, material level as well. This is the poignant reality of life in the physical world. Where there is light, there cannot be dark. Yet material reality itself obstructs the flow of light. Material substances cast shadows, and objects are illuminated in part because shadows limn and define them. Light bounces off materials, enabling vision. The moon is only the example *par excellence* of how most visible objects become apparent to the human eye. Unless it is translucent, an object that receives light also blocks light. Illumination seems to be a zero-sum game: objects come into view at the expense of other objects (or facets of objects). (This is implicit in the word *obiectum*, which means "cast before." An object is necessarily an ob-stacle, its presence an impediment or blockage to one's line of sight).[10] Yet if all objects were wholly occupied by light, they would be difficult if not impossible to see. Humans squint in overwhelming brightness as well as in the dark. In this world at least, too much light inhibits sight. The physical reality here evokes the theological claim of humanity's darkened condition. Natural existence in this world allies humanity to the dark. But what about heavenly existence?

If the darkness cannot comprehend the light, heaven is a land without shadows. The poet portrays the gleaming city in appropriately dazzling terms. The city blazes brightly, through Christ: "Thurgh hym blysned the borgh al bryght" (1048). It is "bryghter" than both the sun and moon (1056). Nothing can compare to the brightness of heaven–but because heaven's brightness differs in kind, not just intensity. In this stanza, the poet undertakes the challenging task of imagining what a city with truly supernatural, Christic light might look like. This leads him into a fantasy of looking, one conceivable only in poetic terms: "Thurgh wowe and won my lokyng yede;/ For sotyle cler noght lette no lyght" (1049, 50). (One might think of the "fabulist" artists Jorge Luis Borges and M. C. Escher, whose visions of impossibility dance between concept and image). "My gaze went through wall and building. For the subtle clarity let the light go unhindered." The transparency that seemed merely to describe the glassy street now, for the poet, imbues all of the heavenly kingdom. This is a miracle

---

[10] See Lawrence Dewan, O.P., "'Obiectum': Note on the Invention of a Word," *Wisdom, Law, and Virtue: Essays in Thomistic Ethics* (New York: Fordham University Press, 2007), 403–43.; Nicola Masciandaro, "Obiectum: Closing Remarks," *Speculative Medievalisms: Discography* (Brooklyn: punctum books, 2013).

of seeing; and since "sight" words metaphorize thought processes, it represents a phenomenological fantasy as well. The Dreamer sees objects without their blocking other objects; he registers them while simultaneously seeing through them. The scandal of particularity is purified but preserved.

This mode of seeing answers to the Dreamer's relationship with his pearl. The barely (but assuredly) recognizable Maiden who first seems so alien is in some sense "the same" as the rest of the heavenly virgins. She is equally loved by Christ, a co-inheritor of his kingdom, one of many Brides—yet the Bride, the Church, one body in the Body, itself Christ's body. The tensile relationship between particularity and sameness is resolved by Christ's all-suffusive light, for it is the unhindered "light" that allows the Dreamer to see through edifices without their becoming invisible. The poignant concluding scene epitomizes this dynamic. Marching with what should be a homogenous mass of Pearl Maidens (a "meyny schene," or "shining company"), the Dreamer's daughter is still recognizable as "my lyttel quene" (1145, 1147). Many "margyryes" equates to one, "several" pearl. In his commentary on Apocalypse, Victorinus of Pettau (third century) insists, "It is one thing to speak of each of the pearls; it is another thing to speak of the one pearl from which they come... this one pearl is our Lord Jesus Christ."[11]

One should not, however, overemphasize the visuality of this poem. The Dreamer temporarily enjoys this fantastic gazing, but the reader apprehends it via poetic de-scription. The same applies to John's vision, of course. The realities of heaven are given in linguistic form. Vision comes by way of words. The city "blysned" brightly because of the lamb. A blaze might be a fiery, auto-illuminative phenomenon, but a blazon is also a pictorial sign—an identifying crest. It is, as well, a poetic description of a holistic entity by means of its individual parts. The poet, following John, blazons heaven, painting it piecemeal with his words. The eternal Word of God enables such blazoning as the living guarantor of meaning for all words: Communion everlastingly underwrites communication.

The poet gives the reader nothing other than a vision of "The hyghe Godes self" sitting upon a throne (1054). How are we to

---

[11] Victorinus of Pettau, "Commentary on Revelation," *Ancient Christian Texts: Latin Commentaries on Revelation, Victorinus of Petovium, Apringius of Beja, Caesarius of Arles, and Bede the Venerable,* ed. and trans. William C. Weinrich (Downers Grove, Illinois: IVP Academic, 2011), 58.

imagine this? By the end of this stanza, we seem to have moved from a vision of the lamb (the wounded, incarnate Second Person) to something more like God's selfsame, substantial glory. How to depict the invisible, all-surpassing Godhead? In poetry, this can be done precisely because it is not being done (cf. Isaiah 6). "As John the appostel [describes] in termes tyghte," so do we "see" God on his throne. These "tight terms" allow us to experience an eschatological reality eluding both physical vision and visual imagination. Poetry renders these hidden things in some way accessible. It insists on their being without their being-visible. The poet invites us into the poem explicitly, shifting abruptly to second-person: "ther moght ye hede (observe)" (1051). In what way might we observe? How can we, like the Dreamer, see "more" of what John describes? Through the mediation of words. Heaven's brightness is a kind of whiteness, like that of parchment (1026). Only on the page can apocalypse (the unveiling of heaven) be witnessed, at least until the sky finally does snap shut like a scroll (Apoc 6.14). Scripture gives textual witness to the Light, but witnesses are not themselves the Light (cf. John 1.8). They reflect it, like the moon.

Stanza III

Heaven's superabundant light is not the only element indicating God's saturating splendor. Water, too, rushes forth from God's throne ("A rever of the trone ther ran outryghte," 1055). This paradisal river surpasses the sun and moon in its glittering beauty (1057), whereas earthly rivers merely reflect those bodies of light. The luminous, living water of heaven represents not a created effect of God's love, but the very source: uncreated grace itself. It gushes forth directly from the "trone" on which God sits just as blood and water flowed from Christ's pierced side (cf. John 3.5). This is no mere trickle, but a "foysoun flode," rushing swiftly through heaven's streets ("thurgh uch a strete," 1059). It has been suggested that this "flood" comprises the very river that separates the Dreamer from the heavenly city.[12] If that is the case, God's cleansing waters provide both the canal leading from earth to heaven as well as the moat separating the two. This topographical metaphor alerts us to a truth about God's uncreated grace (or Holy Spirit). It births a "new creation" while killing the "old man" (2 Cor 5.17, Eph 4.22). Because

---

[12] Rosalind Field, "The Heavenly Jerusalem in Pearl," *The Modern Language Review* 81.1 (1986): 7.

God immediately sources the water, to plunge into it unprepared results in a kind of dream "death." The Dreamer does not make it to the other side. He wakes up.

This image of a river surrounding paradise, both treacherous and full of promise, would have been familiar to the poet and his readers. A contemporary work, *The Book of John Mandeville*, was one of the most widely read texts in the later Middle Ages. *Mandeville* survives in over 250 manuscripts in multiple languages, and the *Pearl*-poet almost certainly "borrowed from it."[13] It doubles as travelogue and pilgrim narrative, and all the lands across which Sir John travels are imprinted with the sacred. His most ultimate goal is Eden itself: the earthly paradise. Like their heavenly counterpart in *Pearl*, the rivers that lead to Eden also render it unreachable. The *Mandeville*-author describes the fantastic topography of the terrestrial paradise in terms similar to the *Pearl*-poet's description of the heavenly paradise. It sits on a mountain so high that Noah's flood could not reach it, and a wall surrounds it (as in *Pearl*). One wall "casteth oute the foure flodes that renne thorowe dyvers londes" (lines 2707–13, p. 92). These "floods" source Eurasia's major rivers, but the closer one follows them to paradise, the less navigable they become. They rage so roughly that some pilgrims die from weariness of rowing, some grow deaf from the waves, and others go blind (2734–35). No one can arrive at paradise without a "special grace of God" (2736). Again, the same goes for the heavenly paradise of *Pearl*: "The yates stoken was never yet, / Bot evermore upen at uche a lone" (1065–66). The gates are never shut against anyone, and yet no one who "beres any spot anunder mone" dares enter (1068). In *Mandeville*, this inaccessibility occasions one of the most famous lines in medieval literature, comical and poignant in its pithiness: "Of Paradyse can I nat speke propirly for I have nat be there, and that angoreth me" (2705–06). The Dreamer of *Pearl* might as well speak that line himself, and the poet most likely read it. As A. C. Spearing says in his foundational study on medieval dream poetry, "The Dreamer is an inadequate vessel for the experience of

---

[13] *The Book of John Mandeville*, eds. Tamarah Kohanski and C. David Benson (Kalamazoo, MI: Medieval Institute Publications, 2007), 1.

his dream."[14] One may not be able to speak properly of Paradise, but that does not stop one from speaking.[15]

Mandeville and *Pearl* share more than an interest in recounting paradise. The protagonists of both are travelers. Both are pseudo-romance questers and pilgrims who seek the face of God in the exotic landscapes in which they find themselves, however haplessly. The practice of journeying to a strange land in order to witness "foreign" epiphanies, then returning to report back, has a long genealogy. In ancient Greece, such religious tourism had an official status in the practice of *theoria*. A *theoros*, either private or civic, traveled beyond his city-state not only to witness, but also to participate in the religious mysteries of another place. He would then return, presumably changed, to share his experiences. Later, Plato and Aristotle metaphorized this cultural practice, using *theoria* to describe philosophical understanding as a "spectacle of truth."[16] In various disciplines, scholars call speculative, abstract, and/or schematic work "theory," participating in a long tradition of philosophical thought. Yet it is easy to forget the origins of this term in itinerant and ritualistic religious praxis, and in the adventure of relationships between alien peoples and persons. As a spiritual traveler to a hyperreal heavenly landscape, one who returns to tell the tale, the Dreamer is a manner of *theoros*. That means that *Pearl* can be called "theoretical poetry." Through language, it draws readers into visions of things that they have not seen—and even "more," could not see with their own eyes.

Stanza IV

In Fitt XVIII, the poet draws the reader into these impossible visions by means of the moon, a figure for flux. An avatar of change itself, the moon is one of the most freighted symbols in premodern literature. Poets associated its round, modest glow with chastity, especially in the figure of Artemis/Diana. Later, Queen Elizabeth

---

[14] Spearing, *Medieval Dream-Poetry*, 126.
[15] Recall Augustine's famous words toward the beginning of his *Confessions*: *Et quid diximus, deus meus, vita mea, dulcedo mea sancta, aut quid dicit aliquis, cum de te dicit? Et vae tacentibus de te, quoniam loquaces muti sunt* (I.iv). The Augustinian "restlessness" of the heart is bound up with the irrepressible desire to acknowledge through speech (i.e. to confess) the greatness of God.
[16] Andrea Wilson Nightingale, *Spectacles of Truth in Classical Greek Philosophy: Theoria in its Cultural Context* (Cambridge: Cambridge University Press, 2004), 40–47.

would share the epithet "Cynthia" with the goddess as an homage to her virginity. Yet the moon's seeming shape-shifting, its movement, and its dark spots also made it a figure of sexual inconstancy, disease, and sin. In Robert Henryson's *The Testament of Cresseid* (fifteenth century), the goddess Cynthia appears "Of colour blak, buskit with hornis twa," and "Hir gyse was gray and full of spottis blak" (lines 255, 260).[17] The crescent moon evoked a cuckold's horns for medievals, and the shadowy craters, the grime of sin. Fitt XVIII of *Pearl* proves a miniature case-study in lunar symbology. Critics never cease to marvel over the rich, non-schematic ways in which its images are working. A white, gleaming orb set in the heavens, the moon would seem an appropriate analogue to a pearl, and to the Pearl Maiden. Yet we see that the moon is "To spotty… of body to grym" to approach or exert itself in the heavenly city (1070). This repeats the point made in the final line of the third stanza, that no one enters heaven with his sin upon him. But the poet then shifts to an astronomical reason for the moon's exclusion. In heaven, "ther ne is never nyght" (1071). Heaven is a land without shadows, always illumined by the lamb-light. As *The Testament of Cresseid* points out, Cynthia is best seen at night (266). Why would she venture to "clym" over heaven's horizon when "that worthly lyght" would render her invisible (1072–73)? This goes for other heavenly bodies as well: the planets are in too poor a plight and the sun is too dim (1075–76). The poem has slipped from a tropological or moral register (too spotty) to a physical one (too weak/poor). This physical weakness collapses gravity and darkness. The natural heavenly bodies cannot make the climb, but the futility stems from their dimness.

As has been shown with the second stanza, God's light is of a supereminently different kind than physical light; it penetrates and suffuses all things while preserving them as discrete entities. Hence, the simultaneous transparency and appearing of heaven's content. Just as there is no darkness in heaven, there is no reflection. Everything shares in and pulses with God's own light. This is why nothing spotty can be said to be in heaven, because God radiates through those souls, purifying and enlightening them. To have a spot or shadow in heaven would be to have a place where God is not,

---

[17] Robert Henryson, *The Testament of Cresseid* in *The Poems of Robert Henryson*, ed. Robert L. Kindrick (Kalamazoo, MI: Medieval Institute Publications, 1997), 163–64.

and what is heaven but abiding in God—enjoying the beatific vision? In Apocalypse, God promises to make all things new: to make a new heaven and a new earth. The New Jerusalem is not entirely Other, but, rather, a transfigured version of the earthly Jerusalem. As crystalline as heaven might seem, it is also strikingly organic. As in Apocalypse, the Tree of Life is present, returning Eden (with a difference) to humanity. Not unlike the "several pearl," the Tree itself is given in the plural ("tres ful schym,/ That twelve frytes of lyf con bere," 1077–78), divided up between the tribes of Israel (and/or Apostles), yet one. The fruits are not a static reality. "Twelve sythes on yer thay beren ful frym,/ And renowles nwe in uche a mone" (1079–80). They grow swollen and ripe, leaving it tantalizingly unclear as to whether they rot, but also leaving one free to assume the miraculous presence of birth/growth without death/decay. These unearthly fruits come to season not once a year, but every month. Immediately after banishing the moon from heaven, the poet tells us that the Tree of Life renews itself in each "mone" (1080). A new heaven requires a new moon. The Pearl Maiden is a cipher for that moon. She possesses her light as a perfect gift from a gracious Lord and avows that gratuitous ownership by invoking the parable of the vineyard. She does not only reflect and refract Christ, she abides in him. She—like the Scripture she cites and evokes—keeps his Word (cf. John 15.7). Despite the moon's spottiness, medieval understandings made it an even more apt metaphor for the Pearl Maiden than our contemporary understanding does. For medievals, the moon served as mediator between earth and the heavens. Itself moved by the upper reaches of the heavens, it could act on the earth in turn.[18] Since God divided the luminaries in the beginning, it was thought that the moon was created full. That and Easter's dependence on the lunar calendar lent the moon a sacrality that belied its reputation for inconstancy and spottiness, associating it with creation and resurrection.[19] Most medievals did not think of the moon as reflecting the sun's rays. They would have followed Averroes, who theorizes, "The sun renders it [the moon] luminescent first, then the light emanates from it in the same way

---

[18] J. D. North, *Stars, Minds and Fate: Essays in Ancient and Medieval Cosmology* (London: The Hambledon Press, 1989), 255–56.
[19] Stephen C. McCluskey, *Astronomers and Cultures in Early Medieval Europe* (Cambridge: Cambridge University Press, 1998), 77–78.

that it emanates from other stars..."[20] The medieval moon is made auto-luminescent through participation in the sun's rays. So does the Pearl Maiden radiate a light uniquely hers by partaking in the Son's grace. Warmed and enlightened by the Son, she is equipped to take up her orbit and illumine those in the outer reaches.

Even the moon's spottiness assumes an illuminative function. How does the moon of *Pearl* appear to its readers? It is received as black markings on a spread of white: letters on a page. The moon's spottiness evokes not only the grime of sin and the darkness of imperfect knowing/seeing (twin evils of postlapsarian reality)–it also evokes the inky stains of writing. The moon spells out seasonal change, dictating the Catholic calendar's moveable feasts with its shifty hieroglyphs. As Augustine struggled to explain and understand, language, too, proves an irreducibly temporal activity.[21] We read through time, moving across the page, and we speak one syllable at a time–the full meaning of which cannot be gleaned (if it ever can) until the utterance is completed. The dark blotches that mar the moon's luminous face are–among other things–the necessary "marks" of signification. Necessary, that is, outside the heavenly city. In heaven, the lamb-light illumines all. When we shift

---

[20] Pierre Duhem, *Medieval Cosmology: Theories of Infinity, Place, Time, Void, and the Plurality of Worlds*, ed. and trans. Roger Ariew (Chicago: University of Chicago Press, 1985) 481 (quoted). See also: B. R. Goldstein, *Theory and Observation in Ancient and Medieval Astronomy* (London: Variorum Reprints, 1985); Robert R. Newton, *Medieval Chronicles and the Rotation of the Earth* (Baltimore: Johns Hopkins University Press, 1972); Francis S. Benjamin, J. R. and G. J. Toomer, eds. *Campanus of Novara and Medieval Planetary Theory* (Madison: University of Wisconsin Press, 1971); Jennifer N. Brown and Marla Segol, eds., *Sexuality, Sociality, and Cosmology in Medieval Literary Texts* (New York: Palgrave Macmillan, 2013); E. Edson and E. Savage-Smith, *Medieval Views of the Cosmos* (Oxford: Bodleian Library, 2004); Rudolf Simek, *Heaven and Earth in the Middle Ages: The Physical World before Columbus*, trans. Angela Hall (Woodbridge, Suffolk: Boydell Press, 1996).

[21] Book XI's famous meditation on temporality analogically distinguishes between created speech and the uncreated Logos. "For it is abundantly clear that your speech was expressed through the motion of some created thing, because it was motion subject to the laws of time, although it served your eternal will. These words, which you had caused to sound in time, were reported by the bodily ear of the hearer to the mind, which has intelligence and inward hearing responsive to your eternal Word... In your Word all is uttered at one and the same time, yet eternally" (Augustine, *Confessions* [London: Penguin Books, 1961], 258–59).

registers from light to Logos or Word, we understand another aspect of heaven. The vision of the Word eclipses and opens earthly words, situated in space and time as they are. Communication becomes Communion. The walls of heaven "glent as glayr" (1025). They gleam like an egg white, a substance used in manuscript illumination.[22] Critics have noted the *Pearl*-poet's white, bright, glossy aesthetic.[23] Heaven appears as a blank page because all that needs saying abides within the Word.

The moon thus serves as a figure for understanding, mediating knowledge. It elaborates the Pearl Maiden's role. She has charitably left the city proper, orbiting it in order to hold an exchange with one on the margin–to enlighten him. Her mien reflects heaven's light; her words refract it, breaking it down into linguistic units the Dreamer can understand. As we have seen, though, this seeming reflection is no reflection at all. Rather, she abides in the original light. Lunar reflection figures the Pearl Maiden's function without exhausting its mysteries. Though her relatively familiar person transmits God's light as a candle might be lit from a wildfire, yet the fire dazzles the eye. Her gloss is not wasted on the Dreamer, though he misunderstands much of it. The dialogue in which they share comments not only on the city before them, but also on Apocalypse as well. Their space is textual, not simply because it is received in the form of a poem, but because their gloss on heaven's white page (1026) evokes the prolific and colorful tradition of medieval marginalia.[24] The Dreamer tries to understand this wordless story from the outside. He and the Maiden proliferate marginalia, glossing the true mysteries with a secondary sheen. In so doing, the Dreamer undergoes a process of lunar understanding, engaged with a

---

[22] *Sir Gawain and the Green Knight, Pearl, Cleanness, Patience*, 39. (See note to line 1026.)

[23] Spearing, *Medieval Dream-Poetry*, 111, note 3: Millard Meiss, *French Painting in the Time of Jean de Berry: The Late Fourteenth Century and the Patronage of the Duke* (London, 1967), 146.

[24] "I could begin, like St Bernard, by asking what do they all mean, those lascivious apes, autophagic dragons, potbellied heads, harp-playing asses, arse-kissing priests and somersaulting jongleurs that protrude at the edges of medieval buildings, sculptures and illuminated manuscripts? But I am more interested in how they pretend to avoid meaning, how they seem to celebrate the flux of 'becoming' rather than 'being'..." (Michael Camille, *Image on the Edge: The Margins of Medieval Art* [London: Reaktion Books, 1992], 9).

mediating entity which, though necessary and beautiful, can only provide a "spotty" account of the immediate glory of the beatific vision. This spottiness derives both from the Dreamer's own earthbound, sinful state, and from the simultaneously revealing and re-veiling quality of linguistic signification. Though the Pearl Maiden is herself spotless, the Dreamer is not yet equipped to see the light in which she abides. For the time being, he sees *per speculum in aenigmate*, through a glass (or mirror) darkly (1 Cor 13.12). He can see only reflected light, and that imperfectly. Yet the *caritas* between his Maiden and him—itself auguring the fulfillment of God's *caritas*—promises he might one day know even as he is known.

Following the Dreamer's dialectical engagement with the mediating Maiden, the poem itself cycles through ideas and motifs, looping back around to explore them with a difference. The poem is formally lunar, aesthetically reproducing the phases of the moon in its structure. Though the Dreamer longs to see the city from within, he acknowledges his need for this commentarial mediation. His longing to enter remains a component of his attachment to his pearl. This attachment, though, points him towards the "several pearl" of which she is a part: the pearl of great price. If it is impossible to enter "without spot," it also proves difficult to gaze without understanding. As the next stanza indicates, staring too long into the light, one might become moonstruck—met with lunacy without understanding. This ravishing madness, however, could initiate a super-linguistic movement across the white space between word and Word. Though not Wisdom itself, the moon is the pearl of wisdom.

Stanza V

In the presence of the Pearl Maiden, the Dreamer is "anunder mone" (1081). This place, however, is beyond what the "fleschly hert... myght endeure" (1082, cf. 1068). He is out of himself—and even, for this stanzaic moment in XVIII, in-sane: he has become a lunatic. And indeed, "lunatic" and "lunacy" derive from connections medievals drew between bouts of madness and the phases of the moon. Similar to the heavenly Maiden, the earthly Dreamer has transcended his own space, but without entering the other's. However perspicacious his sight, he does not pass over into that city of light, to which his daughter gives lunar reference. His vision is studded with sensory impressions, yet he is actually removed from bodily sensation. As with the raptured man of whom Paul speaks, whether the Dreamer is in the body or out of the body, "only God knows" (2 Cor 12.2). But as the lunar mysticism of XVIII makes clear, heavenly enlightenment involves a night of the senses. [25] The Dreamer "felde... nawther reste ne travayle" (1087). The state of *apatheia* is the supreme site of pathos.

The Dreamer's vision was occasioned by wrestling with the departure of his "pryvy perle wythouten spot" (12). But "spot," of course, is not only the stain from which the Dreamer's pearl of supreme goodness and beauty (*kalokagathia*) was wholly free. It is also her place or location. The grassy mound where he fell asleep is, it seems, her grave; through burial and decomposition, it is the site of her disappearance. And this now is the only spot for the pearl, the site of her death. For the Dreamer, death alone "marres a myry juele" (23), even as, for the poet, death disappears as a stain.[26] Death situates and manifests life. The place to which no "I" can testify becomes the place of discovered reality. The fearsomeness of death is perhaps aesthetically undone, but its problematizing reality and phenomenological potentiality are not for that reason (*pace* Epicurus) to be denied. Death is the place of life: if the realm of the dead be conceived as the "underworld," it is thereby foundational.

In meditating on the topos of his pearl's death, the Dreamer has died there the death of sleep, likewise losing his earthly place. From the spot of her death, the Dreamer's "spyryt ther sprang in space" (61). The *theoros* is transported to the place of his pearl, and here, he is truly able to address her, precisely because she most perfectly escapes his possession. Although the mystery of her beatitude is ultimately excessive of his powers–he cannot comprehend where she is, he cannot participate the mystery of her state–he nevertheless speaks with her and she responds to him. In this mystical conversation between Dreamer and Maiden, where

---

[25] "In these lines, with their obvious allusion to St Paul's 'whether in the body, or out of the body, I know not; God knoweth', the Dreamer is claiming that, unlike St Paul, but like St John (in Apocalypse 1:10), he knows that this experience came to him not 'in the body' but 'in the spirit'. ...He describes St John's experience in the Apocalypse as a 'gostly drem' (790), and his own dream can be classed as an equivalent, though less complete, experience. 'Gostly drem' is the Middle English equivalent to what St Augustine calls a *visio spirituale*, a type of vision in which spiritual forces affect the imagination as if they were sensory images..." (Spearing, *Medieval Dream-Poetry*, 117).

[26] Field, 9.

speech has the power to locate, i.e. to address, they are placed in terms of each other's placelessness.[27]

It is in two senses, then, that the Dreamer's pearl springs from him in that spot (13, cf. 61): as earthly loss and as heavenly gain. Because she is incomparable, her purity is unearthly: it is spot-less, place-less. As J. Allan Mitchell writes, it "is a world out-of-bounds."[28] Like the holy city of heaven that the Dreamer espies through her mediation (967–68), she too is unable to be situated or possessed; she cannot be placed or grasped (137–42; cf. 1157–63). And because she cannot be de-fined, she cannot be easily thought, though she must be de-scribed. By losing his mind's place on earth, becoming spotless himself, the forlorn father regains the delight of his daughter's presence, if but for a dreamscape's time. But this presence overwhelms him, utterly exceeding and confounding the categorial evaluation he had imputed to her. With nothing but his pearl's absence of spot to set upon, the Dreamer's ladder is placed upon the site of her dis/appearing. The pseudo-angelic *Pearl*-poet ascends and descends between heaven and earth, describing each realm in terms of the other, sending the Dreamer's and Maiden's words across to each other (cf. Jacob in Gen 28.12, and the Son of Man in John 1.51). The "fresch fygure" of Apocalypse's heavenly city, refracted according to the pearl-in-the-sky's spotless gleam, ravishes the Dreamer (1086, 1088). His reason and his senses are discombobulated. He is become mad. As the Maiden silently and invisibly withdraws from the scene, he is both carried away and yet, his body still resting upon the hillock where he fell asleep, he has not moved anywhere. To be driven crazy with heaven's light is the still point of the turning world, neither flesh nor fleshless, as Eliot sings centuries later. The unoriginated arrow of God's selfsame light, drawn by the moon, targets the Dreamer with nocturnal sublimity. He "stod as stylle as dased quayle" (1085). The lunatic's dazing, here, is not only due to wonder and "merwayle" but also terror. To invoke Coleridge's distinction, the Dreamer encounters not only the beautiful but also the sublime. He finds the sight doubly fearsome ("ferly," 1084, 1086) as he furthermore feels himself hunted,

---

[27] Cf. J. Allan Mitchell, who conceives the dreamer's/maiden's utopia thusly: "Death, the most radical of ontological divisions, separates the two worlds and becomes metonymic of the peculiar epistemological hiatus between 'here' and the otherworld." See Mitchell, "The Middle English 'Pearl': Figuring the Unfigurable," *The Chaucer Review* 35. 1 (2000): 95
[28] Ibid., 106.

mortally pursued. If he sees, it is because he has first been seen; if his gaze penetrates the translucent walls of the heavenly city, it is because he has first been pierced by the glare of the invisible God's glory.

And that which pierces must wound. The Lamb, whose earthly work manifests his incarnate identity as *lumen de lumine*, is necessarily and preeminently a wounded figure that also wounds (cf. 1135, 1142).[29] Nearing his throne, the Dreamer's sight is similarly stricken by all but the blow of death. "Hade bodyly burne abiden that bone, / Thagh alle clerkes hym hade in cure, / His lyf were loste anunder mone." (1090–92). There is only one who has "bodyly burne" this mortal apotheosis: the one, after whose title the Christian takes her name. As for the Dreamer, his near-death experience of wounded marvel, alone out of the entire poem, obtains "consciens sure" (1089). Only earthly insanity can manage heavenly clarity. The "glymme pure" (1088) that drives the Dreamer mad (without moving him) is precisely what gives him knowledge.[30] This "knowledge" is not of this world. Its certainty is therefore uncertain; its wisdom is folly. This knowledge is nothing more (though nothing less) than the assurance that lunar vision defies all bodily life. Here is a species of Augustine's *docta ignorantia*, which Renaissance writers (e.g., Cusanus, Ficino) eagerly take up. To awake, one must fall asleep; to live, one must die; to see, one must dream. This Dreamer is sure that he has seen the *ultima thule*: that which, like his pearl, is beyond all measure, and therefore, beyond all place. But he has not moved anywhere, even as his mind has sprung beyond. Beneath the spotted moon he has been rendered spotless. In suffering the moon's purifying light, the Dreamer has become a theoretical lunatic. The stultifying moonlight has transported him to witness the most sacred and mysterious of all mysteries. "As helde, drawen to Goddes

---

[29] In the Hebrew Scriptures, Jacob, whose dream-ladder stretched between heaven and earth (Gen 28.13), is also wounded in another nocturnal theophany, this one, in terms of wrestling with God or an angel (Gen 35.1–7). (Cf. n. 6, above.) Humanity cannot but come away wounded in its encounter with God. Relevantly, for Christianity, when God's incarnation is claimed to fulfill the encounter between divinity and humanity through the Christ's personal identity, it is "necessary" for him to "suffer and die." The Lamb, therefore, is both wounded and wounding.

[30] "In the dream, the Maiden had described him as 'put in a mad porpose' (267); now he describes as mad those who strive against God's will..." (Spearing, *Medieval Dream-Poetry*, 128).

present, / To mo of his mysterys I hade ben dryven" (1193–94). He has been driven to see the unseeable. Though he ultimately leaves it unparticipated, he is yet still sure of what he has seen. Though his mind and senses cannot comprehend it, he yet still would describe it.

In Conclusion, "More"

As Watts observes, "The Pearl poet not only quotes the Apocalypse but also writes within a tradition of mystic vision shared by his near contemporaries, the English mystics and Dante.... By gradual discipline of contemplation, the mystic comes to a momentary experience of God's light, God's love, or eternal knowing."[31] This tradition's very form thematizes the problem of theological expression, since "the experience passes beyond desire and language even sooner than it passes human understanding." But what and whose "experience passes beyond desire, language, and understanding?" The seer/dreamer's, the poet's, the reader's? Why should the reader of a poem declare that "language" (inter alia) is "passed beyond?" How does visionary experience relate to scriptural/poetic description? How do the seeing and commenting dynamics of Scripture's Apocalypse relate with those of *Pearl*? Apocalypse, after all, is not only the ostensible record of a heavenly vision—it is also a commentary upon other books of the Bible (especially the prophetic books, Isaiah and Ezekiel, themselves containing visionary and even apocalyptic testimonies).[32] Apocalypse is the Bible's own most spectacular gloss. It is the Bible's very own pearl.

As a gloss on Apocalypse, Fitt XVIII uses the moon to explore how words communicate measureless realities for evaluative beings.

---

[31] Watts, 29.

[32] One major theory about the potential origins of biblical apocalyptic finds a notable line in biblical prophecy—whether as a mystical/ethical movement or as a literary form. See, e.g., Paul D. Hanson, *The Dawn of Apocalyptic: The Historical and Sociological Roots of Jewish Apocalyptic Eschatology* (Minneapolis: Fortress, 1979 [1975]). Regardless of theory, the words "prophecy" and "apocalypse" have a certain correspondence. To "prophesy," derived from the Greek, means to "pre-dict" or "say beforehand." Two of the three Hebrew words for "prophet," however, derive from words meaning "to see." The prophet is one who speaks about the beyond because he has seen the beyond. And "apocalypse" is about uncovering hidden things that have been seen by an initiate (see below, n. 32).

In the hands of the *Pearl*-poet, the nature and properties of the moon trope the dynamics of scriptural commentary and mystical vision. Just as the moon draws the earth, leading her tides to cough up pearly treasures, the Bible's Apocalypse draws from the poet the treasure that is *Pearl*—a poetic secret to be rent open and disclosed. In commenting upon Scripture's ultimate book of vision, *Pearl* mirrors how Scripture figures and glosses divine reality. The form of this lunar and specular aesthesis is scriptural apo-calypse: a worded revealing of what is otherwise unimaginable and inconceivable.

"Apocalyptic" or "apocalypse," whose Greek derivation means "un-veiling" or "un-covering," is an ancient Persian and Semitic literary genre. The reality of another hidden time and world is administered to a recipient, typically through the mediation of a trans-worldly being (usually an angel), generally to address a situation of crisis.[33] Apocalypse need not be fungible with accounts of "fire and brimstone." (Such associations proceed not from the Bible's final book, but from its first; see Gen 19.24.) Although the *Pearl*-poet is far-removed from the situation and concerns of traditional apocalypses, a personal crisis occasions the Dreamer's vision, in which the Maiden functions very much like a mediating angel. The poet's gloss upon Apocalypse weaves the aesthetics of Christian Scripture into the fictive Dreamer's experience of it. This gloss upon gloss or lunar mirroring produces *Pearl*'s literary iridescence.

But is not XVIII's lunacy the negative overcoming of theological indication? Is not the Dreamer's silent leave-taking all that remains? Not quite. In the preceding Fitt XVII, the Dreamer recounts his vision just "as John" describes in Apocalypse (cf. 984, 985, 995, 997, 1020, 1032). Then the first line of XVIII announces, "As John hym wrytes yet more I syye" (1033). Contrarily, the seer of Apocalypse swears in conclusion to his book, "If any man shall add to these things, God shall add unto him the plagues written in this book" (Apoc 22.18). The penalty is the blotting-out of one's name from the Book of Life (Apoc 22.19, cf. Ps 69.28 [68.30]). But even if the poet's text is not intended to add more by way of divine inspiration or ecclesial canonicity, the question remains: What precisely is his dreamer's "more" and how is it seen? Perhaps it is

---

[33] See the standard-setting definition in John J. Collins, *The Apocalyptic Imagination: An Introduction to Jewish Apocalyptic Literature*, 2nd ed. (Grand Rapids, MI: William B Eerdmans, 1998 [1984], 5).

the more that remains unapprehended without personal experience and vision. Yet the poet purveys not a vision per se, but words to read or hear—a dreamer's discourse.

Apparently, for the Christian scriptural imagination, there is no experience of vision that is not co-reducible to the hermeneutical experience of a reader/hearer. The poet trades upon the epistemic tension between words and vision, each of which can be prior to the other, and each of which can seem to surpass the other. For example, the poet's Dreamer beholds his pearl in heavenly splendor (1147–52); and yet, because this supernatural order is fundamentally jarring to his earthly sensibility, the Maiden quotes Scripture to him: "In Appocalyppece is wryten ... 'I seghe'" (866–67). To justify a vision, words are cited, which themselves, testify to a vision. Such alternative priority and preeminence between words and vision yields a uniquely refractory discourse for Christian theo-logy, which would articulate how Life is revealed in the Word who is Light (John 1.14, cf. Ps 119 [118].105).[34] Consider the work of *Pearl* more generally apropos Apocalypse and Christian Scripture: the poet writes what the Dreamer sees, which is based upon what Apocalypse describes, testifying to what John sees, which is the opening of the sealed Book, which is accomplished by the Lamb who seems as one slain, being nevertheless the incarnate Logos or Word of Life, whom the Apostles saw, and therefore preached, as they performed great signs and wonders, while the evangelists recorded the Good News, which is ever proclaimed, even as Scripture is ceaselessly glossed. Each of these points is preceded and followed by another, even as each can initiate or follow the rest. Such is the prismatic mystery of scriptural "fulfillment" (see e.g. Matt 5.17).

However the Dreamer and reader of *Pearl* might "see" more than is read in Apocalypse, that "more" lives in the accrual of interrelations between reading/hearing and seeing because a speaker is showing and a reader/hearer is seeing. Like a pearl's ever-accreting layers of nacre, each interval of worded vision adds

---

[34] The great twentieth century literatus-theologian, Hans Urs von Balthasar says the following about the Christian phenomenology of the word: "Scripture is the word of God that bears witness to God's Word. The one Word therefore makes its appearance as though dividing into a word that testifies and into a Word to whom testimony is given." See Hans Urs von Balthasar, "The Word, Scripture and Tradition," chap. 1 in *Explorations in Theology, Vol. 1: The Word Made Flesh*, trans. A. V. Littledale with Alexander Dru (San Francisco: Ignatius Press 1989).

another degree of luminescence. The "more" always divides beyond itself into another space, just as the Dreamer's vision of eschatological increase begins where the "klyfes cleven" the skies (66), and just as the baptismal water that issues from the heavenly city cleaves mortal from immortal life (see e.g. 1157-64). In XVIII, "more" is found in the dark illuminations of the moon whose light is not its own. The moon's "more" captures and chastens the "more and more" of transcendent desire that would be inexorably construed in earthly terms (see III, X). Such earthly terms would ultimately signify, as David Aers reads it, a kind of "suicide." In vaunting the self above all else, the Dreamer actually succumbs to a transcendent lust that is "definitely not... in response to any theocentric yearnings." Rather, "[the Dreamer's] yearning is to terminate desire in the full possession of its (fantasy) object, a possession that dispenses with all mediations, all negotiations, and all language." Perhaps the *Pearl*-poet, however, would save his reader from such supreme "injustice."[35] At any rate, the link-word of XVII, "John," is rightly followed by that of XVIII, "moon," since John writes only what he sees, or, more accurately, de-scribes what is shown and commissioned him to prophesy (see Apoc 1.1-2). The moon is that medium by which one can always say more, since nothing of what is said is formally one's own but the Other's.

The Dreamer finally discovers that the beauty of his pearl is neither her own nor his own (much as the anonymous poet must have thought of his work). His pearl's splendor and the recognition of it participate in a gift that is given from elsewhere, the truly "courteous" grace of a divine "Prince," which is the "ground of all bliss" (see VII, VIII). The "more" of mercy is also the "more" beyond all measure; and this personal, relational gratuity disrupts and reconstitutes all objective, substantial figurings of what is "date" (or "due", see IX). This grace of the Word who is the wounded but glorious Lamb redeems the economy of aesthesis.

The *Pearl*-poet's work is therefore meta-phoric in the strongest sense: his words carry the reader's thesaurus of meaning over into that divine space beyond mortal time, without leaving behind that

---

[35] Here, Aers is reading *Pearl* apposite Chaucer's Troilus, and finds the *Pearl*-poet's "preoccupations... thoroughly individualistic." For Aers, then, *Pearl* is a kind of *pièce de résistance.* See David Aers, "The Self Mourning: Reflections on *Pearl,*" *Speculum* 68.1 (1993): 60, 68, 73.

which has been transcended.³⁶ Through the conceit of a dreamer's vision, the poet's twofold, allegorical sensibility leads beyond itself to much more, that is, to the typological style of an apocalypse–the unveiling of an archetypally destining beyond, which is the Kingdom of friendship between God and humanity. Exceeding all earthly measure, the existence and nature of this paradise (where lamb lies with lion) is not ordinarily conceivable, or even easily metaphorizable, but only transcendentally revealable: faith does not see that for which it hopes (see e.g. Rom 8.24). This unseeable beyond is precisely what the recorded vision of John's *Apocalypse* figures: "Write the things that you have seen!" (Apoc 1.17). And it is John's interlacing of visionary writing and scriptural vision that the *Pearl*-poet glosses, both the text and its textuality. Using this apocalyptic text and trope that intricately interweaves crisis and joy, loss and manifestation, darkness and light, worded witness and envisioned manifestation, the mind of the *Pearl*-poet "springs forth" with words of vision. He pro-phecies vision and apo-calypses Scripture.³⁷ Appropriating and participating apocalyptic text and trope, the poet reveals how words of this world can figure and illumine an unfathomable hope–not through philosophical analogies of metaphysics (though without repudiating them), but through the scriptural metaphorics of personally revealed afterlife: "I saw a new heaven and a new earth" (Apoc 21.1). This apocalyptic theorizing can only take place (as it were) "anunder the mone." And for the earthly mind, to be sure, it is sheer lunacy.

Bruno M. Shah, O.P. is a doctoral student in the Department of Theology at the University of Notre Dame.

Beth Sutherland is a PhD candidate in the English Department at the University of Virginia.

---

³⁶ "The *Pearl* dream-vision thus appears to be a sort of incarnation, which is to say, an embodiment *par excellence* of spiritual facts in human (linguistic) form–in this case, as mediated by the maiden's words, by the dream, and, in the final instance, by the poem itself. The 'figures' (in both senses: tropes and personages) in the poem are therefore simultaneously spiritual and literal, continuous with our world but signifying beyond it" (Mitchell, 90–91).

³⁷ See notes 32 and 33, above.

XIX

DELYT AND DESIRE: WAYS OF SEEING IN *PEARL*

Anne Baden-Daintree

The nineteenth stanza group of *Pearl* marks both the culmination of the heavenly vision and the abrupt ending of the dream, and is held together by the concatenation word '*delyt*'.[1] This term has some resemblance to the modern English 'delight', indicating 'pleasure, joy, gratification felt in a high degree'.[2] As the *Middle English Dictionary* makes clear, in the language of the late Middle Ages this often indicates sensuous pleasure, but in some contexts it might specifically refer to spiritual or intellectual delight.[3] The frequent hints toward the erotic in *Pearl* might then lead us to misread the 'delyt', but its usage simply reflects the common practice in religious texts of the figurative employment of the language of the erotic and a vocabulary of sensuality to indicate spiritual pleasure and joy. In terms of the narrative and dramatic organisation of the poem, the 'blisse' which characterises the seventh stanza group moves from a description of remembered earthly joy and happiness in the father-daughter relationship, towards a depiction of heavenly joy. 'Delyt', in contrast, moves from the heavenly back to the earthly. Furthermore, 'blisse' carries with it a sense of assurance, of the state of experienced joy, and that which is promised; 'delyt' does not always indicate fulfilled desire, but can imply desire itself. So the movement from *blisse* to *delyt* ultimately articulates a movement away from the anticipated joys of heaven.

But this section of the poem is, it turns out, less about the spiritual or sensual pleasures implied by 'delyt', and more about a

---

[1] Apart from one early occurrence of the term 'delyt' in the poem (l. 642, where 'out of delyt' refers to mankind being deprived of joy through the Fall), it only appears in the penultimate stanza group. These occurrences all relate to the vision of the heavenly city, but specifically, as we shall see, to the *inhabited* city.
[2] *OED*, s.v. *delight*, n, 1a.
[3] *MED*, s.v. *delit(e)*, n, 1a, 1b.

series of sense impressions, a succession of moments of awareness and multiple acts of perception which indicate rapid accompanying changes of emotion. Some of these moments are about 'delyt' as pleasurable experience, some play on the secondary meanings of 'delyt' as being about the expectation or yearning toward the pleasurable – something more akin to our modern term 'desire'.[4] It is worth noting that while 'blisse' is generally used to mean pleasure or happiness, it, too, can indicate that state of eager desire (and evidence of such usage is confined to other texts associated with the alliterative revival).[5] So these stanzas encompass both the experience of spiritual joy, and a yearning toward the permanent condition of the joy of salvation.[6] This does not, however, fully account for this stanza group's processes. While translators and editors of this poem tend to employ 'desire' as the nearest equivalent to *delyt*, this not only masks the nuances of meaning which alter with repetition, but 'desire' inevitably carries with it the association of erotic desire. While this might be appropriate to the courtly metaphor which underpins the workings of the poem, it complicates the movement at the end of the poem from spiritual pleasure to a paternal longing expressed through erotic metaphor.

Rather than considering the balance between desire and pleasurable fulfilment, between the spiritual and the sensual, my reading of these five stanzas instead concentrates on the frequent shifts of the Dreamer's attention, guided by the work, in particular,

---

[4] *MED*, s.v. *delit(e)*, n, 1d, 'a desire to have or enjoy something'. The *OED* also shows that in its medieval usage, 'to have delight' was equivalent to the French *avoir envie*, or 'to desire'. *OED*, s.v. *delight*, n, 1b.

[5] *MED*, s.v. *blisse*, n, 2a(b): See *The Siege of Troy*, l. 599; *The Wars of Alexander*, l. 2871.

[6] Malcolm Andrew and Ronald Waldron summarise precisely the purpose of this stanza group in the light of this term's meaning: 'The concatenation word *delyt*, with its overlapping senses of 'delight' and 'desire', suggests the function of this section – to emphasise both the bliss of salvation and the Dreamer's growing desire to cross the water and join the saved'. Malcolm Andrew and Ronald Waldron (eds.), *The Poems of the Pearl Manuscript*, 5th edn. (Exeter: University of Exeter Press, 2007), 105, n. 1093-1152. All quotations from the text will be taken from this edition, however I also draw on the editions by Sarah Stanbury, E.V. Gordon, and Ad Putter and Myra Stokes. *Pearl*, ed. Sarah Stanbury (Kalamazoo, Michigan: Medieval Institute Publications, 2001); *Pearl*, ed. E.V. Gordon (Oxford: Clarendon Press, 1953); *The Works of the* Gawain *Poet*, ed. Ad Putter and Myra Stokes (London: Penguin, 2014).

of Sarah Stanbury, A. C. Spearing, and Alain Renoir.[7] Stanbury's work on focalisation and ocular perception, Spearing's observations on the mimetic processes of dreaming in *The Book of the Duchess*, and Renoir's analysis of cinematic processes in the *Gawain*-poet's descriptive techniques, all inform my reading of these particular stanzas. As Stanbury indicates, this emphasis on the visual, and the direct experience of the narrator, is embedded in the poem's literary processes, the 'structuring [of] descriptive passages according to the mechanics of perception'.[8] As the poem draws to a close, both the dramatic narrative and the descriptive technique turn on acts of perception, with many swift shifts of awareness, and the quick cut cinematic techniques that mimic the process of dreaming. The visual and sensory delights that, prior to the dream, overwhelm the narrator and send him into a state of sleep, here dazzle him with their swift sequence and distract his mind leading to a final error of judgement.

This section of the poem leads from the Dreamer being granted a vision of the New Jerusalem, through to his viewing of the City's inhabitants, culminating in the sight of the Lamb of God, enthroned in majesty. The Dreamer then sees the procession of 144,000 virgins and among them his daughter, the Pearl-maiden. It is this final sight which leads him to attempt to cross the river, 'for luf-longyng in gret delyt' (1148). While this stanza group sees a shift in attention towards the heavenly city and then its inhabitants, and particularly the Lamb of God (before, at its close, the vision moves earthward again) it also demonstrates a number of shifts in its uses of key vocabulary terms. 'Delyt' is, in the first instance, attached to the pearls bound firmly to each maiden's breast, then to the character of their movement through the city (1105, 1116). Subsequently, 'delyt' applies exclusively to the Lamb – the pleasure of his coming (1117), of the experience of loving him (1128), of looking at him (1129), and then, in a rather complicated construction, the contrast of horrified contemplation of his wound which engenders grief rather than delight (1140). The final stanza of the group moves to the Lamb's

---

[7] Sarah Stanbury, *Seeing the* Gawain-*Poet: Description and the Act of Perception* (Philadelphia: University of Pennsylvania Press, 1991); A.C. Spearing, "Literal and Figurative in *The Book of the Duchess,*" *Studies in the Age of Chaucer*, Proceedings, no. 1 (1985): 165-71; Alain Renoir, "Descriptive Technique in *Sir Gawain and the Green Knight,*" *Orbis Litterarum* 13, no. 2 (1958): 126-32.
[8] Stanbury, *Seeing the* Gawain-*Poet*, 2.

own experience of 'delyt' (1141), suggesting, perhaps, that the human emotions previously expressed might merely be reflections of the Divine. And finally the Dreamer's attention is distracted, and the stanza ends with the (ultimately destructive) 'delyt' and longing for his daughter's presence (1152).

Seeing the Heavenly Jerusalem

It has often been noted that the responses of the Dreamer to his viewing of the Heavenly City echo his response to his first sighting of the Pearl-maiden. This is a stunned silence that is articulated through a hunting metaphor, where 'I stod as stylle as dased quayle' (1085) clearly mirrors the earlier expression, 'I stod as hende as hawk in halle' (184). He is now 'rauyste' (ravished) by the radiant light emanating from the City, but this depiction of the qualities of the light of the Heavenly Jerusalem (compared to the dimmer glow of the moon) then continues into the next section with a different figurative emphasis:

> Ryȝt as þe maynful mone con rys
> Er þenne þe day-glem dryue al doun,
> So sodanly on a wonder wyse
> I watz war of a prosessyoun.
> (1093-6)

The emphasis in the first of these five stanzas is on ocular perception, an emphasis which continues, and increases in significance, as the poem progresses. The focus here is on how such acts of perception operate, overlapping and catching the Dreamer unawares. It begins with a simile derived from the impression of the sun and moon appearing simultaneously in the sky. The moon appears within the line of vision before nightfall, when the sun is still strong. And the moon is 'maynful'. Commentators fail to agree on the precise meaning of this term, but it appears to derive from 'main', signifying strength and might, rather than the qualities of brightness and resplendence suggested by the *MED* (largely on the basis of this particular example).[9] The sense, then, is of the moon rising powerfully before the daylight sinks down, and so this simile is about one element overtaking another in prominence. The juxtaposition

---

[9] *MED* s.v. *main; mainful.* Stanbury notes the conventional formula 'myghty and maynful', *Pearl*, ed. Stanbury, 102, n. 1093.

of two opposing elements is the striking image here (and most editors comment on this) but, more than this, the poet wishes to draw our attention to the way in which we appear to be seeing one thing when suddenly another intrudes. The Dreamer has been gazing in wonder at the Heavenly City of Jerusalem, when he notices that the city is, in fact, inhabited:

> Þis noble cité of ryche enpresse
> Watz sodanly ful, withouten sommoun,
> Of such vergynez in þe same gyse
> Þat watz my blysful anvnder croun.
> (1097-1100)

Is it the situation in front of him which has altered, or is it a difference in what he is able to perceive? Have the inhabitants, in fact, been there all along? The Dreamer's sense of being wrong-footed (as he has been several times in the course of his dream) is emphasised by the repetition of 'sodanly': he is suddenly aware of the procession and the city is suddenly full.[10] Where 'sodanly' is used elsewhere by the poet it can include a sense of danger, an action that occurs without warning (as in the destruction of Sodom and Gomorrah, or the surprise attack on Belshazzar as he sleeps, in *Cleanness*).[11] But in *Pearl* the sense of something occurring without warning repeatedly signals the Dreamer's inability to comprehend. 'Sodanly' also refers, in the final stanza group, to his movement out of the dream, and his expulsion from the presence of the heavenly Jerusalem and its inhabitants. It is a painful abruptness: 'Me payed ful ille to be outfleme/ So sodenly of þat fayre regioun' (1177-8). So the repetition of 'sodanly' at the beginning of this stanza group, as the Dreamer views the (now inhabited) City, emphasises his separation from it and prefigures his loss. His repeated failures of perception demonstrate (as the Pearl-maiden has already made clear) a groundedness in the earthly, and an inability or unwillingness to attain the heavenly.[12]

---

[10] Gordon does comment on this aspect, the moon 'appearing as it were miraculously without any warning of its coming. So the procession in the Heavenly City appeared *wythouten sommoun*'. Gordon, *Pearl*, 84, n. 1093-6.
[11] *Cleanness*, 910, 'Sodomas schal ful sodenly synk into grounde'; 1769, 'Now ar thay [i.e. Belshazzar's enemies] sodenly assembled at the self tyme'.
[12] She criticises, for example, his reliance on the visual, his failure to believe anything unless he has seen it: 'Þat leuez noþynk bot 3e hit sy3e' (308).

The kind of perception and realisation that is at play in this stanza is very different, however, from the Dreamer's first sighting of the Pearl-maiden. At that point in the narrative a gradual sense of realisation and recognition is articulated such that we as readers follow the Dreamer's processes of cognition.[13] This culminates in the shock of understanding when the sensory signals and intellectual comprehension result in a message that is incomprehensible: this is his daughter, yet also not the daughter he remembers. In the closing scene of his dream, however, the shock is more muted. While his perceptive faculties have failed him again, he seems to not be unduly troubled by this. By the end of this stanza group, however, further sudden shifts of perception bring everything to conclusion. Although we have seen the Dreamer twice rooted to the spot in desire and wonder, there is no real stability in his 'delyt': it oscillates between the earthly and the spiritual; he is repeatedly swayed, as Stanbury has observed, by the visual.[14] His attention, and his desire, is diverted two more times during the dream: first by the appearance of the Lamb of God, enthroned, at the culmination of the procession, and second, when he is distracted by the sight of his 'lyttel quene'. Both of these sights generate strong emotions.

As this first stanza continues, there is a descriptive emphasis on female physical appearance, although it is very different in tone from the initial description of the Pearl-maiden. This is factual reporting, using the same series of physical attributes that recur repeatedly through the poem (crowned, in white clothing, adorned with pearls):

> And coronde wern alle of þe same fasoun,
> Depaynt in perlez and wedes qwyte;
> In vchonez breste watz bounden boun
> Þe blysful perle with gret delyt.
> (1101-4)

The irony, of course, is that the Dreamer recognises these virgins as being similar in appearance to his daughter, but cannot comprehend that she might be one of them. The account of the procession is

---

[13] 'I knew hyr wel, I hade sen hyr ere' (164) gives way to 'On lenghe I loked [...]/Þe lenger, I knew hyr more and more (167-8).
[14] Stanbury refers to his 'infatuation with physical forms', in *Seeing the Gawain-Poet*, 16.

drawn from Revelation 14.4.[15] But the language of this entire stanza is replete with royal and courtly imagery (*prosessyoun, noble, ryche, croun, coronde*), confirming not only the very material concerns of the poem's figurative range in accordance with the desires of its aristocratic audience, but also the metaphor of heaven as a late medieval court (an approach which has led commentators to assume a direct and literal association with the Ricardian court).[16] The City itself, we might note, was described as 'noble' and of 'ryche enpresse' (great renown) (1097).

While in the seventeenth stanza group the employment of material from the book of Revelation is applied in a straightforward manner, staying close to the Vulgate text (the plainness of the description of the New Jerusalem has been noted by several commentators), the poet draws freely on different sections of Revelation for this account of the interior of the City and its inhabitants.[17] The 144,000 virgins following the Lamb are derived from Revelation 14: 1-5, which also confirms the 'spotlessness' of the Pearl-maiden drawn from the Song of Songs: *sine macula sunt* ('they are without spot', Revelation 14:5). The adornment with white

---

[15] *et nemo poterat discere canticum nisi illa centum quadraginta quattuor milia qui empti sunt de terra/ hii sunt qui cum mulieribus non sunt coinquinatti virgins enim sunt hii qui sequuntur agnum quocumque abierit* (and no man could say the canticle, but those hundred forty-four thousand who were purchased from the earth./ These are they who were not defiled with women: for they are virgins. These follow the Lamb whithersoever he goeth). All Biblical quotations in this essay are from the Latin Vulgate (online version at www.latinvulgate.com) with translations from the Douay-Rheims (drawn either from the same site, or www.drbo.org).

[16] See, for example, John Bowers, "*Pearl* in its Royal Setting: Ricardian Poetry Revisited," *Studies in the Age of Chaucer* 17 (1995): 111-55; John M. Bowers, *The Politics of Pearl: Court Poetry in the Age of Richard II* (Cambridge: D.S. Brewer, 2001).

[17] The construction of the city is based on a close approximation of John's words in Revelation 21, but this section of *Pearl* draws on Revelation 5: 14 (the procession of the 144,000), and 5:21 (the vision of the Heavenly City of Jerusalem), conflating different descriptive and narrative sections. It is worth noting Gordon's observation, however, that in *Pearl*, 'the Heavenly City has all the details of that in Revelation, yet it is imagined in medieval form as *bayle* or *manayre*', (*Pearl*, ed. Gordon, 111). In my reading I also draw attention to the medievalisation of the poet's reading of Revelation, but in terms of social rather than architectural structures, and the specific conception of the heavenly hierarchy as reflective of the medieval court.

clothing and multiple pearls ('depaynt in perlez and wedez qwyte', 1102) confirms the identification of the Pearl-maiden with the 144,000, reinforcing the status of the communal over the binary relationships of father/daughter or bride/bridegroom, but it is also something which connects the followers of the Lamb with the City itself. Several commentators have drawn attention to the associations between the maiden and the City, particularly in terms of the lengthy physical descriptions of each, presented and displayed in their jewel-encrusted finery.[18] This mode of presentation is biblical in origin: Revelation 21:2 describes the Heavenly City as 'prepared as a bride adorned for her husband' (*paratam sicut sponsam ornatam viro suo*), and furthermore, each gate of the Heavenly City is also made of one individual pearl in the biblical account, replayed in the poem as the pearl in each maiden's breast. The account in Revelation of the City's gates: *et duodecim portae duodecim margaritae sunt per singulas et singulae portae erant ex singulis margaritis* ('And the twelve gates are twelve pearls, one to each: and every several gate was of one several pearl'), is transformed into 'In uchones breste was bounden boun/The blysful perle'.[19] The language here indicates an individual distinctiveness ('uchones' and *singulas/singulae/singulis*) that is, paradoxically, enhanced by the concurrent reiteration of sameness (the 144,000 are dressed in identical clothing, as subsequent lines confirm), which chimes with the 'makelez' wordplay in descriptions of the Pearl-maiden.[20]

The following stanza begins with terms that again confirm adherence to the account in Revelation (the golden streets gleaming as glass) while also emphasising the coherence of purpose and appearance ('alle in sute'):

> With gret delyt þay glod in fere
> On golden gatez þat glent as glasse;[21]
> Hundreth þowsandez, I wot þer were,

---

[18] See, for example, Sarah Stanbury, "The Body and the City in *Pearl*," *Representations* 48 (1994): 30-47, Rosalind Field, "The Heavenly Jerusalem in *Pearl*," *The Modern Language Review* 81 (1986): 7-17 (8).

[19] Revelation 21:21

[20] See 780, for example: 'A makelez may and maskellez', where 'makelez' indicates unique, matchless, without peer.

[21] Revelation 21:21 '[...] *et platea civitatis aurum mundum tamquam vitrum perlucidum*' ('And the street of the city was pure gold, as it were, transparent glass')

> And alle in sute her liurez wasse.
> Tor to knaw þe gladdest chere.
>   (1105-9)

The 'liurez' of the processing virgins is the livery which denotes service to a particular lord, and so the ideas of service and of coherence of appearance are also tied to the courtly hierarchy, the identification with one another, and with 'belonging' to this 'lord'.[22] Then the text (and the Dreamer) shifts focus, and we turn to the source of this 'delyt': the Lamb of God. The Lamb with seven horns has a biblical source (Revelation 5:6), but the poet's additional detail of 'red gold' is not related to heraldry or livery, as might be expected, but simply reflects the quality of the gold:[23]

> Þe Lombe byfore con proudly passe
> Wyth hornez seuen of red golde cler;
> As praysed perlez His wedez wasse.
> Towarde þe throne þay trone a tras.
> Þaȝ þay wern fele, no pres in plyt,
> Bot mylde as maydenez seme at mas,
> So droȝ þay forth with gret delyt.
>   (1110-16)

Christ figured as the Lamb of God derives from a number of biblical sources, and, although the primary one here is the apocalyptic vision of the book of Revelation, the other sources also come into play in this stanza group, having already been explicitly paraphrased by the maiden at 801-4 and 822-4:

> Isaiah 53:7 He shall be led as a sheep to the slaughter (*sicut ovis ad occisionem ducetur*)

> John 1:29 Behold the Lamb of God who taketh away the sins of the world (*ecce agnus Dei qui tollit peccatum mundi*)

---

[22] Stanbury describes this as 'the official garb of a group or guild' (*Pearl*, ed. Stanbury, 102, n. 1108). And as the *MED* makes clear, the point here is the 'gifting' of the clothing or 'uniform' by the lord or king to servants or retainers. *MED*, s.v. *livere* n.(3).

[23] *MED* s.v. *red* 1f(a): 'Of the metal gold, gold coins, gold leaf: pure [as shown through becoming red when heated; cp. Pliny *Nat.Hist.*33.59].'

The pain of the Crucifixion and the redemptive powers of Christ underpin his appearance in the New Jerusalem. But the text is fairly static in dramatic and descriptive terms. Putter and Stokes suggest that this picture of the Lamb of God functions as 'emblem rather than a metaphor, a visual image which actually discourages visualisation'.[24] Where much of the text of *Pearl* does provide pictorial detail which encourages 'visualisation', here, in accord with biblical processes, when 'seeing' God we are shown his Divine qualities and attributes rather than his physical appearance. The physicality is restricted, as the poem continues, to contemplation of his wounds, in accord with medieval affective tradition. As with stanza group 17 (where the architectural construction of the City is described), the reliance on biblical source material and the repetitive description of the procession towards the throne slows the pace, inviting the reader to share in the act of contemplation alongside the Dreamer as he enters a state of mesmerised expectation. But the straightforward rendition of biblical terms and the simplicity of the Vulgate's diction nonetheless mask something of the sense of wonder that we are to understand in the Dreamer's act of looking.

The various witnesses to the Lamb's arrival are again derived from biblical sources, where the 144,000 virgins are joined by angels and 'aldermen' in celebrating the presence of the Lamb, and joining in praising him:

> Delyt þat Hys come encroched
> To much hit were of for to melle.
> Þise aldermen, quen He aproched,
> Grouelyng to His fete þay felle.
> (1117-20)

But in *Pearl*'s account we return to the hierarchies of court life as well as the hierarchies of the heavenly realm. The description of the elders of the Heavenly City as 'aldermen' perhaps indicates civic governance more than the strictly courtly, but these men appear to adopt courtly postures when in the presence of royalty (although the prostrate position implied by 'grouelying' occurs in religious texts as often as secular settings). The emphasis on the court is reinforced at the end of this stanza:

---

[24] Putter and Stokes, *Works of the* Gawain *Poet*, 448, n. 835-40.

> Þe steuen moȝt stryke þurȝ þe vrþe to helle
> Þat þe vertues of heuen of joye endyte.
> To loue þe Lombe His meyny inmelle
> Iwysse I laȝt a gret delyt.
> (1125-8)

The image of the Lamb amidst his 'meyny' describes not the hired hands of the parable of the vineyard (542) but that 'moteles meyny' described in St John's Apocalypse (as reported by the Pearl-maiden at 892, 899, 925, 960). These are his followers, his retinue, and he is their lord (a relationship which is figured in terms of courtly hierarchies). However, in between these depictions of the heavenly court, the acts of praise are expressed in an image which adapts a biblical source in a striking metaphor that merges the sensory with the spiritual:

> Legyounes of aungelez, togeder uoched
> Þer kesten ensens of swete smelle;
> Þen glory and gle watz nwe abroched;
> Al songe to loue þat gay Juelle.
> (1121-24)

The biblical source text is Revelation 5:8.[25] As the legions of angels cast about the sweet smelling incense, these scents are figurative representations of the prayers of saints. The poem does not make this explicit: it is concerned instead with extending the metaphor of the containment of spiritual virtues in material objects. As Putter and Stokes explain in their edition of the poem, the unusual word choice, 'abroched', is one associated with the 'broaching' or opening of a wine-cask such that 'glory and gle are allowed to "pour out" like wine'.[26] The vials of prayers (incense) and the casks of glory and joy (new wine) then work together metaphorically to express the idea of an offering.

---

[25] *et cum aperuisset librum quattuor animalia et viginti quattuor seniores ceciderunt coram agno habentes singuli citharas et fialas aureas plenas odoramentorum quae sunt orationes sanctorum* (and when they had opened the book the four living creatures and the four and twenty ancients fell down before the Lamb, having every one of them harps and golden vials full of odours, which are the prayers of saints)

[26] Putter and Stokes, *Works of the* Gawain *Poet*, 461, n. 1123.

Just as we have seen the movement of the term 'delyt' from one object to another, so too, at this point in the poem does the image of the pearl move away from its apparently fixed association with the dead daughter. The Lamb himself is now identified as 'þat gay juelle' (1124) to whom all sing in worship. Both adjective and noun have been previously applied to the Pearl-maiden – she was that 'gracios gaye' (260) and simply 'þat gaye' (433) early in the exchange between Dreamer and Maiden (where 'gay' is used as an adjectival noun), and the Dreamer repeatedly refers to her as 'jewel' (23, 249, 253) and even her words are to him as jewels (277). But then she adopts his metaphor and applies it first to Christ as her heavenly bridegroom (795), and then to the inhabitants of the Heavenly City (929). The poem's processes - the shifting metaphor of the pearl, the shifting meanings of all the concatenation words – only serve to emphasise the insistent references in this poem to interpretation, to perception, to relocating viewpoint. We might also note the opening stanza's use of 'queresoeuer I jugged gemmez gaye' (7): now that the Lamb of God is perceived as the 'gay juelle' the jeweller's ability to 'judge', to appraise or interpret, such 'gemmes' is brought into doubt.

The Wounded Lamb

The more detailed description of the enthroned Lamb of God follows, and concentrates first on demeanour before moving to physical appearance:

> Delit þe Lombe for to deuise
> With much meruayle in mynde went,
> Best watz He, blyþest, and moste to pryse,
> Þat euer I herde of speche spent;
> So worþly whyt wern wedez Hys,
> His lokez symple, Hymself so gent.
> (1129-34)

This formulaic description is misleading, however. While we might want to view the Lamb as exemplifying whiteness (and therefore purity), combining the modest humility of 'symple' with the courtly nobility of 'gent', this image is not straightforward. Moving from the generalised superlatives of character: 'best', 'blyþest' (a range of meanings come into play here such as merciful, gracious, perhaps joyful), 'moste to pryse' (again raising the idea of value and appraisal as well as praise), to the physical appearance which accords with the Pearl-maiden, and with all the inhabitants of the New Jerusalem, a shock awaits both reader and Dreamer:

> Bot a wounde ful wyde and weete con wyse
> Anende Hys hert, þurȝ hyde torente.
> Of His quyte syde His blod outsprent.
> (1135-7)

Why is this shocking when we know the facts of the Crucifixion? This is, after all, the Lamb of Revelation: 'in the midst of the throne [...] stood a Lamb as it had been slain' (Rev 5:6: *in medio throni ... agnum stantem tamquam occisum*). But it still jars in this mood of celebratory 'delyt'.

This portrayal of the Lamb's wound has produced much critical comment. Rosalind Field has drawn attention to the theological inappropriateness of the continued bleeding of the wound once the Lamb is enthroned in majesty, and draws comparisons with pictorial representation in Apocalypse manuscripts.[27] Muriel Whitaker also provides much pictorial evidence from such manuscripts as to the poet's possible sources.[28] Sarah Stanbury, however, finds a psychoanalytical interpretation of the wound.[29] But in theological terms, it is the significance of the presentation of the Lamb of God as bleeding at the point when the Dreamer views him seated on the throne at the heart of the New Jerusalem, which is of concern. Once enthroned in the New Jerusalem the triumphal Lamb should be presented without visible and open wounds.[30] This stain on his

---

[27] Field, "Heavenly Jerusalem," 13: 'the *Pearl* poet might have been expected to introduce the 'Jerusalem Lombe' of Section 15 as the *Agnus Dei*, manifesting the wounds of the Passion, and then to follow the commentators and illustrators in presenting the Lamb in triumph in the New Jerusalem as the *Agnus Victor*, free from such wounds, 'entier quant a sa deité'. In evident contrast to his audience's expectation, the poet does the reverse.'

[28] Muriel Whitaker, "*Pearl* and some Illustrated Apocalypse Manuscripts," *Viator* 12 (1981): 183-201.

[29] Sarah Stanbury, "Feminist Masterplots: The Gaze on the Body of *Pearl*'s Dead Girl," in *Feminist Approaches to the Body in Medieval Literature*, ed, Linda Lomperis and Sarah Stanbury (Philadelphia: University of Pennsylvania Press, 1993), 96-115.

[30] Revelation 5:6 describes 'a Lamb standing, as it were slain' (*agnum stantem tamquam occisum*). Subsequent references to the triumphant Lamb (Rev. 14)

spotless fleece complicates the message, whereby the maiden has already presented to us 'thys Jerusalem Lombe' (841), a lamb with fleece so white, that neither spot nor stain might adhere to it: 'Þat mot ne masklle moȝt on streche' (843).[31] Yet in the Dreamer's subsequent description we see a graphic illustration of his wounds. In line 1137 the whiteness of his side is specifically juxtaposed with the gushing flow of blood, and the significance of the wound is, I think, its persistence. This is the damaged flesh that does not go away, the wound that fails to present itself as healed.[32] In fact, this 'blemish' is at the heart of the poem's conception of grief and salvation. Field demonstrates that it is the perception of this wound, this 'mark of human suffering', that is at stake: if read correctly, 'the mark of death is a cause of joy'.[33] But, of course, the Dreamer is unable to see this. Instead, there is a direct relationship between the wounded Lamb and the 'open wound' of the Dreamer's grief: the reader is invited to see an identification of suffering between the two. That this compassionate awareness of Christ's wounds might be the path to the Dreamer's salvation (even though the point may well be lost on him: his response is presented in terms of his lack of understanding) is indicated by the textual associations of the wound. Suggestive parallels for the poet's emotive focus on the Lamb's wounds are to be found, not in Apocalypse manuscripts (of which Field has only identified one where the Lamb is still presented as bleeding in the New Jerusalem), but in vernacular Passion lyrics, where the frequent calls to gaze upon the wounds of the Crucifixion and the spectacle of Christ's bloodied, damaged body often turn (particularly in later lyrics) toward the wound in his side. The large body of literature based on the contemplation of Christ's wounds refers specifically to the side wound caused by a spear when he was on the Cross, as told in John's Gospel 19:33-4, and the Gospel of Nicodemus. It is also referred to by the Pearl-maiden at the end of stanza group 11, where she mentions blood and water coming out of the wound made by the spear ('glayve') 649-59. The phrase 'wyde

---

and the New Jerusalem (Rev. 21-22) do not mention wounds or marks of slaughter in connection with the Lamb of God.

[31] Field, "Heavenly Jerusalem," 11.

[32] We might also read this in terms of Freud's 'open wound' of melancholic grief as delineated in 'Mourning and Melancholia' (1917), so that the Lamb's sacrificial wound is to be viewed alongside the Dreamer's psychological 'wound'.

[33] Field, "Heavenly Jerusalem," 15.

and weete' appears to be a formulaic alliterative construction occurring elsewhere in the context of describing a wound.[34] Both these descriptive terms are widely used of wounds (particularly Christ's wounds), respectively indicating gaping and bleeding, and also occur in one of the Grimestone lyrics on the Passion: 'wyde weren hus wondis wete'.[35]

The problem in *Pearl*, however, is not the nature of the wound, but rather that the Dreamer can only see the wounded Lamb, not the Lamb triumphant.[36] It is significant that the Dreamer's perception is different from that of the maiden (she does not appear to see or acknowledge the wound): he is still in a state of imperfect understanding. However, the presentation of the wounds of Christ occurring at this particular point in the text (with the potential for access to the Heavenly City), does, in fact, have some biblical authority. In the closing verses of John's Apocalyptic vision comes the simple equation of salvation and redemption from sin, couched in precisely these terms:

> Blessed are they that wash their robes in the blood of the Lamb: that they may have a right to the tree of life and may enter in by the gates into the city.
>
> *beati qui lavant stolas suas ut sit potestas eorum in lingo vitae et portis intrent in civitatem* (Revelation 22: 14)[37]

---

[34] *Destruction of Troy*, 1327-9: The Troiens full tyte were tyrnyt to þe grounde/With batell on bothe halfes, blody beronyn,/Wyde woundes & wete of hor wale dyntes. Source: *The Gest Hystoriale of the Destruction of Troy,* eds. G. A. Panton and D. Donaldson, *EETS* 39, 56 (1869, 1874; reprint as one vol. 1968).

[35] F. J. Furnivall (ed.), *Political, Religious and Love Poems* (Oxford: EETS, 1866, 1903), p. 276, 'In place as man may se', l. 159. MS Adv 18.7.21 (NIMEV 1523).

[36] The *poet*, however, presents both: the Lamb is triumphant *despite* being wounded.

[37] Although the washing 'in the blood of the Lamb' (in the Douay-Rheims translation) is not explicit in the Latin Vulgate text, it is implicit through its association with the opening blessings and salutations of the Book of Revelation: '*Iesu Christo [...] qui dilexit nos et lavit nos a peccatis nostris in sanguine seco*' (Jesus Christ [...] who hath loved us and washed us from our sins in his own blood), Rev. 1:5.; and more directly to Revelation 7:14, where the 'great multitude' who are 'standing before the throne and in sight of the Lamb', 'are they who are come out of great tribulation and have

The bleeding Lamb of God is simply a metaphoric invitation to salvation and redemption from sin, presented to the Dreamer at a point when his resistance to verbal reasoning can only be resolved through visual 'argument'. And of course, this precise image has already been presented verbally by the Pearl-maiden, at the heart of her bridal meditation upon Christ's love:

> In Hys blod He wesch my wede on dese,
> And coronde clene in vergynté,
> And py3t me in perlez maskellez.
> (766-8)

This association between Christ's wounds and redemption from sin was embedded in contemporary liturgical thought and practice, as is made clear from what Miri Rubin describes as 'a most popular' Eucharistic salutation for the elevation of the host: '*O aqua lateris Christi lave me*' (O water from Christ's side, bathe me).[38] That this is returned in *Pearl* to the more problematic biblical image of being washed clean by Christ's blood is entirely consistent with the poem's preoccupations with stains and blemishes (or their absence). And, as the text indicates, compassion for the bleeding Lamb exerts only a fleeting, momentary hold on the Dreamer's attention.[39]

But the shocking contrast of the gush of red blood and the whiteness of Christ's side causes the Dreamer at this point to 'see' the fact of the Crucifixion for the first time. His response is instinctive, engaging with the wounded Christ on a purely human level: Who did this? How could they have hurt you?

> Alas, þo3t I, who did þat spyt?
> Ani breste for bale a3t haf forbrent

---

washed their robes and have made them white in the blood of the Lamb' (*qui veniunt de tribulatione magna et laverunt stolas suas et dealbaverunt eas in sanguine agni*).

[38] Miri Rubin, *Corpus Christi: The Eucharist in Late Medieval Culture* (Cambridge: Cambridge University Press, 1991), 303.

[39] David Aers views this brevity highly critically: 'the dreamer's 'luflongyng' shows no sense of relatedness to anyone but the object of his desire – and that [...] is *not* the processing Lamb of God on whom he bestows three lines of pity before turning away.' David Aers, "The Self Mourning: Reflections on *Pearl*," *Speculum* 68 (1993): 54-73 (72).

> Er he þerto hade had delyt.
> (1135-7)

It is not that the Dreamer was unaware of the Crucifixion before this point, but now, confronted with the physical reality of wounding, he is able to see it clearly for the first time. His apparent lack of comprehension is, in fact, a breakthrough in terms of his deeper understanding, whereby the emotional acknowledgement enhances his intellectual and spiritual engagement. The Dreamer's concerns, we must remember, have been almost entirely earth-bound and literal. And the subsequent stanza continues to describe the Lamb with this naive sense of wonder:

> The Lombe delyt non lyste to wene;
> Þa3 He were hurt and wounde hade,
> In his sembelaunt watz neuer sene,
> So wern Hys glentes gloryous glade.
> (1138-41)

Even though he is hurt and wounded, the Lamb's 'delyt' is evident. While the Dreamer's response to this vicious wounding is instinctive anger and incredulity, the Lamb, in contrast, demonstrates impeccable manners. In the courtly hierarchy which the poet employs as an emblem of heavenly hierarchy, the Lamb is lord or king, and it would not befit him to demonstrate any extreme emotion at this point that might disrupt the celebratory mood of praise. All the followers have demonstrated 'gladest chere', so how could his *sembelaunt* disrupt this? All his 'glentes' (glances) are 'gloryous glade', in accordance with the expressions of his followers.

Desire and Loss

From here, however, we move into the final acts of looking that disrupt the vision, and destroy any illusion of continued relationship between bereaved father and dead daughter. With an abruptness mimetic of the rapid 'scene changes' that typify the process of dreaming, the Dreamer switches his attention away from the Lamb for a moment as he notices the 'meyny' (again, a term which describes the gathering in terms suggesting the household retinue). This is exactly the kind of movement that began this stanza group. Just as the moon rises while the sun is still shining in the sky, now, gazing on the wounded Lamb of God, the sight of his entourage takes precedence in the Dreamer's line of vision:

> I loked among Hys meyny schene
> How þay wyth lyf wern laste and lade;
> Then saȝ I þer my lyttel quene
> Þat I wende had standen by me in sclade.
> Lorde, much of mirþe watz þat ho made
> Among her ferez þat watz so quyt!
> Þat syȝt me gart to þenk to wade
> For luf-longyng in gret delyt.
> (1145-52)

Reading this aloud, it is impossible to ignore the frequent and sudden changes of tone in these few lines. We are carried along with the Dreamer's rapid readjustments as his understanding struggles to catch up with the visual evidence. This section of the poem has a cinematic quality, as, from the Dreamer's perspective, one visual delight overlaps the next in rapid succession. So we move from his conversation with the Pearl-maiden, to the vision of the City, to his shock and compassion at the sight of the wounded Lamb. And then the Dreamer sees the maiden, now inside the City, and his only thought is to join her.

It is the adjective 'lyttel' that intensifies the poignancy of this sighting. She is not just a queen of heaven but a little queen, his little queen, and the force of the father-daughter relationship hits the reader with the shock of remembering that this Pearl-maiden, this queen of heaven, is really the Dreamer's tiny daughter, dead in infancy. His surprise is based on the fact that he thought that she was still standing beside him on the riverbank, but now she is moved further away from him once again, emphasising the inaccessibility of death. She is irredeemably other, but he seems unable to fully accept this. His first comment, as he adjusts his lines of perception, is remarkably upbeat, reflecting on her demeanour with all the pleasure of a proud father:

> Lorde, much of mirþe watz þat ho made
> Among her ferez þat watz so quyt!
> (1149-50)

And while the theological point here is that she is unpeturbed by the Lamb's bleeding wound, and is able to share in his 'delyt' with 'mirthe', from a dramatic perspective it is specifically 'þat syȝt' which causes the Dreamer to step forward out of 'luf-longyng' in his desire to be with her again. 'Luf-longyng', of course, recalls the compound 'luf-daungere' from the opening stanza, both phrases expressive of a desire to breach the distance or divide that separates the man from his object of desire. It is only in the final line of this stanza group that the poem uses 'delyt' to refer to the transformed and transplanted 'pearl'. When he realizes that his maiden is now transplanted into the city, the Dreamer becomes blind to its other inhabitants: as abruptly as he becomes aware of her changed position, all his delight and desires are transferred back to his Pearl-maiden. This moment of transition is the moment from which his multiple failures spin out. He is unable to hold on at once to his spiritual vision and to his earthly desires and needs. But again the complex associations of 'delyt' also complicate our reading of this passage: in this context it appears to speak not of a father overwhelmed by grief, but of a man swayed by the suddenness of sexual desire.[40] While some critics have emphasised this erotic charge, this is not quite, I think, what the poet intends. 'Þat syȝt me gart to þenk to wade' (1151) refers directly back to the Dreamer's thoughts when he first explored the landscape of his dream and stood on the banks of the river, wondering what delights (even Paradise) might be on the other side: 'Bot þe water watz depe, I durst not wade/ And euer I longed aye more and more' (143-4). So the sense of wading across is already associated with longing, with the movement toward sensory experience which alleviates grief and sorrow, and also with a transgressing of boundaries (figuratively associated with ideas of trespass). Each of these could indicate a movement towards either the Heavenly City, or his daughter.

But the Dreamer's emotional state as he embarks on this final act of 'transgression' is ambiguous. The verb 'gart' (from 'geren'), indicates a sense of causing or compelling an action, and the other instance in this poem when it appears to be used in this way is when the Dreamer speaks of the role of the strange landscape in alleviating (or at least temporarily setting aside) his grief: 'The adubbemente of

---

[40] 'Delyt', as Andrew and Waldron have observed, carries with it both desire and its fulfilment, longing and delight. See Andrew and Waldron, 105. Also see *M.E.D.*, s.v. *delyt* 1.d, 'a desire to have or enjoy something'.

þo downez dere/ Garten my goste al greffe forʒete' (85-6). So there is a sense of compulsion arising directly from the sight of the Pearl-maiden. However, 'gart' also carries associations of the other uses of 'geren', and might indicate a getting ready, preparing oneself for action. But the action is slightly deferred – the phrase is 'gart to þenk to wade'. This hesitation, the sight compelling him to think to cross the water (or even the preparing himself to think of that act), cuts against all that we might understand about his impulsive action at this point in the narrative. It all happens so quickly that this divided consciousness is barely apparent. And this is more than a physical stepping forward into the river; it operates on a figurative level, too. To 'wade' also indicates a sense of immersion, a desire to figuratively wallow in 'delyt'. However, the construction 'wade depe', indicating a depth of absorption in love, only occurs in later texts, and so although this indicates the underlying sense of the sentence, it is not implied by the specific term 'wade'. So the Dreamer is distracted by visual 'evidence', and under a sense of compulsion prepares to immerse himself in the pleasures that crossing the water appear to offer. But as we shall see in the final stanza group, the movement towards what might be seen as his primary object of desire ultimately leads the Dreamer to exile from 'that fayre regioun': from the promise of 'blisse', to a perpetual situation of unfulfilled desire.

Anne Baden-Daintree is a Teaching Fellow in English at the University of Bristol. She is currently completing her first monograph, *The Grieving Subject: Loss and the Courtly Dynamic in Late Medieval French and English Poetry*, and is also working on a critical edition of a late medieval household anthology, Lambeth Palace MS 853. Anne has published articles and book chapters on the poetry of Charles d'Orléans, *Pearl*, and the Alliterative *Morte Arthure*. Current research projects include a study of poetry and prayer in the medieval household, and a study of contemporary elegy in terms of its engagement with material culture.

Fitt XX – "Paye"

David Coley

> Þen wakned I in þat erber wlonk;
> My hede vpon þat hylle watz layde
> Þeras my perle to grounde strayd.
>
> *Pearl*, 1171-73[1]

> "Fie on't, ah fie, fie! 'Tis an unweeded garden
> That grows to seed; things rank and gross in nature
> Possess it merely."
>
> *Hamlet*, 1.2.135-37[2]

The end of *Pearl* begins with delight. But while the "delyt" informing Fitt XIX oscillated between communion with the divine ("With gret delyt þay glod in fere" [1105]) and the Lamb's concomitant love for his faithful ("The Lombe delyt non lyste to wene" [1141]), the "delyt" of *Pearl*'s last fitt is manifestly human, a longing that the Dreamer registers as a near physical force. Sensual, fleeting, maddening–this is the delight of the body, of the eye and the ear, of the "manez mynde" (1154). No longer the transcendent love of God, "delyt" here modulates into corruption, human flaw, "spot" (12), "wemme" (221), "mot" (843), "masklle" (843)–those stubbornly terrestrial traits that the Dreamer cannot expunge from his always corporeal, always desiring self.

---

[1] All parenthetical references to *Pearl* and the other poems of MS Cotton Nero A. x, art. 3 are from *The Poems of the Pearl Manuscript: Pearl, Cleanness, Patience, Sir Gawain and the Green Knight*, 5th edition, ed. Malcolm Andrew and Ronald Waldron (Exeter: University of Exeter Press, 2007).

[2] William Shakespeare, *Hamlet*, in *The Norton Shakespeare*, ed. Stephen Greenblatt (New York: Norton, 1996), 1659-1759. *Hamlet* will provide an occasional intertext for my reading of Fitt XX, as the grief expressed by Shakespeare's Danish prince aligns in surprising ways with the grief registered by *Pearl*'s Dreamer.

> Delyt me drof in yȝe and ere,
> My manez mynde to maddyng malte;
> Quen I seȝ my frely, I wolde be þere,
> Byȝonde þe water þaȝ ho were walte.
> I þoȝt þat noþyng myȝt me dere
> To fech me bur and take me halte,
> And to start in þe strem schulde non me stere,
> To swymme þe remnaunt, þaȝ I þer swalte.
> Bot of þat munt I watz bitalt;
> When I schulde start in þe strem astraye,
> Out of þat caste I watz bycalt:
> Hit watz not at my Pryncez paye.
> (1153-64)

George Edmondson describes *Pearl* as a poem in which the "work of mourning, whether understood as personal or impersonal, factual or allegorical, exceeds its immediate object." He further shows how the libidinal desire that *Pearl* stages, a desire inscribed into the poem's elliptical form, "forever [circles] around a lost object that can neither be forgotten, because it embodies the trauma of lack, nor directly recuperated, because it also embodies a residue of impossible enjoyment."[3] The wild delight that dissolves the mind of the Dreamer "to maddyng malte" (1156) and drives him over "meruelous merez" (1166) portends both consummation and exile. If *Pearl* is a poem that eddies around the unattainable object at its center, the Dreamer's ill-fated rush into the river separating life from death marks the point at which it swirls the closest–physically, psychologically, geometrically. And yet, even as the synapse between Dreamer and pearl shrinks, so too does the Dreamer's desire increase, eventually and inevitably becoming a madness that exceeds the will of the Lamb and returns the Dreamer to "þat erber wlonk" (1172). In this respect, the madness to which the Dreamer succumbs has much in common with the "woodnes" described by the author of *The Cloud of Unknowing*, a madness arising from the struggle to experience the spiritual world through always-flawed

---

[3] George Edmondson, "*Pearl*: The Shadow of the Object, the Shape of the Law," *Studies in the Age of Chaucer* 26 (2004): 29-63, at 30, 40.

human faculties.⁴ Indeed, as he attempts to cross the river separating the earthly and the divine, charging into it as though it were a physical barrier to be overcome through force of body and will, the Dreamer becomes one of those who "turne theire bodily wittes inwardes to theire body agens the cours of kynde; and streynyn hem, as thei wolde see inwardes with theire bodily ighen, and heren inwardes with theire eren, and so forthe of alle theire wittes, smellen, taasten, and felyn inwardes ... [and] at the laste thei turne here brayne in here hedes."⁵ His is both a human madness and a visionary one; the crisis that it precipitates–the crisis that begins Fitt XX–is thus fundamentally a crisis born of the Dreamer's own "wreched wylle" (56).

Tellingly, that crisis is marked throughout the stanza by the poet's persistent use of the first person singular, particularly the personal and possessive pronouns. "Quen *I* seȝ *my* frely, *I* wolde be þere, / Byȝonde þe water" (1155-56), the Dreamer declares. It is an assertion that not only restates his claim to "*my* lyttel quene" (1147) from the previous stanza but also, and perhaps more problematically, alludes to his first encounter with the Maiden, in which she corrects him precisely for asking "Art þou *my* perle þat *I* haf playned, / Regretted by *myn one* on nyȝte?" (242-43). Such intimations of the Dreamer's possessive, desiring self redouble throughout the first stanza of Fitt XX: *I* wanted to be there, *I* thought nothing would hold *me* back, *I* was called upon; *my* man's mind, *my* dear one, *my* Prince. Paradoxically, as the Dreamer grows more self referential, so too does the poem increasingly insist upon him as the object of a will outside his own, a will that drives him, fetches him, obstructs him. Simultaneously desiring subject and desired object, the Dreamer registers at the moment of his expulsion both his most strenuous resistance to the Divine will and also the radical impossibility of such resistance. He makes his furthest incursion into the otherworld of the dream even as he confirms the inevitability of his return. David Aers refers to this chiasmic moment as one of "regression," a moment that reveals the Dreamer's "defiant readiness to die in his transgression of boundaries so clearly given

---

⁴ *The Cloud of Unknowing*, ed. Patrick J. Gallacher (Kalamazoo, Mich.: Medieval Institute Publications, 1997), 79, l. 1806. I am grateful to Nicola Masciandaro for pointing out this correspondence.
⁵ *The Cloud of Unknowing*, 79, ll. 1809-14.

him."⁶ I want to suggest that it is precisely in the Dreamer's "regression" that *Pearl* shifts its focus from "delyt" (1153) to the link word for Fitt XX, "paye" (1164).

The two words are near synonyms, but as with so many synonyms in *Pearl*, the anxious disjunctures between them are far more revealing than their surface equivalence. Like "delyt," "paye" can signify pleasure, enjoyment, delight.⁷ The poem's first lines, "Perle plesaunte, to princes paye / To clanly clos in glode so clere"(1-2), offer just such an initial sense. In the luminous but artificial clarity of that opening, in the naïve moments before the poem begins systematically to reveal the shifting and contradictory meanings of its central terms, the pearl appears simply as a beautiful gem, a luxury object whose value lies in its rarity and in the sensual pleasure that it offers.⁸ It is delightful to princes for its sheen, its shape, and its bright gold setting.⁹ To be sure, the *Pearl*-poet is not alone in aligning "paye" with the pleasure of the senses. In the *Confessio Amantis*'s sixth book, which treats the sin of gluttony, Gower uses the word to describe the excessively sensual (and overtly sexual) appetite of the debauched Roman emperor Nero: "And thus what thing unto his pay / Was most plesant, he lefte non. / With every lust he was begon, / Wherof the bodi myhte glade, / For he non abstinence made."¹⁰ "Paye," then, offers shades of the "pleyn delit" in which Chaucer's epicurean Franklin spends his days, the same kind of sensual "delyt" that bewitches *Pearl*'s Dreamer and reduces his "manez mynde to maddyng malte" (1153).¹¹

---

⁶ David Aers, "The Self Mourning: Reflections on *Pearl*," *Speculum* 68 (1993): 54-73, at 68.

⁷ *Middle English Dictionary*, ed. Frances McSparran, University of Michigan, <http://quod.lib.umich.edu/m/med/>, s. v. "pai(e" n. 1(a); "dēlīt(e" n.(1) 1(a).

⁸ See Sarah Stanbury, "Introduction," *Pearl*, ed. Sarah Stanbury (Kalamazoo, Mich.: Medieval Institute Publications, 2001), 1-20, especially 3-7.

⁹ In their edition of the poem, Andrew and Waldron subtly encourage just such a terrestrial reading by leaving the word "prynces" uncapitalized. By the end of the poem, when the now richly metaphorized pearl again serves to "pay þe Prince" (1201), the editors capitalize the word, encouraging a reading that recognizes the prince not as a worldly governor but as God.

¹⁰ John Gower, *Confessio Amantis*, 3 vols., ed. Russell Peck (Kalamazoo, Mich.: Medieval Institute Publications, 2000, 2003, 2004), 6.1208-1212.

¹¹ Geoffrey Chaucer, *The Riverside Chaucer*, 3rd edition, ed. Larry D. Benson (Boston: Houghton Mifflin, 1987), I 336-37. Also consider Chaucer's

But while "delyt" frequently collocates with modifiers like "flesshly" and "foul" in Middle English poetry–the "flesshly delit" that Chaucer's Parson describes husbands and wives taking from one another and the more dubious "foul delyt" that Jason seeks from Medea in the *Legend of Good Women*[12]–"paye" more often attends to the divine, referring not only to the pleasures of the flesh but also to those of the soul and spirit, the pleasure and the will of God, "goddes paye." Thus, while the Dreamer's belated lament, "Hit watz not at my Pryncez paye, " may hint at the temporal delight that the word connoted earlier in the poem, "paye" resonates more strongly in the wake of the Dreamer's vision with Piers Plowman's spiritually attuned assertion "Iich haue ybe his foloware al this fourty wynter / And yserued Treuthe sothly ... / And thow I sey hit mysulf, Y serue hym to paye" or with Hoccleve's admonition to "Do þat right is and good, to goddes pay."[13] In other words, when "paye" returns to *Pearl* in its final fitt, it returns thoroughly recontextualized. The "paye" of *Pearl*'s opening line, like the Dreamer's "delyt" from Fitt XIX, is both contained within the "Pryncez paye" of Fitt XX and contested by it. The internal tension that exists within the word, moreover, is close kin to tensions that the poem animates between the earthly garden and the celestial paradise, between the Dreamer and the Maiden, between the spotty quick and the "mascellez" (732) dead. The Dreamer recognizes too late that his human desire and the Prince's divine will are coterminous but not identical, that while "paye" may, on the one hand, encompass "delyt," it also, on the other, entirely transcends it.

Whether or not the Dreamer ultimately sublimates his human desire into God's divine "paye" remains a central and unresolved question, one that occupies an important place in *Pearl* criticism. For some readers, the Dreamer who emerges blinking from the otherworld of his vision "has progressed from the love of the transitory earthly pearl to longing for eternal bliss," becoming in the

---

Manciple's warning, "men han evere a likerous appetit / On lower thyng to parfourne hire delit / Than on hire wyves" (*CT* XI 189-91).

[12] Chaucer, *The Riverside Chaucer*, *CT* X 904, *LGW* 1380.

[13] William Langland, *Piers Plowman: A Parallel-Text Edition of the A, B, C, and Z Versions*, 2 vols., 2nd edition, ed. A. V. C. Schmidt (Kalamazoo, Mich.: Medieval Institute Publications, 2011), C VII 188-92. Thomas Hoccleve, *The Regiment of Princes*, ed. Charles R. Blyth (Kalamazoo, Mich.: Medieval Institute Publications, 1999), 2498-99. The passage from Hoccleve also appears in the

process a figure whose "will is now completely reconciled to the divine Will."[14] Other readers are more equivocal. Jim Rhodes writes movingly of how the Dreamer "can accept the vision of the eternal world, God's world, and its fulfillment. But he also accepts the fact that there is a real world here and a will to enjoy its pleasures and pains, to understand his purpose in the present life, and to comprehend still further his work here."[15] More darkly, Ross Arthur sees the Dreamer as offering little more than "a confession of his own spiritual inadequacies and of the limitations of his understanding of the truth even when it is displayed to him," a confession that is "perfectly congruent with the man who will later seek even eternity as if it were a physical possession."[16] My own sense of the poem hews more closely to these latter readings. If the Dreamer submits to the will of God, to "þat Pryncez paye," his submission is a grudging one, and it brings with it a dubious comfort.

> Hit payed Hym not þat I so flonc
> Ouer meruelous merez, so mad arayd.
> Of raas þaȝ I were rasch and ronk,
> Ȝet rapely þerinne I watz restayed,
> For ryȝt as I sparred vnto þe bonc,
> Þat brathþe out of my drem me brayde.
> Þen wakned I in þat erber wlonk;
> My hede vpon þat hylle watz layde
> Þeras my perle to grounde strayd.

---

[14] Louis Blenkner, "The Theological Structure of 'Pearl,'" *Traditio* 24 (1968): 43-75, at 68. See also Ann Astell, who sees the Dreamer's experience as leading to "a deeper moral and mystical union with God" (121), Sarah Stanbury, who asserts that "in his spiritual vision of the Lamb of Christ, the Dreamer has seen the beatific vision: he has seen God" (42), and Katherine Terrell, who argues that the Dreamer's "new awareness of eternity allows him to revise his conception of the world's significance and place it in proper perspective (446). Astell, *The Song of Songs in the Middle Ages* (Ithaca, NY: Cornell University Press, 1990); Stanbury, "The Body and the City in *Pearl*," *Representations* 48 (1994): 30-47; Terrell, "Rethinking the 'Corse in clot': Cleanness, Filth, and Bodily Decay in *Pearl*," *Studies in Philology* 105 (2008): 429-45.

[15] Jim Rhodes, *Poetry Does Theology: Chaucer, Grosseteste, and the Pearl-Poet* (Notre Dame, Ind.: University of Notre Dame Press, 2001), 144-45.

[16] Ross G. Arthur, "The Day of Judgment is Now: A Johannine Pattern in the Middle English Pearl," *American Benedictine Review* 38 (1987): 227-42, at 240.

> I raxled and fel in gret affray,
> And, sykyng, to myself I sayd:
> 'Now al be to þat Pryncez paye.'
> (1165-76)

The second stanza contains both the critical moment when the Dreamer awakes from his vision and, perhaps more important, his first verbal utterance outside of it. For readers who see the Dreamer as fundamentally transformed by his experience, this single line of dialogue (or monologue, really, since the Dreamer is alone within the garden) is of central importance. After all, the Dreamer claims to commend "all" to the pleasure of God, including, we must assume, the very pearl that, only moments earlier, he attempted to reach in spite of the Lamb's opposing will. If this declaration stands at face value–if, in other words, we read the Dreamer's ambiguous "sykyng" as a prayerful resignation to God rather than an expression of exasperation or defeat[17]–the Dreamer's abrupt exile from both the New Jerusalem and the redeemed pearl seems to have performed in a single stroke what the Maiden's "gentyl sawez" (278) never managed, impressing a divine perspective upon an all-too-human loss and allowing the Dreamer to surrender his grief to the irresistible (if unfathomable) will of God. The Dreamer is brought into harmony with the divine at precisely the moment he is torn away from it; he is snapped into an appropriately submissive relationship with God with the same suddenness and finality that he finds himself cast out of God's paradisiac otherworld.

Such a sanguine resolution to *Pearl*'s central spiritual crisis is surely, as another grief-stricken dreamer might put it, "a consummation devoutly to be wished."[18] Nonetheless, it is a consummation that can't help but seem, if not cursory, then at least

---

[17] Such a reading might gather support from *Sir Gawain and the Green Knight*, where Gawain sighs to himself before uttering the prayer for deliverance that precipitates the appearance of the Castle of Hautdesert: "And þerfore *sykyng* he sayde: 'I beseche Þe, Lorde, / And Mary, þat is myldest moder so dere, / Of sum herber þer heȝly I myȝt here masse / And Þy matynez tomorne, mekely I ask, / And þerto prestly I pray my Pater and Aue / And Crede'" (753-58). Curiously, Gawain's request for an "herber" where he might he hear mass clearly bears close affinities to the concluding moments of *Pearl*, where the Dreamer returns to his own "erber wlonk" before subsequently attending mass and receiving the Eucharist.

[18] Shakespeare, *Hamlet*, 3.1.65-66.

suspiciously sudden in the face of the Dreamer's continued spiritual uncertainty. Like the Dreamer's equivocal sigh, which resists stable interpretation at the very moment the Dreamer most seeks resolution, the language that marks the transition from visionary sleep to mundane wakefulness hums with a sense of uncertainty and struggle. In the last few moments of his dream, the Dreamer flings ["flonc" (1165)] himself impetuously into the water separating him from the Maiden, springing ["sparred" (1169)] toward the bank in a frenzy of desire only to be "restayed" (1168) by the Lamb like an impetuous child.[19] Upon waking, the Dreamer continues in a state of marked consternation and dismay ["gret affray" (1174)], and his reemergence at the very spot where "*my* perle to grounde strayd" can't help but recall both the possessive language of the previous stanza and the penetrating cry of loss from the poem's opening fitt: "Allas! I leste hyr in on erbere; / Þurȝ gresse to grounde hit from me yot" (9-10). Indeed, looking ahead the poem's final moments, when the Dreamer commends his redeemed daughter to God with "Krystez dere blessyng and *myn*" (1208), the indelible language of possession and desire—the Dreamer insists upon not only Christ's blessing but *his* as well—persists even to the final lines of the poem, revealing a powerful individual will that always resists being sublimated into the will of God. Such contexts complicate the Dreamer's easy assertion "Now al be to þat Pryncez paye" (1176), and they remind us that for all of its investment in God's perfect divine love, *Pearl* is equally invested in an imperfect human love, a spotty, hungry, joyous, tangled emotion that even the recompense of salvation does not entirely displace.

I don't mean by this to suggest that the Dreamer is untouched by his vision; his experience affects him in important, even fundamental ways. I simply want to propose that the terrestrial aftermath of his dream, unlike the crystalline world that he temporarily inhabits during his vision, is necessarily a spotty place,

---

[19] On the Dreamer's childishness: the word "restayed" appears earlier in *Pearl* when the Maiden, drawing from the Gospel of Luke, describes how the disciples of Christ attempted to prevent children from approaching him: "For happe and hele þat fro Hym ȝede / To touch her chylder þay fayr Hym prayed. / His dessypelez with blame 'Let be!' hym bede / And wyth her resounez ful fele restayed" (713-6). Christ, of course, tells his disciples, "Do way, let chylder vnto Me tyȝt; / To suche is heuenryche arayed" (717), or "Suffer children to come to me, and forbid them not: for such is the kingdom of God" (Luke 18:16, Douay-Rheims version)

still interwoven with threads of grief, love, jealousy, desire. In such a world, the Dreamer's sigh strikes a significantly less resigned note. Within the enclosed world of the earthly garden, the Dreamer does not simply accept the Lamb's promise of life eternal as a balm for, to quote again Prince Hamlet, "the heartache and the thousand natural shocks that flesh is heir to," nor does he does blithely accept God's will as a substitute for his own bitter grief.[20] Rather, he accepts God's will within the context of that grief, a mingling of human loss and divine grace that remains as volatile at line 1200 as it did at line 12. "I raxled and fel in gret affray," the Dreamer declares, giving voice to his continued suffering, "*And*, sykyng, to myself I sayd: / 'Now al be to þat Pryncez paye'" (1174-76). The key word in these lines is "and." As with the poem's recursive structure and hypermetaphorical lexicon, the acceptance of loss toward which *Pearl* moves is an additive one, building upon but never entirely replacing the Dreamer's initial loss.[21]

The Dreamer's unfinished (and perhaps unfinishable) struggle to align his desire with God's continues to find expression in the fitt's link word, for even as "paye" speaks strongly to the divine will, it also speaks to another kind of indomitable will, one that is suggestive for both the spiritual and the temporal realms. As Howard Schless has shown, the phrase "Pryncez paye," evokes the legal maxim "quod principi placet legis habet vigorem [the prince's pleasure has the force of law]," an aphorism originating in the Roman *Corpus juris civilis*, codified by Justinian I in the sixth century and rediscovered

---

[20] Shakespeare, *Hamlet*, 3.1.64-65.

[21] In his facing-page translation of the works of the *Pearl*-poet, Casey Finch makes a telling substitution at just this point in the poem when he renders the lines "I raxled and fel in gret affray, / *And*, sykyng, to myself I sayd: / 'Now al be to þat Pryncez paye'" as "My mind was marred with agonies, / *But* sighing to myself I prayed: / 'Let be whatever that Prince please!'" Finch's substitution of "but" for "and" underscores the challenge that the poem presents to its readers: How can human suffering coexist with the love of a benevolent God? Finch's "but" allows the Dreamer to relinquish the former at the moment he fully accepts the latter; however the "and" of the original Middle English offers no such easy resolution, insisting on the fact that both of these seemingly contradictory impulses still exist within the poem. See *The Complete Works of the Pearl Poet*, trans. Casey Finch, ed. Malcolm Andrew, Ronald Waldron, and Clifford Peterson (Berkeley: University of California Press, 1993), 99.

in England in the thirteenth.[22] The presence of this legal commonplace within *Pearl*'s careful series of link words "at once establishes the poem's primary confrontations ... between absolutist and comparative, between New and Old, between divine and human, law."[23] It also carries through a distinctly legalistic discourse within the poem, one that is particularly pronounced in Fitts VI and XII. In the former, which is organized around the word "deme," the Pearl Maiden upbraids her earthly father for proposing to stay with her in the Heavenly City, reminding him both, "Þou most abyde þat He [God] schal deme" (348) and "marre oþer madde, morne and myþe, / Al lys in Hym to dyȝt and deme" (359-60). The verb "demen," like all of the poem's link words, is richly layered, but its primary senses relate to the law: "to judge, to sentence, to condemn, to rule, to ordain."[24] The word "ryȝt," which structures the latter fitt, carries similar connotations, signifying not only that which is morally right but also a legal right, a legal judgment, the law of the land.[25]

When the Maiden argues in Fitt XII that "Þe innocent is ay saf by ryȝt" (720) then, she invokes a divine law that is anathema to the Dreamer's earthbound understanding, one in which "more and lasse" (600) are the same thing, in which 144,000 brides occupy their kingdom with "supplantorez none" (440), and in which a maiden "ful ȝong and tender of age" (412) can be "quen mad on þe fyrst day" (486). The "ryȝt" to which the Maiden appeals is, I would suggest, the same "ryȝt" implicated in the "Pryncez paye" of Fitt XX, one that proposes grace as the foundation of the Lamb's divine law. It is a grace, as *Pearl* reminds us again and again, that operates independent of human logic, that transcends the comparatively localized, culturally determined, and necessarily flawed underpinnings of human law. "Across the stream," as Schless again suggests, "*grace* and *ryght* are one; but for the Dreamer, whose humanity is defined ... by the comparative..., the absolutist doctrine of 'quod principi placet' seems not just a change in degree but a change in kind, a change that ... can only come about through an act

---

[22] From *Fleta*, quoted in Howard H. Schless, "*Pearl*'s 'Princes Paye' and the Law," *Chaucer Review* 24 (1989): 183-85, at 184.
[23] Schless, "Princes Paye," 184.
[24] *MED*, s. v. "dēmen" v., 1(a), 2(a), 3(a, d), 4b, 8(a).
[25] *MED*, s. v. "right" n., 1(a), 2(a), 3(a), 4(a), 5(a).

of grace."²⁶ Insofar as it speaks to the simmering tension between grace and law, the implicit legal valences of "paye" link the Dreamer's unslaked desire for his lost pearl to the poem's elegiac mode, even as they align the Dreamer's uneasy submission to God with *Pearl*'s broader allegorical meditation on Christian soteriology.

Considering the manifold semantic frames developed in *Pearl*, and particularly considering how it develops the legal overtones of both "ryȝt " and "deme," the implied relationship between "paye" and the *Corpus juris civilis* is not wholly unexpected. More subtle is the potential for "paye" to operate in the poem as a bilingual pun, a homonym for the Anglo-Norman "pais," meaning "country" or "land."²⁷ When the Dreamer commends the pearl to the pleasure of the Prince, is he also surrendering her to the land on the far side of the river, to Hamlet's "undiscovered country from whose bourn no traveller returns?"²⁸ Such a secondary meaning comports with the Dreamer's grudging acceptance of his loss, and it affirms the Pearl Maiden's apotheosis as one of "þe meyny þat is withoute mote" (960), the spotless denizens of the New Jerusalem. Clearly, the potential for such bilingual play readily exists in the poem. As a courtly maker writing for an upper class patron–or even, following the groundbreaking work of John Bowers and Michael Bennett, a poet operating within the ambit of Richard II's Royal court²⁹–the *Pearl*-poet could have expected his readers to be comfortable with Anglo-French. Moreover, he occasionally reveals his own knowledge of French and its poetic forms in the other poems of the *Pearl* manuscript, alluding to "Clopyngnel in þe compas of his clene Rose" (*Cl.* 1057) in *Cleanness* and giving Bertilak's castle in *Sir Gawain*

---

²⁶ Schless, "Princes Paye," 184.
²⁷ *Anglo-Norman Dictionary Online*, ed. David Trotter, University of Aberystwyth, <http://www.anglo-norman.net/>, s. v. "pais" n., 1. I am grateful to Geoffrey Morrison for the thought-provoking seminar conversations that helped lead to this insight.
²⁸ Shakespeare, *Hamlet*, 3.1.81-82.
²⁹ See John Bowers, *The Politics of Pearl: Court Poetry in the Age of Richard II* (Cambridge: D. S. Brewer, 2001); Michael J. Bennett, "Sir Gawain and the Green Knight and the Literary Achievement of the North-West Midlands," *Journal of Medieval History* 5 (1979): 63-89, and "The Historical Background," in *A Companion to the Gawain-Poet*, ed. Derek Brewer and Jonathan Gibson (Cambridge: D. S. Brewer, 1997), 71-90.

and the Green Knight the Francophone name "Hautdesert" (*SGGK* 2445), a double pun on "noble wasteland" and "high merit."[30]

It is precisely from the Prince's *pais*–the Prince's "fayre regioun" (1178)–that the Dreamer finds himself "outfleme" (1177) in *Pearl*'s final fitt. Following both the beatific vision of the Lamb and the final glimpse of the Maiden herself, the expulsion pains him, compounding the loss of his pearl with the loss of paradise itself.

> Me payed ful ille to be outfleme
> So sodenly of þat fayre regioun,
> For alle þo syʒtez so quyke and queme.
> A longeyng heuy me strok in swone,
> And rewfully þenne I con to reme:
> 'O perle,' quoþ I, 'of rych renoun,
> So watz hit me dere þat þou con deme
> In þys veray avysyoun!
> If hit be ueray and soth sermoun
> Þat þou so strykez in garlande gay,
> So wel is me in þys doel-doungoun
> Þat þou art to þat Prynsez paye.'
> (1177-88)

The abruptness of the Dreamer's exile from the jewel box of his vision, the jarring return to the garden and to the "body on balke," overwhelms the fitt's third stanza. The Dreamer is outcast "sodenly" (1178), and the longing that comes to him in the moment of waking "strok in swone" (1180). Even the memories that he maintains of the vision itself are described in clipped and harried terms: the sights of the otherworld "so quyke and queme" (1179), the Maiden who "strykez in garlande gay" (1186). Here, rendered almost onomatopoetically, is the shock of return, the eyelids snapping open and the sharp intake of breath, the body reanimated into clothes redolent with sweat and still heavy with sleep.

What does it mean to awake or, in the case of *Pearl*, to be awakened? "Awak!" cries the golden eagle in Chaucer's *House of*

---

[30] *ANDO*, s.v. "halt" (variants "haut," "haute") adv. 1 ("high, high up"), 3 ("nobly, in a venerable way, aristocratically); "desert," n. ("desert, barren, wilderness"); "deserte," n. 1 ("merit, meritorious conduct"), 2 ("reward"). See also Peter J. Lucas, "Hautdesert in *Sir Gawain and the Green Knight*," *Neophilologus* 70 (1986): 319-20.

Fame, and the sudden exhortation leaves poor Geffrey, still within the strange world of his dream, trembling in the bird's "grymme pawes stronge" and watching the ground recede beneath him.[31] In *Piers Plowman*, Will becomes wakeful at the moment that Conscience recommits himself to "gradde aftur grace."[32] In a much later work, Ebenezer Scrooge awakens once to the terrible sound of Marley's shade clattering up from the cellar in Dickens's *A Christmas Carol* and again, more fundamentally, when the Ghost of Christmas Yet To Come gestures toward his neglected headstone.[33] Like these admittedly disparate dream visions, *Pearl* invests the moment of waking with the expectation of transformation, and even if *Pearl*'s Dreamer does not entirely abandon his grief with the promise of the beatific vision—he is no Scrooge, it seems—the poem nonetheless limns the vision's transformative potential. Crucially, what *Pearl* seems to propose at the Dreamer's awakening is not so much a displacement of the Dreamer's desire but a change in its object, a longing not for the return of the pearl but rather a wish that she be fulfilled within "þat Prynsez paye," within His country, His desire, His will, His pleasure. If she is well, the Dreamer asserts, so too is he in the "doel-doungoun" (1186) of earthly life, the dungeon of sorrow that his vision has made of "þat erber wlonk" (1171).[34] It is a painful irony that any consolation the Dreamer takes in his daughter's redemption also brings with it an intensified recognition of the ongoing travails of his own existence. The burden of loss, the poem suggests, must be carried always by the living. It is not for the apotheosized Maiden to relieve the suffering of her earthly father, nor is it for the Edenic otherworld of the Dreamer's vision to offer permanent repose to one still trudging through the mortal world. The Dreamer, it seems, must haul his own pail of water all the way to the very end.

If it contains the potential for transformation, the moment of waking is also riddled with a lingering uncertainty, an uncertainty that has a broad tradition within the Dream Vision genre. Chaucer's

---

[31] Chaucer, *The Riverside Chaucer*, HF 556, 541.

[32] Langland, *Piers Plowman*, C XXII 387.

[33] Charles Dickens, *A Christmas Carol*, ed. Stanley Appelbaum (New York: Dover, 1991), 62.

[34] Even here, Hamlet stalks the margins of *Pearl* in his inky cloak, telling Rosencrantz and Guildenstern that Denmark is a goodly prison, "in which there are many confines, wards, and dungeons" (2.2.241-42).

narrator Geffrey opens *The House of Fame* with an anxious 58-line ramble expressing his continuing doubt over the veracity of his (or any) vision–"God turne us every drem to goode!"[35]–while the irregular rhythms of waking and dreaming that structure *Piers Plowman* make any possibility of resolution seem tentative at best. And of course Scrooge tries to dismiss Marley's ghost as "a fragment of an underdone potato" before he is finally convinced by the gruesome rattling of its heavy chain.[36] In *Pearl*, even as the poem nears its end, the vision of the celestial otherworld that the Dreamer once claimed "bylde in me blys, abated my balez, / Fordidden my stresse, dystryed my painez" (123-24) now serves to diminish the *hortus amoenus* to a prison stew. A resolution seems no nearer at hand.

The Dreamer registers the uncertainty of awakening in his own words, and his caveat in his apostrophe to the pearl, "*If* hit be ueray and soth" (1185), casts his acceptance of God's "paye" in a decidedly conditional light. Ironically, in the preceding line, the Dreamer seems to affirm the truth value of the dream, referring to it as "þys veray avysyoun" (1184), this true vision. Does his subsequent "if," then, suggest that the Maiden herself may be capable of falsehood, even among the redeemed souls of the New Jerusalem? Does it speak to a continued spiritual crisis, a continued uncertainty in the face of loss? Or does the "veray" in the deictic "þys veray avysyoun" simply act as an intensifier – this very vision rather than this true one? Edmondson regards *Pearl* as a work that both recognizes and explores "the troubled intersection of mourning and signification" (32), a poem moreover whose "fascination with language cannot be treated separately from the question of the Dreamer's subjectivity."[37] I would propose that the tour-de-force linguistic play that largely defines the poem is inseparable from the doubt and uncertainty that the Dreamer continues to express, and *vice versa*. The Dreamer can no more cease to doubt and to desire in the wake of his vivid dream than *Pearl* can cease to ply its continually changing metaphors and puns. The Dreamer, fallen as are all those on this side of "þat foysoun flode" (1058), inherits and inhabits a language that is likewise fallen. Thus, even as the poem struggles for transcendence it also circles back toward the signal imperfection–the spot–of its

---

[35] Chaucer, *The Riverside Chaucer, HF* 1.
[36] Dickens, *Christmas Carol*, 12.
[37] Edmondson, "Shadow of the Object," 31, 33.

first stanza, an ouroboros down to its circular form and its looping semantics.

Does the Prince's "paye / pais," then, begin to suggest the "spot," the location or place, of the poem's very first fitt?[38] Does "paye" move toward the idea of Fitt I's "spot," just as Fitt XIX's "delyt" moved toward the idea of "paye" only a few stanzas earlier?

> To þat Pryncez paye hade I ay bente,
> And ȝerned no more þen watz me geuen,
> And halden me þer in trwe entent,
> As þe perle me prayed þat watz so þryuen,
> As helde, drawen to Goddez present,
> To mo of His mysterys I hade ben dryuen.
> Bot ay wolde man of happe more hente
> Þen moȝte by ryȝt vpon hem clyuen;
> Þerfore my joye watz sone toriuen,
> And I kaste of kythez þat lastez aye.
> Lorde, mad hit arn þat agayn Þe stryuen,
> Oþer proferen Þe oȝt agayn Þy paye.
> (1189-1200)

The first half of *Pearl*'s penultimate stanza doesn't seem to foreground "paye" as "pais," though I will argue that the sense does return by the poem's end. The link word here seems clearly to refer to the will of the Prince, and if the bilingual pun on country is present it is only lingering in the background. But even if "paye" doesn't at this moment tend toward "spot" in its sense of "location" or "space," the stanza itself may still gesture toward another primary sense of "spot," as spiritual flaw or blemish. To be sure, what the Dreamer purports to describe in these lines is precisely the flaw that precipitated his ejection from the heavenly city, the "spot" or "weme" that prevented him from experiencing more of God's mysteries. That "spot," the Dreamer claims, that flaw, is that he "ȝerned" more that he was "geuen" (1190). He desired more than he was supposed to.

There can be little doubt that the desire of the Dreamer, or at least a desire within the Dreamer running counter to God's "paye," caused him to be thrust out of the world of his dream. We see such

---

[38] For spot as both "flaw" and "location," see Sylvia Tomasch, "A Pearl Punnology," *Journal of English and Germanic Philology* 88 (1989): 1-20.

desire in him throughout the poem, from his mad dash across the river, to his longing to see the fine "wonez in castel-wal" (917) where he supposes that the Maiden must live, to his consternation that the Maiden has received "to dere a date" (492) for the labor of her short life, to the "longeyng" (244) for the pearl that leaves him "a joylez jueler" (252), to the increasing desire that he registers upon his first glimpse of the paradise of his vision. "Euer me longed ay more and more" (144), a key phrase from Fitt III, utterly defines, even circumscribes the Dreamer throughout the poem. And so, on the one hand, the admission that the Dreamer desired "more þen watz me geuen" (1190) makes perfect sense. But on the other hand, there is something that rings hollow in his easy recognition of his toxic desire, wreathed as it is by still more longing, still more yearning. "If only I had wanted less," the Dreamer moans, "I would have been given more." Particularly in view of the generic expectations of transformation that the dream vision invites, the irony of this final assertion should not be lost on the reader.[39] Even if it slides from the gem to the Maiden to the heavenly city to the mysteries of the Lamb (all of which, within the accretive semantic logic of the poem, register linguistically as the same thing), the desire of the Dreamer remains, excessive, stubborn, and manifestly human.

David Aers, whose psychoanalytically tinged reading of *Pearl* remains an important critical touchstone, is worth quoting at length on this subtle disjunction in the poem's final fitt.

> The narrator maintains that visionary joy and knowledge of God's mysteries was removed from him because he, like humankind in general, coveted more happiness than he was entitled or able to have. However correct this generalization about our inability to accept limits to pleasure, it is a little off the mark as a description of his own motivation as we have been shown it .... This is not a matter of boundaries or degrees on some kind of ladder of perfection. It is rather a question concerning the form of memory and kind of desire.[40]

---

[39] Blenkner offers evidence of such a generic expectation, noting that "the psychic change wrought in the Dreamer is of central importance, and thus *Pearl* is truly an 'interior drama'" ("Theological Structure" 44).

[40] Aers, "The Self Mourning," 69.

Within the broader context of the poem, the question that Aers's analysis implies is clear: does the Dreamer's failure to grasp "mo of His mysterys" reflect a failure to curb his desire, or does it reflect a failure to direct his desire toward a more appropriate object, toward the Lamb rather than toward "*my* lyttel quene" (1147)? The question necessarily informs our understanding of the Dreamer and our sense of his transformation. If the Dreamer's "spot" is, after all, predicated on an overweening love for the lost pearl / Maiden / daughter, then the conclusion of the poem shows the Dreamer beginning to bend to the "paye" of God, shifting his desire from a longing for the riches he one had on earth to a longing for the eternal riches glittering beyond the river of life. Such a shift also echoes the Maiden's own admonition from earlier in the poem, "'Her were a forser for þe, in faye, / If þou were a gentyl jueler. // 'Bot, jueler gente, if þou schal lose / Þy joy for a gemme, þat þe watz lef, / Me þynk þe put in a mad porpose, / And busyez þe aboute a raysoun bref'" (263-68). And the Dreamer will, before the stanza's end, echo the Maiden by referring to himself as "mad" for striving against the "paye" of the Prince, reinforcing her initial diagnosis and further suggesting that perhaps, as one optimistic critic puts it, she "has not instructed in vain."[41]

But if the flaw within the Dreamer is desire itself rather than desire's object, then his transformation is more uncertain. Indeed, the desire to know "mo of [God's] mysterys" seems as powerful for the Dreamer at the end of the poem as his desire for the pearl was at its beginning, and his response to being denied that knowledge– "my joye watz sone toriuen" (1197)–is all but identical to his response to losing the pearl, "I haf ben a joylez jueler" (252). Is a desire to know more of God's mysteries (what a more comic figure might refer to as "Goddes pryvetee"[42]) more licit than a desire for the pearl itself? R. A. Shoaf suggests that within *Pearl* "the desire in man for God is endless, always therefore potentially transgressive, even in its very goodness, and thus it must be chastened by the will to re-frain."[43] Desire is desire; longing is longing; grief over one loss

---

[41] Blenkner, "Theological Structure," 68.

[42] Chaucer, *The Riverside Chaucer, CT* I 3454. The phrase, of course, comes from John the carpenter in *The Miller's Tale,* and his considered opinion that "Men sholde nat knowe of Goddes pryvetee" serves as an interesting counter to the sudden theological longing of *Pearl*'s Dreamer.

[43] R. A. Shoaf, "*Purgatorio* and *Pearl*: Transgression and Transcendence," *Texas Studies in Literature and Language* 32 (1990): 152-68, at 160.

is grief over another. The flaw that marks the Dreamer, the flaw that both prevents him from crossing into the New Jerusalem and precisely makes him human, is not the object of his desire but desire itself. Indeed, *Pearl* provides for this truth of humankind's fallen condition as early as Fitt III, in its use of the linking phrase "more and more" (132) to suggest how the Dreamer both succumbs to the Edenic world of his dream and also recognizes the "mayden of menske" (162) as his lost pearl. It is, however, a truth that the Dreamer himself seems only belatedly to recognize: "Bot ay wolde man of happe more hente / Þen moȝte by ryȝt vpon hem clyuen" (1195-96).

The insatiability of human desire is also a truth, I would argue, that is inscribed in the idiosyncratic poetics of *Pearl*, in its slippery puns and repetitions, its pregnant synonyms and unstable metaphors, its structure and carefully concatenated link words. Indeed, we might ask, what does it mean in *Pearl* to say that the Dreamer desires the pearl? In the poem's opening lines, the pearl is a precious stone "oute of oryent" (3) enclosed in a golden setting, one that slips from the Dreamer's grasp and is lost within a garden. Thus, the Dreamer can be said to desire that valuable jewel. Later, described in terms evoking a ethos of courtly love, the pearl becomes a woman, perhaps a lover, for whom the Dreamer claims to "dewyne, fordolked of luf-daungere" (11); later still, after the pearl has appeared in the vision as both a "faunt" (161) and a "mayden of menske, ful debonere" (162), the Dreamer states that she was nearer to him than aunt or niece (233) and "lyfed not two ȝer in oure þede" (483), thus intimating that that the pearl is his infant daughter. The Dreamer desires these earthly beings as well. But as the poem continues, the pearl takes on spiritual valences. It is the "mascellez" (732) Pearl of Price from the Gospel of Matthew, for which the jeweler "solde alle hys goud, boþe wolen and lynne, / To bye" (731-32).[44] It is the fleece of the Jerusalem Lamb, which "hade neuer pechche / Of oþer huee but quyt jolyf / Þat mot ne masklle moȝt on streche, / For wolle quyte so ronk and ryf" (841-44). It is the Lamb himself, described by the Dreamer as "þat gay Juelle" (1124). And it will be, in the poem's very final line, the redeemed human soul, transcendent and at home in the "paye" of the prince. It is, crucially,

---

[44] "Again the kingdom of heaven is like to a merchant seeking good pearls. Who when he had found one pearl of great price, went his way, and sold all that he had, and bought it." Matt 13:45-46, Douay-Rheims version.

all of these things severally and all of them at all times, daughter and Lamb, lover and jeweler, soul and stone.[45] The metaphorical equivalence upon which the poem insists, an equivalence that is both embedded within its nearly flawless poetic form and fundamental to the motion of its concatenating link words, means that the Dreamer's longing for one is tantamount to the Dreamer's longing for another. Desire for the pearl is desire for the pearl. And that desire, as desire, is an innate part of the human condition, even a defining part of it. To push things even further, we might say that desire is conterminous with living in *Pearl*. To cross the river of life and join the Lamb and "His meyny" is to die on earth. The desire that sends the Dreamer flailing into the river and ultimately prevents him from dwelling forever among those "kythez þat lastez aye" (1998) is, thus, not only transgressive but possibly suicidal. In this respect at the very least, the Dreamer's desire can not be to the "paye" of the Prince.[46]

The dogged humanity of the Dreamer and the impossibility of his struggle make his assertion in the next stanza, the poem's last, particularly puzzling:

> To pay þe Prince oþer sete saȝte
> Hit is ful eþe to þe god Krystyin;
> For I haf founden Hym, boþe day and naȝte,
> A God, a Lorde, a frende ful fyin.
> Ouer þis hyul þis lote I laȝte,
> For pyty of my perle enclyin,
> And syþen to God I hit bytaȝte,
> In Krystez dere blessyng and myn,
> Þat in þe forme of bred and wyn
> Þe preste vus schewez vch a daye.

---

[45] In her introduction to the poem, Sarah Stanbury emphasizes the simultaneity of the pearl's many metaphorical valences within the poem: "The economy of metaphor, or rather its hyper-economy, lies in its uncanny ability to express both equivalence and multiplicity.... The pearl *is* a gem, *is* a two-year old child, *is* a beautiful young woman, *is* the immortal soul, *is* the heavenly city–as well as a collective of the properties that inhere to each term singly."

[46] "O that this too too solid flesh would melt, / Thaw, and resolve itself into a dew, / Or that the Everlasting had not fixed / his canon 'gainst self-slaughter! O God, O God, / How weary, stale, flat, and unprofitable / Seem to me all the uses of this world!" (*Hamlet* 1.2.129-34)

> He gef vus to be His homly hyne
> Ande precious perlez vnto His pay.
> (1201-12)

The word "eþe," often glossed as "easy" but also signifying "comforting" and "agreeable," seems a painfully ironic choice.[47] The Dreamer's own struggle to "pay þe Prince" has proven to be anything but easy, and his exile from God's eternal kingdom suggests that he has, in fact, failed on some level to do so. Moreover, the comfort that the Dreamer receives from the divine is necessarily a cold one, concluding not with a reunion with his beloved pearl but rather with the continued deferral of his desire, even to the point of his own death. Aers calls the Dreamer's assertion "theologically superficial and psychologically superficial"; Stanbury says that it "fails to be fully convincing" since the Dreamer "still seems to believe that he could have stayed in the visionary realm [and is] still unwilling to accept that the condition of living in the world is a condition of exile"; and J. J. Anderson, more simply if no less emphatically, asserts that "the difficulty in taking this statement at face value is that it makes it all sound *too* easy."[48] Similarly unconvincing, I would add, is the progression of epithets that the Dreamer uses to describe the Godhead: "A God, a Lorde, a frende ful fyin." Certainly we see the Lamb as God, and so too, in the strenuous demands that he places upon the Dreamer, do we se him as a lord; however, the phrase "a friend ful fyin"–a true friend[49]–

---

[47] The editions of Andrew and Waldron and Stanbury both gloss the word as "easy" (Andrew and Waldron 110 n. 1201-02; Stanbury 68, gl. 1202). Marie Borroff translates the lines, "To content that Prince and well agree, / Good Christians can with ease incline" (Marie Borroff, *The Gawain Poet: Complete Works* [New York: Norton, 2011], 159).

[48] Aers, "The Self Mourning," 70; Sarah Stanbury, *Seeing the* Gawain-*Poet: Description and the Act of Perception* (Philadelphia: University of Pennsylvania Press, 1991), 32; J. J. Anderson, *Language and Imagination in the* Gawain-*Poems* (Manchester, Eng.: Manchester University Press, 2005), 76. For a counter-opinion, see Jennifer Garrison, "Liturgy and Loss: *Pearl* and the Ritual Reform of the Aristocratic Subject," *Chaucer Review* 44 (2010): 294-323.

[49] I read "fyin" here in the following sense offered by the *MED* s.v. "fīn" adj.: "pure, true, genuine, perfect; faithful; constant, unwavering" (6) The word also links in important ways to other key terms in *Pearl*, as it can mean "Free

stands out here both for the casual relationship it presupposes between Dreamer and God and for the apparent gulf between the epithet "friend" and the figure that the Dreamer has alternately resisted, denied, disobeyed, and raged against over the course of his visionary experience. Even if the vision is granted by God in friendship, even if the intent of the vision is ultimately to instruct and to succor, the summation that the Dreamer provides of both the vision and of God misaligns with his account of his experience in alarmingly underwhelming ways.

Overshadowed by the Dreamer's dubious consideration of how easy it is to accede to God's will is a more subtle but no less important shift in the fitt's link word, which appears for the first time, and powerfully, as an infinitive: "To pay þe Prince" (1201). Earlier in the fitt, the word most frequently appeared as a noun (1164, 1177, 1188, 1189, 1200), just as it did in the poem's opening line. Where "paye" does appear as a verb in Fitt XX, the force of the word is somewhat diminished by the poet's passive construction: "Hit payed Hym not" (1164) and "Me payed full ille" (1177). The infinitive resounds much more strongly, and while its primary sense may still be "to please" (just as the primary sense of the noun is "pleasure") an additional sense emerges clearly: "to pay" as "to render in payment, to pay, to recompense."[50] To pay the Prince is not simply to please him but, quite literally, to make a payment to him. Such a meaning recalls the parable of the Pearl of Price and thus *Pearl*'s soteriological program; however, the reference to payment also reasserts the temporal, social, and mercantile aspects that the poem develops for the Dreamer, aspects grounded in a desire for worldly riches that is anathema to the heavenly economics articulated by the Maiden. A jeweler by trade, the Dreamer sells his wares to customers who are almost certainly his social superiors, mostly members of the aristocracy and the upper reaches of the ecclesiastical hierarchy.[51] He is a capitalist, and his very vocation is rooted in payment for services rendered, not in the Lamb's heavenly

---

of impurities or blemishes" (3.a), as well as "rich, valuable, precious, costly" (1).

[50] *MED* s. v. "paien" v. (3-6).

[51] Heler Barr examines the implications of the Dreamer's identity as a Jeweler in "*Pearl*–or 'The Jeweller's Tale,'" *Medium Ævum* 69 (2000): 59–79. Also useful in this regard is Felicity Riddy, "Jewels in *Pearl*," in *A Companion to the Gawain-Poet*, eds. Derek Brewer and Jonathan Gibson (Cambridge, Eng.: D. S. Brewer, 1997), 143-55.

grace. By subtly reasserting the mercantile exchange that exists at the very core of the Dreamer's earthly identity, the link word "paye" vexes any clear and comfortable sense that *Pearl* might offer of the Dreamer's transformation into a "god Krystyin," insisting instead that his earthly identity and his newfound desire for union with the Lamb continue to mingle with an uneasy friction. The Dreamer is not Saint Francis of Assisi, selling all he has to live a life of service to God. His claim on the Pearl of Price remains uncertain, as does his ability to render the Prince his due, his pleasure, his pay.

It is out of this friction that the poem makes its final, and arguably most unexpected turn. As the Dreamer explicitly looks away from the transcendent and visionary realm of his dream, he specifically locates "liturgical devotion to Christ in the Eucharist [as] the solution to his problems of grief and longing."[52] For some readers, the Dreamer's assertion of the primacy of the Eucharist rings as hollow as the claim that it is "ful eþe" (1202) for a good Christian to please God: John Bowers in particular calls the concluding reference a "gratuitous assertion of the Real Presence" and implies that the *Pearl*-poet may have included it as a salve for orthodox-minded readers in the time of Wycliffism.[53] Jennifer Garrison, countering this view, argues instead that "Eucharistic devotion provides a way for [the Dreamer] to practice emotional and spiritual control," the very control that he so pointedly lacked in his vision.[54] The Eucharist thus becomes not an endpoint but rather part of a process toward becoming "þe god Krystyin" (1202) who pays the Prince with ease, the good Christian that the Dreamer still strives to become. Such a reading has the great advantage of comporting with *Pearl* as a poem more invested in seeking resolution than in resolution itself, a poem that recognizes the inevitability of human desire even as it also recognizes desire's transgressive potential. I want to add to Garrison's ecclesiastically inflected reading by proposing that the sacrament of the Eucharist performs not just important soteriological work for the Dreamer at the poem's end but also important social work. Indeed, inasmuch as the Sacrament of the Altar is fundamental for the individual "god Krystyin," it is still more fundamental as "an essential action within the Church which

---

[52] Garrison, "Liturgy and Loss," 294.
[53] John Bowers, *The Politics of* Pearl: *Court Poetry in the Age of Richard II* (Cambridge, Eng.: D. S. Brewer, 2001), 53.
[54] Garrison, "Liturgy and Loss," 320.

constantly reproduces the Church" and which thus binds together the Christian community itself.[55] By concluding with the Dreamer participating in the communal sacrament of the Eucharist rather than continuing to praise God in the solitude of the garden, *Pearl* both suggests his reintegration into the living (if spotted) community of the faithful and foreshadows a future for him among the spotless and eternal "meyny" (1127) of the Lamb.

The image of the Dreamer receiving "Krystez dere blessyng ... in þe forme of bred and wyn" (1208-09) thus leads naturally to the poem's concluding two lines: "He gef vus to be His homly hyne / Ande precious perlez vnto His pay" (1211-12). It also allows for the fitt's link word to manifest, and all at once, its full semantic range. At its most transcendent, "pay" here suggests that the Dreamer recognizes how God has, through grace, given him the opportunity for eternal life within the heavenly city, his soul, like the pearls set within the Lamb's 144,000 followers, given to the pleasure of the Lord, to God's eternal *pais*, to the "kythez þat lastez aye" (1998). Still in the realm of the spiritual, it also suggests the Dreamer's lingering potential to sell all that he has in order to buy the Pearl of Price, the heavenly kingdom imagined in the Book of Matthew. Communally and socially, "pay" articulates the Dreamer's motion from the isolated and isolating enclosure of the garden toward the living Christian community. And finally, at its most terrestrial, it suggests both the losses associated with the human condition and the costs associated with living in the world, both the incalculable losses, like the loss of the Dreamer's daughter and the loss of paradise itself, and the more readily quantifiable ones: the loss of money, of value, of labor, of goods; the loss of a "Perle plesaunte, to pryncez paye" (1).

David Coley is Associate Professor of English at Simon Fraser University. He is the author of *The Wheel of Language: Representing Speech in Middle English Poetry, 1377-1422* (Syracuse UP, 2012), and his articles have appeared in journals including *Studies in the Age of Chaucer, Exemplaria, Chaucer Review*, and *JEGP*. David is currently working on the relationship between Middle English poetry and the medieval plague pandemic, with a particular focus on the poems of MS Cotton Nero A.x.

---

[55] Catherine Pickstock, "Thomas Aquinas and the Quest for the Eucharist," in *Catholicism and Catholicity: Eucharistic Communities in Historical and Contemporary Perspectives*, ed. Sarah Beckwith (Oxford: Blackwell, 1999), 51.

Glossator publishes original commentaries, editions and translations of commentaries, and essays and articles relating to the theory and history of commentary, glossing, and marginalia. The journal aims to encourage the practice of commentary as a creative form of intellectual work and to provide a forum for dialogue and reflection on the past, present, and future of this ancient genre of writing. By aligning itself, not with any particular discipline, but with a particular mode of production, *Glossator* gives expression to the fact that praxis founds theory.

GLOSSATOR.ORG

www.ingramcontent.com/pod-product-compliance
Lightning Source LLC
Chambersburg PA
CBHW070935180426
43192CB00039B/2185